# The Ways That Never Parted

"A remarkably original and exciting approach to the beginnings of both Christianity and rabbinic Judaism. . . . Rather than Christianity emerging as a repudiation of Judaism, *The Ways That Never Parted* demonstrates that both religions took shape during the same era, influencing one another through close contacts, and that only after 400 C.E. can we speak of two separate religions."

—**Susannah Heschel**
Eli Black Professor of Jewish Studies at Dartmouth College

May 2008

To Taylor Beckering,
Scholar, on the occasion
of your graduation.
    In the hope that I
will someday read your
essays in such a volume!
    Congratulations + best wishes,
        Deborah Goodwin

Gustavus Adolphus College
Saint Peter, Minnesota

# The Ways That Never Parted

## Jews and Christians in Late Antiquity and the Early Middle Ages

*Edited by*

ADAM H. BECKER

*and*

ANNETTE YOSHIKO REED

FORTRESS PRESS

MINNEAPOLIS

THE WAYS THAT NEVER PARTED
Jews and Christians in Late Antiquity and the Early Middle Ages

First Fortress Press edition 2007

Cover design: Jessica Puckett
Cover image: Copyright © Caroline Adams, *Olive Tree Diptych*—aquatint and
    etching —2003. Used by permission.


*Library of Congress Cataloging-in-Publication Data*

Library of Congress Cataloging-in-Publication data is available.

ISBN-13: 978–0–8006–6209–7
ISBN-10: 0–8006–6209–1


The paper used in this publication meets the minimum requirements of American National Standard for Information Sciences—Permanence of Paper for Printed Library Materials, ANSI Z329.48-1984.

Manufactured in the U.S.A.

11   10   09   08   07   1   2   3   4   5   6   7   8   9   10

# Contents

# Foreword

Foreword by MARTIN GOODMAN, SIMON PRICE, AND PETER SCHÄFER

This volume arises from the fortuitous and fortunate coincidence of two originally unrelated events. The first is a series of workshops and colloquia initiated by Peter Schäfer in 2000, with generous funding from John Wilson, formerly Dean of the Princeton University Graduate School. The aim was to foster collaborative research between faculty and doctoral students in the Religions of Late Antiquity subfield of the Department of Religion, while providing the Department's students with unique opportunities for professional development. Each year, two graduate students choose a topic of interdisciplinary interest and, under the guidance of Peter Schäfer, organize a series of workshops on that theme, followed by a colloquium. At each workshop, a graduate student paper is presented, followed by discussion geared towards providing the student with guidance about how best to rework the paper into a formal conference presentation. The student papers are finally presented at the concluding colloquium, alongside papers from the faculty participants and invited scholars from other institutions, who are selected by the two organizers. Following the success of the first colloquium, "In Heaven as it is on Earth: Imagined Realms and Earthly Realities in Late Antique Religion" (January 14–15, 2001),[1] planning soon began for a second workshop and colloquium, this time organized by Adam H. Becker and Annette Yoshiko Reed. For this, they conceived of a timely topic that draws on the special strengths of Princeton's Department of Religion: an exploration of the continued interchange between late antique and early medieval Jews and Christians, which approaches the two religions as "Ways That Never Parted."

The second event was the creation of a formal Research Partnership between Princeton and Oxford in April 2001. One of the first twelve projects approved by that Partnership was on "Culture and Religions of the Eastern Mediterranean." Convened by Simon Price at Oxford and Fritz Graf at Princeton, this project seeks to make use of the ample resources of both universities in the area of late antique religions in order to promote interdisciplinary research and to enhance the excellence of graduate studies through joint projects and graduate student exchanges.[2]

---

[1] The papers from the 2001 colloquium will also be published as a volume: *Heavenly Realms and Earthly Realities in Late Antique Religions,* ed. Ra'anan S. Abusch and Annette Yoshiko Reed (Cambridge: Cambridge University Press, forthcoming).

[2] For more information, see http://www.classics.ox.ac.uk/faculty/oxprinceton.html.

It soon became clear that the "Ways That Never Parted" project was an ideal fit for the new Oxford–Princeton partnership. Martin Goodman and Simon Price organized a seminar on the same topic, involving Oxford students and faculty from a broad range of related fields, and they oversaw the planning for a group of the Oxford participants to travel to Princeton for the culminating conference on January 9–11, 2002.

As the first event in the Oxford–Princeton Research Partnership, the conference brought together faculty and students from Princeton and Oxford, along with selected speakers from other institutions. As part of the unique combination of interdisciplinary research and graduate student training in the "Culture and Religions of the Eastern Mediterranean" project, Martin Goodman and Simon Price also worked with Fritz Graf to arrange two evening workshops during the conference, at which doctoral students from Oxford and Princeton shared their dissertation research with a group of faculty and students from both institutions. Together with the conference itself, these sessions helped to lay the groundwork for further cooperation and collaboration, strengthening the connections between scholars and students from different fields between (and even within) the two universities. The conference itself was organized by the editors of the present volume, under the guidance of Peter Schäfer, and the expenses were met jointly by Princeton and Oxford. The costs of the conference were covered from the fund established to support the yearly workshops and colloquia in Princeton's Department of Religion, while the Oxford visit and graduate student sessions were generously funded by the Oxford–Princeton Research Partnership.

The "Ways That Never Parted" proved to be a wonderful theme for a conference. A great deal of intellectual excitement was generated by the participation of scholars and students from Princeton, Oxford, and other universities, representing an unusually broad array of fields: Jewish Studies, Christianity, and even Paganism. The present book results from this conference. We believe that it successfully conveys the intellectual vigor of this event and, moreover, offers an excellent indication that the Oxford–Princeton project will go from strength to strength, revolutionizing our understanding of the culture and religions of the Eastern Mediterranean world.

# Preface to the Fortress Paperback Edition

It is with great pleasure that we compose the new preface to this volume, which appeared originally as a hardcover published by Mohr Siebeck in 2003. Numerous colleagues have expressed an interest in seeing it published in paperback in order that it might be accessible to a wider audience and more practically useful in classroom settings. We are grateful to Mohr Siebeck and Fortress Press for having made this a reality.

Since this volume's initial publication, interest in interactions between Jews and Christians has continued to grow. It has become increasingly common to examine the relationships between Judaism and Christianity, not just in the first century CE, but also in later periods. In addition, more and more scholars are acknowledging the importance of studying Rabbinic and Patristic sources in concert. The last four years have also seen the publication of a number of major works on the history of Jewish–Christian relations.[1] These include books and articles by many of our volume's contributors. Daniel Boyarin's *Border Lines,* Paula Fredriksen's *Augustine and the Jews,* and Peter Schäfer's *Jesus in the Talmud* attest the ongoing work of the senior scholars who participated in the volume and the conference that inspired it.[2] Inasmuch as the conference and volume grew out of the collaboration between junior and senior scholars at Princeton, Oxford, and beyond,[3] we are especially delighted to report that all of the junior scholars involved in the project have now published books, each of which speaks, in innovative ways,

---

[1] E.g., S. Schwartz and R. Kalmin, eds., *Jewish Culture and Society under the Christian Roman Empire* (Leuven: Peeters, 2003); J. Hahn, *Gewalt und religiöser Konflikt: Studien zu den Auseinandersetzungen zwischen Christen, Heiden und Juden im Osten des Römischen Reiches (von Konstantin bis Theodosius II)* (Berlin: Akademie, 2004); J. Lieu, *Christian Identity in the Jewish and Graeco-Roman World* (Oxford: Oxford University Press, 2004); E. Kessler and N. Wenborn, eds., *A Dictionary of Jewish–Christian Relations* (Cambridge: Cambridge University Press, 2005). Also notable is the much awaited English translation of I. Yuval, *Two Nations in Your Womb: Perceptions of Jews and Christians in Late Antiquity and the Middle Ages,* trans. B. Harshav and J. Chipman (Berkeley: University of California Press, 2006).

[2] D. Boyarin, *Border Lines: The Partition of Judaeo-Christianity* (Philadelphia: University of Pennsylvania Press, 2004); P. Schäfer, *Jesus in the Talmud* (Princeton: Princeton University Press, 2007); P. Fredriksen, *Augustine and the Jews* (New York: Doubleday, 2007).

[3] Specifically, this volume arose from the intersection of two broader projects: Princeton's annual workshops and colloquia on late antique religions and the Oxford– Princeton research partnership on "Culture and Religions of the Eastern Mediterranean"

to parallels, intersections, and interactions between Jewish and Christian cultures in Late Antiquity.[4]

We hope that this volume has contributed, in some small fashion, to the richness and dynamism of current research in these areas. It would be an understatement to say that we have been gratified by its positive reception: the volume has been widely cited as exemplary of the renewed scholarly concern for the overlaps and interactions between Judaism and Christianity in Late Antiquity and the early Middle Ages. Moreover, its critiques of the traditional model of the "Parting of the Ways" have helped to spark further discussion and debate.

Although some have critiqued the volume for not promoting a new model to replace the old, we continue to see its polyphony as one of its strengths. The diversity of its viewpoints reflects the richness of recent specialist research on the interactions between Jews and Christians. It also mirrors, in our view, the stunning variety of approaches to negotiating biblically-based religious identities in Late Antiquity and beyond. Taken together, the contributions in this volume demonstrate the inadequacy of any monolithic model that seeks to theorize the relationships between "Judaism" and "Christianity" without considering the socio-cultural and discursive specificities that shaped interactions between Jews and Christians in different cultural contexts, geographical locales, and social strata.

---

—both creative forums for collaborative, interdisciplinary research that have continued to push research in exciting new directions. Under the guidance of Peter Schäfer, doctoral students in Princeton's Religions of Late Antiquity subfield have organized conferences on central themes in the study of Judaism, Christianity, and Greco-Roman religions. Proceedings of the two most recent conferences are forthcoming with Mohr Siebeck: *Heresy and Self-Definition in Late Antiquity* (ed. E. Iricinschi and H. Zellentin) and *Antiquity in Antiquity: Jewish and Christian Pasts in the Greco-Roman World* (ed. G. Gardner and K. Osterloh); the 2006/2007 project is exploring "Revelation, Literature, and Community." Likewise, the Oxford–Princeton project on "Culture and Religions of the Eastern Mediterranean" has run parallel seminars on "Purity and Pollution in Ancient Religions" (2002/2003), "Society, Wealth and the Divine: Benefactors in Ancient Cities" (2003/2004), "Priesthoods in the Ancient World" (2004/2005), and "Syria in Antiquity" (2005/2006).

[4] A. H. Becker, *Fear of God and the Beginning of Wisdom: The School of Nisibis and the Development of Scholastic Culture in Late Antique Mesopotamia* (Philadelphia: U. of Pennsylvania Press, 2006); R. S. Boustan, *From Martyr to Mystic: Rabbinic Martyrology and the Making of Merkavah Mysticism* (TSAJ 112: Tübingen: Mohr, 2005); A. S. Jacobs, *Remains of the Jews: The Holy Land and Christian Empire in Late Antiquity* (Stanford: Stanford University Press, 2004); A. Y. Reed, *Fallen Angels and the History of Judaism and Christianity: The Reception of Enochic Literature* (Cambridge: Cambridge University Press, 2005); D. Stökl Ben Ezra, *The Impact of Yom Kippur on Early Christianity: The Day of Atonement from Second Temple Judaism to the Fifth Century* (WUNT 163; Tübingen: Mohr, 2004); A. Tropper, *Wisdom, Politics, and Historiography: Tractate Avot in the Context of the Graeco-Roman Near East* (Oxford: Oxford University Press, 2004).

To take seriously recent critiques of the traditional view of the "Part-ing of the Ways" is to accept, in our view, that one can no longer assert that "Judaism" and "Christianity" were separated without also asking where and when, by whom and for whom. No longer can scholars as-sume that there was a single historical moment after which the texts, be-liefs, and practices of Jews became irrelevant to those of their Christian contemporaries–nor the converse. Too much is lost when we study the two in isolation from one another.

With regard to the scholarly temptation to construct monolithic mod-els, it is perhaps telling that some critics of this volume have focused more on its title than its contents. Much to our surprise, some readers misread or misrepresented the volume as denying the existence of any "Jews" or "Christians" in this period; others imagined that we sought to present the religious landscape of Late Antiquity as a hybrid hodge-podge or undifferentiated mélange. In no way did we mean to claim, then or now, that Jews and Christians were always and everywhere the same as one another. To question the retrojection of modern ideas about "Judaism" and "Christianity" into the distant past is not to deny there were ever any differences. It is, rather, to embrace a more textually rig-orous and historically rooted approach that investigates the distinctive ways in which identities were demarcated in specific contexts; rather than imposing modern categories on our pre-modern literary evidence, such an approach is attentive to the anxieties, fluidities, and hybridities in our sources, allowing for a rich and variegated continuum of Jew-ish, Christian, and "Jewish-Christian" identities in dynamic competi-tion, contact, and confli ct. Much recent work in this area, for instance, is marked by renewed attention to local and temporal particularities, whether it be in the appreciation of the Sasanian context of Babylo-nian Rabbinic culture,[5] the investigation of "Jewish Christianity" in its

---

[5] See most recently R. Kalmin, *Jewish Babylonia between Persia and Roman Palestine: Decoding the Literary Record* (New York: Oxford University Press, 2006). Yaakov Elman continues to produce work demonstrating the importance of Middle Persian sources for understanding the Babylonian Talmud; e.g., "'Up to the Ears' in Horses' Necks (N.M. 108a): On Sasanian Agricultural Policy and Private 'Eminent Domain,'" *Jewish Studies, An Internet Journal* 3 (2004): 95–149 [online at http://www.biu.ac.il/JS/JSIJ/]; "Middle Persian Culture and Babylonian Sages: Accommodation and Resistance in the Shaping of Rabbinic Legal Tradition," in *The Cambridge Companion to the Talmud and Rab-binic Literature,* ed. C. E. Fonrobert and M. S. Jaffee (Cambridge: Cambridge University Press, 2007), chap. 8. Junior scholars are following in Elman's footsteps; e.g., G. Her-man, "Ahasuerus, The Former Stable-Master of Belshazzar, and the Wicked Alexander of Macedon: Two Parallels Between the Babylonian Talmud and Persian Sources," AJS Review 29.2 (2005): 283–97.

multiple late antique settings,[6] or the exploration of similar issues of self-definition that arise in the early Islamic period.[7]

With the publication of this volume—and now its reprint—we hope to offer an intervention in an ongoing conversation that has tended to read all textual and material evidence in terms of a unilinear model of the history of Jewish–Christian relations. The traditional scholarly model of the "Parting of the Ways" tells a single and simple story of increased separation and isolation. Our literary and material evidence, however, speaks to the complex dynamics of self-definition among (and between) different kinds of Jews and Christians. While some vehemently asserted the separation of "Judaism" and "Christianity," others ignored their efforts, and still others resisted them. Furthermore, Jewish and Christian communities frequently shared the same social worlds; even when engaged in private and seemingly distinct acts, Jews and Christians often looked over their shoulders at one another.

If this volume succeeds in contributing to the current scholarly discourse on Jewish–Christian relations, we hope that it does so by

---

[6] Fresh attention, for instance, has turned to the late antique Syrian contexts of the redaction of the Pseudo-Clementine literature; see esp. N. Kelley, "Problems of Knowledge and Authority in the Pseudo-Clementine Romance of Recognitions," *JECS* 13.3 (2005): 315–48; eadem, *Knowledge and Religious Authority in the Pseudo-Clementines: Situating the Recognitions in Fourth-century Syria* (Tübingen: Mohr Siebeck, 2006). In addition, P. Piovanelli has drawn attention to the Ethiopian *Book of the Cock*, which preserves anti-Pauline traditions that may shed light on the place of "Jewish Christianity" in late antique Palestine ("Exploring the Ethiopic Book of the Cock, An Apocryphal Passion Gospel from Late Antiquity," *HTR* 96 [2003]: 427–54; idem, "The Book of the Cock and the Rediscovery of Ancient Jewish Christian Traditions in Fifth Century Palestine," in *The Changing Face of Judaism, Christianity and Other Greco-Roman Religions in Antiquity*, ed. I. Henderson and G. S. Oegema [Gütersloh: Gütersloher Verlagshaus, 2006], 318–32. Similarly, Boyarin explores the late antique contexts of heresiological accounts of Ebionites and Nazoreans in *Border Lines*, esp. 207–8. For new insights into "Jewish Christianity," see also P. J. Tomson and D. Lambers-Petry, eds., *The Image of the Judaeo-Christians in Ancient Jewish and Christian Literature* (Tübingen: Mohr, 2003) and O. Skarsaune and R. Hvalvik, eds., Jewish Believers in Jesus: The Early Centuries (Peabody, Mass.: Hendriksen, forthcoming 2007).

[7] For the ongoing reassessment of Islamic origins, see e.g. H. Berg, ed., *Method and Theory in the Study of Islamic Origins* (Leiden: Brill, 2003) and A. Elad, "Community of Believers of 'Holy Men' and 'Saints' or Community of Muslims? The Rise and Development of Early Muslim Historiography," *Journal of Semitic Studies* 47.2 (2002): 241–308, a review of F. M. Donner, *Narratives of Islamic Origins: The Beginnings of Islamic Historical Writing* (Studies in Late Antiquity and Early Islam 14; Princeton: Darwin, 1998). The exact connections between early Islam and Judaism and Christianity are still debated; e.g., most recently, M. E. Pregill, "The Living Calf of Sinai: Orientalism, 'Influence,' and the Foundations of the Islamic Exegetical Tradition" (Ph.D. diss., Columbia University, 2007).

fostering collaborative research, interdisciplinary conversation, and graduate training that crosses the traditional disciplinary boundaries between the study of Judaism and Christianity (as well as so-called "paganism"). In striving towards these goals, we personally have been inspired by the intellectual context of Princeton's Department of Religion, and we owe a great debt to our teachers and advisors: Peter Brown, John Gager, Fritz Graf, Martha Himmelfarb, Elaine Pagels, and Peter Schäfer.

With John Gager's recent retirement, we are poignantly reminded of all he has done to help make Princeton an ideal place for collegial yet rigorous interdisciplinary research. Like Bob Kraft, also recently retired, John has worked to blur the boundaries that once separated the study of Second Temple Judaism, New Testament studies, Late Antiquity, Classics, Rabbinics, and Patristics. Indeed, it is perhaps no coincidence that the era of John's tenure at Princeton and Bob's at the University of Pennsylvania saw so many paradigm shifts in research on Judaism and Christianity. Through their own research no less than their training and mentoring of others, they have pushed scholars of late antique religions to draw on the fruits of contemporary social scientific research, while also compelling scholars of Christianity to study Judaism, scholars of Judaism to study Christianity, and scholars of both to investigate the broader imperial cultures in which the two took form. This volume, we hope, stands as one small example of the value of such approaches, both to shed new light on late antique literature and to dismantle traditional models and trenchant biases in scholarship on Judaism and Christianity.

# Introduction

## Traditional Models and New Directions

by

## ANNETTE YOSHIKO REED & ADAM H. BECKER

For those who seek the origins of our modern conceptions of Judaism and Christianity as ultimately related yet essentially distinct religions, the idea of the "Parting of the Ways" proves powerfully attractive, offering a reassuringly ecumenical etiology of the religious differences between present-day Christians and Jews.[1] In this model Judaism and Christianity are likened to two paths that branched off from a single road, never to cross or converge again.[2] Even as their common origin is affirmed, the allegedly fundamental distinction between the two is explained as a result of a mutual decision, long ago, to part their fates and go their separate ways.

Scholars still debate the determinative catalyst for this "Parting" and whether or not such a split was inevitable.[3] Nevertheless, it is generally agreed that there was a fateful turning point in the first or early second century CE, after which "there were no relations between Jews and Christians except hostile ones."[4] As a result, most research on Late

---

[1] On the place of contemporary ecumenical concerns in the "Parting" model, see Judith Lieu, "'The Parting of the Ways': Theological Construct or Historical Reality?" *JSNT* 56 (1994): 106–9. On the use of various familial metaphors to communicate the same concepts, see Daniel Boyarin, *Dying for God: Martyrdom and the Making of Judaism and Christianity* (Stanford: Stanford UP, 1999), esp. 1–6.

[2] I.e., as illustrated by Figures 1 and 2 in Martin Goodman's piece in this volume, "Modeling the 'Parting of the Ways.'"

[3] See further: James J. D. Dunn, *The Partings of the Ways Between Christianity and Judaism and their Significance for the Character of Christianity* (London: SCM, 1991), esp. 238; idem, ed., *Jews and Christians: The Parting of the Ways, AD 70 to 135* (Cambridge: Eerdmans, 1992), esp. 367–68; Lawrence Schiffman, "At the Crossroads: Tannaitic Perspectives on the Jewish–Christian Schism," in *Jewish and Christian Self-Definition*, vol. 2, *Aspects of Judaism in the Graeco-Roman Period*, ed. E. P. Sanders (Philadelphia: Fortress, 1981), 155–56.

[4] George Dix, "The Ministry in the Early Church," in *The Apostolic Ministry: Essays on the History and Doctrine of Episcopacy*, ed. K. E. Kirk (London: Hodder & Stoughton, 1946), 228. In his view, this situation came into being "after 70."

Antiquity and the early Middle Ages has progressed on the assumptions that (1) Judaism and Christianity developed in relative isolation from one another and (2) the interactions between Jews and Christians after the second century were limited, almost wholly, to polemical conflict and mutual misperception.

Our literary and archaeological data, however, attest a far messier reality than this unilinear spatial metaphor allows. Contrary to the "Parting" model, our sources suggest that developments in both traditions continued to be shaped by contacts between Jews and Christians, as well as by their shared cultural contexts.[5] Even after the second century, the boundaries between "Jewish" and "Christian" identities often remained less than clear, consistent with the ambiguities in the definition of both "Jew" and "Christian."[6] Likewise, attention to the entire range of our extant evidence suggests that the continued diversity of Judaism and Christianity found expression in the variety of ways in which Jews and Christians interacted in different geographical, cultural, and social contexts.[7] Accordingly, a growing number of scholars have begun to challenge the "Parting" model, citing its methodological paucity, its inadequacy as an historical account, and its inability to explain much of our primary evidence.[8] Spurning the simplicity of the notion of a single,

---

[5] See, e.g.: Marc Hirshman, *A Rivalry of Genius: Jewish and Christian Biblical Interpretation in Late Antiquity*, trans. B. Stein (Albany: SUNY, 1996); Israel Yuval, "Easter and Passover as Early Jewish–Christian Dialogue," in *Passover and Easter: Origin and History to Modern Times*, ed. P. Bradshaw and L. Hoffman (Notre Dame: U. of Notre Dame Press, 1999), 98–124; idem, *Two Nations in Your Womb: Dual Perceptions of the Jews and of Christians* (Tel Aviv: Am Oved, 2000) [Hebrew]. Other examples are discussed by Abusch, Koltun-Fromm, Salvesen, Stökl Ben Ezra, and Tropper in this volume.

[6] Ignatius's comments in *Magnesians* 10.3 often serve as the representative example for those who claim that "Jew" and "Christian" became clear-cut and mutually exclusive religious identities in the first century CE. However, counter-examples abound, both from this period and well beyond; see Lieu, "Parting of the Ways," 110–14; Daniel Boyarin, "Semantic Differences; or 'Judaism'/'Christianity'," in this volume.

[7] E.g.: Leonard Victor Rutgers, "Archaeological Evidence for the Interaction of Jews and non-Jews in Antiquity," *AJA* 96 (1992): 101–18; John G. Gager, "Jews, Christians, and the Dangerous Ones in Between" in *Interpretation in Religion*, ed. S. Biderman and B. Scharfstein (Leiden: Brill, 1992), 249–57; W. Kinzig, "'Non-Separatists': Closeness and Co-operation between Jews and Christians in the Fourth Century," *VigChr* 45 (1991): 27–53; R. Kimelman, "Identifying Jews and Christians in Roman Syrio-Palestine" [http://www2.bc.edu/~cunninph/kimelman_identifying.htm]. See also Paula Fredriksen, "What 'Parting of the Ways'? Jews, Gentiles, and the Ancient Mediterranean City," in this volume

[8] Important critiques of this model include Boyarin, *Dying for God*; Lieu, "Parting of the Ways"; P. S. Alexander, "'The Parting of the Ways' from the Perspective of Rabbinic Judaism," in *Jews and Christians*, 1–26; Steven Katz, "Issues in the

early, and decisive separation between the two religions, many have turned to explore new approaches for understanding the relation-ship(s) between Jews and Christians in the centuries after their purported "Parting."[9]

The present volume seeks to further the discussion and debate about the "Parting of the Ways" by demonstrating what we stand to gain by approaching Judaism and Christianity as "Ways that Never Parted" – or, in other words, as traditions that remained intertwined long after the Second Temple had fallen and the dust had settled from the Jewish revolts against Rome. Whereas most treatments of early Jewish–Christian relations focus on the first and early second centuries CE[10] and/or limit their discussions to the conflicts of later centuries,[11] the articles in this volume consider the points of intersection, sites of interaction, and dynamics of interchange between Jews and Christians in the period between the Bar Kokhba Revolt and the rise of Islam. Rather than approaching Judaism and Christianity as monolithic entities that partook in a single act of separation, we here attempt to illuminate the broad range of regional and cultural variation in the encounters between different biblically-based religious groups – including Jews and Christians, but also those so-called "Jewish Christians" and "Judaizers" who so strain the dichotomous definitions of modern scholarship. In the process, we hope to highlight the value of studying Judaism and Christianity as traditions that continued to impact one another, in constantly changing but consistently meaningful ways, throughout Late Antiquity and into the Middle Ages.

---

Separation of Judaism and Christianity after 70 CE: A Reconsideration," *JBL* 103 (1984): 43–76; Martha Himmelfarb, "The Parting of the Ways Reconsidered: Diversity in Judaism and Jewish–Christian Relations in the Roman Empire, 'A Jewish Perspective'," in *Interwoven Destinies: Jews and Christians Through the Ages*, ed. Eugene Fisher (New York: Paulist, 1993), 47–61; John G. Gager, "The Parting of the Ways: A View from the Perspective of Early Christianity: 'A Christian Perspective'," in *Interwoven Destinies*, 62–73. See also Boyarin, Fredriksen, and Becker in this volume.

[9] Lieu, for instance, stresses that "The problem with the model of the 'parting of the ways' is that, no less than its predecessors on the pages of Harnack or Origen, it operates essentially with the abstract or universal conception of each religion, whereas what we know about is the specific and the local" ("Parting of the Ways," 108).

[10] One refreshing exception to this tendency is the volume, *Christian–Jewish Relations through the Centuries*, ed. Stanley E. Porter and Brook W. R. Pearson (Sheffield: Sheffield Academic Press, 2000), in which contributions about Late Antiquity and the Middle Ages bridge the usual gap between discussions of the New Testament and of the modern period.

[11] A recent example: William Horbury, *Jews and Christians in Contact and Controversy* (Edinburgh: T&T Clark, 1998).

## From Supersessionism to Common Origins and "Parted Ways"

In speaking of the "Parting of the Ways" as an historical model, we here
mean to denote the notion of an early and absolute split between Judaism
and Christianity, but also the "master narrative" about Jewish and
Christian history that pivots on this notion. In its basic parameters, this
narrative can be summarized as follows: in the first century CE, Judaism
was characterized by great diversity, and the Jesus Movement was still
negotiating its relationship to Jews and Judaism, both inside and outside
the (still fluid) boundaries of its own communities. As a result, Christ-
believers of both Jewish and non-Jewish ethnicities engaged in a range of
exchanges with non-Christian Jews, such that even the conflicts between
them were typically predicated on close contact and competition. In the
wake of the destruction of the Second Temple and the Bar Kokhba
Revolt, however, the two religions decisively institutionalized their
differences. With the Jerusalem Church's alleged flight to Pella, apostolic
"Jewish Christianity" lost its last bastion of authority, and the church
would thenceforth be dominated by the antinomian "Gentile Christianity"
espoused by the apostle Paul and embraced by non-Jews throughout the
Roman Empire. Concurrent with the church's geographical shift from the
Land of Israel to the urban centers of the eastern Mediterranean,
Christianity emerged as a fully independent system of belief and practice,
self-defined as non-Jewish in its theology, its ritual practice, and the
ethnicity of its adherents. Instead of dwelling on contemporary forms of
Judaism, followers of this religion turned to grapple with their ambivalent
relationship to Greco-Roman culture. From that point onwards, Judaism's
relevance for Christian self-definition would be limited to the Jewish
scriptures that the church appropriated as its Old Testament and to the
"literary Jews" of the Christian imagination, constructed from biblical
paradigms to serve as pawns in intra-Christian debates.

According to this "master narrative," the parallel developments in
Judaism were no less momentous or monolithic.[12] With the rise of the
rabbinic movement, it is asserted that the diversity of Second Temple
Judaism all but disappeared. The "Council of Yavneh," allegedly
convened by Rabban Gamaliel II around 90 CE, put an end to sectarian
disputes among the Jews; not only were the Pharisees/Rabbis empowered
as the leaders of the whole nation, but they expelled the Christ-believers
who remained in their midst by means of the *birkat ha-minim* ("blessing
[= curse] on the heretics"). Under the religious leadership of the Rabbis,
Jews would choose to live in self-imposed isolation from the rest of the

---

[12] For a more extensive account of the (rabbinic) Jewish side of the story of the
"Parting of the Ways," see Schiffman, "At the Crossroads," 115–56.

Greco-Roman world, just as indifferent to Christians and "pagans" as these Gentiles allegedly were to Jews and Judaism. Even when the Roman Empire became Christian and the enemy "Esau/Edom" truly took on the garb of a brother, Christians and Christianity remained far outside the bounds of Jewish concern, interest, or even curiosity, such that classical Judaism successfully resisted any influence from Christian traditions, beliefs, or practices. And hence – according to the view of early Jewish and Christian history that still dominates the scholarly discourse – these two religions came to be separate, conflicting, and categorically different, even despite their common origins in Second Temple Judaism.

The historicity and plausibility of many elements in this account have been questioned in recent years. For instance, the very concept of a mutual "Parting" owes much to the claimed correspondence between rabbinic traditions about the institution of the *birkat ha-minim* at Yavneh (*b. Berakhot* 28b–29a) and early Christian traditions about the expulsion of Christ-believers from synagogues (John 9:22; 12:42; 16:2). However, Peter Schäfer, Daniel Boyarin, and others have convincingly established that the "Council of Yavneh" was a much later construct, rather than an historical event.[13] As such, scholars can no longer point to 90 CE as the end of all early intra-Jewish diversity nor appeal to the *birkat ha-minim* as a Jewish counterpart to (and cause for) Christian anti-Judaism. At the same time, New Testament scholars such as Raymond Brown have shown that the Judaism of the Jesus Movement was hardly limited to a single, Torah-observant "Jewish Christianity" in conflict with a single, anti-nomian "Gentile Christianity," dismissing the traditional assumption that early Christian attitudes towards the Torah were wholly determined by ethnicity.[14] Likewise, Gerd Lüdemann and others have deconstructed the

---

[13] See further: Peter Schäfer, "Die sogennante Synode von Jabne," *Judaica* 31 (1975): 54–64 [1: Zur Trennung von Juden und Christen im 1.–2. Jh. n. Chr.], 116–24 [2: Der Abschluss des Kanons]; Daniel Boyarin, "A Tale of Two Synods: Nicaea, Yavneh, and Rabbinic Ecclesiology," *Exemplaria* 12 (2000): 21–62; idem, "Justin Martyr Invents Judaism," *Church History* 70 (2001): 127–32. Furthermore, Reuven Kimelman has shown that the NT and patristic sources traditionally cited in support are far less univocal on this point than some scholars have made them out to be (*"Birkat Ha-Minim* and the Lack of Evidence for an Anti-Christian Jewish Prayer in Late Antiquity," in *Jewish and Christian Self-Definition*, vol. 2, *Aspects of Judaism in the Graeco-Roman Period*, ed. E. P. Sanders with A. Baumgarten and Alan Mendelson [Philadelphia: Fortress, 1981], 234–40). See also Katz, "Issues," 48–53; Günter Stemberger, "Die sogennante 'Synode von Jabne' und das frühe Christentum," *Kairos* 19 (1977): 14–21.

[14] Raymond E. Brown, "Not Jewish Christianity and Gentile Christianity but Types of Jewish/Gentile Christianity," *CBQ* 45 (1983): 74–79.

myth of the Jerusalem Church's flight to Pella,[15] thereby shedding doubt on the widespread view of the demise of authentically apostolic "Jewish Christianity" during the first Jewish Revolt.[16] Furthermore, a variety of scholars have demonstrated that a critical reading of our late antique and early medieval sources does not support any simple model of separation; for even those authors who most vigorously assert the mutual exclusivity of "Judaism" and "Christianity" provide us with many clues about the continued complexity of the situation "on the ground."[17]

Nevertheless, the notion of the "Parting of the Ways" continues to influence contemporary scholarship, particularly with regard to the relationship between Jews and Christians after the second century. When faced with cases in which Jews and Christians clearly interacted, scholars tend to presume as a matter of course that any post-"Parting" contacts must have been exceptional in nature and polemical in thrust. When common traditions are discovered in Jewish and Christian sources, it is usually assumed that these are isolated examples of the unidirectional "influence" of one self-contained entity on another, as opposed to the products of any substantive intercredal interchange or the fruits of their common participation in a shared cultural or discursive context.[18] Evidence that Judaism continued to hold an attraction for some Christians is typically explained away as the idiosyncratic propensities of isolated and individual Judaizers, who are merely "exceptions to the rule" in a church to which "living" forms of Judaism had long become irrelevant. Likewise, evidence for the existence of authors and groups who blurred

---

[15] See esp. Gerd Lüdemann, "The Successors of Pre-70 Jerusalem Christianity: A Critical Evaluation of the Pella-Tradition," in *Jewish and Christian Self-Definition*, vol. 1, *The Shaping of Christianity in the Second and Third Centuries,* ed. E. P. Sanders (Philadelphia: Fortress, 1980), 161–73. For further references, see Annette Yoshiko Reed, "'Jewish Christianity' after the 'Parting of the Ways'," in this volume.

[16] On the problems with the generalizations about the early demise of "Jewish Christianity," as well as the traditional concept of "Jewish Christianity" more broadly, see the contributions by Frankfurter, Gager, and Reed in this volume.

[17] Note the repeated efforts by certain Christians to discourage others from adopting Jewish practices (e.g., *Didascalia* 26), frequenting synagogues (e.g., Origen, *Homilies on Leviticus* 5.8; Chrysostom, *Homilies Against the Jews*, passim), and even calling themselves "Jews" (e.g., Augustine, *Epistle* 196; Cyril of Jerusalem, *Cat.* 10.16). See further: Judith Lieu, *Image and Reality: The Jews in the World of the Christians in the Second Century* (Edinburgh: T&T Clark, 1996), esp. 39–56; Robert Louis Wilken, *John Chrysostom and the Jews: Rhetoric and Reality in the Late Fourth Century* (Berkeley: U. of California Press, 1983), esp. 66–94; Gager, "Dangerous Ones in Between."

[18] In most modern scholarship, it is only the "mother religion" Judaism that exerts "influence" on the "daughter religion" Christianity. For the methodological problems with this tendency (and the scholarly category of "influence" more broadly), see Peter Schäfer, *Mirror of His Beauty: Feminine Images of God from the Bible to the Early Kabbala* (Princeton: Princeton UP, 2002), 217–43, esp. 229–35.

the supposedly firm boundaries between "Jewish" and "Christian" identities is lumped together under the rubric "Jewish Christianity" and dismissed as an anachronistic remnant of an age long past. In short, our data for the complex relationship between Judaism and Christianity in the late antique and early medieval periods are too often read through assumptions about their "parted ways."

To understand the enduring popularity of the concept of the "Parting of the Ways," it is helpful to consider its origins in the reaction against the supersessionist views that once dominated research on post-biblical Judaism and Christian Origins.[19] In the nineteenth and early twentieth centuries, the academic discourse on these topics was dominated by Protestant Christian voices, and most scholars viewed Jesus as the founder of a new religion that was, from the very moment of its inception, categorically opposed to the Judaism of its time. Reading the triumphalism of ancient Christian literature as an expression of historical fact, they reconstructed post-biblical Judaism in the image of a religion ripe for replacement by emergent Christianity. The result was the so-called *Spätjudentum* ("late Judaism") described by influential historians such as Wilhelm Bousset (1865–1920) and Adolf von Harnack (1851–1930): an allegedly ossified system of belief and practice, a pale reflection of Israel's glorious patriarchal and prophetic past, a legalistic religion purportedly devoid of spiritual value and lacking in any attraction for non-Jews.[20] Inasmuch as this "late Judaism" was dismissed as largely irrelevant to the subsequent growth of the church,[21] it is perhaps not surprising that so few students of Christianity felt any need to peer over – let alone to cross – the disciplinary boundaries that separated

---

[19] On the images of Jews and Judaism in earlier research and their relationship to the often vitriolic anti-Judaism/anti-Semitism of late nineteenth and early twentieth century New Testament scholarship, see George Foot Moore, "Christian Writers on Judaism," *HTR* 14 (1921): 197–254; Susanna Heschel, "The Image of Judaism in Nineteenth Century New Testament Scholarship in Germany," in *Jewish–Christian Encounters over the Centuries; Symbiosis, Prejudice, Holocaust, Dialogue*, ed. Marvin Perry and Frederick M. Schweitzer (New York: Peter Lang, 1994), 215–40.

[20] See Wilhelm Bousset, *Die Religion des Judentums in neutestamentlichen Zeitalter* (Berlin: Ruether and Reichard, 1903); see discussion in Shaye J. D. Cohen, "Adolph Harnack's 'The Mission and Expansion of Judaism': Christianity Succeeds Where Judaism Fails," in *The Future of Early Christianity: Essays in Honor of Helmut Koester*, ed. Birger A. Pearson (Minneapolis: Fortress, 1991), 163–69; and Andrew S. Jacobs, "The Lion and the Lamb," in this volume.

[21] A related trend is the tendency to depict Christianity – even in the apostolic period – as a Greco-Roman cult with no special link to Judaism at all; see the discussion in Stanley E. Porter and Brook W. R. Pearson, "Why the Split? Christians and Jews by the Fourth Century," *Journal of Greco-Roman Christianity and Judaism* 1 (2000): 103–7.

them from their counterparts in the field of Jewish History.[22] And, indeed, in light of the bleak image of Judaism once current in Christian scholarship, the lack of movement in the other direction should surprise us even less.[23]

The metaphor of "parted ways" has some precedent in scholarship from this period: in at least one case – a 1912 collection of essays entitled *The Parting of the Roads* – the title of a work compares post-biblical Judaism and early Christianity to two divergent paths, even as the articles therein remain mired in the supersessionist assumptions of the time.[24] The image of "parting" did not become linked to a competing model until decades later, when questions about the origins of anti-Semitism were brought to bear on the study of the New Testament and early Christianity. For this, the key figure was James Parkes (1896–1981), a British clergyman who over his lifetime produced a number of books on Jewish–Christian relations and the history of anti-Semitism.[25] Parkes' interest in these topics was first sparked in the late 1920s, in reaction to the rise of anti-Semitism among nationalist students across Europe.[26] In 1930 he published the first of his many books: *The Jew and his Neighbor*, an exploration of the history of anti-Semitism, which approaches the

---

[22] Important exceptions include August Friedrich Gfrörer in the nineteenth century (see e.g. *Kritische Geschichte des Urchristentums* [2 vols.; Stuttgart: Schweizerbart, 1835]) and George Foot Moore in the early twentieth (see esp. his seminal article "Christian Writers on Judaism," on which see below).

[23] The most important exception is Abraham Geiger (1810–1874), whose books were widely read by Christian scholars at the time; furthermore, his approach to Jesus and early Christianity in *Das Judentum und Seine Geschichte* (3 vols., Breslau: Schletter, 1864–71) and other works presages many of the "new" postwar developments discussed below; see further Heschel, "Image of Judaism," 225–32; eadem, *Abraham Geiger and the Jewish Jesus* (Chicago: U. of Chicago Press, 1998).

[24] F. J. Foakes Jackson, ed., *The Parting of the Roads: Studies in the Development of Judaism and Early Christianity* (London: Arnold, 1912), cited in Lieu, "Parting of the Ways," 101, as an "anticipation" of the concept of the "Parting of the Ways." Despite the supersessionist stance of the book as a whole, it is notable that the contribution of Ephraim Levine ("The Breach between Judaism and Christianity") attempts "to trace the narrative of religious progress to the point where Judaism and Christianity parted company" (p. 285) and dates this development to 70 CE – contrary to the view of this development as the result of Paul's genius in understanding Jesus' true message as found, for instance, in the introduction to the book (pp. 11–12).

[25] Sidney Sugarman, Diana Bailey, and David A. Pennie, eds., *A Bibliography of the Printed Works of James Parkes, with Selected Quotations* (Southampton: U. of Southampton Press, 1977). On Parkes' broader project, see Robert Andrew Everett, *Christianity Without Antisemitism: James Parkes and the Jewish–Christian Encounter* (New York: Pergamon, 1993).

[26] For Parkes's memoirs on his "Involvement in the Jewish Question," see *Voyages of Discovery* (London: Victor Gollancz, 1969), 111–35, penned under the pseudonym John Hadham.

massacres of Jews during the First Crusade (1096 CE) as the background to the debates about the "Jewish Question" in his own time.[27] For his Oxford doctoral thesis, Parkes sought to uncover the very roots of the phenomenon of anti-Semitism by going back to the period of Christian Origins and by attempting to pinpoint the initial moment of Christianity's separation from Judaism. The result was his influential 1934 book, *The Conflict of the Church and the Synagogue*.[28]

By the time of its publication, Parkes' scholarly work on the prehistory of modern anti-Semitism had become even more relevant to the contemporary situation. On May 1, 1934, the Nazi party periodical *Der Stürmer* issued a special fourteen-page publication accusing Jews of using Christian blood in their Passover baking and other rituals.[29] In the same month of the same year, Parkes began the preface to his book with the following words:

> The publication of a study of the causes of anti-Semitism needs neither justification nor explanation at the present time. But a word may be said of the material offered in the present work. The progress of events from the mediaeval ghetto to modern Europe is fairly well known. That the roots of the present situation lie in the mediaeval past is generally agreed. The present work tries to go a stage further, and to answer the question: why was there a mediaeval ghetto?[30]

Insofar as *The Conflict of the Church and the Synagogue* analyzed the period of Christian Origins as part of a broader inquiry into the causes of modern anti-Semitism, this book represented a radical departure from contemporaneous research on the New Testament, "late Judaism," and early Christianity, which continued to view these topics through the lens of Christian beliefs about the church's deserved status as the new and true Israel. Whereas such studies tended to assume the distinctiveness of Christianity vis-à-vis Judaism even in the lifetime of Jesus, Parkes stressed the continuity of the two in the apostolic age and prioritized the question of the precise moment of their divergence thereafter.

---

[27] James Parkes, *The Jew and his Neighbour: A Study of the Causes of Antisemitism* (London: SCM, 1930). For a more recent investigation of Jews and Christians during the First Crusade, see Robert Chazan, *In the Year 1096: The First Crusade and the Jews* (Philadelphia: Jewish Publication Society, 1996); idem, *European Jewry and the First Crusade* (Berkeley: U. of California Press, 1987).

[28] James Parkes, *The Conflict of the Church and Synagogue: A Study in the Origins of Anti-Semitism* (London: Soncino, 1934).

[29] The Nazi appropriation of the blood libel myth, together with other traditional tropes of anti-Semitism, led many to seek the origins of Nazi anti-Semitism, despite its special virulence, in the Christian past. On this particular myth, see A. Dundes, ed., *The Blood Libel Legend: A Casebook in Anti-Semitic Folklore* (Madison: U. of Wisconsin Press, 1991).

[30] Parkes, *Conflict*, vii.

The resultant account of early Jewish–Christian relations anticipated, in nearly every detail, the "Parting" model that now dominates research on these topics. Most notable is the third chapter, which, in fact, bears the title "The Parting of the Ways."[31] Countering assertions about the inherent theological differences between Judaism and Christianity with a socio-political analysis of the events between the birth of Jesus and the Bar Kokhba Revolt, Parkes concluded that "the definite separation into two religions took place towards the end of the first century,"[32] and he argued that "the end of the first century is the time of the definite emergence of Christianity as a new religion."[33] Although Parkes himself most often spoke of this critical moment as "the separation,"[34] he can be credited with innovating, articulating, and popularizing the concept of the "Parting of the Ways" as we now know it.[35] This model, in short, owes its origins to the integration of the study of Christian Origins into the historiography of anti-Semitism/anti-Judaism, whereby Christian hostility towards Jews (both modern and medieval) forms the impetus and

---

[31] This, to our knowledge, is the earliest attestation of this phrase that reflects its current sense; cf. Lieu, "Parting of the Ways," 101–2, who expresses uncertainty about its exact origins and cites James Dunn's 1991 book as her earliest example. For a critique of Parkes' formulation, see Nicholas de Lange, "James Parkes: A Centenary Lecture," in *Cultures of Ambivalence and Contempt: Studies in Jewish–Non-Jewish Relations*, ed. Siân Jones, Tony Kushner, and Sarah Pearce (London: Vallentine Mitchell, 1998), 42–44.

[32] Parkes, *Conflict*, 91.

[33] Parkes, *Conflict*, 92.

[34] Terms like "the separation" and "the split" would also used by Marcel Simon in his seminal 1948 book *Verus Israel: Étude sur les relations entre Chrétiens et Juifs dans l'Empire Romain (135–42)* (Paris: Editions de Boccard, 1948); English version: *Verus Israel: A Study in the Relations Between Christians and Jews in the Roman Empire, AD 135–425*, trans. H. McKeating (Oxford: Oxford UP, 1986), xiv. Notably, Simon chooses to begin his inquiry "at the moment when the Church became fully conscious of its own autonomy and universal mission" (p. xii), which he dates to 135 CE, arguing against an earlier date of 70 CE (pp. xiv–xvi, plus his response to critiques of this choice in his 1964 Postscript, pp. 386–88).

[35] Already in the 1950s and 1960s, we find the "Parting of the Ways" used in titles of scholarly books and articles about the separation of Christianity from Judaism in the first or early second century CE; see, e.g., Abraham Cohen, *The Parting of the Ways: Judaism and the Rise of Christianity* (London: Lincolns-Prager, 1954), esp. ch. 5; Morton Scott Enslin, "Parting of the Ways," *JQR* 51 (1961): 177–97. More recent examples are cited above. See also: Robert Murray, "The Parting of the Ways," *Christian–Jewish Relations* 20 (1987): 42–44; Richard Bauckham, "The Parting of the Ways: What Happened and Why," *Studia Theologica* 47 (1993): 135–51; Vincent Martin, *A House Divided: The Parting of the Ways Between Synagogue and Church* (New York: Paulist, 1995).

background for inquiries into the very emergence of Christianity as a religion distinct from Judaism.[36]

The horror of the Holocaust prompted even more scholars to seek the ancient roots of modern anti-Semitism and to integrate such concerns into research on the New Testament literature.[37] In the process, Parkes' theories about "the separation" of Christianity from Judaism at the end of the first century CE have become increasingly influential, challenging the

---

[36] Parkes's theories echo the narratives about Jesus and Christianity told by earlier Jewish scholars already in nineteenth and early twentieth centuries (see n. 23 above). Most notable is Heinrich Grätz's influential *Geschichte der Juden von den ältesten Zeiten bis auf die Gegenwart* (first published in 1853–1875; revised English version: *History of the Jews*, trans. B. Löwy [Philadelphia: Jewish Publication Society, 1891–98]). For Grätz, Jesus was an earnest – albeit unlearned and misguidedly messianic – Galilean Jew (2:151–68), and his original followers were observant Jews who differed from other Jews only in their peculiar messianic beliefs (2:168–70). Paul, however, took it upon himself to "destroy ... the bonds which connected the teachings of Christ with those of Judaism" (2:229), and he "conceived Christianity to be *the opposite of Judaism*" (2:230; emphasis added). Nevertheless, the separation of the two did not occur until the original "Judaic Christians" succumbed to the blasphemous errors of their "pagan"/"heathen" counterparts and began to exalt Jesus as more God than man (2:370) – a development that Grätz dates shortly after the destruction of the Temple and the Council of Yavneh. Grätz finds evidence for this break in the composition of the New Testament Epistle to the Hebrews, which he reads as a letter from these "Judaic Christians" to the rest of the Jews, proclaiming their separation (2:371). In his view, it was this that brought an end to "the development of Christianity as a branch of Judaism, drawing sustenance from its roots" (2:365). Although the basic outline evokes the "Parting" model of Parkes and later thinkers, the story of Christianity's emergence as a distinct religion is here told in terms of Paul's creation of a "pagan"/ "heathen" belief-system with no real relationship to Judaism, on the one hand, and the later apostasy of "Judaic Christians," on the other. Notably, we find essentially the same viewpoint in G. Alon's widely-used survey of early Jewish history, *The Jews in their Land in the Talmudic Age, 70–640 C.E.*, trans. G. Levi (Jerusalem: Magnes, 1980–1984); see esp. p. 296 on Paul and the triumph of Pauline Christianity as the "victory that transformed Christianity into a Gentile religion" and pp. 305–7 on the self-separation of "Jewish Christians" from Judaism (which he, like Grätz before him, credits to the "dilution" of their Judaism from increased contact with "Gentile Christians," here adding their alleged refusal to participate in the Jewish Revolt against Rome).

[37] See esp.: Jules Isaac, *Jésus et Israël* (Paris: A. Michel, 1948); idem, *Genèse de l'antisémitisme: Essai historique* (Paris: Calmann-Levy, 1956); idem, *L'enseignement du mépris; vérité historique et mythes théologiques* (Paris: Fasquelle, 1962); Rosemary Radford Ruether, *Faith and Fratricide: The Theological Roots of Anti-Semitism* (New York: Seabury, 1974); Alan Davies, ed., *Anti-Semitism and the Foundations of Christianity* (New York: Paulist, 1979); John G. Gager, *The Origins of Anti-Semitism: Attitudes Toward Judaism in Pagan and Christian Antiquity* (Oxford: Oxford UP, 1985), esp. 11–34; and, most recently, Paula Fredriksen and Adele Reinhartz, eds., *Jesus, Judaism, and Christian Anti-Judaism: Reading the New Testament after the Holocaust* (Westminster: John Knox, 2002).

earlier consensus that Jesus himself (or, alternately, Paul) instituted Christianity's complete independence from Judaism.

This shift has been facilitated by a sea change in the study of post-exilic Judaism, also formulated in response to the events of World War II. Already in 1921, George Foot Moore published a scathing critique of the latent anti-Judaism/anti-Semitism in the scholarly discourse on so-called "late Judaism."[38] Such concerns, however, did not have a real impact on the practice of scholarship until the postwar period – when reflections on the Holocaust intensified scholarly efforts to expose the prejudices of past research and when the foundation of the state of Israel heightened the cognitive dissonance between the bleak image of post-biblical Judaism once prevalent in Western scholarship and our ample evidence for the vitality of the Jewish tradition throughout its history. In response, scholars such as Marcel Simon took on the task of correcting the distorted views of post-biblical – and even rabbinic – Judaism in scholarship on early Christianity, exposing the theological biases that shaped the old stereotypes of the Synagogue as sapped of all spiritual vitality and offering a new view of the Jewish religion as a vital force that continued (at least until Constantine) to compete vigorously with Christianity.[39]

The effects of these developments have been far-reaching and are evident in current research on post-biblical Judaism and Christian Origins.[40] What was once termed "late Judaism" has now been dubbed "early Judaism," in a lexical embodiment of the new sensitivity in postwar scholarship to the full history of Judaism, both before and after the spread of Christianity.[41] Whereas Judaism was once treated as the

---

[38] Moore, "Christian Writers on Judaism," 197–254.

[39] Even a glance at the footnotes of Simon's *Verus Israel* shows his dependence on Parkes' *Conflict* (as well as his use of earlier Jewish treatments of the issue, such as that of Grätz, discussed in n. 36 above). On this work and its relationship to earlier views of Jews and Judaism, see Albert Baumgarten, "Marcel Simon's *Verus Israel* as a Contribution to Jewish History," *HTR* 92 (1999): 465–78.

[40] By "current" we here mean scholarship in the late 1970s, 1980s, 1990s, and the present decade, by which time the earlier developments discussed above truly came to shape the broader scholarly discourse. In our summary of these developments, we do not intend to imply, of course, that the road between World War II and the present day was a smooth one, nor to suggest that traditional biases no longer hold sway in some quarters. See further Shaye J. D. Cohen, "The Modern Study of Ancient Judaism," in *State of Jewish Studies*, esp. 56–58 (section on "Polemics and Apologetics").

[41] On the term "early Judaism," see George W. E. Nickelsburg, with Robert Kraft, "Introduction: The Modern Study of Early Judaism," in *Early Judaism and Its Modern Interpreters*, ed. Robert Kraft and George W. E. Nickelsburg (Atlanta: Scholars Press, 1986), esp. 1–2, 10–11; Martin Jaffee, *Early Judaism* (Upper Saddle River, NJ: Prentice Hall, 1997), 15–20. For our purposes, it is interesting to note that Jaffee chooses to demarcate this period at 200 CE because "The date ... is certainly a convenient point to locate *an irreversible split* between Judaic and Christian religious communities" (p. 19,

deservedly dispossessed heir to the biblical heritage claimed by the church, the earliest Christian communities are now approached as a part of the landscape of first-century Judaism and thus – in a striking reversal of nineteenth-century paradigms – as evidence for the rich diversity and continued vitality of the Jewish tradition in Second Temple times.[42] Many scholars (particularly in Israel, North America, and Great Britain) have profitably revisited the issue of the "Jewishness" of Jesus,[43] and some have even challenged long-held beliefs about Paul's attitudes towards Torah-observance and the chosenness of the Jews.[44] Likewise, New Testament specialists have increasingly strived to resist the temptation to view these writings through the lens of their current status as Christian Scripture; rather than assuming that these texts evince a full-fledged "religion" (i.e., "Christianity"), a growing number of studies now treat

---

emphasis added). Also notable is the term "middle Judaism," on which see Gabriele Boccaccini, *Middle Judaism: Jewish Thought, 300 B.C.E. to 200 C.E.* (Minneapolis: Fortress, 1991).

[42] This shift is perhaps best exemplified by the fascinating fate of Emil Schürer's *Geschichte des jüdischen Volkes im Zeitalter Jesu Christi* (originally published as *Lehrbuch der neutestamentlichen Zeitgeschichte* [Leipzig: J. C. Hinrichs, 1874]; with revised and expanded editions, under the new title published in 1886–1890, 1901– 1909). Although Schürer's own versions are steeped in the stereotypes about "late Judaism" that were prevalent in nineteenth-century German scholarship, a new English version was produced by Geza Vermes and Fergus Millar in 1973 (*The History of the Jewish People in the Age of Jesus Christ (175 B.C.–A.D. 135)* [3 vols.; Edinburgh: T&T Clark, 1973]). Vermes and Millar re-revised, edited, and updated Schürer's work to serve as a reference book for a new scholarly context, and the resultant volumes – now shorn of the anti-Jewish rhetoric of the originals – are used in university courses on early Judaism, as well as in courses on the New Testament.

[43] E.g., David Flusser, *Jesus in Selbstzeugnissen und Bilddokumenten* (Reinbek bei Hamburg: Rowohlt, 1968); Geza Vermes, *Jesus the Jew: An Historian's Reading of the Gospels* (London: Fontana, 1976); E. P. Sanders, *Jesus and Judaism* (London: SCM, 1985); Paula Fredriksen, *From Jesus to Christ: The Origins of the New Testament Images of Jesus* (New Haven: Yale UP, 1988); Bruce Chilton, *Rabbi Jesus: An Intimate Biography* (New York: Doubleday, 2000). As Helmut Koester notes, postwar German scholarship on the historical Jesus and the NT has taken a somewhat different trajectory, due in part to the enduring influence of Rudolf Bultmann ("Epilogue: Current Issues in New Testament Scholarship," in *The Future of Early Christianity: Essays in Honor of Helmut Koester*, ed. Birger Pearson [Minneapolis: Fortress, 1991], esp. 469–73).

[44] See esp.: Krister Stendahl, "Paul and the Introspective Consciousness of the West," *HTR* 56 (1963): 199–215; idem, *Paul among Jews and Gentiles, and Other Essays* (Philadelphia: Fortress, 1976); E. P. Sanders, *Paul and Palestinian Judaism* (Philadelphia: Fortress, 1977); Lloyd Gaston, "Paul and the Torah," in *Anti-Semitism and the Foundations of Christianity*, 48–71; idem, *Paul and the Torah* (Vancouver: U. of British Columbia Press, 1987); Gager, *Origins of Anti-Semitism*, 174–264; idem, *Reinventing Paul* (Oxford: Oxford UP, 2000); Stanley Stowers, *A Rereading of Romans: Justice, Jews, and Gentiles* (New Haven: Yale UP, 1994).

these texts, or strata therein, as evidence for a messianic movement that emerged from within Judaism itself (e.g., the "Jesus Movement").[45]

Postwar developments also paved the way for the new rapprochement between Christian scholars and Jewish scholars in recent years.[46] In this, another contributing factor was the publication of the Dead Sea Scrolls, which helped to open a space in which much needed interdisciplinary dialogue could flourish.[47] In the library of the Qumran community, experts in Second Temple Judaism, early Christianity, and Rabbinics alike have found sources that shed new light on key issues and debates in their respective fields. Furthermore, these newly unearthed sources have exposed the dazzling diversity of Second Temple Judaism and the profound continuities that connect it with *both* rabbinic Judaism *and* early Christianity. Whereas scholars of Jewish history once countered Christian stereotypes about "late Judaism" with claims about a single, normative (and most often Pharisaic) Judaism of pre-rabbinic times that led inexorably to the Mishnah and Talmudim,[48] both Jewish and Christian scholars now speak of "Judaisms" or a "multiform Judaism," of which the

---

[45] E.g., Anthony J. Saldarini, *Matthew's Christian-Jewish Community* (Chicago: U. of Chicago Press, 1994); Bruce Chilton, *Judaic Approaches to the Gospels* (Atlanta: Scholars Press, 1994); Daniel Boyarin, "The Gospel of the Memra: Jewish Binitarianism and the Prologue to John," *HTR* 94 (2001): 243–84. Perhaps most interesting is the fact that many polemical comments in the New Testament literature that were once read as evidence for the rejection of Judaism by even the earliest Christians have now been re-read in terms of intra-Jewish competition, often with the aid of modern sociological theories about the dynamics of religious conversion, the establishment of community boundaries, and the interactions between different religious groups. See, e.g., Douglas Hare, "The Rejection of the Jews in the Synoptic Gospels and Acts," in *Anti-Semitism and the Foundations of Christianity*, 27–46; John W. Marshall, *Parables of the War: Reading John's Jewish Apocalypse* (Waterloo: Wilfrid Laurier UP, 2001); David Frankfurter, "Jews or Not? Reconstructing the 'Other' in Rev 2:9 and 3:9," *HTR* 94 (2001): 414–16.

[46] Much is also owed to prominent Jewish scholars of the New Testament and early Christianity in the postwar period, such as David Flusser.

[47] We here point to the *publication* – and not the *discovery* – of the Dead Sea Scrolls as the key factor, since the controversies attendant on the latter were certainly not conducive to such dialogue.

[48] On the apologetic underpinnings of the view that all pre-rabbinic forms of Judaism – *except* for the Jesus Movement – share a common, normatively "Jewish" core that stands in radical continuity with the rabbinic movement, see Boyarin, *Dying for God*, 1–2; and Alexander, "Parting of the Ways," 2. On the problems with the traditional assumption that rabbinic Judaism evolved solely from Pharisaic Judaism, see e.g. Peter Schäfer, "Der vorrabbinische Pharisäismus," in *Paulus und das antike Judentum; Tübingen-Durham-Symposium im Gedenken an den 50. Todestag Adolf Schlatters*, ed. Martin Hengel and Ulrich Heckel (Tübingen: Mohr Siebeck, 1991), esp. 172–75; also, Shaye J. D. Cohen, "The Significance of Yavneh: Pharisees, Rabbis, and the End of Jewish Sectarianism," *HUCA* 55 (1984): 36–38.

Jesus Movement was a part and from which Christianity only gradually took form.[49]

Although many traces of the old biases still remain,[50] the postwar period has thus seen an unprecedented degree of progress in research about the Jesus Movement's close connections with the Judaism(s) of its time, as well as the copious commonalities shared by Jesus-followers and their Jewish contemporaries. Furthermore, scholars have had much success in locating the emergence of this messianic movement within the religious, cultural, and socio-political landscape of first-century Roman Palestine and in contextualizing its spread within an eastern Mediterranean and Near Eastern world peppered with thriving Jewish communities.[51] Accordingly, it is now practically de rigueur for New Testament scholars to consult works about Second Temple Judaism penned from the perspective of Jewish Studies. Even more striking is the fact that studies on the other side of the disciplinary divide increasingly cite New Testament texts as important evidence for our understanding of early Judaism.[52]

The present popularity of the "Parting" model is very much a product of these postwar developments. In stark contrast to the old supersessionist views, the metaphor of "parted ways" allows for both Judaism and

---

[49] The term "Judaisms" has been popularized by the works of Jacob Neusner (see e.g. his comments in *Studying Classical Judaism: A Primer* [Louisville, KY: Westminster/John Knox, 1991], 33), whereas the term "multiform Judaism" was spread by Robert A. Kraft's seminal article "The Multiform Jewish Heritage of Early Christianity," in *Christianity, Judaism and other Greco-Roman Cults: Studies for Morton Smith at Sixty*, ed. J. Neusner (Leiden: Brill, 1975), 174–99. Further discussion of this issue can be found in Kraft's essay in this volume.

[50] Note, e.g., the treatment of Judaism in W. H. Frend, *The Rise of Christianity* (Minneapolis: Fortress, 1984), esp. 43, 126–28, as well as Ernst Käsemann's widely-used commentary on Paul's Letter to the Romans: *An die Römer* (Tübingen: Mohr, 1973); English version: *Commentary on Romans*, ed. and trans. Geoffrey W. Bromiley (Grand Rapids: Eerdmans, 1980).

[51] To cite one influential example: Wayne Meeks, *The First Urban Christians: The Social World of the Apostle Paul* (New Haven: Yale UP, 1983).

[52] There is a long tradition, beginning already with Geiger and Grätz, of Jewish scholars seeking to integrate the historical Jesus into Jewish history; other influential early works include Claude Montefiore's *The Synoptic Gospels* (2 vols.; London: Macmillan, 1909), Israel Abraham's *Studies in Pharisaism and the Gospels* (2 vols.; Cambridge: Cambridge UP, 1917–24), and Joseph Klausner's *Yeshu ha-Notsri* (Jerusalem: Shtibl, 1922). More recent is the integration of New Testament sources, such as the Gospel of Matthew and Revelation, into studies of early Judaism; see e.g. the inclusion of the former in George Nickelsburg, *Jewish Literature between the Bible and the Mishnah* (Philadelphia: Fortress, 1981), 303–5, and the treatment of the latter in Martha Himmelfarb "'A Kingdom of Priests': The Democratization of the Priesthood in the Literature of Second Temple Judaism," *The Journal of Jewish Thought and Philosophy* 6 (1997): 89–104, esp. 90.

Christianity to be approached as authentic religions in their own right, with equally strong links to the biblical and Second Temple Jewish heritage that they share.[53] As such, this model proves palatable to Jews and Christians alike; the former can affirm the Jewish origins of Christianity even as they deny any Christian influence on the development of classical rabbinic Judaism, while the latter can claim a profound continuity with pre-Christian Jewish history even as they affirm the essential originality of the (Gentile) Christian message. Moreover, the notion of the "Parting of the Ways" fits well with contemporary ecumenical concerns, providing a foundation for inter-religious dialogue and buttressing popular appeals to a common "Judeo-Christian" ethic.

At the same time, however, the theory of a single, pivotal moment of separation has effectively established a boundary between the study of Jewish–Christian relations in the first century and inquiries into Jews and Christians thereafter. If scholars of first-century Judaism and Christianity must now strive to describe a complex reality – in which the boundaries of "Jewish" and "Christian" identities remained fluid and in which neither "Judaism" nor "Christianity" were monolithic entities – scholars of a later period are assured that such problems were already settled by the second century CE. With the "Parting of the Ways," it is alleged that "Jew" and "Christian" became firmly established as categorically distinct communal identities, Torah-observance and Christ-belief became mutually exclusive religious options, and living forms of Judaism became as irrelevant for Christians as Christianity had allegedly always been for Jews. In other words, by the time that the Mishnah was redacted and the early Church Fathers composed their epistles and apologies, "Judaism" and "Christianity" had, at long last, become what we now know them to be: different in essence and by definition.

## Problems with the "Parting" Model

Interestingly, the problems with this particular application of the "Parting" model were already acknowledged by Parkes in the 1930s. In light of the late antique evidence for the ongoing interactions between

---

[53] The "Parting of the Ways" is nevertheless based on a Christian perspective, as Judith Lieu and Martha Himmelfarb rightly stress (Lieu, "Parting of the Ways," 6–10; Himmelfarb, "Parting of the Ways," 47). This is especially clear from fig. 2 in Goodman, "Modeling" – an image that communicates the continuity between current concepts about the "Parting of the Ways" and the traditional Christian theological ideas about Jesus' birth and/or ministry as marking Christianity's radical departure from Judaism. Note also Dunn's characterization of Jesus vis-à-vis the Judaism of his time, as discussed in Fredriksen, "What Parting of the Ways?" n. 1.

Jews and Christians, Parkes qualified his theory of an early "separation" with the following assertion:

> While, therefore, we may correctly date the actual separation from the end of the first and the beginning of the second century, we should be wrong to assume that the distinction which we can now observe between Christians and Jews represents the situation as it appeared to those living at the time.[54]

He thus admits that this initial – yet somehow "actual" – moment of separation did not birth Judaism and Christianity as we now know them. That, in his view, did not happen until much later, during the fourth century CE:

> Though neither [Judaism or Christianity] were born in this century, yet both owe more to its outstanding leaders than to any other similar group of contemporaries, and *both are to this day, in many ways, fourth century religions.*[55]

At the same time that Parkes laid the groundwork for theories about an early and decisive split between the two religions, he thus pointed to the limitations of this schematization of early Jewish–Christian relations and to the problems involved in drawing a sharp dividing line between the pre- and post-"Parting" periods. Even more striking is the fact that his argument for a first-century "separation" already contained the seeds for recent critiques of this model, which frequently point to the fourth century as the critical era for Jewish and Christian self-definition.[56]

As is clear from the discussion above, these qualifications were not heeded by the many scholars who have adopted and developed Parkes' notions about the early and final break between Judaism and Christianity. The apparent reason is somewhat ironic: consistent with his influential assertion of a decisive split in the tannaitic/subapostolic period, few of these scholars have even investigated the relevant evidence from the third century, let alone the fourth. And, when dealing with sources from these eras, they have tended to ask different questions, shaped by different

---

[54] Parkes, *Conflict*, 95. More specifically, he suggests that "there is every reason to believe that the common people were much more friendly with each other than the leaders approved of, and this is reflected in some of the popular literature which has survived, and which lacks the bitterness of the more intellectual theologians" (p. 94).

[55] Parkes, *Conflict*, 153 (emphasis added).

[56] For example, the above cited passage from Parkes is quoted to this effect in Günter Stemberger, *Jews and Christians in the Holy Land: Palestine in the Fourth Century*, trans. R. Tuschling (Edinburg: T&T Clark, 2000), 1. See also: Rosemary Radford Ruether, "Judaism and Christianity: Two Fourth-Century Religions," *Sciences Religieuses/Studies in Religion* 2 (1972): 1–10; Jacob Neusner, *The Three Stages in the Formation of Judaism* (Chico: Scholars Press, 1985), 77; Boyarin, *Dying for God*, 18.

assumptions about the scope, character, and significance of Jewish–
Christian relations.[57]

Even when working with sources from the first and early second
centuries, proponents of the "Parting" model are often faced with the
same problem: much of our evidence simply does not fit into this
appealing and clear-cut narrative, thereby necessitating an increasing
number of qualifications. James Dunn, for instance, takes a theological
approach to the issue in his book *The Partings of the Ways Between
Christianity and Judaism and Their Significance for the Character of
Christianity*; he treats each point of doctrinal difference between the
Jesus Movement and "mainstream" Judaism as one "Parting of the Ways"
among many, which unfolded simultaneously on multiple fronts during
the late first and early second centuries.[58] In his later volume, *Jews and
Christians: The Parting of the Ways, 70–135 CE*, Dunn is forced to tackle
the social and historical questions that such assertions inevitably raise. In
response, he notes that the decisive moment of separation was actually
"bitty" in its progression and that, while an inevitable development, it
may or may not have been inevitable at the time, and it may or may not
have appeared inevitable to those who lived through it.[59] Like the
qualifications posed by Parkes decades earlier, those offered by Dunn
may serve, in the end, to dilute the explanatory power of the model as a
whole – and, as a result, to raise questions concerning its heurism for
historical research and its undue influence on the contemporary practice
of scholarship.

There is no doubt that the metaphor of "parting ways" still proves
helpful when dealing with certain aspects of the relationship between
Jews and Christians in the first centuries of the Common Era. Most
notably, it helps us to grasp the radical impact of the failure of the two
Jewish Revolts against Rome, the destruction of the Second Temple, and
the disappearance of any vestige of a Jewish state on the structure of
Jewish society, Christian attitudes towards their Jewish contemporaries,

---

[57] This is exemplified by Simon, who takes 135 CE as the starting point for his
inquiry into the conflicts between Judaism and Christianity, conceived of as two distinct
entities (*Verus Israel*, xiv–xvii).

[58] See n. 3 above.

[59] See Dunn's conclusion to *Jews and Christians*, esp. 367–68. Faced with Philip
Alexander's emphasis on the historical contingency of the developments that led to the
distancing of the two traditions, in an article in the same volume ("Parting of the
Ways," esp. 24–25), Dunn offers an assertion of the inevitability of Christianity's
"Parting" from Judaism, albeit paired with a question that poignantly exposes the
historically problematic nature of this line of inquiry: "A critical question raised is the
extent to which our judgments on these issues are formed more by hindsight than by
historical data. With the benefits of hindsight, we see that certain developments and
corollaries were inevitable; *but were they so at the time?*" (p. 368; emphasis added).

and Christian biblical interpretation, as well as the perception of Judaism by non-Jews in the Roman Empire. Insofar as this model emphasizes the shared context of historical catastrophe from which both rabbinic Judaism and proto-orthodox Christianity developed, it also draws our attention to ways in which these movements forged their identities in contra-distinction to one another, thereby constructing lasting images of each other as wholly "other."

Although heuristic for some purposes, the "Parting" model frustrates our analysis of many types of evidence concerning Jews and Christians in Late Antiquity and the early Middle Ages. Above, we noted a series of recent findings that have served to shake, if not topple completely, the pillars of proof on which the claimed historicity of this theory is perched.[60] Perhaps more perplexing is the fact that the "Parting" model has remained influential even though most scholars now reject its major presupposition: the equation of rabbinic Judaism and proto-orthodox Christianity with "Judaism" and "Christianity" in a global sense.

Few experts in early church history would now deign to make such sweeping generalizations when discussing inner-Christian developments in the first and second centuries CE, or even the third and fourth. In the decades since Walter Bauer's seminal 1934 book, *Rechtgläubigkeit und Ketzerei im ältesten Christentum* (and particularly since its English translation in 1971),[61] research on early Christianity has increasingly acknowledged the methodological problems involved in treating Western Christian orthodoxy as the only, or even the predominant, form of Christianity in the Roman Empire prior to the Council of Nicaea (or outside the Empire, before or after).[62] The field of Jewish Studies has been somewhat slower to abandon the idea that late antique Judaism consists only of rabbinic Judaism. Nevertheless, recent research has undermined the traditional view of the Tannaim as authoritative figures who immediately succeeded in establishing their vision of Judaism as

---

[60] See further Katz, "Issues," esp. 76.

[61] Walter Bauer, *Rechtgläubigkeit und Ketzerei im ältesten Christentum* (Tübingen: Mohr, 1934); English version: *Orthodoxy and Heresy in Earliest Christianity* (trans. and ed. from the 2nd German edition [1964] by Robert Kraft and Gerhard Krodel; Philadelphia: Fortress, 1971).

[62] Most notable is the new sensitivity to the value of now non-canonical writings for our reconstruction of early Christian culture and to the role of heresiology in the construction of Christian "orthodoxy." See e.g.: Koester, "Apocryphal and Canonical Gospels," *HTR* 73 (1980): 105–30; idem, "Epilogue," esp. 470–76; Rowan Williams, *The Making of Orthodoxy* (Cambridge: Cambridge UP, 1989), esp. 1–23; Elaine Pagels, "Irenaeus, the 'Canon of Truth,' and the Gospel of John: 'Making a Difference' through Hermeneutics and Ritual," forthcoming in *VigChr*.

normative throughout the Land of Israel, let alone the Diaspora.[63] When discussing the relationship between the two religions, however, many scholars of Rabbinics and Patristics are still surprisingly willing to embrace the concept of a global, one-time separation between "Judaism" and "Christianity" in the tannaitic/subapostolic period, which allegedly affected interactions between Jews and Christians across a broad range of geographical locales, social settings, intellectual discourses, and cultural milieux.

No less problematic are the effects of the "Parting" model on the practice of scholarship. As is often the case, the dominant historical assumptions mirror the configuration of disciplinary boundaries, and both have served to reinforce one another. Just as late antique Judaism and Christianity are commonly approached as self-contained entities in conflict, so this split is replicated in the relationship between the fields of Rabbinics and Patristics.[64] The assertion of a decisive "Parting" enables scholars in both fields to continue engaging in their research without serious attention to developments on the other side of the disciplinary divide.[65] In effect, the notion of the "Parting of the Ways" has thus served

---

[63] A more critical reading of the Sages' self-presentation in the classical rabbinic literature, which takes into account both archeological evidence and sociological models, has led to a new emphasis on the limited nature and scope of early rabbinic authority in the second and third centuries CE; see further Catherine Hezser, *The Social Structure of the Rabbinic Movement in Roman Palestine* (TSAJ 66; Tübingen: Mohr Siebeck, 1997), esp. 185–227, 386–404, 460–66; Seth Schwartz, *Imperialism and Jewish Society, 200 B.C.E. to 640 C.E.* (Princeton: Princeton UP, 2001), 110–28. Moreover, like their counterparts in the field of Patristics, scholars of Rabbinics have begun to explore the Sages' efforts at self-definition and their strategies for legitimating their own authority vis-à-vis those who they deemed "heretics"; see Boyarin, "Tale of Two Synods," esp. 21–30; idem, "Justin Martyr," esp. 438–49; idem, *Border Lines: The Invention of Heresy and the Emergence of Christianity and Judaism* (Divinations: Rereading Late Ancient Religions; Stanford: Stanford UP, 2004); Naomi Janowitz, "Rabbis and their Opponents: The Construction of the 'Min' in Rabbinic Anecdotes," *JECS* 6 (1998): 449–62, esp. 449–50, 461; Christine Hayes, "Displaced Self-perceptions: the Deployment of Mînîm and Romans in b. Sanhedrin 90b–91a" in *Religious and Ethnic Communities in Later Roman Palestine*, ed. H. Lapin (Bethesda: U. of Maryland Press, 1998), esp. 254–55.

[64] Perhaps the most ironic example of this tendency is Hershel Shanks, ed., *Christianity and Rabbinic Judaism: A Parallel History of Their Origins and Early Development* (Washington: Biblical Archaeology Society, 1992), a collection of essays that – with the sole exception of James Charlesworth's contribution – approaches the two traditions as completed isolated entities that are only "parallel" insofar as their disparate and unconnected histories can be juxtaposed. See Jacob Neusner's review in *JAAR* (1993): 771–83, esp. 776–81, and Martin Goodman's in *JJS* 44 (1993): 313–14.

[65] On the general lack of contact between the fields of Rabbinics and Patristics, as well as the important exceptions to this pattern, see Burton Visotzky, *Fathers of the World: Essays in Rabbinic and Patristic Literatures* (Tübingen: Mohr, 1995), 5–27. On

to justify and to reify the traditional split between these fields of study in a manner no less marked than older supersessionist models.

It is perhaps not coincidental that, as more and more scholars have sought to bridge this gap,[66] the challenges to the "Parting" model have mounted. Doubts about its heurism and historical soundness have emerged from the fray of various scholarly debates: questions about the "Parting" model have been raised in the ongoing discussions about the exact nature of Christian polemics against Jews and Judaism.[67] During the course of analyzing specific texts, some scholars have been led to seek more sophisticated approaches to comparing Jewish and Christian traditions and new ways to explain the parallels between them.[68] Others, pursuing specialized inquiries into particular figures, groups, and locales, have highlighted a number of specific cases and places for which the "Parting" model proves more misleading than useful.[69] At the same time, an increased awareness about methodological and theoretical advances in the broader academic discourse about human society and culture has led a growing number of scholars to stress the paucity of the "Parting of the

---

the complicity of Patristics and Rabbinics scholars in maintaining this boundary, see Boyarin, *Dying for God*, 7; also Alexander, "Parting of the Ways," 2–3.

[66] One important milestone was the three-volume collection of essays on *Jewish and Christian Self-Definition*, edited by E. P. Sanders (vol. 1) with A. I. Baumgarten and Alan Mendelson (vol. 2) and with Ben F. Meyer (vol. 3), and published from 1980– 1983; although Judaism and Christianity are here treated in separate volumes (i.e., vols. 1 and 2), these collections have facilitated dialogue between scholars in the two fields.

[67] A number of important works have recently been written on the discourse of Christian anti-Judaism, as considered from sophisticated sociological and literary perspectives; see Lieu, *Image and Reality*, esp. 277–90; O. Limor and G. Stroumsa, eds., *Contra Iudaeos: Ancient and Medieval Polemics between Christians and Jews* (Leiden: Brill, 1996). Note also the contributions by Becker, Cameron, Fredriksen, Gibson, and Jacobs in this volume.

[68] E.g., Marc Hirshman, *A Rivalry of Genius: Jewish and Christian Biblical Interpretation in Late Antiquity*; Galit Hasan-Rokem, *Web of Life: Folklore and Midrash in Rabbinic Literature*, trans. B. Stein (Stanford: Stanford UP, 2000), 121–25, 154–57; Charlotte Fonrobert, "The *Didascalia Apostolorum*: A Mishnah for the Disciples of Jesus," *JECS* 9 (2001): 483–509; Schäfer, *Mirror of His Beauty*, 215–43, esp. 229–35. See also Abusch, Koltun-Fromm, Stökl Ben Ezra, and Tropper in this volume.

[69] In terms of locales, the most obvious example is the case of Syriac Christianity and rabbinic Judaism in the Sassanian Empire, as discussed by Naomi Koltun-Fromm and Adam H. Becker in this volume. On Jews and Christians in Rome, see the contribution of Daniel Stökl Ben Ezra, and on Smyrna, E. Leigh Gibson's. As for specific figures, most notable are studies on Origen and Jerome, two proto-orthodox Christians who interacted with Jews; see e.g. Nicholas de Lange, *Origen and the Jews: Studies in Jewish–Christian Relations in Third-Century Palestine* (Cambridge: Cambridge UP, 1976), 50–61, 103–32; Adam Kamesar, *Jerome, Greek Scholarship, and the Hebrew Bible: A Study of the Quaestiones hebraicae in Genesim* (Oxford: Clarendon, 1993), 4–49, 176–91; also Alison Salvesen in this volume.

Ways" as a metaphor for describing the dynamics of religious self-definition and the interaction between groups.[70] By acknowledging that neither tradition was univocal in its stance towards the other, scholars have exposed the fascinating diversity of belief and practice that continued to characterize both Judaism and Christianity, illuminating the broad spectrum that stretched between their respective "orthodoxies" and exploring the persistently complex dynamics of Jewish–Christian relations.

## Beyond the "Parting of the Ways"

In our view, the recent challenges to the "Parting" model hold great potential for enriching scholarship on Judaism and Christianity alike, serving as a necessary corrective to past research and as a constructive basis for future studies. Like any metaphor, the idea of the "Parting of the Ways" proves valuable only insofar as it aids scholars in interpreting the literary and archaeological evidence at hand. But, like too many models, it has gained such an aura of normativity that it is often treated as an axiom or a standard against which our data should be measured, rather than as a conceptual tool whose value rests solely in its usefulness or as a point to be proved (or disproved) from analyses of the relevant data.

With the present volume, we hope to aid in opening the way for a fresh approach to our primary sources and to help to create a space in which new models can be forged. Our choice of title is deliberately provocative. In speaking of Judaism and Christianity as "Ways that Never Parted," we do not intend to imply that the relationships between Jews and Christians remained static, as if somehow frozen in the early first century CE. Neither do we mean to downplay the many conflicts, misperceptions, and polemics that have marred Jewish–Christian relations in both pre-modern and modern times. Rather, we wish to call attention to the ample evidence that speaks against the notion of a single and simple "Parting of the Ways" in the first or second century CE and, most importantly, against the assumption that no meaningful convergence ever occurred thereafter. On one level, our title should thus be read as a challenge to the conventional wisdom: what happens when we approach our evidence from a different perspective, treating the "Parting of the Ways" as a principle that needs to be proved rather than presupposed?

As recent research has shown, the data can support theories about a variety of different "Partings" at different times in different places; even

---

[70] This issue is discussed in a number of the articles herein; see esp. the contributions of Boyarin, Gibson, Kraft, and Jacobs.

with regard to the Roman Empire, a strong case has been made that the fourth century CE is a far more plausible candidate for a decisive turning point than any date in the earlier period.[71] It is, however, perhaps less profitable to debate the exact date of the "Parting" than to question our adherence to a model that prompts us to search for a single turning point that ushered in a global change for all varieties of Judaism and Christianity, in all communities and locales. What proves significant is that attempts to "part" Christianity from Judaism did not cease with the moment of their alleged success, whenever that moment might have been. For example, the essential difference between Judaism and Christianity continued to be asserted and reasserted and reasserted again by proto-orthodox and orthodox church leaders, thereby suggesting that the incompatibility of Jewish and Christian "ways" remained less than clear for others in their midst. Herein lies the second meaning of our title: we suggest that Jews and Christians (or at least the elites among them) may have been engaged in the task of "parting" throughout Late Antiquity and the early Middle Ages, *precisely because* the two never really "parted" during that period with the degree of decisiveness or finality needed to render either tradition irrelevant to the self-definition of the other, or even to make participation in both an unattractive or inconceivable option.

Even more telling, in our view, is the fact that nearly all "partings" in these centuries are followed by new (and often surprising) convergences. Within certain realms, it seems that these two "ways" never fully parted. Even when and where they did, new paths often emerged to mediate new types of interchange between Jews and Christians, and new areas of common ground could be established, thereby posing ever new threats to those who promoted an idealized view of these identities and communities as hermetically sealed off from one another. On another level, one can thus propose that the "ways" never parted inasmuch as developments in Judaism and Christianity still remained meaningfully intertwined long after the second century, parting and joining and parting and joining again for many centuries thereafter.

Even as the "Parting" model still remains regnant, a new understanding of how late antique Jews and Christians related and interrelated with one another is slowly yet steadily developing. It is, however, neither the right time nor the right place to propose a new model to replace the old. As older models are repeatedly dismantled, defended, deconstructed, and debated, new ones will likely emerge to fill their place – and, in fact, several interesting alternatives have already been suggested.[72] As is clear from the example of postwar scholarship on Second Temple Judaism and Christian Origins, the period between the initial voicing of doubts about

---

[71] See n. 56 above.

[72] E.g. Boyarin, "Semantic Differences"; Alexander, "Parting of the Ways," 2.

the conventional wisdom and the emergence of a new *opinio communis* is an important and exciting time that offers unique opportunities to approach familiar sources with fresh eyes, to bring new or overlooked sources into the discussion, to explore untried methodologies, and to bring the findings of specialist research firmly to bear on the musings of the generalist.

It is in this spirit that we offer the present volume. The articles herein express a variety of positions. Some of our contributors accept the basic contours of the "Parting" model but seek to reconfigure its parameters or limit its application to certain cases; others argue that it must be abandoned entirely. In our view, much of the value of the current debates about the "Parting of the Ways" lies in the fact that scholars have free rein to explore issues of interchange, identity, and influence without straining to relate specific texts, figures, and events to any one framework of assumptions (whether old or new). And, whichever way the reader chooses to interpret our title, it is this that we intend to express by our subtitle: the need to focus with renewed energy and intensity on *Jews* and *Christians* in Late Antiquity and the early Middle Ages, before settling on any new generalizations about *Judaism* and *Christianity* during this period.

## Summary of Volume Contents

The volume begins with an article by Paula Fredriksen, aptly entitled "What 'Parting of the Ways'? Jews, Gentiles, and the Ancient Mediterranean City." Fredriksen here demonstrates the inadequacy of the "Parting" model as a description of the lived experience of Jews, Christians, and "pagans" in the Roman Empire and, in the process, opens a new perspective on the Christian *contra Iudaeos* tradition. First, she points to the essential differences between "pagan" anti-Judaism, which was an extension of a more general disdain for foreigners, and Christian anti-Judaism, which was rooted in a reaction against continuing interactions between Jews and Gentiles (both "pagan" and Christian). She then turns to the question of a possible Jewish mission to Gentiles – an idea often conjured by modern scholars to account for the vitriol of Christian anti-Judaism. In light of the intimate setting of the ancient Mediterranean city and the integration of Jews therein, she concludes that active Jewish proselytism is simply not required to explain the continuing Gentile interest in Judaism that so fed the ire of some Christian authors. Next, she considers the balance of "rhetoric" and "reality" in Christian accusations about Jewish participation in "pagan" persecutions of Christians; these statements, she argues, cannot be read simply as reports of events "on the ground" nor generalized into an explanation of

Christian hostility towards Jews, inasmuch as they jar with the social dynamics of ancient urban culture. In the process, Fredriksen highlights the continuity in the interactions between Jews and Gentiles in the centuries between Alexander of Macedon and Augustine of Hippo. She proposes that this situation persisted even after the Christianization of the Empire; in her view, it ended only with the decline of the urban culture of the ancient Mediterranean between the fifth and seventh centuries CE, when socio-political developments led to the gradual erosion of long-lived civic patterns and to the development of a new social reality, built upon the ideology of separation in the *contra Iudaeos* tradition.

Daniel Boyarin's "Semantic Differences, or 'Judaism'/'Christianity'" offers an alternative to the conventional view that "Christianity" was born from a second-century "Parting of the Ways" with "Judaism." Boyarin here considers how the categories of "Judaism" and "Christianity" functioned in antiquity, by integrating recent scholarship on the changing meanings of "Jew" and "Judaism" with theoretical insights from the fields of linguistics and postcolonial criticism. He demonstrates that, prior to Christianity, the term "Jew" was an ethnic appellation, in the same sense as "Greek," the term to which it was most often opposed. The category only became meaningful in a purely "religious" sense when countered with a new opposing term, namely, "Christian." Consequently, there was no static entity "Judaism" from which early Christians could choose to "part ways," precisely because the emergence of "Judaism" as a "religion" (as opposed to a culture of which cult was an inextricable component) only occurred "when Christianity separated religious belief and practice from *Romanitas,* cult from culture." Boyarin then stresses the hybridity of late antique culture and likens the range of biblically-based forms of religiosity in the first centuries of the Common Era to "dialects" that preceded the definition of official "languages." Likewise, the construction of "Judaism" and "Christianity" as mutually exclusive "religions" was initiated by proto-orthodox Christian and early rabbinic Jewish heresiologists, but not actualized or officialized until the Christianization of the Roman Empire.

The practices of definition and categorization also form the focus of Robert A. Kraft's essay, "The Weighing of the Parts: Pivots and Pitfalls in the Study of Early Judaisms and their Early Christian Offspring." In his view, the recent challenges to the conventional wisdom about the early "Parting" of Judaism and Christianity serve as "an invitation to look more closely at the micro-histories behind that 'common knowledge'." Kraft thus questions the selectivity that has lead scholars to deal with the relationship between "early Judaism" and "early Christianity" solely on the basis of their classical forms, and he points to the many more "parts" that need to be "weighed" in an analysis of the religious landscape of Late Antiquity. At the same time, he stresses the limits of modern labels and definitions, and he calls for increased attention to the self-definitions expressed in our ancient sources. Although these methodological caveats pose practical challenges for scholars accustomed to working within clearly delineated subfields, he suggests that these efforts are both valuable and necessary – not least because they open the way to a fuller understanding of the complex process by which classical Judaism and classical Christianity came to become distinct and dominant (at least in the West) from the fourth century onwards.

In "The Lion and the Lamb: Reconsidering Jewish–Christian Relations in Antiquity," Andrew S. Jacobs considers the relevance of Christian comments about Jews for our understanding of the changing dynamics of interchange between Jews and Christians in late antique Palestine. Jacobs begins by surveying the history of research on Christian anti-Judaism, focusing on the debates between those who read the *contra Iudaeos* tradition as mere rhetoric and those who seek a social reality of Jewish–Christian competition behind these sources. Jacobs suggests a possible path out of the present impasse, by introducing insights from the field of post-colonial criticism. Using a discursive analysis that presumes a dialectical relationship between the "rhetoric" and "reality" of Christian anti-Jewish writings, Jacobs examines four examples, spanning the period from the third century CE to the seventh: Origen, Jerome, the Piacenza Pilgrim, and Stratēgios. By focusing on the changing power dynamics between Jews and Christians with regard to "imperial domination and colonial resistance," he offers a fresh reading of their statements about Jews, geared towards "the way in which Christians and Jews constructed their world, reacted to their world, engineered their world through resistant or authoritative discourse."

Debates about the heurism of various models and methodologies for the study of early Jewish–Christian relations are given a new twist in Martin Goodman's contribution. In "Modeling the 'Parting of the Ways'," Goodman presents a series of diagrams, which illustrate different conceptualizations of the relationship between Judaism and Christianity in the first four centuries of the Common Era. When taken together, Goodman's nine diagrams serve to communicate the dangers involved in making generalizations about Judaism and Christianity, apart from an awareness of how the outcome will inevitably be shaped by one's own perspective, the ancient perspective that one chooses to privilege, and the precise topics on which one decides to focus.

Whereas the first five contributions survey evidence from the entire period under discussion, the remaining eleven explore the theme of this volume through close analyses of specific texts, motifs, practices, and locales. We begin in the second and third centuries CE with David Frankfurter's "Beyond 'Jewish Christianity': Continuing Religious Sub-Cultures of the Second and Third Centuries and Their Documents."

Frankfurter here uses an analysis of the *Ascension of Isaiah*, 5 and 6 Ezra, and the *Testaments of the Twelve Patriarchs* to tackle the broader problem of the reification of religious categories in the study of Late Antiquity. Most scholars have responded to the combination of "Jewish" and "Christian" features in these sources by seeking to isolate (early) "Jewish" strata from (later) "Christian" ones. By contrast, Frankfurter undertakes a unified reading of each text, which allows for more complex self-definitions than the anachronistic imposition of a mutually-exclusive understanding of "Judaism" and "Christianity" onto this early period. He suggests that the *Ascension of Isaiah*, 5 Ezra, and 6 Ezra attest the Jewish prophetism of continuous communities that adopted Christ-devotion as an option within Judaism. Likewise, he proposes that the *Testaments of the Twelve Patriarchs* reflects a priestly messianism that resists dichotomous categorization as either "Jewish" or "Christian." Consequently, these texts shed doubt on the existence of "an historically distinct 'Christianity'" already in the second and third centuries, while also exposing the profound inadequacy of the traditional view of "Jewish Christianity" as a singular and self-contained phenomenon.

Like Frankfurter, E. Leigh Gibson shows how our understanding of familiar texts can be enriched by new approaches to Jewish–Christian relations. In "The Jews and Christians in the *Martyrdom of Polycarp*: Entangled or Parted Ways?" she revisits the issue of the date and textual integrity of the *Martyrdom of Polycarp*, with special attention to the references to Jews therein. Whereas such statements have traditionally been taken as evidence for the hostility between Jews and Christians in Smyrna already in the second century, Gibson proposes that the "Jews" of the text are actually Christians, that is, Christ-believers who had different attitudes towards the Jewish Law than the author of this material. Later redactions – such as the version found in Eusebius' *Ecclesiastical History* – bear the marks of changes by tradents who misunderstood this original context; statements about conflicts within a fluid continuum of Jewish and Christian identities were read in terms of later views of the categorical difference between Judaism and Christianity. Likewise, modern scholars have brought to this text their own ideas about the mutual exclusivity of Judaism and Christianity, which echo the concerns of later orthodox Christians but do not fit with the situation in Asia Minor during the first three centuries of the Common Era. Through her reading of the *Martyrdom of Polycarp*, Gibson thus offers a fresh solution to its textual problems, while simultaneously enriching our understanding of the early interchanges and ambiguities among Christians and Jews in Smyrna.

The next article, Amram Tropper's "Tractate *Avot* and Early Christian Succession Lists," raises an important note of caution about comparative projects that analyze parallels between rabbinic Judaism and proto-orthodox Christianity without proper attention to their shared Greco-Roman cultural context. Tropper begins with an analysis of the structure of the chain of transmission in Mishnah *Avot* and investigates its relationship to different types of Greco-Roman succession lists. Only then does he turn to examine their early Christian counterparts. This two-fold comparison leads Tropper to critique attempts by Daniel Boyarin and Shaye J. D. Cohen to liken the purpose and function of *Avot* to contemporaneous Christian lists of similar form. In Tropper's view, both draw upon the same Greco-Roman genre, and they serve a similar apologetic function with regard to the assertion of institutional authority, but there are also notable divergences between them, which prove significant for our understanding of their origins and function in communities shaped by different social structures. He proposes that proto-orthodox Christian succession lists have an exclusionary function aimed outwardly towards so-called "gnostics," whereas the list in *Avot* is more internal than heresiological in function, consistent with the relative lack of concern about *minim* among early Rabbis.

Whereas Tropper stresses the internal orientation of the early rabbinic movement in Roman Palestine, Naomi Koltun-Fromm points to the cultural contacts between rabbinic Jews and Syriac Christians in third- and fourth-century Sassanid Mesopotamia. In "Zippora's Complaint: 'Moses is Not Conscientious in the Deed!' Exegetical Traditions of Moses' Celibacy," Koltun-Fromm shows how Moses served both as a model and as a means for articulating the appropriate way of life for both rabbinic Jews and Syriac Christians. Moreover, these exegetes understood the prophethood of Moses and the role of celibacy in the sanctification of Israel at Sinai in surprisingly similar ways. Koltun-Fromm's analysis reveals that they often focus on the same issues and, at times, even seem to be responding to one another. Her article thus demonstrates the value of a comparative approach to Jewish and Christian biblical interpretation, which does not assume a radical separation between the two communities in all times and places; for, when these two literary corpora from the Semitic Orient are laid side-by-side, one is often able to discern a dialogue between them, shaped by the common discursive-exegetical space shared by Babylonian Rabbis and Christian authors in the same locale.

Annette Yoshiko Reed's contribution considers the continued ambiguities on the borders between "Jewish" and "Christian" identities, even into the fourth century CE. In "'Jewish Christianity' after the 'Parting of the Ways': Approaches to Historiography and Self-Definition in the Pseudo-Clementines," she shows how the modern scholarly discourse about "Jewish Christianity" has been shaped by assumptions about the "Parting of the Ways," such that scholars have stressed the marginalization of "Jewish Christians" in Late Antiquity, even in the face of evidence to the contrary. Rejecting a monolithic concept of "Jewish Christianity," Reed argues for a more nuanced approach to so-called "Jewish-Christian" viewpoints, which regards them as part of a broad and variegated range of attempts to negotiate the relationship between Jewish and Christian identities. These methodological insights are then applied to the Pseudo-Clementine *Homilies* and *Recognitions*, two fourth-century texts that exhibit many so-called "Jewish-Christian" features, including the affirmation of the equal soteriological value of the Torah and the Gospel. Whereas these texts have traditionally been approached as mines for earlier "Jewish-Christian" sources, Reed seeks to recover the value of their redacted forms for our understanding of Judaism and Christianity in the fourth century, proposing that the authors/redactors responsible for the final forms of these texts may be participating in a broader debate about the place of Judaism and Jewish praxis in Christian self-definition.

With the contribution of Alison Salvesen, we turn to focus on two authors who clearly conceived of Christianity as distinct from (and in conflict with) contemporary Judaism: the proto-orthodox/orthodox Christian scholars Origen and Jerome. In "A Convergence of the Ways? The Judaizing of Christian Scripture by Origen and Jerome," Salvesen highlights a case of convergence that is as surprising as it is striking: in the period between the third and fifth centuries – precisely when the authors of Western Christian orthodoxy were establishing theological and hermeneutical traditions in radical distinction from Judaism – the Greek and Latin versions of the Old Testament used by Christians in the Roman Empire were being brought closer to the Hebrew of the Tanakh used by their Jewish contemporaries. In this, Origen and Jerome played key roles, both through their "Hebraization" of Greek and Latin translations of the Bible and through their use of earlier Jewish and/or "Jewish-Christian" Greek versions (esp., Aquila, Symmachus). The precedent that they set, Salvesen suggests, helped to lay the groundwork for Christian Hebraism in following centuries, thereby enhancing the Old Testament's function as a perennial link between Judaism and Christianity.

Just as Salvesen's article starkly demonstrates the value of integrating text-critical research on the Bible into the study of Jewish–Christian relations in Late Antiquity, so the following article, by Daniel Stökl Ben Ezra, draws our attention to another understudied site of interchange: ritual practice and liturgy. In "Whose Fast is it? The Ember Day of September and Yom Kippur," he focuses on the Fast of the Seventh Month, as it was observed in late antique Rome. Earlier scholars limited the possible Jewish background of this festival to an early period, prior to the presupposed "Parting of the Ways," and/or posited that any influence thereafter must reflect Christian encounters with the Old Testament, rather than any response to a local, lived Judaism. By contrast, Stökl Ben Ezra highlights the Fast's close connections with the Jewish festivals of autumn, not just as they appear in the Old Testament, but also as they were practiced by late antique Jews. He notes the prominence of Christians of Jewish heritage within the ancient Roman church and speculates about the Fast's possible origins as a Christianized Yom Kippur. Stökl Ben Ezra then shows that, whatever its roots, the later development of this Christian festival continued to be shaped by Christians' familiarity with the practices of their Jewish contemporaries. As such, this example offers a fascinating case in which contact and competition with Jews continued to inform Christian praxis, even many centuries after the so-called "Parting of the Ways."

Like Tropper and Koltun-Fromm, Ra'anan Abusch highlights the value of new approaches to Jewish–Christian relations for our understanding of late antique Judaism. In "Rabbi Ishmael's Miraculous Conception: Jewish Redemption History in Anti-Christian Polemic," he focuses on a unit preserved within the early medieval Hebrew martyrological anthology, *The Story of the Ten Martyrs*: an "annunciation" scene that claims for Rabbi Ishmael a semi-divine origin. The parallels with Christian claims about Jesus are poignant, particularly in light of its martyrological context. Abusch thus reads this tradition as "a bold act of appropriation" and as a "pointed rejoinder to Christian accounts of Jesus' divine nature and of his uniqueness within human history." Although this function evokes *Toledot Yeshu* traditions, he cautions against assuming a simple polemical aim. Abusch shows how this unit's use of the "contested cultural idiom" of miraculous birth is inextricably intertwined with Jewish martyrological traditions and with the Byzantine Jewish discourse about sexual purity. The latter, in his view, points to the distinct cultural context in which this unit took form. Even as its polemic against Rome may express a Jewish repudiation of Byzantine political power, so its stress on the possibility of paternity through sight raises the possibility that some Byzantine Jews shared the fascination with visuality that shaped Christian culture during the iconoclastic debates of the seventh to ninth centuries.

With Averil Cameron's contribution, we return again to the Christian *contra Iudaeos* tradition. In "Jews and Heretics – A Category Error?" Cameron considers the conflation of the categories of "Jew" and "heretic" in Christian literature from the later Roman Empire and early medieval Byzantium. She shows how various Christian techniques of labeling religious beliefs and practices as "aberrant" developed in tandem with one another, such that Jews, pagans, and "heretics" could be conflated in orthodox Christian genealogies of error. Cameron focuses on the writings of the late fourth-century author, Epiphanius of Salamis. Like earlier heresiologists, Epiphanius does not categorize his enemies, real and imagined, primarily by doctrinal criteria. Rather, he groups them together using a genealogical model, thereby rewriting the history of ancient culture as an account of the divergence from orthodox Christian truth by a diverse set of "others," not limited to those whom we would generally recognize as "Christian heretics." Cameron thus stresses that the scholar engaged with heresiological sources must come to terms with "a mode of thinking, a kind of mindset and a way of describing, that informed Christian self-identity"; for, even as the conflation of categories obstructs our efforts to learn about "real" Jews and "heretics" alike, it tells us much about orthodox Christian heresiology, historiography, and self-definition.

The following article is the third to address the important issue of "Jewish Christianity." In "Did Jewish Christians See the Rise of Islam?" John G. Gager takes as his starting point a debate between Shlomo Pines and Samuel Stern concerning the possibility that a late "Jewish-Christian" document is preserved in the tenth-century *Tathbit* of the Muslim author 'Abd al-Jabbār. Stern dismissed Pines' argument for the "Jewish-Christian" origins of this material, on the grounds that "Jewish Christianity" could not have survived to see the rise of Islam. For Gager, Stern's recalcitrance vis-à-vis Pines' position offers an important lesson about our own presuppositions concerning both the "Parting of the Ways" and the allegedly resultant demise of "Jewish Christianity." These narratives originated in efforts to eradicate an identity that was, according to Gager, far more threatening to orthodox Christians (and perhaps also rabbinic Jews) than that of Christian Judaizers – precisely because they "insisted that there was no need to choose between being Christians or Jews." Modern scholars, then, should be particularly wary, lest we replicate the "conceptual nihilation" of "Jewish Christians" by those ancient elites who had the most to gain from asserting the absolute incompatibility of Judaism and Christianity.

The final paper, Adam H. Becker's "Beyond the Spatial and Temporal *Limes*: Questioning the 'Parting of the Ways' outside the Roman Empire," challenges the scholarly tendency to limit discussions about Jewish–Christian relations to the confines of the Roman Empire. He first focuses on events in the East, which followed a completely different trajectory than those in the West. As many scholars have noted, there seems to have been a post-Constantinian turning-point in Jewish–Christians relations in the Roman Empire; Christians in Mesopotamia, however, remained a minority religious community into the Islamic period. Becker then considers the increase in anti-Jewish literature in those Roman lands conquered by the Arabs in the seventh century, proposing that this development attests to communal boundary problems and, as such, underlines the impact that the formation of a Christian state had on Jewish–Christians relations within the Roman Empire. Nevertheless, the possibility for the development of shared discourses between Jews and Christians remained open. As an example, Becker cites the common space of rational debate shared by early medieval Jews,

Christians, and Muslims within the realm of Islamic dialectical or systematic theology (*kalām*). This, in his view, is an instance where the "ways" in fact converged and, hence, further problematizes a globalized view of the "Parting of the Ways," whether dated to the second century or the fourth.

# Acknowledgements

The editors would be gravely remiss if we did not acknowledge our debt to all those who helped to shape this volume and the conference on which it is based. Neither would have been possible without Peter Schäfer. From the day that we first conceived of the topic in early 2001 to the day that we submitted the manuscript of this volume, Prof. Schäfer has been a constant source of guidance, inspiration, support, and encouragement – both in his capacity as an advisor and as the editor, together with Martin Hengel, of Mohr Siebeck's Texts and Studies in Ancient Judaism series. For all this, we are deeply appreciative.

John F. Wilson, formerly Dean of Princeton University's Graduate School, provided the financial support for the series of workshops and colloquia of which this project is a part. He granted this funding to encourage innovative approaches to facilitating collaboration between graduate students and faculty in the Religions of Late Antiquity sub-field of Princeton's Department of Religion, and we hope that the present volume communicates in some small way the contribution that these workshops and colloquia have made to the intellectual life of students in our sub-field. In addition, Princeton's Program in the Ancient World, Program in Jewish Studies, and Program in Late Antiquity helped to defray the costs involved in the preparation of the present volume.

We would also like to acknowledge those responsible for the Oxford–Princeton cooperation that lies at the very heart of this volume. Fritz Graf first conceived of the idea to integrate the "Ways that Never Parted" workshop and colloquium with the Oxford–Princeton Research Partnership. It was indeed providential that we first discussed our plans for this project with Prof. Graf on the eve of his trip to Oxford University in April 2001 – just in time for him to propose a collaborative endeavor at the initial planning meeting for the joint "Culture and Religion of the Eastern Mediterranean" project, which he convened together with Simon Price.

The logistical challenges of coordinating a trans-Atlantic project were more than outweighed by the great honor and pleasure of working with Martin Goodman and Simon Price, who oversaw the Oxford side of this joint venture: the seminar on the "Ways that Never Parted" at Oxford (Michaelmas term, 2001), at which a number of the articles in this volume were first presented, and the visit of a group of Oxford faculty and students for the culminating conference at Princeton (January 9–11, 2002). Both contributed enormously to the success of the conference itself, while simultaneously laying the groundwork for the ongoing efforts of the broader "Culture and Religion of the Eastern Mediterranean" project. Insofar as this endeavor exemplifies the interdisciplinary approaches to ancient and late antique religions that are so sorely needed at this point in the history of research, we feel especially fortunate that we could be a part of it.

The Oxford–Princeton Research Initiative generously funded the collaborative component of this project. We would also like to express our appreciation to all the graduate students and faculty, on both sides of the Atlantic, who participated in the workshop on the "Ways that Never Parted" at Princeton and in the parallel seminar at Oxford; indeed, the contents of the present volume reflect the lively dialogues and debates that took place in these twin working-groups during fall semester 2001, no less than the conference itself.

Thanks also go to Dr. Henning Ziebritzki, Martina Troeger, and Juliane Haag at Mohr Siebeck, for their patience and efficiency in shepherding this book to publication, and to Paulo Asso, Peggy Reilly, and Kerry Smith for their invaluable aid at various stages of this project. In addition, Adam Becker would like to express his appreciation to Angela Zito and Janine Paolucci at New York University, for providing office space during the summer of 2002 for his work on this project. The editors owe special debts of gratitude to Leyla B. Aker, for her supernumerary but less than remunerative labors on the book, and to Dove C. Sussman, for volunteering his technical prowess and providing constant feedback.

Last but not least, the editors would like to take this opportunity to congratulate John G. Gager on the occasion of his 65th birthday. When we were determining whom to invite to the "Ways that Never Parted" conference, we were rather stunned by the large number of scholars who are on the cutting-edge of research on this topic and who, at some point in their careers, studied with Prof. Gager. From our own experience, we suspect that this is not a coincidence. He has played a major role in inspiring our own research interests in this area, and he has never ceased to push us to look behind and beyond the "master narratives" of modern scholarship, questioning unquestioned assumptions, exposing deeply-ingrained biases, and seeking to recover – to whatever degree that we can – the realities "on the ground." For this, as for so much else, we offer him our warmest thanks.

# What "Parting of the Ways"?

## Jews, Gentiles, and the Ancient Mediterranean City

by

### PAULA FREDRIKSEN

When was the "Parting of the Ways"? At what point did relations between Jews and (Gentile) Christians irretrievably, unambiguously break down?

Until quite recently, scholars of ancient Christianity, particularly of the New Testament, have frequently posed – and just as frequently answered – this question. The options available in the texts of choice have supported such answers as c. 28–30 CE, when Jesus proclaimed a supposedly startling new vision to an indifferent or hostile Israel; c. 50 CE, when Pauline communities are imagined as separate from and independent of Diaspora synagogue communities; c. 70 CE, when the Temple's destruction supposedly untethered Gentile Christianity from its awkward and lingering attachments to Jewish practice; c. 135 CE, after which point Jews were no longer permitted into Aelia, and the leadership of the "mother church" passed from Jewish to Gentile Christians; or, certainly by 200 CE, when Jewish persecutions of Gentile Christians and increasingly effective ecclesiastical organization combined both to articulate and to finalize the "inevitable" break.[1]

---

\* The current essay draws in part on research and arguments advanced in an essay done in collaboration with Doctor Oded Irshai of Hebrew University: "Christian Anti-Judaism: Polemics and Policies, from the Second to the Seventh Century," forthcoming in volume 4 of the *Cambridge History of Judaism*, edited by Steven T. Katz. I gratefully acknowledge support I received for that project from the National Endowment for the Humanities.

[1] "Until recently" should not be taken to imply "but no longer." Much current work in New Testament generally, and in studies of Paul and of the historical Jesus in particular, still operates with this paradigm of separation. James D. G. Dunn's *The Partings of the Ways* (Philadelphia: Trinity, 1991) may be usefully considered in this connection. Rejecting earlier views (such as Baur's, Lightfoot's, and, with a [huge] difference, Sanders') that located the split with Paul, Dunn ultimately settles on the year 135 (p. 238); and then collapses his own point by opining that Jesus, in rejecting distinctions between the righteous and sinners, thereby implicitly rejected the social and ethnic boundary between Jews and Gentiles, on which the vast majority of his co-

The historiography on this issue is now changing. Some scholars currently look much later – to Constantine, perhaps, or to Theodosius – to locate this famous split. That we even ask this question at all, however, is an oblique admission of failure. It gives the measure of the degree to which the concerns of ancient Christian orthodox writers, specifically as manifest in the *contra Iudaeos* tradition, continue to determine the line of approach taken by modern historians. From the vocabulary that we necessarily use to the texts that dominate our investigations[2] to the questions that frame our approaches to the presuppositions that shape our reconstructions, we still work within the terms dictated by history's "winners," those men who successfully finessed their churches' transition to a form of Roman imperial culture, who named their ideological and institutional forebears, and who shaped the canon, both scriptural and patristic.

How can *we* think outside *their* box? How can we come to a less anachronistic, less doctrinally determined view of the past? The short answer is also the obvious one: we need to work contextually. The analytical context of our enquiry coincides with the social context of our ancient subjects, namely, the Mediterranean city. To get some critical

---

religionists insisted (p. 248f). Second Temple Judaism, in brief, could not accommodate the radical inclusiveness of Jesus' message. The Jesus of many prominent "Third-Questers" rejects kashrut, purity rules, Temple offerings, and Jewish "nationalism," thereby functioning as a particular sort of displaced post-second-century Gentile Christian *malgré lui*; see P. Fredriksen, *From Jesus to Christ*, 2nd edition (New Haven: Yale UP, 2000), xxiv–xxviii; eadem, "What You See is What You Get: Context and Content in Current Work on the Historical Jesus," *Theology Today* 52 (1995): 75–97. Locating the "split" with Jesus or Paul, in what is arguably a pre-"Christian" phase of the movement, in part rests on misconstruing the normative coincidence of ethnicity and what we think of as "religion" in antiquity, about which I will say more above. Against reading Paul as breaking from Judaism in any meaningful way, see esp. S. Stowers, *A Rereading of Romans* (New Haven: Yale UP, 1994).

[2] Archaeological, papyrological, epigraphical, and even numismatic data have salubriously confused the tidy picture available from literary evidence alone. See, e.g., on Jews and Christians, L. Rutgers, *The Hidden Heritage of Diaspora Judaism* (Leuven: Peeters, 1998); idem, *The Jews of Late Antique Rome* (Leiden: Brill, n.d.); on Jews and pagan Gentiles, J. Reynolds and R. Tannenbaum, *Jews and Godfearers at Aphrodisias* (Cambridge: Cambridge Philological Society, 1987); E. Gruen, *Heritage and Hellenism* (Berkeley: U. of California Press, 1998); idem, *Diaspora* (Cambridge: Harvard UP, 2002); L. Levine, *The Ancient Synagogue* (New Haven: Yale UP, 2000); on Jews, pagans and Christians, R. Lane Fox, *Pagans and Christians* (New York: Knopf, 1986); S. Schwartz, *Imperialism and Jewish Society, 200 BCE to 640 CE* (Princeton: Princeton UP, 2001); G. W. Bowersock, "Polytheism and Monotheism in Arabia and the Three Palestines," *Dumbarton Oaks Papers* 51 (1997): 1–10; F. Millar, "The Jews of the Graeco-Roman Diaspora between Paganism and Christianity, AD 312–438," in *The Jews among Pagans and Christians*, ed. J. Lieu, J. North, and T. Rajak (London: Routledge, 1992), 97–123.

purchase on the ancient literature (and on its unfortunate ideological afterlife in some modern scholarly discussions), we need to re-incarnate the charged rhetoric of the *contra Iudaeos* tradition within the lived human context of ancient civic life.

The historical origins of the formal *contra Iudaeos* tradition seem to lie in the earlier half of the second century.[3] Its matrix was the intra-Christian disputes of educated, formerly pagan intellectuals. In their effort to make sense of the premier literary medium of Christian revelation, the Septuagint, these Gentile contestants shaped the potent and long-lived hermeneutical idea of the "Jew" – fleshly, hard-hearted, philosophically dim, and violently anti-Christian.[4] As a theological abstraction, this idea had great power, serving by means of the absolute contrast that it constructed between "Jews" and (true or correct) "Christians" to focus and define the desiderata of orthodox identity.[5] This rhetoric of invidious contrast that cast Jews as the Christian anti-type par excellence accordingly came to shape many different sorts of proto-orthodox and orthodox literature: apologies, sermons, heresiological

---

[3] By "formal" I mean an intellectually coherent, coordinate body of polemical and hermeneutical practices. Earlier, retrospectively Christian documents such as Paul's letters and the gospels actually target other Jews, whether Christian or not. Internal targets: false prophets (Mt 7:15–23); false insiders (2 Cor 11:4–5; Gal 2:4 and passim; Phil 3:2). The polemic against other Jews outside of this movement – scribes, Pharisees, Sadducees, and (especially in the Passion narratives) the Jerusalem priests – lies scattered throughout the gospels.

[4] Any number of fine studies of the hermeneutical Jew as a generative element of patristic theology now exist. I have found especially useful the essays collected in Ora Limor and G. G. Stroumsa, eds., *Contra Iudaeos: Ancient and Medieval Polemics between Christians and Jews* (Tübingen: Mohr Siebeck, 1996) and G. N. Stanton and G. G. Stroumsa, eds., *Tolerance and Intolerance in Early Judaism and Christianity* (Cambridge: Cambridge UP, 1998), and the study by J. Lieu, *Image and Reality: The Jews in the World of the Christians in the Second Century* (Edinburgh: T&T Clark, 1996). D. Efroymson analyzed the function of anti-Jewish rhetoric within proto-orthodox, specifically anti-Marcionite polemic in "The Patristic Connection" in *Antisemitism and the Foundations of Christianity*, ed. A. Davies (New York: Paulist, 1979), 98–117. See further Fredriksen and Irshai, "Christian Anti-Judaism," part 1: "The Second-Century Seedbed: Theology, Identity, and Anti-Judaism."

[5] The proto-orthodox do not have the monopoly on such a construction. Both Valentinus and Marcion understood the god of the LXX – a lower kosmokrator identified with the god of Israel (some pagans, too, held this idea) – as Christ's (and thus the high god's) cosmic opposition. They also, accordingly, used "Jews" and "Judaism" as tropes for unenlightened – indeed, drastically mistaken – scriptural communities. But this negative stereotype of the Jew becomes a hallmark particularly of orthodox tradition, which eventually had (and continues to have) an enormous impact on subsequent Western culture. In the current essay, it is this latter community whom I keep especially in view.

tracts,[6] scriptural florilegia, commentaries, histories and historical
fictions, martyr stories, conciliar canons, and eventually, should we chose
to look at them this way, the legal compendia of the later empire, the
*Codex Theodosianus* and *Justinianus*.[7] My question to this body of
writing is simple: what relation does its rhetoric have to (social) reality?

I propose to proceed by looking at some of these writings within their
native social and cultural urban setting. I organize my initial survey
around three issues, often invoked as contributory to the formation of
Christian anti-Judaism, that presuppose clear and principled distinctions,
social and religious, between ancient Jews and their non-Jewish
contemporaries: (1) pagan views on Jews and Judaism, (2) putative
Jewish missions to Gentiles, and (3) pagan and Jewish persecution of
(Gentile) Christians. My conclusion will argue what I hope my prior
presentation will have demonstrated, namely, that to conceptualize
relations between ancient Jews and Christians in terms of a "Parting of
the Ways" is to misconstrue the social and intellectual history of Judaism,
of Christianity, and of majority Mediterranean culture at least up through
the seventh century, and possibly beyond.


## Gentiles on Jews and Judaism

The high-contrast orthodox construct of "Jews" versus "us," besides
affecting historical work on ancient Jews and Christians, has also affected
the historiography on Jews and Gentiles more broadly conceived.
Historians gathering comments by ancient non-Christian Greeks and
Romans have often distinguished these remarks as "pro-Jewish" or "anti-
Jewish," with "anti-Jewish" occasionally characterized as "anti-Semitic."[8]
A similar supposed clarity marks the categorization of ancient Jewish
populations, imagined as "assimilated" or "Hellenized" versus (Jewishly)

---

[6] Thus Tertullian characterizes Marcion as "Jewish" (*adv. Marcionem* III passim);
Origen, the *simpliciores* of his own community who understand apocalyptic passages of
scripture in a millenarian, "fleshly" way (*de Principiis* II.xi,2); Ambrose, his
ecclesiastical opposition (*Ep. Extra coll.* 5 [11].3; Augustine, his (e.g., the Pelagians,
conjured briefly in *ep.* 196,1), and so on (and on). That the word "Jew" could convey
such opprobrium within learned, purely Gentile Christian disputes reveals the degree to
which its meaning became usefully, intrinsically, emphatically negative.

[7] Two invaluable compendia for this material, on which I rely here: A. Linder, *The
Jews in Roman Imperial Legislation* (Detroit: Wayne State UP, 1987); idem, *The Jews
in the Legal Sources of the Early Middle Ages* (Detroit: Wayne State UP, 1997).

[8] Against such an approach as in principle "conceptually flawed," see Gruen,
*Hellenism*, 42–72 and passim.

"orthodox."[9] Actions advocated or taken against ancient Jewish individuals or communities are seen as a species of "religious persecution." And occasionally, their differences notwithstanding, pagan anti-Judaism (granting the construct, for the moment) serves as some sort of explanatory prelude to, or preparation for, later Christian genres.[10] Common to all these modes of thinking is a presumption that something about Jews and Judaism made them in some special way egregious in the ancient context and that this egregiousness accounts for negative remarks by ancient pagans, as well as for the inevitable split (howsoever identified and dated) between "Christians" (conceived primarily as Gentiles) and Jews.

A few general comments about ancient people and ancient religion, before I proceed to consider pagan remarks about Jews. First: in antiquity, gods were local in a dual sense. They attached to particular *places*, whether natural (groves, grottos, mountains, springs) or man-made (temples and altars, urban or rural).[11] And gods also attached to particular *peoples*; "religion" ran in the blood. In this sense, one's *genos* was as much a cult-designation as what we, from a sociological or anthropological perspective, see as an "ethnic" one: ethnicity expressed "religion" (acknowledging the anachronism of both terms for our period), and religion expressed "ethnicity."[12] This generalization holds from the micro-level of domestic deities and ancestors protecting and defining the individual household through the mid-level "family" connections between gods and cities to the macro-level confederations of kingdoms and

---

[9] Against which, J. Barclay, *Jews in the Mediterranean Diaspora from Alexander to Trajan (323 BCE–117 CE)* (Berkeley: U. of California Press, 1996), 82–102.

[10] This material is collected in Menachem Stern, *Greek and Latin Authors on Jews and Judaism*, 3 vols. (Jerusalem: Israel Academy/Dorot, 1974–84). On ancient Jewish populations as "assimilated" or "orthodox," and on pagan anti-Jewish "bigotry," e.g., L. Feldman, *Jew and Gentile in the Ancient World* (Princeton: Princeton UP, 1993); cf. Rutgers, *Hidden Heritage*, 199–234; Barclay, *Jews*, 92–98 and passim. J. Gager, *The Origins of Anti-Semitism* (New York: Oxford UP, 1983) sees pagan and Christian "anti-Semitism" as different in kind. The characterization of pagan–Jewish eruptions as evidence of pagan "anti-Semitism" is questioned both by P. Schäfer, *Judeophobia: Attitudes toward the Jews in the Ancient World* (Cambridge: Harvard UP, 1997), esp. 1–11 and 197–211, and by Gruen, *Diaspora*, esp. 54–83 on the tendency of some scholars to see Gentile Alexandrian actions against Jewish Alexandrians in the tumult of 38–40 CE as "anti-Semitic."

[11] A lively recount of this phenomenon: Lane Fox, *Pagans and Christians*, 11–261.

[12] See the essays assembled in *Ancient Perceptions of Greek Ethnicity*, ed. I. Malkin (Washington, D.C.: Center for Hellenic Studies, 2001), many of which draw attention to Herodotus, *Histories* 8.144.2–3 (where Herodotus speaks of "Greekness" in terms of common blood, gods, cult, and customs). For the ways that political alliances within this culture naturally affected gods and kinship, see C. P. Jones, *Kinship Diplomacy in the Ancient World* (Cambridge: Harvard UP, 1999), esp. ch. 6 on Lycians and Jews.

empires, which added other gods as well as rulers, living and dead, to the pantheon.[13]

The very varied embeddedness of the divine in antiquity means that, in an age of empire, gods bumped up against each other with some frequency, even as their humans did. The greater internal peace and stability permitted by out-sized political units facilitated interior migrations of peoples, and when people traveled, their gods went with them. Also, since different peoples had different gods – as well as different ancestral practices and traditions for honoring their gods and maintaining their people's relationship with them – the larger the political unit, the greater the plurality of gods. In other words, ancient empires did not "practice religious tolerance"; they presupposed religious difference. Put differently: a mark of a successful empire (the subordination of many different peoples to a larger government) was the variety of gods it encompassed (since many peoples meant, naturally, many gods) and accordingly the range of traditional religious practices it accommodated.

Hellenistic and Roman ethnographers and historians commented upon Jewish practices, Jewish people, and the Jewish god. Some of their comments are admiring, others hostile. The positive ones tend to echo what pagans valued about their own culture. Thus, Jews are loyal to their *patria nomima*, as indeed each people should be.[14] They not only keep their traditional rites but know the reasons for them.[15] Further, they are a philosophical people, acknowledging the highest god *sola mente*, without images.[16] Numenius' oft-cited sound-byte sums up this theme tidily,

---

[13] Recent work on gods and families: A. E. Hanson, "The Roman Family," in *Life, Death and Entertainment in the Roman Empire*, ed. D. S. Potter and D. J. Mattingly (Ann Arbor: U. of Michigan Press, 1999), 19–66; on gods and cities, the essays in R. Buxton, ed., *Oxford Readings in Greek Religion* (Oxford: Oxford UP, 2000); on gods, rulers who become gods, and larger political units, S. R. F. Price, *Rituals and Power: The Roman Imperial Cult in Asia Minor* (Cambridge: Cambridge UP, 1984); on civic and imperial piety and the way that it combined especially with athletics and other dedicated competitions, D. S. Potter, "Entertainers in the Roman Empire," in *Life, Death and Entertainment*, 256–325.

[14] E.g., Celsus *apud* Origen, *c. Celsum* 5.2.41 (Jews keep *ton idion nomon*), said while complaining that "others" (that is, non-Jews) abandon their own traditions to adopt Jewish ones; similarly Porphyry, *de abstentia* 4.11 (Jews' obedience to their *nomima*). The story of Plutarch, incubating in the temple of Asclepius, who challenged the god's suggestion that he cure his illness by eating pork, makes the larger point, while alluding to Jewish custom in particular: pagans and their gods respected *patria*, *vita Isidori* (Stern, *Greek and Latin Authors*, vol. 2, no. 549).

[15] Seneca the Younger *apud* Augustine, *de civitate dei* 6.11.

[16] Tacitus, *Historia* 5.5.4, comparing Jewish aniconism, arrived at through the exercise of the mind – two philosophical attributes – with messy Egyptian religion. Tacitus in general is no enthusiast of Jewish virtues. For the broader pagan perception

touching on the prestigious characteristics of wisdom, philosophy, and antiquity: Plato was just an Attic-speaking Moses.[17]

Yet comments on Jewish *amixia* and *deisidaimonia,* on the Jews' *misoxenos bios* and *hostile odium,* likewise abound. Pagans in this connection indict Jewish ancestral practices as the reason for the Jews' odious behaviors and beliefs. Circumcision – a practice viewed with repugnance by majority culture – provided satirists with unending opportunities. The Jews' cultic exclusivism – their general and principled non-involvement with civic and imperial cult – irritated some observers and prompted accusations of impiety and atheism. Worse: In secret rites, claimed some, Jews practiced human sacrifice and even cannibalism. They were lazy (particularly one day out of every seven). Endlessly particular about food, they were sexually profligate. And so on.[18]

Putting insults to Jews within the broader context of insults against ethnic outsiders more generally conceived, historians now incline to interpret this evidence less as ancient anti-Semitism than as ruling-class xenophobia. Egyptians, Scythians, Gauls, Britons, Germans – all came in for similar abuse, because each (like the Jews) had their own ethnic customs which marked them, eo ipso, as un-Roman.[19] Perhaps then the term "xenophobia" also misses the mark; these writers were not fearful of foreigners, only scornful of them. Ruling-class contempt indexes patriotic pride: *our* ways are better than *their* ways, the identity of "them" shifting as needed. Hence too the occasional praise of Jewish loyalty to the *patria ēthē*: Romans (and Hellenes) especially valued that particular virtue too.

The premium placed on ethnic loyalty is also what stands behind the special vituperation occasionally heaped upon not Judaism per se, but on "Judaizing" and, *encore pire,* actual conversion.[20] Adherence to a variety of religious customs was compatible with the sensibility of Mediterranean paganism, which at a practical level was extremely capacious. And the

---

of Jews as a nation of philosophers, infra Schäfer, *Judeophobia*; Gager, *Anti-Semitism*; Feldman, *Jew and Gentile*, 201–32.

[17] *Ti gar esti Platōn ē Mōusēs attikizōn*; apud Clement, *Stromateis* 1.22.150:4; Stern, *Greek and Latin Authors,* vol. 2, no. 363a.

[18] Insults collected, organized, and analyzed in Schäfer, *Judeophobia*; see also Feldman, *Jew and Gentile*, 107–122 (popular prejudice), 123–176 (erudite prejudice). To be fair, Hellenistic Jews made similarly insulting remarks about Hellenistic Gentiles, using them as a "constructed Other" to think with in their own projects of self-definition (i.e., famously, Paul in Rom 1:18–32); see, most recently, Gruen, *Diaspora*, 213–31.

[19] In this connection, Schäfer specifies Tacitus' demeaning comments on Druids (*Hist.* 2.78), Gauls and Britons (4.54; cf. *Annales* 15.30, on human sacrifice), Germans (*Hist.* 4.61; *Germania* 39, on human sacrifice), and Egyptians (*Hist.* 1.11); *Judeophobia*, 187.

[20] By "Judaizing" I mean the voluntary and discretionary adoption of Jewish practices by Gentiles.

idiosyncrasy of any religious culture (special days, special foods, special gods, special rules) was what marked it as specific to a particular people. Seen in this light, the phenomenon of Gentiles' voluntary Judaizing – for which we have evidence in abundance, both well before and well after the development of Christianity – was unremarkable: Gentiles voluntarily assumed whatever foreign practices they wanted (as Juvenal, grumbling about the Orontes, famously complained). But making an *exclusive* commitment to a foreign god to the point of forsaking the gods of one's own people – a condition of conversion unique to Judaism in the pre-Christian period – could be perceived as an act of alarming disloyalty.[21] The prime pagan objection to "God-fearing" (that is, voluntary Judaizing) was not the particular Jewish practices themselves so much as the possibility that they could lead to conversion. And the problem with conversion to *Judaism*[22] was the principled renunciation of all other cult. Though Jewish cultic exclusivism offended, it was also, for Jews, for the most part, accepted, because it met majority culture's twin measure of legal and social respectability, namely, ethnicity and antiquity. But in the convert's case, this exclusivism – voluntary, not customary; adopted, not inherited; foreign, not native – was tantamount to cultural treason. It insulted the "family" (the blood/birth connection of *genos* or *natio*) and placed it at risk (since gods, when disregarded, grew angry).[23]

Despite these tensions, some pagans also evidently favored Jews with the ultimate accolade of intellectual culture: the Jews were a nation of philosophers.[24] Hellenistic Jews not only preserved such comments, but

---

[21] Hence Dio's remarks on Gentile converts who affect *ta nomima autōn* (scil. the Jews), worship a single deity, and do not honor the other gods in *Historia Romana* 37.15.1–2; and, perhaps, Domitian's fury in condemning members of the Roman ruling class for "atheism" and for assuming the *ēthē tōn Ioudaiōn* in 67.14.1–2: conversion is a species of treason.

[22] The point of A. D. Nock's famous and important distinction between "adherence" and "conversion": Judaism and, eventually (and, for contemporaries, confusingly), Christianity were the only two communities in antiquity that admitted of this particular form of voluntary allegiance; *Conversion: The Old and the New in Religion from Alexander the Great to Augustine of Hippo* (New York: Oxford UP, 1961). Since Jews were an ancient *ethnos*, conversion could be understood on the ready analogy of political alliances (joining the *politeia*, e.g., Philo, *de leg. spec.* 4.34.178); see S. J. D. Cohen, *The Beginnings of Jewishness* (Berkeley: U. of California Press, 1999), 125–39, 156–74.

[23] Schäfer, *Judeophobia*, 98, 180–95. Juvenal accuses Roman converts of *Romanas ... contemnere leges/ Iudaicum ediscunt et servant ac metuunt ius* (*Sat.* 14.100f.); Tacitus, of having renounced the *religionibus patriis*, disowning their own gods, country and family (*Hist.* 5.1–2).

[24] The roll-call of such pagans – Theophrastus, Megasthenes, Clearchus of Soli, Hermippus of Smyrna, Ocellus of Lucanus – is sounded in virtually all treatments of

indeed occasionally composed them. In learned forgeries, pagan sibyls hymned Jewish superiority to pagan cult in proper Homeric hexameters; historical fictions recounted pagan kings in quest of Jewish wisdom; literary lions of the classical curriculum – Aeschylus, Sophocles, Euripides – as well as minor comic writers "produced" Judaizing verses, in effect attributing the fundamental aspects of philosophical *paideia* to Jewish virtue, Jewish brains, or the Jewish god.[25] Scholars envisage different intended audiences for this literature, some arguing that it evinces efforts at Jewish "outreach," missionizing to pagan salon-culture, others that such products were for internal consumption.[26] Since I think, and will momentarily argue, that the idea of Jewish missions to Gentiles to convert them to Judaism has been one of the biggest historiographical mistakes of the past century, I incline to the latter position. This is not to say that interested Gentiles may not have picked up and read – or at least heard – such apologetic traditions. Indeed, authentic pagan acclamations of Jewish philosophical achievement may perhaps measure the penetration of such apology.

But I wish to draw attention here to a different point, namely, that such positive assessments of Jewish culture in pagan intellectual terms – be their authors genuine pagans, Jews under false colors, or educated Hellenistic Jews *tout court* – complicates our evaluation of the hostile accusations of Jewish *amixia* in interesting ways. This Jewish control of and commitment to the authors, traditions, and values of gymnasium education restates in a literary key what we know as well from inscriptions, archaeology, and ancient historical writings: Jews lived, and lived thoroughly, in their cities of residence throughout the Diaspora.[27]

---

Hellenistic Judaism; where fragments exist, Stern gives them. See too M. Hengel, *Judaism and Hellenism* (Philadelphia: Fortress, 1974), 1:255–67 and 2:169–77 (notes).

[25] On the "Jewish" sibyllines, see Goodman's discussion in E. Schürer, G. Vermes, et al., *The History of the Jewish People in the Age of Jesus Christ* (Edinburgh: T&T Clark, 1986), 3:618–54; on other such pseudonymous Jewish productions, see pp. 3:654–700. See too the lively appreciations of such "brazen inventiveness" in Gruen, *Diaspora*, 213–31; for analysis, Barclay, *Jews*, 82–102 (terms); 125–230 (texts).

[26] Recent statements: Feldman sees this literature as evidence of missionary effort (*Jew and Gentile*, 305–24); M. Goodman does not (*Mission and Conversion* [Oxford: Clarendon, 1994], 78ff); so too Gruen (*Hellenism,* 221ff; idem, *Diaspora*, 135–231). On the extremely limited social scope of such *salon*-culture productions, and the way that militates against seeing them as "missionary," P. Fredriksen, "Judaism, the Circumcision of Gentiles, and Apocalyptic Hope: Another Look at Galatians 1–2," *JTS* 42 (1991): 533–64, at p. 538.

[27] So too, from a different angle, R. S. Bloch, who notes that neither Tacitus nor other ancient authors refer to Jews as "barbarians," despite being perfectly aware of their distinctive (that is, non-Roman or non-Greek) ethnic identity: Jews were too integrated to be "other" in this way. *Antike Vorstellungen vom Judentum. Der*

Since ancient cities were religious institutions, participation in civic life was itself a form of worship.[28] The workings of government and law, the process of education, the public experience of art and culture in various theatrical, musical, and athletic competitions – all these activities, which we think of as secular and thus religiously neutral, were in fact embedded in the traditional worship of the gods. The gods looked after the city, and the city's residents, to ensure its well-being, looked after the gods. Processions, hymns, libations, blood offerings, communal dancing, and drinking and eating – all these public forms of worship expressed and created bonds that bound citizens together and, by establishing or maintaining the necessary relations with powerful numinous patrons (both imperial and celestial), contributed to the common weal.

Jewish names inscribed as ephebes or members of town councils, Jewish officers in Gentile armies, Jewish Hellenistic literati, Jewish contestants in, patrons of, or observers at athletic, dramatic or musical events (such as Philo and, probably, Paul) – all these give the measure of Jewish participation in pagan worship.[29] Sometimes the wheel squeaks (usually at the point of actual *latreia*: Jews notoriously avoided overt public cult, though essayed to compensate variously through dedications, patronage and prayer); sometimes it doesn't (Jews attended theatrical and athletic events, got good gymnasium educations where they could, joined Gentile armies, and lived public lives as municipal leaders). Acknowledging other gods did not eo ipso entail apostasy; living

---

*Judenexkurs des Tacitus im Rahmen der griechisch-römischen Ethnographie* (Stuttgart: Franz Steiner Verlag, 2002), ch. 4.

[28] A lively description, with comments on how this fact made life complicated for Christians, can be found in H. A. Drake, *Constantine and the Bishops* (Baltimore: Johns Hopkins, 2000), 88–93. (Drake curiously does not include Jews in his musings.)

[29] Primary evidence from the Diaspora is collected and surveyed by F. Millar in Schürer, Vermes, et al., *History of the Jewish People*, 3:1–149; see too Gruen, *Diaspora*, esp. 105–32.

There is no good word for characterizing the Jewish presence in such majority-culture activities. "Worship" underscores the intrinsically religious nature of these activities, but it too readily (and naturally) conjures the term and religious practice that it customarily translates, *latreia*: Worship *as* sacrifice was precisely where ancient Jews generally seem to have – and were thought to have – drawn the line. Christian encounters with the imperial cult present similar ambiguities. Before Constantine, the principled point of resistance or nonconformity seems to have focused on blood sacrifice; after, though all else remained – adoration of the imperial image, incense (a ritual indicator of divine presence or *numen*), priesthoods, feast days, and even the gladiatorial combats – the blood offerings went. At that point, Christians could and did "worship" the emperor. I thank Erich Gruen for helping me fret over this term; we came to no happier terminological proposal, but did see more clearly the problems with this one.

Jewishly did not require isolationism. Ancient Jews, as ancients generally, lived in a world congested with gods, and they knew it.

Hence the dangers of modern constructions of "monotheism" or "religious orthodoxy" when interpreting evidence from ancient Mediterranean monotheists, be these pagan, Jewish, or eventually Christian. In antiquity, the high god stood at the extreme pinnacle of a gradient; he or it was not the austere metaphysical punctilio of modern monotheistic imagination. Worshiping "one god" or "the highest god" or only "our god" did not mean that one doubted the existence of other gods, only that one construed one's obligations to them differently. Moschos son of Moschion, prompted (sometime in the first half of the third century BCE) by two local deities in a dream to manumit his slave, left an inscription attesting to his obedience in their temple. Was this a "defection to paganism or syncretism"? Millar thinks yes; Moschos, from his own perspective, considers and identifies himself simply as *Ioudaios.*[30] Showing respect to a god, by way of obeying a direct command, unquestionably demonstrates common sense; but is this "worship" in the way that Moschos worshiped his own ancestral god? I can only guess, but I would guess not.

To chide ancient Jews for not construing their monotheism in ways that conform to modern constructs – or to standards of rabbinical behaviors eventually enunciated in *Avodah Zarah* – cannot help us to understand them. Herod the Great – so notoriously fussy about food laws (not to mention filial piety) that jokes were made about him, so fastidious in interpreting purity laws that he had *cohanim* trained as masons for the interior sections of his gloriously refurbished Temple in Jerusalem, so personally concerned with purity status that he outfitted his villas with *mikvaot* – also bankrolled pagan temples and prestigious athletic competitions. Does that make him "assimilated"?[31] Was Artapanus – who

---

[30] Millar gives the text of this inscription in Schürer, Vermes, et al., *History of the Jewish People*, 3:65, and judges its religious orientation on p. 138.

[31] On Augustus' reputed play on ὕς/υἱός, see Macrobius, *Saturnalia* II.4:11; on the mason-priests, Josephus, *AJ* 15.11.5–6; on the archaeological evidence for *mikvaot* in Herodian palaces, E. P. Sanders, *Judaism: Practice and Belief* (Philadelphia: Trinity, 1992); on his building-program of pagan (especially imperial) temples, see the copious references and discussion in Schürer, Vermes, et al., *History of the Jewish People*, 1:304–11; on sponsorship specifically of the (dedicated) Olympic games, Josephus, *AJ* 16.5.3; *BJ* 1.21.12. Schürer-Vermes judges "Herod's Judaism ... very superficial" (1:311); Herod and his family were "far removed from Judaism in observance," according to Feldman, *Jew and Gentile*, 157 (a curious judgment in light of the point Feldman ties it to, namely, that Herod insisted that the Arab suitor of his sister Salome first be circumcised [*AJ* 16.7.6]). For an altogether more appreciative, even sympathetic view, see P. Richardson, *Herod: King of the Jews and Friend of the Romans* (Columbia: U. of South Carolina Press, 1996).

proudly credited biblical heroes as fonts of pagan learning, cult and culture – a "syncretist"?[32] What then of the translators of the Septuagint, who altered the prohibition in Ex 22:27 (LXX Ex 22:28) from not reviling "God" (אלהים לא תקלל) to not reviling "the gods" (θεοὺς οὐ κακολογήσεις)? What about those Jews who close pious inscriptions to their god by calling, in routine formulae, on the witness of sky, earth and sun: Zeus, Gē, Helios?[33]

Few ancient monotheists disputed the existence and the powers of other gods; they simply directed their worship particularly toward their own god. Put differently: no ancient monotheist was like a modern monotheist, because the ancient cosmos was imagined differently from the modern, post-Renaissance, disenchanted cosmos. Put a third way: all ancient monotheists were (by modern measure) polytheists.[34] For many Jews and, eventually, for various sorts of Christians, the etiquette for dealing with these other deities and their humans – which for Mediterranean culture meant showing, and being seen to show, appropriate degrees of respect – was necessarily improvised, and it varied across class lines, communities, and historical epochs. (Jews, for example, were always and everywhere exempt from imperial cult, whereas emperor worship, complete with priests, liturgies, gladiatorial contests, incense, adoration of the imperial image – but no blood offerings – continued well after Constantine, who was honored in his eponymous capital as late as the fifth century as ὡς θεός.)[35] Pagan

---

[32] Artapanus, claims Feldman, can scarcely have been "an observant Jew," and on the basis of Artapanus' claims (preserved *apud* Eusebius, *Praeparatio Evangelica* 9.23.4 and 9.27.4, 9, 12) that Joseph established Egyptian temples and that Moses taught music to Orpheus and zoolatry to the Egyptians, he opines that Artapanus was more likely a Gentile (*Jew and Gentile,* 208); cf. Barclay, *Jews,* 127–32 ("a proud Egyptian and a self-conscious Jew"); against such anachronistic assignments of "orthodoxy" and "deviance," pp. 83–102; see also Gruen, *Hellenism,* 87–89.

[33] Manumission inscriptions from the Bosphorus, J.-B. Frey, *Corpus Inscriptionum Judiciarum,* 2 volumes (Rome: Pontificio Istituto di Archeologia Cristiana, 1936–52; repr. New York: Ktav, 1975), vol. 1, nos. 683, 684, 690; comments and literature cited in Levine, *Synagogue,* 114 and notes.

[34] For the ways that ancient metaphysics and astronomical science determined concepts of cosmic intermediation (including Christological ones) – and the ways that modern science has complicated the enterprise – see my essay, "What does Jesus have to do with Christ? What does Knowledge have to do with Faith? What does History have to do with Theology?" in *Christology: Yesterday, Today and Tomorrow* (Maryknoll, NY: Orbis, forthcoming 2003).

[35] Caligula famously resented this Jewish exemption (Philo, *Legatio* 349–67), which continued into the Christian phase of the cult. See esp. G. Bowersock, "The Imperial Cult: Perceptions and Persistence," in *Jewish and Christian Self-Definition,* vol. 3, ed. B. F. Meyer and E. P. Sanders (Philadelphia: Fortress, 1982), 171–82; idem, "Polytheism," whence the reference, p. 7, to Constantine in Philostorgius, *Hist. Eccl. GCS* (1972), 28. By the third century CE, Jewish exemption from public cult was so

monotheists, free of the constraints (howsoever interpreted) that bound biblical communities, had it a little easier.[36]

What relation can we posit, then, between pagan comments about Jews and Judaism and the later, specifically Gentile Christian *contra Iudaeos* traditions? Superficial similarities (such as insulting characterizations of Jews and Jewish customs) should not obscure their basic differences. For some pagans, Jewish exclusivism in particular is what offended; for Christians, such exclusivism, which they shared, could only be admired.[37] Further, pagans, no matter how repugnant Judaism might seem to them, maintained that it befitted Jews,[38] whereas most orthodox Christian thinkers (Augustine excepted[39]) held that Judaism in general and Jewish practice in particular had always and everywhere been religiously wrong, period. Pagan "anti-Judaism," in sum, seems simply an occasional subspecies of a more general contempt for foreign customs and the obverse expression of Graeco-Roman patriotic pride. Converts, not "native" Jews, stimulated the greatest hostility.

By comparison, while Gentile Christian writers might avail themselves of themes first sounded by Gentile pagan counterparts, their negative critique was minutely developed and sweepingly comprehensive, their condemnation broader and more profound, their hostile characterization essential to their own view of themselves. And their ideological ideal of total separation – Christians should not even socialize with Jews, much

---

well established that emperors, attempting to recruit Jews into onerous service in civic *curiae,* stipulated that nothing religiously offensive to them could be requisite to executing the office, and they explicitly excused Jews from emperor-worship; *Digesta Iustiniani* 50.2.3.3, text with comments in Linder, *Imperial Legislation*, 103–7.

[36] See esp. the rich essay by S. Mitchell, "The Cult of Theos Hypsistos between Pagans, Jews, and Christians," in *Pagan Monotheism*, ed. P. Athanassiadi and M. Frede (Oxford: Clarendon, 1999), 81–148.

[37] The insistence, in Christian anti-Jewish writings, that Jews were perennially inclined toward idolatry means that the principle of exclusive worship was itself admired. Origen, *c. Cel.* IV:31, Jews never made images, nor worshiped heaven (the prohibition against which Origen deems "impressive and magnificent"); by hearing the Law on the Sabbath in the synagogue, the entire nation "studied philosophy"; V:7–9 praising Jewish aniconic worship, not to be confused with the worship of heavenly entities; V:43 "The philosophers in spite of their impressive philosophical teachings fall down to idols and daemons, while even the lowest Jew looks only to the supreme God." Augustine, *c. Faust.* 12:13, "It is a most notable fact that all the nations subjugated by Rome adopted the heathenish ceremonies of Roman worship; while the Jewish nation ... has never lost the sign of their law."

[38] E.g., Celsus *apud* Origen, *c. Cel.* V:25–26. More subtly, the insults make the same point: people like this deserve a cult like this.

[39] On Augustine's continuity with, and radical revision of, the traditional anti-Judaism of his church, see P. Fredriksen, "Augustine and Israel: *Interpretatio ad litteram*, Jews, and Judaism in Augustine's Theology of History," *Studio Patristica* 35 (2001): 119–35.

less co-celebrate with them, much less adapt some Jewish customs (actual conversion was utterly, so to speak, beyond the Pale) – contrasted sharply with quotidian reality: Jews continued to be visibly, vigorously integrated in Mediterranean civic life; and Gentiles, whether within the church or without, continued to be drawn to the synagogue. In short, continuing Jewish–Gentile intimacy – which is to say, continuing Mediterranean civic life – itself fostered and amplified the stridency of orthodox rhetoric.

What more can we say about this intimacy, and these patterns of city life?

## Jews, Gentiles, and "Missions"

In the baths and in the schools, in the courts and in the curiae, in theatres, amphitheatres, and hippodromes – where there were Greeks (and, later, Romans) there were Jews.[40] But Jews in the Diaspora had another form of communal life that structured their time and their activities: Jews had the synagogue. A huge body of varied evidence – literary, epigraphical, archaeological – attests to the ubiquity and vitality of this peculiarly Jewish institution, remnants of which have been recovered in settlements stretching from Italy to Syria, from the Black Sea to North Africa. *Synagōgē* might designate the assembly of the local Jewish community itself; *proseuchē* certainly implies an actual building.[41] While no uniform pattern of organization can be teased from the historical record such as it is, certain common activities seem clearly attested. Synagogues served as a type of ethnic reading-house, where Jews could assemble one day out of every seven to hear instruction in their ancestral laws. Pagan rulers granted to some communities the right of asylum. Synagogues sponsored communal fasts, feasts and celebrations; they served as a community archive and as a collecting point for funds to be sent on to the Temple in Jerusalem. They settled issues of community interest – announcing the calendar of festivals, negotiating access to appropriate foodstuffs, adjudicating disputes – and served, as did local pagan temples, as places to enact and record the manumission of slaves. They housed schools, political assemblies, and tribunals. They had officers (women as well as

---

[40] Literary attestation of widespread presence of Jews throughout the Mediterranean, e.g., Strabo apud Josephus, *AJ* 14.114–115; 1 Macc 15:22–23; Acts 2:5–11. Archaeological evidence confirms this, on which see esp. Levine, *Synagogue.*

[41] Other terms for Jewish associations, also adapted from surrounding culture (from where else would Greek-speaking Jews get them?) include *politeuma, collegia, synodos, koinon, thiasos, communitas.* See discussion in Levine, *Synagogue,* 121ff.

men), administrators, and steering committees. They sponsored fund drives; they honored conspicuous philanthropy with public inscriptions.[42]

These donor inscriptions, taken together with our scattered literary evidence, reveal another important datum about Jewish life in the ancient city. Where there was a Jewish community, there was (always? usually?) a synagogue; where there was a synagogue, there were (always? often?) Gentiles, pagan as well as, eventually, Christian. Who were these people? What were they doing there? *How* had they gotten there?

One answer, extremely prominent since the mid-twentieth century, has been that Jews mounted missions to Gentiles to encourage them to convert to Judaism.[43] This explanation has been invoked to account for (1) phenomena as huge and as sweeping as supposed surges in the ancient Jewish population across half a millennium (Where did all these Jews come from? Too many to have been born, they therefore must have been made);[44] (2) phenomena as ubiquitous and highly-charged as the *contra Iudaeos* traditions themselves (Whence all this vituperation? It must be the verbal and psychological run-off from tight competition for the limited Gentile market);[45] and (3) phenomena as minute and incidental as two sentences in the New Testament (Whence Matthew's remarks on

---

[42] Exhaustively: Levine, *Synagogue*; see also Gruen, *Diaspora*, 105–32. Millar points out that, at least in the fourth century in Rome, a synagogue could function as a sort of lending library; see Jerome, *Ep.* 36.1 ("Jews of the Graeco-Roman Diaspora," in *The Jews among Pagans and Christians*, ed. J. Lieu, J. North, and T. Rajak [London: Routledge, 1992], 97–123, at p. 115); further examples in Levine, *Synagogue*, 380–81. The Aphrodisias inscription literally showcases public acknowledgment of benefactions from all groups – native Jews, converts, and God-fearers – to a Jewish fund-drive of some sort; see Reynolds and Tannenbaum, *Godfearers at Aphrodisias*, 92–123; so too Levine, *Synagogue*, 350.

[43] On the historiographical origins of this position, framed initially as a response to A. Harnack's characterizations of Judaism in "Die *Altercatio Simonis Iudaei et Theophili Christiani* nebst Untersuchungen über die antijüdische Polemik in der alten Kirche," *Texts und Untersuchungen sur Geschichte der altchristlichen Litterature* 1/3 (1883): 1–136, see M. Taylor, *Anti-Judaism and Early Christian Identity* (Leiden: Brill, 1995), 7–45; J. Carleton Paget, "Anti-Judaism and Early Christian Identity," *Zeitschrift für Antikes Christentum* 1 (1997): 195–225. In "Jewish Proselytism at the time of Christian Origins: Chimera or Reality?" (*JSNT* 62 [1996]: 65–103), Carleton Paget provides a roadmap of the entire controversy.

[44] See Feldman, *Jew and Gentile*, 293, on what he deems "demographic evidence," on which more below.

[45] Two classic statements of this position: M. Simon, *Verus Israel* (Paris: de Boccard 1948; English translation: H. Keating; New York: Oxford UP, 1986); B. Blumenkranz, *Die Judenpredigt Augustins* (Basel: Helbing & Lichtenhahn, 1946; repr. Paris: Études augustiniennes, 1973, with preface by Simon).

Pharisaic *proselytoi* and Paul's on preaching circumcision? They must stand in a context of ongoing Jewish missions to convert Gentiles).[46]

The so-called "demographic" argument – one of the purest examples of academic *creatio ex nihilo* known to me – rests on the perception of a "dramatic increase in Jewish population" from roughly 150,000 persons at the time of the destruction of the first Temple to roughly four to eight million (*sic*, but who's counting?) in the later mid-first century CE. Birthrate alone cannot account for such an extreme rise, yet these figures "demand further explanation." Answer: aggressive proselytism.

Simply stating this case should be enough to dismiss it. These figures are so speculative as to be ethereal. And they rest on a foundation built by Baron (and before him, Harnack), who combined "a statement by the thirteenth-century chronographer Bar-Hebraeus about the number of Jews at the time of Claudius' census, a comment in Philo (*Flacc.* 43) about the Jewish population in Egypt being a million, and comments in Josephus about the population of Palestine."[47] We do not and cannot know enough about ancient demography of Jews or any group to make this sort of case, period.[48] Its foundation being what it is, the rest collapses: a hypothesis presupposing huge numbers of converts, and then a theory of energetic missionary activity to explain that.

What of the latter two arguments in support of the existence of Jewish missions, namely, intense Christian–Jewish market competition, and the "obvious" readings of Matthew and of Paul? I shall begin by noting that both generate their respective cases almost exclusively from literary texts. What looks like historical explanation turns out, upon examination, to actually be an exercise in exegesis. Rather than engage these arguments at their methodological level – this sort of interpretative argument is endless – I propose that we look instead at what we know of Mediterranean civic life and its culture, and in a sense ricochet off that construct back into the questions that these arguments raise, though cannot answer.

---

[46] Mt 23:15; Gal 5:11. A world of Jewish missions conjured to provide a comfortable context for these statements appears most recently in J. Gager, *Reinventing Paul* (New York: Oxford UP, 2000).

[47] See Feldman, *Jew and Gentile*, 293, for "pro" quotations; observations about Baron's sources from Carleton Paget, "Jewish Proselytism," 70; see also Rutgers' criticisms of Feldman on this point, *Hidden Heritage*, 200–5.

[48] R. S. Bagnell and B. Freier, *The Demography of Roman Egypt* (Cambridge: Cambridge UP, 1994), 53–57 (with further bibliography) make this point nicely. Although expansion of Hasmonean sovereignty entailed consolidation by means of joining other local Semitic peoples, like the Idumeans, to the Judean commonwealth, such "conversions" (if that is the correct term) would still not be adequate to account for this putatively huge increase in the total number of Jews; see further discussion in Cohen, *Jewishness*, 110–19.

Both socially and religiously (co-extensive terms in ancient culture), in practice and in principle, the Diaspora Jewish community was extremely permeable. This was due to the visibility of ancient religious celebration generally. As with contemporary Mediterranean paganism, much of ancient Jewish religious activity (dancing, singing, communal eating, processing, and – as Chrysostom mentions with some irritation – building and feasting in *sukkot*) occurred out-of-doors, inviting and accommodating the participation of interested outsiders.[49] No special effort at recruitment, such as that presupposed by a theory of missions, was necessary.[50] The spectrum of this pagan affiliation was very broad. Through donor inscriptions we glimpse socially prominent pagans – Julia Severa, noblewoman and priestess of the imperial cult; Capitolina, a wealthy woman and self-identified *theosebēs*; the nine *bouleutai* among Aphrodisias' God-fearers – who made significant benefactions to Jewish institutions; some of these benefactors chose to involve themselves in the specifically religious activities of these communities.[51] At a lower end of the social spectrum, magicians invoked garbled biblical stories and "magic" Hebrew in recipe books compiled for serious professionals: this knowledge could have been easily picked up by hearing Scripture – read

---

[49] A tiny sampling: Philo mentions the celebration on the beach at Pharos, "where not only Jews but also multitudes of others cross the water, to do honor to the place [the site of the 72 translators' labors] ... and also to thank God" (*de vita Moysis* 2.41– 42); Tertullian, in *de Ieiunio* 16, mentions that Jews gather on fast days to worship out of doors, by the sea. Chrysostom, in his notorious sermons *Against the Judaizers*, complains of Christians co-celebrating Jewish rituals, fasts, and feasts (4.376: "When have they ever celebrated the Pasch with us? When have they shared the day of Epiphany with us?"; 1.844: "Many who belong to us ... attend their festivals and even share in their celebrations and join their fasts"). On Jews dancing on Shabbat, see Augustine, *s.* 9.3.3; *in Ioh. Tr.* 3.19; *in Ps.* 32,2; 91.2; D. Sperber, "On Sabbath Dancing," *Sinai* 57 (1965): 122–26 [Hebrew]; on the public celebration of the Purim festival, *C. Th.* XVI. 8,18.

[50] Noted rightly by G. F. Moore: "When [Judaism] is called a missionary religion, the phrase must ... be understood with a difference. The Jews did not send out missionaries .... They were themselves settled by thousands in all the great centers and in innumerable smaller cities .... Their religious influence was exerted chiefly through the synagogues, which they set up for themselves, but which were open to all whom interest or curiosity drew to their services," *Judaism in the First Three Centuries of the Christian Era*, 3 vols. (Cambridge: Harvard UP, 1927–30), 1:323–24.

[51] On Julia, Capitolina, and other such benefactors, see Levine, *Synagogue*, 111, 121, 479–83; on the town councilors, Reynolds and Tannenbaum, *Godfearers at Aphrodisias*. On the general openness of urban Jewish culture, the essays collected in S. Fine, ed., *Jews, Christians and Polytheists in the Ancient Synagogue* (London: Routledge, 1999). Levine notes, "the interest of pagans in the synagogue is indicative of the institution's accessibility as well as its importance and centrality in the Jewish community" (p. 121). All these studies cite numerous pertinent collections of inscriptional materials.

in the vernacular – in synagogues.[52] Other, less socially locatable
Gentiles, vaguely designated as "God-fearers" went even further, and
voluntarily assumed certain Jewish practices; ancient data speak (or
complain) most often of dietary restrictions, the Sabbath, and festivals.[53]
Those pagans who did convert fully to Judaism (and, particularly during
its first generation, to the Christian movement) most likely emerged from
among these voluntary Judaizers collected within the penumbra of
Diaspora synagogues.[54]

For pagan Gentiles, multiple religious allegiances were entirely
normal; indeed, traditional polytheism encouraged this sort of openness.
These Gentiles freely assumed as much or as little of Jewish practice as
they wished, while continuing unimpeded in their own cults. For the
Jews' part, welcoming the material support and encouraging interest, and
even admiration, among those of the host Gentile majority simply made
good sense, politically and socially. In the open city of antiquity, no
fences made good neighbors. Exclusive for insiders (Jews in principle
should not worship foreign gods), the synagogue was inclusive for
outsiders (interested Gentiles were welcomed). Thus pagans *as pagans*
could be found together with Jews in the Diaspora synagogue. So too,
until 66 CE, could they be found in Jerusalem, in the largest court of the
Temple, a house of *avodah/latreia* for Israel, a house of prayer for all the
nations.[55] No formal constraint, whether from the pagan or from the

---

[52] E.g., *PMP* ll. 3,007–3,085; Origen, *c. Cel.* IV:33 asserts that the Jewish god was
invoked not only by Jews "but also by almost all of those who deal in magic and
spells"; cf. V:50. Philip S. Alexander, "Jewish Elements in Gnosticism and Magic, c. CE
70 – c. CE 270," in *Cambridge History of Judaism,* vol. 3, *The Early Roman Period,* ed.
William Horbury, W. D. Davies, and John Sturdy (Cambridge: Cambridge UP, 1999),
1052–78.

[53] B. Wander, *Gottesfürchtige und Sympathisanten* (WUNT 104; Tübingen: Mohr
Siebeck, 1998); Feldman, *Jew and Gentile,* 483–501; J. Lieu, "The Race of the God-
fearers," *JTS* 46 (1995): 483–501; Cohen, *Jewishness,* 175–97.

[54] So, famously, Juvenal: *Quidam sortiti metuentem sabbata patrem ... mox et
praeputia ponunt; ... Iudaicum ediscunt et servant ac metuent ius:* the God-fearing
father had not only kept the Sabbath, but also avoided pork, *Satires* 14.96–101; Stern,
*Greek and Latin Authors,* vol. 2, 102–7. Acts routinely presents Paul encountering
Gentiles in Diaspora synagogues (13:16; 14:1; 16:14; 17:1–4, etc). Paul himself
nowhere mentions a synagogue context for his mission, but his reliance on arguments
drawn from Scripture certainly supports the inference: in the mid-first century CE, the
synagogue would have been the only means for Gentiles to have the familiarity with
scripture that Paul presupposes.

[55] Blood sacrifices represented (and enacted) shared meals between gods and
humans. Given the "kin" relationship between gods and their *genos,* the hot zone of
ritual activity around the altar was often restricted, as in Jerusalem, to members of the
god's family. The shrine to the founder of the Delians, similarly, forbade entry to the
*xenos,* though Delos was otherwise famous for religious tourism that attracted (and
encouraged) hosts of non-Delians to its site. On this us/them distinction in

Jewish side, abridged this ad hoc, improvised, and evidently comfortable arrangement.

Faced with this great sea of already-interested potential recruits, why didn't these Jews swing into action, turning their neighbors to the exclusive worship of the true god? For a moment, a tiny sub-culture of Hellenistic Jews did try. They seem to have been actively repudiated by their host synagogues, run out of town by irate Gentile citizens, and occasionally punished by Roman authorities attempting to keep the peace.[56] I speak, of course, of Jews like Paul, whose convictions (especially that of knowing what time it was on God's clock, e.g., Rom 13:11) led him and other like-minded colleagues to attempt to convince Gentiles to make a unique commitment to the god of Israel and to cease their traditional practices, living as if they were Jews without in fact converting to Judaism. I'll return to the first generation of this radioactively apocalyptic Jewish movement in a moment. For the most part, however, in the arc of centuries that span the period from Alexander to Islam and beyond, most Jews, evidently, made no such attempt.

Why not? Again we return to the ubiquitous respect accorded to antiquity and ethnicity as the bedrock of law, religion, and culture – and to the universal conviction that proper religion was an inherited characteristic. This respect was what enabled Jews to win the concessions to their own customs that they negotiated with their various local governments, mirrored eventually in later imperial (even Christian imperial) law.[57] Ancient Jews, themselves participants in this same

---

Mediterranean cult, see C. Sourvino-Inwood, "Further aspects of *Polis* Religion," in Buxton, *Greek Religion*, 38–55; on Delos in particular, see p. 50.

[56] Paul lists his woes, variously from Jews, Gentiles, and specifically Romans, in 2 Cor 4:8–9; 6:4–5; 11:24–26; cf. Acts 13:50; 14:2, 4–6, 19; 16:20–24 (in v. 21, pagans complain to magistrates about Paul and Silas, "They are Jews and are advocating customs that are not lawful for us as Romans to adopt or observe"); 17:5–9; 18:12–17 before Gallio in Corinth; 19:23–41 a tumult in Ephesus. The relation of the scenes in Acts to the historical Paul is beside the main point: these are vividly plausible Jewish and pagan responses to such a socially disruptive mission.

[57] The Roman decrees cited by Josephus, *AJ* 16 passim, consistently name "ancestral custom" as the reason for cities in Asia Minor to permit funds collected by Jews to be sent to Jerusalem; cf. too his rendition of Claudius' directives to Alexandria in 19.283–91. Centuries later, with the empire de facto divided, Honorius tried to prohibit the patriarch's collection of donations from synagogue communities (*CTh* 8.14, in 399 CE); within five years he rescinded his own order in light of the antiquity of this privilege, a reference to protection of the Temple tax (*CTh* 8.17). The Syrian legate, Vitellius, coming to Antipas' aid in 39 CE against Aretas, took the long road around and avoided cutting through Judea lest his army's standards, which bore images, offend Jewish "tradition" (*AJ* 18.120–22). Not everyone was as patient as the legate. "If the Jews wish to be citizens of Alexandria," complained Apion, "why don't they worship

culture, likewise respected pagan religious difference: as LXX Ex 22:28 implies and as numberless biblical and extra-biblical passages plainly state, the nations have their gods, the nation of Israel, Israel's god. This universal presumption, reinforced by daily reality – different peoples with their own gods, good relations with Gentile neighbors, the occasional hefty benefaction from a pagan sympathizer – sufficiently explains both why Diaspora Jews would welcome Gentile participation, and why they would impose no demand of exclusive worship (given to them alone by their god) on interested pagan neighbors.

Two last considerations, one more theoretical, one more practical, might provide more purchase on this question of Jews, Gentiles, and missions. The first relates to speculations concerning the ultimate fate of Gentiles, a theme arising within apocalyptic or messianic Jewish traditions. These traditions, and this theme, appear variously in literature ranging broadly in period, provenance, and genre: the classical prophets, apocrypha and pseudepigrapha, Philo and Paul, synagogue prayers, rabbinic disputes in the Bavli.[58] Nonetheless, this textual attestation cannot provide any information on whether and to what degree such speculations had any impact or influence on the day-to-day life of ancient Jews and their various Gentile associates. We cannot, for example, extrapolate Jewish missions from prophetic statements about Israel as a light to the nations, or about Israel's god as the god of the whole universe. Further, while speculations about the Gentiles' ultimate fate do appear throughout this literature, they diverge. Some texts speak of the ultimate subordination of Gentiles to Israel (or their destruction, dejection, defeat); others, of their participation with Israel at the End (such as worship at the Temple mount, or observing some mitzvot). These traditions – as we would expect – are not univocal, and single documents can express many, sometimes opposing, views.[59]

Those texts, finally, which do evince a positive orientation toward "eschatological Gentiles," speak only of Gentile *inclusion, not conversion.* The "righteous Gentile" of rabbinic discussion abandons his idols in this life; the proselyte, a former Gentile, "counts" eschatologically as a Jew.[60] But the Gentiles of these apocalyptic

---

the Alexandrian gods?" *c. Apionem* 2.65; cf. the similar complaint from cities in first-century Asia Minor, *AJ* 12.126.

[58] See citations and analysis in Fredriksen, "Circumcision of Gentiles," 533–48.

[59] Surveyed and analyzed in E. P. Sanders, *Jesus and Judaism* (Philadelphia: Fortress, 1985), 212–21.

[60] Christianity aside, absent conversion, non-idolatrous Gentiles were theoretical Gentiles: rabbinic remarks on this score are speculative ("What would a 'good Gentile' look like, and for what scriptural reasons?") not prescriptive, *b. Sanh.* 56–60 (cf. *Jubilees* 7:20ff. and Acts 15:20). See D. Novak, *The Image of the Non-Jew in Judaism: An Historical and Constructive Study of the Noahide Laws* (Toronto Studies in

scenarios cling to their idols literally right to the End, repudiating them only once the Lord of Israel has revealed himself in glory. And even at that point, these Gentiles *do not convert* to Judaism; rather, they turn from their own (false) gods and acknowledge, as Gentiles, Israel's god.[61] Far from serving as a likely inspiration for Gentile missions, then, this inclusive tradition may bespeak rather what Jews thought it would take to get most Gentiles to abandon their traditional worship: nothing less than a definitive and final self-revelation of God.[62] Taking this view in conjunction with the virtually universal Jewish opinion that the Law was the defining privilege of Israel (so too Paul, Rom 9:4), a theological impetus for mounting missions to Gentiles becomes difficult to reconstruct.

This theoretical consideration – that ancient Jews would have little ideological or theological reason to feel that they should attempt to convince Gentiles to become Jews – leads to a second, practical one: the balance within the religious ecosystem of the ancient city. Jews won exemptions from civic and imperial cult through persistence and negotiation. Majority culture tolerated their exclusivism out of its general respect for ancestral traditions. To have actively pursued a policy of alienating Gentile neighbors from their family gods and native civic and imperial cults would only have put the minority Jewish community at risk.[63] Pagan communities and civic authorities were for the most part willing to adjust to and respect Jewish religious difference, even to the point – remarkably – of tolerating former pagans who, as converts to Judaism, sought the same rights and exemptions as "native" Jews.[64] But,

---

Theology 14; New York: E. Mellen, 1983); cf. M. Bockmuehl, *Jewish Law in Gentile Churches* (Edinburgh: T&T Clark, 2000). On converts to Judaism "counting" as Israel in the eschatological round-up, see Fredriksen, "Circumcision," 545f.

[61] E.g., Tobit 14:5–6, Sib. Oracles 3:715–24; Justin, *Dial.* 122–23; Fredriksen, "Circumcision of Gentiles," 544–48.

[62] This is precisely Paul's point: that Gentiles-in-Christ now abandon idols and *porneia* is a sign that the End (identified with Christ's return) was at hand; the full argument can be found in P. Fredriksen, *Jesus of Nazareth, King of the Jews* (New York: Knopf, 1999), 125–54.

[63] Valerius Maximus suggests that (some) Jews were expelled from Rome in 139 BCE because *Romanis tradere sacra sua conati sunt* or *Sabazi Iovis cultu Romanos inficere mores conati erunt*. Does this refer to missionary activity? Astrologers were likewise expelled: see Stern, *Greek and Latin Authors,* vol. 1, nos. 147a–b and discussion on p. 359f. Gruen attempts to put this datum, together with the similar remarks of Dio on Roman Jews under Tiberius, in a political context: Dio, *Hist. Romana* 57.18.5a (Stern, *Greek and Latin Authors,* vol. 1, no. 419); Gruen, *Diaspora,* 15–53. Also, receiving converts (which Jews undoubtedly did) is different from soliciting them (that is, missionizing).

[64] Again, keeping Domitian's actions in mind (above, n. 21), social rank – thus, civic and cult responsibilities – might set the limits of such tolerance.

as the early Gentile churches found out, when Christians began conspicuously to insist on exercising Jewish religious prerogatives without themselves becoming Jews, this tolerance ran out.

To sum up this section: Jews and pagans lived amidst and among each other in the cities of the Diaspora. Their mutual awareness of difference did not compromise their equally mutual interest and participation in the activities of their respective communities. Jews did not need to advertise their activities to incite pagan interest, and the missionary position is both untenable and unnecessary as an explanation for it. Some scholars want to argue that, while perhaps not all Jews missionized most of the time, some Jews missionized some of the time.[65] Whatever this more modest proposal might gain in plausibility, however, it loses in explanatory value for our larger question: supposed Jewish missions that were only sporadic and local cannot have provided the white-hot competition that supposedly accounts (according to Simon Blumenkranz, *et alii*) for the ubiquity and hostility of the *contra Iudaeos* tradition.

## Hostility, Identity, and Martyrdom

This point brings us to our final question on the relation of Christian anti-Jewish rhetoric to social reality, and thus to the larger question of the so-called "Parting of the Ways." What role, if any, did Jews play in the (pagan) persecutions of (Gentile) Christians?[66] And how did this role, perceived or actual, contribute to the theologically-freighted *contra Iudaeos* tradition?

Historians conventionally divide the empire's anti-Christian persecutions into two phases, the first, roughly from the late first to the mid-third century CE; the second, from Decius in 249 to Diocletian in 303. In the later period, emperors mandated uniform participation in acts of public cult. Jews (and, thus, Jewish Christians) were explicitly exempted;[67] Gentile Christians who refused were targeted for harassment, imprisonment, even death. The persecutions of the first phase, however,

---

[65] Carleton Paget's proposal, "Jewish Proselytism," 102.

[66] The floggings that Paul both initiated (Gal 1:13) and endured (2 Cor 11:24) are not relevant to this discussion, since the principals in both instances were Diaspora Jews.

[67] J. B. Rives, "The Decree of Decius and the Religion of Empire," *Journal of Roman Studies* 89 (1999): 135–54; Jewish exemption, *y. Avodah Zarah* 5.4.44 d; Eusebius, *HE* 6.12.1 (a Gentile Christian considers converting to Judaism – thereby remaining a Christian? – to avoid imperial harassment). A. M. Rabello, "On the Relations between Diocletian and the Jews," *JJS* 35 (1984): 147–67.

random and sporadic, arose at local rather than imperial initiative, and their actual legal grounds remain obscure.[68]

Popular rumors of the Christians' debauchery and cannibalism, and their self-exemption from imperial cult, doubtlessly contributed to the churches' local visibility. Visible, too, was their non-participation in the civic cults of those gods who were theirs by birth and blood.[69] Such behavior threatened to rupture the *pax deorum*, the pact or peace between heaven and the human community. Deprived of cult, the gods grew angry; when gods were angry, humans suffered. Thus, "when the Tiber overflows or the Nile doesn't," when plague or earthquake struck, Christians could find themselves sitting targets for local anxieties.[70] Once before the magistrate (frequently the Roman governor on his assize rounds), Christians would be ordered to sacrifice. Refusal often meant death.[71] The pagan context of these persecutions dominates the accounts; yet some historians claim that the Jews, "either in the background or in the foreground," also played an important role, spreading malicious rumors, stirring up trouble, participating actively and enthusiastically in local outbreaks of anti-Christian violence.[72]

Evidence cited in support of this claim includes some statements found in patristic writings, and some episodes given in *acta martyrum*. In his *Dialogue*, Justin accused the Jews of murderous harassment of Christians, extending back to the crucifixion itself: "Your hand was lifted high to do evil, for even when you had killed the Christ you did not repent, but you

---

[68] H. Musurillo, *Acts of the Christian Martyrs* (Oxford: Clarendon, 1972), lvii–lxii; the now-classic exchange of de Ste. Croix and Sherwin-White, "Why were the Early Christians Persecuted?" *Past and Present* 26 (1963) and 27 (1964).

[69] Tertullian vividly (and disapprovingly) describes these festivals, during which residents brought "fires and couches out into the open air," feasted from street to street, turned the city into a tavern, made mud from wine (whether through libations or indecorous behavior), and in general celebrated a city-wide party; *Apology* 35.

[70] Tertullian, *Apology* 40.2; on Christian withdrawal from cult and the anxieties that it occasioned, see Price, *Rituals and Power*, 123–26.

[71] See, e.g., the martyrdoms of Polycarp 9; Perpetua 6; Scillitan martyrs (where the proconsul complains of their forsaking the *mos Romanorum*); also the procedure sketched in Pliny, *ep.* 10.

[72] A. Harnack, *Expansion of Christianity in the First Three Centuries* (New York: G. P. Putnam's Sons, 1904), 64–67; W. H. C. Frend, *Martyrdom and Persecution in the Early Church* (New York: New York University Press, 1967), e.g., 178 (malice), 194 (troublemaking), 215 (active part in persecutions). Taylor notes that Frend "so takes the hostility and malice of the Jews for granted, that they occasionally overshadow the pagan officials in his descriptions of the persecutions" (*Anti-Judaism*, 84). This interpretation continues, more recently, in Lane Fox, *Pagans and Christians*, 487, and G. W. Bowersock, *Martyrdom and Rome* (Cambridge: Cambridge UP, 1995), 56. Cf. F. Millar's review of Frend in *Journal of Roman Studies* 56 (1966): 231–36; Taylor, *Anti-Judaism*, 78–114.

also hate and murder us" (133.6). Likewise, Tertullian characterized synagogues as *fontes persecutorum* (*Scorpiace* 10), and Origen suggested that Jews stood at the source of popular anti-Christian calumnies about ritual murder, cannibalism, and promiscuous sex (*c. Cel.* VI.27; cf. VI. 40). Jews also figure prominently in the martyr stories of Polycarp and of Pionius: "the entire mob of pagans and Jews from Smyrna" roar, enraged, demanding Polycarp's death in the arena (*Poly.* 12); later, when "the mob" collects wood for his pyre, "the Jews (as is their custom) zealously helped them with this" (13). Later, the Jews together with their pagan neighbors frustrate the Christian community's efforts to retrieve Polycarp's body (17–18). A century later, again in Smyrna, Pionius and his companions are watched on their way to the tribunal by a great crowd of Greeks, women, and also Jews ("on holiday because it was a great Sabbath"; *Pionius* 2–3), who importune Christians in the crowd to come into their synagogues (13).[73]

This is a slim dossier, and one that reveals the rhetorical and retrospective nature of these indictments. These sources present contemporary Jews as standing in the long line of persecutors of the righteous extending back to the first generation of the church, to Jesus himself, and before him to the prophets. The Jewish presence described in these documents, in other words, is a narrative restatement of the "trail of crimes" motif in orthodox anti-Jewish hermeneutic,[74] wherein allegations of such persecutions serve to reaffirm orthodox Christian identity and the

---

[73] James Parkes argues that the Smyrnaean Jews attempted to offer these Christians refuge in *Conflict of Church and Synagogue* (Cleveland: World Publishing Company 1961; orig. pub. 1934), 144–45; if so, this would cohere with Eusebius' report of Jewish sympathy toward persecuted Christians in *Martyrs of Palestine* 8.1. Others see evidence of hostile intent; e.g., Lane Fox, who paints a lurid picture of Jews and pagans together "gloating at the Christians from their city's colonnades" (*Pagans and Christians*, 487; full discussion on pp. 479–87); exhaustively, *Le martyre de Pionios*, ed. L. Robert, G. W. Bowersock, and C. P. Jones (Washington, D.C.: Dumbarton Oaks, 1994). I warmly thank these last two colleagues for their efforts to dissuade me from the view I present here, and regret that I must defer a fuller consideration of their objections to a later essay.

[74] Thus, for example, Tertullian's famous remark on the synagogues continues, "before which the apostles endured the scourge" – a clear reference to episodes described or predicted in various NT texts. Parkes comments, "The statement of Jewish hostility in general terms is based on theological exegesis [of OT and NT texts] and not on historical memory"; *Church and Synagogue*, 148. For general discussion and analysis of this literature, see pp. 121–50; Taylor, *Anti-Judaism*, 91–114, cf. Carleton Paget, "Anti-Judaism," 215f; J. Lieu, "Accusations of Jewish Persecution in Early Christian Sources, with Particular Reference to Justin Martyr and the *Martyrdom of Polycarp*," in *Tolerance and Intolerance*, 279–95.

orthodox understanding of contested biblical texts.[75] It is the rhetoric of these texts, "the literary and theological nature and function of such accusations" that demands investigation. "Thus the initial question must not be about the Jews – 'Did they persecute Christians?' – but about the Christians – 'Why did they perceive Jews as persecutors?'"[76]

Does this literary framing mean that real Jews were most likely not involved in these persecutions? No historical evidence can prove a negative, but consideration of other factors can help assess relative plausibility or implausibility. First, these charges of Jewish anti-Christian aggression arise specifically within orthodox Christian documents, which are the showcases of the erudite *contra Iudaeos* tradition. Here it must be recalled that more than the orthodox perished in these outbreaks of violence. "Heresies" – rival Gentile Christian churches with quite different orientations toward the Septuagint, thus with identities independent of Jewish constructions of "Israel" – also produced martyrs. It is difficult to frame a Jewish resentment sufficiently broad to account for both anti-orthodox and anti-Marcionite aggression.[77] Second, as attested by the cry awkwardly attributed to the Smyrnaean Jews in the *Martyrdom of Polycarp*,[78] such anti-Christian actions focused on the issue of public cult. Were Jews on these volatile occasions to have made themselves so conspicuous, they would have risked emphasizing, on precisely the same issue, their own degree of religious difference from majority culture.

---

[75] E.g., "Anonymous" response to Montanism's challenge to "orthodox" identity and scriptural practices: "They used to dub us 'slayers of the prophets,' because we did not receive their prophets .... [But] is there a single one of these followers of Montanus ... who was persecuted by Jews or killed by lawless men? Or were any of them seized and crucified for the sake of the Name? Or were any of the[ir] women ever 'scourged in the synagogues' of the Jews or stoned?" in *Eusebius, HE* 6.16.12; the passage resonates with references to Mt 23:31–37.

[76] Lieu, "Accusations," 280. I would rephrase the question: not why did these authors "perceive" Jews as persecutors, but why were they compelled to present them in this way. See too eadem, *Image and Reality*. Perhaps the target of this rhetoric was internal, i.e., synagogue-going Christians: E. L. Gibson, "Jewish Antagonism or Christian Polemic: The Case of the *Martyrdom of Pionius*," *JECS* 9 (2001): 339–58.

[77] Pionius is burned next to a member of Marcion's church, 21.5; "Anonymous" complains about the "immense number" of martyrs from "heretical" churches, naming specifically Montanists and especially Marcionites; Eusebius, *HE* 5.16.20–21. See also R. MacMullen, *Christianizing the Roman Empire, AD 100–400* (New Haven: Yale UP, 1984), 29f. and n. 13.

[78] "The whole crowd of Gentiles and Jews dwelling in Smyrna cried out in uncontrollable anger and with a great shout, 'This is the teacher of Asia, the father of the Christians, the destroyer of our gods, the one who teaches many to neither sacrifice nor worship!'"; *Pionius* 12.2; D. Boyarin, *Dying for God: Martyrdom and the Making of Christianity and Judaism* (Stanford: Stanford UP, 1999), 127–130.

Finally, to either side chronologically of these persecutions, we consistently find vigorous complaints of excessive intimacy between Gentile Christians and their Jewish neighbors. These thread throughout orthodox writings of many genres – sermons, letters, commentaries, conciliar canons. These sources speak regularly of Christians frequenting synagogues, keeping Sabbath or feast days with Jewish friends, soliciting Jewish blessings, betrothing their children to Jews or, indeed, marrying Jews themselves.[79] This is not to say that relations were always sunny, and Jewish anti-Christian polemic dates from this period, too.[80] But polemic is not persecution. If Jews had actually played – *or even been commonly thought to have played* – a vigorous role in the persecution of Gentile Christians, then this abundant and continuous evidence of intimate social interaction becomes extremely difficult to account for.

When focusing on ancient Jewish–Christian relations, the lived social context of these relations too often falls outside of consideration. These two minority communities lived within cities that were both structured and celebrated by the majority religious culture. An abiding aspect of that culture was its deep respect for the *mos maiorum*, inherited religious tradition, the cornerstone of both law and piety.[81] It is this deep respect alone that accounts for the extraordinary privileges and exemptions granted uniquely to Jewish communities in virtue of the ethnicity and antiquity of their own ancestral way of life. And these exemptions in turn allowed Hellenistic Jews, without compromising those things funda-mental to their own religious identity, to attain their remarkable degree of social and cultural integration in the ancient city. Despite the evidence of the *contra Iudaeos* tradition – indeed, on the evidence of the *contra Iudaeos* tradition, including the ways in which it is manifest in the law

---

[79] Christians going to synagogue, e.g., Origen, *In Lev. hom.* 5.8; *Sel. in Exod.* 12.46; notoriously, Chrysostom's sermons against Judaizers. Christians keeping the Sabbath, Augustine, *ep.* 54.2, 3; going to a Jew for a cure, *de civ. Dei* 22.8.21. Conciliar canons continuously legislate against Christian interest in Judaism and interactions with Jews, e.g., Elvira (303 CE) condemns intermarriage (c.16), soliciting Jewish blessings for fields (c. 49), accepting Jewish hospitality (c. 50), and sexual relations (c. 78). For such legislation, attesting to Jewish–Christian mixing well up through the Visigothic period, see Linder, *Legal Sources.*

[80] Horbury, *Controversy*; on the *birkat ha-minim*, besides Horbury, see S. Wilson, *Related Strangers: Jews and Christians, 70–170 C.E.* (Minneapolis: Fortress, 1995), 183–193; Carleton Paget, "Anti-Judaism," 217 n. 98, 221. Boyarin, *Dying for God*, 93–126; J. Z. Pastis, "Jewish Arguments against Christianity in the *Dialogue of Timothy and Aquila*," in *A Multiform Heritage: Studies on early Judaism and Christianity in honor of Robert A. Kraft*, ed. B. G. Wright (Atlanta: Scholars Press, 1999), 184 n. 4; for the earlier period, see C. Seltzer, *Jewish Responses to Early Christians: History and Polemics, 30–150* (Minneapolis: Fortress, 1994).

[81] T. D. Barnes, "Legislation against the Christians," *Journal of Roman Studies* 58 (1968): 32–50.

codes of the late empire – Jews retained their place on this social map for as long as the ancient city remained relatively intact. And this placement meant that their non-Jewish neighbors, whether pagan or Christian, continued in their social (including religious) interactions with them.

## Conclusions

When, then, did "the ways" part? Our answer – and indeed, the question itself – depends upon what evidence we consider. An awareness of separation, even a principled insistence upon separation, seems clearly attested in some early to mid-second century writers (Ignatius, Marcion, Justin); equally clearly, we see strong indications of persistent, intimate interactions. Despite the tendencies of imperial law, the eruptions of anti-Jewish (and anti-pagan, and anti-heretical) violence, the increasingly strident tone and obsessive repetition of orthodox anti-Jewish rhetoric, the evidence – indeed, precisely *this* evidence – points in the other direction: on the ground, the ways were *not* separating, certainly not fast enough and consistently enough to please the ideologues.

While Constantine's patronage eventually empowered orthodox bishops, the conduits and authors of the *contra Iudaeos* tradition, they had little effect on long-lived civic social patterns. Religious and social mixing between different types of Jews and Christians, between Christians of different sorts, and between Christians, Jews and pagans all continued.[82] Indeed, the vitality of this habitual contact accounts in part for the increasing shrillness of anti-Jewish invective. As orthodox identity, enabled especially under Theodosius II, becomes enacted in Mediterranean cities, the volume and the vituperation of the *contra Iudaeos* tradition increases. Together with the laws preserved in the *Codex Theodosianus* and the canons in various conciliar corpora, this literature at once relates the prescriptions of the governing elites and provides glimpses of the social reality that they condemn or attempt to regulate: Jews, pagans, and Christians of many different stripes continue

---

[82] E.g., Constantine's efforts to break up the "interfaith" fair (pagans, Jews, and Christians of various sorts) held at Mamre; Eusebius, *Vita Constantini* 3.51–53. Laodicea (fourth century), c. 37 attempts to prevent the orthodox from receiving festal gifts from Jews and heretical Christians; Vannes (465?) tried to legislate against orthodox *clerics* eating with Jews, c. 12; Epaone (517), forbidding clerics to fraternize with heretical clergy and with Jews, c. 15. The Piacenza pilgrim's story of the miraculous bench in the synagogue at Nazareth may very well be evidence of sixth-century Christian–Jewish co-operation for the benefit of the tourist trade; *Antoninio Placentini Itinerarium* 5 (*CCL* 175:130–31); J. Taylor, *Christians and the Holy Places* (Oxford: Clarendon, 1993), 228–29.

to mix and mingle.[83] Church and state did collaborate in the Christianization of Late Roman culture, but no direct correspondence between law, theology, and society can be presumed. Indeed, the constant reiteration of civil and ecclesiastical legislation suggests the opposite: legal prescription cannot yield social description.[84]

Squeezed by Visigoths and Franks in the West, and eventually by Muslims in the East, Mediterranean society in the fifth through seventh centuries became increasingly brutalized as ancient traditions of urban civility waned. In this new climate of violence, the church's tremendous moral prestige legitimated the coercion of all religious outsiders. By this point, in learned Christian imagination, "the Jew" represented the religious outsider par excellence. In time, within this changed context, the rhetoric of the ancient *contra Iudaeos* tradition would create a new social reality; and, indeed, the social experience of Jewish communities within Roman culture seems to change more dramatically in the century and a half between Augustine and Isidore of Seville than it had for the seven plus centuries between Alexander and Augustine.[85] But actual, effective segregation (which will facilitate targeted aggression) lies outside our period, well off into the Middle Ages.

By controlling the transmission of earlier texts and traditions, the orthodox ideologues of separation not only (eventually) changed the future; they also changed the past, which we still see, despite ourselves, too much from their vantage point. The ideology of separation was initially an optative principle, intimately and immediately allied to textual practices, articulated and developed by an intellectual minority (redundancy intended) beginning, perhaps, in the early second century CE.[86] It was an ideal vociferously – or, depending on our degree of empathy for

---

[83] Summarized in Parkes, *Conflict*, 379–86.

[84] Except, perhaps, *à l'inverse*. So too Schwartz, *Imperialism and Jewish Society*, 195–99, noting a sixth-century inscription from Calabria attesting to a Jewish *patronus civitatis*; David Noy, *Jewish Inscriptions of Western Europe* (Cambridge: Cambridge UP, 1993), vol. 1, no. 114; M. Williams, "The Jews of Early Byzantine Venusia: The Family of Faustinus I, the Father," *JJS* 50 (1999): 47–48.

[85] Fredriksen and Irshai, "Christian Anti-Judaism," part 5: "The End of Mediterranean Antiquity."

[86] Intolerance of its own diversity characterizes late Second Temple Judaism, and accounts for much of its sectarian literary production. The intra-group vituperation and intense debate about authority, behavior, and biblical interpretation that marks canonical and extra-canonical paleo-Christian texts (Paul's letters, the gospels, Barnabas [perhaps], Revelation) are some of the most Jewish things about them. These texts were read in support of the *contra Iudaeos* tradition by later Gentile Christians; they do not directly witness to it. (Cf. Ruether, *Faith and Fratricide*, criticized on exactly this historiographical point by the authors assembled in Davies, *Anti-Semitism*.)

figures like Chrysostom, perhaps plaintively – urged in the fourth.[87] It was a policy ineffectually legislated, in pockets of the old Roman world, in the sixth.[88] It was never in this culture, for the entire period from the coming of Christianity to the coming of Islam, a native reality universally lived. How, then, can we best respond to the question, "When was the Parting of the Ways?" Only with another question: "What Parting of the Ways?"

---

[87] The continuing value of Simon's great *Verus Israel*, thus, is less its historical reconstruction than its comprehensive review of this literature, which Simon took as socially descriptive rather than prescriptive.

[88] For this later legal material, see Linder, *Legal Sources*; for continuities in Roman culture, R. A. Markus, *Gregory the Great and his World* (Cambridge: Cambridge UP, 1997); discontinuities in Iberia, P. D. King, *Law and Society in the Visigoth Kingdom* (Cambridge: Cambridge UP, 1972); P. Heather, *The Goths* (Oxford: Clarendon, 1996); on the decline of urban culture, the magisterial study by J. H. W. G. Liebeschuetz, *The Decline and Fall of the Roman City* (Oxford: Oxford UP, 2001).

# Semantic Differences; or, "Judaism"/"Christianity"

by

## DANIEL BOYARIN

*For Chana*

> The role of the intellectual is not to tell others what they have to do. By what
> right would he do so? ... The work of an intellectual is not to shape others'
> political will; it is, through the analysis that he carries out in his field, to
> question over and over again what is postulated as self-evident, to disturb
> people's mental habits, the way they do and think things, to dissipate what is
> familiar and accepted, to reexamine rules and institutions and on the basis of this
> re-problematization (in which he carries out his specific task as an intellectual)
> to participate in the formation of a political will (in which he has his role as
> citizen to play).
>
> – Michel Foucault[1]

A recent writer in a popular context was surely representing what is
postulated as self-evident – people's mental habits, the way they do and
think things – when he wrote the following sentence: "Christianity's
parent religion, Judaism, is actively hostile to celibacy, one of
monasticism's chief institutions."[2] This is precisely the sort of self-
evidence that my work as an intellectual sets out to question, disturb, and
dissipate. Judaism, I will argue (and so do many other scholars today), is
not the parent religion to Christianity; indeed, in some respects the
opposite may be as true. Nor can we speak of a religion, Judaism, at all in
the sense of a bounded institution existing before the Christian era (and
even fairly deep into that era), of which it could be said that it was hostile
to any one thing. The issue of celibacy actually provides an instructive
example. Various groups that we can only call Jewish were very friendly
indeed to celibacy in the period just before and at the time of the

---

\* I wish to thank Erich Gruen and Chana Kronfeld for their help in thinking through
the issues in this paper and especially Prof. Gruen, who has been instrumental in saving
me from several lamentable errors (perhaps not as many as he would have liked).

[1] Michel Foucault and Lawrence D. Kritzman, *Politics, Philosophy, Culture:
Interviews and Other Writings, 1977–1984*, ed. and trans. Lawrence D. Kritzman
(London: Routledge, 1988), 265.

[2] Diarmaid MacCulloch, "Solitaries in Community," *TLS* 5107 (16 Feb 2001): 10.

emergence of Christianity,[3] and *rabbinic* Jewish hostility to celibacy is almost surely a product of the Christian era (and arguably a response to Christianity).

An increasing number of cutting-edge scholars are referring to the "fourth century as the first century of Judaism and Christianity."[4] If we are not to speak of Judaism as the parent of Christianity, how, then, shall we speak of the emergence of two religions, Judaism and Christianity, as two religions, as we know them in our modern world? The first major theoretical assumption I adopt is that, as postcolonial theorist David Chidester has put it, "Religions have been reopened as invented traditions or as imagined communities." No less than with the study of the idea of the "nation," the idea of the "religion" – as in the Jewish religion, the Christian religion – the question can be asked: where and when did this idea emerge? Moreover, as Chidester points out as well, "rather than bounded cultural systems, religions are intrareligious and interreligious networks of cultural relations."[5] It is on the borders, at the contact zones, that we find "religions" being produced (rather like the production of continents at the borders between tectonic plates). As Homi Bhabha has written: "It is the 'inter' – the cutting edge of translation and negotiation, the *in-between* space – that carries the burden of the meaning of culture."[6] Studying such borders should be a productive way of thinking about the construction of "religions" and thus, in this case, of Judaism and Christianity.

This is an inquiry into how language produces social "facts" and how social facts produce language. It is about how "Christianity" and "Judaism," as the names for a difference that we call "religions," came into being. I am attempting a sort of social history of ideas as material

---

[3] Steven D. Fraade, "Ascetical Aspects of Ancient Judaism," *Jewish Spirituality from the Bible through the Middle Ages*, ed. Arthur Green, World Spirituality: An Encyclopedic History of the Religious Quest (New York: Crossroad, 1986).

[4] Jacob Neusner, *The Three Stages in the Formation of Judaism*, Brown Judaic Studies (Chico, Calif.: Scholars Press, 1985), 77; Rosemary Radford Ruether, "Judaism and Christianity: Two Fourth-Century Religions," *Sciences Religieuses/Studies in Religion* 2 (1972): 1–10; James William Parkes, *The Conflict of the Church and the Synagogue: A Study in the Origins of Antisemitism* (Cleveland: World Pub. Co. Jewish Publication Society of America, 1961), 153; Günter Stemberger, *Jews and Christians in the Holy Land: Palestine in the Fourth Century* (Edinburgh: T&T Clark, 1999), 1.

[5] David Chidester, *Savage Systems: Colonialism and Comparative Religion in Southern Africa* (Charlottesville: UP of Virginia, 1996), 260.

[6] Homi K. Bhabha, *The Location of Culture* (London: Routledge, 1994) 38–39, and see Chidester, *Savage Systems*, xv.

facts.[7] One of the outstanding theoretical issues with which I struggle is the question of language as social practice.[8] The problem is to find a theoretical model for understanding the situation in which Judaism and Christianity are existent realities but not defined nor clearly distinguished ones, that is, a situation of hybridity.

## Linguistic Histories

At the beginning of the Christian era, people in the Mediterranean area seem most often to have named themselves in ethnic terms, and not as adherents of what we would call a religion. The name "*Ioudaios*" by and large meant "Judean," as did its Hebrew cognate, יהודי.[9] There was no *Ioudaismos*, as the name of the Jewish religion, before there was *Christianismos*. Although the term "*Ioudaismos*," of course, existed before the Christian Era, it meant something else than what we call Judaism. In its earliest use, in 2 Maccabees 2:22 of the second century B.C.,[10] the term "*Ioudaismos*" is contrasted with "*Hellenismos*": the ways of the Judeans (or of the Jewish state) as opposed to the ways of the foreigners.[11] According to this text, there are those who "vie with one another in fighting manfully for *Ioudaismos*" (2 Macc 2:21). This means

---

[7] "I shall therefore say that, where only a single subject (such and such an individual) is concerned, the existence of the ideas of his belief is material in that *his ideas are his material actions inserted into material practices governed by material rituals which are themselves defined by the material ideological apparatus from which derive the ideas of that subject*"; Louis Althusser, "Ideology and Ideological State Apparatuses (Notes Toward an Investigation)," in *Mapping Ideology*, ed. Slavoj Zizek (London: Verso, 1994), 127 [emphasis in original]; earlier publication: Louis Althusser, "Ideology and Ideological State Apparatuses (Notes Towards an Investigation)," *Lenin and Philosophy, and Other Essays* (London: New Left Books, 1971), 127–86.

[8] For a very useful presentation of the notion of language as practice, see Pierre Bourdieu, *Outline of a Theory of Practice*, Cambridge Studies in Social Anthropology (Cambridge: Cambridge UP, 1977), 96–97.

[9] Shaye J. D. Cohen, "Ioudaios: 'Judaean' and 'Jew' in Susanna, First Maccabees, and Second Maccabees," *Geschichte – Tradition – Reflexion: Festschrift für Martin Hengel zum 70. Geburtstag*, ed. H. Cancik, H. Lichtenberger, and P. Schäfer (Tübingen: Mohr Siebeck, 1996), 1.211–20.

[10] Throughout my work, I shall be using the terms "B.C." and "A.C." instead of the customary "B.C.E." and "C.E." The latter seem to me hardly an improvement (from the perspective of Jews) on the older B.C. and A.D., since the term Common Era is just as imperialistic as the traditional usage. The virtue of B.C. and A.C. (imitating the French manner) is that it simply names the Era without making a judgment, theological or cultural, about it.

[11] Jonathan A. Goldstein, trans. and ed., *II Maccabees: A New Translation with Introduction and Commentary*, The Anchor Bible 41a (New York: Doubleday, 1983), 192.

fighting not for the defense of the faith but, as the text puts it, to preserve "the temple, the city, and the laws."

That *Ioudaismos* here is not the name of a "religion" can be argued philologically with a certain degree of plausibility (if not ineluctably). In the same work, at 4:13, "*Hellenismos*" means, according to Jonathan Goldstein, "the aping of Greek manners." In the Greek of the time, "*Medismos*" meant aping of Persian manners and with it "Greek collaboration with the Persian enemy." In the ostracisms of Athens in the early decades of the fifth century BC, "*Medismos*" indicated disloyalty to the city.[12] "*Hellenismos*" in the Maccabees text (4:13) occupies the semantic role of *Medismos* in those Athenian anathemas. It indicates disloyalty to the city, together with its temple and its laws, as well as the miming of Greek ways. The opposite of *Medismos* in Greek usage was, seemingly, "*Hellenismos*," meaning remaining loyal to the Greek cause and the Greek ways.[13] It follows, therefore, if Goldstein is correct, that "*Ioudaismos*" (2 Macc 8:1) in the Jewish text, which occupies the semantic position of *Hellenismos* in the Greek texts, means what *Hellenismos* means in those: remaining loyal to the ways of the Judeans and the political cause of Jerusalem.[14] It is not a name, then, for what we would identify as "Judaism," the Jewish religion. Indeed, we habitually differentiate between "Judaism" and "Jewishness" to mark something like this distinction. That very distinction that we make between Judaism and Jewishness could only appear after, in the words of historian Seth Schwartz, the "emergence of religion as a discrete category of human experience."

Although conversion to "Jewishness" was already a possibility, this move constituted a sort of naturalization into the Jewish People more than it did a conversion in the later, religious sense. "Conversion" in the first century still seems semantically and socially more like becoming an Athenian or a Roman citizen, than it was like becoming a Christian.[15]

---

[12] See also Jonathan M. Hall, *Ethnic Identity in Greek Antiquity* (Cambridge: Cambridge UP, 1997), 46–47.

[13] Goldstein, *II Maccabees*, 230, who is careful to remind us that *Hellenismos* is not necessarily attested in this meaning, but that it is the "implied" antonym of *Medismos*.

[14] Goldstein's own evidence and argument, therefore, militate against his translation of the term as "the Jewish religion" (*II Maccabees*, 300). Admittedly 14:38 (on Razis) seems to lean a bit more in that direction but can also easily be explained as referring to loyalty to the cause of the Jews and fealty to their traditional ways, and not the religion "Judaism." For a similar conclusion, see also Cohen, "Ioudaios," 219: "Thus Ioudaismos should be translated not 'Judaism' – 'religion' is not the focus of the term – but 'Jewishness' (Judaeaness?).... It is a conflict between 'Judaism' the ways of the Ioudaioi, and the 'Hellenism,' the ways of the Greeks."

[15] Similar, but not identical, as there was no formal citizenship in "Israel," and, presumably, one could be both a member of Israel and a citizen of a polis. I would be

When Paul was writing, "Greek" and "Jew" were as incompatible as identities for a single person at a single moment as "male" and "female" or "slave" and "free" (Gal 3:28).[16] Similarly, in the somewhat later *Acts of Pilate*, Pilate asks the Jewish leaders, "What are proselytes?" to which the answer comes: "They were born children of Greeks, and now have become Jews."[17] The semiotic opposition is still Greek/Jew. On the other hand, "Christian" and "Jew" were compatible identities in Paul's formulation, as well as for centuries thereafter. Most, if not all, Christians of the first, second, and perhaps even third centuries considered themselves and were considered by others as Jews. "Jew," accordingly, is a member of the paradigm that includes "Greek," while "Christian" identifies another semantic field – perhaps one that included such entities as "Pharisee," "Sadducee," and "Essene." Becoming a Jew was like becoming a Spartan or an Athenian (not in the full political sense of these latter, as there was no formal civic identity of "Jew").[18] "Jew" was clearly an ethnic identity, even if a mutable one. Of course, entry into the community carried with it the requirement that one behave according to the mores of one's new

---

thus hard-put to describe what happened to Paul as a conversion in the religious sense, pace Alan F. Segal, *Paul the Convert: The Apostolate and Apostasy of Saul the Pharisee* (New Haven: Yale UP, 1990).

[16] Although it is much earlier, the following example discussed by Cohen is instructive. The earliest evidence we have for a "Greek Jew" is an inscription by a certain "Moschos," from the third century B.C., David M. Lewis, "The First Greek Jew," *Jewish Social Studies* 2 (1957): 264–66. The extraordinary thing about this Moschos is that, although he is identified in the inscription as a *Ioudaios*, his "religion" is clearly that of Greek gods. He may be a Greek Jew from our historical perspective, but from his own he is just a *Ioudaios* and not a Greek (for that is how he identifies himself), whatever his religious practice, thus anticipating Paul's usage in which Greek and Jew are as incompatible identities as man and woman. See Shaye J. D. Cohen, *The Beginnings of Jewishness: Boundaries, Varieties, Uncertainties*, Hellenistic Culture and Society 31 (Berkeley: U. of California, 1998), 97–98. See also pp. 134–35, where the point is made that one could not be both Greek and Jew because these were competing cultural identities, not genealogical ones, which makes sense but still surely does not lead to the conclusion that they were religions, as Cohen himself argues (cf. Cohen, "Ioudaios," 219). Paul, in seeking to break down this boundary in Christ, certainly does not mean that followers of Jesus will be both Greeks and Jews religiously. Cf. Hans Dieter Betz, "Christianity as Religion: Paul's Attempt at Definition in Romans," *Journal of Religion* 71 (1991): 315–44, and see discussion in Birger Pearson, "The Emergence of the Christian Religion," *The Emergence of the Christian Religion: Essays on Early Christianity* (Harrisburg, Pa: Trinity Press International, 1997), 15.

[17] Felix Scheidweiler, ed. and trans., "The Gospel of Nicodemus, Acts of Pilate and Christ's Descent Into Hell," *New Testament Apocrypha*, ed. Wilhelm Schneemelcher and R. McL. Wilson; English edition, ed. Edgar Hennecke (Philadelphia: Westminster, 1991), 1:508. See also Cohen, *Jewishness*, 159–60 and correct reference there, n. 68.

[18] Cohen, *Jewishness*, 160.

community. It, nevertheless, remained a matter of essentially ethnic or national identification and identity-formation.

I have been arguing that *"Ioudaismos"* could not have meant Judaism, the religion, in the period before and just after the advent of Christianity, by observing the sets of semantic oppositions (or lexical paradigms) within which the term then functioned. Signifiers, as we have known since Saussure, only function differentially, that is, by virtue of their difference from other signifiers within a signifying system such as a language. Consequently, a "term" in a signifying system exists only when there are others which it is not. This is not a psychological point about identity (e.g., Freud's "narcissism of minor differences") but a theoretical claim that by now is both unexceptional and unexceptionable. However, its implications for the history of religions have not been taken seriously. Insofar as the semiotic system did not include other "religions" to which Jews might adhere, there could be no name that means the "proper" Jewish religion. The oppositional term to the various religions of the Ancient Near East with which the Israelites were in contact has to have been "the Israelite cult," in the broadest sense of "cult/ure," not because of substantive difference between this and the religion that we call Judaism (although there is, of course, such and much), but because this was what it was: the cult, in all of its various forms and subvarieties, of the ethnic group called Israel, and not a "religion." The other terms within the paradigm to which this signifier belongs are "the cult/ure of Assyria," "the cult/ure of Egypt," "the cult/ure of Canaan," and ultimately "the cult/ure of Greece" as well. As the terms of this paradigm suggest, the set of oppositions that it comprised was peoples and their lands and the practices and beliefs associated with them, not religions and *their* beliefs, practices and so forth.[19] Although in all of these formations (and in Israelite and early Ioudaistic cult/ure as well), elements of what we call religion were prominent (that's the point of the virgule in the middle of the word), "religion" was not a dominant and independent variable, "a discrete category of human experience" – to use Schwartz's formulation – disembeddable from the culture as a whole.

It is, therefore, meaningless semiotically as well as historically to claim that Judaism existed before there was another term in the semiotic system, the names of religions, for it to be *not* that, and there is no point

---

[19] However, it must not be thought that these ethnic groups, themselves, just existed. They are also constructed identity formations that arise in particular historical circumstances. For discussion of the construction of Israel as "ethnicity" in antiquity, see Regina M. Schwartz, *The Curse of Cain: The Violent Legacy of Monotheism* (Chicago: U. of Chicago Press, 1997) and Ilana Pardes, *The Biography of Ancient Israel: National Narratives in the Bible,* Contraversions (Berkeley: U. of California, 2000). For ancient Greece and its ethnicity/ies, see Hall, *Ethnic Identity.*

in even attempting to define a pre-Christian "Judaism" or Judaisms.[20] In other words, *Ioudaismos* in the sense of "Judaism" could only appear after *Christianismos* had appeared. *Christianismos* too, as the name for a religion, can only appear in opposition to *Ioudaismos* as the name for another religion, and that, as we shall see, has had important material consequences. A strong analogy to this point is that heterosexuality and homosexuality could only have come into the world together, and together as elements in a new paradigm called "sexualities." Similarly, I claim, Judaism and Christianity as the names of religions could only come into the world together as elements in that paradigm, "religions."

It should be emphasized that *Ioudaismos*, even before it became a "religion," nevertheless constituted a cultural complex that had important religious elements. The argument, then, is that, following the epistemic shift for which I am arguing, *Ioudaismos* was transformed into a religion containing important national, ethnic and cultural elements.

The coming of Christianity, it would seem, made the difference. The most dramatic innovation that Christianity introduced into the world was the making of a new kind of identity, "religion." It would follow from this that it was this invention, moreover, that produced the Jewish religion as well. Accepting the positions of such scholars as Wilfred Cantwell Smith[21] and, more recently, Talal Asad,[22] that our modern concept of religion is a historical product of Christianity, I will suggest a revision to this thesis, proposing that this historical production does not belong to the eighteenth century but was in process from nearly the beginnings of certain parts of the Jesus movement and largely complete – whatever that might mean precisely – by the beginning of the fifth century. Late antique historian Seth Schwartz has strikingly phrased this point by referring to

---

[20] This goes further, then, than the approach of Jonathan Z. Smith, who took us pretty far indeed when he wrote, "All three [Gnosticism, Judaism, Apocalypticism] have most usually been treated as reified, substantive nouns (indeed, as proper names); I would like to reduce each to the status of qualifying adjectives. There is no essence of Gnosticism, Judaism or Apocalypticism. Rather there is a shifting cluster of attributes which, for a particular purpose and in terms of a given document, makes one or another of these labels appropriate" (*Map is not Territory: Studies in the History of Religions* [Chicago: U. of Chicago Press, 1993], x). Smith's approach already makes it virtually impossible to speak of Judaism or even of Judaisms; I suggest, further, that these labels function only as signifiers within a signifying system in which they are differentiated from others semiotically. Thus we have to determine the synchronic structure of the semantic field at any given time and space. For the period under question in this research, until there is "Christianity" in the semiotic system as something that is not-Judaism, then there cannot be "Judaism" either.

[21] Wilfred Cantwell Smith, *The Meaning and End of Religion* (London: SPCK, 1978).

[22] Talal Asad, *Genealogies of Religion: Discipline and Reasons of Power in Christianity and Islam* (Baltimore: Johns Hopkins UP, 1993).

"Christianization, and what is in social-historical terms its sibling, the emergence of religion as a discrete category of human experience – religion's *disembedding*."[23] What Schwartz is claiming and what my work here will support is that the production of Christianity, and thus the production of Judaism as a religion in this sense, is itself the invention of religion as such a discrete category. The production of such a category does not imply that many elements of what would form religions did not exist before this time but rather that the particular aggregation of verbal and other practices that would be named now as constituting a religion only came into being as a discrete category as Christianization.[24] Tracing a similar trajectory lexically, Maurice Sachot has argued that the term *religio*, in the sense in which we use it, is entirely the product of Christianity.[25] Schwartz has written that the disembedding of religion that constitutes the very invention of religion "had a direct impact on the Jewish culture of Late Antiquity because the Jewish communities *appropriated* much from the Christian society around them."[26]

In other words, when Christianity separated religious belief and practice from *Romanitas,* cult from culture, Judaism as a religion came into the world as well. The Rabbis articulated their own sense of identity and definition in part through "appropriation," not of course at this period owing to any power or dominance that "Christianity" – even if it made sense to claim the existence of such an entity – possessed, but owing to the compelling force of the question of identity asked by at least some early Christians. The partial (not parodic, but partial and in some sense strategic) "appropriation" referred to by Schwartz is not, then, on the interpretation to be offered here, a mimesis of or the product of the

---

[23] Seth Schwartz, *Imperialism and Jewish Society from 200 B.C.E.. to 640 C.E.* (Princeton: Princeton UP, 2001), 179.

[24] For a similar argument with respect to the emergence of sexuality as such a discrete category, see David M. Halperin, "How to Do the History of Male Homosexuality," *GLQ: A Journal of Lesbian and Gay Studies* 6.1 (2000): 87–123.

[25] Maurice Sachot, "Comment le christianisme est-il devenu religio?" *Revue des sciences religieuses* 59 (1985): 95–118; Maurice Sachot, "«Religio/Superstitio». Historique d'une subversion et d'un retournement," *Revue d'histoire des religions* CCVIII.4 (1991): 355–94. See also Eric Laupot, "Tacitus' Fragment 2: The Anti-Roman Movement of the Christiani and the Nazoreans," *VigChr* 54.3 (2000): 233–47, who argues that the word "religio" has been substituted for an original "superstitio" in a Tacitean fragment reproduced in Sulpicius Severus' *Chronicles*. See also the interesting formulation of Frend, "After circa A.D. 100 there was less of a tendency for Christians to claim to be Israel and more of a tendency to contrast Christianity and Judaism as separate religions. Christianity claimed to be heir to the universalist claims of Judaism. 'Catholic' or 'universal' was applied to the church for the first time. One can recognize the transition in Ignatius' letters" (*The Rise of Christianity* [Philadelphia: Fortress, 1984], 124).

[26] S. Schwartz, *Jewish Society*, 179.

influence of Christianity on Judaism. It should be read, I will argue, as a kind of mimicry (in the technical post-colonial sense) and thus as an act of resistance in the sense articulated by Bhabha:

> Resistance is not necessarily an oppositional act of political intention, nor is it the simple negation or exclusion of the 'content' of another culture, as a difference once perceived. It is the effect of an ambivalence produced within the rules of recognition of dominating discourses as they articulate the signs of cultural difference and reimplicate them within the deferential relations of colonial power – hierarchy, normalization, marginalization and so forth.[27]

Schwartz has given us, too, a further and more fine-grained statement of his notion of "appropriation":

> We should not be debating whether some pre-existing Jewish polity declined or prospered, or think only about relatively superficial cultural borrowing conducted by two well defined groups. In my view, we should be looking for *systemic change*: the Jewish culture which emerged in Late Antiquity was radically distinctive, and distinctively late antique – a product of the same political, social and economic forces which produced the no less distinctive Christian culture of Late Antiquity.[28]

Schwartz, appropriately for the purposes of his book, does not further specify those forces but does set a major agenda for my own work. By entirely revisioning the problematic of the so-called "Parting of the Ways,"[29] thinking it as a much later and very different process from that which is usually portrayed, we find the formations of Judaism and Christianity ineluctably bound up in the question of Christianization, Peter Brown's "great society going over a watershed," the "systemic change" to which Schwartz refers. If Christianity becomes, then, the symbolic religious marker of the place of the Universal, transcendent, and translocal in the making of Imperial power, then Judaism becomes the place-holder of the very other of that Universal, the particular, the ethnic, the local.[30] One of the important constructive hypotheses of my work is that *both* Orthodox Christianity and "Orthodox" rabbinic Judaism, or perhaps better put, the system of orthodoxies that comprised both the church and the rabbinic formation, was an element in that aspect of the history of Roman Imperial power that was concerned with the discourse

---

[27] Bhabha, *Location of Culture*, 110–11.

[28] S. Schwartz, *Jewish Society*, 184.

[29] For a fine discussion of the problems of this very formulation of the historical issue, see Judith Lieu, "'The Parting of the Ways': Theological Construct or Historical Reality?" *JSNT* 56 (1994): 101–19.

[30] David Brakke, "'Outside the Places, Within the Truth': Athanasius of Alexandria and the Localization of the Holy," *Pilgrimage and Holy Space in Late Antique Egypt (and Its Mediterranean Neighbors)*, ed. David Frankfurter (Leiden: Brill, in press). And see as well David Brakke, "Jewish Flesh and Christian Spirit in Athanasius of Alexandria," *JECS* 9.4 (2001): 453–81.

of religion, that aspect of the history that is conventionally denominated
as Christianization.


## Thinking Hybridity in Language

In my 1999 work, *Dying for God*, I suggested that we might think of
Christianity and Judaism in the second and third centuries as points on a
continuum from the Marcionites, who followed the second-century
Marcion in believing that the Hebrew Bible had been written by an
inferior God and had no standing for Christians, and who completely
denied the "Jewishness" of Christianity, on one end, to many Jews on the
other end for whom Jesus meant nothing. In the middle, however, there
were many gradations that provided social and cultural progression across
this spectrum. In other words, to use a linguistic metaphor, I proffered a
wave-theory account of Christian-Jewish history, in which innovations
disseminate and interact like waves caused by stones thrown in a pond, an
account in which convergence was as possible as divergence, as opposed
to the traditional *Stammbaum* or family tree model, within which virtually
only divergence was possible – after 70 A.C. in some versions, or after
135 A.C. in others. I argued the case via a close analysis of Christian and
Jewish texts about martyrdom produced in the second, third, and fourth
centuries and proposed that the best way to account for many features of
these texts was the assumption of shared cultural, religious innovations
flowing in both directions, providing social contiguity and contact and
even cultural continuity between the two religious groups in formation.[31]
To put the same point in terms drawn from postcolonial studies, we must
imagine, I think, a "contact zone," a space of "transculturation," where,
as Mary Louise Pratt defines it, "disparate cultures meet, clash, grapple
with each other, often in highly asymmetrical relations of domination and
subordination."[32] The advantage of the wave-theory model for my
purposes here is that it does not presuppose an originary separateness of
the two cultures in question, which the colonial description tends to.[33]

---

[31] It should be emphasized that wave theory is the historical or diachronic
complement of dialect geography. For discussion of the latter and the fuzzy boundaries
that it indicates between dialects, see William Labov, "The Boundaries of Words and
Their Meanings," *New Ways of Analyzing Variation in English*, ed. Charles-James N.
Bailey and Roger. W. Shuy (Washington, D.C.: Georgetown UP, 1973), 344–47.

[32] Mary Louise Pratt, *Imperial Eyes Travel Writing and Transculturation* (London:
Routledge, 1992).

[33] For other versions of problematization of "pure precolonial" selves as
projected by certain versions of postcolonial analyses, see Ania Loomba,
*Colonialism/Postcolonialism*, New Critical Idiom (London: Routledge, 1998), 181–82.
See too, "Bhabha's notion of 'hybridity' implies that the colonial space involves the

The religious dialect map is a hybridized one, and the point is that the hybridity extends even to those religious groups that would consider themselves "purely" Jewish or "purely" Christian in their self-understanding. This shift in model is significant, not only for purely scholarly reasons, by which I mean that it provides a better, "truer" description of "facts," but also because it represents a shift in fundamental understandings of human difference and its meanings. Writing in an analogous context, Robert Young has said: "We may note here the insistently genetic emphasis on the metaphor of 'families' of languages, and the oft-charted language 'trees' which were to determine the whole basis of phylogenetic racial theories of conquest, absorption and decline – designed to deny the more obvious possibilities of mixture, fusion and creolization."[34] It is, then, no minor matter to revise our basic metaphors for understanding how "religions" – Christianity, Judaism, and Paganism – came into being.[35]

The wave-theory analogy can be productively extended in ways that I hope will clarify my approach to modeling the hybridity of the late ancient religious world and narrating the history of the emergence of Judaism and Christianity in Late Antiquity. Jonathan M. Hall has undertaken a critical rethinking of the use of ancient genealogical texts for the reconstruction of archaic Greek history.[36] Among the other issues and methods that Hall has employed in his investigation are linguistic ones, in particular *Stammbaum* vs. Wave Theory. Traditional historiography of Greek ethnicity has assumed that the various Greek groups, as well as their dialects (Ionian, Dorian, and so forth) derived from a once unified proto-Greek. Assuming this original unity and subsequent divergence has enabled historians to construct narratives of tribal migrations and invasions in the pre-archaic period. Hall mounts a critique of this methodology. Hall's argument, however, could have been enhanced by a

---

interaction of two originally 'pure' cultures (the British/European and the native) that are only rendered ambivalent once they are brought into direct contact with each other"; Richard King, *Orientalism and Religion: Postcolonial Theory, India and the Mystic East* (London: Routledge, 1999), 204. While I am somewhat doubtful as to whether this critique is properly applied to Bhabha, it does seem relevant to me in considering the postcolonial model for reading Judaism and Christianity in antiquity, which are surely always/already hybridized with respect to each other, as it were.

[34] Robert Young, *Colonial Desire: Hybridity in Theory, Culture, and Race* (London: Routledge, 1995), 65.

[35] The perspective outlined in Daniel Boyarin, *Border Lines: The Invention of Heresy and the Emergence of Christianity and Judaism*, Divinations: Rereading Late Ancient Religions (Stanford: Stanford UP, 2004) is generally similar to that of Mary Beard, John A North, and S. R. F. Price, *Religions of Rome* (Cambridge: Cambridge UP, 1998), 307–12.

[36] Hall, *Ethnic Identity*.

sharper articulation of Wave Theory itself. Clarifying the difference between his and my understanding may prove an effective way for me to propose a first rough draft of the theory that I am developing in my work. Hall believes that Wave Theory, just as much as *Stammbaum* theory, presupposes primal linguistic (cultural) uniformity and merely explains the differences between dialects as owing to diffusion of innovations over various parts of the language area.[37] However, it is the virtue of Wave Theory, as usually understood by historical linguists, that it does *not* presuppose a unified proto-language at any point in time and imagines dialects in contiguous geographical areas becoming more like each other than previously, not less, and thus producing dialect groups. Wave Theory is, thus, more akin to the situation that Hall himself imagines as the historical origin of groupings such as Dorian in archaic Greece, where once unrelated groups became more like each other, linguistically and otherwise, and agglomerated into the "ethnic" groups known from the archaic period.

This is a model to which I appeal as well. I am not claiming an undifferentiated "Judaism" that formed itself into Judaism and Christianity through the "borrowing" of various religious traits but rather an assortment of religious "dialects" throughout the Jewish world that gradually developed structure as clusters through diffusion and were eventually organized as "languages" (religions) through processes very much analogous to those by which national languages, such as French and Italian, were also formed. In other words, I am not denying that in the second, third, and fourth centuries there were religious groups that were more Christian than others (I shall immediately below be talking about what this comparative might mean), nor that there were groups that were not Christian at all, but rather that the various Christian groups formed a dialect cluster within the overall assortment of dialects that constituted Judaism (or perhaps, better, Judaeo-Christianity) at the time.

Hall himself argues that "the clustering of dialects within dialect groups is 'a scholars' heuristic fiction'." Linguist William Labov has also written: "But in regard to geographical dialects, it has long been argued that such gradient models are characteristic of the diffusion of linguistic features across a territory and the challenge has been to establish that boundaries between dialects are anything but arbitrary." However, Labov goes on to state: "Nevertheless, even in dialect geography, most investigators agree that properties do bundle, and that it is possible to show boundaries of varying degrees of clarity even when all variable features are superimposed upon a single map."[38] In other words, one can model a

---

[37] To be sure, he is careful to ascribe this version of Wave Theory to a single scholar, W. F. Wyatt; see Hall, *Ethnic Identity*, 166.

[38] Labov, "Boundaries of Words," 347.

situation in which there will be persons or groups who will clearly be "Christian" or "non-Christian Jewish," that is, who will form definable clusters of religious features, while the boundaries between the two categories will remain undefinable. The eventual triumph (or even partial triumph) of orthodoxies in defining a separate identity for the two "religions," is much like the formation of national languages. Remarking that many dialects of Italian are more understandable by French speakers than by other Italians, and citing other similar phenomena, Hall writes:

> What allows for this at first sight surprising phenomenon is the fact that a "national language" is seldom a higher order linguistic category which embraces and subsumes its constituent dialects. It is, rather, an invention which rarely precedes the nineteenth century and which owes its existence to reasons "that are as much political, geographical, historical, sociological and cultural as linguistic." From a linguistic point of view, there is little or no difference between a standardised national language and a dialect in terms of their hierarchical ranking within the historical structure of a language.[39]

Adding only the proviso, following Labov, that dialects do group eventually into dialect clusters, analogous to Judaism and Christianity in formation, I suggest, once more, that this provides a powerful analogy for thinking about the history of these nascent "religions." Not via a separation, a "Parting of the Ways," but via choices made by different groups of different specific indicia of identity,[40] and the diffusion and clustering of such indicia (such as, eventually, non-compliance with the Law – hardly an essential "Christian" trait[41]) were groups gradually congealing into Christianity and Judaism, but it was only with the mobilizations of temporal power (via Ideological State Apparatuses and Repressive State Apparatuses[42]) in the fourth century that the process can be said to have formed "religions." One might say that Judaism and Christianity were invented in order to explain the fact that there were Jews and Christians.

---

[39] Hall, *Ethnic Identity*, 172.

[40] "What an ethnic group does is actively and consciously to select certain artefacts from within the overall material cultural repertoire which then act as emblemic indicia of ethnic boundaries. In the words of Catherine Morgan, 'ethnic behaviour affects only those categories of artefact selected to carry social or political meaning under particular circumstances, rather than the totality of a society's material culture'"; Hall, *Ethnic Identity*, 135. In this case, religious ideas and practices are the equivalent of artefacts. One example of this point is the identification of "modalism" and its opposite as variation within Judaeo-Christian theology that was eventually chosen to be among the most significant of indicia for Christian and Jewish separate religious identity.

[41] It was Jack Miles who originally suggested to me that the conflict over the Law animated every page of the New Testament and that, therefore, "rejection" of the Law could not be made part of an "intensional" definition of Christianity over-against Judaism.

[42] For this distinction, see Althusser, "Ideology."

In suggesting that Judaism and Christianity were not separate entities until very late in Late Antiquity, I am, accordingly, not claiming that it is impossible to discern separate social groups that are in an important sense Christian/not-Jewish or Jewish/not-Christian from fairly early on (by which I mean the mid-second century). In order to make the opposite claim, even if I believed it, I would have to do a very different kind of historical research from what I am doing here. Indeed, although I do not know quite how one would show this, such "separatist" groups may have been statistically dominant much earlier than the fifth century. Thus I cannot answer empirical questions such as: how much were Christian and other Jewish congregations mixed at any given time or place? Or, what was the social status of Jewish-Christian groups; were they accepted as Jews, as Christians (by whom?), or neither at any given time?

Instead, the question that I pose is a theoretical one, or at least an interpretative one: Even if we grant the statistical dominance (and perhaps a certain power dominance, although, once more, I don't know how we would show or know this) of the separatists, in terms of the semantics of the cultural language, the discourse of the time, are there sets of features that absolutely define who is a Jew and who is a Christian in such wise that the two categories will not seriously overlap, irrespective of the numbers of members of the blurring sets? I think not.

The perspective adopted here is not unlike that of Beard, North, and Price, who write:

> Our last section in this chapter does investigate the degrees of religious continuity in these cults traceable across the Roman world. By and large, however, in discussing the religions of the empire we have tried to avoid thinking in terms of uniformity, or in terms of a central core 'orthodox' tradition with its peripheral 'variants'; we have preferred to think rather in terms of different religions as clusters of ideas, people and rituals, sharing some common identity across time and place, but at the same time inevitably invested with different meanings in their different contexts.[43]

Another body of theory may help us make progress in understanding a situation in which there are recognizably separate entities within a given field but no way to articulate the borders between them. Mobilizing some recent thought in semantics might help us in thinking about this issue. These theories begin with Wittgenstein's notion of family resemblance in the formation of semantic fields.[44] In Chana Kronfeld's succinct formulation: "Members of one family share a variety of similar features: eyes, gait, hair color, temperament. But – and this is the crucial point –

---

[43] Beard, North, and Price, *Religions*, 249.

[44] Partially anticipated by Beard, et al, who cite R. Needham, "Polythetic Classification: Convergence and Consequences," *Man* n.s. 10 (1975): 349–69.

there need be no one set of features shared by all family members."[45]
There is, perhaps, one feature that constitutes all as members of the
Judaeo-Christian semantic family: appeal to the Hebrew Scriptures as
revelation. In all other respects, the category of Jews/Christians
constitutes a family in which any one sub-group might share features with
any other (on *either* side of that supposed divide) but not all features with
any, and there is no one set of features that uniquely determines a
Christian group (except, of course, for some appeal to Jesus, which is
simply an analytic statement and therefore tautologous) over and against
a non-Christian Jewish group.          needless repetitron

Kronfeld's work, of course, has been devoted to an entirely different
classificatory problem, namely, the description of "modernism" as a
literary movement, but it is a relevant one for my inquiry in that it has to
do with groups of people and their practices and the ways that they and
others (including "scholars") array the people and the practices into
named categories (as opposed, for example, to the ways that people
[including scholars/scientists] categorize plants, animals, or colors).[46] The
problems and solutions that she has envisioned will, therefore, be useful
for me. Kronfeld has written:

> Despite the overwhelming evidence that modernism defies reduction to simple
> common denominators, one study after another, after asserting the complexity
> and heterogeneity of the various manifestations of modernism, proceeds to
> attempt the impossibly positivist task of providing a definition of modernism;
> and this usually means, explicitly or tacitly, an attempt at what logicians call an
> intensional definition – namely, a list of necessary and sufficient conditions for
> all modernist trends .... While it would be nice for a theory of modernism to
> have the explanatory power that an intensional definition can facilitate (by
> showing clearly what makes all the branches of modernism part of one
> distinctive movement or trend), such an approach would force us to restrict
> severely the extension of what we could term modernist. Many important works,
> authors, and even entire groups that identified themselves as modernist and that
> are commonly perceived to be subsumed under this admittedly tattered and
> oversized umbrella would have to be kept out. There simply is no set of
> distinctive features that can apply to all the subgroupings of modernism (from

---

[45] Chana Kronfeld, *On the Margins of Modernism: Decentering Literary Dynamics*,
Contraversions (Berkeley: U. of California, 1996), 28. I wish specifically to thank Prof.
Kronfeld for suggesting this direction which has proved very fruitful for me and for
much much else.

[46] Just in case, my formulation has not done so already, I wish to make absolutely
clear that the distinction that I am drawing here is not between "folk" and "scientific"
modes of classification but between the classifications of groups of people and things
that people do and the classifications of non-human objects. These are related cognitive
tasks, of course, but also significantly different. See also Robert D. Baird, *Category
Formation and the History of Religions* (The Hague: Mouton, 1971).

futurism to surrealism) and separate them from all nonmodernist groupings (classicism, baroque, romanticism, and so forth).[47]

The problem with Judaism/Christianity is somewhat different, but analogous enough for this statement of the issue to be useful for me. While, as I have said, there is one (analytic) feature that could be said to be common to all groups that we might want to call (anachronistically) "Christian," namely some form of discipleship to Jesus, this feature hardly captures enough richness and depth to produce an interesting category, for in so many other vitally important ways, groups that follow Jesus and groups that ignore him are similar to each other. Or, put another way, groups that ignore (or reject) Jesus may have some highly salient other religious features (for instance, logos theology) that binds them to Jesus groups and disconnects them from other non-Jesus-Jews, or some Jesus-Jews may have aspects to their religious lives (to wit, following Pharisaic halakha) that draws them closer to some non-Jesus-Jews than to other Jesus People.[48] Moreover, some Jesus groups might relate to Jesus in ways phenomenologically more similar to the ways that other Jewish groups relate to other prophets, leaders, or Messiahs than to the ways that other Jesus groups are relating to Jesus, and the reverse: some non-Jesus-Jews might very well have had in their religious lives elements similar to the belief in an incarnated or present mediator from God.[49] The model of family resemblance that Kronfeld develops for talking about modernism seems, therefore, apt for talking about Judaeo-Christianity as well. "[Judaeo-Christianity] can remain one clear category even though no two subtrends within it may share the same features."[50]

There is, however, another issue for my project that can be illuminated via Kronfeld's version of semantic categorization, because there is another problem that I face here. I am not only trying to describe a category called "Judaeo-Christianity" (I would prefer just to call it Judaism), but also to account for a division within this category that will ultimately produce a binary opposition between categories, namely between Christianity and Judaism. The part of the theory that seems relevant for this works with what is called the "prototype theory of

---

[47] Kronfeld, *On the Margins of Modernism*, 27.

[48] Albert I. Baumgarten, "Literary Evidence for Jewish Christianity in the Galilee," *The Galilee in Late Antiquity*, ed. Lee I. Levine (New York: Jewish Theological Seminary of America, 1992), 39–50.

[49] For the general perspective, see Alan F. Segal, *The Other Judaisms of Late Antiquity*, Brown Judaic Studies 127 (Atlanta: Scholars Press, 1987).

[50] Kronfeld, *On the Margins of Modernism*, 29 For an interesting use of family-resemblance semantics (without mentioning it explicitly) in an important problem in late antique religious history, see Nathaniel Deutsch, *Guardians of the Gate: Angelic Vice Regency in Late Antiquity*, Brill's Series in Jewish Studies (Leiden: Brill, 1999), 14.

categorization."[51] The *"prototype*, in the technical sense developed by Rosch and others, is a member of the category (for example, birds) which is considered a 'best example' of that category (sparrow, swallow, or robin, but not turkey, penguin, or chicken)."[52]

Prototype semantics makes, moreover, distinctions between categories, however family-resemblance-like, that have clear boundaries and categories that don't. Some things may be prototypical birds, and indeed different birds can be more or less central to the category – this is called the "centrality gradience" – but in the end a given object is either a bird or it isn't. The category "bird" is not, seemingly, one with "extendable boundaries" like the categories "number" or "game." Thus, George Lakoff has written with respect to Eleanor Rosch's work:

> For example, take her results showing prototype effects within the category bird. Her experimental rankings shows that subjects view robins and sparrows as the best examples of birds, with owls and eagles lower down in the rankings and ostriches, emus, and penguins among the worst examples. In the early to mid 1970's ... such empirical goodness-of-example ratings were commonly taken as constituting a claim to the effect that membership in the category bird is graded and that owls and penguins are less members of the bird category than robins .... It later became clear that that was a mistaken interpretation of the data. Rosch's ratings ... are consistent with the interpretation that the category bird has strict boundaries and that robins, owls, and penguins are all 100 percent members of that category. However, that category must have additional internal structure of some sort that produces these goodness-of-example ratings.[53]

Similarly, there may be "best examples" (prototypes) of "Jew" and "Christian" already in the second or third century with, however, an internal structure to the category that will allow other-than-best examples to be members of the group as well.[54] This is the semantic analogue of Labov's point about dialect grouping in language geography: Are there or are there not "objective" criteria with which such distinctions can be made? This is particularly relevant, I think, when there are different political actors in antiquity and in the present as well (both in "scholarship" and outside of it) attempting to make such determinations. "Best example" is itself a context-bound,[55] historically shifting, and therefore political category. In a situation such as the one under investigation, moreover, it can be (and is) a contested one. Another way

---

[51] For a good general introduction to this theory, see George Lakoff, *Women, Fire, and Dangerous Things: What Categories Reveal About the Mind* (Chicago: U. of Chicago Press, 1987) 12–58.

[52] Kronfeld, *On the Margins of Modernism*, 29.

[53] Lakoff, *Women, Fire, and Dangerous Things*, 44–45.

[54] The situation of law-observing "Jewish Christians" in Justin's *Dialogue* would be a case in point. "People of the Land" in rabbinic parlance is another.

[55] As Kronfeld remarks, "turkey" is the best example of bird on Thanksgiving.

*Daniel Boyarin*

of putting this is to say that I am inquiring whether an emu would have a different sense of what the best example of a bird is than a robin would, and, moreover, do robins get to judge what a bird is?

There is, moreover, a further wrinkle. Another kind of category has "unclear boundaries," and then, in addition to a centrality gradience, there is a "membership gradience" as well. *Judaism* and *Christianity*, I want to claim, are categories more like *red* and *tall* than like *bird* (or perhaps a fuzzy category of categories somewhere on the boundaries between categories like "bird" and categories like "tall"): "It seems to me that (modernism) [Judaism/Christianity] present(s) so many difficulties for the (literary theorist) [historian of religions] partly because in its different constructions it involves both centrality and membership gradience."[56] As Lakoff has argued,

> Prototype effects are superficial. They may result from many factors. In the case of a graded category like *tall man,* which is fuzzy and does not have rigid boundaries, prototype effects may result from degree of category membership, while in the case of *bird,* which does have rigid boundaries, the prototype effects must result from some other aspect of internal category structure.[57]

Lakoff does not emphasize (at least at that juncture) that there is another consequence of this difference between types of categories. One cannot be both a *bird* and a *fish,* but one can be both a *tall* man and a *short* man. Moreover, I suspect that this latter form of category is typically the case for the human construction of categories of the human and that much human violence is generated simply by resisting the fuzziness of our own categories of socio-cultural division. Just as certain entities can be more or less tall or red, I wish to suggest they can be more or less Christian (or Jewish) as well. And just as certain entities can be tall and short given different perspectives, so too can certain people or groups be Christian or Jewish from different perspectives, or both.[58]

---

[56] Kronfeld, *On the Margins of Modernism*, 30.

[57] Lakoff, *Women, Fire, and Dangerous Things*, 45.

[58] Another riveting analogy comes to the fore: Kronfeld writes, "My investigations of Hebrew and Yiddish modernist poetry have consistently presented a fascinating paradox: that although many modernists defined very clearly their poetic principles (typically formulated in rather strong terms by group manifestoes or individual aesthetic credos), the best examples – or prototypes – that came to represent these trends (individual poets or even individual works) are often quite atypical of or only marginally consistent with the principles of the group" (*On the Margins of Modernism*, 31), to which one might revealing compare, I think, a paradox uncovered by Shaye Cohen who shows that the prototypical converts to Judaism (from "paganism") in the Talmuds do not follow the explicit rules laid down for conversion; Cohen, "The Conversion of Antoninus," *The Talmud Yerushalmi and Graeco-Roman Culture*, ed. Peter Schäfer, TSAJ 71 (Tübingen: Mohr Siebeck, 1998), 167 and passim. Cohen could have made, I think, further progress on analyzing this paradox (to which

Indeed, the determination itself will be a matter of contention. Jerome's very important notice that the sect of Nazarenes are to be found "in all of the synagogues of the East among the Jews" and that they consider themselves both Christians and Jews but are really "neither Christians nor Jews," is emblematic of this point.[59]

Let us imagine that "Jew" and "Christian" are both categories with gradation of membership. Moreover, while both have "central" members (which can be different at different times and even at the same time for different groups), there will be a semantic (and in this case, therefore, social[60]) chain that connects the most central and salient members to others:

> Another case is where I call *B* by the same name as *A*, because it resembles *A*, *C* by the same name because it resembles *B*, *D*... and so on. But ultimately *A* and

---

he basically merely points) by considering comments such as the following: "Focusing on these modernist prototypes tends to foreground one or two highly salient poetic features which fulfill or match some particular (artistic, linguistic, ideological, or social) need. In each case, there are specific reasons, which need to be reconstructed and analyzed, why a particular feature came to be perceived as exemplary within the particular conditions for the creation and reception of a particular brand of modernism at a particular historical and cultural juncture. This contextually motivated salience raising creates, among other things, a series of 'deviant prototypes,' artistic paragons and exemplary texts that do not centrally belong to any trend but have nevertheless come to represent it" (Kronfeld, *On the Margins of Modernism*, 31–32).

[59] Jerome, *Correspondence*, ed. Isidorus Hilberg, Corpus Scriptorum Ecclesiast-icorum Latinorum (Vienna: Verlag der Osterreichischen Akademie der Wissenschaften, 1996), 55:381–2.

[60] One of the interesting phenomena about religious categories is the ways that sub-groups will mutually deny each other's salience or centrality as member of the group. We might think that "Pharisee" is a Jew if anyone is a Jew (just as integer is a number if anything is a number), but it seems that (on the Talmud's account itself), there were others who would have denied that claim, because by believing the resurrection of the dead, Pharisees were rendering themselves less Jewish than others! Interestingly, this feature, believing in resurrection of the dead is taken as absolutely necessary for being a Jew by some non-Christian Jews and for being a Christian by some Christians and denied by some of both. In other words, we have a doubly complicated system here, for while a group such as the Fox Indians (example from Lakoff, *Women, Fire, and Dangerous Things*, 23–24) may have complicated rules for determining who is an "uncle" with graded salience of prototypicality in the category, in our case there are, in effect, competing groups claiming the right to be called "uncle" or not or to be "better" uncles than others. The semantic situation remains, nevertheless, the same. It is fascinating that one of the characteristic claims of heresiologists is that they are "Christians" while others are hyphenated in some way, e.g., Valentinian Christians; in other words that the claim is that "we" are the prototype itself. Similarly the Rabbis call "heretics," "kinds" [מינים], in my view, to imply that "we" are the prototype of Jew, while they, by being "kinds" of Jews are less salient, less centrally members of the category. This kind of semantics gives us tools for understanding the complexity of the discourses of religious categorization.

say *D* do not resemble each other in any recognizable sense at all. This is a very common case: and the dangers are obvious when we search for something "identical" in all of them![61]

The net result will be that there might indeed be people who are prototypes of *Jew* but also *Christian* (say a Pharisee who observes all of the Pharisaic laws and rules but believes that Jesus is the Messiah) and, moreover, that the "best example" of *Jew* and *Christian* would almost definitely be both a politically charged and a diachronically varying category. Further, while there would be *Jews* who would not recognize certain other Jews as such, there might be ones whom they would recognize as Jews who would recognize in turn those others as Jews, setting up the possibility of chained communion or communication. An example of this phenomenon (from the other "side") would be Justin, who recognizes as Christians precisely those Jewish Christians to whom Jerome, much later of course, would deny the name *Christian*, even though Jerome would have certainly recognized Justin as Christian. Those so-called Jewish Christians surely thought of themselves as both Jews and Christians, and some non-Christian Jews may very well have recognized them as Jews as well.

Therefore, with respect to religious history we must add yet another factor, which may be less relevant to a literary movement like modernism (although probably equally salient for something like "Marxism"), to wit, the activities of writers/speakers who wish to transform the fuzzy category into one with absolutely clear borders and the family resemblance into a checklist of features that will determine an intensional definition for who is in and who is out of the group as it defines itself and, therefore, its others.[62] Returning to the wave-theory metaphor, these are the legislators who wish, as well, to determine and enforce clear

---

[61] J. L. Austin, *Philosophical Papers* (Oxford: Clarendon, 1961), 72.

[62] Note the contrast between this account and Lakoff's statement that "we even have a folk model of what categories themselves are, and this folk model has evolved into the classical theory of categorization. Part of the problem that prototype theory now has, and will face in the future, is that it goes beyond our folk understanding of categorization. And much of what has given the classical theory its appeal over the centuries is that it meshes with our folk theory and seems like simple common sense" (*Women, Fire, and Dangerous Things*, 118). I am suggesting that for the categories Jew and Christian it is distinctly possible that "folk models" worked more like prototype or experiential real categories for centuries, while it was precisely the work of certain "experts" to attempt to impose "traditional" or "objective" categorization upon them. For something like this claim, working however out of a somewhat different theoretical model, see Galit Hasan-Rokem, "Narratives in Dialogue: A Folk Literary Perspective on Interreligious Contacts in the Holy Land in Rabbinic Literature of Late Antiquity," *Sharing the Sacred: Religious Contacts and Conflicts in the Holy Land First–Fifteenth Centuries CE*, ed. Guy Stroumsa and Arieh Kofsky (Jerusalem: Yad Ben Zvi, 1998), 109–29.

boundaries between languages, to decide what is orthodox French and what is orthodox Italian. These are the writers whom we know of now as heresiologists. The discursive practice known as heresiology was crucial in the formation of Judaism and Christianity as religions for all that it appeared in very different textual guise in each of these cultures.[63]

---

[63] Boyarin, *Border Lines*.

# The Weighing of the Parts

Pivots and Pitfalls in the Study of Early Judaisms
and their Early Christian Offspring

by

ROBERT A. KRAFT

In the study of early Christianity, we often hear references to the "Parting of the Ways" as the process or result of Christianity declaring itself independent of its Jewish origins, and of Judaism reciprocally rejecting Christianity.[1] It is quite obvious that the "ways" that led to classical Christianity and rabbinic Judaism did indeed "part" by the fourth century CE. This becomes true simply by definition, since in those classical Christian and classical Jewish communities, each understood the other as "other." To be a "Christian" involved in part not being a "Jew," and vice versa. They came to understand themselves as exclusively different "religions," and/or perhaps also, at times, exclusively different cultural options.

But the path to such a simple and clear answer is littered with the sorts of complexities that surround all historical and social developments, that is, all human developments; these complexities get masked by the urge to make and keep things clear and simple. It was doubtless with this in mind that the organizers of the Princeton colloquium selected the confrontational title, "The Ways that Never Parted: Jews and Christians in Late Antiquity and the Early Middle Ages." To issue such a challenge to "common knowledge" (or exclusive definition) may appear, on the surface of things, to be a bold step, but it constitutes an invitation to look more closely at the micro-histories behind that "common knowledge" in order to determine what other trajectories may be ascertained. A challenge is offered to a unilateral development model. Ockham's razor is blunted if not shattered, and one of the major results is to explore quite closely the interrelationships of the various parts and participants and

---

[1] See, for example, James D. G. Dunn, *The Partings of the Ways Between Christianity and Judaism and their Significance for the Character of Christianity* (London: SCM, 1991); also idem (ed.), *Jews and Christians: The Parting of the Ways, AD 70 to 135* (the second Durham-Tübingen Research Symposium on Earliest Christianity and Judaism, Durham, September 1989; Cambridge: Eerdmans, 1992).

particularities that in various ways produced the familiar medieval/classical landscape. In an obvious attempt to be clever, I've christened this deconstructive exploratory process "The Weighing of the Parts." Although there is a rash of modern literature that is relevant to this subject, I will make no attempt to survey it extensively or directly, but will pay some attention, by way of footnotes, to aspects of two recent contributions, from Gabrielle Boccaccini and Seth Schwartz.[2]

Several points need to be made, some methodological and others evidentiary. Since effective methodology cannot take place in a vacuum (true by definition; otherwise it would not be considered "effective"), these aspects of method and data cannot always be separated. One of the first lines of attack on traditional assumptions and arguments is the recognition of how many "parts" there are to be "weighed"! It is fashionable in some scholarly circles today to speak of "Judaisms" (rather than simply "Judaism") in the period prior to the ever increasing success of "rabbinic" authority;[3] regarding Christianity, we hear fewer voices speaking of "Christianities" in the early period, but the same recognition is captured with the oft heard references to early Christian "varieties," including discussions of whether such varieties as "gnosticism" can be considered legitimately "Christian."[4] The vocabulary used is perhaps less crucial than the situation it attempts to represent – there are many "parts" to be recognized and weighed in the close study of these materials! And,

---

[2] Most recently, Gabrielle Boccaccini, *Roots of Rabbinic Judaism: An Intellectual History, from Ezekiel to Daniel* (Grand Rapids, MI: Eerdmans, 2002), especially the "Introduction: The Intellectual Quest of Rabbinic Origins and Roots"; and Seth Schwartz, *Imperialism and Jewish Society, 200 B.C.E. to 640 C.E.* (Princeton: Princeton UP, 2001).

[3] The use of "Judaisms" became popularized by the anthology entitled *Judaisms and their Messiahs at the Turn of the Christian Era* (Cambridge: Cambridge UP, 1987), edited by Jacob Neusner, William Scott Green, and Ernest S. Frerichs. Boccaccini is sympathetic: "Neusner's approach has already left its clear imprint on Judaic studies ('from Judaism to Judaisms') and the indication of a much promising method of studying rabbinic origins and roots as a comparison of systems of thought that 'took place in succession to one another'" (*Roots of Rabbinic Judaism*, 14; citing Jacob Neusner, *The Four Stages of Rabbinic Judaism* [London: Routledge, 1998]). Schwartz emphasizes the variety without embracing the plural terminology: "It is difficult to imagine any serious scholar ever again describing the Judaism of the later Second Temple period as a rigorous, monolithic orthodoxy, as was still common only a generation ago" (*Imperialism and Jewish Society*, 4–5); or again, "In this book I assume that ancient Judaism was complex, capacious, and rather frayed at the edges," although not "multiple" (p. 9).

[4] For example, James D. G. Dunn, *Unity and Diversity in the New Testament: An Inquiry into the Character of Earliest Christianity* (London: SCM, 1990–2); Walter Bauer, with Georg Strecker, *Orthodoxy and Heresy in Earliest Christianity* (trans. and ed. from the 2nd German edition, 1964, by Robert Kraft and Gerhard Krodel; Philadelphia: Fortress, 1971).

indeed, this multifaceted situation does not automatically disappear with the "victory" of the respective classical forms of these religions. There continue to be variant, sometimes competing, forms within and sometimes somewhere between each tradition (e.g. Samaritans, Karaite Judaism, Cathar Christianity, Mandeans, Manicheans, "mysticism" of various sorts).

In some ways, there is little that is new in these observations. The presence of "Jewish" groups and/or perspectives labeled Sadducees, Pharisees, Essenes, and more, comes straight from the ancient sources. Modern supplementation, by attempting to give actual social reality to ancient Jews with apocalyptic, wisdom, Enochic, Hellenistic, or other foci, simply increases the possible "parts" we need to deal with.[5] On the Christian side of the ledger, our ancient reporters mention especially "docetics" and "gnostics" of various stripes, and more vaguely "Judaizers" as well as "chiliasts" and the like; modern study has refined things further by categorizing the "parts" as Pauline, Johannine, syncretistic, reformist (e.g., Cynics), and so forth.[6] The naming process is relatively easy. Weighing the parts in relation to each other and to the respective surrounding worlds is quite another matter.[7]

---

[5] Boccaccini provides an excellent example of an attempt to isolate various tendencies and socio-religious interests within Judaism, especially in the period that he labels "middle Judaism" – see his *Middle Judaism: Jewish Thought, 300 B.C.E. to 200 C.E.* (Minneapolis: Fortress, 1991), followed by *Beyond the Essene Hypothesis: The Parting of the Ways between Qumran and Enochic Judaism* (Grand Rapids, MI: Eerdmans, 1998), and now *Roots of Rabbinic Judaism* (2002).

[6] For a general overview of the earliest Christian materials, see Bart D. Ehrman, *The New Testament: a Historical Introduction to the Early Christian Writings* (Oxford: Oxford UP, 2000[2]). See also above, note 4.

[7] In the opening chapter of his *Roots of Rabbinic Judaism*, entitled "Introduction: The Intellectual Quest of Rabbinic Origins and Roots," Boccaccini attempts to survey the work of his recent predecessors, including: E. P. Sanders ("covenantal nomism" as the common denominator or "essence" of Judaism); Lawrence H. Schiffman (an "evolutionary model" in which "the essence of Judaism is its history," which leads to the rabbinic stage); Shaye J. D. Cohen and Martin S. Jaffee (a more ethnocentric model in which "Judaism is the history of its people"); and Jacob Neusner ("the history of Judaism is the history of Judaisms"). Seth Schwartz, whose book appeared after Boccaccini's, would probably fit somewhere between Schiffman's "evolutionary" approach and Neusner's "skepticism," and he uses a large measure of the emphasis on variety and change attributed to Cohen and Jaffee. Schwartz argues for a general "coherence" around "the three pillars of ancient Judaism – the one God, the one Torah, and the one Temple" within which there was "messiness, diversity, and unpredictability of the effects of this system in Jewish Palestinian society in the first century." He also notes "the existence of a subsidiary ideological system – basically, a mildly dualistic mythological narrative – that implicitly contradicted the main one." For Schwartz, "the main sects were in fact an integral part of the Torah-centered Judaean mainstream elite ... the three main sects are evidence not simply of Judaism's diversity but also of the

Definitions and assumptions play crucial, often unrecognized roles in such discussions. If "Judaism" really is taken to be meaningful only in some sort of direct relationship with what it became in its later classical forms (I hesitate to oversimplify even here and say "form") – a definitional assumption that seems to be alive and thriving even in some contemporary scholarly circles – then some aspects of the ancient evidence will be privileged over others (e.g. legal and ritual interests, "biblical" connections, separatism, roots-awareness).[8] It becomes difficult, for example, to imagine someone, or some group, being at the same time "Jewish" and uninterested in aspects of ritual law (e.g. circumcision, food restrictions). Were there such people? Of course. Why should that world be so different from ours? Are they important for purposes of understanding historical developments and processes? Of course. To ignore them or pretend they didn't exist is to neglect an aspect of the real world that creates both attraction and reaction, perhaps revulsion, at the very least. Philo is well aware of such situations, and he tries to tread a fine line between them. For him, understanding meanings is crucial, but he is wary of throwing out the baby with the bath water in failing to find an appropriate balance between meanings and the activities that they interpret.[9] Probably his nephews, Marcus Julius Alexander and Tiberius Julius Alexander, were less committed to such compromise. Would that make them less "Jewish"?

For fruitful pursuit of all such discussions, clear and consistent definition is basic. In my experience, most "arguments" about this subject area are actually valid or invalid (successful or unsuccessful) "by definition." That is, if the definitions being used for "Jewish" or "Christian" were clear and explicit, arguments about whether this or that individual or text or phenomenon could be considered "Jewish" (or "Christian") would simply become unnecessary. If my understanding of "Jewish" does not permit me to apply that term to data in which Jesus is

---

power of its ideological mainstream. For their part, the Christians illustrate the proposition that there were limits to acceptable diversity in ancient Judaism, for those who remained Jewish did so by affirming their adherence to the Torah and at least the idea of a temple, while the rest in short order ceased to regard themselves as Jews" (*Imperialism and Jewish Society*, 49).

[8] As noted above, the most important categories for Schwartz's treatment of Palestinian Judaism in the "second temple" period are God–Torah–Temple (but with lots of variations), which he finds compatible with Sanders' "covenantal nomisim." Some would add the idea of election/peoplehood and the "promised land" (e.g. Dunn, *Partings of the Ways*; see also Boccaccini's presentation of the Cohen-Jaffee approach).

[9] The classic Philonic passage is from *Migration of Abraham* 86–93. Philo sometimes seems caught between his epistemological idealism (attention to essences and meanings) and his socio-political realism (avoiding conflicts or criticisms that weaken community) – a dilemma doubtless encouraged by his Platonic orientation.

uniquely and self-consciously revered, it may be necessary to explore the extent to which a given historical witness does or does not reverence Jesus; when that has been determined, the choice of labels will be self-evident. In such an approach the parts may still be in need of weighing, but that will take place inside of the boundaries imposed by the definition.[10]

But the practice of imposing definitions upon material is not the only possible approach, and in my estimation it is less satisfactory, for historical purposes, than attempting to let the materials define themselves. Admittedly, such relativizing of labels (i.e., definitions) can lead to confusing situations in which self-identifications ("I am a Jew") may be in conflict with assessments made in the same world ("You are not really a Jew"). Even then, however, we can learn more about the historical situation by recognizing the apparent confusion than we can by ignoring it or defining it away. For our "Parting of the Ways" and/or "Weighing of the Parts" perspectives, historical self-identification (explicit or suspected) may force the modern scholar to develop new categories and vocabularies that are more satisfactory for the task. If, in their own understandings, Herod the Great and his successors were "Jewish" – as were Philo and his nephews, Jesus and his opponents, Paul and the other "apostles," Hillel and Shammai, Josephus and Bar Kokhba, etc. – our task as would-be "insiders" is to refine our categories in order to enable better

---

[10] Interestingly, in his otherwise provocative and instructive treatment of Palestinian Judaism's relationship to "Imperial Power," Schwartz seems carefully to avoid proposing or establishing any definition of "Judaism" beyond his rather fuzzy (and largely assumed rather than argued!) triad of God–Torah–Temple, over against which he sees various shades of deviation – for example, "how can the centrality of God–Temple–Torah in Jewish self-definition be proved? What about the Judaean settlements at Elephantine or, more chronologically relevant, at Leontopolis in Egypt? Or the worshipers of the Most High God settled in the Cimmerian Bosporus? Did these Jews, too, if that is what they were, live in symbolic worlds whose central components were the Temple and the Torah?" (*Imperialism and Jewish Society*, 50). He then argues that the centrality of Torah–Temple are "not a priori an eternal truth of Jewish identity, uncontingent on changing social and political conditions" (p. 50) but the result of a process, and that originally "pagan" areas in Palestine that "passed under Judean rule all now became in some sense Jewish" (p. 51) and "had by and large internalized some version of the ideology that was centrally constitutive of Judaism, [but] we must not assume that their Judaism was indistinguishable from that of the Judaeans" (p. 52). Further on, Schwartz mentions the Diaspora, where the legal and social contexts were different, and notes that "it is in the Diaspora that one finds clearest evidence of radically anomalous types of Judaism, as well as a constant trickle of people both in and out of Judaism" (p. 74). He does not show any awareness or provide any discussion of the value of definitions for his project, and it is clear that although he recognizes the value of "self-identification" as an important factor, he does not limit himself to it as the central definitional criterion. These aspects of his otherwise very instructive study are, I think, distressingly problematic.

understandings of the situation(s). This holds similarly for the "Christianity" of such people as Marcion, Montanus, Mani, Valentinus, and the
like. And this requires a whole lot of "weighing" within the historical
contexts that produced the available evidence (and with an awareness of
our own motives and contexts). What issues were important to the
historical participants, and how do those issues affect our historical
understandings?

Complexity is the normal state of human social existence, and
complexity is certainly the rule with reference to the situations under
examination here. Prior to the emergence of self-conscious "Christianity,"
and even after that, there was significant diversity within the seedbed
from which classical Judaism emerged. And from its very start within that
seedbed, Christian varieties would also be expected to be in evidence – is
it likely that all of the earliest followers of Jesus as Messiah/Christ shared
the same attitudes to such things as Jewish ritual, or eschatological
expectations, or sources of authority, or the value of material/physical
existence? Is there any reason to expect such conceptual "unity" at the
earliest period of what comes to be called "Christianity"?[11] While it is
clear that the definitional simplicity of mutually exclusive self-
understandings ("Jewish" means, among other things, not "Christian,"
and vice versa), where it exists, shows parted ways, it is not clear that
historically, every user of these terms "Jewish" or "Christian" (or their
functional equivalents) would accept the exclusivist element. At the start
of the fourth century, Jerome scoffs at those whom he claims to have
encountered in the Syro-Palestinian region who would accept both
designations (for Jerome, "they are neither"!),[12] and we are left to

---

[11] Schwartz acutely observes, without attempting further detail: "Jesus was the
figure expected to usher in the end of the dominion of evil and the beginning of the rule
of God; he and his followers were renowned for their ability to manipulate demons and
free people from their influence. It was a movement, or rather a loose collection of
related groups, that took shape around a distinctive understanding of the
[eschatological] myth complex, a movement in which the Torah was not ignored (it
could not possibly have been) but was definitely of secondary importance" (*Imperialism
and Jewish Society*, 91).

[12] Jerome, *Epistle* 112.13, to Augustine (apparently also designated "Epistle 79" in
some sources) [PL 22.0924/746–747]: *Quid dicam de Ebionitis, qui Christianos esse se
simulant? Usque hodie per totas Orientis synagogas inter Judaeos haeresis est, quae
dicitur Minaeorum, et a Pharisaeis nunc usque damnatur: quos vulgo Nazaraeos
nuncupant, qui credunt in Christum Filium Dei, natum de virgine Maria, et eum dicunt
esse, qui sub Pontio Pilato passus est, et resurrexit, in quem et nos credimus: sed dum
volunt et Judaei esse et Christiani, nec Judaei sunt, nec Christiani.* [Why do I speak
about the Ebionites, who pretend that they are themselves Christians? To this very day,
throughout all the eastern synagogues, there is a heresy/sect among the Jews which is
called "of the Minim" and is condemned even now by the Pharisees. Those people are
commonly designated "Nazarenes," who believe in Christ as Son of God, born of the

speculate whether their multisidedness is indicative of a self-understanding that had continuity from the very outset of "Christianity." Various clues are scattered along the path (e.g. Justin in his dialogue with Trypho on the reception of "Jewish" believers in "Christian" communities;[13] the traditions of Elisha ben Abuya ["Aher," the "other" oriented one];[14] Tertullian on Christians as a "third race"[15]), but it is difficult to connect the dots with any confidence or consistency. And why, after all, should we care?

Some of us are simply nosy, inquisitive. We want to know as many of the "why?"s as we can handle. We are uncomfortable with overly comfortable answers. Some of us may want to explore different solutions to old problems. If Judaism and Christianity were not always mutually exclusive by definition, perhaps some sort of contemporary rapprochement can be recreated with reference to the historical developments; history provides basic justification for trying to reset the clock to a more favorable time and situation. Some of us revel in the unusual, in what seems to challenge the accepted norms. Some of us are looking for evidences of "influence," to try to trace the various tides and ripples on the troubled sea of human history. Some want to focus on the continuities of history, to trace the roots of what has survived to the present. Whatever our motives, we collect the clues and sift the variegated sands to recreate or recapture what we think is a more accurate picture of this aspect of our historical past, which also is to some degree our historical heritage.

How can we proceed responsibly in such difficult waters? We are driven partly by reaction to commonly accepted oversimplifications, although we are always in danger of making the same mistakes in our own reformulations. To be aware that mono-directional models need to be avoided is one thing, actually to avoid them is another. We are also forced to make much use of arguments from analogy – what we can see in our own worlds clearly happening elsewhere or elsewhen may provide us

---

virgin Mary, and they acknowledge that he is the one who suffered/died under Pontius Pilate and was resurrected, in whom we also believe. But while they wish to be both Jews and Christians, they are neither Jews nor Christians!]

[13] Justin, *Dialogue with Trypho* 46–47.

[14] E.g. *b. Ḥagigah* 15a; see also Alan Segal, *Two Powers in Heaven: Early Rabbinic Reports about Christianity and Gnosticism* (Leiden: Brill, 1977) and the discussions it engendered.

[15] E.g. Tertullian, *Scorpiace* 10: *Illic constitues et synagogas Judaeorum, fontes persecutionum, apud quas Apostoli flagella perpessi sunt, et populos nationum cum suo quidem circo, ubi facile conclamant, "Usquequo genus tertium?"* (PL) [Will you plant there both synagogues of the Jews – fountains of persecution – before which the apostles endured the scourge, and heathen assemblages with their own circus, forsooth, where they readily join in the cry, "Death to the third race?" (NPNF)]

with the possibility, other things being similar, that the same sorts of things happened in the period or materials we study. Thus we build up probabilities on the basic assumption that individuals and groups operating under similar conditions will operate similarly. To the extent that our impressions about what is similar are accurate, and to some degree persuasive, we fill in some of the missing blanks in the historical records. And we operate on sort of a spiral of exploration, which comes around to the same questions and subject matter every so often but with fresh insights and sometimes even new evidence that has been acquired since the previous time around, thus moving the discussion to a new level. Since we can't all be expert in everything that is significant or necessary for our investigations, a major factor in this weighing and reweighing process is the identification of trustworthy partners and resources in the process. Whom do you trust in areas outside of your expertise? And why?

What does all this have to do with the "Parting of the Ways" or "The Weighing of the Parts" in exploring the respective developments of those complexities covered by the terms "early Judaism" and "early Christianity" – and what followed them in both the "classical" formulations and also otherwise? Our most basic definitions and assumptions tell us that at a most obvious level ("the big picture"), the ways did part, although perhaps at different times and under different circumstances in different locations in the course of history. But by weighing the parts – that is, by recognizing the immense diversity that existed (and to some extent still exists) within and between the targeted traditions and attempting to understand how the representatives interacted, or perhaps refused to do so – we may be able to begin to understand more fully, if not more clearly, what was involved in the various processes out of which classical Judaism and classical Christianity shaped themselves and gradually became dominant (at least from the perspective of traditional Western history) and definitionally mutually exclusive from the fourth century onward.

# The Lion and the Lamb

Reconsidering Jewish–Christian Relations in Antiquity

by

ANDREW S. JACOBS

A lion's whelp is Judah: from the prey, my son, you rose up.

– Genesis 49.9

Here is the Lamb of God who takes away the world's sin.

– John 1.29

The Lion and the Lamb have long been potent symbols of Judaism and Christianity. Although Judah is not the only son prophetically compared to an animal in his father Jacob's prophetic testament,[1] the image of the Lion of Judah has long persisted in the religious imagination of Jews and others.[2] The lure of Judah's lion as an icon of Jewishness may simply be

* Versions of this essay were presented to the Christianity In Antiquity reading group at the University of North Carolina, Chapel Hill; the Department of Religious Studies at the University of California, Riverside; the North American Patristics Society annual meeting (2001); and the Society of Biblical Literature annual meeting (2001). I would like to thank my diverse audiences for their thoughts and suggestions, especially Paula Fredriksen, who had to hear it twice and offered gracious support both times. Thanks also to Annette Yoshiko Reed and Adam H. Becker for inviting me to include my essay in this collection.

[1] Issachar is a donkey, Dan is a snake, Naphtali is a doe, and Benjamin is a wolf (Gen 49.14, 17, 21, 27).

[2] On the image of the lion (particularly the "lion of Judah") in Jewish art and nomenclature in antiquity, the Middle Ages, and early modernity, see the entry "Lion" in *Encyclopedia Judaica* 11 (1972): 262–76 (including many plates of lion imagery), as well as Cecil Roth's study of Jewish heraldry ("Stemmi di famiglie ebraiche italiane," in *Scritti in memoria di Leone Carpi: Saggi sull'ebraismo italiano*, ed. Daniel Carpi, Attilio Milano, and Alexander Rofé [Jerusalem: Sally Mayer/Milan: Scuola Superiore di Studi Ebraici, 1967], 165–84). The verses to Judah in Genesis 49 provided Martin Luther with a bountiful exegesis in his stunningly vitriolic treatise, *On the Jews and their Lies* (written in 1543). The lion has reappeared in ancient and Christian interpretation as a Christological symbol (due mainly to the confluence of the lion of Judah and the Lamb of God in Rev 5.5–6) and was used by the Ethiopian emperor Haile Salaisse.

due to the fact that the people who considered themselves Jacob's physical and spiritual descendants came to be named after his son Judah (*Yehudim, Ioudaioi, Iudaei, Jews*). Or perhaps there has been something more compelling in the image of the fearsome lion slinking down by his prey, and commanding the obedience of many peoples.

The biblical lamb in my epigraph enters into view in the Gospel of John, between the cosmological opening and the account of Jesus' earthly ministry, when John the Baptist is being questioned by the "Jewish authorities." As the unfolding narrative of the gospel makes clear, the "Lamb of God" takes away the world's sin through a gesture of unparalleled self-sacrifice.[3] Although the Son of God in John's gospel possesses ultimate power and authority, he submits to the most excruciating and humiliating death. This image of reversal and submission, like the warlike image of the Lion of Judah, has also persisted in the religious imagination of Christians and others.[4]

It would be rewarding, I think, to explore how these iconic images – the Lion of Judah and the Lamb of God – have served to shape, or at times disrupt, the self-understanding of Jews and Christians throughout their histories. This essay, however, will not take that route. Instead, I invoke these iconic moments of speech in order to begin thinking about how imaginative historical reconstructions have shaped the modern scholarly discourse on Jews and Christians in antiquity, and to suggest ways we might shift that discourse. In recent decades scholars have taken to framing their historical reconstructions of contacts between Jews and Christians in the first centuries CE as "relations."[5] The term suggests interplay, interaction, discussion, debate, exchange, as well as the notion of being somehow "related," like brothers, or sisters, or parents and children.[6] In some of the more irenic scholarship, "relations" has come to

---

[3] John R. Miles, "Lamb," *Anchor Bible Dictionary* (1992), 4:131–34, contextualizes John's lamb with prophetic passages on sacrifice.

[4] Typical patristic readings can be found in Origen, *Commentary on John* 1.37; John Chrysostom, *Homily 17 on John* 1; and Augustine, *Tractates on John* 4.10. See also "Lamb" in *The Oxford Companion to Christian Art and Architecture*, ed. Peter and Linda Murray (Oxford: Oxford UP, 1996), 267–68 and "Lamm, Lamm Gottes," in *Lexikon der christlichen Ikonographie*, ed. E. Kirschbaum (Rome: Herder, 1971), 3:7–14, which includes literary as well as material references through early modernity.

[5] The term "Jewish–Christian relations" in its various forms (including "Beziehungen" or "Rapports") was certainly used in earlier scholarship, but I would suggest it has become a recognizable "subfield" only in the postwar period.

[6] Probably the most fruitful use of the "familial" ties of early Christianity and (especially rabbinic) Judaism recently is Alan Segal's *Rebecca's Children: Judaism and Christianity in the Roman World* (Cambridge: Harvard UP, 1986). See also the discussion in Daniel Boyarin, *Dying for God: Martyrdom and the Making of Christianity and Judaism* (Stanford: Stanford UP, 1999), 1–16 and 133–44 (notes).

connote something like religious diversity or interfaith dialogue. By bringing the symbolic weight of the Lion and the Lamb to bear on this scholarly trend, I hope to suggest that the theoretical underpinnings of the study of "Jewish–Christian relations" might be in need of some imaginative rethinking.

I shall first explore the context in which this idea of "relations" has come to predominate in modern scholarship, exploring the double bind of ethical and historiographic concerns within which scholars of Jewish–Christian relations have been operating. An ethically checkered historiographic tradition has resulted in the decisive, and perhaps problematic, theoretical divide between rhetoric and reality in the study of late antique religious identities. I shall then suggest how other theoretical scholarly positions that seek to reintegrate rhetorical and "realistic" historiographies might productively be brought to bear on the study of Jewish–Christian relations. I shall focus here specifically on postcolonial criticism, the emphases of which I feel can be especially helpful in reimagining religious and cultural contacts in the first several centuries CE. In the third section, I shall present a few readings of scenes of imperial domination and colonial resistance in the Roman Empire, focusing, as many studies of "Jewish–Christian relations" do, on the provinces of Palestine. Applying some of the theoretical insights of new reading practices may provide a historiographically viable reimagining of Jewish–Christian relations.

## Shifting Historiographies: From Supersession to "Relations"

There is presently a sort of academic stalemate among scholars of ancient Judaism and Christianity, a contest about power and powerlessness, about uplifting truths and demeaning fictions, about rhetoric and reality. The sides of this contest can be rehearsed fairly quickly. We begin with the view scholars held roughly a century ago about the "relations" between Jews and Christians – or, as they were more apt to consider it, between *Judaism* and *Christianity*. The professional historians of that time, meticulously trained in the study of ancient languages and texts (as well as in Christian theology), framed their historical studies of Judaism and Christianity in thinly veiled supersessionist terms. They imagined Judaism as progressively fading in significance through antiquity, until the first century when it was poised to be superseded and replaced wholesale by Christianity. These scholars juxtaposed the moral and spiritual exhaustion of Judaism with the fresh and revitalizing movement inaugurated by Jesus.[7] The Jewish Lion of Judah, they imagined, was rather mangy and toothless, not to mention ritualized and legalistic, by the first century CE.[8] They called this *Spätjudentum*, "late Judaism," a religion on the decline.[9] By contrast, the Christian "Lamb of God" was quite spry and frisky, youthful and regenerative, breathing new life into the spiritually moribund Mediterranean world.[10]

A major proponent of this view was Adolf von Harnack, whose works in the decades before and after the First World War are still considered foundational for the study of early Christianity.[11] Harnack could not imagine any vital contact between Jews and Christians once the lively Lamb of God arrived on the scene. Whatever "real" religious vigor the Jews had possessed, he thought, did not survive the destruction of their Jerusalem Temple in 70 CE, or their refusal of the call to universalism embraced by Christianity:

> The Jewish people (*das jüdische Volk*), by their rejection of Jesus, disowned their calling and administered the death-blow to themselves; in their place came

---

[7] Recent scholarship has begun to examine some of the intrinsic links between the rise of historical critical methods of religious scholarship in European and American universities and the emergence of particular notions of historical, theological, and cultural evolution. See, for instance, the recent dissertation of James Pasto, "Who Owns the Jewish Past: Judaism, Judaisms, and the Writing of Jewish History" (Ph.D. diss., Cornell University, 1999), some arguments of which appear in "Islam's 'Strange Secret Sharer': Orientalism, Judaism, and the Jewish Question," *Comparative Studies in Society and History* 40 (1998): 437–74.

[8] Julius Wellhausen's pioneering work in redaction criticism of the Hebrew Bible (following W. De Wette) enshrined a historical trajectory from lively and moral prophetic wisdom to a calcified and uninspiring ritualism (coincidentally ripe for invigoration by Jesus): see discussion in Pasto, "Islam's 'Strange Secret Sharer,'" 442–47.

[9] According to Martin Jaffee, *Early Judaism* (Princeton: Prentice-Hall, 1997), 22, the term *Spätjudentum* was likely coined by German historian Wilhelm Bousset in his *Die Religion des Judentums in neutestamentlichen Zeitalter* (Berlin: Ruether and Reichard, 1906 [originally 1903]); see pp. 1–2 where Bousset defines "late Judaism" as the period from the Maccabean revolt (*ca.* 160 BCE) to the Bar Kokhba revolt (or, as he calls it, the "Hadrianic War," *ca.* 130 CE). Bousset is also credited with this ideologically laden neologism by Anders Runesson, "Particularistic Judaism and Universalistic Christianity? Some Critical Remarks on Terminology and Theology," *Journal of Greco-Roman Christianity and Judaism* 1 (2000): 120–44, at 120.

[10] See the rather chill representation of this viewpoint (presented for critique) by Shaye J. D. Cohen in his textbook of ancient Judaism: "'Late Judaism' was a sterile, lifeless organism, waiting in vain for the infusion of spirituality that only Christianity could provide. After the birth of Christianity 'late Judaism' lost all importance and could be ignored by scholars and Christians alike" (*From the Maccabees to the Mishnah*, Library of Early Christianity [Philadelphia: Westminster, 1987], 19).

[11] See L. Michael White, "Adolf Harnack and the 'Expansion' of Early Christianity: A Reappraisal of Society History," *Second Century* 5 (1985–86): 97–127.

the new people of the Christians (*das neue Volk der Christen*), who took over the entire tradition of Judaism. What was unserviceable in it was either reinterpreted, or allowed to drop away .... Yet gentile Christianity only brought to a conclusion a process which had begun long before in part of Judaism: the unbounding (*Entschränkung*) of the Jewish religion, and its transformation into a World Religion (*Weltreligion*).[12]

Such leftover dregs of Judaism could not "relate" to Christianity, nor did Christianity have any need to "relate" to the Jews. The Jewish Lion was toothless, and the Christian Lamb had found more satisfying pasture on which to graze.

Harnack brought this vision of a listless Judaism withering on the vine to his study of early Christian literature, particularly those Christian texts that recounted "debates" between Jews and Christians.[13] These "debates," as well as most Christian writings about Jews, were usually, according to Harnack, thinly veiled fictions: these Jews were "imaginary (*gedachter*) opponents," devil's advocates, stereotypes bearing absolutely no relation to real Jews or real Judaism.[14] Christians writing about Jews, Harnack

---

[12] Adolf von Harnack, *Die Mission und Ausbreitung des Christentums in den ersten drei Jahrhunderten*, 2 vols., 3rd ed. (Leipzig: J.C. Hinrichs, 1915), 1:70–71. The English translation of the first edition (from which this paragraph remains more or less unaltered) is rather loose (see Adolf von Harnack, *The Mission of Early Christianity*, trans. J. Moffatt, 2 vols. [New York: G. P. Putnam, 1904–5], 1:81–82). See the critical evaluation of Shaye J. D. Cohen, "Adolph [*sic*] Harnack's 'The Mission and Expansion of Judaism': Christianity Succeeds Where Judaism Fails," in *The Future of Early Christianity: Essays in Honor of Helmut Koester*, ed. Birger A. Pearson with A. T. Kraabel, G. W. E. Nickelsburg, and Norman R. Petersen (Minneapolis: Fortress, 1991), 163–69.

[13] One of Harnack's earlier works (in 1883) was a careful philological study of the *Debate between Simon the Jew and Theophilus the Christian*, one example of a "debate" genre that was mildly popular among early Christians (*Die Altercatio Simonis Iudaei et Theophilii Christiani nebst Untersuchungen über die antijüdische Polemik in der alten Kirche*, Texte und Untersuchungen 1.3 [Leipzig: J.C. Hinrichs, 1883]). The only other major extant text of such a type is Justin Martyr's *Dialogue with Trypho the Jew*, which is the main showpiece in discussions of historicity and "Jewish–Christian relations." We know of the existence of other dialogues from the first centuries (such as the "Dialogue of Jason and Papiscus") and the continuation of the genre well into the Byzantine period (see the rhetorical analysis of David M. Olster, *Roman Defeat, Christian Response, and the Literary Construction of the Jew*, Middle Ages Series [Philadelphia: U. of Pennsylvania, 1994], esp. his discussion in pp. 4–29 on the use of such "dialogues" in the history of Jewish–Christian relations).

[14] Harnack, *Altercatio*, 56–91, comprises an "introduction to anti-Jewish literature in the ancient church." A typical statement: "Der Gegner ist hier [i.e., in Christian 'polemic'] in der That nur ein *gedachter*, er besitzt keinen anderen Horizont als sein Widerpart; eben darum ist er nicht der Jude, wie er wirklich war, sondern der Jude, wie ihn der Christ fürchtete" (p. 63, author's emphasis). Specifically he notes that the opponents in these dialogues (Simon, Trypho, Jason) were "most likely invented freely" by the Christian authors (p. 80).

concluded, engaged in a "specious polemic,"[15] making Christians look
smart and triumphant to themselves and their pagan neighbors.[16] Any
vital interaction that was taking place in Christianity's first centuries was
with the intellectuals of the Hellenistic and Roman worlds, not the
increasingly spiritless Jews.

Some of Harnack's contemporaries challenged the view of an ancient
Judaism sapped of all vitality,[17] but his supersessionist historical vision
remained quite strong until World War II. As in so many areas of
historical inquiry, the racialized and religious violence of World War II
must be viewed as a watershed in religious historiography, as John Gager
thoughtfully noted in the 1980s:

> The study of relations between Judaism and early Christianity, perhaps more
> than any other area of modern scholarship, has felt the impact of World War II
> and its aftermath. The experience of the Holocaust reintroduced with
> unprecedented urgency the question of Christianity's responsibility for anti-
> Semitism: not simply whether individual Christians had added fuel to modern
> European anti-Semitism, but whether Christianity itself was, in its essence and
> from its beginnings, the primary source of anti-Semitism in Western culture.[18]

A new note of historical responsibility was henceforth sounded among
historians of religion. In the light of the Holocaust, scholars realized the
ethical impact of their work outside the academy. To vacate the spiritual
vitality of ancient Jews might be to justify the violence perpetrated
against them – then as well as now. The sympathetic study of "Jewish–

---

[15] That is, "sheinbare Polemik": Harnack, *Altercatio*, 64.

[16] See Harnack, *Altercatio*, 64: "Es ist oben bemerkt worden, dass er gegen den
Juden gerichtet ist, *wie ihn der Christ sich dachte*. Der Jude aber, wie der Christ ihn
sich dachte, *ist der Heide*" (author's emphasis).

[17] In the pre-war period we can point to Jean Juster, *Les Juifs dans l'Empire
Romain: Leur condition juridique, économique et sociale* (Paris: Paul Geuthner, 1914);
Wilhelm Bousset, *Religion des Judentums* (see above, n. 9); and A. Lukyn Williams,
*Adversus Judaeos: A Bird's-Eye View of Christian* Apologiae *until the Renaissance*
(Cambridge: Cambridge UP, 1935). It is significant that each of these scholars (in the
French, German, and British spheres, respectively) evince entirely different motives for
his infusion of ancient Judaism with such liveliness: Juster is apologetic (see pp. vi–
vii), Bousset presses the "syncretistic" agenda of the *Religionsgeschichtliche Schule*
(see esp. pp. 540–94), and Lukyn Williams is overtly missionizing (see pp. xv–xvii).
Kim Haines-Eitzen has also directed my attention to the particular work and influence
of formative English Quaker text critic James Rendel Harris: Kim Haines-Eitzen,
"Ancient Judaism Imagined Through the Lens of Early Christianity: The Work of James
Rendel Harris, 1852–1941" (manuscript). I thank Dr. Haines-Eitzen for sharing her
initial work with me.

[18] John Gager, *The Origins of Anti-Semitism: Attitudes Toward Judaism in Pagan
and Christian Antiquity* (Oxford: Oxford UP, 1985), 13.

Christian relations" may be said to have emerged, in part, from the shadow of Nazi death camps.[19]

Possibly the most significant scholar of this new, postwar view of "relations" was Marcel Simon; his work *Verus Israel: A Study of the Relations between Christians and Jews in the Roman Empire (135–425)* was originally published in French in 1948 and has appeared in various versions up to the most recent English edition in the mid-1980s.[20] It is worth noting not only the ways in which Simon sought to revise previous scholarly supersessionism, but also the assumptions and presuppositions central to that ideology that he let stand. Like Harnack, Simon accepted that the vitality (or feebleness) of ancient Jews related directly to the historicity (or falsity) of Christian texts depicting Jewish–Christian interaction. Simon read the situation quite differently, however, and asked Harnack (posthumously): "Do men rage so persistently against a corpse?"[21] Simon's answer was "no": there could not be so much rhetorical smoke without a real fire somewhere. He demonstrated in as painstaking detail as Harnack – both men were thoroughly meticulous in their scholarship – the ways and degrees in which "relations" among Jews and Christians determined the levels of debate and conflict between them. He relied heavily on the early Christian writings about Jews that Harnack had dismissed as "imaginary." Simon concluded:

> The problem of Jewish–Christian relations in antiquity was not a fictive problem. The two religions confronted each other, in a conflict the principal aspects of which I have attempted to determine. Judaism, from one end to another of the period under consideration, did not cease to bother the Church.[22]

---

[19] Equally significant in the decades following World War II was the issuing of the papal decretum *Nostra aetate* in 1965 (out of the second Vatican Council), which condemned anti-Semitic and anti-Jewish language in the Church and called for "fraternal dialogues" (*fraternis colloquiis*) between Catholics and Jews (as well as Buddhists, Hindus, and Muslims) (Latin text of the decretum found in the *Acta Apostolicae Sedis* 59 [1966]: 740–44).

[20] See Albert I. Baumgarten, "Marcel Simon's *Verus Israel* as a Contribution to Jewish History," *HTR* 92 (1999): 465–78; he points out that the original French version included a preface that directly acknowledged the postwar, post-Holocaust context of this study (in which Simon is rather equivocal on the relation between history and theology). The preface was not included in the English translation.

[21] Marcel Simon, *Verus Israel: A Study in the Relations Between Christians and Jews in the Roman Empire (135–425)*, trans. H. McKeating (Oxford: Oxford UP, 1986), 140. (I am citing from this 1986 English translation.) The original French is perhaps more vivid (and less gendered): "S'acharne-t-on avec une telle obstination sur un cadavre?" (Marcel Simon, *Verus Israel: Étude sur les relations entre Chrétiens et Juifs dans l'Empire Romain (135–42)*, Bibliothèques des écoles françaises d'Athènes et de Rome [Paris: Editions de Boccard, 1948], 171).

[22] My translation from the French: Simon, *Verus Israel*, 433. McKeating's English translation reads: "the problem of Jewish–Christian relations in the ancient world is a

In Simon's historiography, the Jewish Lion has regained his claws, and the Christian Lamb does not frolic so carefree across the meadows of the ancient Mediterranean.

Simon's revision of ancient Jewish–Christian "conflict" responded to a perceived need for a more fair and judicious evaluation of post-Temple Judaism, and it has remained highly influential.[23] The decades following the appearance of *Verus Israel* witnessed a renewed interest in the Christian literature Harnack had deemed historically worthless, and a renewed appreciation for its utility in recovering the vital relations of Jews and Christians. Often the spoken or tacit understanding was that a more fair and ethical treatment of ancient Judaism would result from such efforts.[24] Archaeological evidence from the ancient Mediterranean added another boost, insofar as scholars could identify with more certainty those places in which Jews and Christians both lived and most likely inter-acted.[25] But scholars' understanding of the nature of these inter-actions ("relations") still relied (and continues to rely) heavily on Christian literature. There has remained a certain consensus that, without the willingness to read Christian literature as a type of historical evidence, a reflection or record of real interactions, there would be little or no way to judge how and on what terms Jews and Christians "related" at all. Were such texts nothing but "specious" rhetoric, they would perforce be dismissed as historically invalid, resulting in an ethically harmful Jewish

*of minority*

---

real one [n'est pas un faux problème]. The two religions did confront each other, in a conflict whose principal aspects I have attempted to delineate. From beginning to end of the period we have been considering, Judaism did not cease to trouble the Church" (English *Verus Israel*, 369).

[23] Simon himself remarked on the durability of his thesis in a postscript written in 1964: *Verus Israel*, 385, 390, 395, and 406 (references to the English translation) all note the validation or confirmation of various major theses of the original work. This postscript also broadly treats six issues: the vitality of Judaism, Jewish proselytism, the question of "anti-Semitism" in the early church, Jews in the Roman Empire, the identity of the *minim* (Jewish "heretics"), and the problem of "Jewish Christianity." All of these, incidentally, remain centrally debated subjects in the history of ancient Judaism and early Jewish–Christian relations, as any recent bibliography on the subject will demonstrate.

[24] Some studies of note operating (explicitly or implicitly) from Simon's perspective are: Nicholas de Lange, *Origen and the Jews: Studies in Jewish–Christian Relations in Third-Century Palestine*, University of Cambridge Oriental Publications 25 (Cambridge: Cambridge UP, 1976); S. G. Wilson, *Related Strangers: Jews and Christians 70–170 C.E.* (Minneapolis: Fortress, 1995); William Horbury, *Jews and Christians in Contact and Controversy* (Edinburgh: T&T Clark, 1998).

[25] See, for instance, the recent overview of Thomas Braun, "The Jews in the Late Roman Empire," *Scripta Classica Israelica* 27 (1998): 142–71, who surveys literary and archaeological evidence. The assumption remains, however, that Jewish "vitality" leads inexorably to "relations."

history. Issues of historical ethics became intertwined with the needs of historical reconstruction, and in this context "Jewish–Christian relations" came alive: suddenly we saw the Lion wrestling with the Lamb.[26]

The new discourse of "Jewish–Christian relations" has not been without its own critique. The most incisive criticism in recent years has been Miriam Taylor's 1995 monograph, *Anti-Judaism and Early Christian Identity: A Critique of the Scholarly Consensus*. Through her own particular post-World War II lens, Taylor returned to the idea that much of Christian anti-Jewish literature was not real but rhetorical. For Harnack, the rhetorical nature of these texts had indicated the emptiness of ancient Judaism and the spiritual triumph of Christianity. For Taylor, reading these texts as rhetorical signaled the deeply symbolic and abiding nature of Christian anti-Judaism. Historians such as Simon (whom she singles out in her work as representative, if not the inaugurator, of the "scholarly consensus") in fact replayed this anti-Jewish tendency by giving the Jewish Lion claws with which to fight against and provoke the Christian Lamb. As Taylor characterized their approach:

> The focus on Judaism as stimulator of antagonism effectively succeeds in shifting the focus away from internal soul-searching in the Christian camp, in order to distribute the blame and divide the responsibility in accounting for the generation of prejudice. For if anti-Judaism is described as emerging out of a social conflict, then it can be characterized as the by-product of an historical rivalry in which both parties might be said to be equally involved, and equally responsible.[27]

Despite noble intentions, Taylor claims, the result of this reading is a sort of "they-asked-for-it" theory of anti-Semitism that places a significant portion of the blame for anti-Jewish language (and, implicitly, behavior) on the Jews themselves.

Taylor's "critique" has repolarized the debate about Jewish–Christian relations. Articles and conference papers have been dedicated to

[26] An additional shift in scholarly discourse has been the "Third Quest" of Historical Jesus scholarship, which has sought (among other things) to emphasize the thorough Jewishness of Jesus' context, prompting more nuanced and theologically sympathetic studies of Jews in the first centuries CE and their "relations" to Christians. This seems to be the context in which the Society of Biblical Literature produced its first "consultation on Early Jewish/Christian Relations" in 1988 (later a "group" and now a "section"): see Jeffrey S. Siker, "A Brief Social History of Jewish/Christian Relations in the Society of Biblical Literature," paper delivered at the 2001 SBL/AAR Southeastern Regional Meeting (I thank Dr. Siker, one of the founders of the Early Jewish/Christian Relations Group, for sharing this paper and his recollections with me).

[27] Miriam S. Taylor, *Anti-Judaism and Early Christian Identity: A Critique of the Scholarly Consensus*, Studia Post-Biblica 46 (Leiden: E. J. Brill, 1995), 195.

responding to her criticism.[28] In addition to criticizing her reading of primary and secondary texts, respondents have also decried Taylor's "either-or" stance: why must all of the literature be rhetorical? Can't careful scholarship be the answer, distilling fact from fiction, debate from polemic, reality from rhetoric?[29] Taylor's view, some warn, risks a return to a harmful Harnackian historiography, stripping ancient Jews of their vitality and agency.[30] The orientation of these scholars is ultimately clear: they still prefer to dig "beneath" the rhetoric for evidence of Jewish–Christian relations, while attending to the rhetorical nature of the writings separately.[31] Rhetoric and reality remain ethically and historiographically opposed perspectives.

This aspect of the debate, from Harnack onward, has remained constant: the implicit division between "rhetoric" and "reality."[32] Even in the most recent scholarship since Taylor, there remains the sense that real

---

[28] Among the many reviews of the monograph, see Wolfram Kinzig, "Review of *Anti-Judaism and Early Christian Identity*," *JTS* n.s. 48 (1997): 643–49. A recent thorough response is James Carleton Paget, "Anti-Judaism and Early Christian Identity," *Zeitschrift für Antikes Christentum* 1 (1997): 195–225. A more sympathetic presentation of Taylor and Simon may be found in Baumgarten, "Marcel Simon's *Verus Israel*," 474–76. Acknowledgment of Taylor's critique has become a commonplace in studies of "Jewish–Christian relations," ranging from tepid, to uninterested, to intrigued, to hostile.

[29] See Stephen J. Shoemaker, "'Let Us Go and Burn Her Body': The Image of the Jews in the Early Dormition Traditions," *Church History* 68 (1999): 775–823; Carleton Paget, "Anti-Judaism," 222–24; and Judith Lieu, *Image and Reality: The Jews in the World of the Christians in the Second Century* (Edinburgh: T&T Clark, 1996), the arguments of which are rehearsed (with more attention to the current historiographic context) in "History and Theology in Christian Views of Judaism," in *The Jews Among Pagans and Christians in the Roman Empire*, ed. Judith Lieu, John North, and Tessa Rajak (London: Routledge, 1992), 79–96.

[30] See Shoemaker, "'Let Us Go,'" 786–88; and Timothy Horner, "The Adversus Judaeos Tradition: Window or Mirror? A Discussion of Some of the Methodological Issues in Determining Early Christian/Jewish Relations," paper presented at the 1996 SBL Annual Meeting (I thank Dr. Horner for sharing some of this paper with me).

[31] Certainly the most vivid example of this historiographic strategy in Patristics is Robert Wilken, *John Chrysostom and the Jews: Rhetoric and Reality in the Late 4th Century*, Transformation of the Classical Heritage 4 (Berkeley: U. of California, 1983).

[32] See the evaluation of Guy G. Stroumsa, "From Anti-Judaism to Antisemitism in Early Christianity?" in *Contra Iudaeos: Ancient and Medieval Polemics between Christians and Jews*, ed. Ora Limor and Guy G. Stroumsa, Texts and Studies in Medieval and Early Modern Judaism 10 (Tübingen: Mohr Siebeck, 1996), 1–26; he contrasts the "conflict theory" (reality) and "Christian discourse approaches" (rhetoric) (p. 16) with his own contextualization of Christian anti-Jewish writings within the pluralistic "market situation" of the later Roman Empire (a concept he derives from John North, "The Development of Religious Pluralism" in Lieu et al., *Jews Among Pagans and Christians*, 174–93). Also see Judith Lieu, "'The Parting of the Ways': Theological Construct or Historical Reality?" *JSNT* 56 (1994): 101–19.

evidence must be distilled from false rhetorical "images." Furthermore, this choice between rhetoric and reality carries implicit ethical obligations on the historian: "real" readings of this literature will create a Jewish Lion with some teeth – the lion of Genesis 49 – even if that means in the process that the Christian Lamb must become a little bloodied – like the lamb of John 1. "Rhetorical" readings, on the other hand, risk conceding "truth" to supersessionist Christian images of Jewish decline, essentially plucking the Lion's mane and leaving him weak and defenseless while the Lamb trots in a now somewhat sinister manner through fields unchallenged. Rhetoric or reality seems to be the choice; the Jewish Lion's strength and the Christian Lamb's innocence are made to depend on it.

## A New Historiography: Past the Reality–Rhetoric Divide

This confrontation of ethics and history, of rhetoric and reality, resonates with other spheres of academic inquiry that originated in politically self-conscious attempts to change how we understand the past and/in the present. Women's studies, black studies, hispanic studies, subaltern studies, gay and lesbian studies, and other similarly constituted fields have all grappled with what one historian has called the "text–context conundrum."[33] That is, how can we write responsible history from biased literary documents? How can we ethically and fairly derive the social from the rhetorical? How can we recover the history of an oppressed or minority group from literature that sets out to distort, demean, or even erase that group?

To take an example familiar to historians of religion: in the political climate of the 1970s and 1980s, feminist historians enjoyed an initial heyday of "discovering" and celebrating female personalities in early Christian or Jewish history.[34] In the 1990s, however, many of these same historians became acutely aware of the fact that they were often attempting to extract historical information about women from highly rhetorical, male-authored texts. These same texts that gave precious

---

[33] Gabrielle Spiegel, "History, Historicism, and the Social Logic of the Text in the Middle Ages," *Speculum* 65 (1990): 75. See my discussion (in relation to the history of early Christian women) in "Writing Demetrias: Ascetic Logic in Ancient Christianity," *Church History* 69 (2000): 719–48.

[34] See the discussions, among others, of Susan Niditch, "Portrayals of Women in the Hebrew Bible," in *Jewish Women in Historical Perspective*, ed. Judith Baskin, 2nd ed. (Detroit: Wayne State UP, 1998), 25–45; and Elizabeth A. Clark, "The Lady Vanishes: Dilemmas of a Feminist Historian After the 'Linguistic Turn,'" *Church History* 67 (1998): 1–31.

biographical data on ancient Christian and Jewish women were also grounded in the religious misogyny feminist historians were seeking to overturn. The irony attendant upon this "linguistic turn" of post-structuralist history was acute: it seemed that, even centuries later, the biases of male authors were serving to silence women and their histories.[35] I suggest that the history of "Jewish–Christian relations" has reached a similar conundrum: if we rely on one-sided and highly rhetorical Christian texts *about* Jews for our understanding of how Jews and Christians "related," how do we acknowledge the literary nature of the evidence?[36] Do we not risk internalizing and replicating the very biases of Christian rhetoric? Can real Jews emerge from the rhetoric of early Christians?

The problem seems particularly acute when we try to engage Jews and Christians in their social and political context of the Roman Empire, especially in the post-Constantinian period. From about 325–550 CE, some of the most rhetorical and strident literature imaginable about Jews came from the styluses of ancient Christian authors. At the same time, however, Jews were notably quiet on the subject of Christian "triumph" and imperial rule. What scholars have been able to deduce from the Jewish literature of this era about Romans and Christians is veiled in symbolic, often coded language, couched in biblical metaphors that are patently disinterested in historical reportage.[37] The Jewish Lion seemed to be remarkably lamblike, while the Christian Lamb, once cloaked in Roman imperial power, was on a leonine rampage.

One avenue worth pursuing out of the "text-context conundrum" might be presented by postcolonial criticism (a route that feminist historians, among others, have also taken).[38] Broadly defined, postcolonial criticism

---

[35] See Clark, "Lady Vanishes," and eadem, "Holy Women, Holy Words: Early Christian Women, Social History, and the 'Linguistic Turn,'" *JECS* 6 (1998): 413–30.

[36] My example of early Christian and Jewish women is deliberately chosen to invoke (if only in a footnote) the ongoing debate over the extent to which feminist Christian historiographies (and theologies) have internalized anti-Jewish rhetoric in the service of a recovering a positive feminist history from biased Christian texts: see the helpful overview of Ross Kraemer, "Jewish Women and Christian Origins: Some Caveats," in Ross Kraemer and Mary Rose D'Angelo, *Women and Christian Origins* (Oxford: Oxford UP, 1999), 35–49 and the thorough analysis and critique of Amy-Jill Levine, "Second Temple Judaism, Jesus, and Women: Yeast of Eden," *Biblical Interpretation* 2 (1994): 8–33.

[37] See the discussion of rabbinic literature and "history" in Yosef Yerushalmi, *Zakhor: Jewish History and Jewish Memory*, The Samuel and Althea Stroum Lectures in Jewish Studies (Seattle: U. of Washington, 1982), 1–52.

[38] See the essays on gender and feminism in *Colonial Discourse and Postcolonial Theory: A Reader*, ed. Patrick Williams and Laura Chrisman (New York: Columbia UP, 1994). For the sake of convenience I choose the label "postcolonial criticism," although

is a distinct set of reading practices that seeks to uncover the cultural processes of domination and appropriation that are intimately interwoven with the politics of empire.[39] Empires are built not only on economic and military might and exploitation, but also on more widespread forms of social and material domination at home and "in the colonies." Postcolonial critics engage the subtle processes of cultural construction to illuminate how imperial identities come into existence through the multifaceted subordination and appropriation of colonized subjects. Additionally, these critics explore how the colonized devise methods of exploiting and resisting the instabilities of imperial practice. There is a distinct political edge to postcolonial criticism; critics analyze these colonialist practices in order to show how they might be unmasked and, potentially, resisted by the objects of this power: the colonized subjects themselves.[40] The material of such analyses is often imperial literature, or, more rarely, literature produced by colonial subjects under the constraints of imperial regimes. The approach of postcolonial criticism towards this "evidence" can, I think, be instructive and elucidating to historians of religion. At the risk of overly schematizing a diverse and rich theoretical enterprise, I want to give a rapid overview of the foundational assumptions of postcolonial criticism, before moving on to some specific readings of the ancient literature that might suggest how this new perspective might help us reconsider Jewish–Christian relations in antiquity.

A central premise of many postcolonial analyses is that discourse – by which I mean not just *words* but also authoritative structures of meaning and action – does not reflect the "real world" of its participants, but rather constructs that world.[41] When the empire speaks, it speaks from a position of authority and determination. In writing "the subaltern," the figure of colonial appropriation, the imperial writer institutes an ideological world in which things can only be a certain way. When imperial subjects speak authoritatively, we cannot dismiss it as "mere rhetoric." Nor, however, can we benignly condone imperial language as "merely reflective" of

---

a variety of other theoretical labels might suit as well: postcolonial theory, postcolonial studies, colonial discourse analysis, colonial criticism, and so forth.

[39] In this sense it is not a metanarrative theory, like Marxism or Freudianism, but rather a loosely affiliated array of critical stances with regard to colonialism, politics, literature, and history.

[40] See also Bart Moore-Gilbert, *Postcolonial Theory: Contexts, Practices, Politics* (London: Verso, 1997), 12: "a distinct set of reading practices ... preoccupied principally with analysis of cultural forms which mediate, challenge, and reflect upon the relations of domination and subordination – economic, cultural and political – between (and often within) nations, races or cultures."

[41] See the discussions in Edward Said, *Orientalism* (London: Penguin, 1991) and idem, *Culture and Imperialism* (London: Chatto & Windus, 1993).

conflict between imperial and colonial subjects, thereby flattening the imbalance of power that defines colonial existence.[42] As one colonial historian has noted: "Domination is a relationship."[43] The rhetoric of empire should not then be kept distinct from reality; such rhetoric produces reality, determines in what manner reality can come to be. The discursive analysis of empire demonstrates how the rhetoric–reality divide begins to evaporate.

Like many aspects of imperial administration, the forceful construction of colonial identity is a sobering idea, invoking Orwellian images of totalitarian thought-control. What saves this notion of "rhetoric producing reality" from seeming to be yet another form of political domination, intractable and irresistible, is a second useful idea prominent in postcolonial criticism: the idea of imperial ambivalence. Postcolonial theorists have traced the ways in which imperialist language, while authoritative and dominating, is also unstable and fluid and so always vulnerable to colonial resistance. At the moment in which the imperial subject "creates" the colonial object, he has also conjured up his own inerasable "other," constantly present and potentially threatening. As he fantasizes about her, he fears her; as he controls her, he reminds himself that she constantly *necessitates* control, that only his imperial authority prevents her from overturning his dominion. At the moment she is conjured into his imperial world, the colonial object resists her place in that world by exploiting this lack of imperial coherence. In the discursive analysis of empire, imperial identities themselves constantly shift, and authority, power, and control rest on no stable ground.

A further assumption of postcolonial theory that historians should find useful is the focus on the material consequences of colonialist discourses. Empires are not metaphors; they are real sites of physical domination and political resistance. Colonial subjects are not ideas; they are people. The material foundation and effects of colonialism provide a salutary response to those who perceive "literary" criticism to be too ephemeral or evanescently rhetorical. Discourses of control and resistance materialize. Even when colonial existence has been arbitrarily and, at times, brutally directed by imperial control, the economic and administrative machinery of imperialism ensures that colonial subjects cannot be "thought" out of existence. The reality produced by ambivalent imperial rhetoric is fixed in the material world in which people eat, sleep, and live.

---

[42] Ania Loomba, *Colonialism/Postcolonialism*, The New Critical Idiom (London: Routledge, 1998), 37: "no human utterance could be seen as innocent .... The place of language, culture and the individual in political and economic processes could no longer be seen as simply derivative or secondary."

[43] Patrick Wolfe, "History and Imperialism: A Century of Theory, from Marx to Postcolonialism," *American Historical Review* 102 (1997): 412.

## Religion, Culture, and Empire: The Lamb Writes the Lion

From the vantage point of postcolonial criticism, I want to reexamine some of the literary materials of "Jewish–Christian relations." These are all moments of contact found in Christian writings about Jews from the holy land. Such a geographic restriction can allow us both to narrow the scope of inquiry and to ground it in a particularly rich and meaningful site. Taking my cue from the discursive and material analyses of postcolonial theory, I shall read this material not as the raw data of historical reconstruction – as transparent reality – nor as the discardable fantasy of the Christian psyche – as mere rhetoric. Instead, from within these episodes I want to trace the utility of four common "themes" of postcolonial criticism: colonial mimicry, imperial hybridity, the inscription of domination, and the ultimate instability of imperialist discourses. My hope is that these familiar scenes and new thematic frameworks can provide at least one new theoretical perspective from which we might imagine how Jewish reality and Christian rhetoric were simultaneously produced, contested, and reformulated in the late antique world.

### Origen and Colonial Mimicry

I begin in the third century, a period when Christianity was a minority sect in the wide-ranging Roman Empire. The fantasy of the sacrificial Christian lamb was widespread during this period: Christians in the second and third centuries imagined themselves as paradigmatic "sufferers," the martyred elect facing off against an antagonistic empire.[44] In this context Origen is credited by ancients and moderns alike with infusing the early Christian movement with a new strain of erudite intellectualism. Origen spent much of his life as a preacher in Palestinian Caesarea Maritima, where he became notable for his attempts to learn Hebrew in order to understand better the Christian Old Testament, as well as for his supposed interactions with the learned Jews of his day. Origen's biblical commentaries and sermons are peppered with references to "what a Jew taught me" and "what the Jews say."[45] Modern scholars interested in "Jewish–Christian relations" have made prolific use of this material in

---

[44] See the study of Judith Perkins, *The Suffering Self: Pain and Narrative Representation in the Early Christian Era* (London: Routledge, 1995).

[45] See Gustave Bardy, "Les traditions juives dans l'oeuvre d'Origène," *Revue Biblique* 34 (1925): 217–52 and the detailed treatment of de Lange, *Origen and the Jews*, 20–28, 89–102.

order to reconstruct Jewish intellectual life and its relation to Christianity.[46]

For my part, I do not think that Origen is lying or maliciously planting red herrings for scholars to chase. I do, however, propose that this straight reading of Origen's accounts of his conversations and debates with contemporary Jews should be examined in a more critical light. If we read Origen's notices of debates and interaction neither as evidence of rhetorical fancy nor as objective reportage, we might instead perceive how the religious politics of empire are being at once reified and contested. In Origen's day, Jews enjoyed a cultural and political legitimacy (as tenuous as it may have been) that Christians did not.[47] Their odd and sometimes unsettling beliefs and practices (such as monotheism and circumcision) had legal protection, and Jews had the benefit of a long and rich ethnic history to grant them some cultural legitimacy. Origen relates his Christian identity to this Jewish legitimacy in the interests of cultural and religious resistance against the Roman Empire.

Origen's framing of Roman, Jewish, and Christian political power becomes particularly clear in his correspondence with Julius Africanus. Africanus had been present at a public debate between Origen and some "ignoramus" (as Africanus calls him) during which Origen made reference to the story of Susanna from the book of Daniel. As Africanus points out to Origen, this story is not found in Hebrew versions of the book of Daniel, only in Greek versions (which most Christians used); what's more, it seems likely (to Africanus as well as modern scholars) that the story of Susanna was a later addition, composed in Greek and added to Daniel at a later date. Africanus is writing to ask how Origen, who knows Hebrew and knows real Jews, could make reference to this apocryphal biblical story.[48]

---

[46] E. E. Urbach, "The Homiletical Interpretation of the Sages and the Expositions of Origen on Canticles, and the Jewish Christian Disputation," *Scripta Hierosolymitana* 22 (1971): 247–75; de Lange, *Origen and the Jews*, 39–47, elaborated by Reuven Kimelman, "Rabbi Yohanan and Origen on the Song of Songs: A Third-Century Jewish–Christian Debate," *HTR* 73 (1980): 567–95; Hayim Lapin, "Jewish and Christian Academics in Roman Palestine: Some Preliminary Observations," in *Caesarea Maritima: A Retrospective after Two Millennia*, ed. Avner Raban and Kenneth G. Holum, Documenta et monumenta orientis antiqua 21 (Leiden: E.J. Brill, 1996), 496–512; Simon, *Verus Israel*, 173–75. One critique of Taylor's book has been her insufficient treatment of Origen; see Carleton Paget, "Anti-Judaism," 197–98 n. 25 and 203.

[47] See, for instance, the discussion of Amnon Linder, *The Jews in Roman Imperial Legislation* (Detroit: Wayne State UP, 1987), 54–86.

[48] Julius Africanus, *Epistula ad Origenem* 2, 5, 7. Text and French translation in *Origène: Sur les écritures; Philocalie, 1–20; Lettre à Africanus sur l'histoire de*

In response, Origen simultaneously affirms his intellectual "relations" to Jews *and* his own position of intellectual resistance on the margins of the Roman Empire. First, Origen says flatly, "learned Jews" have told him that the story is authentic and that Jews really did act as they are portrayed in the story of Susanna.[49] Furthermore, Origen has lived for a "long time" among the Jews and knows how powerful and dangerous they can be: "Why even now, while Romans run their empire (*basileuontōn*) and Jews pay the drachma tribute to them, with Caesar's agreement their Ethnarch rules over them as if he were still the king of this nation (*basileuontos tou ethnous*)."[50] By using the same term to characterize the dominion of the Romans and the Jews – *basileia*, sovereignty – Origen positions himself as the object of their imperial authority. By "dialoguing" and debating with the Jews,[51] Origen, the suffering Christian Lamb, succeeds in credibly articulating Christian resistance. The "relation" between Jew and Christian in Origen's writings is perhaps not the scholarly exchange of ideas that, perhaps, some modern academics wistfully project backwards. It might instead be a rare instance in which "the subaltern speaks" (to borrow Gayatri Spivak's now famous phrase):[52] the object of imperial authority creates for himself a voice from the very position of cultural and political inferiority in which he has been constructed.

It is useful to imagine Origen as the clever Christian Lamb that has learned to *mimic* the Jewish Lion's roar.[53] In postcolonial criticism, mimicry signals the ways in which a colonial subject both appropriates and subverts dominant modes of cultural authority: the cunning (and fearsome) ability to become almost-but-not-quite, to approach the limits of sameness in order to exploit the possibilities of cultural difference. It is a mode of identity construction that appears conciliatory, but operates

---

*Suzanne*, ed. Nicholas de Lange, Sources Chrétiennes 302 (Paris: Editions du Cerf, 1983), 514–21.

[49] Origen, *Epistula ad Africanum* 11–12. Text and French translation in *Origène: Sur les écritures; Philocalie, 1–20; Lettre à Africanus sur l'histoire de Suzanne*, ed. Nicholas de Lange, Sources Chrétiennes 302 (Paris: Editions du Cerf, 1983), 522–73, here pp. 538–40.

[50] Origen, *Epistula ad Africanum* 20 (de Lange, *Origène*, 566).

[51] Origen describes the interaction of Christians and Jews as "dialoguing" (*dialegoumenoi*) and "debate" (*zētēsis*): *Epistula ad Africanum* 9 (de Lange, *Origène*, 534).

[52] See Gayatri Spivak, "Can the Subaltern Speak?" originally in *Marxism and the Interpretation of Culture*, ed. C. Nelson and L. Grossberg (Basingstoke: MacMillan, 1988), 271–313; cited here from Williams and Chrisman, *Colonial Discourse*, 66–111. See now also Gayatri Spivak, *A Critique of Postcolonial Reason: Toward a History of the Vanishing Present* (Cambridge: Harvard UP, 1999), esp. chs. 2–3, where she significantly nuances her earlier discussion of the "foreclosure of the native informant."

[53] On colonial "mimicry" see Homi K. Bhabha, *The Location of Culture* (London: Routledge, 1994).

subversively (like racial "passing"). Jews, in this period, had a recognizable voice in the Roman Empire; Christians did not. By correlating his illegitimate Christianness to their legitimate Jewishness, Origen creates a space in which to assert Christian resistance. This does not mean Origen and Jews did *not* have contact of the type that Origen implies; it also doesn't confirm that they did. It is rather the *way* Origen positions himself and the Jews within the intellectual climate of the Roman Empire that tells us something about how a minority group might achieve a measure of cultural legitimacy despite political disenfranchisement; it informs us about the political and intellectual situation of Jews and Christians in the Empire.

## *Jerome and Imperial Hybridity*

Jerome, living in Palestine 150 years after Origen, is often compared to Origen for his "zealous" learning of Hebrew and his interactions and debates with local Jews.[54] Much, of course, had changed in 150 years: Christianity had inverted its position in the Roman Empire, from marginal and illicit to central and powerful. In this religious and cultural climate, Jerome moved to Bethlehem in the 380s, and there for close to thirty years produced biblical translations, commentaries, and sermons in which he explicitly relied on Jewish informants and teachers. Yet if we might read Origen's rhetoric of Jewish knowledge from the standpoint of colonial mimicry, we might configure Jerome instead as the imperial hybrid: the agile arbiter of knowledge and power, negotiating between disgust of and desire for the "other," the imperial subject produced from within the colonial margins.[55]

When Jerome describes his interactions with Jews, he does not, like Origen, allow them any upper hand, any *basileia*. Instead, he fashions them into Christian "tools," living dictionaries or reference manuals that he can adeptly handle.[56] He has paid good money, he tells one friend, to

---

[54] Such comparisons begin with Jerome himself: see Mark Vessey, "Jerome's Origen: The Making of a Christian Literary Persona," *Studia Patristica* 28 (1993): 135–45. A thorough comparison of Origen's and Jerome's study of Hebrew is found in Adam Kamesar, *Jerome, Greek Scholarship, and the Hebrew Bible: A Study of the Quaestiones Hebraicae in Genesim*, Oxford Classical Monographs (Oxford: Clarendon, 1993).

[55] My understanding of hybridity also relies on Bhabha, especially "Signs Taken for Wonders: Questions of Ambivalence and Authority Under a Tree Outside Delhi, May 1817," in *Location of Culture*, 102–22; see also Robert Young, *Colonial Desire: Hybridity in Theory, Culture, and Race* (London: Routledge, 1995).

[56] Kamesar, *Jerome*, 181, refers to the rabbinic "informants" of Jerome as part of a series of translational and exegetical "tools" at his disposal. On Jerome's particular use of Jewish "informants" as tools, see my "The Place of the Biblical Jew in the Early Christian Holy Land," *Studia Patristica* 38 (2001): 417–24.

get the best Jewish teacher of Hebrew available to come to his monastic cell to help him with translations.[57] Jerome appears to unite his Christian superiority with the dominating privilege of empire: he can interact with, and even read and speak like a Jew by nature of his imperial superiority. In Jerome's dominating language, however, we begin to see how assertions of power summon the threat of cultural contamination: the perilous slide from imperial knowing to colonial becoming. Unease surrounds his casual handling of Jewish knowledge from real Jews. His friends (and even more so his enemies) ask him whether this is such a good idea, consorting with Jews, reading and speaking Jewishly. Jerome must write to some friends in Rome to assure them that he's not "going native":

> Back in Jerusalem and Bethlehem, with what trouble and at what cost I acquired Bar Haninah as my night-time teacher! He so feared the other Jews that he showed himself as a second version of Nicodemus .... If it is expedient to hate any men and to detest any nation, I have a notable hatred for the circumcised [i.e., Jews]. Even into the present day they persecute our Lord Jesus Christ in the synagogues of Satan. Yet can anyone object to me for having had a Jew as a teacher?[58]

Jerome's assertions of imperial control ironically invoke the threat of colonial contamination: Bar Haninah, the local Jewish teacher smuggled in at night to Jerome's monastery, carries the implicit threat of "the synagogues of Satan." The reader is asked to believe that Jerome's particular mastery can allow him to appropriate the knowledge while avoiding the peril. This swaggering attitude is typical of colonialist discourses of cultural conquest; we might imagine Sir Richard Burton successfully "passing" as a Muslim in order to view the sacred stone at the shrine of Mecca.[59] But the swagger also covers over the cultural danger of contamination, of crossing that line between imperial and colonial

---

[57] Jerome, *Praefatio in libro Iob* 20–23. Line numbers follow the editions of the prefaces found in *Biblia sacra iuxta Vulgatam versionem*, ed. R. Weber et al., 2 vols. (Stuttgart: Würtembergische Bibelanstalt, 1964), here 1:731.

[58] Jerome, *Epistula* 84.3.2. Text in *Sancti Hieronymii Eusebii Epistulae*, ed. I. Hilberg and M. Kamptner, Corpus Scriptorum Ecclesiasticorum Latinorum 54–56 (Vienna: Verlag der Österreichischen Akademie der Wissenschaften, 1996), here vol. 55, p. 123. The cautious trepidation of Jerome's friends in Rome (to whom he writes here) is polemically amplified by his Origenist opponent and erstwhile friend, Rufinus of Aquileia, who calls Bar Hanina "Barabbas" (*Apologia contra Hieronymum* 2.15).

[59] An episode explored to great effect by Edward Said, *Orientalism* (New York: Vintage Books, 1978), 195–96: "So what we read in his prose is the history of a consciousness negotiating its way through an alien culture by virtue of having successfully absorbed its systems of information and behavior" (p. 196). Burton's accounts of this "passing" are recorded in his *Personal Narrative of a Pilgrimage to al-Madinah and Meccah*, ed. Isabel Burton, 2 vols. (1893; repr. New York: Dover Publications, 1964).

subject. The dominance in fact emerges precisely from the danger of that tight-rope walk: to claim the mastery of empire is to risk closeness to the colonial other. For Jerome, to be an imperial Christian means to risk Jewishness. If Origen's representation of "Jewish–Christian relations" articulated Christian resistance by mimicking Jewish privilege, Jerome's representation constructs the simultaneously perilous and triumphant posture of imperial Christianity over the resistant Jews. Deriving knowledge from the frontier of colonial existence elicits both the desire of cultural conquest and the fear of cultural contamination, what theorists have called the double-faced, hybrid quality of imperial identity.[60] We might imagine Jerome, then, as the Christian Lamb parading around in the freshly skinned Lion's pelt.

## The Piacenza Pilgrim and the Inscription of Power

Another example of a "Jewish–Christian interaction" that has fueled the imagination of modern scholars comes from a lively pilgrimage text of the mid-sixth century (about 150 years after Jerome). From the author known as "the Piacenza Pilgrim" (about whom we know little except for his departure point in northern Italy[61]) we can discern some of the ways in which Christian domination could be viewed on and inscribed into an expressly "other" landscape. Sometime between 560 and 570 CE, our pilgrim traveled throughout the holy land and down to Egypt to visit the sites associated with Jesus and the Christian saints. In his account we see Palestine becoming fully and truly the holy land: a fantasy land of religious sights, sounds, wonders, and experiences that are produced by the locals and consumed by his pious gaze.

His tour group's first stops are the cities of Galilee, where Jesus and his mother Mary supposedly grew up. In one city he sees the "breadbasket" Mary used as a little girl; in the village of Cana he sees the jugs in which Jesus turned water into wine.[62] In the village of Nazareth, the first place he visits is the Jewish synagogue:

> In the synagogue there is kept the book in which the Lord wrote his ABCs, and in this synagogue there is a bench on which he sat with other children. Christians can lift the bench and move it about, but the Jews are completely unable to move it, and cannot drag it outside. The house of Saint Mary is now a basilica, and her clothes are the cause of frequent miracles. The Jewesses of this city are better looking than any other Jewesses in the whole country. They declare that this is

---

[60] Bhabha, "Signs Taken for Wonders," 116.

[61] On the pilgrim see Celestina Milani, *Itinerarium Antonini Placentini: Un viaggio in Terra Santa del 560–570 d.C.*, Scienze filologiche e letteratura 7 (Milan: Università Cattolica del Sacro Cuore, 1977).

[62] *Itinerarium Antonini Placentini* 4–5. Text in *Itineraria et alia geographica*, ed. P. Geyer, Corpus Christianorum, Series Latina 175 (Turnhout: Brepols, 1965), 130.

Saint Mary's gift to them, for they also say that she was a relative of theirs. Though there is no love lost between Jews and Christians, these women are full of kindness. This province is like paradise.[63]

A few historians have imagined what sort of situation (other than a bona fide miracle) might have prevented Jews from moving the furniture in their own synagogue, or why the Jewish women of Nazareth (the prettiest in the land) should be so sweet to these foreign tourists. One scholar used this story to argue for the autonomy and even authority of Jews in some cities of Galilee: she suggests that Jews must have operated this "tourist site," laughing (as it were) behind their hands as Christians paid over precious "tourist dollars" for the privilege of moving benches and making eyes at the local girls.[64] The hyper-romantic novelist and poet Robert Graves incorporated this incident into his Byzantine story *Count Belisarius*. He attributed the bench-moving scheme to an unscrupulous huckster who swindled the Christian tourists and paid off the Jewish locals.[65] Other scholars resort to in those elusive "Jewish Christians," stalking the conceptual border between both religions and handily resolving such moments of difficulty.[66]

Yet if we focus on the manner in which the pilgrim narrates this encounter, instead of gauging its falsifiability, we find yet another situation in which "Jewish–Christian relations" are staged in the context of cultural colonialism. The literature of pilgrimage proves especially effective in this staging of dominance. The doubled nature of travel writing as both descriptive – "what I saw" – and prescriptive – "what you too will see" – illuminates the ways in which the Christian text frames a particular Jewish reality in the holy land. For the writer and reader, this becomes a real synagogue with real Jewish locals and real Christian tourists. Whether or not the incident occurred as narrated (if, indeed, it occurred at all), the process of textual repetition and circulation inscribes and produces these particular Jewish–Christian relations as real: a discourse of religious and imperial domination is inscribed and, henceforth, scripted (for future travelers), and the Nazareth synagogue has become the natural stage on which this religious domination is played out. To keep to my metaphor, in the world of the Piacenza Pilgrim, the

---

[63] *Itinerarium Antonini Placentini* 5 (Geyer, *Itineraria*, 131).

[64] Joan E. Taylor, *Christians and the Holy Places: The Myth of Jewish Christian Origins* (Oxford: Clarendon, 1993), 228–29.

[65] Robert Graves, *Count Belisarius* (London: Penguin, 1954), 44–45: "[Barak the relic-seller] had a Jew or two always within call to prove the truth of one-half of this assertion; the pilgrims themselves could prove the other half, if they paid for the privilege."

[66] "Jewish Christians" are implausibly suggested by Simon Mimouni, "Pour une définition nouvelle du judéo-christianisme ancien," *NTS* 38 (1992): 171–82.

Christian Lamb has become something of a flamboyant Lion-tamer, whip and chair in hand.

## *Stratēgios and the Instability of Empire*

My final example comes from the seventh century, perhaps sixty years after the Piacenza Pilgrim visited Palestine, and gives us keen and, perhaps, disquieting insight into the ultimate instability of these colonialist and imperialist discourses. A Christian monk named Stratēgios was living near the city of Jerusalem when that city was attacked and stormed by soldiers from the neighboring Persian Empire in the year 614. Stratēgios wrote an account of the sack of the holy city, focusing on the tyranny of the barbarians and the cruelty of the local Jews.[67] Stratēgios narrates how Jews opened the gates of the city to the Persian enemies of the Roman Christians.[68] The Christians who were not deemed economically valuable by the Persian generals were confined to a nearby lake, where they slowly starved and drowned. When the Jews heard of this, according to Stratēgios, they were delighted and went to see:

> The Jews approached the edge of the lake and proclaimed to God's children, the Christians, as they were in Lake Mamila: "Whoever among you wants to be made a Jew, come up to us, and we will buy you from the Persians." But their evil scheme was not accomplished by them, and their work was in vain. Moreover, the children of the Christians chose for their bodies to perish and for their souls not to die, and that no part of their lives should be with the Jews. When the Jews saw the true faith they burned with a fierce anger, and their barking was like that of dogs. They devised another plan: as if buying Christ with Judas' coins, they wanted to buy the Christians from the lake with coins. And like lambs to be slaughtered, the Christians were purchased by the Jews from the Persians, and they were slaughtered. But the Christians rejoiced greatly when they were slaughtered for Christ's faith.[69]

---

[67] The account survives in Georgian and Arabic recensions of a Greek original: G. Garrite, *La prise de Jérusalem par les Perses en 614*, Corpus Scriptorum Christianorum Orientalium 202–3 (Louvain: CSCO, 1960); idem, *Expugnationis Hierosolymae* A.D. *614 Recensiones Arabicae*, Corpus Scriptorum Christianorum Orientalium 340–41, 347–48 (Louvain: CSCO, 1973–74); the Georgian versions are probably an earlier witness of the Greek original. Stratēgios is sometimes confused with another Christian monastic narrator of these events, Antiochus: see G. W. Bowersock, "Polytheism and Monotheism in Arabia and the Three Palestines," *Dumbarton Oaks Papers* 51 (1997): 9–10.

[68] Another contemporary witness of these events was Sophronius, later patriarch of Jerusalem, who refers to the Jews of this period as "friends of the Persians" in one of his recondite poems: *Anacreontica* 14.61 (text in *Sophronii Anacreontica*, ed. M. Gigante [Rome: Gismondi, 1957], 105).

[69] Stratēgios, *Expugnatio Hierosolymae* 11 (cited here from the Latin rendering of one of the Arabic recensions).

Scholars enmeshed in the historical debates of "Jewish–Christian relations" still wrangle over the historical facts of this narrative.[70] Did Jews *really* hand over the city of Jerusalem to the Persians (like vicious dogs)? Did they *really* violently mistreat the Christians, forcing them to choose between conversion and death or slavery (like submissive lambs)? Those scholars who favor a "rhetorical" reading of Christian literature, disregarding Christian bias in favor of ethical representation of Jews, say "no."[71] Those scholars who seek the reality behind the rhetoric are often forced, in this instance, to affirm Christian bias and Jewish savagery and say "yes."[72] In terms of colonial and religious domination and resistance, replicated throughout the period of Late Antiquity, we might respond that this brutal narrative makes a sort of sense. From the intellectual resistance of Origen to the cultural appropriation of Jerome and the casual privilege of the Piacenza Pilgrim, we can trace the asymmetrical relations of culture and politics, of religious domination in the Empire. This episode, perhaps more than any other, encapsulates the challenges and benefits of historiographic readings that refuse to separate rhetoric from reality. We see here how the colonizer and the colonized reproduce and contest each other, embody and resist their constructed positions. Jew and Christian "relate" in a manner we may not have previously imagined, as subjects and objects of endlessly shifting and reorienting power relations firmly embedded in their material worlds. Out of these shifting relations emerges the possibility of fear, of desire, of control, of resistance and, in the end, of extraordinary violence, which may or may not be real with historical certainty, but remains chillingly real in its potential.

I am not reconstructing historical data for use in some great tribunal of accountability; I am tracing discourses that never ceased to produce new truths.[73] At this moment of imperial decline and catastrophe, it makes a sort of cultural sense for the colonized Jewish Lion of Judah to burst from its cage and rise up against the weakened Christian Lamb of God; by acknowledging that cultural sense, we can start to comprehend the manner of religious life, culture, and contact in the ancient world, even if its actual twists and turns are lost to us.

---

[70] See the perceptive study of Elliott Horowitz, "'The Vengeance of the Jews Was Stronger Than Their Avarice': Modern Historians and the Persian Conquest of Jerusalem in 614," *Jewish Social Studies* 4.2 (1998): 1–39.

[71] Such as Averil Cameron, "The Jews in Seventh-Century Palestine," *Scripta Classica Israelica* 13 (1994): 75–93.

[72] As, for instance, by Robert Wilken, *The Land Called Holy: Palestine in Christian History and Thought* (New Haven: Yale UP, 1992), 203–4.

[73] See Loomba, *Colonialism/Postcolonialism*, 240: "we can abandon the grand narratives which once dominated the writing of history without also abandoning all analysis of the *relationships* between different forces in society."

## Conclusions and Suggestions

My foray into "Jewish–Christian relations" in the holy land is meant to be more suggestive than definitive. My goal has not been to dismiss the critical scholarship of students of Jewish–Christian relations, nor to suggest that the theoretical patch of postcolonial criticism can be used to iron over the ethical and historiographic dilemmas facing scholars in this field. I do think, however, that we gain some insight by viewing some familiar stories from a new theoretical lens:

> It will be clear by now that such questions are not unique to the study of colonialism but are also crucial for any scholarship concerned with recovering the histories and perspectives of marginalised peoples – be they women, non-whites, non-Europeans, the lower classes and oppressed castes – and for any consideration of how ideologies work and are transformed.[74]

Taken together, these somewhat imaginative permutations of the Jewish Lion and Christian Lamb do not allow us to peer through the literature on Jews by Christians into a stable and "real world," but they do, perhaps, give us useful intellectual grist to mill questions of precisely the sort of "ideological work" that Jewish–Christian relations have had difficulty facing.

I am not arguing for the reality of representations but rather am attempting to disclose *how* that reality was produced, scripted, and resisted through linguistic representations. We witness, in these "relations" between Christians and Jews, the way in which Christians and Jews constructed their world, reacted to their world, engineered their world through resistant or authoritative discourse. Like Gayatri Spivak,

> what I find useful is the sustained and developing work on the *mechanics* of the constitution of the Other; we can use it to much greater analytic and interventionist advantage than the invocations of the *authenticity* of the Other.[75]

Scholars historically and ethically enmeshed in the debate over rhetoric versus reality may find the abandonment of "the Other's authenticity" a difficult pill to swallow. But we do not lose any political or scholarly traction when we turn to the "mechanics" of that Other's construction; instead we attend more astutely to the ways in which we might comprehend the significant and all-too-real interplays and consequences of politics and culture, of religion and identity.

---

[74] Loomba, *Colonialism/Postcolonialism*, 231.
[75] Spivak, "Can the Subaltern Speak?" in Williams and Chrisman, *Colonial Discourse*, 90.

# Modeling the "Parting of the Ways"

by

## MARTIN GOODMAN

Much of the disagreement in modern scholarship about when, how, why, and indeed whether, the ways of Judaism and Christianity parted in antiquity derives from confusion about differences of perspective. The relationship of one group to another may be seen quite differently by members of the two groups, and differently again by the modern observer. Thus, for instance, someone considered Jewish by a Christian might not consider himself or herself Jewish, and might or might not be considered as a Jew by non-Christian Jews. It is unreasonable to expect ancient authors always to have made the clear distinctions which historians now seek to discover: the relationship between Jews and Christians may generally have been important for Christians as part of their self-definition, but it was much less crucial for Jews, who could ignore for much of Late Antiquity what Christians thought and did.[1] At the same time, occasional contact and conflict between members of distinct groups, and their sharing of theological notions or liturgical practices, need not imply any lack of clarity for the ancient participants of each group about the differences between them: if modern scholars find it hard to decide whether the author or intended readers of a particular text were Jews or Christians, it does not follow that those who produced and used the text in antiquity were similarly in doubt.

In illustrations of these varieties of perspective I drew up, for the last of the seminars held in Oxford before the Princeton colloquium, a series of schematic diagrams for the seminar participants to refine. Crude copies of the revised diagrams were distributed at the start of the Princeton meeting, where they were subjected to further alteration. They were amended yet again in the light of comments by a group in Cambridge and in reaction to the alternative models proposed by the student leaders of

---

[1] See further M. Goodman, "The Function of Minim in Early Rabbinic Judaism," in *Geschichte – Tradition – Reflexion, Festschrift für Martin Hengel zum 70*, vol. 1, *Judentum*, ed. P. Schäfer (Tübingen: Mohr Siebeck, 1996), 501–10; S. Stern, *Jewish Identity in Early Rabbinic Writings* (Leiden: Brill, 1994); and A. Tropper's article in this volume.

the seminar held in Oxford after our return from Princeton. The final versions presented here are thus very much the product of joint endeavor.

All models are inexact representations of an elusive reality. In the course of discussing these diagrams many useful suggestions were made of what might better represent the complex relationships between Judaism and Christianity on which all are agreed. There was much enthusiasm, for instance, for a three-dimensional model, which might give greater prominence to synchronic variation in religious practice and belief in different places and to the varying significance of the different streams – the idea is attractive, but hard to represent on the page. A water-filled construction to represent the wave model, based on language formation, as proposed by Daniel Boyarin in this volume, is similarly impractical for mass distribution.

If no image is perfect, some images are more useful than others. In any case, models should only be used as heuristic devices for finding out more about the import of the ancient evidence. It is in that minimal spirit that the diagrams are reproduced here, expertly transformed from my incompetent artistic efforts through Jeremy Boccabello's expertise in computer design.

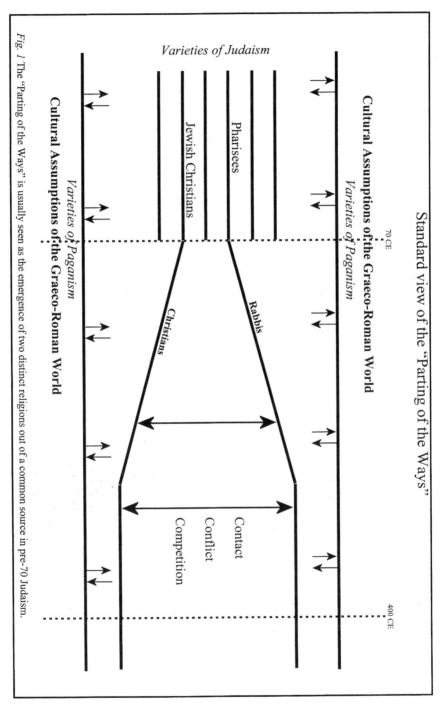

*Fig. 1* The "Parting of the Ways" is usually seen as the emergence of two distinct religions out of a common source in pre-70 Judaism.

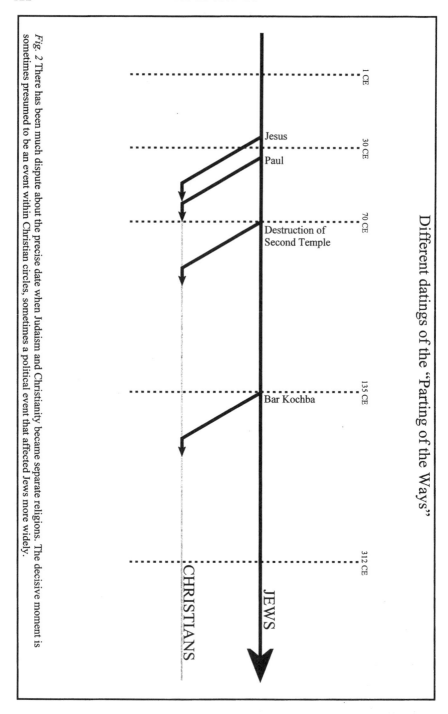

Different datings of the "Parting of the Ways"

1 CE
30 CE
Jesus
Paul
70 CE
Destruction of
Second Temple
135 CE
Bar Kochba
312 CE
CHRISTIANS
JEWS

*Fig. 2* There has been much dispute about the precise date when Judaism and Christianity became separate religions. The decisive moment is sometimes presumed to be an event within Christian circles, sometimes a political event that affected Jews more widely.

## Jews and Christians as seen by pagans in antiquity

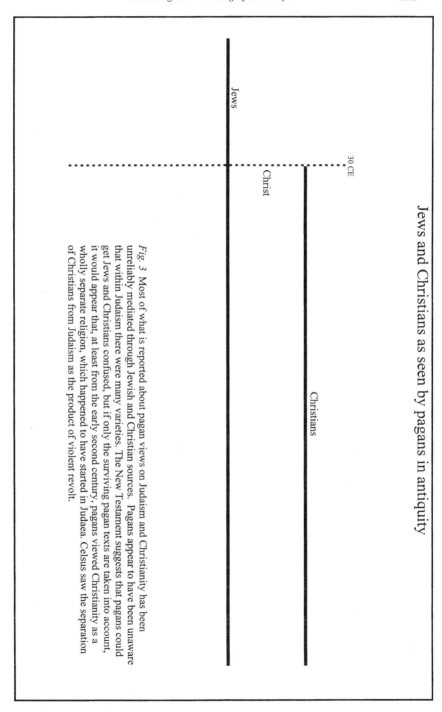

*Fig. 3* Most of what is reported about pagan views on Judaism and Christianity has been unreliably mediated through Jewish and Christian sources. Pagans appear to have been unaware that within Judaism there were many varieties. The New Testament suggests that pagans could get Jews and Christians confused, but if only the surviving pagan texts are taken into account, it would appear that, at least from the early second century, pagans viewed Christianity as a wholly separate religion, which happened to have started in Judaea. Celsus saw the separation of Christians from Judaism as the product of violent revolt.

Jews

30 CE

Christ

Christians

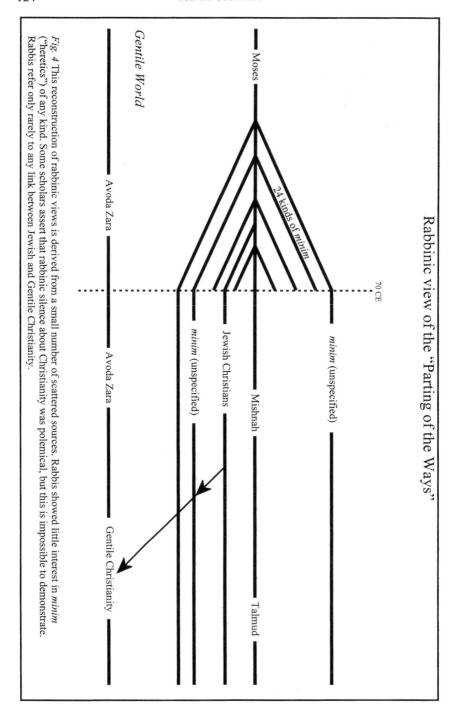

Rabbinic view of the "Parting of the Ways"

*Fig. 4* This reconstruction of rabbinic views is derived from a small number of scattered sources. Rabbis showed little interest in *minim* ("heretics") of any kind. Some scholars assert that rabbinic silence about Christianity was polemical, but this is impossible to demonstrate. Rabbis refer only rarely to any link between Jewish and Gentile Christianity.

Moses

24 kinds of *minim*

70 CE

Gentile World

Avoda Zara

Avoda Zara

Avoda Zara

Gentile Christianity

*minim* (unspecified)

Jewish Christians

Mishnah

Talmud

*minim* (unspecified)

Eusebius' view of the "Parting of the Ways"

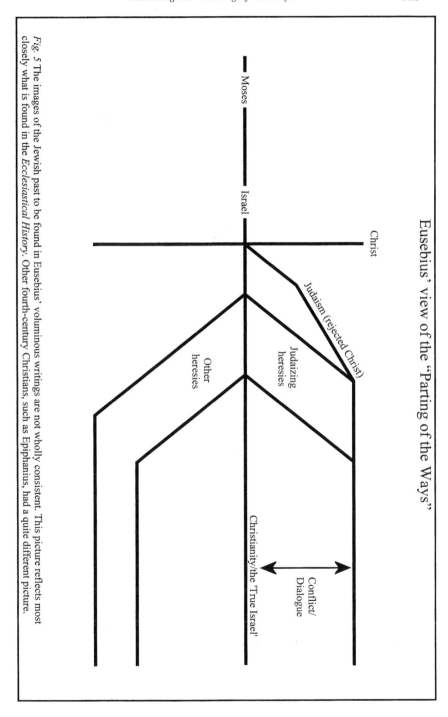

*Fig. 5* The images of the Jewish past to be found in Eusebius' voluminous writings are not wholly consistent. This picture reflects most closely what is found in the *Ecclesiastical History*. Other fourth-century Christians, such as Epiphanius, had a quite different picture.

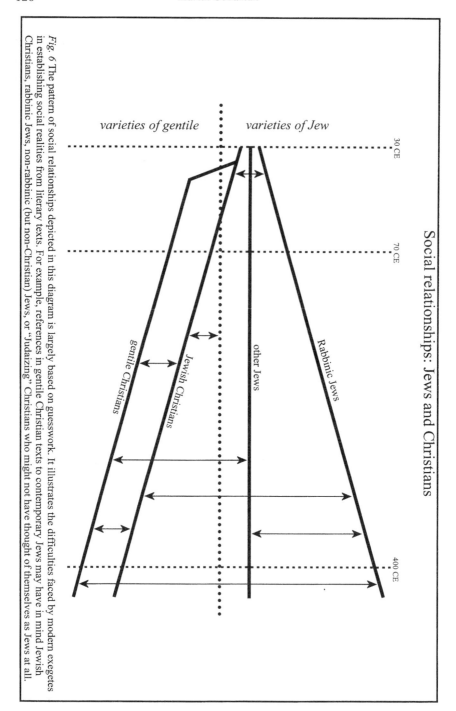

Social relationships: Jews and Christians

*varieties of gentile*     *varieties of Jew*

30 CE

70 CE

gentile Christians

Jewish Christians

other Jews

Rabbinic Jews

400 CE

*Fig. 6* The pattern of social relationships depicted in this diagram is largely based on guesswork. It illustrates the difficulties faced by modern exegetes in establishing social realities from literary texts. For example, references in gentile Christian texts to contemporary Jews may have in mind Jewish Christians, rabbinic Jews, non-rabbinic (but non-Christian) Jews, or "Judaizing" Christians who might not have thought of themselves as Jews at all.

Self-perceptions

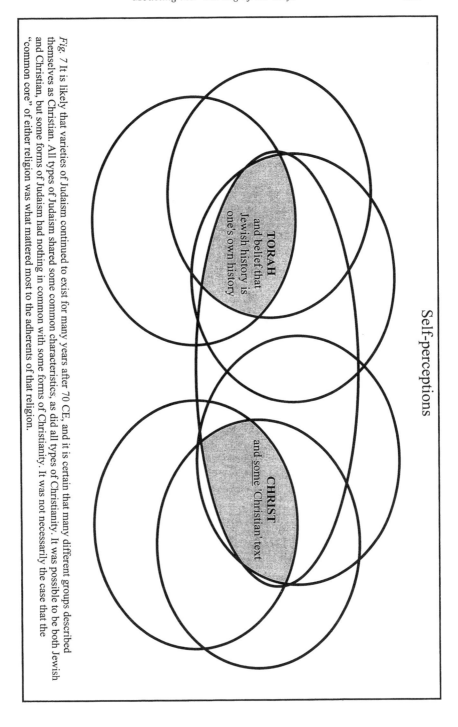

*Fig.* 7 It is likely that varieties of Judaism continued to exist for many years after 70 CE, and it is certain that many different groups described themselves as Christian. All types of Judaism shared some common characteristics, as did all types of Christianity. It was possible to be both Jewish and Christian, but some forms of Judaism had nothing in common with some forms of Christianity. It was not necessarily the case that the "common core" of either religion was what mattered most to the adherents of that religion.

The two shaded regions are labeled:

**TORAH** and belief that Jewish history is one's own history

**CHRIST** and some Christian text

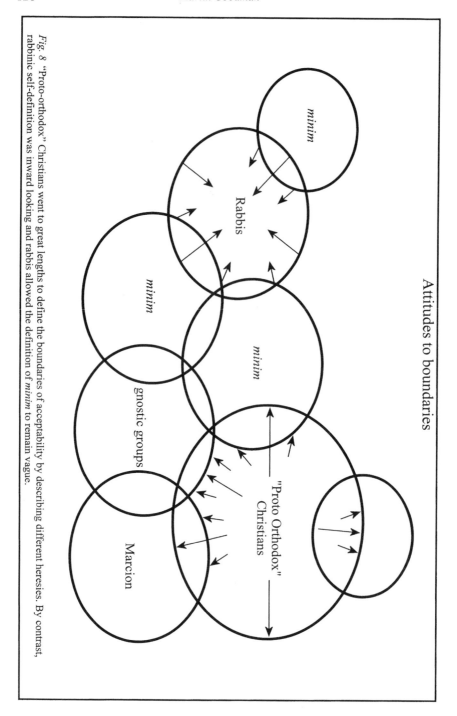

Attitudes to boundaries

*Fig. 8* "Proto-orthodox" Christians went to great lengths to define the boundaries of acceptability by describing different heresies. By contrast, rabbinic self-definition was inward looking and rabbis allowed the definition of *minim* to remain vague.

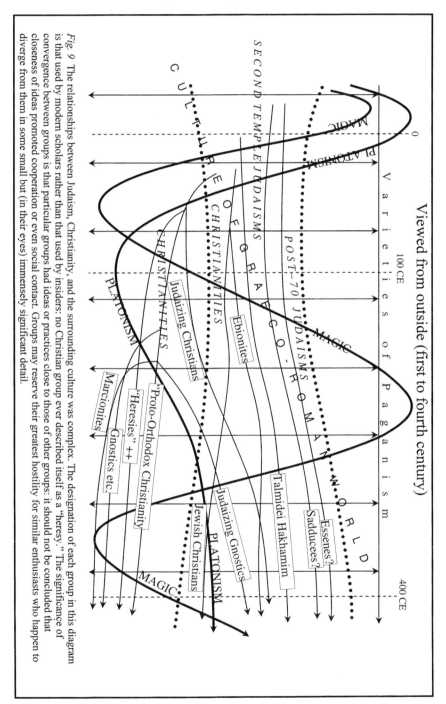

Viewed from outside (first to fourth century)

*Fig. 9* The relationships between Judaism, Christianity, and the surrounding culture was complex. The designation of each group in this diagram is that used by modern scholars rather than that used by insiders: no Christian group ever described itself as a "heresy." The significance of convergence between groups is that particular groups had ideas or practices close to those of other groups; it should not be concluded that closeness of ideas promoted cooperation or even social contact. Groups may reserve their greatest hostility for similar enthusiasts who happen to diverge from them in some small but (in their eyes) immensely significant detail.

# Beyond "Jewish Christianity"

## Continuing Religious Sub-Cultures of the Second and Third Centuries and Their Documents

by

### DAVID FRANKFURTER

## Documents that Challenge Categories

Scholarship on ancient Mediterranean religions continues to be inhibited by its dependence on theological categories. Use of the word "pagan," for example, an ancient term of bias for the unconverted rustic, has inevitably led to false contrasts between "pagans" and "Christians" and, despite contemporary scholars' earnest efforts to qualify their terminology, to the erroneous reification of two essential religious "halves" in Late Antiquity.[1] Such reifications produce further errors: for example, discussions of "Christian-*ity*," "Juda-*ism*," and "Mithra-*ism*" as historical entities have succumbed to post-Reformation notions that religiosity in antiquity was a matter of belief and doctrine rather than practice and place.[2] So with the terms "Christianity" and "Judaism": not only have they been conceived of largely doctrinally, but the image of two essentially *exclusive* religious ways from the beginning of the first millennium CE has led the majority of New Testament scholars to retroject modern anxieties about religious clarity and orthodoxy onto a period of blur and flux in religious boundaries.

---

[1] See the careful attempts to generalize a "paganism" despite admission of utter diversity by Ramsay MacMullen, *Paganism in the Roman Empire* (New Haven: Yale UP, 1981), and Robin Lane Fox, *Pagans and Christians* (New York: Knopf, 1987), 30–36. Cf. rejections of the term as ultimately misleading by David Frankfurter, *Religion in Roman Egypt: Assimilation and Resistance* (Princeton: Princeton UP, 1998), 33–36, and James J. O'Donnell, review of Salzman, *The Making of a Christian Aristocracy*, *Bryn Mawr Classical Review* 2002.06.04 [http://ccat.sas.upenn.edu/bmcr/2002/2002-06-04.html].

[2] See in general Charles Robert Phillips, "The Sociology of Religious Knowledge in the Roman Empire to A.D. 284," *ANRW* II.16.3 (1986): 2677–773.

However, "history, rightly done, must err on the side of radical nominalism," as Jacob Neusner once said,[3] and nowhere has this challenge to old categories and their reification been more necessary, and more productive, than in the traditional model of a "Christianity" *emergent and separate* from a "Judaism." For there was not only an immense diversity *within* these two religious clusters but also a mutual influence persisting through Late Antiquity. And most importantly for this paper, there is evidence for a degree of overlap in self-definition that, all things considered, threatens almost every construction of an historically distinct "Christianity" before at least the mid-second century.[4]

I am interested specifically in the nature of these "overlaps" in self-definition: situations where there is ritual or interpretive attention in some form to Christ practiced entirely within a Jewish self-definition. Allegiance to Christ in these cases is conceived as a devotional orientation *within* a world of Torah observance and Jewish identity, sometimes even of a sectarian nature. This kind of Jewish Jesus-devotion has emerged as a primary historical model in new scholarship on Paul,[5] on the Gospel of Matthew,[6] and more recently on the book of Revelation.[7] In extolling a priestly degree of purity in the life of the Elect, and in vilifying those who teach the lightening of halakhic purity restrictions, the book of Revelation belongs not to an amorphous "Christianity," but to an extreme, purity-oriented sect of Judaism.[8]

---

[3] Jacob Neusner, *Judaism: The Evidence of the Mishnah* (Chicago: U. of Chicago, 1981), 23.

[4] See in general Daniel Boyarin, *Dying for God: Martyrdom and the Making of Christianity and Judaism* (Stanford: Stanford UP, 1999).

[5] E.g., W. D. Davies, *Paul and Rabbinic Judaism: Some Rabbinic Elements in Pauline Theology* (2nd ed.; London: SPCK, 1955); E. P. Sanders, *Paul and Palestinian Judaism* (Philadelphia: Fortress, 1977); John Gager, *The Origins of Antisemitism* (New York: Oxford UP, 1983), and *Reinventing Paul* (Oxford: Oxford UP, 2000); Daniel Boyarin, *A Radical Jew: Paul and the Politics of Identity* (Berkeley: U. of California, 1994); Markus Bockmuehl, *Jewish Law in Gentile Churches: Halakhah and Beginning of Christian Public Ethics* (Edinburgh: T&T Clark, 2000).

[6] E.g., Anthony J. Saldarini, *Matthew's Christian-Jewish Community* (Chicago: U. of Chicago, 1994), and David C. Sim, *The Gospel of Matthew and Christian Judaism: The History and Social Setting of the Matthean Community* (Edinburgh: T&T Clark, 1998).

[7] See David Frankfurter, "Jews or Not? Reconstructing the 'Other' in Rev 2:9 and 3:9," *HTR* 94 (2001): 403–25, and John W. Marshall, *Parables of the War: Reading John's Jewish Apocalypse*, Studies in Christianity and Judaism 10 (Waterloo, Ont.: Wilfred Laurier UP, 2001).

[8] See Frankfurter, "Jews or Not" and Stephen Goranson, "Essene Polemic in the Apocalypse of John," in *Legal Texts and Legal Issues*, ed. Moshe Bernstein, Florentino Garcia Martinez, and John Kampen (Leiden: Brill, 1997), 453–60.

As we begin to adjust our model for Christ-worship within distinctively Jewish contexts, a substantial corpus of literature outside the Christian canon gains greater importance: the Christian Pseudepigrapha. These documents, *attributed to* Jewish heroes, express varying degrees of affiliation with or origin in Judaism but were preserved in Christian scribal milieus. Some of these texts, such as *First* and *Second Enoch, Jubilees, Apocalypse of Abraham*, are certainly Jewish in origin, even if the best manuscripts come from Ethiopian or Eastern European monasteries.[9] Others are more complex, for example, *Ascension of Isaiah*, the *Testaments of the Twelve Patriarchs, Apocalypse of Elijah,* and *Testament of Abraham*. The explicit references to Christ in these documents mean that Christians took a special interest in them, but did they write them or merely edit earlier Jewish compositions?

The usual approach to these documents holds that Jewish texts were edited by Christians and interpolated with new material, *rather than* written from scratch within a Christian milieu.[10] Why has this approach been preferable? There seem to be theological reasons, such as the triumphalist notion that scribes would update Jewish texts to show their fulfillment rather than that they would promote Christ from the points of view of Jewish heroes and alongside the reassertion of Jewish identity.[11] Another theological reason for viewing Christian materials as a distinct, separate stage in a text's development would be that such Christian details are somehow *prohibitive* of Jewish identity. That is, Christ's very presence in heaven or the world to come is deemed such an unusual, arresting feature that it could only indicate the text's shift to an entirely *new* religious worldview. The alternative perspective – that the authors may not have regarded these details as a shift out of Judaism in any way –

---

[9] See M. A. Knibb, "Christian Adoption and Transmission of Jewish Pseudepigrapha: The Case of 1 Enoch," *JSJ* 32 (2001): 396–415.

[10] See, e.g., James H. Charlesworth, "Christian and Jewish Self-Definition in Light of the Christian Additions to the Apocryphal Writings," in *Jewish and Christian Self-Definition*, vol. 2, *Aspects of Judaism in the Graeco-Roman Period*, ed. E. P. Sanders, A. I. Baumgarten, and Alan Mendelson (Philadelphia: Fortress, 1981), 27–55. For the older, "default" position that texts should be considered Jewish unless proven otherwise, see Émil Schürer, *The History of the Jewish People in the Age of Jesus Christ*, 2nd ed. rev.; ed. Geza Vermes, Fergus Millar, and Martin Goodman (Edinburgh: T&T Clark, 1973–87), vol. 3.2, 771 n.17. For critiques see Robert A. Kraft, "The Pseudepigrapha in Christianity," in *Tracing the Threads: Studies in the Vitality of Jewish Pseudepigrapha*, ed. John C. Reeves (Atlanta: Scholars Press, 1994), 55–86; idem, "Setting the Stage and Framing Some Central Questions," *JSJ* 32 (2001): 371–73; and Marinus de Jonge, "The So-Called Pseudepigrapha of the Old Testament and Early Christianity," in *The New Testament and Hellenistic Judaism*, ed. Peder Borgen and Søren Giversen (Aarhus: Aarhus UP, 1995), 59–71.

[11] See, e.g., Marcel Simon, "Les Saints d'Israël dans la dévotion de l'Église ancienne," *Revue d'Histoire et de Philosophie Religieuses* 34 (1954): 98–127.

is deemed unimaginable. Finally, the rather chauvinistic, even sectarian, Jewish ethics of some of the Pseudepigrapha have struck some scholars as incompatible with a Christian (or proto-Christian) ecumenism that they imagine prevailed in the first centuries CE.[12] Thus, rather than imagining a genus of Christ-devotee who embraced, say, priestly purity traditions as a central feature of self-definition, scholars proposed redactional stages whereby a narrowly Jewish text might be "opened up" to ecumenical Christian values.

There were ancient groups, of course, that had no particular historical connection to Jewish culture, like the authors of the Egyptian Christian *Apocalypse of Elijah* or *Testament of Isaac*. For these authors, the claim to biblical authority was a kind of *invented tradition*, an appropriation of symbolism from a culture with which they had no intrinsic association.[13] Robert Murray labeled this phenomenon "Hebraistic Christianity" to distinguish it from Christian milieus that showed some cultural continuity with Judaism.[14]

This paper, however, involves those texts that reflect a sectarian Jewish identity while at the same time positioning Christ as a central part of the heavenly world. What happens in the discussion of these texts if one *abandons* the category "Christian" – as a distinct stage in these texts' composition and, implicitly, as a distinct religious mentality? What if we were to look at these texts, rather, as the work of *continuous* communities of halakhically-observant Jewish groups – perhaps of a sectarian nature –

---

[12] Cf. Daniel C. Harlow, *The Greek Apocalypse of Baruch (3 Baruch) in Hellenistic Judaism and Early Christianity*, SVTP 12 (Leiden: Brill, 1996), who finds in 3 Baruch an ecumenism that eschews an earthly temple for God's general accessibility and uses this observation to place the text in a new "placeless" Judaism of individual piety (esp. 71–76, 157–62). The model of this ecumenical Judaism bears a remarkable resemblance to Protestant notions of placeless, individualized spirituality. Ecumenism was not, of course, unimaginable in antiquity, even in those groups that drew upon Jewish apocalyptic traditions: see, e.g., David Frankfurter, "Apocalypses Real and Alleged in the Mani Codex," *Numen* 44.1 (1997): 60–73, esp. 65–68.

[13] See Eric Hobsbawm and Terence Ranger, eds., *The Invention of Tradition* (Cambridge: Cambridge UP, 1983), and for the ancient world, David Frankfurter, "The Consequences of Hellenism in Late Antique Egypt: Religious Worlds and Actors," *Archiv für Religionsgeschichte* 2.2 (2000): 162–94, esp. 184–92.

[14] Robert Murray, "Jews, Hebrews, and Christians: Some Needed Distinctions," *NovT* 24 (1982): 194–208. See also David Frankfurter, *Elijah in Upper Egypt: The Apocalypse of Elijah and Early Egyptian Christianity* (Minneapolis: Fortress, 1993), 58–77, 270–98, and Joan K. Taylor, "The Phenomenon of Early Jewish-Christianity: Reality or Scholarly Invention?" *VigChr* 44 (1990): 313–34. On the appropriation of "Jewish" religious identity by culturally unaffiliated groups, compare the American sects of Black Hebrews, discussed in Hans A. Baer and Merrill Singer, *African American Religion in the Twentieth Century: Varieties of Protest and Accommodation* (Knoxville: U. of Tennessee, 1992), 113–18.

that incorporated Jesus into their cosmologies and liturgies while retaining an essentially Jewish, or even *priestly*, self-definition? This is certainly what is going on in Revelation, where matters of purity are at least as important as celebrating Christ.

The four texts considered in this paper are the *Ascension of Isaiah*, the two prophecies included in the 2 Esdras corpus and now designated *5* and *6 Ezra*, and the *Testaments of the Twelve Patriarchs*. Each of these texts has caused considerable problems for commentators trying to identify the Jewishness or Christianness of the authors or later editors. In two cases, the problems were resolved by positing that the texts originated in a Jewish sect, like Qumran, and were later subject to Christian redaction. But more recent scholarship in each case has shown that these texts were *entirely* compositions of Christ-believers. This paper will discuss the implications of this conclusion for identifying subcultures of *Jewish* Christ-believers.

## Documents of Continuing Jewish Prophetism

The *Ascension of Isaiah* contains two ostensibly discrete stories: one of Isaiah's sufferings under Manasseh, culminating in his being sawed in two (chs. 1–5); and the other of Isaiah's ascent through the seven heavens to behold an enthroned figure delicately referred to as the *Beloved* (6–9) and to watch him descend into the world *incognito*, be born of Mary, and undergo crucifixion (10–11). Seams and repetitions abound in the extant Slavonic, Ethiopic, and Latin texts, and the "Ascent" portion of the text apparently circulated independently at some point. It is not certain, however, that the seams, repetitions, and modular components of the text have anything to do with religious affiliation. This was, of course, the proposal of early scholars of the Pseudepigrapha, who sought discernible seams between the materials that retold the Isaiah story and the materials revealing Christ.[15]

The most recent studies by Robert Hall and Enrico Norelli have offered a more unitary historical setting: a guild of prophets imagining themselves in the model of biblical *nevi'im* but oriented towards Christ in

---

[15] David Flusser, "The Apocryphal Book of Ascensio Isaiae and the Dead Sea Sect," *IEJ* 3 (1953): 34–47, and Schürer, *History of the Jewish People* 3,1: 337–38. A new historiographical entry on "Martyrdom of Isaiah" is much more circumspect about the possibility of excising Jewish sources: Albert-Marie Denis and Jean-Claude Haelewyck, *Introduction à la littérature religieuse judéo-hellénistique* (Turnhout: Brepols, 2000), vol. 1, 633–57.

some way.[16] This guild's adherence to the notion that biblical prophetic authority continued in their group seems to indicate some relationship with Jewish culture. Indeed, there are insinuations in the text that biblical prophecy is being revitalized among some "in-group" but *denied* by some opposing group that is distinctive for having a hierarchy of offices (3.21–31) and that bears a remarkable resemblance to the ecclesiasticism advocated by Ignatius of Antioch (*Smyrnaeans* 8–10; *Trallians* 2–3) and the Pastoral Epistles (1 Timothy 3; Titus 1).[17] The "in-group's" authority, Hall has argued, revolves around some prophet's claim to have ascended to heaven, beheld the divine throne, and observed Christ; but even the imagery of Christ and his advent in the world are somewhat secondary to the general claim of heavenly ascent. That is, Christian imagery is presented not apologetically – as if by "Christians" to outsider Jews – but rather as a *quality* of a Jewish apocalyptic heaven; it is the authority to reveal this heaven that is under dispute.[18] The opposing group's incredulity at this vision, indeed, is deemed utterly evil and ascribed to several Satanic forces.[19]

---

[16] Robert G. Hall, "The Ascension of Isaiah: Community, Situation, Date, and Place in Early Christianity," *JBL* 109 (1990): 289–306; Enrico Norelli, *Ascension d'Isaïe* (Turnhout: Brepols, 1993), 87–99, and *L'Ascensione di Isaia: Studi su un apocrifo al crocevia dei christianesimi* (Bologna: EDB, 1994), 235–48; compare the more derivative work of Jonathan Knight, *Disciples of the Beloved One: The Christology, Social Setting and Theological Context of the Ascension of Isaiah*, JSPSupp 18 (Sheffield: Sheffield UP, 1996), 197–205. Further on *Ascen. Is.* in the history of early Christian prophetism, see Richard Bauckham, *The Climax of Prophecy: Studies on the Book of Revelation* (Edinburgh: T&T Clark, 1993), 89–91.

[17] See Norelli, *Ascension d'Isaïe*, 95–99.

[18] Robert Hall, "Isaiah's Ascent to See the Beloved: An Ancient Jewish Source for the Ascension of Isaiah," *JBL* 113 (1994): 463–84. *Ascen. Is.*'s implicit docetism and general care to label the heavenly figure "Beloved" indicates a disinclination to identify him closely with the earthly Jesus and, rather, an inclination to preserve God's features as essentially transcendent. (The account of the virgin birth in 11.2–16 does not really contradict the docetism implicit in the descent of the Beloved in 10.17–31, since events in this lower world do not change the meaning of the text's essential heavenly truths). Revelation's series of christological manifestations is similar. Both stem from Jewish apocalyptic traditions of envisioning God (cf. Gedaliahu G. Stroumsa, "Form(s) of God: Some Notes on Metatron and Christ," *HTR* 76.3 [1983]: 269–88, and Jarl Fossum, "Jewish-Christian Christology and Jewish Mysticism," *VigChr* 37 [1983]: 260–87) and seem to be opposed by Ignatius of Antioch's anti-docetic statements (*Magn.* 11; *Trall.* 9–10; *Smyrn.* 1; 6.1).

[19] On the basis of *Ascen. Is.* 3.8–10 Knight adds to the author's enemies a quasi-rabbinic Jewish establishment that opposed the Isaianic vision on "Mosaic" grounds (*Disciples of the Beloved One*, 190–96). Resembling J. Louis Martyn's reasoning about Jewish aggression in *History and Theology in the Fourth Gospel* (2nd ed.; Nashville: Abingdon, 1979), Knight's proposition depends not only on an over-reading of the text but also on the same false Judaism/Christianity binary discussed above: legalistic and mundane Jews opposing spiritually-minded Christians on grounds of Torah.

Thus, while the text properly considered shows little evidence of a separate Jewish *Vorlage*, it does reflect a type of Christ-devotion that is Jewish enough in frame of reference – particularly in its details of heavenly ascent and prophetic authority – that calling it "Christian" or "Jewish" in a *mutually exclusive* sense will not suffice.[20] Nor does the term "Jewish-Christian" (however one defines it) offer greater clarity.[21] Texts like *Ascension of Isaiah* thus challenge us to reconstruct historical nuances of identity that these theological categories just cannot capture.

In trying to situate this text in a real religious milieu I have found it useful to link it to the book of Revelation, which, although normally dated a half-century or so earlier, bears striking resemblances to it.[22] Each text focuses on revealing the heavenly world; each depends deeply on Jewish apocalyptic visionary traditions; each is concerned with prophetic authority, its incipient rivalries, and their typological references in biblical tradition.[23] Revelation should certainly be read as a Jewish document – even despite certain "novelties" in its heavenly world (i.e., christological spins on the manifestation of God). Its concern for sexual purity (2:14, 20; 5:10; 14:4), apparently in response to certain (Pauline?) leaders' call for greater freedom in sexual relations (2:14, 20; cf. 1 Cor 7), is best understood in relation to Jewish priestly purity traditions.[24] The *Ascension of Isaiah* does not address issues of purity to the extent that Revelation does, but rather focuses its diatribes against a movement apparently trying to replace prophets with hierarchy (3.21–31). Yet this same hierarchical movement is specifically envisioned as "abandon[ing] the prophecy of the twelve apostles, and their faith and their love and their purity" (3.21) and as driven by "the spirit of error and of *porneia* and of vainglory and of the love of money" (3.28). This catalogue of sins

---

[20] Cf. Knight, *Disciples of the Beloved One*, 268–71, on continuities with Jewish scribal traditions.

[21] Where Marcel Simon's definition of "Judeo-Christianity" emphasized the continuity of Jewish halakhic practice ("Réflexions sur le Judéo-Christianisme," *Christianity, Judaism, and Other Greco-Roman Cults: Studies for Morton Smith at Sixty*, ed. Jacob Neusner, SJLA 12 [Leiden: Brill, 1975], 2.53–76), that of Jean Daniélou revolved around apocalyptic, visionary ("theological") features (e.g., *The Theology of Jewish Christianity*, trans. John A. Baker [London: Darton, Longman, & Todd, 1964]). See Robert A. Kraft, "In Search of 'Jewish Christianity' and its 'Theology': Problems of Definition and Methodology," *RSR* 60 (1972): 81–92.

[22] See now Richard Bauckham, "The Ascension of Isaiah: Genre, Unity and Date," *The Fate of the Dead: Studies on the Jewish and Christian Apocalypses*, NovTest Supp. 93 (Leiden: Brill, 1998), 363–90, esp. 384, on an attempt to date *Ascen. Is.* to the later first century.

[23] E.g., Revelation's biblically-inspired labels "Jezebel" (2:20) and "teachings of Balaam" (2:14), like *Ascen. Is.*'s depiction of ancient false prophets opposing Isaiah and Elijah (2.12–3.5); see Norelli, *L'Ascensione di Isaia*, 93–113.

[24] Frankfurter, "Jews or Not?" 410–18.

recalls Revelation's anti-Pauline ideology of strict sexual purity and prophetic hegemony.[25]

Might the *Ascension of Isaiah* be Jewish in the same way as Revelation? Each text would thus emerge from a guild of self-defined prophets maintaining visionary traditions within some Jewish milieu who at some point in the later first century arrive at the conclusion that Christ is the visible portion of God. Yet it is not Christ per se that preoccupies them in these texts, but the defense of their prophetic authority and the identification of evil.

A similar social setting appears to lie behind *5* and *6 Ezra*, the rather breathless prophetic tracts that sandwich the great first-century Jewish apocalypse *4 Ezra*. As Ted Bergren has noted, both texts drew upon sources or language typical of Jesus-believers – Matthew and Revelation, for example – yet neither even mentions Christ or describes heaven at all.[26] They both appear to be prophetic discourses steeped in biblical lore and discourse. They both promote prophetic authority, even to the point of martyrdom (*5 Ez* 1:32; 2:18; *6 Ez* 15:1–4). And they each have a strong sense of a privileged Elect, who will undergo persecution (*6 Ez* 16:68–76) and be gathered together and sealed (*5 Ez* 2:38–45). Resemblances to Revelation are striking: *5 Ezra* envisions the sealing of the Elect on Mt. Zion; *6 Ezra* warns that the Elect might be forced to eat unkosher meat (16:68–69) but must keep God's "commandments and rules [*mandata et praecepta*]" (16:76).[27] Once again, the prophetic concerns and self-definition of the authors of these texts seem "Christian" only in a limited sense but "Jewish" in their more basic appeal to a religious frame of reference and authority. Even references to the rejection of Israel are heir

---

[25] Likewise, the appeal to the authority of the Twelve to ground prophecy would seem implicitly to endorse a Jewish framework for the Jesus movement and to repudiate maverick apostles like Paul, whose opinions on prophecy (1 Cor 12–14) were remembered as lukewarm. In general on 3.21–31 see Enrico Norelli, ed., *Ascensio Isaiae: Commentarius*, CSSA 8 (Turnhout: Brepols, 1995), 212–14 (taking Greek προφητεία as the original reading over Ethiopic *temhert* [teachings]: ibid., 212). Knight (*Disciples of the Beloved One*, 192–93) proposes that *Ascen. Is.* actually opposed Torah-observance (including purity traditions) altogether, because it neglects the Torah in a list of scriptures supporting prophecy (4.21–22). But it is unclear why the Torah would have been mentioned anyway in this context.

[26] Michael E. Stone and Theodore Bergren, "2 Esdras" in *Harper's Bible Commentary*, ed. J. L. Mays (San Francisco: Harper & Row, 1988), 776; Bergren, *Fifth Ezra: The Text, Origin and Early History*, SCS 25 (Atlanta: Scholars Press, 1990), 269–70; ibid., "Prophetic Rhetoric in 6 Ezra," in *For a Later Generation: The Transformation of Tradition in Israel, Early Judaism, and Early Christianity*, ed. Randal A. Argall, Beverly A. Bow, and Rodney A. Werline (Harrisburg: TPI, 2000), 29.

[27] G. N. Stanton, "5 Ezra and Matthean Christianity in the Second Century," *JTS* 28 (1977): 75–76; Bergren, *Fifth Ezra*, 269–70, and idem, *Sixth Ezra: The Text and Origin* (Oxford: Oxford UP, 1998), 15–16.

to older biblical traditions and can be read as actually upholding the observance of Torah.[28]

Indeed, for Revelation, *Ascension of Isaiah*, and *5* and *6 Ezra*, larger religious affiliations do not concern the authors nearly as much as prophetic authority – its biblical lineage, and its powers to see and warn against threats from rivals, the impure, and the demonic world. As much as Christ may have been imagined as a significant part of cosmology and liturgy, identity in these texts seems to emerge from a Jewish frame of reference. Jewish culture – it seems unwise to speak of a "Judaism" – defines what a prophet is, what heaven consists of, and what religious practices determine an Elect.[29]

The concept of a "continuous community" seems apt here as a historical-social model, for the term proposes a continuity between these Jewish prophet-guilds oriented towards Christ and some earlier period when, one might suppose, they were not so oriented. Bob Kraft once offered the term "evolved literature" to describe these kinds of materials,[30] but rather than focusing on the evolution of the literature itself, it is perhaps time to shift to the social settings *behind* the literature. Thus, far from a Christian "importation" of Jewish texts, or even a self-consciously "Christian" appropriation of Jewish traditions, we should posit a multiform "prophetic sectarianism" that continued with a fairly consistent identity and impulse from a Jewish stage into a Jewish and Christ-oriented stage.[31] And this prophetic sectarianism makes best sense in Asia Minor, since *5* and *6 Ezra* and *Ascension of Isaiah* overlap considerably with Revelation and such religious trends as the New Prophecy ("Montanism").[32]

But it is the continuity of a religious phenomenon under the umbrella of Judaism that is at issue here, not the sociology of prophetism per se. It

---

[28] *5 Ezra* 1:24–2:11 – esp. 1:26 and 34 versus 1:31. Cf. Stanton, "5 Ezra and Matthean Christianity," 73–79; Bergren, *Fifth Ezra*, 316–21.

[29] On this general cultural inheritance among many Jesus-sects, see Simon, "Les Saints d'Israël," (above, n.11) and "Réflexions sur le Judéo-Christianisme" (above, n. 21).

[30] "The Multiform Jewish Heritage of Early Christianity," in *Christianity, Judaism, and Other Greco-Roman Cults* (above, n. 21), 3.185; cf. 180.

[31] See David Frankfurter, "The Legacy of the Jewish Apocalypse in Early Christian Communities: Two Regional Trajectories," in *The Jewish Apocalyptic Heritage in Early Christianity*, CRINT 3.4, ed. James C. VanderKam and William Adler (Minneapolis: Fortress, 1996), 141–42.

[32] Frankfurter, "Legacy of the Jewish Apocalypse," 132–42, and "Early Christian Apocalypticism: Literature and Social World," *Encyclopedia of Apocalypticism*, vol. 1, *Jewish and Christian Origins of Apocalypticism*, ed. John J. Collins (New York: Continuum, 1998), 426–30, 434–40; cf. Stanton, "5 Ezra and Matthean Christianity," 81–83; Christine Trevett, *Montanism: Gender, Authority, and the New Prophecy* (Cambridge: Cambridge UP, 1996), 80–87; and Norelli, *L'Ascensione di Isaia*, 243–48.

is quite significant, for example, that none of these texts rail against non-Christ-believing outsider-Jews but only against those who persecute them: a combination of hegemonic forces in the world and intimate opponents in the prophetic or Christ-believing subculture. We can infer from this feature that forging a macro-identity is not nearly as important in these texts as establishing internecine boundaries and authority.[33]

*Conflict within a group*

## Documents of Continuing Priestly Messianism

If "continuity" in this last subculture revolves around Jewish prophets, in the case of the *Testaments of the Twelve Patriarchs* it revolves around the scribal preservation of Jewish traditions. Here again, the bulk of scholarship has sought passionately to disengage Jewish *Vorlagen* from the obviously Christ-oriented sentiments of the finished project, which consists of the last words of each of the sons of Jacob.[34] But the Dutch scholar Marinus de Jonge has tirelessly insisted on the unity of the text and even on its historical distance from any kind of prior Jewish versions of patriarchs' testaments. De Jonge's approach has begun to prevail, and rightly so, since it engages the *Testaments'* status *between* "Jewish" and "Christian."[35]

*implore*

The ethics in the *Testaments* lie somewhere halakhically to the right of the Gospel of Matthew, adjuring the sons of Israel to cleave to the Torah (*T. Reu.* 3.8, 6.8; *T. Levi* 13.1–4, 16.3; *T. Jud.* 23.5), to avoid the evils brought by women and the demonic Beliar, to exalt the Levite priesthood (*T. Levi* 2–8; *T. Jud.* 21.1–4), and even to lament the incipient intermarriages of Levitical priests (*T. Levi* 14.6).[36] A second- or third-century composition, the *Testaments* clearly seek to revitalize some assortment of Jewish values under the aegis of the twelve tribes of Israel. Yet there is concern for the status of Gentiles as well, and this is apparently where Christ comes in: as the savior who brings Gentiles into the promises of Israel (*T. Levi* 4.2–4; 14; *T. Jud.* 24.6; *T. Zeb.* 9; *T. Dan.*

---

[33] See Frankfurter, "Jews or Not?" 424.

[34] See Schürer, *History of the Jewish People,* 3,2: 770–72, and Denis and Haelewyck, *Introduction à la littérature religieuse judéo-hellénistique* 1:275–76, 281–85.

[35] Cf. John J. Collins, "The Testamentary Literature in Recent Scholarship," in *Early Judaism and Its Modern Interpreters,* ed. Robert Kraft and George Nickelsburg (Atlanta: Scholars Press, 1986), 270–76.

[36] On the castigation of intermarriage in *T. Levi* see Martha Himmelfarb, "Levi, Phinehas, and the Problem of Intermarriage at the Time of the Maccabean Revolt," *JSQ* 6, 1 (1999): 11–12, and more generally on matters of priestly purity and intermarriage in Palestinian Jewish culture of the Roman period, eadem, "Sexual Relations and Purity in the Temple Scroll and the Book of Jubilees," *DSD* 6, 1 (1999): 11–36.

6.6ff; cf. Tobit 14.5–7). Christ's authority lies in his fulfilling the lineages of the patriarchs Judah and Levi and presenting himself to the world as a priestly savior. Gentiles have not replaced Israel but have been absorbed into it; "Christians" do not exist as a separate category; and "Judaism," a combination of patriarchal inheritance and arcane ethical pronouncements, is neither abstracted nor opposed.[37] For these reasons, De Jonge has pointed out the inadequacy of the labels "Jewish" and "Christian" to describe the composition. The text rather seems to represent a moment in the evolution of some community or scribal conventicle:

> [T]he present text of the eschatological passages seems to suppose a relatively long process of redaction activity, quite possibly starting with a pre-Christian stage in the history of the Testaments. The stages in this process can no longer be distinguished; not only are we unable to determine what Christian scribes changed or added, we are also not in a position to say anything with certainty about possible developments in Jewish circles.[38]

De Jonge rightly emphasizes the "scribal" nature of the *Testaments*. Just as the Asia Minor texts invoke the authority of prophetic *performance* – the vision as reported orally (e.g., *Ascen. Is.* 6) – the *Testaments* invoke the authority of *literature*: books of Enoch, old literary genres, and the mystique of literary transmission. Most of the individual testaments are introduced as a "copy [ἀντίγραφον] of the words of [the patriarch] to his sons."[39]

It is a self-consciously scribal world in which the author situates himself and promotes his teachings. And it seems likely that this scribal world, with its typically preservationist, *archaistic* tendencies, must be another context in which a Jewish subculture could open itself to Christ-interpretations while still remaining essentially identified with traditional forms of authority and practice. Such scribal worlds, as we know from other cultural settings, habitually combined the archaic with the novel.[40] With this scribal model it is easier to allow some general literary

---

[37] Marinus De Jonge "The Future of Israel in the Testaments of the Twelve Patriarchs," *JSJ* 17 (1986): 196–211, and "The Transmission of the Testaments of the Twelve Patriarchs by Christians," *VigChr* 47 (1993): 17–19.

[38] De Jonge, "The Testaments of the Twelve Patriarchs: Christian and Jewish," *Jewish Eschatology, Early Christian Christology, and the Testaments of the Twelve Patriarchs* (Leiden: Brill, 1991), 241; cf. "Transmission of the Testaments of the Twelve Patriarchs," 14–15.

[39] The Asia Minor texts, to be sure, show a concern for the written word, instructing that prophecies be written down – fixed for posterity – in Revelation (1:3, 11, 19; 22:7, 18–19) and *6 Ezra* (15:2) and imagining heavenly books in *Ascension of Isaiah* (9:22).

[40] Cf. François Daumas, "Littérature prophétique et exégétique égyptienne et commentaires esséniens," in *A la rencontre de Dieu: Mémorial Albert Gelin, Bibliothèque de la faculté catholique de théologie de Lyon* 8 (Le Puy: Mappus, 1961), 203–21.

continuity between the world of the *Testaments* and prior Jewish scribal
worlds with similar testamentary or visionary materials (like Qumran),
even without assuming direct dependence.[41] Even if we cannot safely
propose that a single group of Jewish scribes historically came to
incorporate Christ-devotion in their editorial pursuits, we can conclude
that the kind of scribal world that the *Testaments* reflect could well
entertain both Christology and the strict observance of Jewish traditions.
It seems likely, given the *Testaments'* Levitical-priestly interests, that it
was composed in a region where the authority and destiny of temple
priests might still have been a cultural issue even in the late second
century: that is, Palestine.[42]

## Conclusions

We thus have two types of social worlds in which Christ-orientation was
a feature of the belief system, but Judaism deeply informed practice,
sense of group boundaries, and the discourse of authority, whether in
visions or literary composition. Moreover, the literature of these social
worlds – such as we have it – did not regard Christ as the raison d'être for
texts or even as the singular focus of ideology. Other concerns, claims,
and problems seem to have preoccupied the authors besides apologetics
for Christ or Christian identity. What were these concerns and problems?

The cluster of prophetic texts here attributed to Asia Minor revolve
principally around the claims and problems of prophetic milieus: (1)
visions of and access to the heavenly world; (2) the authority a prophet
claims *from* such experiences; (3) the prophet's *general* authority to
clarify the nature of present crises and afflictions; and (4) the inevitable
conflicts over purity, status, and rival authorities in a prophetic
subculture. For these prophetic milieus, Judaism provides the framework
for imagining the heavenly world and gaining entry to it, for constructing
prophetic authority and its heroes, for prophetic speech, and for the
notions of the purity of the Elect and the sins of the enemy.

For the author of the *Testaments of the Twelve Patriarchs*, the main
concern in constructing the twelve-fold collection is to show the
persistence of the "tribal" inheritance among Jews – the continuing
legacy of the twelve tribes, with particular attention to the exalted lines of

---

[41] H. W. Hollander and Marinus de Jonge, *The Testaments of the Twelve Patriarchs:
A Commentary*, SVTP 8 (Leiden: Brill, 1985), 24–27, and De Jonge, "The Testaments
of the Twelve Patriarchs and Related Qumran Fragments," *For a Later Generation*
(above n. 26), 63–77, esp. 66.

[42] See Frankfurter, "Early Christian Apocalypticism," 424. On matters of distinctively priestly halakhah, see above, n.36.

Levi and Judah. The author couches the culminative status of Christ for Judah and Levi in a larger demonstration of the authority of the patriarchs over current issues. He also reasserts the authority of books attributed to Enoch; perhaps it was a period when their marginalization was of general concern. The problems he addresses in his immediate world are more abstract than those of the Asia Minor prophets: demonology, for example, the status of Gentiles, the status of the Levitical line, and the status of Christ within the patriarchal inheritance. Judaism for this author provides the framework for the traditions of Levi and the priesthood, for the construction of patriarchal authority, and for the admission of Gentiles into the patriarchal traditions.

In examining some ways in which Jewish culture continued to embrace Christ-worship and Christ-worship continued to assume Jewish practice and identity, we must not preclude situations where non-Jews really did appropriate Jewish traditions: that is, the "Hebraistic Christian" movements mentioned above – particularly in Egypt and Syria – whose members might have cultivated a "Hebrew" or "Israelite" identity and practice for centuries after the separation or disappearance of the ethnic, traditional Jews who might have had a part in their formation.[43] It is thus quite possible for non-Jewish adherents to the Asia Minor prophet guilds to have prevailed in some places and taken the cults in hybrid directions, with new – even indigenous, *non*-Jewish – notions of prophecy and ritual practice. In this regard, placing Asia Minor's New Prophecy movement in relationship to a Jewish prophet subculture becomes a special challenge; for New Prophecy was as beholden to Jewish prophetic tradition as it was a departure from Jewish observance for the flush of otherworldly intimacy.[44] And yet this challenge of "placing" New Prophecy gains much through suspending overly reified categories of Judaism and Christianity.

---

[43] See Frankfurter, "Regional Trajectories," 181–85, on Egyptian holy men and devotion to Hebrew saints.

[44] See images of prophetic performance in Vis. Perp. 4, 7–8, 20; Tertullian, *De anima* 9; and Hippolytus, *Ref.* 8.12. A prophetess in early third-century Cappadocia claims to be from "Judea and Jerusalem" and to be returning there (Cyprian, *Ep.* 75 [from Firmilian], 10.2–5). In general on the relationship of New Prophecy to Jewish prophetic tradition see Trevett, *Montanism*, 80–87, 140–45.

# The Jews and Christians in the *Martyrdom of Polycarp*

## Entangled or Parted Ways?

by

## E. LEIGH GIBSON

As Laurence Broadhurst reminds us in a review of Daniel Boyarin's impressive essay, *Dying for God*, "This idea of an indistinct border [between Judaism and Christianity] for several centuries is not entirely novel but Boyarin's dedicated pursuit of it is."[1] In this chase, Boyarin accomplishes two most laudable tasks. One, he dissects the metaphors scholars employ to characterize the relationship between Judaism and Christianity, revealing in some cases their inability, and in other cases their reluctance, to allow for an extended period of exchange between the two traditions. In contrast, Boyarin asserts that rabbinic Judaism and Christianity crystallized only through an interaction that he likens to the intersecting of waves.[2] Two, Boyarin profitably applies this insight to rabbinic martyr stories – texts that at first glance might appear uncooperative – and uncovers a discourse intimately engaged with Christianity.

On these and many other counts, *Dying for God* is a remarkable book. Students of Christianity, however, may lament that Christian martyrologies do not receive the same original and sustained analysis from Boyarin as do the rabbinic martyr stories. In this paper, I address this gap by renewed attention to the *Martyrdom of Polycarp* (henceforth *MPoly*), the well-known second-century account of the final days of Polycarp, the bishop of Smyrna. Although Polycarp flees Smyrna upon the advice of his friends when the persecution of Christians begins, two slaves reveal his whereabouts and the police ultimately bring him to the stadium and

---

* Earlier versions of this paper had been previously presented at the Institute for Advanced Study, Hebrew University, and the Philadelphia Seminar on Christian Origins. On both occasions, and again at "The Ways that Never Parted" colloquium, I have benefited greatly from questions and comments.

[1] Laurence Broadhurst, review of Daniel Boyarin, *Dying for God: Martyrdom and the Making of Judaism and Christianity*, *JECS* 8 (2000): 598.

[2] Daniel Boyarin, *Dying for God: Martyrdom and the Making of Judaism and Christianity* (Stanford: Stanford UP, 1999), 8–11.

present him to the authorities. Rejecting their invitations to swear allegiance to the emperor, Polycarp defiantly proclaims, "I am a Christian." Only after a crowd said to include Jews demands that he be burnt alive do the reluctant officials act. The crowd then turns its attention to preparing his pyre, a task in which the Jews participate eagerly. The fire, however, is unable to consume Polycarp's body, forcing an executioner to pierce him with a dagger, thereby releasing a dove and a quantity of blood so great that it extinguishes the fire. In the final scene, the Jews intervene against the Christians attempting to recover Polycarp's body; in the end the Christians collect only the ashes of his cremated corpse. By revisiting the issue of date and textual integrity of *MPoly* and utilizing fresh studies on other Smyrnaean texts and on Jewish interest in the remains of the dead, I argue that *MPoly* does not document active Jewish hostility against Christians but rather is a remnant of the battle within second-century Smyrnaean Christianity about the implication of Jesus-following for the observation of Jewish custom.

## Changing Historiographic Context

The several appearances of the Smyrnaean Jewish community in *MPoly* have long been read as transparent references to the hostility that Smyrnaean Jews bore for local Christians. This interpretation has been bolstered by widespread acceptance of the text as a faithful account of events and by its consonance with other evidence for the Jewish community of Smyrna. Neither aspect, however, can fully sustain this interpretation.

Attempts to reconcile the extant manuscripts of *MPoly* and the version preserved in Eusebius' *Ecclesiastical History* have long complicated efforts to date Polycarp's death and its associated textual tradition.[3] In a survey of this literature, Dehandschutter, a long-time student of the text,

---

[3] For a discussion of the manuscript traditions, see Boudewijn Dehandschutter, "The Martyrium Polycarpi: A Century of Research," *ANRW* II.27.1 (1993): 488–90.

Newly published Coptic fragments, known as the Harris fragments (Frederick Weidman, *Polycarp and John: The Harris Fragments and Their Challenge to the Literary Tradition*, Christianity and Judaism in Antiquity Series, vol. 12 [Notre Dame: U. of Notre Dame, 1999]), suggest that a retelling of Polycarp's death was integrated into a larger story of the apostle John's work in Asia Minor. In this poorly preserved story, Polycarp is subordinated to John, whose peaceful end is seen as problematic for an apostle of Jesus; the martyrdom of Polycarp is then cast as a substitute or replacement for John's uneventful death. Although the fragments include some previously unattested elements, they appear dependent on *MPoly*. As a result, at least at this early stage in their scholarly discussion, the fragments do not figure in this discussion.

reiterates the widespread consensus that has pinned Polycarp's death to the mid-150s CE with the written account following within the year.[4] This conclusion may be scholars' best guess, but it becomes problematic when it is paired with verdicts on the document's historical reliability. If the text followed quickly on Polycarp's death, then *MPoly* is reliable as an account of second-century events; however, it is time to revisit the dating of this text. As David Satran has aptly observed, "like many a consensus, these conclusions remain largely unproved."[5]

The current consensus relies heavily on the chronological information cited in *MPoly* 21:

> The blessed Polycarp was martyred on the second day at the beginning of the month of Xanthicus, seven days before the kalends of March, a great Sabbath, at the eighth hour. He was arrested by Herod when Philip the Trallian was high priest and Statius Quadratus proconsul, but our Lord Jesus Christ is king forever; to whom be glory, honor, majesty, and an eternal throne from generation to generation. Amen.[6]

The above chapter, however, follows several verses that appear to conclude the letter: "Now you asked for a detailed report be made to you; for the present we have made this summary available through our brother Marcion ... Greet all the saints. Those with us and Evarestus, the scribe, with all his house greet you" (20). This casts suspicion on *MPoly* 21 as possibly a secondary addition. Nonetheless, many judge the chapter to be an early addition and have continued to use it as evidence. To complicate matters further, each of the three main chronological clues in *MPoly* 21 – the day and month, the reference to the high priest, and the reference to the proconsul – points to a different date in the second half of the 150s.[7]

---

[4] B. Dehandschutter, "Martryrium Polycarpi," 497–501.

[5] David Satran, *Biblical Prophets in Byzantine Palestine: Reassessing the Lives of the Prophets* (Leiden: Brill, 1995), 1.

[6] Unless otherwise noted, translations of *MPoly* are those of William R. Schoedel, *Polycarp, Martyrdom of Polycarp, Fragments of Papias*, in *The Apostolic Fathers: A New Translation and Commentary*, ed. Robert M. Grant (Camden, N.J.: Thomas Nelson, 1967), 51–82.

[7] Placing Polycarp's death "on the second day at the beginning of the month of Xanthicus, seven days before the kalends of March, a Great Sabbath, at the eight hour" yields possible dates of 155 and 166, years in which "seven days before the kalends of March" falls on a Saturday. If the reference to a "*Great* Sabbath" [emphasis added] is also taken into account, another obstacle arises: what is a "great Sabbath"? Intuition would perhaps suggest the Sabbath before Passover, but no appropriate lunar dates coincide with "seven days before the kalends of March," that is, February 23. Other possibilities include Easter and Purim, but at this point how the "Great Sabbath" fits into the picture remains unresolved. For many years W. Rordorf served as the standard reference on this issue; see Rordorf, "Zum Problem des »grossen Sabbats« im Polykarp und Pioniusmartyrium," in *Pietas: Festschrift für Bernhard Kötting*, ed. Ernst Dassmann and K. Suso Frank, Jahrbuch für Antike und Christentum. Ergänzungsband 8

But accepting any date in the 150s has serious implications because it would dismiss the dating of Eusebius, who seems to have been unaware of, or to have ignored, the dating information contained in *MPoly* 21 when he placed Polycarp's death during the reign of Marcus Aurelius (161–180 CE).[8] Since Eusebius' *Ecclesiastical History* is the earliest witness to the document *MPoly*, the widely conceded date of the 150s, though plausible, does not account for all – or, dare I say, even most – of the available evidence.

Dating *MPoly* is further complicated by differing assessments of the text's integrity. The poles of the discussion on textual integrity have remained largely unchanged for more than a century: some advocate the view that the text was written within a year of Polycarp's death and was preserved mostly intact in the manuscript tradition, while others suggest a multi-stage redaction with the final form postdating Polycarp's death by a century or more. The standard-bearer for the latter view is Hans von

---

(Münster: Aschendorff, 1980), 246–51. His work has perhaps been replaced by Judith Lieu's treatment of the question; see Lieu, *Image and Reality: The Jews in the World of the Christians in the Second Century* (Edinburgh: T&T Clark, 1996), 70–79.

The remaining two dating clues (references to the high priest and the proconsul) are prosopographical and their usefulness depends on finding other datable references to these individuals. *MPoly* 21.1 names Philip the Trallian as high priest when Polycarp was martyred. Immediately, a problem emerges: the only Philip identified in the body of the document is Philip, the Asiarch, but this has not hindered scholars from using the epigraphic evidence associated with this name to set the parameters of the possible date of Polycarp's death because some think the titles may have been interchangeable. Epigraphic evidence records a Gaius Julius Philippus several times in the mid-second century, and he can be most precisely placed as an Asiarch in 149. For full details see Timothy D. Barnes, "A Note on Polycarp," *JTS* 18 (1967): 434.

Although the proconsul figures prominently in the text in *MPoly* 9–10, he is only identified by name, Statius Quadratus, in *MPoly* 21. Using this name to date Polycarp's martyrdom more precisely, we turn to the *Fasti*, which places Quadratus as consul in 142. Since the time between a consulship and a proconsulship can vary, this date can only establish the 150s as a likely time for Quadratus to have served as proconsul. The complicated chronologies of Aelius Aristides have often been invoked to date Quadratus' service more precisely. Waddington painstakingly established Quadratus' term as proconsul as occurring in 154–55, providing an appealing overlap with the fact that the 23rd of February fell on a Saturday in 155; see William Henry Waddington, "Vie du rhéteur Aelius Aristide," *Mémoires de l'Institut royal de France, Académie des inscriptions et belles-lettres* 26 (1867): 232–41. Although Grégoire has explained how an ancient writer, eager to pin down a more precise date for the death of a famous martyr, could build on clues existing in the body of the narrative to write such an epilogue, this possibility has been ignored, and a date in the mid-150s is now widely accepted; see H. Grégoire, "La véritable date du martyre de S. Polycarpe (23 février 177) et le 'corpus polycarpianum,'" *Analecta Bollandiana* 69 (1951): 1–38.

[8] Even within the corpus of this one author, the evidence is not fully consistent: Eusebius dates Polycarp's death in various relationships to the reign of Marcus Aurelius. For further discussion, see Barnes, "A Note on Polycarp," 436.

Campenhausen. His analysis hinges on the differences between the version of the story preserved in the manuscript tradition and that preserved in Eusebius' *Ecclesiastical History*. For large portions of text, the story proceeds in almost word-for-word agreement, interrupted occasionally by relatively minor changes in tense, mood, or voice – an agreement that would indicate considerable faithfulness to *MPoly* or a shared source. But a set of striking omissions mars the correspondence between *MPoly* and Eusebius' account. Working from this data, Campenhausen proposed a series of redactions. Those elements absent from Eusebius' account were not, Campenhausen argued, omitted by careless copying or from a desire to condense the account. Rather, Eusebius' source did not include those passages. Moreover, he argued, these elements form a striking pattern: they introduce or emphasize parallels between the narrative of Jesus' death in the gospels and the narrative of Polycarp's martyrdom; Campenhausen dubbed them the handiwork of "the evangelizing redactor."[9]

Many have found Campenhausen's arguments compelling because he brought greater rigor to suspicions that had been long harbored against the integrity of the text. Others, however, have offered retorts. Leslie Barnard's counter is widely regarded as among the most persuasive. His work stresses that the majority of gospel parallels are shared by Eusebius and *MPoly* and therefore predate Campenhausen's hypothesized redactor. Furthermore, the instances of gospel imitation preserved only in *MPoly* are heavy-handed and hardly worthy of "the evangelizing redactor." Instead, Barnard sees gospel imitation as a common phenomenon in Christian literature as early as the second century and concludes that "the literal conformity of Polycarp's sufferings to the sufferings of Christ was present in the earliest account [of *MPoly*]."[10]

Regardless of the document's composition history, the first document produced must be dated. Most advocates of an integral document begin with *MPoly*'s internal chronological indicators, emphasizing this key passage located before the first conclusion in *MPoly* 20:

> And there, in so far as it is possible, the Lord will grant that we welcome together with joy and gladness and celebrate the birthday of his martyrdom both in memory of those who have contended in former times and training of those who will do so in the future. (18.3)

---

[9] Based on the awkwardness in the narrative flow of the chapter concerning Quintus a Phrygian, *MPoly* 4 – a chapter that Eusebius also includes – Campenhausen postulates a pre-Eusebian redaction with an anti-Montanist bent. Hans von Campenhausen, "Bearbeitungen und Interpolationen des Polykarpmartyriums," in *Aus der Frühzeit des Christentums* (Tübingen: Mohr Siebeck, 1963), 268.

[10] L. W. Barnard, "In Defence of Pseudo-Pionius' Account of Polycarp's Martyrdom," in *Kyriakon. Festschrift Johannes Quasten*, vol. 1, ed. P. Granfield and Josef A. Jungmann (Münster: Aschendorff, 1970), 196.

Although this passage is often read as suggesting that the Smyrnaean community wrote this document to encourage commemoration of the first anniversary of Polycarp's martyrdom, it cannot firmly anchor the text to the first year after his death. The concluding phrases seem to present the perspective of someone writing at a distance from the event, someone who recognizes that in times to come many will have to train for the same sort of battle. The writer hopes that the Lord will grant future celebrations of the birthday of Polycarp's martyrdom, but this hope would not have been limited to the first year after his death.

The center of scholarly judgment, which places Polycarp's death in the mid-150s, is the best approximation of the date of his persecution, but it is an equivocal and insufficient foundation from which to prejudge other important issues. Neither the consensus with respect to *MPoly*'s date nor its integrity are so sound that the text can be regarded as a transparent account of Christian life in Smyrna and certainly not of relations between Jews and Christians, especially given revisions recently proposed.

# New Interpretations of Relations between Jews and Christians in Smyrna

Recent studies of two other texts with connections to Smyrna – the book of Revelation and the *Martyrdom of Pionius* – have challenged long-held views that the Jews of Smyrna instigated hostilities against Christians, replacing them with readings of these texts as complex documents that incorporate remnants of this community's struggle over the place of its Jewish inheritance. In *Parables of War: Reading John's Jewish Apocalypse*, John Marshall has demonstrated that only through double-jointed exegetical gymnastics have interpreters been able to read Rev 2:9–10 ("I know the slander on the part of those who say that they are Jews and are not, but are a synagogue of Satan. Do not fear what you are about to suffer") as the product of a dispute between Jews and Christians. Instead, he suggests that the conflict was among Jesus-followers with different stances in respect to food laws.[11] Building on Marshall's work, David Frankfurter identifies John of Patmos' opponents as Gentile Jesus-followers who were inspired by Paul's teachings but who related more loosely to purity laws than John would have preferred.[12] As for the *Martyrdom of Pionius*, I have argued elsewhere that scholarly convictions

---

[11] John W. Marshall, *Parables of the War: Reading John's Jewish Apocalypse*, Studies in Christianity and Judaism/Études sur le christianisme et le judaïsme 10 (Waterloo, Ont.: Wilfrid Laurier UP, 2001).

[12] David Frankfurter, "Jews or Not? Reconstructing the 'Other' in Rev 2:9 and 3:9," *HTR* 94 (2001): 414–16.

about Jewish–Christian tensions in Smyrna are so entrenched that the target of the text's anti-Jewish rhetoric has been consistently misunderstood as hostile Jews even though Pionius directly addresses the issue of Judaizers.[13]

Marshall's and Frankfurter's work on Revelation and my own on the *Martyrdom of Pionius* share a common conclusion: that the issue of Jesus-followers' participation in Jewish communal life plagued the Smyrnaean Christian community in the first and third centuries. Long misread as polemics against outsiders, these texts address communities of Jesus-followers who do not agree on the status of their Jewish inheritance, an issue that also appears in Ignatius' *Letter to Smyrna*, which addresses "Christ's saints and believers, whether among the Jews or among the Gentiles in one body of the church" (1.2). From this new perspective on relations between Jews and Christians in Smyrna, let us now return to the depiction of Jews in *MPoly*.

## The Jews in the *Martyrdom of Polycarp*

The references to the Jews in this text are a little odd in the settings in which they appear. The Jews first appear in *MPoly* 12, where they, along with the Gentiles, gather in the stadium and angrily respond to Polycarp's confession, exclaiming, "This is the teacher of Asia, the father of the Christians, the destroyer of *our gods*, the one who teaches the many not to sacrifice nor to worship" (12.2 [emphasis added]). This lament, with its reference to multiple gods, is said to have come from Jews.[14] Beyond this cry, the simple appearance of the Jews at this point in the narrative is striking: they are not consistently described as part of the crowd. For example, in chapter 16 only the "lawless pagans" (οἱ ἄνομοι) are amazed that the pyre could not consume Polycarp's body (16.1).[15]

---

[13] E. Leigh Gibson, "Jewish Antagonism or Christian Polemic: The Case of the *Martyrdom of Pionius*," *JECS* 9 (2001): 339–58.

[14] Gospel echoes have been identified for two aspects of this scene. Polycarp's death by conflagration and not by wild beasts (*MPoly* 12) may imitate the failure of Jesus to be stoned in John 18 and his crucifixion instead in fulfillment of his prediction in John 12.32–3. The depiction of the Jews shouting for Polycarp's death has sometimes been thought to echo the Jews' enthusiasm for Jesus' death in Luke 23.

[15] In a preface to the account of Polycarp's death, the Philomelians learn that Germanicus, another martyr, bravely pulled the animals onto himself to speed his end. At this incredible display, "the whole multitude (πᾶν τὸ πλῆθος), amazed at the nobility of the godly and pious race of Christians began shouting: 'Away with the atheists! Let Polycarp be sought!'" (3.2). No Jews are specified as spectators. And when Polycarp arrives in the stadium, "the whole crowd of lawless heathens in the stadium" (εἰς πάντα τὸν ὄχλον τὸν ἐν τῷ σταδίῳ ἀνόμων ἐθνῶν) again participates in the

The Jews next appear on the "Great Sabbath,"[16] eagerly collecting wood and fuel for Polycarp's pyre (13). While the nature of Sabbath worship in second-century Asia Minor remains uncertain, these activities give the reader pause, for the collection of wood and the kindling of fire are among the few acts specifically prohibited by Torah on the Sabbath (Ex 35:3, Num 15:32–36).[17]

The last appearance of the Jews – the only one where they act independently of the crowd (*MPoly* 17–18) – may be particularly helpful in unraveling the logic behind their clumsy and hostile depiction. In this passage, the crowd has just recognized that Polycarp's body cannot be consumed by the pyre. An otherwise unidentified "evil one," usually understood to be connected with the Jews, sets out to thwart Christian access to Polycarp's "holy flesh" by inciting Nicetes, father of the police captain, to influence a magistrate (*MPoly* 17–18).[18]

| | |
|---|---|
| 17.1 Now when the jealous, envious, and evil one, enemy of the race of the just, saw that his martyrdom had been illustrious and his life irreproachable from the beginning, that he was crowned with the crown of incorruption and had carried off the incontestable prize, he set about preventing even his poor body being taken by us, *though there were many who wanted to do this and to have fellowship with his holy flesh.* | 17.1 Ὁ δὲ ἀντίζηλος καὶ βάσκανος καὶ πονηρός, ὁ ἀντικείμενος τῷ γένει τῶν δικαίων, ἰδὼν τό τε μέγεθος αὐτοῦ τῆς μαρτυρίας καὶ τὴν ἀπ᾽ ἀρχῆς ἀνεπίληπτον πολιτείαν, ἐστεφανωμένον τε τὸν τῆς ἀφθαρσίας στέφανον καὶ βραβεῖον ἀναντίρρητον ἀπενηνεγμένον, ἐπετήδευσεν ὡς μηδὲ τὸ σωμάτιον αὐτοῦ ὑφ᾽ ἡμῶν ληφθῆναι, καίπερ πολλῶν ἐπιθυμούντων τοῦτο ποιῆσαι καὶ κοινωνῆσαι τῷ ἁγίῳ αὐτοῦ σαρκίῳ. |
| 17.2a *So he suggested to Nicetes, the father of Herod and the brother of Alce, to beg the magistrate not to give up his body.* 17.2b *"Lest," he said,* | 17.2a ὑπέβαλεν γοῦν Νικήτην τὸν τοῦ Ἡρώδου πατέρα, ἀδελφὸν δὲ Ἄλκης, ἐντυχεῖν τῷ ἄρχοντι ὥστε μὴ δοῦναι αὐτοῦ τὸ σῶμα· 17.2b μή, |

---

unfolding drama, demanding Polycarp's death (9.2). Jewish participation in this exclamation seems precluded by the description of the onlookers as exclusively heathens. Nonetheless, the content of the exclamation better suits the Jews than the one discussed above.

[16] As I have already noted, there is considerable debate about the proper identification of the "Great Sabbath." Some take it to be solely the product of gospel imitation while others look for a specific Jewish holiday that might have born this name. See note 7 for further discussion. For our purposes, we can sidestep this complicated issue and focus on the simple fact that the activities occurred on a Sabbath.

[17] Robert Goldenberg, "The Jewish Sabbath in the Roman World Up to the Time of Constantine the Great," *ANRW* 19.1 (1979): 414.

[18] Square brackets denote material missing in two manuscripts. Italics mark interpolations according to Campenhausen, "Bearbeitungen und Interpolationen des Polykarpmartyriums." Underlined text marks possible interpolations according to Schoedel, *Polycarp, Martyrdom of Polycarp, Fragments of Papias.*

*"they abandon the Crucified and begin to worship this man."* 17.2c *And with the Jews suggesting and urging these things, the Jews who watched as we were about to take him from the fire;* 17.2d *[they did not know that we shall never find it possible either to abandon Christ who suffered for the salvation of those saved in all the world, the blameless for the sinners, or to worship any other.* 17.3 *For him we worship as the Son of God; but the martyrs we love as disciples and imitators of the Lord, as they deserve because of their incomparable loyalty to their own King and Teacher. May it also be granted to us to become their partners and fellow disciples.]*

φησίν, ἀφέντες τὸν ἐσταυρωμένον τοῦτον ἄρξωνται σέβεσθαι. 17.2c καὶ ταῦτα ὑποβαλλόντων καὶ ἐνισχυόντων τῶν Ἰουδαίων, οἳ καὶ ἐτήρησαν μελλόντων ἡμῶν ἐκ τοῦ πυρὸς αὐτὸν λαμβάνειν, 17.2d ἀγνο-οῦντες ὅτι οὔτε τὸν Χριστόν ποτε καταλιπεῖν δυνησόμεθα τὸν ὑπὲρ τῆς τοῦ παντὸς κόσμου τῶν σωζ-ομένων σωτηρίας παθόντα ἄμωμον ὑπὲρ ἁμαρτωλῶν οὔτε ἕτερόν τινα σέβεσθαι. 17.3 τοῦτον μὲν γὰρ υἱὸν ὄντα τοῦ θεοῦ προσκυνοῦμεν, τοὺς δὲ μάρτυρας ὡς μαθητὰς καὶ μιμητὰς τοῦ κυρίου ἀγαπῶμεν ἀξίως ἕνεκα εὐνοίας ἀνυπερβλήτου τῆς εἰς τὸν ἴδιον βασιλέα καὶ διδάσκαλον, ὧν γένοιτο καὶ ἡμᾶς κοινωνούς τε καὶ συμμαθητὰς γεν-έσθαι.

18.1 When the centurion, then, saw the contentiousness caused by the Jews, he put him in the center, as they usually do, and burned him. 18.2 Accordingly, we later took up his bones, more precious than costly stones and finer than gold, and deposited them in a suitable place. And there, so far as it is possible, the Lord will grant that we come together with joy and gladness and celebrate the birthday of his martyrdom both in memory of those who have contended in former times and for the exercise and training of those who will do so in the future.[19]

18.1 Ἰδὼν οὖν ὁ κεντυρίων τὴν τῶν Ἰουδαίων γενομένην φιλονεικίαν, θεὶς αὐτὸν ἐν μέσῳ, ὡς ἔθος αὐτοῖς, ἔκαυσεν. 18.2 οὕτως τε ἡμεῖς ὕστερον ἀνελόμενοι τὰ τιμιώτερα λίθων πολυτελῶν καὶ δοκιμώτερα ὑπὲρ χρυσίον ὀστᾶ αὐτοῦ ἀπ-εθέμεθα ὅπου καὶ ἀκόλουθον ἦν. 18.3 ἔνθα ὡς δυνατὸν ἡμῖν συν-αγομένοις ἐν ἀγαλλιάσει καὶ χαρᾷ παρέξει ὁ κύριος ἐπιτελεῖν τὴν τοῦ μαρτυρίου αὐτοῦ ἡμέραν γενέθλιον εἴς τε τὴν τῶν προηθληκότων μνήμην καὶ τῶν μελλόντων ἄσκησίν τε καὶ ἑτοιμασίαν.[20]

This muddled passage, although at first glance appearing to address the Jews' actions and reactions, is ultimately shaped by an issue relevant only to Christians: How should Christians relate to the remains of martyrs? How should their worship of Christ differ from their reverence for martyrs? From the Roman perspective, whether Christians insist they are "Christian" or "Polycarpian" does not matter so long as they continue to refuse to sacrifice to the emperor. From a Jewish perspective, it makes

---

[19] Translation adapted from Schoedel, *Polycarp, Martyrdom of Polycarp, Fragments of Papias*, 73–76.

[20] Greek text from Karl Bihlmeyer, *Die apostolischen Väter: Neubearbeitung der funkschen Ausgabe* (3rd ed.; Tübingen: Mohr Siebeck, 1956), 1.129–30.

little difference whether Christians think that Jesus or Polycarp is a messiah figure. Indeed, the premise of the scene – that the Jews wish to prevent the Christians from collecting Polycarp's remains – is almost farcical. It makes little sense to vilify Jews for thwarting worship of Polycarp's relics, a practice the text itself seeks to circumscribe. The exact logic of this passage may never be entirely clear, but a closer examination of, respectively, its strained coherence, its syntactical confusion, and its textual variation yields surprising results.

The passage's roughness is evident in its opening sentence. It is unclear who or what this "evil one" is: he is identified by a string of substantives that allows multiple parsings ('Ο δὲ ἀντίζηλος καὶ βάσκανος καὶ πονηρός, ὁ ἀντικείμενος τῷ γένει τῶν δικαίων).[21] The "evil one" also does not directly oppose the Christians; rather, he seeks the help of Nicetes, who is himself awkwardly introduced by his relationship to two family members. References to his son Herod, information that appeared earlier in the story,[22] and to his brother Alce, who does not figure elsewhere,[23] slow the narrative at a pivotal moment. In addition, Nicetes, to ensure that Polycarp's body is not turned over to the Christians, prevails upon yet another individual, the "ἄρχων"; however, no character under this title has been previously introduced (MPoly 17.2).[24] Finally, the Jews, not mentioned since MPoly 13, suddenly reappear.

The syntax of this passage is similarly strained. MPoly 17.2b begins with an abrupt shift into direct speech to introduce the concern that the Christians might give up Christ to worship Polycarp. The subject of φησίν, the verb that introduces the direct speech, however, is unclear: the "evil one," Nicetes, and the archon are all possibilities. Presumably looking back to this direct speech, MPoly 17c's "καὶ ταῦτα" ("and these things") raises the expectation that the speaker will be identified. But

---

[21] Francis X. Gokey summarizes the major commentators' position on the various parsings in *The Terminology for the Devil and Evil Spirits in the Apostolic Fathers* (New York: AMS, 1981), 905–6. Bihlmeyer's compact notes summarize the considerable manuscript variation, some of which tries to impose greater order on the passage (*Die apostolischen Väter*, 1.129).

[22] Herod appears in the narrative at *MPoly* 6.2, where the police captain that brings Polycarp to the stadium is identified as "Herod," and at *MPoly* 8.2, when "the police captain, Herod, and his father, Nicetes" transfer Polycarp into a carriage to take him into the stadium.

[23] Alce may be a Smyrnaean Christian of some repute, as Ignatius and Polycarp both mention an "Alce" in their respective correspondences (*Letter to the Smyrnaeans* 13.1 and *Letter to Polycarp* 8.2).

[24] In one manuscript, however, Nicetes targets as his coconspirator the proconsul (ἀνθύπατος), the official Polycarp has dealt with but who has been off-stage, so to speak, since *MPoly* 12, when the Asiarch took the lead in punishing Polycarp. Eusebius calls the official "ἡγεμών" (*Ecclesiastical History* 4.15.41).

"καὶ ταῦτα" is the object in a genitive absolute clause in which the Jews are the subject (καὶ ταῦτα ὑποβαλλόντων καὶ ἐνισχυόντων τῶν Ἰουδαίων, "and with the Jews suggesting and urging these things"). For a careful reader, it is a disorienting transition, clumsily forging a connection between the Jews and the evil one through the repetition of the verb ὑποβάλλω, "suggest."

Interestingly, these stressors to the syntax and coherence of the passage coincide with instability in the textual tradition. Eusebius, the earliest witness to the story, forges more tightly the connection between the activities of the "evil one" and the Jews. Returning to 17.2a, Eusebius changes the first occurrence of ὑποβάλλω, "suggest," from a singular, ὑπέβαλεν, to a plural, ὑπέβαλον, and supplies an indefinite plural pronoun, τινες, a pronoun whose nearest referent would be the Jews of 17.2c.[25] With these changes, Eusebius inserts the Jews into the story far earlier, making them responsible for a greater portion of the ensuing action. At the transition to direct speech, Eusebius again inserts a plural verb (εἶπον) so that "Lest they abandon the Crucified and begin to worship this man" becomes the concern of the Jews.

Variations in the manuscript tradition also plague this passage and, although they have not figured prominently in its analysis, can cast new light on this vexing passage. Two manuscripts omit 17.2d and 17.3, resulting in this text:[26]

> ... 17.2a So he incited Nicetes, the father of Herod and the brother of Alce, to beg the magistrate not to give up his body, 17.2b "Lest," he said, "they abandon the Crucified and begin to worship this man." 17.2c And with the Jews suggesting and urging these things, the Jews who watched as we were about to take him from the fire. 18.1 When the centurion, then, saw the contentiousness caused by the Jews, he put him in the center, as they usually do, and burned him ...

Without the lengthy theologizing about the proper reverence for Christ and the martyrs, the passage flows more smoothly, yet it is still marred by the syntactical problem associated with the introduction of the Jews at 17.2c and by the wordy identification of Nicetes. As a result, William Schoedel brackets this sentence, along with the portion omitted in two manuscripts, as a possible interpolation. His text reads:

> 17.1 Now when the jealous, envious, and evil one, enemy of the race of the just, saw that his martyrdom had been illustrious and his life irreproachable from the beginning, that he was crowned with the crown of incorruption and had carried

---

[25] While the Loeb of Eusebius prints the plural form, ὑπέβαλον, Kirsopp Lake translates it as a singular; see Eusebius, *The Ecclesiastical History,* vol. 1, trans. Kirsopp Lake, Loeb Classical Library (Cambridge: Harvard UP, 1926), 457.

[26] Manuscripts c and v according to Bihlmeyer's labeling (*Die apostolischen Väter,* 1.120).

off the incontestable prize, he set about preventing even his poor body being taken by us, though there were many who wanted to do this and to have fellowship with his holy flesh. 18.1 When the centurion, then, saw the contentiousness caused by the Jews, he put him in the center, as they usually do, and burned him. 18.2 Accordingly, we later took up his bones ...

In this condensed version, the evil one makes it his business to thwart the Christians' access to Polycarp's remains, an initiative that the centurion completes. Although the overall flow of the story has improved, the Jews still appear abruptly as the cause of φιλονεικία, a term that can have negative or positive valences, either "to be contentious and fond of strife" or "to be eager and to desire to emulate." Translators have preferred the former, but in Schoedel's shortened text this option presents difficulties, as those with whom the Jews are contending are not identified. The positive valence of φιλονεικία suggests a different and intriguing possibility: that the Jews vied with the Christians not to thwart Christian access but to win the remains for themselves.

Although Jews have been long thought to have shunned contact with the remains of the dead (Num 19:11–22; 31:19–24), a growing body of scholarship suggests that some Jews collected the bones of revered persons and buried them at places of religious significance.[27] In Palestine, tombs of national heroes were most likely to be treated in this way, but scholar of ancient Judaism Jack Lightstone extends this practice to the Diaspora as well. There, he suggests, "the manner of dying [instead of status as a national hero] might win *post mortem* sacrality for the deceased for his or her tomb."[28] His primary example is the remains of the Maccabean martyrs installed beneath a synagogue in Antioch. From this Lightstone concludes,

> The assimilation of the tombs of the Maccabean martyrs to the synagogue and its sacral function provides the clearest statement regarding the mediatory character of the 'graves of the saints.' Just as prayer could be more efficacious at Ancient Israel's altars (I Sam 1), so now the effects of the synagogue liturgy are enhanced by the tombs under the synagogue floor. At both the altar and the tomb, heaven and earth meet; here the commerce between the earthly and divine realms may best transpire.[29]

If this suggestion could be extended to Smyrna, might Jews have sought the remains of Polycarp for their own purposes? At first glance it remains

---

[27] Jack N. Lightstone forcefully advances this view in *The Commerce of the Sacred: Mediation of the Divine among Jews in Graeco-Roman Diaspora* (Chico, Calif.: Scholars Press, 1984) and in "The Dead in Late Antique Judaism: Homologies of Society, Cult and Cosmos," in *Survivre ... la religion et la mort*, ed. Raymond Lemieux and Réginal Richard, Cahiers de recherches en sciences de la religion 6 (Montreal: Bellarmin, 1985), 51–79.

[28] Lightstone, "The Dead in Late Antique Judaism," 64.

[29] Lightstone, "The Dead in Late Antique Judaism," 65.

difficult to understand why Jews would want to claim Polycarp's remains; after all, he was a man famous for his confession of Christianity. But interest in Polycarp on the part of Judaizing Christians – followers of Jesus who also embraced observance of Jewish law – is more easily understood. Polycarp's *Letter to the Philippians* and the commentary about Polycarp preserved in Eusebius' *Ecclesiastical History* help explain why.

In the *Letter to the Philippians*, Polycarp ranges widely over a variety of problems that have arisen in Phillipi, among them avarice, sexual licentiousness, and Docetism. A concern for purity appears at several points (ἁγνεία in 4.2 and 5.3 and its Latin translations *castus*, 11.1 and *castitas*, 12.3). While the roots of this term in cultic purity are often conceded, the natural and intriguing possibility that Polycarp is advocating observance of specifically Jewish law has not been widely investigated.[30] This oversight is all the more surprising given Polycarp's preference for observing Easter on the Jewish Passover. In an important discussion concerning the date of Easter – whether it was to coincide with Passover, a practice known as "quartodecimanism" – Eusebius quotes two authors (Polycrates and Victor) who identify Polycarp as a quarto-deciman.[31] Indeed, the text of *MPoly* may itself echo the importance of Passover to this Christian community when it places Polycarp's arrest on the Great Sabbath, a holiday most scholars are inclined to link with the Sabbath before Passover.[32]

I would like to refine Judith Lieu's observation that *MPoly* 17–18 seems to reflect "an inner-Christian debate under the guise of objections made by Jews or pagans,"[33] by suggesting that the insertion of Jews into the passage regarding Polycarp's remains reflects a practice Christians employed in other contexts: "thinking with Jews" about Judaizers. Although the best-known example of this is John Chrysostom's fourth-

---

[30] For general discussion of ἁγνεία, see Gerhard Kittel, *Theological Dictionary of the New Testament*, trans. Geoffrey W. Bromiley (Grand Rapids, Mich.: Eerdmans, 1964–76), 1.122–23; for further discussion of this terminology in the context of the *Letter to the Philippians*, see J. B. Lightfoot, *The Apostolic Fathers Part II: S. Ignatius, S. Polycarp* (London: MacMillan, 1885), 2.2.925, and Schoedel, *Polycarp, Martyrdom of Polycarp, Fragments of Papias*, 31–32. Harry Maier's emphasis on Polycarp's references to purity is on the mark but limited. Maier notes the close connection between Polycarp's views of avarice and Jewish apocalyptic literature, but he does not investigate whether ἁγνεία may additionally reveal the nature of the boundary, i.e., that Polycarp endorsed observance of Jewish purity laws; Harry Maier, "Purity and Danger in Polycarp's Epistle to the Philippians: The Sin of Valens in Social Perspective," *JECS* 1.3 (1993): 229–47.

[31] Eusebius, *Ecclesiastical History* 5.24.

[32] For further discussion of the great Sabbath, see Boyarin, *Dying for God*, 12–14 and Lieu, *Image and Reality*, 70–79.

[33] Lieu, *Image and Reality*, 67.

century sermons (long called *Against the Jews* even though it was the synagogue-attending members of his Antiochene Christian congregation who precipitated his attacks), the technique is also employed in the other Smyrnaean martyr text, the third-century *Martyrdom of Pionius*.

Finally, inserting Judaizers into the text addresses the dead end that Lieu's nuanced reading eventually confronts. She herself identifies the problem, writing that *MPoly* reflects contacts "that are far more specific than can be assigned to 'tradition' or 'thought-world' and demand some explanation within the historical setting of the document," an explanation that she struggles to supply.[34] A Jewish–Christian continuum with disputed or porous boundaries fits the bill. Indeed, *MPoly*'s uneven attempt to cast Jews as enemies in a text straining for coherence is perhaps explicable only when the fully formed and distinct categories of "Jews" and "Christian" are rejected as not reflecting the more complex spectrum of beliefs and groups in first- through third-century Asia Minor.

Thus *MPoly*, Revelation, and the *Martyrdom of Pionius* embed prescriptions about the boundaries of Christian identity in their narratives. In other words, a contributor to *MPoly*, wanting to claim Polycarp's legacy for his brand of Christianity, uses a hostile depiction of Jews as a surrogate for criticizing Judaizing Christians. In this contributor's avoidance of a more direct attack, the original target, the Judaizers, recedes as the original context of the polemic shifts over time. Eventually, tensions over the place of Jewish law within the Christian community diminish and are replaced by those between Jews and Christians, producing the vexing interpretative challenge we have just examined.

The Smyrnaean evidence is a valuable resource for investigating when and how Christianity and Judaism came to part ways. Not only does it demonstrate the exchange of ideas between Jews and Christians, but it also hints at the social context in which this exchange would have occurred: not between a Christian community fully opposed to a Jewish community but within a Jesus-following community struggling with its Jewish inheritance. That is, entangled ways have been misunderstood as parted ways.

---

[34] Lieu, *Image and Reality*, 70.

# Tractate *Avot* and Early Christian Succession Lists

"Difference makes a comparative analysis interesting; similarity makes it possible." Thus writes F. J. P. Poole in his examination of the comparative project in the anthropology of religion.[1] In a similar vein, the twin premises of this essay are that rabbinic Judaism and proto-orthodox Christianity share more than enough common ground to render a comparative analysis possible, while they are sufficiently different to make this comparison interesting. On the basis of these premises, I attempt to construct below a comparative analysis between the rabbinic chain of transmission in Tractate *Avot* and the apostolic succession as it appears in several roughly contemporary Christian texts. My interpretation of this comparison will suggest that each of these two groups employed the same literary genre, sometimes in a strikingly similar manner, within the context of two distinct (though mutually interacting) histories. I will contend, in addition, that even though both groups may have employed the same literary genre in pursuit of certain similar political strategies, the relative significance of such strategies may well have varied within the context of these two burgeoning religious movements.

## The Structure of *Avot*

It has been known for many centuries that the sixth chapter of Tractate *Avot* is in fact a late addition,[2] and therefore the original text of the tractate, in contrast to the *Pirkei Avot* of later fame, consists of only five chapters. Although some modern scholars delay the final editing of the

---

[1] F. J. P. Poole, "Metaphors and Maps: Towards Comparison in the Anthropology of Religion," *JAAR* 54:3 (1986): 417.

[2] Chapter six of *Avot*, otherwise known as "Kinyan Torah," is also found in *Kallah Rabbati* and *Seder Eliahu Zuta*. The Geonim explicitly refer to this chapter as an appended unit (see Ch. Albeck, *Shishah Sidrei Mishnah*, vol. 4 [Jerusalem: Bialik Institute & Dvir, 1953], 351); the preface of the chapter implies that it does not belong to the Mishnah.

original text to the late third and even the early fourth century CE, the
evidence seems to suggest that the traditionalists were correct to regard
*Avot* as a Mishnaic tractate.[3] Thus, the patriarch R. Judah ha-Nasi, or one

---

[3] A. Guttmann offers the following four arguments in favor of a redaction date for
*Avot* at the turn of the fourth century ("Tractate Abot – Its Place in Rabbinic
Literature," *JQR* 41 [1950]: 181–93): (1) The absence of a *Tosefta* for *Avot* may be
logically explained by the claim that *Avot* had not yet come into existence when the
*Tosefta* was being redacted in the mid-third century. (2) The tendency in the Babylonian
Talmud to cite *Avot* sayings without introductory formulas (as indicative of a *baraita*)
and to quote *baraita* parallels of *Avot* sayings (rather than the mishnaic versions) is
thought to imply that the Rabbis were unaware of the existence of a *Mishnah Avot*. (3)
It is claimed that the earliest references to *Avot* sayings as *mishnayot* in both Talmuds
are attributed to fourth generation *amoraim*. (4) The placement of *Avot* alongside the
non-Talmudic Small Tractates in the Munich manuscript of the Talmud is viewed as a
reflection of *Avot*'s true status as a non-tannaitic composition. Although Guttmann's
arguments certainly deserve a more thorough treatment and rebuttal (see A. Tropper,
"Tractate Avot in the Context of the Graeco-Roman Near East" [Ph.D. diss., Oxford
University, 2001], ch. 3; idem, *Wisdom, Politics and Historiography: Tractate Avot in
the Context of the Greco-Roman Near East,* forthcoming, ch. 3), A. J. Saldarini has
noted that Guttmann's arguments are based on evidence which "is all external, late, or
from silence" (*Scholastic Rabbinism: A Literary Study of the Fathers According to
Rabbi Nathan* [Chico, CA: Scholars Press, 1982], 138). However, for a different
assessment, see G. Stemberger, "Die innerrabbinische Überlieferung von Mischna
Abot," in *Geschichte – Tradition – Reflexion: Festschrift für Martin Hengel zum 70,* ed.
M. Hengel, H. Cancik, H. Lichtenberger, and P. Schäfer [Tübingen: Mohr Siebeck,
1996], 511–27). B. Z. Dinur argues that the House of Gamaliel literary unit was
compiled during the tenure of Rabbi Judah Ha-Nasi since, he maintains, its contents
reflect the contemporary tension between the patriarch and the Sanhedrin ("The
Tractate Aboth [Sayings of the Fathers] as an Historical Source," *Zion* 35 [1970]: 34, I).
As M. B. Lerner points out, however, Dinur's attempts to link *Avot* teachings to specific
historical contexts are not convincing ("The Tractate *Avot*," in *The Literature of the
Sages,* ed. S. Safrai [Philadelphia: Fortress, 1987], 275). A sixth argument for a late
redaction date for *Avot* suggests that certain sages mentioned in *Avot* flourished only
after the editing of the Mishnah; see Z. Frankel, *Introduction to the Mishna* (Leipzig,
1859; repr. Tel Aviv: Sinai, 1959), 226–28 [Hebrew]; E. Z. Melammed, *Essays in
Talmudic Literature* (Jerusalem: Magnes, 1986), 212 [Hebrew]. Close examination
reveals, however, that most, if not all, of the sages mentioned in *Avot* were active
during the tannaitic period, and the possible exception or two may simply have been
later interpolations (see Albeck, *Mishnah,* vol. 4, 348 n. 4; Tropper, *Wisdom,* ch. 3).
Moreover, the literary analysis of *Avot* supplied below suggests that an unfinished
redaction of *Avot* was most probably edited by R. Judah ha-Nasi or one of his
successors in the early to mid-third century. Although P. Schäfer has suggested that the
existence of many variants in a manuscript tradition may reflect a dynamic process
"which does not allow any neat division between pre- and post-redactional history"
("Once Again the Status Quaestionis of Research in Rabbinic Literature: An Answer to
Chaim Milikowsky," *JJS* 40 [1989]: 90; see also idem, "Research in Rabbinic
Literature: An Attempt to Define the Status Quaestionis," *JJS* 37 [1986]: 139–52), I
believe that the relative uniformity amongst *Avot* manuscripts in reference to its
structure and contents, if not to its language, suggests that an unfinished redaction of

of his successors, most probably edited *Avot* in the early to mid-third century CE.

The rabbinic chain of transmission provides the overarching structure for chapters one and two of *Avot* and the following schematic will demonstrate this structure.

> 1:1: Moses *received* (קבל) the Torah from Sinai and delivered it to Joshua, and Joshua to the elders, and the elders to the prophets, and the prophets delivered it to the Men of the Great Assembly.
> 1:2: Simeon ha-Zaddik was of the remnants of the Great Assembly.
> 1:3: Antigonus of Sokho *received* (קבל) [the Torah] from Simeon ha-Zaddik.
> 1:4: Yose ben Yoezer of Tseredah and Yose ben Yohanan of Jerusalem *received* (קבלו) from them.[4]
> 1:6: Joshua ben Perahyah and Nittai of Arbela *received* (קבלו) from them.
> 1:8: Judah ben Tabbai and Simeon ben Shetah *received* (קבלו) from them.
> 1:10: Shemaiah and Avtalyon *received* (קבלו) from them.
> 1:12: Hillel and Shammai *received* (קבלו) from them
> 1:16:       Rabban Gamaliel said ...
> 1:17:       Simeon his son said ...
> 1:18:       Rabban Simeon ben Gamaliel said ...
> 2:1:        Rabbi (i.e. R. Judah ha-Nasi) said ...
> 2:2:        Rabban Gamaliel ben Rabbi Judah ha-Nasi said ...
> 2:4: Hillel said ...
> 2:8: Rabban Johanan ben Zakkai *received* (קבל) from Hillel and from Shammai. Five disciples were there to Rabban Johanan ben Zakkai and these are they: Rabbi Eliezer ben Hyrcanus, and Rabbi Joshua ben Hananiah, and Rabbi Yose ha-Cohen, and Rabbi Simeon ben Nethanel and Rabbi Eleazar ben Arakh.
> (2:15: R. Tarfon said ... )

The keyword, which connects multiple links in this chain of transmission, is the word "received," "קבל". Just as Moses receives (קבל) the Torah on Mt. Sinai, so the five Pairs of sages (or זוגות, as they are commonly called) from Second Temple times receive (קבלו) the Torah.[5] The keyword skips over the sayings of Gamaliel the Elder and his descendants (1:16–2:2 [2:4]),[6] appearing one final time in reference to Rabban

---

*Avot* may be assigned to the rabbinic period (see Ch. Milikowsky, "The Status Quaestionis in Rabbinic Literature," *JJS* 39 [1988]: 201–11). Although the somewhat fluid manner in which the language of rabbinic texts was transmitted implies that we may never be able to reconstruct the precise language of *Avot*'s Ur-text, it appears that an original tradition, which determined the structure and contents of *Avot*, resonates strongly throughout the manuscript evidence.

[4] See MS Kaufmann and MS Parma for the preferred reading "from him."

[5] See *Ḥagigah* 2:2. According to rabbinic tradition, these five pairs were leaders of the people during the period of the Second Temple.

[6] The "Hillel" in *Avot* 2:4 has been identified either as R. Hillel, the grandson of R. Judah ha-Nasi, or as Hillel the Elder. For supporters of the former position, see J. N. Epstein, *Introduction to the Mishnaic Text* (Jerusalem and Tel Aviv: Magnes and Dvir, 1948), 1182–83 [Hebrew]; S. Sharvit, "Textual Variants and Language of the Treatise

Johanan ben Zakkai. Then, despite the absence of the word "קבל," the story of the transmission continues with Rabban Johanan ben Zakkai's five disciples' preservation of Torah traditions. Chapter two concludes with the sayings of R. Tarfon, yet another disciple of Rabban Johanan ben Zakkai, and with him the direct line of transmission terminates.[7]

The absence of the keyword "קבל" in reference to the members of the house of Gamaliel highlights a break in the literary flow that coincides with the violation of the strict chronological order of the chain of transmission. Chronologically speaking, Rabban Johanan ben Zakkai, rather than the second- and third-century descendents of Gamaliel, should have followed Hillel in chapter one. Further reason to believe that the house of Gamaliel sayings were interpolated into an already existing chain stems from the fact that the House of Gamaliel lineage is not part of the early textual substratum which served as the basis for *Avot de-Rabbi Nathan*, a rabbinic text apparently based on an earlier version of *Avot*.[8] Thus, *Avot*'s editor inserted the dynastic lineage of the House of Gamaliel immediately after the sayings of Hillel and Shammai and, at first glance, one might assume that the connection between the Gamaliel genealogy and Hillel and Shammai is simply that Gamaliel received the Torah traditions from the final Pair and then passed on these traditions to his family. However, since the House of Gamaliel insertion traces a familial genealogy rather than a series of non-familial successors in a chain of transmission, the insertion would have been more smoothly integrated into the text if it could also have been linked to the original chain of transmission by means of a family connection.

Indeed, rabbinic literature preserves traditions which claim that Hillel was Gamaliel's ancestor, and this family connection would be a central reason for the placement of the House of Gamaliel genealogy immed-

---

Abot and Prolegomena to a Critical Edition" (Ph.D. Diss., Ramat Gan, 1976), 144 [Hebrew]; M. Kister, *Studies in Avot de-Rabbi Nathan: Text, Redaction and Interpretation* (Jerusalem: ha-Universitah ha-Ivrit, ha-Hug le-Talmud: Yad Yitshak Ben-Tsevi, ha-Makhon le-heker Erets Yisrael ve-Yishuvah, 1998), 117–21 [Hebrew]. For supporters of the latter position, see L. Finkelstein, *Introduction to the Treatises Abot and Abot of Rabbi Nathan* (New York: Jewish Theological Seminary of America, 1950), 40 n. 64 [Hebrew]; E. E. Urbach, *The Sages: Their Concepts and Beliefs* (Jerusalem: Magnes, 1975), 713 [Hebrew]; idem, *The Halakhah* (Givatayim: Masadah, 1984), 152 [Hebrew]. Y. Sussman has recently stated that this unresolved matter is still in need of a thorough investigation ("The Scholarly Ouevre of Professor Ephraim Elimelech Urbach," in *E. E. Urbach: A Bio Bibliography, Supplement to Jewish Studies* 1 [1993]: 76 n. 149). I have attempted to resolve this matter (in favor of Hillel the Elder) in Tropper, *Wisdom*, ch. 3.

[7] Akavya ben Mahalalel, who appears in 3:1, was not a disciple of Rabban Johanan ben Zakkai.

[8] See Finkelstein, *Introduction*, 6–7; Albeck, *Mishnah*, vol. 4, 347; Saldarini: *Scholastic Rabbinism*, 10–11; Kister, *Studies*, vii.

iately after the sayings of Hillel and Shammai.[9] The juxtaposition of the House of Gamaliel with the final Pair links the Gamaliel lineage to their legendary forefather, Hillel, and the House of Gamaliel becomes, in effect, the House of Hillel.[10] Given that this House of Hillel genealogy vastly enhances the profile of the members in the genealogy, it is not unlikely that a member of the genealogy inserted the interpolation and edited *Avot*. Not surprisingly, the editor of the Mishnah, R. Judah ha-Nasi, is the penultimate member of the genealogy, and therefore it seems reasonable to conclude that he, or one of his descendants, interpolated the genealogy of the patriarchate when editing *Avot*.

In contrast to the explicit line of transmission in these first two chapters, chapters three and four do not show obvious signs of an overarching structural principle. There is no keyword to highlight the chronological structure of these chapters, and the sages are not cited in a teacher-student schema as they were in chapters one and two. As a result, many commentators and scholars surmise that the chronological order of tradents terminated in chapter two.[11] A few scholars, however, have recognized that chapters three and four also adhere to a chronological structure but employ a generational rather than a teacher-student schema.[12] Thus, chapter three opens with statements attributed to sages from the end of the Second Temple period and then cites sages from the first three generations of the tannaitic period with only a few minor exceptions. Chapter four picks up with a few sages from the third generation of Tannaim, and then records statements attributed, for the

---

[9] See *b. Shabbat* 15a; D. Goodblatt, *The Monarchic Principle* (Tübingen: J. C. B. Mohr, 1994), 143–175, 210. Whether or not Hillel was actually Gamaliel's father or grandfather is irrelevant to the *Avot* rhetoric, just as it is irrelevant whether Antigonus of Sokho actually received Torah traditions from Simeon ha-Zaddik. The only significant factor is whether or not such claims were believable, and the evidence seems to indicate that they were.

[10] In this vein, Maimonides blends the House of Hillel genealogy with the chain of transmission in the introduction to his commentary on the Mishnah (see J. Kapah, *Mishnah with the Commentary of Maimonides*: *Zeraim* [Jerusalem: Mossad Harav Kook, 1963], 15–16).

[11] See, for example, R. T. Herford, *Pirke Aboth* (New York: Jewish Institute of Religion, 1945), 7; Albeck, *Mishnah*, 4:347; Saldarini, *Scholastic Rabbinism*, 16–17; Y. Frankel, *Darkhei ha-Aggada weha-Midrash* (Givatayim: Yad la-Talmud, 1991), 429 [Hebrew].

[12] See Finkelstein, *Introduction*, 64; B. Z. Dinur, "The Tractate Aboth (Sayings of the Fathers) as an Historical Source," *Zion* 35 (1970): 1–2 n. 3 [Hebrew]; M. B. Lerner, "The Tractate *Avot*," in *The Literature of the Sages*, ed. S. Safrai (Philadelphia: Fortress, 1987), 267.

most part, to sages from the fourth and the fifth generation of Tannaim.[13] Consequently, though the chain of transmission neither follows an explicit teacher-student schema nor adheres meticulously to chronology, the rough, generational schema of chapters three and four suggests that these two chapters were designed to continue the chain of tradition down through the tannaitic period. The fifth and final chapter of *Avot* adheres to a literary structure apparently unrelated to the chain of transmission, and it is therefore not relevant to our discussion of *Avot*'s chain of transmission.

In short, the preceding discussion offers two levels of analysis for the first four chapters of *Avot*. An overall view of the text reveals the continuous historical theme of all four chapters, while a closer examination shows that the historical theme is developed in two ways: the explicit transmission of the Torah in the first two chapters and the implicit transmission in the latter two chapters.

Since *Avot*'s chain of transmission leads up to the rabbinic sages who are also the Tannaim of the early rabbinic period, it seems that its overarching literary structure legitimates the tannaitic sages and the Torah traditions of their community in Palestine. Indeed, a comparison to similar chains in other tractates of the Mishnah only reinforces this notion.

*Yadayim* 4:3: Rabbi Eliezer wept and said, The counsel of the Lord is with them that fear him: and His covenant, to make them know it. Go and tell them: Do not have any apprehension on account of your voting. *I received a tradition from R. Johanan b. Zakkai who heard it from his teacher, his teacher from his teacher, and so back to a halachah given to Moses from Sinai*, that Ammon and Moab must give tithe for the poor in the seventh year.

*Pe'ah* 2:6: Nahum the Scribe said: *I have a tradition from R. Me'asha, who received it from Abba, who received it from the zugoth, who received it from the prophets as a halachah of Moses from Sinai*, that a man who sows his field with two kinds of wheat and makes it up into one threshing-floor must give one pe'ah, if two threshing floors, [he gives] two pe'ahs.

*Eduyyot* 8:7: R. Joshua said: *I have received a tradition from Rabban Johanan b. Zakkai, who heard it from his teacher, and his teacher [heard it] from his teacher, as a halachah [given] to Moses from Sinai*, that Elijah will not come to pronounce unclean or to pronounce clean, to put away or to bring near, but to put away those brought near by force and to bring near those put away by force.

Whereas the chains of transmission in these other tractates serve to ground a single law, the chain of transmission in *Avot* offers a blanket

---

[13] Of the forty-two sages cited in chapters three and four, only five or six figures truly violate the rough chronological order. In addition, most if not all of the "problematic" sages were cited because their sayings naturally fit into the immediate context.

justification for the tannaitic interpretive project as a whole.[14] In this manner, *Avot* offers a meta-legal, historical justification for the host of extra-biblical Torah traditions practiced by the rabbinic community.

## The Genre of *Avot*'s Chain of Transmission

In light of the structure of the first four chapters of *Avot* just described, let us turn now to the question of genre. Prior to Elias Bickerman's seminal article "La Chaîne de la Tradition Pharisienne,"[15] Louis Finkelstein had argued that the chains of transmission in *Avot* and in *Avot de-Rabbi Nathan* were modeled on a traditional genealogy of High Priests, since a fourteen-generation schema is common to all three lists. Finkelstein then reasoned that the first-century stratum of *Avot* must have been designed to counter the priestly genealogy and to commend the sages, in lieu of the priests, as the authentic authorities of Torah.[16] However, Bickerman

---

[14] Though it is unclear whether *Avot* posited the concept of an Oral Torah delivered at Sinai, the context demands, in any event, that the Torah of the chain of transmission include the extra-Scriptural traditions of the rabbinic sages. *Sifre Devarim* attributes the theory of a dual Torah, in which an Oral Torah stands alongside the Written Torah, to an early tanna (351, ed. L. Finkelstein, *Sifre on Deuteronomy* [Berlin: Gesellschaft zur Föderung der Wissenschaft des Judentums, 1939; Reprint. New York: JTS, 1969], 408–9), but *Avot* offers no indication whether it subscribes to this point of view. (See Saldarini, *Scholastic Rabbinism*, 6–7; Jacob Neusner, *Torah: From Scroll to Symbol in Formative Judaism* [Philadelphia: Fortress, 1985], 51–53). Moreover, the standard rabbinic term for the Oral Torah, תורה שבעל פה, does not appear in the Mishnah at all (see Peter Schäfer, "Das Dogma von der mündlichen Torah im rabbinischen Judentum," in *Studien zur Geschichte und Theologie des rabbinischen Judentums* [Leiden: Brill, 1978], 153–97; Y. Blidstein, "A Note on the Term Torah She-be-al Peh," *Tarbiz* 42 [1973], 496–98 [Hebrew]). It is therefore possible that *Avot* views extra-biblical rabbinic traditions simply as products of the authentic biblical exegesis inherited from Moses.

[15] E. Bi[c]kerman[n], "La Chaîne de la Tradition Pharisienne," *Revue Biblique* 59 (1952): 44–54.

[16] See Finkelstein, *Introduction*, 9–11. Since there is no complete priestly genealogy in the Bible, Finkelstein was forced to reconstruct this genealogy on the basis of various biblical texts. There is no textual evidence, however, that Finkelstein's reconstructed genealogy ever existed. In addition, Finkelstein discusses similarities between *Avot* and the genealogy of Jesus related in Matt 1:1–17, but it must be stressed that unlike this New Testament passage, *Avot* does not consist of a genealogy for the most part. (A good response to Finkelstein's claims regarding the supposed importance of the fourteen stages in the rabbinic chain in light of Matthew's 3 x 14 scheme may be found in M. D. Johnson, *The Purpose of the Biblical Genealogies With Special Reference to the Setting of the Genealogies of Jesus* [2nd ed.; Cambridge: Cambridge UP, 1988], 205–7.) That said, the genealogy that does exist in *Avot* may have been designed to link R. Judah ha-Nasi to the House of David (via Hillel) just as the Christian genealogies in Matthew and Luke (3:23–38) explicitly trace Jesus' lineage back to David.

pointed out a critical factor which distances *Avot* from this supposed biblical precedent. Whereas the priestly genealogy records a family line, *Avot*'s chain (excluding the House of Hillel) traces a non-familial succession. Since pre-rabbinic Jewish writings do not seem to offer a compelling literary precedent for this type of succession,[17] Bickerman suggested that Hellenistic scholastic successions had served as the literary model for the chain of transmission in *Avot*.

The genre of Hellenistic succession lists originated within the history of philosophy but eventually had far-reaching ramifications for the historiography of intellectual disciplines throughout the ancient world. In reconstructing the history of a discipline, succession lists served two important and interrelated goals. Firstly, successions embodied the political and institutional realities upon which they were initially modeled. The institutional succession of scholarchs therefore reflected the history of authority in philosophical academies and may have also served to justify a contemporary figure who was placed in a line of succession.[18] Secondly, a succession, as popularly understood in the classicizing atmosphere of the Second Sophistic (i.e., the cultural renaissance in the Greek-speaking east of the Roman Empire from the mid-first to mid-third centuries CE), outlined the transmission of proper doctrine over the course of history. The founder's successors continued his legacy and viewed the interpretation of his writings as the unfolding of his ideas. In a scholastic or intellectual succession list, the central factor was the belief that the founder's heirs transmitted proper doctrine; their role as institutional successors was far less prominent. In effect,

---

[17] J. L. Crenshaw has suggested that *Avot*'s chain of transmission stems from a similar ancient Babylonian conception of wisdom (*Old Testament Wisdom: An Introduction* [Louisville: Westminster John Knox, 1998], 5), but it seems unlikely that this motif would have lain dormant throughout Hebrew wisdom literature only to appear in *Avot* for the very first time. Ben Sira (46–48), Eupolemus (in Eusebius *Praep. Ev.* 9.30), and Josephus (*Apion* 1.39–41) all employ the concept of a non-familial succession (see Bickerman, "La Chaîne," 133–134; M. Hengel, *Judaism and Hellenism: Studies in their Encounter in Palestine during the Early Hellenistic Period*, trans. J. Bowden [2 vols.; Philadelphia: Fortress, 1974], 136), but they do not present a teacher-disciple succession schema in a scholastic setting as found in *Avot*. In contrast to these pre-rabbinic writings, the chains of transmission in the Mishnah cited above do reflect a teacher-disciple succession and *Avot* essentially presents a generalization of those chains. However, the mishnaic chains of transmission and the chain of transmission in *Avot* differ in respect to chronological structure. Whereas the mishnaic chains begin in the present and then trace the transmission of a law into the past, *Avot*, like Hellenistic succession lists, begins in the ancient past and traces the transmission of the Torah through the forward flow of history down to the present.

[18] See Diogenes Laertius, *Lives of Eminent Philosophers* 9.116; J. Glucker, *Antiochus and the Late Academy*, Hypomnemata 56 (Göttingen: Vandenhoeck & Ruprecht, 1978), 349–356.

political and intellectual dimensions were often intertwined because the continuous transmission of tradition established the successors as the authentic interpreters of the classical heritage and thereby justified their power over their schools.

Although various Jewish writers employed the concept of a non-familial succession before the editing of *Avot*,[19] *Avot* is the earliest extant Jewish text that locates a succession within a scholastic, teacher-disciple setting and seems to be modeled on the succession literary genre. As Bickerman pointed out, *Avot*'s chain of transmission appears to be a succession list because it opens with a legendary sage and then follows with the transmission of Torah through a list of successors.[20] Indeed, the popularity of succession lists in the ancient world makes it likely that the creator of *Avot*'s original chain of transmission would have been aware of this genre from the Hellenistic cultural environment of Roman Palestine and adapted it to suit his own particular needs.[21] Moreover, the revival of the genre in the second and third centuries[22] coincides nicely with the patriarch's updated edition of this rabbinic succession.

If the succession literary genre was selected as a central structuring element in *Avot*, it stands to reason that it was chosen because it reflected or enhanced specific features and claims of the rabbinic movement. In particular, I would like to suggest that the scholastic and institutional dimensions of the successions discussed above may shed further light on the meaning of Avot's chain of transmission. The succession genre was probably employed not merely for its literary and aesthetic contributions, but because the ideas associated with this literary form were relevant to the world of the Tannaim. In particular, the scholastic and institutional dimensions of the successions discussed above may shed further light on the meaning of *Avot*'s chain of transmission.

In respect to the scholastic dimension of succession lists, scholastic successions highlighted the teacher-disciple chain which supposedly guaranteed the continuity of a school. Similarly, *Avot* opens with Moses receiving the Torah on Sinai and then transmitting it to Joshua. This link

---

[19] See n. 17 above. The mishnaic chains of transmission discussed probably reflect the same tannaitic thinking which underlies the chain in *Avot*.

[20] See Bickerman, "La Chaîne," 134.

[21] See below for a more detailed analysis of the origins of the succession list in *Avot* and in early Christian writings.

[22] This revival is attested to by the successions in Diogenes Laertius' *Lives of Eminent Philosophers* and by the teacher-disciple structure of Philostratus' *Lives of the Sophists* (see S. Swain, *Hellenism and Empire: Language, Classicism and Power in the Greek World AD 50–250* [Oxford: Clarendon, 1996], 97). In addition, perhaps the revival was reinforced by the renewal of the institutional successions in philosophy in 176 CE (Philostratus, *Lives of the Sophists* 566; Dio Cassius, *Roman History* 72.31; Lucian, *The Eunuch* 3).

then becomes the first of many in the chain of transmission of the Torah through Jewish history. The links in the chain, however, are not merely famous personalities from the past, but figures whom the Rabbis considered their intellectual predecessors. Consequently, the scholastic message of *Avot* is that the Torah traveled across history in the capable hands of its caretakers, the most recent of whom were the Tannaim.

I turn now to the second dimension of succession lists: institutional leadership. Although the scholarch successors of philosophical succession lists were initially recognized office-holders, the succession literary model was applied, in time, to settings in which an institutional succession had never existed. In this manner the literary model allowed the authors of these lists to project an institutional aura onto a non-institutional setting, and it appears that the explicit succession list in the first two chapters of *Avot* functioned in just this way.[23]

*Avot* 1:1 opens with the biblical tradents who were the official leaders of the Jewish people and concludes with the Men of the Great Assembly. Although the nature of this institution is unclear, the context intimates that (at least in rabbinic eyes) they were a group akin to the elders and the prophets who were thought to have succeeded them. Simeon ha-Zaddik follows in *Avot* 1:2 and, despite his tenure as High Priest, *Avot* connects him to the illustrious body of the Great Assembly. Antigonus of Sokho follows Simeon, but his official capacity is not revealed. Nonetheless, since he is preceded and followed by political leaders, it stands to reason that he was probably regarded as a leader as well. The five Pairs, who are described as *Nesi'im* (i.e. princes or presidents) and Fathers of the Court in *Hagigah* 2:2,[24] then succeed Antigonus of Sokho.[25] Setting aside the

---

[23] When relating to the first-century stratum of *Avot*, J. Glucker argues that "the whole point of the succession, from the Great Assembly onwards, is that the Law was handed down through recognized holders of office. Only such a succession of recognized holders of office would constitute an answer to the Sadducees, who had a near monopoly on the office of the High Priest" (*Antiochus*, 358 n. 83). Though Glucker's conjecture is theoretically possible, there could have been other targets for *Avot*'s chain of transmission (such as Qumran sectarians and early Christians) in a first-century setting. In addition, it is highly questionable whether there is any evidence that the Sadducees "had a near monopoly on the office of the High Priest." In any event, I have chosen to focus my discussion on the meaning of the leadership succession in the final version of *Avot*, rather than attempt to reconstruct the role of an earlier version of *Avot* in a first-century setting.

[24] This mishnaic depiction of the Pairs as *Nesi'im* and Fathers of the Court is not corroborated by earlier sources and appears to function as the tannaitic reconstruction of the history of Jewish leadership during the Second Temple period. Moreover, D. Boyarin suggests that this description of the Pairs belongs to a late layer of the Mishnah ("The Diadoche of the Rabbis, or, The Apostolic Succession and the Invention of Judaism," paper delivered at the conference "Jewish Culture and Society in the Christian Roman Empire," Jewish Theological Seminary, New York, March 13-15,

insertion of the House of Gamaliel for the moment, the next tradent is the tannaitic leader, Rabban Johanan ben Zakkai. With Rabban Johanan ben Zakkai, the list of leaders comes to a close and, in *Avot* 2:8, the text moves from the leadership succession to Rabban Johanan ben Zakkai's five disciples. Thus, the chain of transmission of the first two chapters contains a succession list of the Jewish leaders from Moses until the early tannaitic period. These leaders were considered the official transmitters of Torah; thus, their role as leaders was entwined with their role as the guardians of authentic Torah interpretation.

Seen in this light, the insertion of the Gamalielite genealogy into the first two chapters of *Avot* is even more striking. Since the original succession mechanism in the first two chapters is the teacher-disciple link, the sudden appearance of a familial genealogy would have been jarring if the sole purpose of these chapters was to demonstrate that the teacher-disciple relationship is the guarantor of Torah knowledge. However, since the chain of transmission of the first two chapters is also a succession of leaders, the editor apparently reasoned that the leadership context would naturally harmonize with his insertion. In other words, while the explicit chain of transmission presented a list of Jewish leaders from Moses until the first century CE, the patriarch inserted his family in order to present them as the Jewish leaders of the tannaitic period. Just as Sextus Empiricus apparently tacked on a succession of Empiricists to a doubtful Pyrrhonian succession,[26] so the patriarch enhanced his own reputation by inserting his family's genealogy into a succession of Jewish leaders.

The institutional succession list of chapters one and two terminates when Rabban Johanan ben Zakkai transmits his teachings to five students, rather than to an institutional successor. The image of a teacher

---

2000. This paper forms the basis for the forthcoming article, "The Diadoche of the Rabbis: or, Rabbi Judah at Yavneh," in *Jewish Culture and Society under the Christian Roman Empire*, ed. R. Kalmin and S. Schwartz [Louvain: Peeters, 2002]; see also Boyarin's chapter on "Naturalizing the Border: Apostolic Succession in the Mishna," in his forthcoming book *Border Lines: The Invention of Heresy and the Emergence of Christianity and Judaism*, Divinations: Rereading Late Ancient Religions [Stanford: Stanford UP, 2004]). If he is correct then perhaps R. Judah ha-Nasi himself introduced this reconstructed history into *Ḥagigah* in order to transform his intellectual predecessors (presented in *Avot*) into the leaders of the Second Temple period.

[25] As Glucker notes (*Antiochus*, 359 n. 84), it makes no difference whether the Pairs actually served in leadership positions during the Second Temple period; what is important is the rabbinic understanding that these were the official Torah authorities of that period.

[26] See n. 18 above. Sextus Empiricus' list concludes with his disciple just as the genealogy in *Avot* terminates with R. Judah ha-Nasi's son (assuming the Hillel of *Avot* 2:4 is Hillel the Elder). If R. Judah ha-Nasi edited *Avot*, then in both cases the lists were probably designed to show that the successions would continue into the future.

surrounded by his students emerges from the mishnayot involving Rabban Johanan ben Zakkai, and this image of a disciple circle seems to have served as the model for the subsequent two chapters. In other words, chapters three and four present a few sages or students for each generation of Tannaim, suggesting that the transmission of knowledge occurred in a scholastic setting apparently devoid of institutionalized leadership.[27] This generational schema captures the scholastic dimension of succession lists but lacks the direct line of successors typical of the genre. Consequently, the transition from the institutional succession list of chapters one and two and the implied scholastic succession of chapters three and four demands an explanation.

Two factors may explain why the overview of the tannaitic period in chapters three and four does not include a teacher-disciple succession list. First, perhaps an institutional, teacher-disciple succession list for the tannaitic period would have been too obvious a fabrication since *Avot*'s audience would have known that tannaitic Judaism was not the product of a single, centralized, rabbinic academy. In reference to the classical golden age of Second Temple times, the Rabbis could imagine that the Pairs served as successive national leaders and, as a result, could more easily project the succession genre into the distant past. However, the Rabbis were well aware that this utopian state of affairs did not continue into the post-Temple period. Although the Mishnah assigned Rabban Johanan ben Zakkai a leadership role, none of his disciples inherited his mantle. Scattered disciple circles, rather than a functioning, centralized academy, characterized the rabbinic social structure in the tannaitic period.[28] (In a similar manner, Hellenistic writers projected the succession paradigm back to the early days of philosophy, before the advent of academies; when the disciple circles replaced the Peripatos and Academy in the first century, the succession lists were no longer continued.[29]) Second, and more important, the institutional dimension of

---

[27] See S. J. D. Cohen, "The Rabbi in Second-Century Jewish Society," in *The Cambridge History of Judaism*, vol. 3, *The Early Roman Period*, ed. W. Horbury, W. D. Davies, and J. Sturdy (Cambridge: Cambridge UP, 1999), 950–56.

[28] The difference between a disciple circle and an academy has been described as follows: "An academy is a permanent institution whose corporate identity transcends the existence of any single individual. It has faculty and students, officers and ranks. It might hold its sessions in a building or some other specific place. A disciple circle is much more fluid, with no permanence or corporate identity. A single master has around him a handful of apprentices who attend their master like servants in order to learn from his every action. When the master dies, the circle disbands and the students are left to fend for themselves"; Cohen, "The Rabbi in Second-Century Jewish Society," 951.

[29] See J. M. Dillon, "Philosophy," in *The Cambridge Ancient History*, vol. 11, *The High Empire A.D. 70–192*, ed. A. K. Bowman, P. Garnsey, and D. Rathbone (2nd edition; Cambridge: Cambridge UP, 2000), 924–25.

the rabbinic succession list – that is, the leadership of the tannaitic period – had already been outlined in chapters one and two. In other words, Gamaliel the Elder and his descendants were portrayed as the recognized office-holders when their dynastic lineage was interpolated into the succession list of chapters one and two. Since the patriarch presented his family as the authentic leaders of the first two centuries, there was no need to fabricate a teacher-disciple leadership succession for the tannaitic period. Thus, chapters three and four of *Avot* present the continuation of the scholastic dimension of the chain of transmission within disciple circles, while chapters one and two point to Rabbi Judah ha-Nasi's family as the authentic political successors of the leaders from the classical past.[30]

## The Apostolic Succession in Early Christian Writings

In light of the institutional and scholastic dimensions of succession lists discussed above, let us look at how these two dimensions were put to work in the apostolic successions of Christianity. In my attempt to provide an historically contextualized analysis, I will present a short overview of some relevant literary material roughly contemporaneous with *Avot*, material from writings dating from the late first to the early fourth century CE. The analysis of this Christian material will then be brought to bear on *Avot* in an attempt to decipher similarities and differences between *Avot* and its early Christian literary counterparts.

One important function of the apostolic succession in early Christianity was the legitimation of church authority; evidence of this function appears rather strikingly in 1 Clement (of the late first or early second century[31]). In response to a schism in Corinth involving a group of young men who deposed the established leadership of the church, the leaders (or a leader) of the church in Rome intervened by sending a letter of protest condemning the innovators. Since there is no explicit indication that the rift in the Corinthian church was caused by a disagreement over doctrine, most scholars are inclined to believe that some non-doctrinal

---

[30] Although the importance of a distinguished lineage was clearly important to Jews in earlier periods as well, it is worth noting that, in Greek culture, one might enhance one's social or professional status by publicizing one's relationship to a famous or important ancestor, or even by fabricating a lineage. See S. B. Pomeroy, *Families in Classical and Hellenistic Greece: Representations and Realities* (Oxford: Clarendon, 1997), 143–59.

[31] See C. N. Jefford, K. J. Harder, and L. D. Amezaga, *Reading the Apostolic Fathers* (Peabody, MA: Hendrickson, 1996), 104; S. Tugwell, *The Apostolic Fathers* (Harrisburg, PA: Morehouse, 1990), 90.

matter, such as a break in church discipline, inspired the schism.[32] However, even if a disagreement over doctrine caused the younger generation to revolt, Clement's condemnation focuses on the dispossession of the Corinthian elders. As part of his rationale for condemning this subversive activity, Clement stresses the importance of the continuous succession of Christian leaders (although he does not actually formulate a succession list). With communities scattered all over the Roman Empire and an as yet primitive and limited bureaucracy in many places, church leaders such as Clement of Rome sought to reinforce the power of the small clerical establishment by tracing the succession of church officials back to the apostles.

Like Clement of Rome at the turn of the first century, Cyprian used the institutional (or episcopal) succession to ground the authority of church leadership in the third century. Cyprian "never appeals to this succession to guarantee the soundness of his doctrine nor of his tradition because he sees no necessity to produce authority from any source except the Bible and because he does not believe in any tradition outside the Bible."[33] Just as Clement of Rome had commended the leadership of the Corinthian church on the basis of an institutional succession, Cyprian also employed an institutional succession to justify church leadership and discipline against supposed innovators and schismatics in North Africa in the third century.

A second, and perhaps more widespread, function of the apostolic succession was its role in the defense of religious doctrine.[34] Within the

---

[32] In claiming that Clement "found no doctrinal deviation" in Corinth, H. Chadwick (*The Early Church* [London: Penguin, 1993], 42) presents the consensus view. (For a description of the movement in Corinth as a schism, see 1 Clement 46:9.) See also Frend, *The Rise of Christianity*, 134; H. von Campenhausen, *Ecclesiastical Authority and Spiritual Power in the Church of the First Three Centuries*, trans. J. A. Baker (Peabody, MA: Hendrickson, 1997), 86–88. Some suggest, however, that certain chapters may hint at disagreements over doctrine (see P. F. Beatrice, "Clement of Rome," *Encyclopedia of the Early Church* [1992], 181) and a review of the scholarship on the various interpretations of the Corinthian schism is presented in H. O. Maier, *The Social Setting of the Ministry as Reflected in the Writings of Hermas, Clement and Ignatius* (Waterloo, Ont.: Published for the Canadian Corporation for Studies in Religion by Wilfrid Laurier University Press, 1991), 87–94.

[33] R. P. C. Hanson, *Tradition in the Early Church* (London: SCM, 1962), 159. See Cyprian, *Epistulae* 33.1.1, 45.3.2, 66.4.1.

[34] The crystallization of orthodoxy and heresy in early Christianity developed over the course of the first few centuries. As M. Goodman notes, religious variety "was treated by Church historians in later antiquity, such as Eusebius, as the product of the implantation of heretical error into the originally pristine Church. More recent scholarship has argued, on the contrary, that an insistence on uniformity of belief and practice emerged only in the second century, and that the first Christians were tolerant of great diversity. The truth probably lies between these two extremes" ("The

context of 2 Timothy's "handbook for church leaders,"[35] apparently designed to combat what its author considered false teachings,[36] Paul is said to have given the following command:

And what you have heard from me through many witnesses entrust to faithful people who will be able to teach others as well.[37]

Although this passage does not elaborate on its message, the sentiment expressed resembles the notion of the apostolic succession as it was developed by second-century apologists. Unlike Clement of Rome and Cyprian, who emphasize that church leaders derive their authority from their position in an apostolic succession, the apologists wed tradition to the apostolic succession and thereby maintain that tradition is transmitted through the proto-orthodox ministry. In this manner, they argue that only the established "apostolic" churches maintain true doctrines and authentic traditions. Whereas Clement of Rome admonishes the Corinthian "schismatics" with an institutional succession, later apologists use a doctrinal succession to refute the gnostics, who claim that their knowledge is comprised of secret apostolic traditions passed down through a succession of teachers. In fighting the "false doctrines" of his own day, perhaps the author of 2 Timothy articulates the germ of the idea which later second-century opponents of gnosticism developed into the doctrinal theory of succession.[38]

Within proto-orthodox Christianity, the second-century church historian Hegesippus was apparently the first to have compiled an apostolic succession list. Although the idea of the apostolic succession appears in earlier writings, Hegesippus was apparently the first proto-orthodox Christian to compile a list of an apostle's successors. According to Eusebius, Hegesippus wrote about his travels to Corinth and Rome while remarking on 1 Clement. In this context, Hegesippus is said to have written the following sentence.

Having arrived in Rome, I established a succession until Anicetus.[39]

Hegesippus then mentions the names of a few of the later members of the Roman succession list and states that the members of every church

---

Emergence of Christianity," in *A World History of Christianity*, ed. A. Hastings [London: Cassell, 1999], 21).

[35] A. T. Hanson, *The Pastoral Letters* (Cambridge: Cambridge UP, 1966), 16.

[36] Hanson, *Pastoral Letters*, 16.

[37] 2 Tim 2:2.

[38] See Campenhausen, *Ecclesiastical Authority*, 155–56.

[39] Eusebius, *Historia Ecclesiastica* 4.22.3. On the proper reading of this passage see *Histoire Ecclésiastique*, trans. G. Bardy (Paris: Editions du Cerf, 1952–1960), ad loc.; F. S. Barcellon, "Hegesippus," *Encyclopedia of the Early Church* (1992), 371; Campenhausen, *Ecclesiastical Authority*, 165.

succession in every city agree on issues of doctrine. Thus, Hegesippus connected church succession lists with universal agreement on doctrine, perhaps in the hope of demonstrating the truth of proto-orthodox Christian doctrine.

A critical difference between Hegesippus' notion of succession and the gnostic notion is that Hegesippus did not refer to mere teachers, but to official Christian leaders. Even though, like gnostic successions,[40] his succession is primarily concerned with tracing the transmission of doctrine and tradition, Hegesippus ascribed the links in the chain to consecutive members in the church administration. In this manner, Hegesippus seems to have conflated Clement of Rome's idea of successsive, authoritative leaders with the notion of an unbroken chain of transmission and thereby created a succession list designed to justify official church doctrine.

Shortly after Hegesippus devised his succession list, the classic formulation of the Christian doctrinal chain of transmission appeared in the writings of Irenaeus. In his work *Adversus Haereses*, which was written between 175 and 189 CE,[41] he opposes gnostic sects by refuting their claims to possess oral traditions of Jesus' secret teachings. Irenaeus claims that the apostles had taught oral traditions to church leaders and that each generation of church leaders passed on these traditions to the next generation of leaders.[42] He contends, moreover, that if the apostles had known any hidden mysteries, they would have taught these secrets to the very people to whom they were committing the church.[43] Irenaeus concludes that since the church leaders never taught any secret traditions, no such traditions had ever existed. Instead, the church maintained both scripture and oral tradition through a continuous succession of recognized

---

[40] There is no extant second-century gnostic text that outlines a succession list; the evidence for these successions can only be gathered from the writings of non-gnostic Christian authors. These authors refer to chains of transmission which certain gnostic sects had apparently formulated in order to legitimate their secret traditions (see Epiphanius, *Panarion* 33.7.9; Clement of Alexandria, *Stromateis* 7.106.4; Hippolytus, *Philosophoumena* 5.7.1; Origen, *Contra Celsum* 5.62). For example, Hippolytus states that Basilides claimed to have been Matthew's disciple and that Matthew had supposedly learned secret lore from Jesus (see Hippolytus, *Philosophoumena* 7.20.1).

[41] See R. M. Grant, *Irenaeus of Lyons* (London: Routledge, 1997), 6.

[42] J. N. D. Kelly notes that Irenaeus' polemic against gnosticism "led him to apply the word 'tradition' in a novel and restricted sense, specifically to the Church's oral teaching as distinct from that contained in Scripture" in *Early Christian Doctrines* (2nd ed.; New York: Black, 1960), 37. It is disputed, however, whether these traditions referred to kerygmatic and doctrinal traditions alone or included customary law (such as the date of Easter) as well. See Chadwick, *Early Church*, 84–85; W. Rordorf, "Tradition," *Encyclopedia of the Early Church* (1992), 848.

[43] See Irenaeus, *Adversus Haereses* 3.3.1.

leaders. For Irenaeus, Christian oral tradition was assured through this succession and was likened to precious money deposited in a bank.[44]

Irenaeus did not merely state that the doctrinal succession exists; he even offered an example of one such list. After explaining that a presentation of the succession lists of each and every church would become tedious, Irenaeus presents the succession list of the church he considered most holy – the church of Rome.

> The blessed apostles, then, having founded and built up the Church, committed into the hand of Linus the office of the episcopate ... To him succeeded (διαδέχεται) Anacletus; and after him, in the third place from the apostles, Clement was allotted the bishopric ... To this Clement there succeeded (διαδέχεται) Evaristus. Alexander followed Evaristus; then, sixth from the apostles, Sixtus was appointed; after him, Telephorus ... then Hyginus; after him, Pius; then after him, Anicetus. Soter having succeeded (διαδεξαμένου) Anicetus, Eleutheris does now, in the twelfth place from the apostles, hold the inheritance of the episcopate. In this order, and by this succession (διδαχῇ [διαδοχῇ]), the ecclesiastical tradition from the apostles, and the preaching of the truth, have come down to us.[45]

According to Irenaeus, this list of Roman church leaders, or a comparable list from any other apostolic church, demonstrates that the church has received the authentic apostolic traditions and then preserved them in an unbroken chain of succession. Moreover, like Hegesippus, Irenaeus emphasizes that all apostolic churches agree on matters of doctrine because the successions in each church guaranteed the accurate transmission of apostolic doctrine.[46]

In short, Irenaeus offers the first clear and explicit illustration of the synthesis of tradition and succession in proto-orthodox Christianity. Despite the similarities between the kinds of apostolic succession articulated by Clement of Rome and by Irenaeus, it is vital to bear in mind that second-century apologists like Irenaeus revolutionized the notion of apostolic succession by using it to justify doctrine rather than to ground the authority of Christian leadership.[47] In this vein, Tertullian

---

[44] See Irenaeus, *Adversus Haereses* 3.2.2; 3.4.1. In addition, Irenaeus mentions a "charisma veritatis certum" (4.40.2) that is granted to the church leaders, though scholars are divided on the proper interpretation of this phrase. See Grant, *Irenaeus of Lyons*, 194 n. 13.

[45] Irenaeus, *Adversus Haereses* 3.3.2–3 in *The Ante-Nicene Fathers*, vol. 1 (trans. A. Roberts & W. H. Rambaut; Grand Rapids, Mich.: Eerdmans, 1989).

[46] See Irenaeus, *Adversus Haereses* 1.2–3.

[47] Even though the links in Irenaeus' succession lists are church leaders, their public role is important to his argument only insofar as the apostles chose to entrust the true doctrines to the church leadership. Their actual function as bishops, however, is irrelevant to this argument since, for Irenaeus, the essential factor is the transmission of orthodox doctrine. In fact, Irenaeus did not even believe that a position in the succession automatically guaranteed the accuracy of one's teachings, for he listed

follows Irenaeus' general approach[48] but reduces the importance of the individual bishop by focusing instead on the succession of church generations,[49] and Clement of Alexandria located the transmission of traditions not in the established church leadership but in gifted teachers.[50] For these Christian thinkers, the factor of central importance was the continuous transmission of doctrine rather than the authoritative status of the individual transmitters.

A third function of the succession list in early Christianity was the historical use, as in Eusebius' writings. In the course of his *Ecclesiastical History*, one encounters several kinds of succession, not all of them apostolic. The succession of prophets, Jewish rulers, high priests, emperors, and teachers at the School of Alexandria are all cited. Eusebius appears to have been interested in these various successions because they all help to give a sense of historical continuity and the passage of time.[51] Moreover, the central role of the apostolic succession in the structure of his composition demonstrates that, for Eusebius, the apostolic succession reflects both the continuity and the divine preservation of the church.

Robert Grant has noted that "as a schoolman Eusebius was aware of the importance of legitimate succession, especially in the teaching of philosophy." Grant accordingly suggests "that along with Eusebius' primary emphasis on episcopal succession there is a clearly identifiable emphasis on school succession, which actually existed, in his view, at Alexandria and Caesarea."[52] Even if Alexandria was not home to an established Christian school, Eusebius lent it the aura of an academy by employing the Hellenistic succession genre. In addition, the institutional and scholastic successions in his *History* intersect in Dionysius of Alexandria, who was both a bishop and the head of the Christian school in Alexandria. For Eusebius, the institutional succession of church leaders reflects the history of Christian leadership, while the scholastic

---

additional attributes, such as holiness, which an authentic teacher must also possess (*Adversus Haereses* 4.42.1). Rather, the succession list "functioned negatively to mark off the heretics" (E. Ferguson, "Apostolic Succession," *Encyclopedia of Early Christianity* [1990], 77) since their traditions were never entrusted to the proper church leadership.

[48] See Tertullian, *De Praescriptione Haereticorum* 20–26, 32–36.

[49] See, for example, Tertullian, *De Praescriptione Haereticoum* 20.5–6; Hanson, *Tradition in the Early Church*, 158.

[50] See Clement of Alexandria, *Stromateis* 6.7.61.3.

[51] See R. Trevijano, "Succession, Apostolic," *Encyclopedia of the Early Church* (1992), 798.

[52] Grant, *Eusebius*, 46.

succession of the school reflects the Christian intellectual tradition; these two streams merge in the person of Dionysius of Alexandria.[53]

In sum, the apostolic succession assumed various functions within early Christian literature. Certain writers emphasize the continuous transmission of authentic doctrine by demonstrating the unbroken transmission of Christian tradition via the succession of church leaders (Irenaeus), churches (Tertullian), or teachers (Clement of Alexandria). Other writers ground the authority and power of the Christian leaders in their position in institutional church successions (Clement of Rome and Cyprian). These unbroken successions of church leaders were employed to bolster the authority of the church and counter the claims of schismatics who disagreed with the church on non-doctrinal matters. As a church historian, Eusebius stressed a third aspect of the successions: their reflection of historical continuity. Moreover, in presenting Dionysius of Alexandria as a member of both an institutional succession and a scholastic succession, Eusebius reveals his vision of the synthesis of Christian teaching with Christian leadership.

## The Succession List Genre in *Avot* and in Early Christianity

Considering the parallel appearance of the succession literary genre in *Avot* and in early Christian writings, scholars have questioned why members of these different communities employed the same device to trace the history of their respective traditions. One might suggest that the similarities are purely coincidental or, alternatively, that similar ideas of tradition and succession are inevitable "in all religions which profess to be wholly and solely based on a revelation, fixed and final, embodied in certain books."[54] Perhaps an investigation into the historical settings from which these lists emerged will offer a less arbitrary and more historically plausible solution.

One approach to the matter suggests that an early version of *Avot*, or some comparable rabbinic oral traditions, served as the paradigm or

---

[53] For Dionysius as head of the school, see *Historia Ecclesiastica* 6.29.4 (τῆς τῶν αὐτόθι κατηχήσεως τὴν διατριβὴν διαδέχεται Διονύσιος), and as bishop, see 6.35 (see also Grant, *Eusebius*, 47). Eusebius writes that Dionysius "was a disciple of Origen and that, before succeeding Heraclas as bishop, he succeeded him as head of the city's *didaskaleion*; but the idea that the Alexandrian church had a higher school of *catechesis*, similar to the philosophical schools of Athens and endowed like them with a succession of eminent teachers, is an artifice which has led Eusebius to force his texts, so that his claim about D. cannot be certain" (P. Nautin, "Dionysius of Alexandria," *Encyclopedia of the Early Church* [1992]: 238).

[54] G. F. Moore, *Judaism in the First Centuries of the Christian Era* (Cambridge, MA: Harvard UP, 1927), 1:257–258.

inspiration for the early Christian succession lists.[55] A second approach
turns the first on its head and suggests that the succession lists of early
Christianity served as a model for *Avot*.[56] A third approach imagines that
both the Rabbis and the Church Fathers were adapting an idea from their
shared Jewish heritage, whether the genealogy of the High Priest[57] or
Josephus' idea that religious traditions were guaranteed by the succession
of priests and prophets who transmitted the lore of the past. A fourth
approach minimizes the relevance of the Jewish setting for the creation of
the apostolic succession lists and argues instead that proto-orthodox
Christians acquired the doctrinal succession from the gnostics, who, in
turn, had modeled their chains of transmission on the Hellenistic school
traditions (though some suggest that the gnostics acquired this succession
from the proto-orthodox).[58] However, a critical flaw shared by all of these

---

[55] Perhaps Eusebius' claim that Hegesippus knew Jewish unwritten traditions
(*Historia Ecclesiastica* 4.22.8) may indicate that, in creating the first apostolic
succession list, Hegesippus was influenced by a second-century version of *Avot*. (For a
similar claim regarding Justin, see A. Le Boulluec, *La notion d'hérésie dans la
littérature grecque IIe–IIIe siècles* [Paris: Études augustiniennes, 1985], 1:84–91). This
is certainly a possibility, but the unwritten traditions Hegesippus supposedly knew were
not necessarily rabbinic oral traditions. W. Telfer maintains that Hegesippus was a
Greek-speaking Christian who encountered Jewish Christians whom he considered
orthodox, "and he discovered that they attributed their orthodoxy to the fact that down
to their dispersal, they had had a succession of *desposyni* (kinsmen of Christ) as heads
of their church for most of the time" ("Was Hegesipus a Jew?" *HTR* 53 [1960]: 149).
This is certainly a suggestive revisionist reading of Eusebius, but it is also highly
speculative.

[56] Boyarin entertains this possibility, though not too seriously. See Boyarin,
"Naturalizing the Border."

[57] In light of Eusebius' remark that Hegesippus was of Jewish descent, A. Ehrhardt
contends that Hegesippus was the conduit through which the Jewish genealogy of the
High Priest entered Christianity to become the model for Christian succession lists (*The
Apostolic Succession in the First Two Centuries of the Church* [London: Lutterworth,
1953], 63–66). However, Hegesippus' list is not a familial genealogy like the genealogy
of the High Priest. As far as other Jewish succession precedents are concerned, no pre-
rabbinic source presents a succession list or the concept of succession as found in *Avot*,
and there is no evidence that Josephus' or Eupolemus' exposition influenced the
creation of *Avot*'s chain of transmission (see n. 17 above).

[58] Campenhausen stresses what he believes are the gnostic origins for Hegesippus'
list and claims that it is most likely that the doctrinal succession would have first
appeared among a minority group such as gnostics (*Ecclesiastical Authority*, 159). A.
Hastings, however, argues that the doctrinal succession reflects an early Catholicism
that predates gnosticism ("150–250," in *A World History of Christianity*, ed. A.
Hastings [London: Cassell, 1999], 29). In contrast to these decisive positions, R.
Trevijano acknowledges the connection between gnostics and the doctrinal succession
but, since the evidence is late, states that "we cannot prove that the idea of doctrinal
transmission appeared first in the milieu of gnosis" ("Succession, Apostolic," 798). As I
will argue below (along the lines of A. Brent, "Diogenes Laertius and the Apostolic

approaches is their attempt to trace a unidirectional channel of influence (often through a specific individual) when the evidence is simply too sparse to support such robust hypotheses. In addition, J. Z. Smith cautions that in a careful comparative analysis, "the question is not 'which is first?', but rather, 'why both, at more or less the same time?'"[59] Therefore, perhaps one should abandon the attempt to draw a line of influence from one group to another, but focus instead on the broad historical setting, on the discursive space which all these communities shared.[60]

When comparing a rabbinic text with certain Christian texts, one risks forgetting that rabbinic Jews and proto-orthodox Christians were also participating in the broader cultural discourse of their times and that their discursive space was not necessarily occupied only by Jews and Christians. It is therefore worth stressing that the succession literary genre was well known throughout Hellenistic and Roman antiquity and that the classicizing tone of the Second Sophistic (of the early Common Era) apparently enhanced the importance of these lists for the historical reconstruction of an intellectual discipline. In other words, rather than speculating how one particular succession list (or one particular religious tradition's succession discourse) may have served as the origin for another, we should envision the wider role of Hellenistic succession lists as setting the stage for the creation of rabbinic, proto-orthodox Christian, and gnostic successions.

Having described the literary relationship between *Avot* and proto-orthodox apostolic successions, let us consider the extent to which the succession list functioned in a similar manner within the context of rabbinic Judaism and early Christianity. Since, as discussed above, the refutation of heresies and the bolstering of institutional authority against

---

Succession," *The Journal of Ecclesiastical History* 44 [1993]: 367–89), I think it is futile to attempt to discern a single immediate source for the succession list; instead, one should consider the broader cultural and discursive atmosphere of the period.

[59] J. Z. Smith, *Drudgery Divine: On the Comparison of Early Christianities and the Religions of Late Antiquity* (London: U. of London, 1990), 114.

[60] See P. Schäfer, *The Talmud Yerushalmi and Graeco-Roman Culture*, vol. 1 (Tübingen: Mohr Siebeck, 1998), 16, who quotes J. Culler, *The Pursuit of Sign: Semiotics, Literature, Deconstruction* (London: Routledge, 1981), 103. Consider also M. Goodman's comment (review of H. Shanks [ed.], *Christianity and Rabbinic Judaism: A Parallel History of their Origins and Early Development, JJS* 44 [1993]: 314): "The question is whether disparateness is necessary, since there are of course common themes which run through Jewish and Christian history in this period, not least attitudes to a shared text. But perhaps the best way to view Jews and Christians together would be a study of the world of Late Antiquity itself .... It can be argued that rabbinic Judaism and early Christianity are best understood not only on their own terms, as in this book, but also as part of the general religious change of Late Antiquity which accompanied the apogee and collapse of the Roman Empire."

schismatics were apparently the two primary functions of the apostolic succession, it is worth investigating the degree to which succession lists served these same functions in the rabbinic setting as well.

If we consider first whether *Avot* could have refuted the ideas of groups considered heretical by the Rabbis, it is clear that by legitimating one particular group, *Avot* (at least implicitly) rejected the claims of any and all other groups. Scholars have applied this reasoning to different stages in the history of the text, and they have suggested that an early version of *Avot* may have been used to combat Sadducees or other sectarians, and that the custom to read *Avot* on the afternoon of the Sabbath may have arisen in the Geonic period in order to counter the heretical claims of the Karaites. However, the question still remains as to how *Avot* functioned in the third-century Palestinian setting in which it was edited.

S. J. D. Cohen, taking a clear stance on the issue, argues that *Avot* functioned as an integral component of a polemic against heterodoxy in the same way that apostolic successions functioned in second-century Christian apologetics. Linking *Avot* to a group of rabbinic texts which parallel Christian arguments employed against heretics, Cohen suggests that "for both Rabbis and fathers the error of heresy is documented by its rejection of the true tradition, the unity, and the universal consensus of the catholic church/synagogue."[61] Though Cohen admits that "unlike the church fathers, the Rabbis were not faced by organized sects" (or, at least, they do not discuss them as organized), he maintains nonetheless that *Avot* and apostolic successions authenticated orthodoxy by appealing "to an accurate tradition deriving from the founder of the faith."[62]

In a related stance, D. Boyarin argues not only that *Avot* was designed as a rabbinic polemic, but that it helped create the discourse of heresiology by disenfranchising anyone not included in the rabbinic chain of transmission. Boyarin also links *Avot* to a number of other rabbinic sources and claims that, as a group, these texts comprise the rabbinic counterparts to the major elements in the emergence of catholic Christianity.

> Three major events constitutive for the ultimate emergence of catholic Christianity take place in the second century: the emergence of the discourse of heresiology, the notion of the rule of faith, and the invention of the idea of the apostolic succession. Three threads in the fabric of rabbinic history that also seem to be woven together in the late second century, as evidenced by the literary product of that period, the Mishna, parallel these: The invention of *minut*, the first Jewish term for "heresy," the promulgation of the Pharisaic

---

[61] Cohen, "A Virgin Defiled: Some Rabbinic and Christian Views on the Origins of Heresy," *Union Seminary Quarterly Review* 36 (1980): 5.

[62] Cohen, "A Virgin Defiled," 2–4.

*regula fidei* as well as practices for the exclusion of the *minim* from the House of Israel, and the publication of a list of "apostolic succession" for rabbinic Judaism, Tractate Avot.[63]

Thus, for Boyarin, *Avot* helped invent the discourse of rabbinic heresiology and laid the rhetorical groundwork for the eventual domination of rabbinic Judaism. However, Boyarin stresses that even though *Avot* is a central component in the invention of the discourse of rabbinic Jewish orthodoxy, this is not "to suggest that at that time it became hegemonic, any more than Justin's discourse of orthodoxy or even Irenaeus' became hegemonic in their time."[64]

In short, both Cohen and Boyarin believe that *Avot* is startlingly similar to the apostolic succession because both were designed to distinguish heresies and to combat them. However, these two scholars differ in respect to the significance which they assign to *Avot*'s supposed apology since each fits *Avot* into his own view of the evolution of rabbinic Judaism. For Cohen, the distinctive characteristic of early rabbinic Judaism is that the Rabbis had agreed to disagree and therefore "had no need for elaborate ecclesiological theories or precise creeds and rules of faith which would serve as touchstones to distinguish the true Jew from the heretic." Nonetheless, since certain seemingly polemical texts like *Avot* are present in rabbinic literature, Cohen suggests that these texts preserve relics from the Rabbis' sectarian past.[65] In contrast, Boyarin rejects the notion of an irenic tannaitic disposition and argues that the Rabbis' agreement to disagree is actually a feature of later amoraic Judaism. For Boyarin, the Tannaim believed in an exclusive rather than a pluralistic religion "in which rabbinic authority was produced through acts of exclusion not entirely dissimilar from the heresiology of contemporaneous Christianity."[66] Within this framework, Boyarin believes that *Avot* functioned as the rabbinic equivalent to the apostolic succession as used in the heresiological setting.

Although Cohen and Boyarin present a similar front, the technical features of their arguments as well as their overarching interpretations are quite different and therefore deserve to be evaluated independently. For Cohen, *Avot* is a polemical treatise because it belongs to a set of arguments found in rabbinic literature that parallel arguments which the early Church Fathers employed against heretics. However, Cohen uses

---

[63] Boyarin, "The Diadoche of the Rabbis," 13. From the single chapter of Prof. Boyarin's forthcoming book that I have had the privilege to read, it seems to me that the argument cited here will function as a prominent element therein.

[64] Boyarin, "Naturalizing the Border."

[65] Cohen, "A Virgin Defiled," 2–3.

[66] Boyarin, "A Tale of Two Synods: Nicaea, Yavneh, and Rabbinic Ecclesiology," *Exemplaria* 12 (2000): 46.

primarily late rabbinic material to develop this picture of the Rabbis and it is questionable if legends from sources such as *Avot de-Rabbi Nathan*, the Babylonian Talmud, and Midrash Tanhuma reflect the third-century Palestinian environment within which *Avot* was edited. Moreover, it is even more difficult to imagine that Cohen's selected rabbinic sources, including *Avot*, are merely vestiges of a sectarian past rather than active reflections of the rabbinic present. Nonetheless, Cohen's central point is well taken in that, by asserting that the Torah was transmitted to the Rabbis alone, *Avot* implies that the Rabbis alone held a monopoly on authentic religious tradition.

In contrast to Cohen, Boyarin reconstructs a rabbinic heresiology from the Mishnah alone and dates this rabbinic invention to roughly around the time that the Mishnah was edited. Accordingly, Boyarin does not conflate literary sources from different periods, nor does he claim to be able to specify which rabbinic statements preserve the relics of a long-past sectarian experience. Instead, Boyarin relates *Avot* to the period in which it was edited and claims that, just as the notion of apostolic succession "was a crucial invention for the promulgation of Christian orthodoxy, so I claim, it was for the development of rabbinic authority as well."[67]

From a literary or rhetorical point of view, Boyarin's interpretation of *Avot* and the comparison he draws to the creation of the discourse of heresiology in the Christian world are enlightening. Through his reading, *Avot* emerges as a central element in a matrix of tannaitic sources which invent a rhetoric of legitimation that will eventually justify a rabbinic monopoly over religious discourse in the Jewish world. If Boyarin has identified the existence of a potential rhetorical parallel in the function of *Avot* and apostolic successions, I would like to investigate the difference in this function in the rabbinic and the Christian settings. Though *Avot* may be interpreted as part of a heresiological discourse which prioritizes the Rabbis as sources of religious knowledge, I wonder if, in its original third-century context, *Avot* would have served as a polemical tool in the same way as did the apostolic successions of the writings of the apologists of the second and third centuries. In other words, to what extent may one apply the heresiological model derived from early Christianity to *Avot* and to the evolution of the rabbinic movement in the third century?[68]

---

[67] Boyarin, "Naturalizing the Border."

[68] Both Cohen and Boyarin qualify their comparison of the rabbinic context to that of the Christian heresiologists. Boyarin (as cited above) cautiously states that the acts of exclusion designed to justify rabbinic authority were not "entirely dissimilar" to the heresiological approach of the early Christians, while Cohen argues that the Rabbis had no need "for the anger and vitriol of the Christian heresiologists who catalogued the odious features of so many schisms and heresies" ("A Virgin Defiled," 3). Given this

According to the dominant and mainstream paradigm in scholarship on the early rabbinic period, rabbinic Judaism – certainly by the late second century – was a relatively confident movement which faced little serious opposition and therefore did not often engage in polemics. A rough caricature of this standard view may be portrayed as follows: the priests and Sadducees lost their power base with the destruction of Jerusalem; the Essenes were wiped out with the destruction of Qumran; Jewish Christians, gnostics, and other assorted heretical groups were marginal minorities; and the powerful Pharisees of the Second Temple period were transformed into the popular Rabbis of the rabbinic period. These Rabbis promoted (supposedly) traditional Jewish practices that did not depend on the existence of the Temple, and at Yavneh in the late first and early second centuries, they immediately ejected all non-rabbinic Jews from the fold.[69] Alternatively, S. J. D. Cohen has offered a highly influential argument which claims that the critical shift in the rabbinic period occurred when the Rabbis at Yavneh "agreed to disagree," and with this liberal stance essentially absorbed most significant dissenting groups.[70] In either view, however, the Rabbis quickly emerged as the most popular religious group in Palestine; the relatively little explicit evidence of polemic in rabbinic literature is thought to attest to their confident and virtually unrivaled position.[71] Without the need for a strident heresiology in the early third century, the Rabbis, according to these mainstream views, would have probably assigned far less value to the polemical function of *Avot* than their Christian contemporaries clearly assigned to apostolic successions.

However, there is a growing revisionist trend in scholarship today which questions the viability of this mainstream paradigm. It has been argued that Sadducees and Essenes may have continued to flourish during the tannaitic period,[72] that supposedly marginal groups may only appear as such because of the biases of rabbinic and Christian literature, and that

---

recognition that heresiology does not assume an identical role in rabbinic Judaism and in proto-orthodox Christianity, it is my intention to explore the nature of what I take to be a critical difference in the role of heresiology within these two contexts.

[69] For a summary of this position and references to various works which set it forth, see S. J. D. Cohen, "The Significance of Yavneh: Pharisees, Rabbis, and the End of Jewish Sectarianism," *Hebrew Union College Annual* 55 (1984): 28 n. 2.

[70] See Cohen, "Significance of Yavneh," 27–53.

[71] See, for example, S. G. Wilson, *Related Strangers: Jews and Christians 70–170 C.E.* (Minneapolis, MN: Fortress, 1995), 34–35, 170–172; S. Krauss, *The Jewish–Christian Controversy: From the Earliest Times to 1789*, vol. 1, *History* (rev. ed. W. Horbury; Tübingen: Mohr Siebeck, 1996), 7–11.

[72] See M. Goodman, "Sadducees and Essenes after 70 CE," in *Crossing the Boundaries: Essays in Biblical Interpretation in Honour of Michael D. Goulder*, ed. S. E. Porter, P. Joyce, and D. E. Orton (Leiden: Brill, 1994), 347–56.

the perception of the Tannaim as a popular group is also a product of the bias of rabbinic literature. In addition, scholars continue to identify more encoded dialogue with, and polemic against, non-rabbinic groups in rabbinic literature; this evidence is interpreted as reflecting a rabbinic community more engaged with competing religious groups, such as Christians.[73] According to this new paradigm, "it may be that what became rabbinic majority Judaism was at one time only one of many legitimate alternatives within Judaism,"[74] and therefore the possibility arises that the Rabbis may have defined themselves through a heresiological process much like their Christian contemporaries.

It has been suggested, however, that even proponents of this new paradigm must be very careful when applying the heresiological model of Christian self-definition to the rabbinic movement. Despite the possible existence of many alternative religious groups, and the likely existence of much encoded polemic in rabbinic literature, rabbinic literature still presents a picture strikingly different from the one presented in the writings of the early Christian heresiologists. As M. Goodman has argued, the term *"min"* (i.e. heretic) assumes a vague meaning in tannaitic literature without specifying any particular heresy, and the tannaitic reaction to heresy does not seem to have gone beyond "attempts by Rabbis to protect themselves from quasi-infection." These features of tannaitic Judaism, Goodman argues, contrast sharply with the history of early Christianity in which "theology and practice both developed to a large extent through polemic against deviants. St. Paul and heresiologists like Irenaeus advised their flocks on correct action and belief through highly effective rhetoric against specific heresies."[75] As a result,

---

[73] For discussions on one or more of these various issues (primarily in reference to Christianity), see A. Marmorstein, *Studies in Jewish Theology*, ed. J. Rabbinowitz and M. S. Lew (Oxford: Oxford UP, 1950), 198–220; L. Teugels, "The Background of the Anti-Christian Polemics in Aggadat Bereshit," *JSJ* 20:2 (1999): 178–208; D. Boyarin, *Dying for God: Martyrdom and the Making of Christianity and Judaism* (Stanford: Stanford UP, 1999), 8–18; C. E. Fonrobert, "The Didascalia Apostolorum: A Mishnah for the Disciples of Jesus," *JECS* 9:4 (2001): 484–87; I. J. Yuval, "Easter and Passover as Early Jewish–Christian Dialogue," in *Passover and Easter: Origin and History to Modern Times*, ed. P. F. Bradshaw and L. A. Hoffman (Notre Dame: U. of Notre Dame, 1999), 103–4. A critique of the mainstream view of the nature of the relationship between rabbinic Judaism and Christianity and a presentation of the new, revisionist view appear in I. J. Yuval, *Two Nations in Your Womb: Perceptions of Jews and Christians* (Tel Aviv: Am Oved, 2000), 40–45 [Hebrew].

[74] See P. Sigal, "Early Christian and Rabbinic Liturgical Affinities: Exploring Liturgical Acculturation," *NTS* 30 (1984): 64.

[75] M. Goodman, "The Function of Minim in Early Rabbinic Judaism," in *Geschichte – Tradition – Reflexion, Festschrift für Martin Hengel zum 70*, ed. M. Hengel, H. Cancik, H. Lichtenberger, and P. Schäfer (Tübingen: Mohr Siebeck, 1996), 506.

Goodman questions whether the same Christian modes of self-definition may be attributed to the Tannaim.[76]

If Goodman's exposition is convincing, however, the revisionists are faced with the question of why the rabbinic treatment of *minim* differs so greatly from the parallel treatment of the Christian heresiologists. It seems unlikely that the Tannaim hid their objections to other religious groups out of fear (as Jews may have in later periods[77]), because it does not seem likely that any of their potential competitors were particularly powerful at this point in time. Goodman himself suggests that the Rabbis thought that "the best way to deal with a potential problem is often simply to ignore it" and therefore just ignored heretics.[78] Alternatively, S. Stern has described rabbinic self-definition as self-referential, arguing that "the solipsistic and centripetal stance of Jewish identity is not necessarily a protective strategy against an external threat, but is related to the general ontology and *habitus* of Jewish (male and, particularly female) experience."[79] Yet even if one is convinced by Goodman's or Stern's interpretation, one may still wonder if there are any other historical conditions which may help to explain why the Rabbis, unlike their Christian contemporaries, did not "hound out of the fold particular deviants whose continued presence was believed to threaten the health of the body politic."[80]

I would like to suggest that the greater weight attributed to heresiology and polemics in the Christian context as compared to the tannaitic context may be, in no small part, a result of the differing social structures of the two movements. Whereas the early Church Fathers were religious leaders seeking to maintain their communities and to convert others, the sages of the tannaitic period flourished in disciple circles and were occupied with studying Torah.[81] If the institutionalized church may be viewed as the offensive force and heresiology as its rhetorical and defensive counterpart in the expansion of the proto-orthodox Christian community,[82] the

---

[76] Goodman, "Function of Minim," 506 n. 23.

[77] See Yuval, *Two Nations*, 41.

[78] See Goodman, "Function of Minim," 509.

[79] S. Stern, *Jewish Identity in Early Rabbinic Writings* (Leiden: Brill, 1994), 247.

[80] Goodman, "Function of Minim," 508.

[81] For a relatively recent study which explores in detail the nature of the social structure of the rabbinic movement, see C. Hezser, *The Social Structure of the Rabbinic Movement in Roman Palestine* (Tübingen: Mohr Siebeck, 1997).

[82] See W. Bauer, *Orthodoxy and Heresy in Earliest Christianity,* ed. R. A. Kraft and Gerhard Krodel (2nd English edition; Mifflintown, PA: Sigler Press, 1996), 231: "Rome confidently extends itself eastward, tries to break down resistance and stretches a helping hand to those who are like-minded, drawing everything within reach in to the well-knit structure of ecclesiastical organization. Heresy, with its different brands and peculiar configurations that scarcely even permitted it to be united in a loose

rabbinic movement, with its informal network of disciple circles, may not have felt the need to develop the heresiological counterpart to institutionalization. Thus, whereas early Christian heresiology was designed to bolster and spread proto-orthodox beliefs, tannaitic literature, intended for the sages and students of the relatively small and elite rabbinic gatherings, would have been preaching to the converted.

In short, I believe that both Cohen and Boyarin were correct to point out the connection between the polemical function of apostolic success-sions and *Avot* since, by its very nature, *Avot* legitimates the Rabbis at the expense of everyone else. However, I also believe that the heresiological function of the succession list was a far more prominent feature in the Christian context than in the rabbinic one. For the small groups of rabbinic disciple circles, there was no need to direct *Avot* against any specific heresy and thus, unlike Christian texts by writers such as Irenaeus, *Avot* does not explicitly inform the reader of any polemical purpose of the rabbinic succession list. Instead, perhaps the Rabbis employed *Avot* as they did the term *"min"* – as a general argument against all those whose ideas they considered unacceptable.

Turning now from the rejection of heresy to the bolstering of authority against schismatics, the literary reading of *Avot* presented above seems to indicate that that the treatise legitimates the authority of the Rabbis in general and of the patriarchate in particular. Moreover, in establishing the authority of the patriarchate, *Avot* apparently points to R. Judah ha-Nasi's Mishnah as the authentic compilation of tannaitic traditions. If this appraisal is accurate, then perhaps the role of the apostolic succession in Clement of Rome's and Cyprian's disputes with schismatics supplies an illuminating parallel to *Avot*. When in conflict with schismatics, Clement of Rome and Cyprian employed apostolic successions not to fight heretical doctrines but to justify the rights and rule of institutional leadership. In a similar manner, the first two chapters of *Avot* review the institutional succession of Jewish leadership in order to legitimate rabbinic and, more importantly, patriarchal leadership. This legitimation may have served to bolster the patriarch's reputation both within the rabbinic movement itself and, perhaps, Jewish society in general.

Beyond the issues of refuting heresies and combating schismatics, other features of Christian apostolic successions may be relevant to *Avot*. For example, Irenaeus' conception of a "deposit" passed down from generation to generation is not unlike the impression conveyed by *Avot*'s

---

association reflecting common purpose, had nothing corresponding to this by way of similar offensive and defensive force with which to counter .... The form of Christian belief and life which was successful was that supported by the strongest organization."

chain of transmission.[83] In addition, both Rabbis and Christians thought that this precious deposit was passed down through a scholastic succession. The scholastic dimension of *Avot*'s succession is highlighted in chapters three and four of the work, which seem to trace the history of the tannaitic "school."[84] In a similar vein, gnostics and Clement of Alexandria traced the transmission of the gnosis through teachers and, although his apostolic succession was comprised of church leaders, Irenaeus, too, was primarily interested in their role as the public teachers of the apostolic tradition. Thus, both Rabbis and early Christians adapted for their own purposes the scholastic dimension of the Hellenistic succession lists.

For Eusebius, the scholastic and institutional successions of Christianity were independent streams which intersected in the person of Dionysius of Alexandria; operating independently for hundreds of years, the successions eventually intertwined in a unique and incomparable figure of the third century CE. In a fascinating comparison, one finds a very similar intersection in *Avot*. As discussed above, R. Judah ha-Nasi was the penultimate member in the Gamalielite genealogy of chapters one and two, but he is also the penultimate sage mentioned in chapter four.[85] The appearance of a sage's name more than once in *Avot* is a rarity, so R. Judah ha-Nasi's double appearance is certainly striking. The very last sage in chapter four is Rabbi Eliezer ha-Kappar, who was probably chosen to close the chapter because his extended, poetic rumination on divine justice serves as a fitting conclusion. The final position in the work having been sacrificed for literary purposes, R. Judah ha-Nasi appears in the penultimate position of the implicit chain of transmission. In light of Eusebius' portrayal of Dionysius of Alexandria, perhaps R. Judah ha-Nasi's double appearance in *Avot* may be interpreted in a similar manner: R. Judah ha-Nasi's position in the institutional succession of chapters one and two establish that he was the rightful heir to the Jewish leadership while his position in the scholastic succession in chapters three and four validates his position in the rabbinic school. Thus, in a world without a functioning priesthood, R. Judah ha-Nasi was portrayed as the heir to the other two crowns: the crowns of Torah and kingship.[86]

---

[83] Whereas the Christian "deposit" referred to proper doctrine, the Rabbis transmitted Torah law.

[84] Interestingly, the generational schema of chapters three and four is comparable to Tertullian's focus on the succession of generations in the church.

[85] See *Avot* 4:20. Some witnesses record "R. Meir" rather than "Rabbi," but "Rabbi" dominates and appears in most superior manuscripts (such as MS Parma and MS Cambridge). In addition, J. N. Epstein (*Introduction to the Mishnaic Text* [Jerusalem: Magnes, 1948], 1203–4 [Hebrew]) explains that "Rabbi" was often changed to "Rabbi Meir."

[86] On the three crowns, see *Avot* 4:13.

## Conclusion

The similarity between *Avot* and Christian apostolic successions demands comparison, and this comparison in turn illuminates their difference. In the broadest sense, the literary genre employed within both religions to assert continuity with the past apparently inhabited the religious and intellectual discursive space of the contemporary Graeco-Roman culture. Implicitly, *Avot* may have functioned as a polemical treatise against all non-rabbinic groups, but I suspect that the heresiological role of the apostolic succession was more significant than any such role played by *Avot* in the early third century.

However, the role that episcopal successions played against threatening schismatics may indeed reflect a power struggle akin to the one implicit in *Avot*'s institutional succession. Both the patriarch and some early Christians employed an institutional succession in order to establish the religious and historical grounds upon which their authority could be justified. In a related vein, the intersection of an apostolic succession with the scholastic succession in Eusebius' presentation of Dionysius of Alexandria finds a suggestive rabbinic counterpart in *Avot*'s portrayal of R. Judah ha-Nasi. Thus the claim was made amongst both Tannaim and early Christians that a contemporary public figure embodied both the intellectual and the political traditions of the past.

# "Jewish Christianity" after the "Parting of the Ways"

## Approaches to Historiography and Self-Definition in the Pseudo-Clementines

by

ANNETTE YOSHIKO REED

What is "Jewish Christianity," and how do we know a "Jewish-Christian" text when we see one? Our answers to these questions tell us as much about our own assumptions concerning the definition, development, and interrelation of Judaism and Christianity as about the broad continuum of biblically-based approaches to belief and worship in Late Antiquity.

From our literary and archaeological evidence,[1] we know of a variety of texts and groups that cannot be readily categorized as either "Jewish" or "Christian" – at least not by a modern schema that treats the two as different by definition and uses rabbinic Judaism and Western Christian orthodoxy as the standards for judging "Jewishness" and "Christianness." For, contrary to our understanding of early Christian self-definition as inextricably tied to supersessionism, triumphalism, and antinomianism, some late antique authors and communities appear to have accepted Jesus as a special figure in salvation-history, without seeing this belief as inconsistent with Torah-observance and/or the continued validity of God's eternal covenant with the Jews.[2] And, contrary to the tendency to treat the Rabbis as the sole arbiters of halakha in late antique Judaism, some of these same individuals seem to have been no less preoccupied with matters such as dietary restrictions and ritual purification.[3]

---

[*] I am grateful to Adam H. Becker, John Gager, Martha Himmelfarb, Bob Kraft, Peter Schäfer, Dove C. Sussman, and the participants in the Princeton University workshop on "The Ways that Never Parted" for their helpful comments on this piece in its various incarnations.

[1] Most recently, the bulk of our evidence for post-apostolic "Jewish Christianity" has been surveyed in Simon Claude Mimouni's weighty volume *Le Judéo-christianisme ancien: Essais historiques* (Paris: Cerf, 1998); see esp. his treatment of non-literary sources on pp. 317–452. For the relevant patristic references, see A. F. J. Klijn and G. J. Reinink, *Patristic Evidence for Jewish-Christian Sects* (Leiden: Brill, 1973), 95–281.

[2] See below for examples from the Pseudo-Clementine literature.

[3] Note, for instance, the instructions in the Pseudo-Clementine *Homilies* 7.8 for Gentiles not only "to be baptized for the remission of sins," but also "to abstain from

Scholars most often use the label "Jewish Christian" (as opposed, for instance, to "Judaizing" Christian or simply "Christian") to designate ethnically Jewish and/or Torah-observant Christ-believers[4] – albeit with varying degrees of sensitivity to the problematic presupposition that the two categories are coterminous, as well as to the difficulties involved in defining "Christian."[5] For the purposes of the present volume, the vexed

*having the same scope or duration*

_____

the table of devils – that is, from food offered to idols – from dead carcasses, from animals that have been suffocated or caught by wild beasts, and from blood" and "not to live any longer impurely; to wash after intercourse; that the women on their part should keep the law of purification [i.e., after menstruation]." For other examples from the Pseudo-Clementine literature, see, e.g., *Epistula Petri* 4.1–2; *Recognitions* 2.71–72; 6.9–11; 7.29, 34; 8.68; *Homilies* 11:28–30; 13:4, 9, 19.

[4] A handy survey of scholarly attempts at definition can be found, together with analysis and recent bibliography, in J. Carleton Paget, "Jewish Christianity," in *The Cambridge History of Judaism*, vol. 3, *The Early Roman Period*, ed. William Horbury, W. D. Davies, and John Sturdy (Cambridge: Cambridge UP, 1999), 733–42. To summarize, "Jewish Christian" has been typically taken to mean: (1) a Christ-believing Jew (i.e., using the adjective "Jewish" primarily in an ethnic sense, although usually with a qualification to include Jews by conversion); (2) a person of any ethnicity who combined elements of Judaism and Christianity (most frequently with the former consisting of Torah-observance and the latter of belief in Jesus as the Messiah – "Jewish" in practice and "Christian" in belief – so as to distinguish this approach from the combinations thereof accepted as "orthodox" in the "Great Church"); and/or (3) a person who articulates his/her Christianity in Jewish cultural or literary forms (a category that encompasses Jean Daniélou's radically broad definition of "Jewish Christianity" as "l'expression de christianisme dans les formes du *Spätjudentum*" in *Théologie du Judéo-Christianisme* [Paris: Desclée & Cie, 1958], 19, but also more widespread views, such as the notion that to be "Jewishly" Christian is to have a low Christology). Most often, we find combinations and conflations of the three (esp. due to the often unquestioned assumption, in much research on the NT and early Christianity that only an ethnic Jew would voluntarily choose to keep the precepts of the Torah). Each of these three modes of definition, as Carleton Paget and others have shown, is methodologically problematic in its own way – not least because #1 is the only criteria that clearly distinguishes these "Jewish Christians" from Judaizers (esp. #2) or Christians in general (esp. #3).

[5] Accordingly, some recent scholars have eschewed the use of the term "Jewish Christianity," citing both its vagueness and its problematic use as a rubric under which to conflate of a broad variety of different groups, texts, and figures, primarily on the basis of our own inability to fit them into (our own) categories of "Jew" and "Christian"; see, e.g., Joan Taylor, "The Phenomenon of Early Jewish-Christianity: Reality or Scholarly Invention?" *VigChr* 44 [1990]: 313–34 and David Frankfurter in this volume. There is no doubt a problem in using this label to denote a cohesive movement or phenomenon, as made clear by the reception of Jean Daniélou's *Théologie du Judéo-Christianisme*, particular after its translation into English (*The Theology of Jewish Christianity* [trans. J. Baker; London: Darton, Longman, & Todd, 1964]); see esp. A. F. J. Klijn, "The Study of Jewish-Christianity," *NTS* (1973–74): 419–31; Robert A. Kraft, "In Search of 'Jewish Christianity' and its 'Theology': Problems of Definition and Methodology," *Recherches de Sciences Religieuse* 60 (1972): 81–96. Personally, I

question of definition proves less pressing than the fact that, by their very existence, these texts, groups, and figures complicate commonplace assumptions about Christianity's so-called "Parting of the Ways" from Judaism. Whether we speak of "Jewish Christianity" or "Jewish Christianities,"[6] distinguish the former from "Christian Judaism,"[7] or limit our discussions to specific groups like Nazarenes/Nazoraeans and Ebionites,[8] it remains that the sources traditionally studied under the rubric of "Jewish Christianity" shed doubt on any tidy narrative about an unavoidable, mutual, and final split between Christianity and Judaism in the first or second century CE.

The "Parting of the Ways" is typically depicted as an inexorable development from Jesus' revolutionary teachings, Paul's preaching of a law-free Gospel for the Gentiles, and/or the de-Judaization of the church's base of converts in the wake of the Jewish revolts against Rome. To these proposed catalysts for the purported "Parting," many add the alleged demise of "Jewish Christianity,"[9] opining that this movement lost

---

am not quite ready to jettison the term. I feel that it still holds some value, not least of all as a heuristic irritant; for, when read with some awareness of the scholarly debate about "Jewish Christianity," the term serves to disturb – literally by definition – any unquestioned assumptions that we might harbor about the essential incompatibility and inevitable "parting" of Judaism and Christianity, while also reminding us that we have yet to settle some basic definitional issues about "Judaism" and "Christianity" and that our scholarly categories (even the ones with ancient counterparts) are exactly that: categories shaped by our scholarly aims and modern experiences that we choose to impose, for better or worse, on our ancient evidence.

[6] See, e.g., Marcel Simon, *Verus Israel: A Study of the Relations between Christians and Jews in the Roman Empire, AD 135–425* (trans. H. McKeating; London: Littman Library of Jewish Civilization, 1996), 240; Burton Visotzky, "Prolegomenon to the Study of Jewish-Christianities in Rabbinic Literature" in *Fathers of the World: Essays in Rabbinic and Patristic Literatures* (Tübingen: Mohr Siebeck, 1995), 130.

[7] See, e.g., Bruce Malina, "Jewish Christianity or Christian Judaism: Toward a Hypothetical Definition," *JJS* 7 (1976): 46–50.

[8] This approach is admirably sensitive to the fact that the term "Jewish Christianity" is a wholly modern invention, whereas our ancient accounts speak of specific groups. Yet, the task of reconstruction proves difficult, due to the tendentious, muddled, and inconsistent nature of our second-hand testimonies to these groups (i.e., writings of Christian heresiologists), from which it proves difficult to draw any concrete conclusions; see discussion in Klijn and Reinink, *Patristic Evidence*, 67ff.

[9] Interestingly, this is especially the case in accounts of the "Parting of the Ways" as approached from the Jewish perspective. See, e.g., Gedalia Alon's chapter on this theme – aptly entitled: "Jewish Christians: The Parting of the Ways" – in *The Jews in their Land in the Talmudic Age, 70–640 C.E.* (trans. G. Levi; Jerusalem: Magnes, 1980–1984), 288–307; Lawrence Schiffman, "At the Crossroads: Tannaitic Perspectives on the Jewish–Christian Schism," in *Jewish and Christian Self-Definition*, vol. 2, *Aspects of Judaism in the Graeco-Roman Period*, ed. E. P. Sanders (Philadelphia: Fortress, 1981), 156; P. S. Alexander, "'The Parting of the Ways' from the Perspective of

its single stronghold either during the first Jewish Revolt (66–70 CE), when members of the Jerusalem Church reportedly fled to Pella,[10] or after the Bar Kokhba Revolt (132–35 CE), when a defeated Jewish Jerusalem became a pagan city closed to all Jews.[11] Some go on to speculate that the "Jewish-Christian" message was simply rendered obsolete with the establishment of the mutual exclusivity of Christ-belief and Judaism, as allegedly proclaimed from both sides (i.e., by proto-orthodox Christians and early rabbinic Sages, each of whom are presumed to speak for all of their respective co-religionists).[12] Others go even further, suggesting that, by the close of the first century, "Jewish Christianity" had already ceased to be a viable and vital religious option that could compete with the rabbinic movement for Jewish adherents or, for Gentile converts, with the law-free forms of Christianity proclaimed in the name of Paul.[13]

Our extant evidence for so-called "Jewish Christianity," however, frustrates scholarly attempts to tell the story of Christian origins as simply a tale of the inevitable separation of Christianity (in all its varieties) from its theological, social, and cultural ties to Judaism (both

Rabbinic Judaism," in *Jews and Christians: The Parting of the Ways, A.D. 70 to 135*, ed. J. Dunn (Grand Rapids: Eerdmans, 1992), 3, 20–24.

[10] The notion of a flight to Pella is based on Eusebius, *HE*, 3.5.3; Epiphanius, *Pan.* 1.29.7–30.7; *Mens.* 15. Although this tradition has long been a mainstay of scholarly reconstructions of the history of "Jewish Christianity," some scholars question its historicity; e.g., Gerd Lüdemann, "The Successors of Pre-70 Jerusalem Christianity: A Critical Evaluation of the Pella Tradition," in *Jewish and Christian Self-Definition*, vol. 1, *The Shaping of Christianity in the Second and Third Centuries*, ed. E. P. Sanders (Philadelphia: Fortress, 1980), 161–73, idem, *Opposition to Paul in Jewish Christianity* (Minneapolis: Fortress, 1989), 200–12; J. Verheyden, "The Flight of Christians to Pella," *Ephemerides theologicae lovanienses* 66 (1990): 368–84; Taylor, "Phenomenon," 315–16; Johannes Munck, "Jewish Christianity in Post-Apostolic Times," *NTS* 6 (1959): 103–4. Cf. Marcel Simon, "La migration à Pella: Légende ou réalité?" *Recherches de science religieuse* 60 (1972): 37–54; J. Wehnert, "Die Auswanderung der Jerusalemer Christen nach Pella – historische Faktum oder theologische Konstruktion?" *Zeitschrift für Kirchengeschichte* 102 (1991): 321–55; Carleton Paget, "Jewish Christianity," 746–48.

[11] So Schiffman, "At the Crossroads," 155–56.

[12] See, e.g., Carleton Paget, "Jewish Christianity," 750. Here, when concluding his summary of our evidence for "Jewish Christianity" (see pp. 742–50), J. Carleton Paget admits that "we know little about the historic fate of Jewish Christianity," notes that proto-orthodox/orthodox Christian heresiological comments are "not, of course, proof positive that they were perceived in such a way [i.e., as 'heretics'] everywhere," and even allows for the possibility that groups like the Nazarenes "might in certain quarters have been regarded as orthodox [i.e., orthodox Christians] even up to the middle of the fourth century." It is thus particularly striking that he goes on to assert: "What is clear is that, excluded from both Church and synagogue ... it [i.e., Jewish Christianity] declined dramatically" – and, moreover, associates this decline with "the late second century onwards" (or, as he further specifies on p. 752: "by the 160s").

[13] E.g., Simon, *Verus Israel*, 268–69.

without and within). Following the "Parting" model, for instance, one would expect a proto-orthodox Christian like Justin Martyr – who wrote so soon after the Bar Kokhba Revolt and who so strenuously argued the church's supersession of the "old" Israel – to denounce those who retained Jewish observance alongside a belief in Christ, as part of his own construction of a Christianity in radical distinction from Judaism. Justin, however, readily embraces such individuals as authentic Christians (*Dial.* 47).[14] However tempting it is to imagine that early Christian polemics against Judaism were accompanied by equally strident efforts to purge the church of "Jewish Christianity," our sources make clear that the situation was not so simple.[15]

Modern theories about the early split between Christianity and Judaism might also lead us to imagine that our evidence for "Jewish-Christian" groups should be strongest for the first two centuries of Christianity and then progressively peter off, as Christ-believing Jews were replaced by new Gentile converts to an increasingly dominant orthodoxy and as "living" forms of Judaism were allegedly rendered irrelevant for the Christians of all stripes. This, indeed, is the story told by most historians.[16] It remains the case, however, that much of our extant data about "Jewish Christians" – both firsthand and secondhand – comes from the third, fourth, and fifth centuries CE.[17]

---

[14] Notably, Justin here expresses concern that some Christ-believing Jews wish to convert Gentiles to a Torah-observant Christianity.

[15] Indeed, in the second and third centuries CE, it seems that Marcion's complete rejection of Christianity's Jewish heritage was perceived as much more of a threat by proto-orthodox Christian authors than so-called "Jewish Christians"; see e.g., Justin, *1 Apol.* 26.5–8; 58.1; *Dial.* 38.6 (also Irenaeus, *AH* 4.6.9, on Justin's no longer extant treatise against Marcion); Irenaeus, *AH* 1.1.2–4, 3, 23, 30.9; 3.3.4, 4.3, 11.2; 4.8–13, 29–34; Tertullian, *Adv. Marc.*

[16] Not surprisingly, the classical formulation of this perspective can be found in Adolf von Harnack's influential works (see, e.g., *The Mission and Expansion of Christianity in the First Three Centuries* [Gloucester: P. Smith, 1972], 44–72). For a summary of the history of scholarship on "Jewish Christianity," see, e.g., Carleton Paget, "Jewish Christianity," 731–75; Klijn, "Study," 419–26; Simon Claude Mimouni, "Le Judéo-Christianisme ancien dans l'historiographie du XIXème et du XXème siècle," *Revue des Etudes Juives* 151 (1992): 419–28; Gerd Lüdemann, *Opposition to Paul in Jewish Christianity* (trans. E. Boring; Minneapolis: Fortress, 1989), 1–34.

[17] From even a glance at the collection of Klijn and Reinink (*Patristic Evidence*), it is clear that our secondhand data cluster in these centuries. It is notable that the first author to mention the Nazoraeans/Nazarenes is Epiphanius (*Pan.* 29); it is no less striking that authors of his time seem far more preoccupied with the Ebionites than their heresiological predecessors (note, e.g., Irenaeus' very brief comments about this group [*AH* 1.26.2; 3.11.7, 21.1; 4.33.4; 5.1.3], in contrast to his copious comments about Marcionites, Valentinians, etc.). Moreover, the *Didaskalia Apostolorum* appears to date from the third century, whereas the Pseudo-Clementine *Homilies* and *Recognitions* are both from the fourth (see discussion below).

This makes it especially ironic that regnant assumptions about the "Parting of the Ways" are perhaps nowhere more evident than in research on "Jewish Christianity." Most striking is the contrast between scholarly approaches to "Jewish-Christian" tendencies in the NT literature and approaches to post-apostolic evidence exhibiting the same tendencies.[18] When dealing with the pre-"Parting" period, scholars (now, at least) see "Jewish-Christian" characteristics as authentic, widespread, and even normative, viewing them as important evidence for the Jewish heritage of the church and the vibrant diversity of the earliest Christ-believing communities. After the second century CE, however, "Jewish Christianity" becomes a problem for the church historian: a phenomenon

---

The three "Jewish-Christian gospels" that scholars have reconstructed from comments of proto-orthodox/orthodox Christian authors – the so-called *Gospel of the Nazoraeans*, *Gospel of the Ebionites*, and *Gospel of the Hebrews* – are all commonly dated to the first half of the second century (so Philip Vielhauer and Georg Strecker, "Jewish-Christian Gospels," in *NTA* 1:134–78, esp. 159, 169, 176). But, as with the evidence for these gospels in general, their early dating is based on a very particular reading of a set of data that admits multiple explanations and enables very little certainty (as clear from the summary in Vielhauer and Strecker, "Jewish-Christian Gospels," 1:136–151). For instance, the second-century dating of the *Gospel of the Ebionites* is based on the statements of Irenaeus (ca. 180 CE) about the Ebionites' use of a Hebrew version of the Gospel of Matthew redacted to fit their own beliefs (*AH* 1.26.2; 3.11.7, 21.1; 5.1.3). Arguments about a similarly early date for the *Gospel of the Nazoraeans* and the *Gospel of the Hebrews* are based on Eusebius' statement that Hegesippus (ca. 180) must be a convert from Judaism since "he quotes from both the Gospel according to the Hebrews and the Syriac" (*HE* 4.22.8). In light of the widespread traditions about Matthew composing his gospel in Hebrew and the early Christian application of the label "Gospel of/according to the Hebrews" to a broad variety of works – including the Gospel of Matthew itself (Epiphanius, *Haer.*, 30.3.7) and Tatian's *Diatesseron* (Epiphanius, *Haer.* 46.1) – none of these arguments prove terribly persuasive, particularly if we follow Klijn, Reinink, and others in questioning the overconfidence with which some scholars reconstruct the beliefs and practices of the Ebionites and the Nazoraeans/Nazorenes from our heresiological witnesses (see *Patristic Evidence*, esp. 67ff). Rather, what is striking about the secondhand evidence adduced by Vielhauer and Strecker is that so many Christian authors in the centuries following the so-called "Parting of the Ways" (i.e., especially the fourth and fifth centuries, but even well into the Middle Ages) seem to know of gospels written in Hebrew or Hebrew letters (i.e., Hebrew or Aramaic), gospels circulated among "the Jews," and gospels that generally strike them as τὸ Ἰουδαϊκόν.

[18] This is perhaps most clear in the work of Jean Daniélou. As mentioned above, Daniélou offers a very broad definition of "Jewish Christianity." Nevertheless, he still remains firm in limiting this phenomenon to the period before mid-second century CE. Afterwards, in his view, there could only be "secondary contributions, Jewish traditions incorporated into a whole that was no longer Jewish" (*Theology*, 8–10). Hence, he treats the evidence for later attempts to combine Jewish and Christian elements under the title "Heterodox Jewish Christianity," and he deems these efforts significant only insofar as they "preserve certain elements which they had in common with Jewish Christianity (i.e. the earlier, orthodox variety)" (p. 55).

in need of explanation, whose spread and influence can ideally be limited to a narrow geographical scope or constrained into tiny "heretical" sects huddled on the periphery of the "Great Church."[19]

Underlying most modern studies of "Jewish Christianity" after the "Parting of the Ways," one can thus sense a striking sense of disbelief at the possibility that, after the second century CE, anyone might be attracted to varieties of Christianity that still "clung" to Jewish observance – let alone the possibility that there could be varieties of Judaism that granted some special role to Jesus.[20] Even Marcel Simon (who so incisively critiqued the tendency to see "Jewish Christianity" as "an aberrant manifestation of early Christianity" and who stressed the diversity of "Jewish-Christian" groups and the diversity of the Judaism from which they drew) described late antique "Jewish Christianity" as a "fossilized form of Christianity," a stunted "survival" left in the wake of the decisive evolution of the church away from its Jewish origins.[21] The implications are striking: Christianity's early "Parting" from Judaism was allegedly so decisive as to transform certain normative variations in biblically-based belief and practice into bizarre anachronisms, at best, and pernicious heresies, at worst. In other words, the narratives told in modern research echo proto-orthodox/orthodox Christian historiography in asserting that "Jewish-Christian" forms of belief and worship should have never survived – let alone thrived – long beyond the apostolic age. Accordingly, scholars largely follow the lead of the heresiologists, by minimizing, marginalizing, and explaining away the evidence to the contrary.

---

[19] On the traditional tendency to insist upon the limited regional scope of "Jewish-Christian" tendencies and their complete lack of influence on orthodox Christianity, see Klijn, "Study," esp. 421–25. Here too we can discern the influence of Harnack, who accepted the existence of a variety of "Jewish-Christian" groups in both the apostolic and post-apostolic periods, but stridently emphasized that they had no impact on the "Great Church" (see, e.g., *Lehrbuch der Dogmengeschichte* [Tübingen: Mohr, 1909; repr. Darmstadt, 1965], 317).

[20] It should be noted that "Jewish Christianity" has usually been studied as a variety of Christianity, rather than a variety of Judaism; an important exception is Charlotte Fonrobert, "The *Didascalia Apostolorum*: A Mishnah for the Disciples of Jesus," *JECS* 9 [2001]: 483–509. See further Visotzky, "Prolegomenon," 129–49, and recent studies of rabbinic traditions about *minim* ("heretics" or "sectarians" – a category that sometimes includes "Jewish Christians"), particularly: Daniel Boyarin, "A Tale of Two Synods: Nicaea, Yavneh, and Rabbinic Ecclesiology," *Exemplaria* 12 (2000): 55–60; idem, "Justin Martyr Invents Judaism," *Church History* 70 (2001): 438–49; Boyarin's much anticipated forthcoming book, *Border Lines: The Invention of Heresy and the Emergence of Christianity and Judaism* (Stanford: Stanford UP, 2004); also Richard Kalmin, "Christians and Heretics in Rabbinic Literature of Late Antiquity," *HTR* 87 (1994): 155–69, esp. 163–65.

[21] Simon, *Verus Israel*, 238–44.

Insofar as the "Problem of Jewish Christianity" resonates with very basic questions about how assumptions about religious identity shape the modern categorization of ancient groups (as well as the scholarly reconstruction of the relationships between them), this issue proves particularly relevant for our present efforts to explore the value of approaching Judaism and Christianity as "Ways that Never Parted." Towards this goal, I will here focus on the Pseudo-Clementine *Homilies* and *Recognitions*, two fourth-century texts widely recognized as our most important and extensive sources for reconstructing a first-hand account of "Jewish Christianity."[22] I will begin by considering how assumptions about the "Parting of the Ways" have shaped modern scholarship on the Pseudo-Clementines. Then, I will turn to examine three selections from the *Homilies* and *Recognitions* (R 1.27–71; 4–6; H 8–11), attempting to elucidate the self-understanding of their final authors/redactors. Finally, I will try to locate these texts in their late antique context, offering some tentative suggestions about their broader significance for our under-standing of the history of Jewish–Christian relations more broadly.

Due to the complex literary-history of the Pseudo-Clementines, this inquiry will raise more questions that it can answer. Nevertheless, I here hope to highlight the diversity of viewpoints that the modern category of "Jewish Christianity" conflates, by drawing attention to the range of perspectives expressed and preserved, even within a single corpus. In the process, I hope to show the special value of so-called "Jewish-Christian" sources – and the Pseudo-Clementines in particular – for a fresh approach to the relationship between Judaism and Christianity in Late Antiquity, pursued apart from traditional assumptions about their allegedly "parted ways." New approaches, I will argue, are nowhere more needed than in the study of late antique "Jewish Christianity," due to the dissonance between our ancient evidence and the modern frameworks used to interpret it. And, for precisely this reason, the sources studied under the rubric of "Jewish Christianity" may provide particularly heuristic foci for forging and testing fresh approaches to the interactions between Jews and Christians – and the continuing ambiguities in "Jewish" and "Christian" identities – in the multiple geographical, social, intellectual, and political worlds of Late Antiquity.[23]

---

[22] For an extensive, accessible, and generally invaluable survey of the scholarship on this literature, see F. Stanley Jones, "The Pseudo-Clementines: A History of Research," *Second Century* 2 (1982): 1–33, 63–96.

[23] This potential is tapped, to brilliant effect, by Fonrobert in her article "*Didascalia Apostolorum*" (see esp. her comments on pp. 484–87, 508–9). As Fonrobert rightly stresses, "Our understanding of the formation of Jewish and Christian collective identities as separate identities depends on developing an intelligible way of discussing the phenomenon called 'Jewish Christianity,' one that is not marred by Christian

# The "Parting of the Ways" and the History of Scholarship on the Pseudo-Clementine Literature

In form, the *Homilies* (henceforth H) and *Recognitions* (henceforth R) are composite texts that integrate ample material from earlier sources. Insofar as H and R share the same basic structure and contain many parallels, most scholars accept that they rework the same Basic Source (henceforth B), which most scholars date to the early third century CE.[24] The earlier of the two appears to be H (ca. 300–320 CE), for which the original Greek is still extant.[25] R is commonly dated to the middle of the fourth century, but it only survives in full in Rufinus' Latin translation (ca. 406 CE).[26] The Syriac version of the Pseudo-Clementines integrates selections from both H and R (i.e., R 1–4.1.4; H 10–14) and is extant in a manuscript from 411 CE.[27] In addition, we have later epitomes of H and/or R in Greek, Arabic, Georgian, and Armenian, as well as fragments in Slavonic and Ethiopic.[28]

Both H and R legitimize their teachings by means of an overarching narrative about the conversion and early career of Clement of Rome. In both, exhortations and instructions are attributed to Clement's distinguished mentor, the apostle Peter. Among these are statements emphasizing the importance of Moses, the Torah, and halakhic observance (especially ritual purity and dietary laws), asserting the

---

theological prejudices, nor by unexamined assumptions about either 'Jewish' identity formation or its 'Christian' counterpart" (p. 484).

[24] See further Jones, "Pseudo-Clementines," 8–14. This source is generally dated to before 220 CE, due to its apparent dependence on Bardaisan's *On Fate*.

[25] For the text of H: Bernhard Rehm, *Die Pseudoklementinen*, vol. I: *Homilien* (GCS 42; Berlin: Akademie-Verlag, 1969), on which all citations in this article are based. The edition is prefaced with a discussion of H's date and provenance, the relationship between the two extant Greek MSS ("P" and "O") and the two Greek Epitomes ("e" and "E"), and its text-history (pp. vii–xxiii).

[26] For the text of R: Bernhard Rehm, *Die Pseudoklementinen*, vol. 2, *Rekognitionen in Rufinus Übersetzung* (GCS 51; Berlin: Akademie-Verlag, 1969), on which all citations in this article are based. Notably, R is extant in a greater number of MSS than is H (i.e., over a hundred, dating from the fifth to fifteenth centuries; see pp. xvii–xcv, cix–cxi).

[27] I.e., British Museum add. 12150. For the Syriac of this and a later MS, together with reconstructed Greek, see Wilhelm Frankenberg, *Die syrischen Clementinen mit griechishem Paralleltext: Eine Vorarbeit zu dem literargeschichtlichen Problem der Sammlung* (TU 48.3; Leipzig: J. C. Henrichs, 1937). It is notable that the selections from R 1–4 in this version seem to come from a different translator than the selections from H 10–14 (pp. viii–ix). On the importance of this understudied version for our knowledge about the Greek *Vorlage* of Rufinus' Latin R, see Jones, *Ancient Jewish Christian Source*, 39–49.

[28] See Jones, "Pseudo-Clementines," 6–7, 80–84, and references there.

continued chosenness of the Jews, and depicting the Mosaic Torah and the teachings of Jesus as equal sources of salvific knowledge.[29] In addition, H and R appeal to the authority of this apostle to promote an account of early church history that counters the epistles of Paul and the Book of Acts.[30] Most notably, they exalt James and Peter as the true guardians of Jesus' message and the authentic leaders of the apostolic community, while condemning Paul and the law-free mission associated with him.[31]

Although the literary-history of the Pseudo-Clementines is notoriously complex, almost all scholars thus acknowledge that some "Jewish-Christian," or specifically Ebionite, strata are imbricated therein.[32] Different scholars, however, have identified these strata and have reconstructed their sources (and the sources for their sources) in different ways,[33] depending in large part on their assumptions about the development of Judaism, Christianity, and "Jewish Christianity" after the "Parting of the Ways." In judging the "Jewish Christianity" of the Pseudo-Clementines and reconstructing the "Jewish-Christian" stages in their redaction-history, most scholars have imposed external criteria upon H and R either from (1) heresiological comments about the Ebionites (especially Epiphanius, *Pan.* 30)[34] or (2) scholarly reconstructions of the history of "Jewish Christianity," such as the theory that late antique "Jewish-Christian" groups are remnants of the Jerusalem Church which, after the flight to Pella, regrouped into small sects in Syria and Palestine.[35]

---

[29] See discussion below.

[30] This is most obvious in the *Epistula Petri*, now affixed to H, in which Peter purportedly writes to James to complain against those who "pervert my words by various interpretations, as though I taught the abolition of the Law" (2.4; cf. Acts 11:4–17; Gal 2). R 1.27–71 is also notable in that its literary relationship to Acts has been established and explored by F. Stanley Jones in "An Ancient Jewish Christian Rejoinder to Luke's Acts of the Apostles: Pseudo-Clementine Recognitions 1.27–71" in *Semeia 80: The Apocryphal Acts of the Apostles in Intertextual Perspectives* (ed. R. Stoops; Atlanta: Scholars Press, 1990), esp. 239–44.

[31] See Lüdemann, *Opposition to Paul*, 171–94.

[32] For the history of scholarship on this issue, see Georg Strecker, *Das Judenchristentum in den Pseudoklementinen* (TU 70[2]; Berlin: Akademie-Verlag, 1981), 1–34; Jones, "Pseudo-Clementines," 84–96. On the Pseudo-Clementines and the Ebionites, see esp. Hans Joachim Schoeps, *Theologie und Geschichte des Judenchristentums* (Tübingen: Mohr, 1949) and the revised English version of this work, *Jewish Christianity: Factional Disputes in the Early Church* (trans. D. Hare; Philadelphia: Fortress, 1969).

[33] See discussion in Jones, "Pseudo-Clementines," 84–96

[34] For a survey of the other patristic evidence concerning the Ebionites, see Klijn and Reinink, *Patristic Evidence,* 19–43.

[35] See, e.g., Schoeps, *Jewish Christianity,* 18–37. See n. 11 above .

The former has led some scholars to follow the heresiologists in determining the "Jewish Christianity" of different strata primarily on the basis of doctrinal issues, such a christology,[36] and perhaps to overstate the importance of Epiphanius' comments about the Ebionites for our understanding of the Pseudo-Clementine literature (and "Jewish Christianity" in general).[37] The latter helps to explain the inordinate amount of attention given to the material about James, Peter, Paul, and the primitive church in scholarship on H and R.[38] Although this research has proved invaluable for supplementing (and interrogating) the canonical depiction of the apostolic age found in Acts, it has often been pursued with the assumption that the scholarly value and religious authenticity of the "Jewish-Christian" material in H and R stands contingent on proof for its continuity with a form of Christianity that existed prior to the "Parting of the Ways."

In a sense, the influence of Ferdinand Christian Baur still looms large. Baur first brought the Pseudo-Clementines to prominence as a neglected source for the conflicts of the apostolic age. Not coincidentally, he was also largely responsible for formulating and popularizing the concept of "Jewish Christianity" as we now know it.[39] Baur's reconstruction of apostolic history revolved around the dichotomy between the "Jewish Christianity" of James, Peter, and the Jerusalem Church, and the "Gentile Christianity" of Paul and the Diaspora communities that he founded.[40] His interests in recovering the former led him to draw attention to later heresiological comments about "Jewish Christian" groups, but also to H and R. Just as he traced a straight trajectory of (d)evolution from the Jerusalem Church to the Ebionites mentioned by Irenaeus and Epiphanius, so he posited that H and R were second-century texts, which preserve precious remnants of the "Jewish Christianity" that was soon

---

[36] So Schoeps, *Jewish Christianity,* 59–73.

[37] See discussion in F. Stanley Jones, *An Ancient Jewish Christian Source on the History of Christianity: Pseudo–Clementine Recognitions 1.27–71* (Atlanta: Scholars Press, 1995), 35–37. Although the attempt to correlate the literary-history of the Pseudo-Clementines with Epiphanius' description of the Ebionites has dominated both source-critical and textual scholarship on this corpus, the result has been an almost total lack of unanimity.

[38] See, e.g., Schoeps, *Jewish Christianity,* 38–58; Robert E. Van Voorst, *The Ascents of James: History and Theology of a Jewish-Christian Community* (SBL Dissertation Series 112; Atlanta: Scholars Press, 1989).

[39] Although the term was used prior to Baur, he is widely credited as the father of the modern study of "Jewish Christianity" (see, e.g., S. K. Riegel, "Jewish Christianity: Definitions and Terminology," *NTS* 24 (1978): 411; Mimouni, *Judéo-christianisme ancien,* 419; Klijn, "Study," 419; Carleton Paget, "Jewish Christianity," 731).

[40] See esp. F. C. Baur, "Die Christuspartei in der korinthischen Gemeide, der Gegensatz des petrinischen and paulischen Christentums in der alten Kirche, der Apostel Petrus in Rom," *Tübinger Zeitschrift für Theologie* 5 (1831): 61–206.

doomed to be usurped by the "Gentile Christianity" at the heart of the "Great Church."[41]

In short, the modern study of the Pseudo-Clementine literature and the very concept of "Jewish Christianity" emerged hand-in-hand on the scholarly scene and were, moreover, products of discussions about early apostolic history. Now, over a century later, it seems almost superfluous to speak of "Jewish Christianity" in the first century CE, and it seems strange to limit "Jewishness" to only one group or stream of the Jesus Movement: in Helmut Koester's words, "[E]veryone in the first generation of Christianity was Jewish-Christian."[42] Furthermore, scholars have since sought to move beyond Baur's simple dichotomy between "Jewish Christianity" and "Gentile Christianity," turning instead to recover from the NT literature a range of attitudes towards the Torah and Jewish chosenness, as espoused by multiple groups of Christ-believing Jews and their Gentile converts.[43] As a result, some scholars now reserve the label "Jewish-Christian" only for texts and groups in the post-apostolic period, when Christianity had purportedly "parted" from Judaism, thus becoming non-Jewish enough in orientation and self-definition that the designation actually proves meaningful.[44]

Although H and R are now known to date from this later period, scholarship on the Pseudo-Clementine literature still operates largely within the parameters set by Baur back in the 1830s. Most notably, it is still widely assumed that the "Jewish Christian" material in H and R is only worthy of study insofar as it can tell us something about the primitive church.[45] Indeed, it is perhaps not coincidental that, after scholars such as Charles Biggs and Hans Waitz demonstrated the fourth-century dates of both H and R,[46] research on these texts has been

---

[41] Baur, "Die Christuspartei in der korinthischen Gemeide," 114–17.

[42] Helmut Koester, "ΓΝΩΜΑΙ ΔΙΑΦΟΡΟΙ: The Origin and Nature of Diversification in the History of the Early Church," *HTR* 53 (1965): 380.

[43] See esp. Raymond Brown, "Not Jewish Christianity and Gentile Christianity but Types of Jewish/Gentile Christianity," *CBQ* 45 (1983): 74–79.

[44] Mimouni, for instance, reserves the term "Jewish Christian" for groups after 135 CE (*Judéo-christianisme ancien*, 475–93).

[45] Jones describes two tendencies in scholarship on the "Jewish Christianity" of the Pseudo-Clementines: "(1) the tendency to maintain Baur's evaluation by dating the Jewish Christian element early in the literary history of PsCl and by emphasizing the importance of Jewish Christianity for the history of the church and (2) the tendency to refute Baur's evaluation of the PsCl either by denying the Jewish Christian element in the PsCl or by relativizing its importance through the assignment of a late date to the Jewish Christian influence or through denial of the seriousness of this influence" ("Pseudo-Clementines," 86).

[46] The fourth-century dating, which is now commonly accepted, was argued by Charles Biggs on the basis of H's apparent familiarity with the Arian controversy and the occurrence of certain Syriac words therein ("The Clementine Homilies," in *Studia*

dominated by source-critical inquiries. Rather than studying H and R for their own sake, scholars have focused their efforts on reconstructing the early sources that may lie *behind* their (also non-extant) source B.[47] In effect, those who take seriously the "Jewish Christianity" of H and R still search, like Baur, for second-century heirs to the Jerusalem Church of James and Peter.

Accordingly, critics of this approach, who deny any continuity between the Pseudo-Clementines and apostolic "Jewish Christianity," tend either to downplay these texts' "Jewish-Christian" elements or to dismiss them as late, "heretical"/"heterodox" accretions that prove largely irrelevant to our understanding of this literature and the late antique church more broadly.[48] In both cases, the scholarly approach to the "Jewish Christianity" of the Pseudo-Clementine literature has been inextricably shaped by the broader tendency to treat the post-70/post-135 survival of "Jewish Christianity" as merely a footnote to a narrative about early Christian history in which its alleged demise functions as a necessary contrast to the triumphant rise of "Gentile Christianity" and as a necessary corollary to the "Parting of the Ways" with Judaism.

*Consequence drawn from a true proposition*

---

*biblica et ecclesiastica*, vol. 2 [Oxford: Clarendon, 1890], 191–92, 368–69). On R, see Hans Waitz, *Die Pseudoklementinen: Homilien und Rekognitionem: Eine quellen-kritische Untersuchung* (TU 10.4; Leipzig: J. C. Hinrichs, 1904), 372.

[47] Proposed sources of B include: a *Kerygma Petrou* or *Kerygmata Petrou* related to the text of that name quoted by Heracleon; a *Praxeis Petrou* somehow related to the extant Acts of Peter; a version of *Anabathmoi Jakobou* related to the text mentioned by Epiphanius in *Haer.* 3.16; and Bardaisan's *Book of the Laws of the Countries* (esp. R 9.19–29). In this endeavor, modern scholarship on the Pseudo-Clementines has been inextricably shaped by the foundational work of Georg Strecker (see further Jones, "Pseudo-Clementines," 14–33, and idem, *Ancient Jewish-Christian Source*, 20–36). Some recent scholars, however, have expressed their doubts about how methodologically sound it is to, in Gerd Lüdemann's words, "reconstruct a source used by a document [i.e. B] that itself must be reconstructed as a source for our existing documents" (*Opposition to Paul*, 169–70).

[48] An important example is Johannes Munck, "Primitive Jewish Christianity and late Jewish Christianity: Continuation or Rupture?" in *Aspects du Judéo-Christianisme: Colloque de Strasbourg, 23–25 avril 1964* (Paris: Presse Universitaires de France, 1965), 77–94. Munck here observes that, "In the case of the Pseudo-Clementine writings, we have to try to make our way back to the second century – if we can – by means of a complicated classification of sources, about which no two scholars are in complete agreement" (p. 106). Together with his judgment that "fragments of the so-called Jewish-Christian gospels ... do not contain Jewish-Christian features linking them with primitive Christianity," this leads him to conclude that (1) we cannot "learn anything about primitive Jewish Christianity from sources other than the New Testament writings," (2) "primitive Jewish Christianity ceased to exist at the destruction of Jerusalem," and (3) "all later Jewish Christianity [which he terms 'heretical Jewish Christianity'] has its origin in the Gentile-Christian Church of the post-apostolic period" (pp. 107, 114).

## Historiography and Identity in the Pseudo-Clementines

Here, I will approach H and R with a different set of assumptions. In my
opinion, the notion of an early and decisive "Parting" between
Christianity and Judaism is neither plausible nor heuristic, due to our
evidence for the continually complex and charged relationships between
Jews, Christians, and "Jewish Christians" in the centuries that followed.
This model fits with the assertions of some proto-orthodox Christians and
rabbinic Jews, but it errs in reading the rhetoric, polemics, and normative
claims of these groups as historical statements. In light of recent research
on the early rabbinic movement and new perspectives on "orthodoxy" and
"heresy" in early Christianity, we can no longer write the history of Jews
and Christians in Late Antiquity as merely a tale about the triumphant
emergence of these twin "orthodoxies" out of the ashes of the Second
Temple. It is now clear that, even in the second and third centuries CE,
neither group held the authority that they so vociferously claimed for
themselves. And, just as we cannot assume that their writings are
representative of "Judaism" and "Christianity" more globally, so we
should be wary of the attractive but simplistic image of an early "Parting"
between the two religions, conceived in monolithic terms.[49]

Furthermore, recent research has suggested that the elite authors of
these "orthodoxies" remained so preoccupied with, and so vehement
about, the boundaries between "Judaism" and "Christianity" precisely
because these boundaries were still being constructed, negotiated,
contested, and blurred "on the ground" – not only in the second century
CE, but also, with growing intensity, in the third and fourth centuries (and
even beyond, particularly in some locales). If we can no longer presume
that "Jew" and "Christian" were firmly established as mutually-exclusive
religious identities by the close of the second century CE, then we also
cannot assume as a matter of course that the so-called "Jewish Christians"
of Late Antiquity were transgressing a clear-cut boundary between
"normative" Judaism and "normative" Christianity or forging a hybrid
identity based on universally accepted notions of "Jew" and "Christian."[50]

Some scholars now point to the fourth century as the critical era for the
establishment of these identities as socially, religiously, and definitionally
distinct (at least in the Roman Empire).[51] This raises the intriguing

---

[49] My co-editor, Adam H. Becker, and I discuss these issues in more detail in the
introduction to this volume.

[50] On the methodological problems involved in treating "Jewish Christianity" as
simply the "middle ground" between two well-defined entities, see Visotzky, "Prolegomenon," 129–30.

[51] See esp. Daniel Boyarin, *Dying for God: Martyrdom and the Making of Christianity and Judaism* (Stanford: Stanford UP, 1999), 18.

possibility that the authors/redactors of H and R were participating in a broader discourse about the relationship between "Christianity" and "Judaism," rather than simply deviating from a set norm. Consequently, it is perhaps most prudent to revisit the question of the "Jewish Christianity" of the Pseudo-Clementines, reconsidering these sources in light of the new scholarly sensitivity to the diversity of biblically-based forms of religiosity, even after the so-called "Parting of the Ways." Towards this goal, I will here focus on the late antique authors/redactors of this literature, exploring the efforts at self-definition found within H and R in their extant, redacted forms.[52] Rather than judging their "Jewish Christianity" in terms of modern models or other external criteria, I will attempt to highlight the texts' own attempts to define proper belief and practice, by focusing on their accounts of the origins of both proper and improper modes of worship.[53]

Like Gentile Christian writers from Luke to Justin Martyr to Eusebius, the authors/redactors of H and R use biblically-based historiography to situate the true believer in relation to Jews and Gentiles, the Torah and the Gospel, the demonic and the divine. Within H and R, we find three passages that use the early history of humankind to expound the origins of sin and the path(s) to salvation. R addresses this theme twice, first in the context of Peter's initial instructions to Clement (R 1.27–71) and then in the context of their sojourn at Tripolis (R 4–6). In H, the theme occurs once, in the parallel to R 4–6 at H 8–11.

In light of the large quantity of shared material between H 8–11 and R 4–6, it is probable that both of them recast the corresponding section of B. By contrast, there is no counterpart in H to R 1.27–74. Since this unit also contains many divergences from H and the rest of R,[54] it has been widely recognized as preserving a special source of either B or R.[55] From

---

[52] I here follow Jones' approach in *An Ancient Jewish Christian Source*, where he attempts to move beyond the multiplication of hypothetical sources (and conflicting scholarly hypothesis about them) in previous research on the Pseudo-Clementines by focusing upon the internal literary features of the text itself, rather than emphasizing its hypothetical relationship to the non-extant texts mentioned by Epiphanius, Hegesippus, and others (see esp. pp. 35–37).

[53] Fonrobert similarly stresses that "In each case, we need to question what 'Christian' and 'Jewish' means to the author(s) of such 'Jewish-Christian' texts, since 'Christian' is not a stable category until late into the period of the Christianization of the Roman imperial power and the consolidation of political-institutional Christian power" ("*Didascalia Apostolorum*," 485).

[54] See Jones, *Ancient Jewish-Christian Source*, 129–31.

[55] Portions of R 1.27–71 have been identified with a variety of non-extant sources, most notably the *Kerygma Petrou* or *Kerygmata Petrou* (e.g., Waitz, Cullman) and *Anabathmoi Jakobou* (e.g., Bousset, Schoeps, Strecker, Lüdemann, Van Voorst). For a summary of the history of scholarship on this issue, see Jones, *Ancient Jewish-Christian*

his analysis of internal criteria in R 1, F. Stanley Jones has recently argued that R 1.27–71 reflects a source that B integrated *en bloc*, with only minor revisions and additions, and that this source was written by a "Jewish Christian" living in Judaea around the year 200 CE.[56] Whatever the precise date and provenance of R 1.27–71, we here have a discrete unit that can be labeled "Jewish-Christian," but – as we will see – differs notably from H and the rest of R on key issues pertaining to the relationship between the Torah, the Gospel, and Jesus' place in salvation history.

To illuminate the historiographical construction of religious identity in these three passages, this inquiry will consider their attitudes towards three key issues: (1) the status of Jesus in comparison to Moses, (2) the status of Gentiles in comparison to Jews, and (3) the path(s) to salvation. We will begin with R 1.27–71, which uses a summary of Jewish history from Creation to the death of James to argue that Jesus' teachings fulfill and correct those of Moses. Then, we will proceed to examine the Gentile-oriented histories in R 4–6 and H 8–11. After analyzing two parallel passages that assert the absolute equality of the Torah and the Gospel (R 4.5; H 8.5–7), we will explore the ways in which R 4–6 and H 8–11 rework their shared source material (i.e., B), thereby expressing strikingly different attitudes towards the relationship between Jews, Gentiles, and those who follow the teachings of Jesus.

*Jews, Gentiles, and Salvation-History in R 1.27–71*

The review of history attributed to Peter in R 1.27–71 presents an apt starting point for our inquiry.[57] This unit appears to embody two criteria that scholars sometimes use to define texts or persons as "Jewish-Christian": (1) the notion of the "Jewish-Christian" as an ethnic Jew who believes in Jesus and (2) the idea that "Jewish Christianity" can be identified with the type of Christianity first promulgated among Jews in the Jerusalem Church, in contrast to the type commonly associated with Paul and his mission to the Gentiles.

As for the first criterion, the pseudepigraphy of this source frustrates any certainty about the identity of its author. It is notable, however, that the pseudo-Peter of R 1.27–71 stresses his own Jewish ethnicity (R 1.32.1) and exalts Hebrew as the original tongue of humankind and the language "pleasing to God" (Syriac R 1.30.5) or "divinely given" (Latin

---

*Source,* 4–33. A handy table listing the major theories about this unit can be found in Van Voorst, *Ascents of James,* 25 (Table 1).

[56] See Jones, *Ancient Jewish Christian Source,* 157–68.

[57] All English translations of R 1.27–71 follow Jones' parallel translations of the Syriac and Latin versions, as well as Armenian fragments, in *Ancient Jewish-Christian Source,* 51–109.

R 1.30.5). Moreover, the author of this text depicts the Christian community as one of a number of competing Jewish sects that debate questions of belief amongst themselves (e.g., resurrection, the identity of the Messiah), but he makes no mention of any variance with regard to practice. In fact, the author explicitly states that there is only one difference between Christians and other Jews: the Christians identify Jesus as the Messiah, whereas some Jews think John the Baptist is the Messiah, and other Jews are still waiting for this savior to appear (R 1.43.2; 1.50.3; also 1.44.2; 1.60; 1.62.4). Although it is impossible to be certain, these features suggest that the author himself self-identified as Jewish.

At the very least, R 1.27–71 has been shaped by a concern to depict the followers of Jesus as a group *within* Judaism, akin to the Pharisees, the Sadducees, and the followers of John the Baptist.[58] As in many pre-rabbinic and rabbinic Jewish sources, the Sadducees and Samaritans are the main objects of the author's criticism.[59] The former receive condemnation on the basis of their rejection of resurrection (1.54.2–3; 1.56.1; see Mt 22:23/Mk 12:18/Lk 20:27), and the latter are said to share this terrible error, which is compounded by their claims about the primacy of Mt. Gerizim (1.54.4–5; 1.57.1). The depiction of the Pharisees is more complex – but also more intriguing. Whereas the Sadducees and Samaritans are paired by means of their rejection of resurrection and their links to Dositheus (1.54.3, 5),[60] the Pharisees are associated with the followers of John the Baptist (1.54.7–8). They are credited with being baptized by John (cf. Mt 3:7–10) and with possessing "the word of truth received from Moses' tradition (*verbum veritas tenentes ex Moysi*

---

[58] Notably, the contrast is not between "Christian" and "Jew" but between true Judaism and Jewish "sects" (i.e., parallel to the role of *minim* [lit. "kinds"] in the Sages' promotion of rabbinic Judaism as simply "Judaism"). The author even offers an aetiology of Second Temple sectarianism: when "the Slanderer" saw that the Messiah would soon be coming, he "created sects and division" to frustrate his acceptance by his own people (R 1.54.1, see also 1.54.9). Consistent with this view, the Syriac version stresses that "the gospel will be made known to the nation as a witness for the healing of the schisms that have arisen so that also your separation [from them] will occur" (R 1.64.2; contrast the Latin version: "so that your unbelief may be judged on the basis of their belief").

[59] On the rabbinic parallels and their significance, see Albert Baumgarten, "Literary Evidence for Jewish Christianity in the Galilee," in *The Galilee in Late Antiquity,* ed. L. Levine (New York: Jewish Theological Seminary of America, 1992), 42–43.

[60] Interestingly, both Dositheus and Simon Magus are here said to have been Sadducees, thus evoking the treatment of Sadducees as a paradigmatic group of *minim* in early rabbinic sources (see esp. *m. Niddah* 4.2; also ARN[A] 5); note also the polemics against those who deny resurrection (e.g., *m. Sanh.* 10.1; *BerR* 53.12).

*traditione*)" that is "the key to the kingdom of heaven."[61] Even though they are critiqued for hiding this key (cf. Mt 23:13), the latter – as Albert Baumgarten notes – is a surprising affirmation of one of the most radical and controversial characteristics of Pharisees and/or early Rabbis: their claim to preserve a tradition no less ancient than the (written) Torah itself.[62]

Similarly ambivalent is the portrayal of their relationship with Jesus' followers. Consistent with the Pharisees' special connection to Moses, it is a Pharisee who here contests the equality of Moses and Jesus (R 1.59.1; see below). Yet R. Gamaliel is portrayed positively as the leader of the nation and as a secret believer in Jesus, working behind the scenes to aid James and his community (R 1.65.2–68.2).[63] Even as the author appeals to the apostolic heritage cherished by other Christians, he may also, as Baumgarten suggests, view "the Jewish past in much the same way as the Pharisees and/or their rabbinic heirs did."[64]

The second criterion – continuity (real or claimed) with the Jerusalem Church – is unquestionably present in R 1.27–71. In his statements about Jesus and early apostolic history, the author counters the narrative in Acts by depicting James as the true leader of the authentic community of Christians (see e.g., R 1.66). Moreover, the martyrdom of the Jewish James here replaces the martyrdom of the Gentile Stephen in Acts 7, with notable ramifications for the place of Jew and Gentile in Christian salvation-history.[65] In this, the anti-Paulism that many scholars associate

---

[61] In both cases, the author integrates traditions from the Gospel of Matthew, but revises them towards a more positive characterization of the Pharisees. In Mt 3:7–10, John turns away the "scribes and Pharisees" who wish to be baptized by him; here, they are baptized. In place of the enigmatic reference to the Pharisees "sitting on the seat of Moses" (Mt 23:1) and the accusation that they shut "the kingdom of heaven against humankind" (Mt 23:13) – which, in Matthew, is followed by a series of increasingly fierce denunciations (vv. 15–32) – it is here stressed that they truly possess "the word of truth received from Moses' tradition," and their concealment thereof does not occasion further condemnations.

[62] I.e., the claims at the heart of the later distinction between the Oral Torah and the Written Torah. See Baumgarten, "Literary Evidence," 42.

[63] Cf. Acts 5:34; 22:3. On late antique Christian traditions about R. Gamaliel – e.g., the tale about the discovery of Gamaliel's tomb in 415 CE in *Epistula Luciani* (PL 41.807ff) and the fifth-/sixth-century *Gospel of Gamaliel* – and their possible link to "Jewish-Christian" traditions, see Günter Stemberger, *Jews and Christians in the Holy Land: Palestine in the Fourth Century* (trans. R. Tuschling; Edinburgh: T&T Clark, 2000), 108–12; M.-A. van den Oudenrijn, "The Gospel of Gamaliel," in *NTA* 1:558–60.

[64] Baumgarten, "Literary Evidence," 43. Notably, Baumgarten does not here distinguish between H and R, let alone any strata therein. His evidence for this assertion, however, comes from only two units: R 1.27–71 (esp. 54) and H 11 (esp. 28; on which see below).

[65] On R 1 and Acts 7, see Jones, "Ancient Christian Rejoinder," 241.

with "Jewish Christianity" plays a key role: not only is Paul held responsible for the martyrdom of James, but he is blamed for the failure of the Christian mission among the Jews.[66] After a seven-day sermon defending the authenticity of Jesus' claim to be the Messiah to his fellow Jews, James had finally succeeded in persuading "all the people together with the high priest" to be baptized (R 1.69.8). At that very moment, however, the "enemy" Paul violently burst into Temple, accused James of being a magician, and provoked the priests into joining him in slaughtering James and many of his followers (R 1.70). This necessitates the Christian mission to the Gentiles, since the number of the chosen remains unfilled (see R 1.50). Rather than aetiologizing the Gentile mission with reference to the Jews' "hard-heartedness" or their perennial persecution of prophets, the author here points to the alleged scheming of a figure celebrated in proto-orthodox Christian circles as "The Apostle" and, perhaps more importantly, embraced by Marcion.

The message is clear: the real enemy of Jesus' followers is not the Jewish nation that now remains unconvinced, but rather Paul. The end of this unit poignantly describes Paul promising the high priest Caiaphas to "massacre all those who believe in Jesus" and then setting off "for Damascus, to go as one carrying letters from them, so that when he got there the non-believers might help him and might destroy those who believe" (R 1.71.3). Although this passage echoes Acts 9:1–2 (also 22:5), we here find no hint of Paul's subsequent vision of the risen Christ or his commission as the "apostle of the Gentiles" (Acts 9:3–22; 22:6–16). In fact, the narrative setting – Peter's account of apostolic history to Clement, well after these events took place – serves to imply that Paul is *still* "the enemy" of James and the authentic Christian community, thereby suggesting that Paul's apostleship and preaching are the deceptive continuation of his failed efforts to destroy them through violence.

Are these features sufficient to make R 1.27–71 "Jewish-Christian" (as opposed, for instance, to merely anti-Pauline)? It is hardly a coincidence that, by a certain definition, the material about Jesus and the apostles at the end of this review of history (i.e., R 1.39–71) is paradigmatically "Jewish-Christian," since these very passages proved central to Baur's reconstruction of apostolic "Jewish Christianity." Consequently, we must further ask whether this unit's description of the rest of human history depicts the ideal believer as simultaneously Jewish and Christian in a sense that differs from the negotiation of these identities that is usually accepted as "Christian."

---

[66] Cf. Eusebius *HE* 2.9. See further Lüdemann, *Opposition to Paul*, 183–85.

Does the preceding treatment of early human history (i.e., R 1.24–38)
depart notably from similar accounts in other early Christian sources?
The author here begins by enumerating the twenty-one generations before
Abraham and recounts the progressive decline of humankind with special
appeal to the spread of non-monotheistic worship. Here, the first
transgression was not the sin of Adam but rather the unnamed sins
promulgated by the "sons of God" of Gen 6:1–4, here interpreted
euhemeristically as righteous men who became corrupted by lust (R
1.29). This leads to the Flood, from which only Noah and his family were
saved, and it prompts God's "first commandment": the prohibition
against eating blood (1.30). The subsequent degradation of humankind is
marked by the spread of fire-worship and idolatry (see esp. R 1.30), and
this moral decline continues unhindered until the birth of Abraham, the
father of "our race, the Hebrews, who are also called the Jews" (Syriac R
1.32.1).[67] The assertion that the "prophet of truth" revealed "everything"
to Abraham (R 1.33) represents the only possible clue to the "Christian"
nature of this narrative,[68] which otherwise resembles – and draws heavily
from – Second Temple Jewish writings like *Jubilees*.[69]

The material that follows, however, is dominated by one main theme:
the polemic against animal sacrifice. The author achieves this goal
through a careful argument that distances the biblical precepts related to
the Temple cult from the rest of the Torah given by God at Mount Sinai.[70]
Moses himself is exalted as a prophet (R 1.34.4; 1.36.2),[71] but he is here
held responsible for the institution of sacrifice among the Jews – albeit
begrudgingly and for solely pragmatic aims: after the incident with the
Golden Calf,[72] Moses realizes that the Jews must be distracted at all costs

---

[67] Latin R 1.32.1: "Abraham, from whom the race of us Hebrews is descended"

[68] I say "possible" because the designation "true prophet"/"prophet of truth" is not
quite as clear as we might wish. We can readily interpret this "true prophet"/"prophet of
truth" as Jesus (1.44.6), who appears first to Abraham (1.33.1) and then to Moses
(1.34.3 in Latin and Armenian). The Syriac version of the latter, however, refers to
Moses too as the "prophet of truth" (see also Syriac 1.34.6 in contrast to Armenian and
Latin), thus evoking the doctrine of a single "true prophet" who entered into a
succession of figures (e.g., Adam, Moses, Jesus) in H 1.19, 3.17–28; on the latter, see
further Strecker, *Judenchristentum*, 145–53.

[69] On the use of *Jubilees* in this unit, see Jones, *Ancient Jewish Christian Source*,
138–39.

[70] Notably, the author also privileges the Ten Commandments over the rest of the
Torah (R 1.35.2).

[71] See parallel comparison of Syriac, Armenian, and Latin translations in Jones,
*Ancient Jewish Christian Source*, 61.

[72] Cf. Stephen's speech in Acts 7, for which the Golden Calf incident also serves as
the key turning point – in this case, the point at which "God turned away from them and
handed them over to worship the host of heaven" (7:42). See Pier Cesare Bori, *The*

from the desire to practice the idolatry that tainted them in Egypt (R 1.35–36), and he therefore sets aside a single place for his people to sacrifice to the one God (R 1.36–37, 39). The author sees the rest of Jewish history as God's attempt to wean the Jews off of sacrifice, by periodically exiling them to other lands in order to encourage their adoption of other forms of monotheistic worship (R 1.37.3–4).

Notably, this argument recalls the proto-orthodox/orthodox polemic against the Jewish sacrificial cult, albeit with important distinctions: rather than singling out the Jews as a "hard-hearted," disobedient, and sinful people who are particularly prone to the idolatrous worship of demons (e.g., Justin, *Dial.* 19; 22; 92; Irenaeus, *AH* 4.15.2; Tertullian, *Adv. Marc.* 2.18),[73] the author here takes pains to associate these practices with the Canaanites and Babylonians (R 1.30.2, 4, 7) and to depict the Jews' temptations to idolatry as a result of their "evil upbringing with the Egyptians" (Syriac R 1.36.1; see also 1.35.1, 5–6).[74] Furthermore, the polemic against sacrifice in R 1.27–71 is pursued apart from any broader denigration of Jewish Torah-observance.[75]

Nevertheless, the issue of sacrifice proves central to the author's assertion that Jesus' teachings are the fulfillment and completion of those of Moses. In his view, this is the main reason that God sent the "true prophet" Jesus: to abolish sacrifice and to preach, in its place, baptism for the remission of sins (see esp. R 1.39.1). According to this retelling of Jewish history, Moses himself anticipated the coming of a second prophet when he instituted the Temple and sacrificial laws (1.37); he took on the first half of the task of instituting proper worship among his people (i.e., cleansing his people of Egyptian idolatry), with full knowledge that a "prophet like me" would come in the future to complete the second half (i.e., the abolishment of sacrifice and promulgation of baptism).

Within the account of apostolic history, Jesus' superiority to Moses is stated explicitly, in the context of debates between his followers and other Jews (R 1.59.1–3):

> Hearing this, a certain Pharisee chided Philip because he put Jesus on a level with Moses. Answering him, Bartholomew boldly declared that we do not only say that Jesus was equal to Moses, but that he was greater than him (*quidam non*

---

*Golden Calf and the Origins of the Anti-Jewish Controversy* (trans. D. Ward; Atlanta: Scholars Press, 1990).

[73] See further Simon, *Verus Israel*, 167–69.

[74] The gist of the Latin is the same, although its rhetoric is softer: "When Moses, that faithful and wise steward, perceived that the vice of sacrificing to idols had been deeply ingrained into the people *from their association with the Egyptians* ...."

[75] Cf. Justin's argument that the laws about sacrifice, circumcision, food, festivals, and Shabbat are only in the Torah because God used these measures to punish the Jewish people and to set them apart as a pariah among the nations (*Dial.* 16–22).

*dicimus Iesum aequalem Moysi, sed maiorem*),[76] because Moses was indeed a
prophet – as Jesus was also – but Moses was not the Messiah/Christ, as Jesus
was. And therefore he is doubtless greater who is both a prophet and the
Messiah/Christ, as opposed to he who is only a prophet.

Just as the polemic against sacrifice can be read as a pro-Jewish variant of
an anti-Jewish trope of proto-orthodox/orthodox Christian historiography
(see esp. Justin, *Dial.* 19; 22),[77] so this statement about Moses and Jesus
evokes the supersessionist attitudes common among proto-orthodox
Christians.[78]

Yet it is significant that the author consistently describes and defends
Jesus as "the image of Moses that had previously been announced by
Moses" (see R 1.36.2, 1.40.4–41.1) and, moreover, makes no attempt to
argue that God has disowned His chosen nation in favor of the Gentiles.
In fact, he paints a surprisingly sympathetic portrait of non-Christian
Jews. The priests – those who benefit most from the Jewish sacrificial
cult – are said to have recognized how much they stood to lose if "the
entire people came to our faith" (R 1.43.1), and they thus scheme against
both Jesus and his followers. By contrast, the majority of the Jewish
people did not recognize the truth of Jesus' teachings simply because
"they had been educated to believe these things [about the Temple and

---

[76] In light of R 1.60 (discussed below), it may be significant that Bartholomew here
frames the superiority of Jesus to Moses as something that "we say," rather than simply
asserting it.

[77] Oskar Skarsaune has argued that Justin draws this and other traditions from a
"Jewish-Christian" source related to the Pseudo-Clementines (*Proof from Prophecy*,
316–20; so too David Rokéah, *Justin Martyr and the Jews* [Jerusalem: Dinur Center,
1998], 34–39 [Hebrew]). We should not, however, close off the possibility that this
author may instead be dependant on Justin's writings and rework his arguments in order
to paint a different picture of the Jews – just as he recasts traditions from Acts to
counter its account of early apostolic history.

[78] This becomes even clearer as the passage continues: "After following out this
train of argument, he [i.e. Bartholomew] stopped. After him, James the son of Alphaeus
gave an address to the people, with the aim of showing that we are not to believe in
Jesus on the ground that the prophets foretold concerning him, but rather that we are to
believe that the prophets were really prophets, because the Messiah/Christ bears
testimony to them; for it is the presence and coming of Christ that shows that they are
truly prophets, since testimony must be borne by the superior to his inferiors, not by the
inferiors to their superior." Interestingly, this passage has many parallels with R 1.60,
which records a debate on the relative status of John the Baptist and Jesus: "And,
behold, one of the disciples of John asserted that John was the Christ, and not Jesus,
inasmuch as Jesus himself declared that John was greater than all men and all prophets.
'If,' he said, 'he is greater than all, then he must be held to be greater than Moses and
than Jesus himself. And, if he is the greatest of all, then must he be the
Messiah/Christ.'" For the surprising conclusion to this debate, see below.

sacrifice] for so long" (Latin R 1.40.2).[79] Even in the course of describing the Jews' rejection of Jesus, the author makes efforts to stress that belief in Jesus is the only difference between Christians and other Jews (R 1.43.2). Moreover, non-Jews are here granted the chance for salvation because Paul undermined the Jews' acceptance of the inheritance that was rightly theirs. And, even as the text describes the failure of James' (almost successful) conversion of the Jewish people in its entirety, it refrains from suggesting that individual Jews cannot or will not number among the chosen.[80]

Seen from an inner-Christian perspective, R 1.27–71's review of history can be read as an attempt to articulate a vision of Christianity that is not dependant on the denigration of Jews or the severing of the church's traditional ties to Judaism. Is it also possible, then, to read this source as a Jewish text? Most significant in this regard is the primacy of the author's polemic against animal sacrifice. In its emphasis on this particular issue, R 1.27–71 fits well in the context of Jewish attempts to come to terms with the tragic events of 70 and 135 CE (e.g., 4 Ezra, 2 Baruch).[81] Furthermore, the polemic in R 1.27–71 not only presupposes that the Gentiles' idolatrous and polytheistic worship is far worse, but it also chooses to critique the Jews for something that they – at the time of the author – simply no longer do.

Although the author's argument about sacrifice rests on a reading of the Torah as a combination of God's eternal precepts and Moses' own attempts to guide his people,[82] his choice to depict *this* issue as the primary area in which Jesus corrects the Mosaic covenant ironically has

---

[79] Contrast the Syriac version, which here states: "For they are people who are more wretched than any, who are willing to believe neither good nor bad for the sake of virtue." That both versions go on to condemn the non-believing majority without condemning "the Jews" *en tout* (see esp. R 1.40.3) suggests that the Latin is closer to the original Greek.

[80] See also the Syriac version of R 1.64.2, as discussed above.

[81] Whereas proto-orthodox Christian authors like Justin connect the Roman destruction of the Temple and the establishment of Aelia Capitolina to the Jews' alleged violence against Jesus (e.g., Justin, *Dial.* 25.5; 26.1; 92; 108.3; *1 Apol.* 32.4–6; 47–49; 53.2–3), this source associates these tragedies with their "sacrificing after the end of the time for sacrificing" (e.g., R 1.64.1–2). Accordingly, the blame for the Jews' refusal to listen to Jesus' message is placed particularly on the priests, as is clear from the account of Peter's prediction of the destruction of the Temple and the erection of an "abomination of desolation in its place" in R 1.64–65. The priests grow quite irate after Peter's statements, but R. Gamaliel calms them, saying: "Leave these men alone, for if this matter is of human origin, it will come to nothing. But if it is of God, why are you transgressing in vain and achieving nothing?"

[82] Cf. the theory of the false pericopes found elsewhere in the Pseudo-Clementines (e.g., H 2.38), which posits that the Torah contains some later emendations; see further Strecker, *Judenchristentum*, 166–86.

the effect of downplaying the differences between him and his non-Christian Jewish contemporaries. Inasmuch as the author repeatedly stresses that Christ-belief is the only thing distinguishing James' community from other Jews, it is difficult to imagine any radical differences in praxis existed between them;[83] indeed, even the addition of baptism can be readily situated in a broader Jewish discourse about purity and piety in the absence of the Temple, particularly since R 1.27–71 promotes this practice as a substitute for sacrifice (see esp. R 1.39.2).

Also notable is the attitude implied in R 1.60, which depicts Jesus' followers and other Jews arguing about the identity of the Messiah. One might expect the argument to end with the unquestioned victory of Jesus' followers, but the author portrays the groups as coming to an absolute impasse. To this, Barnabas offers a surprisingly tolerant solution:

> Barnabas... began to exhort the people that they should not regard Jesus with hatred, nor speak evil of him. For it is much more proper for the one who does not know Jesus, or is in doubt concerning him, to love rather than hate him (*multo enim esse rectius, etiam ignoranti vel dubitanti de Iesu, amare eum quam odisse*; Latin R 1.60.6).

Although the author is firm in his opinion that Jesus is the Messiah, he appears to understand why some Jews might not think so – not only on the grounds of ignorance, but also because of doubt.[84] Rather than condemning them outright, he encourages them to embrace Jesus in a more limited capacity (i.e., like the followers of John, who are said to accept him as a prophet).[85] Seen from this perspective, the author's

---

[83] Notably, the author is not forthcoming on the question of primary concern for modern scholars: must the Gentile converts undergo circumcision? Strecker tentatively posits a positive answer with appeal to R 1.33.5, which – in the context of explaining how the practice of circumcision amongst "some of the Indians and the Egyptians" was the result of the travels of Abraham's progeny – calls circumcision "the proof and sign of purity" (*Judenchristentum*, 251). By contrast, Schoeps dismisses the reference as "only decorative elements in the historical narrative" (*Anti-Paulism*, 182). Jones similarly downplays its significance: he identifies R 1.33.5 as part of B's additions to the original source (*Ancient Jewish Christian Source*, 160) and goes on to speculate that "the very notion of calling the nations to complete the number shown to Abraham (R 1.42; compare R 1.63.2, 64.2) contradicts the view that these Gentiles should first have to convert to Judaism (e.g., submission to circumcision) before entering Christianity" (p. 164). Even if we accept Jones' text-critical argument, the latter proves problematic; we know too little to conflate so confidently the support of a Gentile mission with the acceptance of non-circumcised Christ-believers, especially since the Gentile mission accepted by the author is so firmly distinguished from the Pauline one. Although the text's own lack of interest in this issue precludes any certainty on our part, Strecker's view strikes me as more plausible.

[84] Interestingly, the latter option is omitted in the Syriac version of this verse.

[85] It is notable that the negative exemplar is the high priest Caiaphas, who is here portrayed as hating Jesus (R 1.61–62).

Christian supersessionism looks a lot like Jewish messianism, and his viewpoint does indeed seem both "Jewish" and "Christian," insofar as he portrays the ideal Christian as a Jew who accepts Jesus as the Messiah, without wholly condemning those Jews who do not.

*Two "Teachers of Truth": Moses and Jesus in H 8.5–7 and R 4.5*

Many of the same issues are addressed by the parallel accounts of Peter's sojourn in Tripolis in H 8–11 and R 4–6. Here, however, we find very different explanations of the relationship between the Torah and the Gospel, which fit different modern definitions of "Jewish Christianity."

Both accounts can be divided according to the different audiences depicted therein. In each, Peter first speaks to his followers about the equality of Moses and Jesus (H 8.5–7 = R 4.5) and then proceeds to preach a series of sermons to gathered crowds of Gentiles. In H 8–11 and R 4–6 alike, Peter's initial words to his Jewish and Gentile followers function to contextualize his public preaching to non-believing Gentiles by offering a broader perspective on the relationship between Jewish and Gentile paths to salvation. Here, both H and R articulate a soteriology that can be termed "Jewish-Christian" insofar as it appeals to the equality of Moses, Jesus, and their respective teachings to assert the equality of the Torah and the Gospel as paths to salvation.[86]

In R 4.5 and H 8.5–7, Peter first cites the Jews' special dispensation through Moses, as a "teacher of truth." In R 4.5.1–5, the apostle uses this assertion as the basis for his argument that Gentiles too have now been given the chance for salvation, through their very own "teacher of truth":

> For so also it was given to the people of the Hebrews from the beginning, that they should love Moses and believe his word, as it is written: "the people believed God and His servant Moses" (Ex 14:31). What was therefore a special gift from God toward the nation of the Hebrews, we see now to be given also to those who are called from among the Gentiles to the faith (*quod ergo fuit proprii muneris a deo erga Hebraeorum gentum, hoc nunc videmus dari etiam his qui ex*

---

[86] Especially since scholars are often tempted to see "universalism" as a "Christian" characteristic and "particularism" as a "Jewish" characteristic, we should note that the concept of two different paths to salvation fits far better with Jewish tradition than with Christian tradition. Within the former, we find some affirmations that righteous Gentiles will have a place in the World to Come, as well as discussions about the more limited requirements for righteousness (i.e., the Noachite commandments) that God places upon Gentiles (see, e.g., *t. Avodah Zarah* end; *t. Sanhedrin* 13.2). By contrast, the vast majority of Christian soteriological traditions are emphatically "one way": peoples of different ethnicity can be saved, but only if they follow the one, single path opened by Jesus. Seen from this perspective, Christianity is much more "particularistic" and Judaism more "universalistic," thereby underlining the profoundly problematic nature of the dichotomy. See further Anders Runesson, "Particularistic Judaism and Universalistic Christianity? Some Critical Remarks on Terminology and Theology," *Journal of Greco-Roman Christianity and Judaism* 1 (2000): 120–44, esp. 125–27.

*gentibus convocantur ad fidem).* The method of works is put into the power and will of everyone, and this is their own. But to have an affection towards a teacher of truth, this is a gift of the heavenly Father (*desiderium vero habere erga doctorem veritatis, hoc a patre caelesti donatum est*). And, salvation is in this: that you do the will of one whom you have conceived a love and affection through the gift of God; lest that saying of his, which he spoke, be addressed to you: "Why do call you me 'lord, lord,' and do not what I say?" (Lk 6:46). It is thus the special gift bestowed by God upon the Hebrews that they believe Moses, and the special gift bestowed upon the Gentiles is that they value Jesus (*est ergo proprii muneris a deo concessi Hebraeis, ut Moysi credant, gentibus autem, ut Iesum diligant*).

The contrast with R 1.27–71 is striking. This passage does not exalt Jesus over Moses, but neither does it depict Jesus as the true Messiah of the Jews. Instead, Jesus is portrayed as the teacher of the Gentiles, just as Moses is the teacher of the Jews.

The parallel passage in H focuses on the issue of proper praxis. In H 8.5, the assertion of the Jews' special dispensation through Moses functions as the basis for pseudo-Peter's argument that the salvation of the Gentiles is dependant on their good works:

For even the Hebrews who believe Moses but do not observe the things spoken by him are not saved, unless they observe the things that were spoken to them ... Since, therefore, both for the Hebrews and for those who are called from the nations (Ἑβραίοις τε καὶ τοῖς ἀπό ἐθνῶν κεκλημένοις), to believe in teachers of truth is from God, while good deeds are left to each one to do by his own judgment, the reward is justly bestowed upon those who act well. For, there would have been no need of Moses or of the coming of Jesus, if they would have understood of themselves what is reasonable (οὔτε γὰρ ἀν Μωυσέως οὔτε τῆς τοῦ Ἰησοῦ παρουσίας χρεία ἦν, εἴπερ ἀφ' ἑαυτῶν τὸ εὔλογον νοεῖν ἐβούλοντο). Neither is there salvation in believing in teachers and calling them "lords" (cf. Mt 7:21; Lk 6:46).

Interestingly, the version in H emphasizes proper praxis to such a degree that *this* pseudo-Peter even downplays the importance of Moses and Jesus. For, according to H's authors/redactors, God sent both teachers to reassert what human beings should have already known to be true and rational. As a result, mere faith in these teachers as exalted figures is sorely misguided, as H 8.5 asserts by alluding to the saying of Jesus quoted in R 4.5.4 (i.e., Luke 6:46).

In both cases, the example of Moses is used to explain the importance of Jesus for the Gentiles. Interestingly, however, H 8.5 appears to presuppose what R 4.5 must assert with a scriptural prooftext, namely, that the Jews were granted long ago the salvation now accessible to Gentiles. In arguing that the Gentiles who believe in Jesus should follow the example of the Jews in following their "teacher of truth" through their actions and in seeing this teacher as a pedagogical figure, instead of a soteriological one, the authors/redactors of H assume that its audience already accepts the (continued) chosenness of the Jews and, moreover, sees them as a model for monotheistic piety.

Both R and H then turn to the topic of Jewish and Gentile salvation. In R 4.5.5–6, pseudo-Peter cites another saying of Jesus to expand on its "two-ways" model of salvation:

> For this also the master (*magister*) intimated when he said, "I will confess to you, O Father, Lord of heaven and earth, because you have concealed these things from the wise and prudent, and you have revealed them to babes" (Mt 11:25/Lk 10:21). By which it is certainly declared that the people of the Hebrews, who were instructed out of the Law, did not know him (*per quod utique declaratur, quia Hebraeorum populus qui ex lege eruditus est, ignoravit eum*).[87] But the people of the Gentiles have acknowledged Jesus and venerate him, on which account they too will be saved (*populus autem gentium agnovit Iesum et venerator, propter quod et salvabitur*), not only by acknowledging him, but also by doing his will.

Although the ignorant "wise and prudent" of Mt 11:25/Lk 10:21 are here identified with the Jews and the knowing "babes" with the Gentiles, the authors/redactors of R do not use this saying to critique non-Christian Jews, nor to depict them as dispossessed heirs to God's promises. Rather, R 4.5.6 explains this saying to mean simply that "the people of the Hebrews, who were instructed out of the Law, did not know him (i.e., Jesus), but the people of the Gentiles have acknowledged Jesus and venerate him." The text goes on to assert that believers – among both the Jews and the Gentiles – should strive to accept both teachers:

> But he who is of the Gentiles and who has it from God to value Jesus should also have it of his own purpose to believe Moses too (*debet autem is qui ex gentibus est et ex deo habet, ut diligat Iesum, proprii habere propositi, ut credat et Moysi*). And again, the Hebrew, who has it from God to believe Moses, should have it also of his own purpose to believe in Jesus (*et rursus Hebraeus qui ex deo habet, ut credat Moysi, habere debet ex proposito suo, ut credat in Iesum*) – so that each of them, having in himself something of the divine gift and something of his own exertion, may be perfect by both (*sit ex utroque perfectus*). For concerning such a one our lord (*dominus noster*) spoke, as of a rich man, who brings forth from his treasures things new and old (R 4.5.7–9; cp. Mt 13:52)

By distinguishing between the divine gift of salvation and human efforts at perfection, R 4.5 deftly avoids condemning either Jews who do not accept Jesus or Gentiles who do not accept Moses. Nevertheless, R here encourages both Jew and Gentile to recognize the two as equally "teachers of truth" – and clearly asserts the superiority of those who do.

---

[87] Cf. Paul's critique of those Jews who "rely on the Law and boast of your relation to God, and know his will, and determine what is best because you are instructed from the Law (κατηχούμενος ἐκ τοῦ νόμου)" in Rom 2:17–19.

The parallel passage in H 8.6 also expounds on the relationship between Jews, Gentiles, Moses, and Jesus with appeal to Mt 11:25/Lk 10:21, albeit with different results:

> For this reason, Jesus is concealed from the Hebrews who have taken Moses as their teacher (ἀπὸ μὲν Ἑβραίων τὸν Μωυσῆν διδάσκαλον εἰληφότων καλύπτεται ὁ Ἰησοῦς), and Moses is hidden from those who have believed Jesus (ἀπὸ δὲ τῶν Ἰησοῦ πεπιστευκότων ὁ Μωυσῆς ἀποκρύπτεται). For, since there is a single teaching by both (μιᾶς γὰρ δι᾽ ἀμφοτέρων διδασκαλίας), God accepts (ἀποδέχεται) one who has believed either of these. But, to believe a teacher (τὸ πιστύειν διδασκάλῳ) is for the sake of doing (ἕνεκα τοῦ ποιεῖν) the things spoken by God. And our lord himself says that this is so: "I thank you, Father of heaven and earth, because you have concealed these things from the wise and prudent, and you have revealed them to sucking babes" (Mt 11:25/Lk 10:21). Thus God Himself (αὐτὸς ὁ θεὸς) has concealed a teacher from some, who foreknew what they should do (τοῖς μὲν ἔκρυψεν διδάσκαλον ὡς προεγνωκόσιν ἃ δεῖ πράττειν), and He has revealed [him] to others, who are ignorant about what they should do (τοῖς δὲ ἀπεκάλυψεν ὡς ἀγνοοῦσιν ἃ χρὴ ποιεῖν).

Jesus' saying about the "wise" and "ignorant" (Mt 11:25/Lk 10:21) is here interpreted to mean that God concealed Jesus from the Jews precisely because they already know "what they ought to do." When considered in light of H's previous assertion that neither Moses nor Jesus would have been sent if humans had simply done what they know to be rational, the ramifications are striking. Above, we noted that R 1.27–74 excuses those Jews who do not recognize Jesus as Messiah by placing the blame on the evil Paul. H here goes even further, explaining the rejection of Jesus by Jews as the result of God's own choice to hide him from this people and send him only to the Gentiles.

H then goes on to explain its theory of concealment. First, it stresses that neither Jews nor Gentiles are condemned for their ignorance of the "teacher" of the other, since this division of labor conforms with God's will; "God accepts one who believes in either," so neither is superior to the other. The authors/redactors add, however, two important qualifications: (1) all must do the things commanded by their own teacher, and (2) they must not "hate him whom they do not know" (H 8.7.1–2).[88] H then comments on each qualification with appeal to a saying of Jesus.

On the topic of proper practice, H's pseudo-Peter appeals to the same saying quoted in R 4.5.4 (i.e., Lk 6:46) to stress that "it is not saying that will profit anyone, but doing; by all means, therefore, is there need of

---

[88] Does this mean that Jews must accept Jesus as the Messiah? Interestingly, the theme of "hating" is not present in R 4 and thus likely not present at this point in their shared source, B. Here, H appears to have integrated a portion of R 1.27–71, which it otherwise omits: Bartholomew's statements in R 1.60 (see above).

good works!" (H 8.7.4). On the value of recognizing both the Torah and the Gospel, H then alludes to Mt 13:52 (as quoted in R 4.5.8) and concludes by exalting the one who "has been thought worthy to recognize by himself both as preaching one doctrine (καταξιωθείη τοὺς ἀμφοτέρους ἐπιγνῶναι ὡς μιᾶς διδασαλίας ὑπ' αὐτῶν κεκρυγμένης)" and who thus "has been counted rich in God, understanding both the old things as new in time, and the new things as old" (H 8.7.5). Whereas the parallel in R 4.5 encourages Jews and Gentiles to perfect themselves by supplementing the knowledge of their own teacher with knowledge about that of the other, H 8.7 implies that few are worthy enough to realize that the two teachings, new and old, are really the same.

Both H 8 and R 4 exalt those whom some scholars might call "Jewish Christians" (or even "Christian Jews"),[89] in the sense of people who view the Torah and the Gospel as equal in soteriological value. In this, both H 8 and R 4 depart from R 1.27–71, which depicts Jesus as the Jewish messiah, Christianity as the correct sect of Judaism, and Gentile believers as filling the slots for the saved left empty by unbelieving Jews (a point that remains significant, even if it is a result of the malicious mechanizations of Paul). Nevertheless, the two parallel texts themselves express different perspective on the relationship between the followers of Moses ("Hebrews"/"Jews") and the followers of Jesus (whom we might, although the text does not, call "Christians").

For both H and R, any exaltation or worship of a teacher is misplaced, since God's purpose lies in the encouragement of good works among his creatures. Of the two, H develops the more coherent (and more radical) argument. Whereas R proposes that Moses and Jesus opened two separate paths to salvation through praxis, H asserts that the teachings of the two are essentially the same and, moreover, consist of the proclamation of principles that are inherent to all humankind. For H, this means that neither Jew nor Gentile can be condemned for not knowing the teacher meant for the other – not only because God has chosen to conceal Jesus from the Jews, but also because Moses and Jesus are really two messengers with the exact same message.

---

[89] Bruce Malina, for instance, suggests that from a purely terminological standpoint, the label "Jewish Christian" more aptly describes proto-orthodox and orthodox Christianity, which (in contrast to Christians like Marcion) actively integrates Jewish elements into their Christian belief. Those who saw the Torah and the Gospel as two equal parts of the same message, without subordinating the former to the latter or claiming that the church superseded Israel, are – in his view – better termed "Christian Jews" ("Jewish Christianity or Christian Judaism," 46–50).

*Demons, Jews, and the Salvation of Gentiles in H 8–11 and R 4–6*

The differences between H 8–11 and R 4–6 become even more apparent when we consider their subsequent descriptions of Peter's public preaching to non-believing Gentiles. In contrast to R 1.27–71's account of the history of the Jews, these units focus on the history of the Gentiles and the demons that enslave them. In both, Peter attempts to correct the Gentiles' ignorance about the supernatural influence that guides them and the illnesses that infect them by describing the origins, spread, and methods of the demons. Towards this goal, the apostle associates the demons with the fallen angels (H 8.7ff; R 4.26; cf. R 4.8); recounts the long history of their corruption of humankind through innovations in improper worship (e.g., H 9.2–7); and explains how they infiltrate the human mind by pretending to be gods (H 9.13, 9.16; R 4.19) and how they sneak into the body through the wine and meat that has been consecrated to the idols of these false gods (H 8.20, 9.8–10; R 4.16), thereby causing suffering and disease (e.g., H 9.12). Both texts depict that idolatry as the root cause of all human wickedness and suffering (R 4.31, 5.2–4; H 9.14, 11.15), and they proclaim baptism and monotheism as the ways for Gentiles to free themselves from the demons (R 4.17–18; H 8.22, 9.11, 9.19) and thereby return to their original state as the "image of God" (e.g., H 10.6, 11.7).

In light of the ample thematic and linguistic parallels, it is likely that the two units are both based on the same parts of B. It is notable, however, that these sections are marked by formal and structural differences between H and R.[90] As such, the two versions of Peter's Tripolis sermons provide us with an ideal opportunity to see how each set of fourth-century authors/redactors recast, reshaped, and supplemented B according to their own views about the "pagan" past, the salvation of the Gentiles, and the relative status of Gentiles and Jews after the earthly sojourn of the "true prophet."[91]

---

[90] E.g., H structures the material into four sermons, whereas R has only three. See further Strecker, *Judenchristentum*, 70–75, and esp. the chart on p. 75.

[91] Source-critical inquiries into H and R are often based on the tacit assumption that the authors/redactors responsible for composing H, R, and even B are mere tradents and compilers of earlier material. In my view, this proves problematic, due to the nature of Jewish and Christian literary production in Late Antiquity. Contrary to our modern concept of the "author" as an autonomous creative agent and the resultant tendency to view all later literary hands as only adulterating the purity of the "original" text, the literary practices of authorship, redaction, collection, and reproduction were not always so clear-cut prior to the invention of the printing press; just as the named authors of pre-modern times often integrated large selections from earlier texts and drew heavily from source-collections, so redactors, compilers, and anthologists often displayed an "authorial" creativity that significantly shaped the meaning of texts in their final form.

Their distinct approaches to Gentile salvation are perhaps most evident in their demonologies. H, consistent with its earlier assertion that the teachings of Moses and Jesus are one, depicts baptism and the abandonment of idols as the means by which Gentiles can become more like Jews, who are not enslaved by demons. In H 9.16, for instance, Peter argues for the causal connection between idolatry and demonic possession by citing the "fact" that the demons "do not appear to the Jews." After explaining to the Gentile crowds how baptism can empower them against these evil creatures (H 9.19), this pseudo-Peter assures them:

> Do not then suppose that we do not fear demons on this account, that we are of a different nature. For we are of the same nature (φύσεως), but not of the same worship (θρησκείας). Therefore – being not only much but altogether superior to you – we do not begrudge you becoming like us (ὄντες καὶ ὑμᾶς τοιούτους γενέσθαι οὐ φθονοῦμεν). Rather, we counsel you, knowing that all these [demons] honor and fear beyond measure those who are reconciled to God (H 9.20.1–2).

From the comment in H 9.16, it is clear that Peter's "we" refers to "we Jews." In stark contrast to the proto-orthodox/orthodox Christian demonization of the Jews, the authors/redactors here exalt them as the only ones from whom the demons cower, due to their superior mode of worship. Accordingly, baptism[92] is presented as a means by which Gentiles can "become like us," free from demons and reconciled to the one God.

When the text later returns to this argument (H 11.16), pseudo-Peter admits that there are some exceptions. He explains them by clarifying his definition of "Jew," a category that, for him, encompasses the Gentile "God-fearer":

> But no one of us can suffer such a thing; they themselves are punished by us, when, having entered into anyone, they entreat us so that they may go out slowly. Yet, someone will perhaps say: "Even some of the God-fearers (θεοσεβῶν)[93] fall under such sufferings [i.e. diseases caused by demons]." I say that is impossible! For I speak of the God-fearer who is truly God-fearing, not

---

[92] Notably, "baptism" is here conceived as regular ritual ablutions, both for the remission of sins and for the purification of the body after defilement; see H 11.26–30.

[93] The term θεοσεβής can simply denote any pious person (including Jews), but it is also used in a more technical sense to designate those Gentiles who affiliate themselves with Judaism without undergoing full conversion (i.e., like the Hebrew equivalent יראי שמים – "those who fear Heaven [= God]"; e.g., *Mekh. Nezikin* 18; BerR 53.9). The latter is particularly fitting in the present context: Peter's attempts to persuade the Gentile crowds to give up idolatry and turn to the one God, so that they can become more like Jews. See discussion in Joyce Reynolds and Robert Tannebaum, *Jews and God-Fearers at Aphrodisias: Greek Inscriptions with Commentary* (Cambridge: Cambridge Philological Society, 1987), 48–66.

one who is such only in name, but one who really fulfills the commandments of the Law that has been given him (ὁ δὲ ὄντως ὢν τοῦ δοθέντος αὐτῷ νόμου ἐκτελεῖ τὰς προστάχεις). If anyone acts impiously, he is not pious. And, hence, if a foreigner keeps the Law, he is a Jew, but he who does not is a Greek (ἐὰν ὁ ἀλλόφυλος τὸν νόμον πράξῃ, Ἰουδαῖός ἐστιν, μὴ πράξας δὲ Ἕλλην). For the Jew, believing in God, keeps the Law (ὁ γὰρ Ἰουδαῖος πιστεύων θεῷ ποιεῖ τὸν νόμον). But he who does not keep the Law is manifestly a deserter through not believing God. And thus – as no Jew, but a sinner (ἁμαρτωλὸς) – he is on account of his sin brought into subjection to those sufferings that are ordained for the punishment of sinners (R 11.16.1–4).

The authors/redactors go on to explain how the "punishment of sinners" differs from God's punishment of the Jews (and, by extension, of Gentile "God-fearers"): the latter is simply a "settlement of accounts" by which God mercifully permits Jews to be "set free of eternal punishments" (R 11.16.5–6).[94]

Here, H redefines the category of "Jews" to include Torah-observant monotheists of non-Jewish ethnicity and, accordingly, condemns idolatrous and non-observant Gentiles as "sinners," together with non-observant Jews. It is unclear, however, whether the former category (i.e., true "Jews") can be simply mapped onto our category of "Christian"; for instance, the authors/redactors tie freedom from demonic possession not to belief in Jesus as Christ but rather to worship of the one God. This is consistent with the rest of H 8–11, which repeatedly stresses the need for faith in God as the only God, while treating Jesus as a "teacher" (e.g., H 11.20) and as the "prophet of truth" whom God sent to tell Gentiles what to do and believe (e.g., H 10.3–4, 11.19).

By contrast, R has reworked the material in B to express a different demonology, historiography, and soteriology, based on different ideas about those who are free from demonic influence. There is no parallel to H 9.16, and the smug "we" in the parallel to H 9.20 at R 4.33 appears to refer to those who believe in Jesus as Christ. For instance, the statements about "our" freedom from the demons are directly followed by a description of the temptation of Jesus by the Devil (i.e., R 4.34). H treats

---

[94] In effect, H here outlines a principle for the interpretation of Jewish history that differs markedly from the proto-orthodox/orthodox Christian approach; for, following this theodical principle, the historical tragedies of the Jewish nation are not signs of God's abandonment of an allegedly sinful and "hard-hearted" people, but rather emblems of their righteousness, continued chosenness, and their inheritance in the World to Come. Cf. BerR 33.1, which attributes to R. Akiva the statement, "He [God] deals strictly with the righteous, calling them to account for the few wrongs that they commit in this world, in order to lavish bliss upon and give them a fine reward in the World to Come; He grants ease to the wicked and rewards them for the few good deeds that they have performed in this world in order to punish them in the future world" (see also *b. Qiddushin* 40b; *b. Taʿanit* 11a). On God's punishment of the Jews as distinct from the nations, see also 2 Macc 6:12–17; EkhaR 1.35; *b. Yevamot* 63a.

this theme in another context (see H 8.21), introducing the incident as an instructive example (see H 8.20) and concluding with Jesus' assertion that "You shall fear the Lord your God, and you shall serve *only Him*" (cp. Mt 4:10/Lk 4:8). Although R's version also integrates this saying, its authors/redactors stress that Jesus is the one through whom the Devil will be destroyed – thereby expressing a demonology more consonant with that of proto-orthodox/orthodox Christians.

Likewise, R's parallel to H 11.16 does not focus on the meaning of being a true "Jew," but rather what it means to be a "worshipper of God" (*dei cultor*):

> But some one will say, "These passions sometimes befall even those who worship God." It is not true! For we say that he is a worshipper of God who does the will of God and observes the precepts of His Law (*etenim nos illum dei dicimus esse cultorem, qui voluntatem dei facit et legis praecepta custodit*). For in God's estimation he is not a Jew who is called a Jew among men, nor is he a Gentile who is called a Gentile, but he who, believing in God, fulfils His Law and does His will, even though he is not circumcised (*etiamsi non sit circumcisus*). He is the true worshipper of God (*verus dei cultor*),[95] who not only is himself free from passions but also sets others free from them; although they are so heavy that they are like mountains, he removes them by means of the faith with which he believes in God .... Yet he who seems to worship God, but is neither fortified by a full faith nor by obedience to the commandments, is only a sinner .... (R 5.34)

R here dismisses both "Jew" and "Gentile" as meaningless categories – and adds that circumcision is not a precondition for adherence to God's Law and will. And, even as this passage retains some of the emphasis on proper praxis that we have seen above in R 4.5, it also stresses the need for "a full faith" and freedom from the passions. Accordingly, this passage ends with a treatment of the theme of different kinds of punishment, which revolves around the contrast between believers and unbelievers, with no reference to the Jews or their special status in the eyes of God.

Furthermore, R 4–6 is marked by an exaltation of Jesus' soteriological role that is absent in H's version of the Tripolis sermons. This is most evident in R 5.10–13, which has no parallel in H. Here, the authors/redactors describe Jesus as the "true prophet in all that he spoke," but then state that "the sayings of the Law ... were fulfilled in him; and the figures of Moses and of the patriarch Jacob before him bore in all respects a type of him" (R 5.10). Through the mouth of Peter, R goes on to contrast the Jews, who still wait for the Messiah, with the Gentiles, to

---

[95] Note that Rufinus does not use the Latin equivalent of θεοσεβεῖς, in the sense of a Gentile affiliated with Judaism (i.e., *metuentes*), but rather chooses a rendering based on its more generic denotation of piety.

whom "all things which are declared concerning him are to be transferred" (R 5.11.3):

> The Jews from the beginning had understood by a most certain tradition that this man should at some time come, the one by whom all things should be restored. And they are meditating daily and looking out for his coming. However, when they saw him amongst them, accomplishing the signs and miracles – as had been written of him – they were blinded with envy and could not recognize him (*ubi adesse eum viderunt et signa ac prodigia, sicut de eo scriptum fuerat, adimplentem, invidia excaecati agnoscere nequiverunt praesentem, in cuius spe laetabantur absentis*; R 5.11.4).

R's pseudo-Peter concludes with a qualification: "Nevertheless, the few of us who were chosen by him understood it" (*intelleximus tamen pauci nos qui ab eo electi sumus*; R 5.11.4). The context, however, suggests that this statement refers primarily to the Jewish disciples selected by Jesus, rather than to the Jews of R's own time. Even as the authors/redactors remain acutely aware of the apostle Peter's own Jewishness, they here equate the Gentiles' salvation through Jesus with the disinheritance of the Jews.

The subtle difference between their references to James may also prove significant. In the parallel units in which both R and H warn their audiences about the demonically-inspired forgeries of the Gospel, R's pseudo-Peter asserts that one should only believe those who bring the testimonial of either "James, the brother of Jesus" or those in his line of succession (R 4.35). The version in H is more expansive. Here, James is not only called "the brother of my Lord," but also the one "to whom was entrusted to administer the *church of the Hebrews* in Jerusalem" (H 11.35). In effect, H takes this opportunity to emphasize that all true followers of Jesus stem from his Jewish disciples.

That H 8–11 views the close connections between Jews and Jesus' Gentile followers as not merely artifacts from the apostolic age is also suggested by its treatment of the Pharisees. In the course of stressing the need for both moral and physical purity (H 11.28–30), the text quotes a saying of Jesus that critiques this group for their preoccupation with only outer purity (i.e., Mt 23:25). Rather then reading this as a blanket denunciation of the Pharisees (or of the Jews more broadly), H's authors/redactors specify that Jesus spoke "the truth with respect to 'the hypocrites' among them, *not with respect to all of them*," and stress that "To some, he said that obedience should be rendered, because they were entrusted with 'the chair of Moses'" (H 11.29 on Mt 23:2).

Interestingly, the main point of the passage is not the importance of moral purity, but rather the need for converted idolaters to partake in regular ritual ablutions with water, particularly after intercourse, and to avoid copulation with women rendered impure by menstruation, "for thus the Law of God commands" (H 11.28, 30). As Baumgarten notes, these passages may reveal H's familiarity with, and respect for, rabbinic culture.[96] To this, we might add that the authors/redactors of H self-consciously participate in a Jewish discourse about halakha, even as their focus falls on issues pertaining to Gentile impurity and purification.[97]

### *"Jewish Christianity" in H 8–11 and R 4–6*

Insofar as the soteriology of H 8–11 is more consistent with the shared material about Moses and Jesus (i.e., R 4.5 = H 8.5–7), it is possible that R's version of the Tripolis sermons reflects redaction of their shared source B towards consonance with proto-orthodox/orthodox Christian traditions. Comparison with this shared material also suggests that the authors/redactors of H enhanced and developed those very features of B that R chose to downplay. If the authors/redactors of R 4–6 did indeed seek to neutralize the "Jewishness" of B, then those responsible for H seem to have done the opposite.

Of course, all such theories remain speculative in the absence of B, and no firm source-critical conclusions can be drawn only from the Tripolis material alone. Moreover, for our present purposes, the precise relationship of H and R to B proves less significant than the contrast between their final forms, which attests the divergent concerns of different fourth-century authors/redactors. As we have seen, H 8–11 and R 4–6 both fit the label "Jewish-Christian," albeit in different ways. The authors/redactors of H 8–11 appear to conceptualize Christianity as essentially the transformation of "pagans" into God-fearers and/or Jews, as made possible by Jesus' (re-)revelation of the same teachings as Moses. Here, it proves significant that H 8–11 defines a "Jew" as one from any ethnicity who "keeps the Law" and describes "baptism" as the first step in a continual process of purification by washing, both for the remission of sins and for the removal of physical defilement (H 11.28–29). In this sense, one could call H 8–11 "Jewish-Christian," but one could also call it a Jewish missionary text that uses the sayings of Jesus to encourage Gentiles to abandon their idolatry, free themselves of the impurity that clings to "pagans," and adopt a praxis that serves the one, true God.

It proves more challenging to characterize R 4–6. As we have seen, Peter's sermons are here prefaced by his assertion of the equality of the

---

[96] Baumgarten, "Literary Evidence," 47.

[97] On rabbinic attitudes towards Gentile impurity, see Christine Hayes, *Gentile Impurities and Jewish Identities: Intermarriage and Conversion from the Bible to the Talmud* (Oxford: Oxford UP, 2002), 107–98, esp. the discussion on pp. 107–44 concerning the ritual impurity of Gentiles and rabbinic debates about the defilement associated with idolatry, on the one hand, and the seminal and menstrual emissions of non-Jews, on the other.

Torah and the Gospel as paths to salvation. What follows, however, is a series of sermons in which Jesus is described as necessary for salvation and the Gentiles are said to be the true heirs of God's biblical promise to the Jews. Nevertheless, it proves significant that R 4–6 requires from Gentile Christ-believers a level of Torah-observance similar to H (see e.g. R 4.36), thus evoking yet another common scholarly criterion of "Jewish Christianity": the combination of Jewish practice with Christian belief.

One could thus characterize R 4–6 as a "catholicizing" redaction of "Jewish-Christian" material that chooses to retain a critique of the antinomianism associated with Paul. This, however, evades a more puzzling question: if "Jewish Christianity" was – as many scholars believe – so marginalized after the "Parting of the Ways" and thus so irrelevant to the majority of Christians, why would a fourth-century Christian wish to rework and transmit this material in the first place? And, more puzzling still, why would Rufinus translate it into Latin?

## The Pseudo-Clementines in Their Late Antique Context

These questions, in my view, may be the key to determining the significance of the so-called "Jewish-Christian" material in H and R for our understanding of Judaism and Christianity as "Ways that Never Parted." As noted above, most research into the Pseudo-Clementines has been devoted not to understanding H or R but rather to reconstructing the sources of B; instead of considering the fourth-century context in which the texts were composed, scholars have focused on the non-extant sources that allegedly stand *behind* their non-extant third-century source. Even if we accept the historical and text-critical value of using hypothetical sources to fill the gap between our NT evidence for "Jewish Christianity" and our patristic evidence for "Jewish-Christian" groups,[98] we can still question the heurism of using the latter only to reconstruct the former. As noted above, source-critical inquiries into H and R serve to neutralize the tension between this late antique evidence for "Jewish Christianity" and the modern scholarly model of the "Parting of the Ways," either by projecting the "Jewish-Christian" elements of H and R into an earlier era or by dismissing them as later "heretical"/"heterodox" accretions to an originally "orthodox"/"catholic" core. In the process, such studies evade important questions about the function of "Jewish-Christian" material in the final forms of these texts: as fourth-century products of creative acts

---

[98] Note also J. Wehnhar's critique of this approach on linguistic grounds ("Literar-kritik und Sprachanalyse: Kritische Anmerkungen zum gegenwärtigen Stand der Pseudoklementinen-Forschung," *Zeitschrift für die Neutestamentliche Wissenschaft* 74 [1983]: 268–301).

of composition, compilation, and redaction (shaped by choices about the inclusion of material, no less than choices about excision and supplementation); and as books that proved surprisingly popular with a late antique Christian readership.[99]

Whatever the validity of the dazzling variety of hypotheses about B's sources,[100] it remains that H and R both date from the fourth century CE, and they were transmitted, read, epitomized, and translated in the fifth century CE and beyond.[101] If these texts do indeed integrate very early "Jewish-Christian" material, then they also serve as important evidence for the continuous preservation of such traditions, for centuries after the "Parting of the Ways" allegedly rendered "Jewish Christianity" irrelevant for both Christians and Jews.

Although it is difficult to make sense of this data using the "Parting" model, new approaches to Jewish–Christian relations in Late Antiquity may prove more helpful. Eschewing the sociological and methodological simplicity of the idea of a single, early separation between the two religions, scholars such as Daniel Boyarin, John Gager, Judith Lieu, and Israel Yuval have stressed the need for a more critical reading of our sources, one which is sensitive both to the elite status of their literate authors and to the gaps between their rhetoric and the social realities "on the ground."[102] In the process, these and other scholars have demonstrated that Jewish and Christian efforts at self-definition remained intimately interconnected, charged with ambivalence, and surprisingly fluid, long after the so-called "Parting of the Ways." Contrary to traditional assumptions about the complete independence and isolation of late

---

[99] Did these books also reach a Jewish readership? This idea should not be dismissed out of hand, and further inquiries into their parallels with rabbinic literature (see below) should also leave open the possibility that these texts may have influenced Jewish traditions, whether by written or oral channels.

[100] See further Jones, "Pseudo-Clementines," 14–33 and idem, *Ancient Jewish-Christian Source*, 20–36.

[101] Interestingly, the third-century *Didascalia* was similarly translated into both Syriac and Latin in the fourth century CE.

[102] See, e.g.: Boyarin, *Dying for God*, esp. 6–19, and articles cited above, as well as his contribution in this volume; John G. Gager, "Jews, Christians, and the Dangerous Ones in Between," in *Interpretation in Religion*, ed. S. Biderman and B. Scharfstein (Leiden: Brill, 1992), 249–57; idem, "The Parting of the Ways: A View from the Perspective of Early Christianity," in *Interwoven Destinies: Jews and Christians through the Ages*, ed. Eugene J. Fisher (New York: Paulist, 1993), 62–73; Judith Lieu, "'The Parting of the Ways': Theological Construct or Historical Reality?" *JSNT* 56 (1994): 101–19; Israel Yuval, "Easter and Passover as Early Jewish–Christian dialogue," in *Passover and Easter: Origin and History to Modern Times*, ed. P. Bradshaw and L. Hoffman (Notre Dame: U. of Notre Dame Press, 1999), 98–124; idem, *Two Nations in Your Womb: Dual Perceptions of the Jews and of Christians* (Tel Aviv: Am Oved, 2000) [Hebrew].

antique Christianity from post-Christian Judaism and vice versa, it seems that interactions between Jews and Christians hardly ceased in the second century; accordingly, the relationship between Judaism and Christianity was negotiated in different ways in different social contexts, intellectual discourses, and geographical milieux – including but not limited to the nascent academies of the rabbinic movement and the proto-orthodox/orthodox Christian churches of the Roman Empire. In short, both were still in the process of formation, usually in a generative tension with one another, even (and perhaps especially) in the fourth century.

For our purposes, these insights prove consequential insofar as they may point the way to a fresh approach to H and R, which recovers the significance of the texts' final forms by exploring the significance of their composition/compilation, transmission, translation, and reception for our understanding of the ongoing discourse about Christian and Jewish identities in Late Antiquity. Needless to say, time and space do not permit a detailed investigation of these issues. For now, I would like to offer several suggestions about potentially fruitful directions for future investigation.

Foremost is the need to integrate the study of H and R, together with other so-called "Jewish-Christian" sources, more fully into research on late antique Judaism and Christianity. Within modern scholarship, the label "Jewish-Christian" too often functions to marginalize texts like the Pseudo-Clementines and to ensure that they are studied in relative isolation from broader discussions. Simply stated, such works are treated as evidence for "Jewish Christianity," but not for Christianity or Judaism. This selectivity is inculcated by the traditional view of the former as a monolithic phenomenon with no real relevance for our understanding of post-70 developments in the "mainstream" of either religion. Yet, as Stephen Wilson observes, "The evidence seems to point neither to their rapid marginalization nor to their continuing dominance after 70 CE but rather to their survival as a significant minority."[103]

Likewise, theories about the post-70/post-135 decline of "Jewish Christianity" are insufficient to explain the integration of such viewpoints in both H and R[104] – let alone the widespread circulation of these and other Pseudo-Clementine compositions in the centuries that followed. A different approach to the question of the "Jewish Christianity" of this

---

[103] Stephen G. Wilson, *Related Strangers: Jews and Christians, 70–170 C.E.* (Minneapolis: Fortress, 1995), 158.

[104] Schoeps, for instance, uses the Pseudo-Clementines and its hypothetical sources (in this case, the *Kerygmata Petrou* and the *Anabathmoi Jakobou*) to reconstruct the Ebionites' "Jewish Christianity." Yet, even by his calculation, a specifically Ebionite origin can only be proposed for about 25% of this corpus (*Jewish Christianity,* 17).

literature is suggested by Georg Strecker's characterization of their shared source, B:

> Noch nachdem die Orthodoxie den Sieg über die Häretiker endgültig errungen hatte, mußte Johannes Chrysostomus die Homilien „Adversus Judaeos" halten, um die Christen seiner Gemeinde von dem Besuch der jüdischen Synagogen (PG 48 Sp. 850) und dem Feiern der jüdischen Fast- und Festtage (ebd. Sp. 844. 849) zurückzuhalten. Dies – das ungeklärte Verhältnis zwischen Judentum und Christentum – ist das Milieu, in dem ein Buch wie die pseudoklementinische Grundschrift entstehen und gelesen werden konnte.[105]

Strecker limits this conclusion to the third-century B and to the Syrian cultural context in which this source likely originated. In light of recent research on Judaism and Christianity in the fourth century, Strecker's observations about B – as reflecting not "Jewish Christianity" *per se* but rather the unresolved relationship between Judaism and Christianity – may prove no less relevant for our understanding of H and R, as well as the subsequent circulation of both (especially R in Latin translation) far beyond the bounds of Syria.

With regard to the early history of Jewish–Christian relations, Daniel Boyarin has proposed that our data are best approached, not in terms of a simple contrast between a "Judaism" derived from the classical rabbinic literature and a "Christianity" derived from the writings of the Church Fathers, but rather in terms of a continuum, marked on one end by Marcion's construction of a Christianity severed of all connections to Judaism and, on the other, by Jews for whom Jesus was similarly irrelevant.[106] Following this approach, Western Christian orthodoxy represents only one of the many possible solutions to mapping a middle ground between these two poles. The various churches of the East articulate other solutions, which would prove no less theologically and practically feasible. Likewise, so-called "Jewish-Christian" sources may attest to the continued existence (and ongoing emergence) of a variety of groups, which offered still other answers to the same questions in the centuries before political and social developments enabled a more final resolution.[107]

There are reasons to believe that these ambiguities persisted into the fourth century,[108] forming an important part of the cultural landscape from which both H and R emerged. The debates about the place of Judaism and Jewish praxis in Christian identity may have even

---

[105] Strecker, *Judenchristentum*, 260.

[106] Boyarin, *Dying for God*, 8.

[107] This occurred in different places at different times; see Becker in this volume.

[108] See Fredriksen in this volume. On the archeological evidence for ongoing interactions, see Leonard Victor Rutgers, "Archaeological Evidence for the Interaction of Jews and non-Jews in Antiquity," *AJA* 96 (1992): 101–18, 110–15.

intensified, concurrent with the beginning of the Christianization of the Roman Empire and the (possibly resultant) consolidation of rabbinic power in Roman Palestine.[109] The former would eventually empower orthodox ecclesiarchs to promote, institutionalize, and legislate their own particular concept of Christianity as a religion that had co-opted the biblical heritage from the Jews and thus stood in absolute conflict with post-Christian forms of Judaism. This, however, seems to have been a rather challenging task, which encountered not a little resistance.

In the fourth and fifth centuries, we find an increase in orthodox Christian polemics against Judaizers and so-called "Jewish-Christian" sects, as well as a rise in the violent tenor of Christian anti-Judaism.[110] This evidence likely speaks to orthodox Christian efforts to establish the mutual exclusivity of Judaism and Christianity, but it may also hint at the reception of such efforts: Joan Taylor, for instance, suggests that the fourth century was also marked by "widespread interest in Jewish praxis by Gentile members of the church and a variety of groups exhibiting 'Jewish-Christian' characteristics."[111] If so, then it is possible that some Christians reacted to these ecclesiastical efforts by articulating and defending different approaches to Christianity's Jewish heritage vis-à-vis Christian praxis, based both on the OT and on contacts with their Jewish contemporaries (not to mention the NT accounts of Jesus and his own observance of Torah).

When we locate H and R within this broader context, their so-called "Jewish-Christian" features take on a new significance. Studies of H and R have shown that their authors/redactors actively engaged in the Christological debates that raged during the fourth century and culminated in the denunciation of Arianism at the Council of Nicaea (325 CE). Through their integration and reworking of "Jewish-Christian" material, they may also participate in the no less heated discussions concerning Christianity's relationship with pre-Christian and post-Christian Judaism – as also evinced by the decision, at the same council, to calculate the date of Easter independently from the Jewish festival of Pesach and to condemn all Quartodecimani as "heretics."[112]

In the case of H, the authors/redactors appear to promote a vision of Judaism and Christianity as two equal paths to salvation, acknowledging

---

[109] On the latter, see Seth Schwartz, *Imperialism and Jewish Society, 200 B.C.E. to 640 C.E.* (Princeton: Princeton UP, 2001), 179–289.

[110] See Robert Louis Wilken, *John Chrysostom and the Jews: Rhetoric and Reality in the Late Fourth Century* (Berkeley: U. of California Press, 1983), esp. 66–94; Gager, "Jews, Christians, and the Dangerous Ones in Between," 249–57.

[111] Taylor, "Phenomenon," 327.

[112] See Wolfgang Heber, *Passa und Ostern: Untersuchungen zur Osterfeier der alten Kirche* (Berlin: Töpelmann, 1969), esp. 1–88.

and accepting those who view these religions as different by definition. This proves particularly intriguing insofar he is clearly familiar with proto-orthodox/orthodox Christian traditions and may also be in close cultural contact with rabbinic Jews. With regard to the latter, further research is needed and to determine the precise scope and nature of his familiarity with contemporary form(s) of Judaism and to confirm that the Jews with whom he seems to interact can indeed be identified with the Rabbis. Notably, this task is facilitated by H's fourth-century context, which makes inquiries into its parallels with rabbinic sources like the *Tosefta*, *Talmud Yerushalmi*, and *Bereshit Rabbah* far less problematic than the usual scholarly attempts to correlate early Christian references to Jews with statements from the classical rabbinic literature.[113]

If we can in fact draw such connections, then H's theories about the concealment of Jesus from the Jews may function as an aetiology of the assertion of the mutual exclusivity of Judaism and Christianity by rabbinic Jews and Christian ecclesiarchs in the Roman Empire – the two groups to whom we owe our modern conceptions about the "Parting of the Ways." Even as the authors/redactors of H stress that both will be saved and explain their perception of difference with reference to God's will, they critique both of them alike by promoting the combination of the two as superior to either alone; for H, the ideal Gentile Christian is a Torah-observant God-fearer, whereas the ideal Jew is one who recognizes Jesus as a teacher of the same divine precepts revealed to Moses. If these authors/redactors are responding to rabbinic Jewish and proto-orthodox Christian efforts to "part" Christianity from Judaism, they do so with a poignant combination of acceptance and resistance, which hints at their participation (or desire for participation) in both religious spheres.

By contrast, R couples its claims about the equality of the Torah and the Gospel with supersessionist statements about Gentiles and Christ. That R incorporates material that expresses different stances towards the relationship between Judaism and Christianity is also demonstrated by its inclusion of R 1.27–71, which the authors/redactors of H evidently chose to exclude from their Clementine pseudepigraphon. In R's final form, this unit functions as Peter's initial explanation to Clement concerning how the Christians came to proselytize among the Gentiles, whereas R 4–6 is set in the context of Clement's travels with Peter on this mission. In

---

[113] It is indeed an apt time to take another look at the parallels between the Pseudo-Clementines and the classical rabbinic literature compiled by earlier scholars such as J. Bergman ("Les éléments juifs dans les pseudo-clementines," *REJ* 46 [1903]: 89–98) and A. Marmorstein ("Judaism and Christianity in the Middle of the Third Century," *HUCA* 10 [1935]: 223–63). As noted above, Baumgarten has made an important contribution to this task ("Literary Evidence," 39–51), but his conflation of evidence from H and R makes his findings preliminary.

effect, the account of Jewish history in R 1.27–71 is juxtaposed with the exploration of Gentile history in R 4–6, such that the Jewish heritage of the church is positively affirmed even as the focus falls on the Gentile mission. Together, they offer an alternative account of Christianity's separation and supersession of Judaism that eschews the fierce denigration of Jews, Judaism, and Jewish Law found in contemporaneous treatments of this theme in favor of a stress on the sinfulness of "pagans" and on the continuity between authentic Christianity and its Jewish heritage, both pre-Christian and apostolic.

Unlike H, R appears to operate mainly in a Christian cultural context. Yet this text can also be read as a critique of other fourth-century Christian approaches to the relationship between Judaism and Christianity. The authors/redactors not only chose to include both R 1.27–71 and Peter's discussion of the equality of the Torah and the Gospel in R 4.5, but they consistently stress the need for good works and articulate the ideal Christian praxis as a combination of moral and ritual purity. In the process, they promote their own synthesis of Judaism and Christianity as the only authentically apostolic way to adhere to Jesus' teachings. The result is a text that challenges the importance of Paul for proto-orthodox/orthodox articulations of the church's relationship to Judaism, while simultaneously severing, with varying degrees of success, the assertion of the truth of Christianity from the antinomianism and anti-Judaism of the nascent orthodoxy.

Rufinus' translation of this book may have been motivated primarily by its status as "proof" for Clement's close connections with Peter and, hence, of the authentic apostolicity of the Roman church. Nevertheless, it is striking that he was not more troubled by its anti-Pauline stance and its refutation of the apostolic history in the Book of Acts, nor (despite his notorious abhorrence of Judaizing) by the so-called "Jewish-Christian" features discussed above. We might speculate that Rufinus viewed these characteristics merely in terms of historical verisimilitude, as a faithful record of the opinions of the Jewish apostle Peter and perhaps also of the important place of ethnically Jewish Christians in the early Roman church.[114] But, in any case, Rufinus ironically ensured that the so-called "Jewish Christian" material therein would circulate widely in the Roman Empire for many centuries to follow, presented as the words of Peter himself. An understanding of the influence of this material on the later readers must await further research into the reception-history of R.

To conclude, I would like to pose a variation of the question with which I began: how should we define "Jewish Christianity" in light of new perspectives on Judaism and Christianity? In our analysis of

---

[114] The latter is discussed by Daniel Stökl Ben Ezra in this volume.

selections from H and R, we have seen how the variety of viewpoints that can be fit under this rubric strains the heurism of the category. Rather than seeking a single "Jewish Christianity" that stands in a direct line of development from the Jerusalem Church, it may be more prudent to view the persistence of so-called "Jewish-Christian" modes of belief and worship as a natural extension of Christianity's origins within Judaism, Christians' continued contacts with Jews, and the church's use of the Jewish Scriptures,[115] as well as the long and rich tradition of messianic speculation within Judaism itself.

Likewise, our discussion of the history of scholarship has shed doubt on the traditional approach to "Jewish Christianity" as a self-contained phenomenon, distinct from all varieties of "Gentile Christianity." As A. F. J. Klijn notes, our term "Jewish-Christian" encompasses all those who combined Judaism and Christianity in ways that differed from the combination(s) that ecclesiarchs in the Roman Empire eventually succeeded in promoting as "Christian."[116] This, however, may tell us more about the formation of Western Christian orthodoxy than about the phenomenon that we term "Jewish Christianity." Just as the notion of "heresy" was a product of efforts to construct "orthodoxy" and never remained a static category, so the idea that some Christ-believers were too "Jewish" to be "Christian" arose in the course of discussions about the precise nature of the Jewish heritage of the church and its exact ramifications for Christian practice. As with other modes of heresiology, the critique of "too Jewish" Christian groups has roots in the first and second centuries but appears to reach an apex in the fourth and fifth. Far from evincing the marginalization of "Jewish-Christian" viewpoints after 70 or 135 CE, the evidence traditionally studied under this rubric may instead help us to illuminate their relevance for a broader discourse about Christianity's relationship to Judaism, which continued to shape Christian self-definition for centuries after the so-called "Parting of the Ways."

---

[115] See, e.g., Patricia Crone, "Islam, Judeo-Christianity and Byzantine Iconoclasm," *Jerusalem Studies in Arabic and Islam* (Jerusalem: Magnes, 1980), 2:93, and John G. Gager's discussion thereof in this volume.

[116] Klijn asserts that we can only "speak of the 'Jewish Christianity' of a particular writing or of a particular group of Christians" in the sense that "we can detect ideas having a Jewish background and which were not accepted by the established Church" ("Study," 431). When commenting on Daniélou's efforts to reconstruct a single, coherent "theology of Jewish Christianity," Klijn similarly emphasizes that "we are dealing with one Christian movement in which the Jewish ideas and practices and the Jews themselves play a part in Jerusalem and Rome, Ephesus and Alexandria. For this reason it is impossible to define the term 'Jewish Christian' because it proved to be a name that can readily be replaced by 'Christian'" (p. 426).

# A Convergence of the Ways?

## The Judaizing of Christian Scripture by Origen and Jerome

by

### ALISON SALVESEN

The present essay argues that, at a period when distinctively Christian theology was being developed out of and even away from the originally Jewish Scriptures, thus taking Christianity away from its Jewish roots, important links were periodically reestablished with the Bible of Judaism. This meant that in this era of Christian and Jewish self-definition, and almost in spite of itself, Christianity never completely lost its grounding in Judaism. Similar movements occurred in later periods, but the precedent was established early on, principally by two great Christian scholars based in Palestine who were in contact with rabbinic Jews. This essay will first demonstrate that such rapprochements did take place and then look at what caused them.

Until fairly recently, translation and interpretation of the Bible, especially of the Old Testament, was not accorded much attention by Patristics scholars, except where it had a bearing on developments concerning Christian belief. The history of Christianity from the second to fifth centuries of the Common Era has traditionally been presented as a series of creeds, ecumenical councils, and key writers, representing milestones in the shaping of a distinctively Christian theology. Statements of faith expressing the nature of Christ and the relationships between the Persons of the Trinity were developed, based on Scripture as far as possible, though given the subject matter, the New Testament was the main basis for doctrinal statements. The creeds did not help define Christianity against Judaism so much as establish a party line against variant and supposedly aberrant forms of Christian belief, yet they prove how different a religion the ex-Jewish sect of Christianity had become.[1]

---

[1] Credal formulation, it is probably safe to say, is a peculiarly Christian idea: it is hardly found in Judaism and Islam, where the Shema and the Fatihah serve as expressions, but not as exclusive definitions, of faith. The attempt to define the nature of God is fraught with difficulties. It was, however, deemed necessary in the face of certain teachings that seemed to contradict Scripture and the experience of the church. Although there were already statements about the person of Christ within the New

The ties that continued to bind Christianity to Judaism largely involved, as they still do, what Christians call the Old Testament.[2] In a Greco-Roman society suspicious of innovation, especially in matters of religion, it was important to stress Christianity's ancient origins in the Jewish religion, and in dialogue with Jews it was commonplace to allege that contemporary Judaism was a tradition that had lost its continuity with the truth revealed to the Hebrews and Israelites. Paul's statement, "Christ died for our sins, according to the Scriptures," (1 Cor 15.3) expresses the belief that the significance of the death of Jesus arises from the Jewish Scriptures. In fact, the setting and self-understanding of Jesus, and of Paul and the other apostles, is entirely Jewish and intimately connected with their ancestral holy writ. Difficult as the Old Testament was for Christians to interpret from the perspective of an increasingly non-Jewish church, it was necessary to do so in order to make the connection between Christian faith and Hebrew religion.[3] Christian tradition had many resources on which to draw, but exegetical tools were often borrowed from Jews, who had first tackled the problem of interpreting the ancient writings of their ancestors for their own times and religion, often in quite varied ways.

When examining the role of Scripture in Judaism and Christianity, the first question to arise concerns the canon: which books are to be considered as Scripture, fundamental for doctrine and practice? By the patristic period there were already many more Greek works that could be considered scriptural than existed in Hebrew. Various lists and groupings of books are mentioned in passing in works from the Maccabean period onwards, but the idea of a canonical list is a late one in both faiths.[4] But whenever the number of books in the Jewish biblical canon was finally settled, it was smaller than any list of authoritative books in the Old Testament among Christians in antiquity. The Four Gospels and the

---

Testament literature, these needed to be clarified and given some coherence. Patristics textbooks rightly focus on doctrinal and ecclesiastical developments of this period, but other issues, such as the translation and interpretation of the Bible, are often overlooked as a result.

[2] Since this essay is largely concerned with the biblical text in different languages, to prevent confusion the term "Hebrew Bible" will be avoided, except when referring to the Bible *in Hebrew*.

[3] At least according to their detractors, Marcion and Mani are two examples of thinkers who could not reconcile Jewish Scripture with the life of Jesus, and so rejected the former altogether (e.g. Irenaeus, *adv. Haer.* I.25.1; Tertullian, *adv. Marc.* I.2.2–3; Augustine, *c. Faustum*, passim).

[4] In the tannaitic period there was some discussion of whether or not certain books "defiled the hands" (*m. Yadaim* 3.5; 4.5). Doubts were expressed as to whether Song of Songs or Ecclesiastes rendered the hands unclean. But the discussion in the Mishnah is primarily concerned with the physical form of the Scriptures, rather than on their theological content: they have to be in Assyrian (square) script, on leather and in ink.

writings of the New Testament were quoted as authoritative by many Christians from the late second century onwards.[5] However, the term "New Testament" does not appear regularly until the time of Origen, and there was no generally accepted canon (in the sense of an inclusive and exclusive list) of New Testament books until the late fourth century.[6] Much Jewish literature of the Second Temple period was also read by Christians, such as Wisdom of Solomon, Ben Sira, Baruch, and Maccabees. But there was a host of further possibilities for the Christian reader: revelations and acts and apocalypses of figures known from older scriptural books.

Discussions of what was authoritative were common but indecisive in this period, and Christians were therefore interested in the contents of the Jewish canon. Pressed by a correspondent some time between 160 and 180 CE, Melito of Sardis presents a list of Old Testament books he has found out "from the east ... the place where it all happened, and the truth was proclaimed."[7] The list corresponds to the contents of the rabbinic biblical canon except for the omission of the book of Esther.[8] However, Melito does not explicitly mention Jews or Hebrews in connection with the list. In the next century, in the introduction to his commentary on Psalm 1, Origen also provides a list of the canonical books according to Jewish tradition, which does include Esther, and gives their Hebrew titles, but he explicitly says that Maccabees is excluded.[9] Origen notes in his letter to Africanus that the Hebrews did not use Tobit or Judith, and that they did not exist in Hebrew, nor were they included among the Jewish apocryphal books. But he remarks that Tobit is used in the churches, and he implies that it is of value by using information in it to support the

---

[5] However, Tatian's *Diatesseron*, or Gospel harmony, played an important role for some time, especially in the Syriac church.

[6] See J. G. Dunn, "New Testament," in *Oxford Companion to Christian Thought*, ed. A. Hastings, R. Mason, and H. Pyper (Oxford: Oxford UP, 2000), 473–76. I am grateful to Prof. Elaine Pagels for giving me a copy of her article "Irenaeus, the 'Canon of Truth,' and the *Gospel of John*: Making a Difference through Hermeneutics and Ritual," to be published in *Vigiliae Christianae*.

[7] In Eusebius, *Hist. Eccl.* IV.26.

[8] The scroll of Esther was accepted as canonical in rabbinic circles by the end of the second century CE and read in the synagogue on the feast of Purim (*m. Megillah* 1.1). Moreover, Esth 2.22 is cited in *m. Avot* 6.6.

[9] Also cited in Eusebius, *Hist. Eccl.* VI.25. Origen actually omits the Minor Prophets, includes 1 Esdras and the Epistle of Jeremiah, and only has twenty-one books in his list. A. C. Sundberg believes that he was confused by the Hebrew titles and muddled 1 Esdras and the Epistle of Jeremiah with the Hebrew Ezra and Nehemiah (*The Old Testament of the Early Church,* Harvard Theological Studies 20 [Cambridge: Harvard UP, 1964], 135).

authenticity of the story of Susannah, an addition to the Greek book of Daniel.[10]

The exact content of the Christian canon continued to be ill-defined, and even today there are great differences between the canons of different churches, but it is noteworthy that some Christians in the patristic age wanted to know which books were accepted by Jews. This was sometimes so that they could use the parts of Scripture that were common to both Jews and Christians for religious debate, as Origen admits in his letter to Africanus.[11] But perhaps there was additionally a sense of the priority of the Hebrew canon. In contrast, Jerome accepted the Hebrew canon, very often remarking on whether or not a certain book was read "*apud Hebraeos*," and he declared all other books apocryphal: edifying, but not authoritative for doctrine.[12] Yet he continued to cite these non-canonical books, though it is debatable whether he still considered them to be Scripture.[13] He translated Tobit and Judith into Latin, in each case from Aramaic originals and with Jewish help, but this was apparently under pressure from his patrons.[14]

Another issue of importance to Christians was how to understand the Old Testament and interpret it for their contemporary setting. For Greek-speaking Christians who used the Septuagint (= LXX), the easiest means of access to the Old Testament writings, including their cultural and historical significance, were the writings of Hellenistic Jews. These include Philo and Josephus, the minor Hellenistic writers such as Demetrius, Eupolemus, Artapanus, and Ezekiel the Tragedian. Such authors had already adapted and systematized Scripture for a Hellenistic setting, in the Greek language. The minor Jewish Hellenistic writers were excerpted by Alexander Polyhistor in the mid-first century BCE, in his work "Concerning the Jews." In turn, the Christian writers Clement of Alexandria and Eusebius of Caesarea recycled many extracts that they

---

[10] Origen, *Ep. ad Afr.* 13.

[11] Origen, *Ep. ad Afr.* 5.

[12] *Prologus Galeatus, Praef. in Ezra, Praef. in Reg.*, and *Ep.* 53.8. In *Ep.* 107.12, addressed to the parents of a girl dedicated to virginity from her infancy, Jerome recommends that she should avoid the apocrypha (*cavet omnia apocrypha*), and if she does read them occasionally, it should be out of reverence for the miracles, not for the truth of their teaching. He notes their pseudonymity and says that much faulty material is included, so that great prudence is required to sift the gold from the mud.

[13] D. Brown, *Vir Trilinguis: A Study in the Biblical Exegesis of St. Jerome* (Kampen: Kok Pharos, 1992), 65–70, and J. Braverman, *Jerome's Commentary on Daniel*, CBQMS 7 (Washington, DC: Catholic Biblical Association of America 1978), 45. See Jerome's remarks about Tobit in his preface to his *Commentary on Jonah.*

[14] See his prefaces to the translations of Tobit and Judith, as well as his comments on the additions to Daniel in his preface to the *IH* version of that book. At the end of the preface to his *Commentary on Habbakuk*, he gives the reader the choice of accepting or rejecting the parts which are not read "among the Hebrews."

found in Alexander Polyhistor's work, mainly for apologetic purposes against pagans and thus at times with some degree of distortion.[15] Josephus was a popular choice for Christian readers. In his twenty books of *Jewish Antiquities*, he presented Old Testament history in a format familiar to his non-Jewish contemporaries from works like Dionysius of Halicarnassus' twenty books of *Roman Antiquities*. One passage testifies to the earthly existence of Christ, but part or all of this piece, which is known as the *Testimonium Flavianum* and is quoted in Eusebius' *Hist. Eccl.* I.11, is likely to have been fabricated by Eusebius.[16] Nonetheless, the forgery contributed to the preservation of Josephus' works by the church. Philo Judaeus provided allegorical, spiritual interpretations of the Pentateuch, following the technique of the Homeric allegorists: ancient texts that were central to one's culture but problematic for interpretation could be read in such a way as to uncover the hidden, spiritual meaning behind the rebarbative and even barbarian exterior. This technique proved immensely useful to Christians, in particular to Origen of Alexandria and his successors in the Alexandrian tradition. Finally, there was the Jewish literature available in Greek from the period of the Second Temple, which was important for the history and religious developments among the Jews from the time of Ezra until the time of Christ. The books of Maccabees were popular among Christians, both for historical information and for encouragement at times of persecution by the Roman or Persian authorities. The Wisdom of Solomon spoke of divine wisdom and the possible immortality of the soul, Tobit and Judith were stories of human bravery and divine aid. Moreover, the Hebrew book of Ben Sira had been translated into Greek by the author's grandson and, as the book of Ecclesiasticus, was widely quoted by Christian authors. In all these cases, Jewish works were taken over by Christians, and preserved by the church, to understand and defend their faith even after rabbinic Judaism had largely discarded them.[17]

---

[15] Cf. S. Inowlocki, "The Citations of Jewish Greek Authors in Eusebius of Caesarea's *Praeparatio Evangelica* and *Demonstratio Evangelica*," M.Litt. Thesis, Oxford University, 2001.

[16] *Ant.* XVIII.63–64. For a recent, negative evaluation of the excerpt's authenticity, see K. A. Olson, "Eusebius and the *Testimonium Flavianum*," *CBQ* 61 (1999): 305–22.

[17] There is no trace of an original Hebrew text of Judith, though Jerome says that he knew an Aramaic version. He says that it was regarded by Palestinian Jews ("Hebraeos") as apocryphal (*Praef. Iudith.*). Tobit is attested in Aramaic at Qumran, and Jerome translated it into Latin from Aramaic. But both Origen and Jerome say that it was unknown in Hebrew and not read among the "Hebrews" (Origen, *Ep. Ad Afri.* 13; Jerome, *Praef. Tobit*). The First Book of Maccabees is believed to have had a Semitic original but, as noted earlier, Origen says that it was not part of the Hebrew canon, even though he knew a Semitic title for it (in Eusebius, *Hist. Eccl.* VI.25). The other books of Maccabees and the book of Wisdom were all written in Greek, and not recognized by

In contrast to Alexandrian Christian writers, those of the Antiochene school preferred a more literalist and historical approach to Scripture.[18] Syriac-speaking Christians, who used the Peshitta, the Syriac translation of the Hebrew Bible, tended to adopt methods similar to the Antiochenes. In the fourth century, the two earliest influential Syriac writers, Aphrahat, whom tradition locates in the region of what is now Mosul, and Ephrem, from Nisibis and Edessa, show familiarity with a Jewish haggadic approach to Scripture, filling in the apparently missing details of biblical narrative and harmonizing apparent discrepancies. Sometimes they agree with specific lines of interpretation known from rabbinic midrash, sometimes they explicitly disagree with them. But probably because of the common Aramaic language and culture, these early Syriac writers tend to follow established Semitic, rather than Hellenistic, Jewish methods of interpretation, in places where there are no precedents set by the New Testament's interpretation of the Old Testament and no christological capital to be made from the passage under comment.

## Origen, the Hexapla, and the Three

So Hellenistic Jewish writers and Aramaic Jewish tradition were used by Christians to interpret the content of the Old Testament. But sometimes it was the Old Testament text itself, specifically the LXX, that seemed to be the problem. According to the pseudonymous work the *Letter of Aristeas*, the LXX Pentateuch was translated, by Gentile royal decree under Ptolemy Philadelphus (285–247 BCE), from the best manuscripts available in Jerusalem, by the most qualified translators representing the twelve tribes of Israel, with the approval of the high priest, and was acclaimed by the whole of the Jewish community of Alexandria.[19] This wondrous

---

rabbinic Judaism. In contrast, the Hebrew book of Ben Sira, though not part of the traditional Hebrew canon, is cited by the Rabbis, from the Mishnah (*m. Avot* 4.4) to Saadya Gaon, and fragments of it have been found in the Cairo Genizah.

[18] For a recent, more nuanced view of the distinction between Antiochene and Alexandrian exegesis, see F. Young, *Biblical Exegesis and the Formation of Christian Culture* (Cambridge: Cambridge UP, 1997).

[19] The account of the translation reads very much like propaganda for its authority. See S. P. Brock, "The Phenomenon of Biblical Translation in Antiquity," *Alta: the University of Birmingham Review* 2/8 (1969), reprinted in *Studies in the Septuagint: Origins, Recensions, and Interpretations: Selected Essays with a Prolegomenon*, ed. S. Jellicoe (New York: Ktav, 1974), 541–71.

The Greek text of the *Letter of Aristeas*, edited by H. St.-J. Thackeray, can be found in *An Introduction to the Old Testament in Greek*, ed. H. B. Swete, rev. R. R. Ottley (Cambridge: Cambridge UP, 1914), 533–606. An introduction and English translation is provided by Andrews in *The Apocrypha and Pseudepigrapha of the Old Testament in*

pedigree was accepted by many Hellenistic Jews and embellished even further by Christians, who extended the legend to encompass the whole Greek Bible and viewed the translation of the LXX as a special dispensation to enable Gentiles to receive revelation.[20] But Jews who knew both Greek and Hebrew had become dissatisfied with the LXX very early on, even before the turn of the Common Era, and were producing revisions and improvements to bring the Greek closer to the text and current interpretation of the emerging standard Hebrew text.[21]

Such developments did not go unnoticed by Christians, and the first references to Jewish revisions of the Greek text of Scripture reflect the suspicion that they aroused. Origen, who lived in the period between

---

*English*, vol. 2, *Pseudepigrapha*, ed. R. H. Charles (Oxford: Clarendon Press, 1913), 83–122. Dr. Sylvie Honigman of Tel Aviv University is currently engaged in writing a monograph on the *Letter of Aristeas* (*The Septuagint and Homeric Scholarship in Alexandria: Studies in the Narrative of the "Book [Letter] of Aristeas"*; to be published by Routledge).

[20] Josephus paraphrases the account found in Aristeas in *Ant.* XII.7–118. Philo, *De vita Mosis* II.40 sees the translators as "priests (ἱεροφάντες) and prophets" who were in harmony with the spirit of Moses. The experienced translator Jerome disagreed: *in una basilica congregatos contulisse scribant, non prophetasse ... aliud est enim vatem, aliud esse interpretem* (*Praef. in Pent*; cf. *Praef. in Paralip.*).

The first embellishment by Christians occurs in the *Cohortatio ad Graecos* 13: the translators are placed in seventy *separate* cells and miraculously produce identical renderings of the Hebrew. Irenaeus, Eusebius, Clement of Alexandria, Tertullian, and Augustine have similar versions, while Epiphanius has the translators working in pairs in thirty-six cells. For references, see the introduction by Andrews in R. H. Charles, ed., *Apocrypha and Pseudepigrapha*, 2:92–93. For the idea that the LXX was a "Bible for the Gentiles," see A. Kamesar, *Jerome, Greek Scholarship, and the Hebrew Bible: A Study of the Hebraicae Quaestiones in Genesim*, Oxford Classical Monographs Series (Oxford: Clarendon, 1993), 29–34.

[21] Revision of the Greek text, either stylistically or towards the proto-Hebrew text, started in Jewish circles long before Origen or even the versions of Theodotion, Aquila, and Symmachus. See N. Fernández Marcos, *The Septuagint in Context: Introduction to the Greek Versions of the Bible* (Leiden: Brill, 2000), 247–52; P. W. Skehan, "4QLXXNum: A Pre-Christian Reworking of the Septuagint" *HTR* 70 (1977): 39–50; J. W. Wevers, "An Early Revision of the Septuagint of Numbers" *Eretz-Israel* 16 (H. M. Orlinsky Volume) (1982), *235–*239; J. W. Wevers, "Pre-Origen Recensional Activity in the Greek Exodus," in *Studien zur Septuaginta – Robert Hanhart zu Ehren aus Anlaß seines 65. Geburtstages*, ed. D. Fraenkel, U. Quast, and J. W. Wevers, Mitteilungen des Septuaginta-Unternehmens XX (Göttingen: Vandenhoeck & Ruprecht, 1990), 121–39. Ulrich is inclined to see the 4QLXXLev^a fragments as closer to the original Septuagint ("Old Greek") version, and the text as presented in Wevers' edition as a revision towards the proto-Masoretic Text ("The Septuagint Manuscripts from Qumran: A Reappraisal of their Value," in *Septuagint, Scrolls and Cognate Writings. Papers Presented to the International Symposium on the Septuagint and its Relations to the Dead Sea Scrolls and Other Writings (Manchester, 1990)*, ed. G. J. Brooke and B. Lindars, SCSS 33 [Atlanta: Scholars Press, 1992], 49–80).

these two pairs of Fathers, was much less defensive, even though as the prime espouser of Philonic exegesis he could have ignored the revisions and used only allegory to explain apparent difficulties in the LXX. Because Origen lived in Caesarea in Palestine, where there was a certain amount of dialogue with Jews who knew Hebrew, he would have been aware that there was more to Jewish revision of Greek Scripture than the desire to produce anti-Christian renderings.[22]

It is well known that Origen was profoundly dissatisfied with the state of LXX manuscripts and attempted to "heal" (ἰάσασθαι) them.[23] Certainly he would have found many sloppily copied Greek biblical manuscripts and discrepancies in the wording of different texts, and noticed that the transmission of LXX manuscripts fell short of the norms established in his native Alexandria for texts of the classics. It is also likely that during his time in Palestine he became aware of the care with which Hebrew manuscripts were copied and how the best exempla were chosen for transmission. Using tools from both of these superior textual traditions, the rabbinic and the classical, Origen produced a revised LXX text. Taking the Hebrew text current in his day as the criterion, he supplied a Greek text annotated with the Aristarchian signs used by classical scholars.[24]

---

[22] Origen's own knowledge of Hebrew was very limited and depended heavily upon the renderings of the Three. His proficiency fell very far short of Jerome's. See N. R. M. de Lange, *Origen and the Jews* (Cambridge: Cambridge UP, 1976), 21–23.

[23] *Comm. in Matt.* 15.14. There has been some controversy over whether Origen intended his revised LXX text to serve an apologetic or a scholarly purpose. Much depends on how one weighs what he says about his work in *Comm. Matt.* 15.14 compared with his remarks in *Ep. ad Afri.* 2–5, and how one interprets the fact that Origen generally quotes from the non-revised LXX text in his works from his later years. See the following studies: S. P. Brock, "Origen's Aims as a Textual Critic of the Old Testament" in *Papers Presented to the Fifth International Conference on Patristic Studies held in Oxford 1967 = Studia Patristica* X, ed. F. L. Cross, TU 107 (Berlin: Akademie-Verlage, 1970), 215–18; reprinted in *Studies in the Septuagint: Origins, Recensions, and Interpretations,* ed. S. Jellicoe, 343–46; P. Nautin, *Origène. Sa Vie et son Oeuvre,* Christianisme antique 1 (Paris: Beauchesne, 1977), 345–53; N. R. M. de Lange, *La Lettre à Africanus sur l'Histoire de Suzanne,* SC 302 (Paris: Cerf, 1983), 493–98; de Lange, *Origen and the Jews,* 51–52. Most recently J. Schaper has argued persuasively that, since Origen was both scholar and apologist, the revised LXX text was intended to serve both scholarly and apologetic purposes ("The Origin and Purpose of the Fifth Column of the Hexapla" in *Origen's Hexapla and Fragments,* ed. A. Salvesen, TSAJ 58 [Tübingen: Mohr Siebeck, 1998], 3–15).

[24] Working from different angles, Geoff Jenkins and Gerard Norton have both shown that Origen's synopsis of scriptural versions, the Hexapla, originally had a first Hebrew column which formed the matrix upon which the other columns were ordered (presumably the Hebrew column was supplied by a Jewish scribe). From the few, late folios copied from the Hexapla that have come down to us, it seems clear that the first column consisted of the Hebrew text written out one word per line in its biblical order.

Origen never got as far as the notion of the "*Hebraica veritas*," the idea that the Hebrew biblical text was the ultimate source of authority in terms of the *meaning* of Scripture as well as its shape. Yet it is clear that he regarded the Hebrew text as important, not obsolete – as the rest of his Christian contemporaries did – from the fact that he used it as a quantitative yardstick against which to compare his revised LXX text. This was because he assumed that the Hebrew text used by Jews of his day was exactly the same as that used by the original translators of (all) the books of the LXX. He may have made this assumption through observing the care taken by Jewish scribes over the copying of Hebrew manuscripts and the apparent lack of variation between Hebrew texts of Scripture, and supposed, erroneously, that such faithful copying went back to the original text of each biblical book. In fact, as we now know from fragments of biblical books at Qumran, and suspect from the shorter versions of some LXX books, there were several layers of editing and redaction in the Hebrew, and scribes were not always as careful as they later came to be. But of course Origen could not have known this. The Aristarchian signs were therefore used in the fifth column of Origen's Hexapla to highlight the comparison of the two texts, Hebrew and Greek, while preserving the best LXX text of the church.[25] Anything present in the Hebrew but absent in the LXX was filled in with help from the later Greek revisions of the LXX and marked with asterisks. Obeli showed the reader where the Greek had something over and above what appeared in the Hebrew.[26] It was the "Three," the three Jewish Greek revisions of Aquila, Symmachus, and Theodotion, which indicated whether there were pluses or minuses vis-à-vis the Hebrew.[27]

The Hexapla was such a vast work that only parts of it tended to be copied, and it seems to have disappeared in the upheavals of mid-seventh-

---

See R. G. Jenkins, "The First Column of the Hexapla: the Evidence of the Milan Codex (Rahlfs 1098) and the Cairo Genizah Fragment (Rahlfs 2005)" and G. J. Norton, "Observations on the First Two Columns of the Hexapla," both in *Origen's Hexapla and Fragments,* ed. Salvesen, 73–87, 88–102.

[25] On the presence or absence of signs in the fifth column, see the discussion in Schaper, "Origin and Purpose," 6–9.

[26] Origen, *Comm. Matth.* 15.14, and Jerome, *Ep.* 106.7, *Praef. in Pent.*; I. Soisalon-Soininen, *Der Charakter der asterisierten Zusätze in der Septuaginta,* Annales Academiae Scientiarum Fennicae, ser. B, 114 (Helsinki: Suomalainen Tiedeakatemia, 1959), 193–97, notes how mechanically these passages from the Three are added, with no attempt to change the original or added text, often resulting in some incongruity.

There has been some difference of opinion over whether the fifth column of the Hexapla represented Origen's revised text or whether this column contained only a "standard" LXX text, as a preliminary to Origen's production of a revised LXX text. Schaper argues for the former ("Origin and Purpose," 6–9).

[27] *Comm. Matt.* 15.14: κριτηρίῳ χρησάμενοι ταῖς λοιπαῖς ἐκδόσεσιν ... τὴν κρίσιν ποιησάμενοι ἀπὸ τῶν λοιπῶν ἐκδόσεων ....

century Palestine.[28] Not all copyists were conversant with the Aristarchian signs, and so the Hexapla's LXX column incorporating the material from the Jewish Greek revisions began to be transmitted without them.[29] From the point of view of textual criticism of the Bible, this muddied the waters more than a little: one French scholar has characterized Origen's revisional activity as "catastrophique," since the Hexaplaric text tended to influence other LXX text-types.[30] So the witness of the LXX to the ancient Hebrew texts that preceded the standard rabbinic "Masoretic" text became distorted by Origen's attempt to bring the Greek Bible in line with the Hebrew text of the third century CE. However, Origen's textual work, regarded as a tragedy by modern textual critics, did bring the Old Testament of the Greek Church closer to the Hebrew Bible of the Jews. Origen had an additional, apologetic motive for conforming the LXX to the Hebrew text, in that it would make debates with Jews easier if everyone was using the same text (i.e. Christians would not be trying to argue points from passages that did not appear in Hebrew or in the latest Jewish Greek Bible versions). But whether from scholarly or apologetic motives, the effect was the same: to rein in LXX tradition from its own Christian trajectory and move it back towards the Jewish Bible. Eugene Ulrich speaks of Origen's work as effecting the Christianization of the Jewish Bible, but I would see it as a Hebraization of the Christian Bible.[31]

As for the actual extent of this "Hebraization," it is hard to gauge precisely for a number of reasons. First, we have very few texts of the Greek Old Testament that predate Origen's recension, and this makes comparison with later manuscript tradition difficult. Those that we do possess display considerable textual variety, as we might expect from Origen's own observation about διαφωνία among exempla in the mid-

---

[28] But not before Paul of Tella translated the whole of it into Syriac in 616–17. This version became known as the Syrohexapla and influenced the subsequent history of the Old Testament text in Syriac. However, since the standard Old Testament text used in the Syriac churches, the Peshitta, had been translated directly from Hebrew manuscripts in the first and second centuries CE, the effect of the Syrohexapla was to bring Greek influence into Syriac textual tradition rather than to make the Syriac Scriptures closer to the Hebrew text of the Rabbis.

[29] As Jerome notes in *Ep.* 106.22, 55.

[30] D. Barthélemy, "Origène et le texte de l'Ancien Testament," in *Epektasis. Mélanges patristiques offerts à Cardinal Jean Daniélou,* ed. J. Fontaine and C. Kannengiesser (Paris: Beauchesne, 1972), 247–61 (247). Reprinted in D. Barthélemy, *Etudes d'histoire du texte de l'Ancien Testament,* OBO 21 (Göttingen: Vandenhoeck & Ruprecht, 1978), 203–17.

[31] Eugene Ulrich, "The Old Testament Text of Eusebius: The Heritage of Origen," in *Eusebius, Christianity and Judaism,* ed. H. W. Attridge and G. Hata (Leiden: Brill, 1992), 543–63 (558).

third century.[32] It is equally hard to find manuscripts that faithfully represent his revised LXX text. Their witness varies from book to book. For instance, in Isaiah the best representatives of Origen's recension are the fourth-century codex Vaticanus (which in other books is free from Hexaplaric influence), the eighth-century codex Venetus, three medieval minuscules, the Syriac rendering of Origen's LXX column known as the Syrohexapla, and the Syro-Palestinian version.[33] But in Exodus, the main Hexaplaric witnesses are the fourth-century uncial G, five medieval minuscules, and the Syrohexapla again. A further hindrance to perceiving the influence of Origen's recension on subsequent Greek textual history is the tendency to regard modern scholarly editions of LXX as representing *the* Septuagint. Critical editions such as the Göttingen series naturally aim to recover the earliest possible stage of the text, and diplomatic editions like the Larger Cambridge edition reproduce a single early manuscript, usually the fourth-century Vaticanus, chosen precisely because it is relatively free from later recensional activity.[34] Neither scholarly edition gives as its main text a common-or-garden medieval manuscript of no particular pedigree, but it is precisely this sort of text that would be most likely to contain readings that have filtered down from Origen's recension, along with many others. If one is not in a position to delve into collections of manuscripts, evidence for those readings that reflect the rabbinic Hebrew text can be found in the apparatus of the critical editions along with the evidence for other recensional activity such as the Lucianic/Antiochene.[35]

It would be a lifetime's work to list every detail of every manuscript reading that is probably due to Origen's attempts to bring the LXX in line

---

[32] *Comm. Matth.* 15.14.

[33] Ed. J. Ziegler, *Isaias,* Septuaginta Vetus Testamentum Graecum, Auct. Acad. Scient, Gottingensis editum 14 (2nd ed.; Göttingen: Vandenhoeck & Ruprecht, 1969), 36–38.

[34] *Septuaginta: Vetus Testamentum Graecum* (Göttingen: Vandenhoeck & Ruprecht, 1931–); *The Old Testament in Greek according to the text of Codex Vaticanus, supplemented from other uncial manuscripts, with a critical apparatus containing variants of the chief ancient authorities for the text of the Septuagint,* eds. A. E. Brooke, N. McLean, and H. St. J. Thackeray (Cambridge: Cambridge UP, 1906–40).

[35] K. H. Jobes and M. Silva, *Invitation to the Septuagint* (Grand Rapids, Mich.: Baker Academic, 2000), chapters 6 and 10, give helpful explanations of how to carry out the analysis of individual manuscript readings, and the examples given note the presence of possible Hexaplaric readings that reflect the Hebrew Masoretic Text.

In contrast to the position with the Origenic recension, there is more than one recent edition of the Lucianic/Antiochene recension: N. Fernández Marcos and J. R. Busto Saiz, *El texto antioqueno de la Biblia Griega,* Textos y Estudios "Cardenal Cisneros" 50, 53, 60 (3 vols.; Madrid: C.S.I.C., 1989–96), and B. A. Taylor, *The Lucianic Manuscripts of 1 Reigns,* Harvard Semitic Monographs 50–51 (2 vols.; Atlanta: Scholars Press, 1992–93). This recension was largely a stylistic, inner-Greek one.

with the Hebrew text of his day.[36] For the purposes of this essay, the examples of Origen's influence can be most clearly seen in the passages where large "minuses" existed: places where the ecclesiastical LXX had verses missing compared with the Hebrew text of Palestinian Jews. Origen filled these in, often from the revisions of the "Three." As noted above, although he marked such passages with asterisks, they were often omitted by copyists. Consequently the passages were read as if they were the original work of the Seventy translators.[37] For the nature of the smaller additions and changes to match the Hebrew, the study of Ilmari Soisalon-Soininen is invaluable; he presents the texts of Numbers 1.1–20, Joshua 9–10, and Ezekiel 34–35 along with an analysis of the Origenic recension of those chapters.[38]

The LXX text of Exodus in chapters 35–40, especially 36.8–39.23, differs markedly from that of the standard Masoretic Hebrew text (MT).[39] However, there are manuscripts which undoubtedly represent the Origenic revision, since they present a text that is close to MT. These are manuscripts F[b] G ckm Arm Eth[c] and Syh, and their text of 36.8–39.23 is so different that the Larger Cambridge edition places it in an appendix at the end of the volume, while the Göttingen edition incorporates it in the first apparatus.[40]

Another place where Origen's recensional activity can be easily seen, because it involves sizeable additions, is the book of Job. The original LXX text is much shorter, and Origen appended the "missing" material largely from Theodotion, as the study of Gentry has shown.[41] However, as Gentry notes, while the modern editions indicate this additional material with asterisks, as Origen had done, the ecclesiastical texts often

---

[36] As a New Testament textual critic, Bruce Griffin, remarked to the present writer.

[37] This tended to happen even when the signs were still present, as Jerome notes in his *Praef. in Job.* Jerome speaks of Origen "mixing" (*miscuit*) the LXX with Theodotion's version (*Praef. in Pent., Praef. in Paralip.*).

[38] Soisalon-Soininen, *Der Charakter der asterisierten Zusätze.*

[39] The reason for the difference between the original LXX ("Old Greek") and the standard Masoretic Hebrew text (MT) has been explained in different ways. See D. W. Gooding, *The Account of the Tabernacle Translation and Textual Problems of the Greek Exodus* (Cambridge: Cambridge UP, 1959), 105, and A. Aejmelaeus, "Septuagintal Translation Techniques – A Solution to the Problem of the Tabernacle Account," in *Septuagint, Scrolls and Cognate Writings. Papers Presented to the International Symposium on the Septuagint and its Relations to the Dead Sea Scrolls and Other Writings (Manchester, 1990)*, ed. G. J. Brooke and B. Lindars, SCSS 33 (Atlanta: Scholars Press, 1992), 381–401.

[40] J. W. Wevers, *Septuaginta Vetus Testamentum Graecum*, II,1: *Exodus* (Göttingen: Vandenhoeck & Ruprecht, 1991), 51–54.

[41] P. J. Gentry, *The Asterisked Material in the Greek Job*, Septuagint and Cognate Studies 38 (Atlanta, Ga.: Scholars Press, 1995). Origen comments specifically on the quantitative differences between the Jewish and Christian texts of Job in *Ep. ad Afr.* 6.

lacked the signs, and these additions, made to conform to the rabbinic Hebrew text, passed into church tradition more or less unnoticed.[42] The result is, as Gentry says, "a genetic monstrosity, hybridized from apples and oranges ... [it] results from patching together the Old Greek translation of Job (OG) and a later revision or translation attributed by textual witnesses to θ', i.e. Theodotion."[43] Similarly, Claude Cox speaks of the disastrous exegetical consequences of Origen's work on Job, describing the Origenic text there as "a veritable hodgepodge of two very different translations."[44] Cox criticizes the Göttingen edition of Job, edited by Ziegler, for providing the Hexaplaric text as the main text in the edition, since this is not the earliest recoverable Greek text of Job.[45] However, while this was a questionable thing to do from the text-critical angle, it does provide a good picture of the way in which the current Hebrew tradition became part of the Greek Christian tradition of this book.

Why is the witness to the Origenic, Hebraizing recension so widely disseminated but not more unified? We have evidence that some ecclesiastical authorities made a deliberate attempt to diffuse the Origenic recension. Eusebius reports that he himself provided fifty copies of the Scriptures for the new churches in Constantinople at the Emperor's request; these were undoubtedly based on Origen's revised LXX column,[46] and there are scholia and colophons in several manuscripts which refer to the "edition" of Origen's text made by Eusebius and Pamphilus, a fact also mentioned by Jerome.[47] But a wider acceptance of this recension was probably hindered by the hostility towards Origen's doctrine that had begun by 400 CE.[48] Individual readings from his revised LXX did trickle down through the manuscript tradition and permeated it fairly thoroughly. Very rarely would readers be aware of their origin, unless this was indicated by a scholion, colophon, or critical sign. It must

---

[42] Gentry, *Asterisked Material,* 10–11. Jerome mentions in his preface to his *Iuxta Hebraeos* version of Job that the asterisked portions were read out in church as if they were the work of the Seventy, so even when the signs were included, their significance was overlooked.

[43] P. J. Gentry, "The Place of Theodotion-Job in the Textual History of the Septuagint" in *Origen's Hexapla,* ed. Salvesen, 199.

[44] C. Cox, "Origen's Use of Theodotion in the Elihu speeches," *Second Century* 3 (1983): 89–98 (97).

[45] Cox, "Origen's Use of Theodotion," 98 n.20, in *Septuaginta Vetus Testamentum Graecum* XI/4: *Isaias,* ed. J. Ziegler (Göttingen: Vandenhoeck & Ruprecht, 1982).

[46] Eusebius, *Vita Const.* IV.34–37. This is the conclusion of M. Caloz, *Étude sur la LXX Origénienne du Psautier,* OBO 19 (Fribourg: Universitätsverlag, 1978), 447–49.

[47] *Praef. in Paralip.*

[48] Fernández Marcos, *Introduction,* 196–97. (N.B.: The name "Theodotion" in the third paragraph on p. 197 is an error: the text should read "Origen.")

be remembered that, far from bringing textual variety to an end, Origen's work proliferated it still further: he merely added another, albeit major, stream to the swirling waters of LXX manuscript tradition, already replete with theological and stylistic revisions and scribal corruptions.[49]

One spin-off of Origen's work on the Hexapla was the greater availability of the minor Jewish Greek revisions of the LXX, especially those of the Three. Irenaeus was aware of Aquila and Theodotion before Origen's time, but since he only cites their rendering of Isaiah 7.14,[50] we cannot be sure that these revisions were circulating among Christians in their entirety, rather than as individual readings pertinent to Christian theological concerns. Certainly Origen was able to acquire whole revisions for use in the Hexapla, not just those of the Three, but other unnamed versions referred to as Quinta, Sexta, Septima, and so on.[51] Scholars using the library at Caesarea were able to note the most interesting readings of individual versions, which then turn up in commentaries, notably those of the Cappadocian Fathers, Didymus the Blind, and Theodore of Mopsuestia. They also appear in the margins of some LXX manuscripts, including the Syrohexapla, the Syriac rendering of Origen's Hexapla made in 616–17 by Paul of Tella. From the Syrohexapla these minor Greek versions became known to Syrian Orthodox scholars and even to writers in the Church of the East, notably Isho'dad of Merv in the ninth century.[52] Their Jewish provenance was known, and generally in Christian commentaries, catenas, and scholia their readings are not used to replace the word used by LXX (or by the Syriac Peshitta) but to accompany the familiar biblical text of the church in order to elucidate difficulties in the meaning.[53]

Christian scholars made some use of the Jewish Greek revisions, yet they were suspicious of them. To Christian eyes, the revisers were individuals working alone and at variance; they were Jewish or Judaizers; they probably wanted to harm the church by their interpretations and conceal the truth of Christ; their work implied that the LXX translation was inadequate or imperfect and therefore not inspired. Irenaeus suggests that Aquila and Theodotion had anti-Christian motives for their rendering of Isaiah 7.14, "a *young woman* [not, "virgin"] shall conceive and bear a

---

[49] Cf. Ulrich, "The Old Testament Text of Eusebius," 557; and M. Harl, G. Dorival, and O. Munnich, *La Bible Grecque des Septante* (Paris: Cerf, 1986), 165–67.

[50] Irenaeus, *adv. Haer.* III.21 (23).

[51] Eusebius, *Hist. Eccl.* VI.16. Apparently one was found in a jar near Jericho in the time of Antoninus son of Severus.

[52] See A. Salvesen, "Hexaplaric Readings in Isho'dad of Merv's Commentary on Genesis," in *The Books of Genesis in Jewish and Oriental Christian Interpretation: A Collection of Essays,* ed. J. Frishman and L. Van Rompay, TEG 5 (Leuven: Peeters Press 1997), 229–61.

[53] See Kamesar, *Jerome,* 34–38.

child,"[54] and Eusebius of Caesarea says that Symmachus attacked Matthew's Gospel.[55] Epiphanius' account in *de Mensuris et Ponderibus* 16 is much fuller and impugns the motives behind the work of the Three. Aquila, according to Epiphanius, was a relative of Hadrian. He converted first to Christianity, but was rejected by the church because he practiced astrology. He converted again, this time to Judaism, learned Hebrew, and produced his translation to attack the LXX. (Modern study has borne out Jerome's observation that Aquila's translation mirrors the Hebrew word order and etymology.[56]) Epiphanius says that Theodotion was another convert to Judaism, in this case from Marcionism, and, at the beginning of the third century, produced a translation close to that of the LXX. However, this account does not fit the facts: readings like Theodotion's are known much earlier than this.[57] It could be that if a historical person called Theodotion lived, he adopted and revised an earlier version. Since Theodotion's version differs little from the LXX, Epiphanius does not offer much criticism of it, but he does describe the work as carried out ἰδίως, "in an individual manner," implying a contrast with the divinely inspired band of the Seventy translators of the Septuagint, whom he believes worked in thirty-six pairs, each producing an identical translation. As for Symmachus, Eusebius says he was an Ebionite, a Jewish-Christian sectarian. This must have arisen out of a misunderstanding of what Irenaeus states in *adv. Haer.* III.21 (23) about Ebionites agreeing with Aquila and Theodotion's rendering of Isaiah 7.14.[58] In contrast, Epiphanius suggests that Symmachus was a Samaritan convert to Judaism, who lived at the end of the second century and who translated in order to combat Samaritan interpretations. Symmachus' translation style is much more elegant than that of Aquila, and he is more interested in the sense of the Hebrew rather than in producing a literalistic rendering.[59]

---

[54] Irenaeus, *adv. Haer.* III.21 (23); cf. Justin Martyr, *Dial.* 71.1.

[55] Eusebius, *Hist. Eccl.* VI.17.

[56] Jerome, *Ep.* 57.11. See J. Reider and N. Turner, *An Index to Aquila*, VTSup 12 (Leiden: Brill, 1966), and K. Hyvärinen, *Die Übersetzung von Aquila*, CBOTS 10 (Lund: Liber Läromedel–Gleerup, 1977).

[57] See, for example, D. Barthélemy, *Les Devanciers d'Aquila*, VTSup 10 (Leiden: Brill, 1963).

[58] D. Barthélemy, "Qui est Symmaque?" *CBQ* 36 (1974) (*Patrick Skehan FS*), 451–65 (460), republished in *Etudes d'Histoire du Texte*, OBO 21 (Fribourg: Universitätsverlag, 1978), and A. van der Kooij, *Der Alten Textzeugen des Jesajabuches. Ein Beitrag zur Textgeschichte des Alten Testaments*, OBO 35 (Fribourg: Universitätsverlag, 1981), 221–57.

[59] Recent studies on Symmachus include J. R. Busto Saiz, *La Traducción de Símaco en el Libro de los Salmos*, Textos y Estudios Cardenal Cisneros 22 (Madrid: Instituto Arias Montano C.S.I.C., 1978); J. González Luis, "La Version de Símaco a los Profetas

25

Given this hostility towards the Three, it is all the more remarkable that Origen took them seriously enough to include them in his Hexapla. In spite, or perhaps because, of his minimal knowledge of Hebrew, he seemed to have thought that the later Greek versions were useful guides to the Hebrew text. This is something that Epiphanius, for one, seems to have misunderstood: he believed that Origen compiled the Hexapla in order to show that the LXX of the church was the superior text compared to the later revisions and the Hebrew![60]

Regardless of the concern about their origins, readings of the Three were used by Christian writers not only to explain obscurities in the LXX text, but also to display their knowledge and wide reading – this is certainly true of Isho'dad of Merv. But Adam Kamesar believes that the Three had a great impact on Jerome in particular and that he was drawn to the "Hebrew truth," at least in part through these minor versions, which demonstrated that there were legitimate alternative renderings of the Hebrew besides the LXX.[61]

## The Work of Jerome

This leads us to the most prominent figure in this survey of Christian use of Jewish tools and Hebrew learning in the study of the Old Testament. Towards the end of his life Jerome claimed that he originally set out to learn Hebrew as means of bringing his sinful thoughts under control during his time in the desert of Chalcis (375–77 CE).[62] His first teacher was a Jewish convert to Christianity, and other, unconverted Jews often served him as paid language teachers and explained rabbinic

---

Mayores," Ph.D. diss., Madrid, 1981; A. Salvesen, *Symmachus in the Pentateuch,* JSSMS 15 (Manchester: U. of Manchester, 1991).

[60] *de Mens. et Pond.* 2–3, 17.

[61] Kamesar, *Jerome,* 44, 59–61, 72. Kamesar points out that Jerome may have had contact with the versions of the Three independent of the Hexapla initially, since they also circulated separately (p. 72 n.118).

[62] Kamesar, *Jerome,* 38, suggests that it is more likely that Jerome's decision to learn Hebrew was based on "a simple aesthetic need to read decent literature," but it is unclear how he would have known that the Hebrew Bible was satisfying to read from a literary point of view before he had a solid grasp of the language. Perhaps the intellectual and linguistic challenge appealed to him: after all, he had already learnt some spoken Syriac from the monks in Chalcis (*Ep.* 7.2), which may have given him the confidence to embark on the study of Hebrew when he encountered a Jewish convert who could teach him (*Ep.* 125.12). Cf. J. Barr, "St. Jerome's Appreciation of Hebrew," *BJRL* 49 (1966–67): 281–302 (285–86), and J. N. D. Kelly, *Jerome: His Life, Writings, and Controversies* (London: Duckworth, 1975), 49–50.

interpretations to him.[63] He even got them to borrow books from the synagogue for him to copy.[64] He also made extensive use of Aquila, Symmachus, and Theodotion. These were the only tools for Christians to learn Hebrew in an era before written vocalization of the consonantal script, before grammars and dictionaries. His appreciation of the Hebrew text grew the more he studied the language, during the time he was in Constantinople in 380, in Rome from 382–85, and of course in Palestine from 386 until his death in 420.

But Jerome's dawning recognition of the "Hebrew truth" – that the Hebrew Bible represented the original and ultimate inspired text of Scripture – was a process that took many years. He uses the term explicitly in 391–92, but the notion appears several years earlier in his writings. Adam Kamesar argues that it was Jerome's own position as a Latin-speaker that made him dissatisfied not only with the Old Latin version of the Old Testament, a poorish series of translations of the LXX, but also with the LXX itself.[65] Native Greek-speakers were invariably monolingual, like many native English speakers today, and chauvinistic and incurious about other languages. But Jerome was aware of the gap between translation and original because he was familiar with Latin versions of Greek works, and he was scornful of the exaggerated claims concerning the inspiration of the LXX translation.[66] Rather than revise the Old Latin version according to the Hexaplaric LXX, as he had originally set out to do, he wanted to go back to the *fons et origo* of the LXX, the Hebrew. It is difficult in this day and age to imagine a time when the church did not revere the Hebrew text and automatically turn to it as *the* Old Testament. But the belief that the LXX was divinely inspired, even in its differences from the Hebrew, and had been designated by God to bring revelation to the Gentiles, was very deeply entrenched among Christians in this period. It is difficult to discern Jerome's real motives for producing his *Iuxta Hebraeos* version, which one day became the backbone of the Latin Vulgate. This is because he answers his detractors with arguments that would convince them, rather than stating the reasons which had convinced him of the importance of the Hebrew. One of the most common lines of argument that he used in favor of the "Hebrew truth" was that the Apostles' quotations of the Old Testament are not always from the LXX, but are often from Hebrew, even when prophecy concerning Christ is involved.[67] This is not actually correct: the Old

---

[63] *Epp.* 18.10; 84.3 (*quo labore, quo pretio Baraninam nocturnum habui praeceptorem!*); *Praef. in Daniel.*

[64] *Ep.* 36.1.

[65] Kamesar, *Jerome*, 43–47.

[66] *Apology against Rufinus* 2.25, *Praef. in Pent.*, *Comm. Ezek.*

[67] E.g. *Praef. in Pent.*, *Praef. in Iosue.*

Testament citations in the New are often from the LXX, some are
influenced by the Hebrew, and many agree with neither.[68] But Jerome
knew that his fellow Christians would only regard the Hebrew text as
acceptable if it was legitimized by use in the New Testament by the
Apostles and Christ himself.[69] Somewhat provocatively, he says that the
Seventy rendered their translations so as to hide the Trinitarian mysteries
in the Hebrew text from the monotheist monarch, and not in order to
reveal the truth to Gentiles. As Kamesar observes, this resembles the
Jewish tradition of the alterations made to the LXX for King Talmai (*b.
Meg.* 9a) in order to prevent a polytheistic interpretation![70] So while their
translation was providential and inspired, Jerome implies, it hid some of
the truth, which could not be revealed until after the coming of Christ.[71]
Like Origen, he is critical of the state of the churches' texts, which
become more corrupt the further they are from the Hebrew, with scribes
altering the text as they see fit.[72] To Rufinus' claim that Origen only
produced the Hexaplaric LXX in order to argue with Jews, not to
supersede the traditional LXX of the church, Jerome could reply that the
asterisked passages (supplied from the Three) were read in churches,
which implied both that they were valid and that the LXX was at times
defective.[73] It is inconsistent, he says, to accept Origen's work and not his
own.[74] Another point he makes is that his labors are to avoid Jewish
criticism of the churches' Scriptures.[75] The concluding argument in
several cases is that the "Hebrews," i.e. living and learned Jews
conversant with Hebrew, can verify what Jerome has written since they
have testimonies of Christ that do not appear in the Old Latin.[76]

---

[68] See Kamesar, *Jerome,* 64.

[69] Braverman, *Jerome's Commentary on Daniel,* 32.

[70] Kamesar, *Jerome,* 64–67. Jerome attributes this idea to "Iudaei prudenti," who
say that this concealment was done by agreement between them in order not to publish
the "arcanum fidei" (*Praef. in Pent.*).

[71] He claims only to be building on the work of others, such as the Seventy and
Origen, and not to be condemning them (*Praef. in Pent., Praef. in Iosue, Praef. in Iob*).

[72] *Praef. in Pent.: emendatiora sunt exemplaria latina quam graeca, graeca quam
hebraea!*; *Praef. in Iosue: maxime cum apud Latinos tot sint exemplaria quot codices,
et unusquisque pro arbitrio suo vel addiderit vel subtraxerit quod ei visum est.* Cf.
*Praef. in Iob, Praef. in Paralip.*

[73] Rufinus, *Apol. c. Hier.* II.40; Jerome, *Praef. in Iosue: cur ea quae sub asteriscis
et obelis vel addita sunt vel amputata, legunt et non legunt?* Cf. *Praef. in Iob* and *Praef.
in Ezra.* on the reading in churches of the Three, who are Jews or Judaizers, because
they were included in the Hexaplaric recension.

[74] *Praef. in Iob.*

[75] *Praef. in Isaia.*

[76] E.g. *Praef. in Pent.: sicubi tibi in translatione videor errare, interroga Hebraeos,
diversarum urbium magistros consule: quod illi habent de Christo, tui codices non
habent*; *Praef. in Ezra: interrogent Hebraeos et ipsis auctoribus translationi meae vel*

Jerome's lack of transparency when defending the "Hebrew truth" is not merely deviousness on his part. It has to be remembered that the late fourth and early fifth centuries were a period when imperial legislation was restricting Jewish relations with Christians and the holding of certain posts by Jews.[77] There was both triumphalism and insecurity in the church after the long years of persecution and difficulty for Christians, the short, sharp shock of Julian's reign, and the restoration of Christian rule. Augustine thought Jerome's new version would split the Latin and Greek churches, since the Scriptures of the former would be based on the Hebrew and not the LXX, and Rufinus accused him of promulgating Jewish alterations to the biblical text.[78]

In some respects it is easier to perceive the enormous influence of the Hebrew text and the Three in Jerome's *Iuxta Hebraeos* version than in Origen's version. For instance, Jerome follows the order of material that he finds in the rabbinic Hebrew texts of Jeremiah and Exodus.[79] On the other hand, the seams and incongruities in Origen's Hebraizing recension are not found: Jerome did retain much of the LXX and Old Latin where he could, but he aimed for a consistent literary style within each book.

Assessing the precise extent to which Jerome made use of the Jewish Greek revisers is more difficult, because there are very few places where we have extensive extracts from any of the Three with which to compare the *Iuxta Hebraeos*. We do, however, have fragments of a copy of the Hexapla of Psalms to facilitate comparison in that book.[80] Colette Estin's study of Jerome's Psalms *Iuxta Hebraeos* uses different fonts to present in visual form how he interwove interpretations from the various Greek versions in his own work.[81] She notes that he relies much on Aquila, with Symmachus as "second best," but he avoids Aquila's literalistic style.[82] Elsewhere one has to rely on the preserved readings of Aquila,

---

*adrogent vel derogent fidem*; *Praef. in Regum*: *interroga quem libet Hebraeorum*. See n. 90 below.

[77] As C. T. R. Hayward notes (*Jerome's Hebrew Questions on Genesis,* Oxford Early Christian Studies [Oxford: Clarendon, 1995], 1).

[78] Augustine, *Ep.* 71A, and Rufinus, *Apol. c. Hier.* 2.36–41.

[79] *Praeterea ordinem visionum, qui apud Graecos et Latinos omnino confusus est, ad pristinam fidem correximus* (*Praef. in Ier.*). Jerome could not have know that the conflicting order arose from the existence of two different editions of the Hebrew of Jeremiah, one reflected in the MT, and the other in the Old Greek and in the Qumran fragments of Jeremiah (4QJer[b,d]).

[80] Published by G. Mercati, *Psalterii Hexapli Reliquiae ... Pars Prima = Codex Rescriptus Bybliothecae Ambrosianae O 39 sup. phototypice expressus et transcriptus* (Città del Vaticano: Bibliotheca Apostolica Vaticana, 1968).

[81] *Les Psautiers de Jérôme à la lumière des traductions juives antérieures* (Rome: San Girolamo, 1984), 37–105. Estin surveys only those psalms which are found in the Mercati fragments of the Hexapla.

[82] *Les Psautiers de Jérôme,* 205–6.

Symmachus, and Theodotion, and even when there appears to be a coincidence between the interpretation in the *Iuxta Hebraeos* version and one of the Three, one cannot rule out the possibility that the source was in fact one of Jerome's Jewish informants. However, this is less likely since it was easier to consult a written text than to approach learned Jews in secret. It is possible that Jerome arrived independently at a certain reading, while verifying his translation from one of the Three. Bearing all this in mind, a few examples from the Pentateuch clearly demonstrate the influence of the Jewish Greek revisers on Jerome's Latin version:[83]

a) Aquila's rendering is closest to Jerome's in Gen 1.2 κένωμα *vacua*; Gen 3.15 προστρίψει *conteret*; Gen 6.4 δυνατοί *potentes*; Gen 41.6, 2 ἐφθαρμένοι τῷ καύσωνι *percussae uredine*; Ex 34.35 κεκράτωτο *cornutam*; Num 24.17 ὄψομαι ... προσκοπῶ αὐτὸν αλλ' οὐκ ἐγγύς *videbo ... intuebor illum sed non prope*.

b) Symmachus seems to have provided the basis for Jerome's rendering in Gen 2.23 ἀνδρίς *virago*; Gen 3.17 ἐν τῇ ἐργασίᾳ σου *in opere tuo*; Gen 4.7 ἡ ὁρμὴ αὐτῆς *appetitus eius*; Ex 1.19 μαῖαι γάρ εἰσι καὶ πρὶν εἰσελθεῖν τὰς μαίας τίκτουσιν *ipsae enim obstetricandi habent scientiam et priusquam veniamus ad eas pariunt*; Ex 14.20 καὶ ἦν ἡ νεφέλη σκότος μὲν ἐκεῖθεν φαίνουσα δὲ ἐντεῦθεν *et erat nubes tenebrosa et inluminans noctem*; Ex 28.5, etc. κόκκινος δίβαφος *coccum bis tinctum*; Ex 32.25 εἶδεν δε Μωυσῆς τὸν λαὸν ὅτι γεγύμνωται προέδωκεν γὰρ αὐτὸν Ααρὼν εἰς κακωνυμίαν *videns ergo Moses populum quod esset nudatus spoliaverat enim eum Aaron propter ignominiam sordis*; Deut 8.15 φυσήματι καίων *flatu adurens*; Deut 33.8 τελειότης καὶ διδαχή σου ... ὃν ἐπείρασας *perfectio tua et doctrina tua ... quem probasti*.

c) Theodotion's translation is closest to Jerome's in Gen 3.17 μετα μόχθου *in laboribus*; Gen 4.7 οὐκ ἂν ἀγαθῶς ποιεῖς δεκτόν *nonne si bene egeris recipies*; Gen 15.2 ὁ υἱὸς τοῦ ἐπὶ τῆς οἰκίας μου *filius procuratoris domus meae*.

It should be remembered that Jerome often retained the rendering of the LXX or Old Latin where he felt that it was compatible with the Hebrew text.

The Hebrew and Jewish learning that Jerome acquired was disseminated through the Latin Church not only through his *Iuxta Hebraeos* Latin version, but also through his commentaries on the Old Testament and his letters. In these latter, the Hebrew text and language, along with

---

[83] See Salvesen, *Symmachus in the Pentateuch*, 265–81. Older works include J. Ziegler, "Die jüngeren griechische Übersetzungen als Vorlagen der Vulgata in den prophetischen Schriften," *Beilage zum Personal- u. Vorlesungsverzeichnis d. Staatl. Akademie zu Braunsberg/Ostpr. WS* (1943/44), 1–92, M. Johannessohn, "Hieronymus und die jüngeren griechischen Übersetzungen des Alten Testaments," *TLZ* 73 (1948): 145–52, and idem, "Zur Entstehung der Ausdrucksweise der lateinischen Vulgata aus den jüngeren griechischen alttestamentlichen Übersetzungen," *ZNW* 44 (1952–53): 90–102.

the knowledge gleaned from Jewish interlocutors and his familiarity with Palestine, are used to explain various points, especially those involving topography, flora, and fauna.[84] Where the Hebrew apparently conflicts with the Greek, Jerome often tries to reconcile the readings, as in *Comm. Ionam* 2.1a, where the Hebrew has "great fish" ("piscem grandem ... dag gadol") and both the LXX and Christ himself speak of a whale ("cetum"). Jerome says that there is no doubt that the former signifies the latter. Elsewhere he places the readings side by side, as alternatives, apparently giving the reader a choice.[85] He does not always explain why the two readings differ, as in *Comm. Ionam* 1.9, where the Hebrew has "Hebraeus ego sum," and the LXX "servus Domini ego sum." The reason lies at the text-critical level: the Masoretic Text, an early version of which Jerome must have used, has עברי, whereas the LXX translator either had עבדי in his Vorlage or read it as such. Graphic similarity has resulted in confusion somewhere along the line. In other places Jerome seems to be aware of text-critical problems, but here he makes no attempt to explain the discrepancy.[86]

Given the anti-Jewish hostility of the time, how was it that Jerome's Latin version of the Hebrew Bible, the *Iuxta Hebraeos*, eventually became so widely accepted that it formed the major part of the Vulgate, the "widely used" version?[87] Jerome's reputation as a scholar increased after his death (he was eventually proclaimed a Doctor of the Church), and this must have played a part. It was easier for Latin readers to accept

---

[84] The position is similar in the *Iuxta Hebraeos*: "It is most likely that whenever Jerome's translation radically departs from the older versions that preceded him, especially in the identification of the biblical fauna and flora, that he is following current Jewish interpretation"; Braverman, *Jerome's Commentary on Daniel*, 6. The most well-known example must be the plant that sprang up over Jonah, about which Jerome and Augustine disagreed. In his Commentary on Jonah 4.6, Jerome offers a long disquisition on the habits of the Palestinian "ciceion," which has no exact equivalent in Latin.

[85] E.g. *Comm. Ionam* 13b: sive *mercedem navis, id est subvectionis eius, iuxta* hebraicum, sive *naulum pro se, ut septuaginta transtulerunt* .... *Et* vel *descendit in eam, ut proprie continetur in hebraico ('iered' enim descendit dicitur), ut fugitivus sollicite latebras quaeret,* vel *ascendit, ut scriptum est in editione vulgata* [= LXX], *ut quocumque navis pergeret perveniret* [emphasis added].

[86] Recent studies of the influence of the Greek versions and Hebrew text on Jerome's commentaries include those of P. Jay (*L'exégèse de saint Jérôme d'après son 'Commentaire sur Isaïe'* [Paris: Cerf, 1985]), Jenny Dines ("Jerome's Methodology in his Commentary on Amos," in *Origen's Hexapla*, ed. Salvesen, 421–436), Adam Kamesar (*Jerome*), and Robert Hayward (*Jerome's Hebrew Questions*).

[87] Isidore of Seville in the seventh century declared that it was the clearest translation and, because it was carried out by a Christian, it was more faithful (*Etymol.* VI.4). For a recent assessment of Jerome's achievement in the *IH* and its relation to the Vulgate, see C. Brown Tkacz, "'Labor tam utilis': The Creation of the Vulgate," *VigChr* 50 (1996): 42–72.

the *Iuxta Hebraeos* version, since no one had claimed inspiration for the Old Latin version(s) it replaced. Moreover, the literary style of its Latin was evident, especially when compared with the Old Latin based on LXX. Adam Kamesar thinks that one factor that drew Jerome to study Hebrew in the first place was the literary quality of the Jewish Scriptures, though to be honest, one has to know a good deal of Hebrew grammar and vocabulary even to begin to appreciate this. The beauty of the Hebrew Scriptures was a substitute for that of the pagan classics that Jerome had forsworn, thinks Kamesar, and he was keen to reproduce its effect as far as possible in his Latin translation.[88] It is doubtful that faithfulness to the Hebrew original was something that readers of the *Iuxta Hebraeos* particularly favored, but they do seem to have liked its good Latin. The Vulgate remained the authoritative Old Testament version of the Catholic Church until relatively recently. Once again, the Christian Old Testament had been brought more closely in line with Jewish Scripture, rather than moving gradually further away from it through lack of care in transmission and a desire to elucidate difficulties by Christian means only.[89] Benjamin Kedar says of Jerome's achievement:

> Israelite and Jewish emotion and thought from earliest beginnings on down to the times of Jesus, were passed on unto the new centres of civilization and their letters. Dozens of fundamental phrases and a thousand phrases were transferred from Hebrew into Latin, and then from Latin into modern tongues. The Hebraic spirit, its essence and its form poured into Latin molds put its imprint on all subsequent human affairs.[90]

That last phrase goes too far, as one has to bear in mind that for all its deficiencies, the LXX did represent Hebrew language and concepts quite well already, and the Old Latin conveyed some of the original Hebraism, despite being poured into the third jar, as Jerome put it.[91] Western Christianity would not have been wholly devoid of Hebrew and Jewish influence if Jerome (and Origen) had not lived, but Jerome did bring the Latin Christian Bible closer to the Jewish Bible. A more negative evaluation, this time from a Christian scholar, comes from the late

---

[88] Kamesar, *Jerome*, 47–48.

[89] The term "Vulgate" was first used in the sixteenth century for Latin Bibles that contained Jerome's translation from the Hebrew text and the Greek Gospels. The rest of the New Testament and those books outside the Palestinian Jewish canon were translated by others. In 1979 the Vatican issued the new official Latin translation of the Bible, which had been produced by the Pontifical Commission for the Neo-Vulgate, set up in 1965. This is a revision of the Vulgate according to the Hebrew and the Greek.

[90] "The Latin translations," in *Miqra: Text, Translation, Reading and Interpretation of the Hebrew Bible in Ancient Judaism and Early Christianity,* ed. M. J. Mulder and H. Sysling (Assen: Van Gorcum, 1988), 335.

[91] *In tertium vas confusa* (*Praef. in Salom.*).

Dominique Barthélemy, who disparagingly refers to Jerome as "nouveau riche de la culture hébraïque frotté de vernis rabbinique" and the *Iuxta Hebraeos* version as "une Bible des rabbins."[92] However, it is doubtful that any fourth century rabbi would have recognized it as such. The Christian, Latin influence is still very strong in the text.[93]

# Conclusion

So it is clear that, at various points in the formative centuries of Christian belief, while Christianity was striding off in its own direction, in the area of Old Testament Scripture it took some shuffling steps back, both towards its origins and even towards contemporary Judaism. *Why* it did this is a much more complex problem. Were the continuing contacts with Judaism and Hebrew accidental or providential, or were they necessitated by the origins and nature of Christianity itself? This paper has tended to imply that Christianity was a monolithic entity, but of course it was not, as the dissension and schisms of the fourth and fifth centuries prove. Individual great scholars were reasonably free to develop ideas, some of which were later discarded or anathematized, as happened in the case of Origen, who was later regarded as a heretic because of his doctrines concerning the soul and the Trinity. The biblical scholarship of Origen and Jerome, and the preservation of Jewish traditions and writings by Eusebius, Clement of Alexandria, and others, did remain. Again, this might not have been the case. Christianity could have opted for myths and philosophies to interpret, denigrate, or replace the Old Testament, especially given the church's hostility towards Jews and Judaism. But deep down there must have been a strong pull towards its own origins in first-century Judaism and the Jewish Scriptures, perhaps with some reluctance because of the many ordinary Christians who were tempted to Judaize (Aphrahat, Ephrem, and John Chrysostom bear witness to this phenomenon). Additionally, polemic against pagans demanded that Christians acknowledge their Jewish roots in order to establish their legitimacy and antiquity.

There is no one reason for the continuing contact with Judaism, which of course could be seen in later periods: the use of Maimonides by Aquinas, Nicholas of Lyre's knowledge of Jewish interpretations, Erasmus' use of Jewish biblical scholars, and the movement of Christian

---

[92] D. Barthélemy, "L'Ancient Testament a mûri à Alexandrie," *ThZ* 21 (1965): 358–70 (370).

[93] C. Tkacz, "Classical allusions in the Vulgate," *American University Studies Series 7, Theology and Religion* 207 (1999): 93–104.

Hebraists generally.[94] And reliance on Jewish learning rarely went hand
in hand with a respect for Jews and Judaism. Jerome says some revolting
things about contemporary Jews, and one suspects this was not only to
fend off criticism of his pro-Hebraic scholarly line.[95] But since
contemporary Jews were Christ-deniers, they were seen in a very negative
light.[96] Eusebius of Caesarea uses Hellenistic Jewish sources on the Bible
principally to show the antiquity and importance of the Hebrews, from
whom Christians had evolved, and to prove that Christians, not Jews,
were the true heirs of Hebrew religion, that Christians were not a
breakaway group from Judaism. But stressing the continuity of
Christianity with Judaism, even in this obviously supersessionist way,
had the effect of turning Christian attention to the Old Testament and the
preservation of Jewish Greek works as a testimony to the propriety of
Christian origins.

Jerome sometimes refers to his translation activities as making the
secrets of Hebrew erudition available for Latin speakers.[97] This may have
been to boost his own role, or to make Hebrew seem glamorous and
mysterious rather than barbarous. Or was there perhaps a widespread
belief among Christians in antiquity that the Jews still had a secret line on
biblical truth, since their ancestors had been heralds of divine revelation?
It is a question that I have not sought to address here since it would merit

---

[94] See W. McKane, *Selected Christian Hebraists* (Cambridge: Cambridge UP,
1989), for the work of Andrew of St. Victor, William Faulke, Gregory Martin, Richard
Simon, and Alexander Geddes.

[95] Remarks such as those in *Ep.* 84.3 – *si expedit odisse homines, et gentem aliquam
detestari, miro odio adversor circumcisos* – have to been seen in context, however. In
the latter case, Jerome is defending himself against criticism for having an unconverted
Jew as teacher. Of relevance is a paper given at SBL in Denver, 2001, by Matthew
Kraus, "Jerome as an ethnographer of the Jews." Besides, Jerome's invective against a
variety of targets, not just Jews but also heretics, pagans, and erstwhile friends, can be
seen as part of the classical tradition of satire: D. S. Wiesen, *St. Jerome as a Satirist,*
Cornell Studies in Classical Philology (Ithaca, NY: Cornell UP, 1964), 188–95.

[96] Sabrina Inowlocki surveys the use of the term "Hebrew" versus "Jew" by
Christian writers in antiquity. She notes that in Eusebius, Philo, Josephus, and
Aristobulos they are referred to by the complimentary term "Hebrews" because of their
"witness" to the truth of the gospel, but the writer's Jewish contemporaries are called
"Jews," a pejorative name in this context ("Citations of Jewish Greek Authors," 48–71,
108–18; cf. de Lange, *Origen and the Jews,* 31–32). Jerome's approach in this matter is
similar to that of Eusebius, although more nuanced. He uses "Hebraeus" to denote any
of his learned informants, and even "Iudaeus" occasionally occurs in a positive context,
as in "Iudaei prudenti" (*Praef. in Pent.,* see n. 65 above).

[97] E.g. *Comm. Zech.* 6. 9–15: *Semel proposui arcana eruditionis Hebraicae, et
magistrorum synagogae reconditam disciplinam, eam dumtaxat, quae scripturis sanctis
conuenit, Latinis auribus prodere.* Contrast the more ambivalent comment in *Comm.
Zech.* 10.11–12: *Haec ut ab Hebraeis nobis tradita sunt, nostrae linguae hominibus
expressimus, fidem dictorum ad eos a quibus sunt dicta referentes.*

an essay in its own right. The work of Origen and Jerome did much to disseminate in the Greek and Latin churches the Hebrew and Jewish learning that was otherwise inaccessible (effectively "arcana") because of the linguistic gulf. They were also responsible for laying solid foundations for Christian Hebraism in future generations, which was instrumental in opening up lines of communication between the two faiths. So it is not overstating the case to say that, in respect of the role of Hebrew learning in the church, there was some convergence of "the ways."

*Alison Salvesen*

## Figure 1. The "Hebraization" of Greek and Latin Scripture

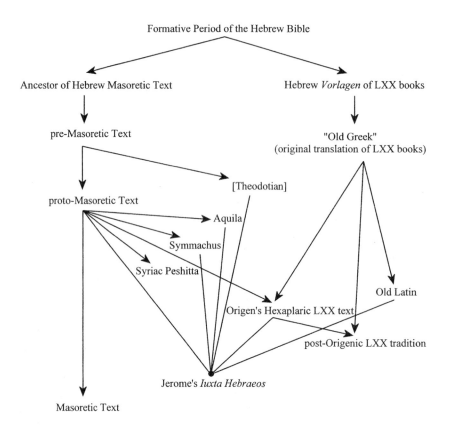

# Whose Fast Is It?

## The Ember Day of September and Yom Kippur

by

### DANIEL STÖKL BEN EZRA

Confidently encouraging you with fatherly counsels, dearly beloved, we preach the Fast dedicated in the Seventh Month to the exercises of common devotion, sure that what was first the Jewish fast will become Christian by your observance.[1]

With these words Pope Leo the Great (440–461 CE) opens a sermon on the Fast of the Seventh Month, the so-called "Ember Day" of September.[2]

---

[*] I would like to express my gratitude to the participants in the colloquium and the workshop that preceded it for the very helpful discussion. I am particularly indebted to Annette Yoshiko Reed and Adam H. Becker for improving my argumentation and straightening out my English.

[1] Leo the Great, *Sermon* 90:1, English translation by A. J. Conway and J. P. Freeland, *St. Leo the Great: Sermons* (The Fathers of the Church 93; Washington, D.C., 1996), 379. Latin edited by A. Chavasse, *Sancti Leonis Magni Romani Pontificis Tractatus Septem et Nonaginta* (2 vols.; Corpus Christianorum Series Latina 138, 138A; Turnholt, 1973), here 138A, 556:1–4.

[2] The literature on the fast is extensive. See the analyses by: G. Morin, "L'origine des Quatre-Temps," *Revue Bénédictine* 14 (1897): 337–46; L. Fischer, *Die kirchlichen Quatember. Ihre Entstehung, Entwicklung und Bedeutung in liturgischer, rechtlicher und kulturhistorischer Hinsicht* (Veröffentlichungen aus dem kirchenhistorischen Seminar München IV. Reihe Nr. 3; München, 1914); K. Holl, "Die Entstehung der vier Fastenzeiten in der griechischen Kirche," in *Gesammelte Aufsätze,* vol. 2, *Der Osten* (Tübingen, 1928), 155–203; J. Schümmer, *Die altchristliche Fastenpraxis, mit besonderer Berücksichtigung der Schriften Tertullians* (Münster, 1933); J. Daniélou, "Les Quatre-Temps de septembre et la fête des Tabernacles," *La Maison-Dieu* 46 (1956): 114–36; J. Janini, *S. Siricio y las cuatro temporas. Una investigacion sobre las fuentes de la espiritualidad seglar y del Sacramentario Leoniano. Leccion inaugural del curso 1958–59* (Valencia, 1958); G. G. Willis, "Ember Days," in *Essays in Early Roman Liturgy* (Alcuin Club Collections 46; London, 1964), 49–97; A. Chavasse, "Le sermon III de saint Léon et la date de la célébration des Quatre-Temps de septembre," *Revue des sciences religieuses* 44 (1970): 77–84; T. J. Talley, "The Origin of the Ember Days. An inconclusive postscript," in *Rituels* (*Mélanges P.-M. Gy*), ed. Paul De Clerck and Eric Palazzo (Paris, 1990), 465–72; J.-L. Verstrepen, "Origines et instauration des Quatre-Temps à Rome," *Revue Bénédictine* 103 (1993): 339–65. Also see: A. Chavasse, "Les Quatre-Temps," in *L'Église en Prière: Introduction à la Liturgie,* ed. A. G.

Interestingly, the bishop of Rome openly portrays this Roman Christian fast as a transformed version of the Jewish fast of Yom Kippur. The last person to offer a revised, scholarly version of this traditional view was Ludwig Fischer in the beginning of the last century.[3] Fischer's thesis, however, was not accepted.[4] The most knowledgeable living scholar on the Roman Fasts, Antoine Chavasse, expresses the current *opinio communis* that the Christian fast reflects "the perspective of a fourth-century Roman who reread the Old Testament in order to be inspired concerning the regulations of a celebration taking place during the 'Seventh Month'."[5] In his view, the Fast of the Seventh Month was inspired by the Old Testament and developed independently from contemporary Judaism.

Both views derive from the widespread conception of an early and absolute "Parting of the Ways" between Christianity and Judaism, after which there would have been no contact aside from the polemical. Fischer allows for Jewish influence on the Christian fast, but he places this influence in the time *before* the "Parting of the Ways" sometime in the first or second century.[6] Chavasse, who situates the emergence of the Christian fast on a much later date, suggests a Biblical or "bookish"

---

Martimort (Paris, 1965), 758–67; H. Auf der Maur, *Feiern im Rhythmus der Zeit. Herrenfeste in Woche und Jahr* (Gottesdienst der Kirche. Handbuch der Liturgiewissenschaft 5/1; Regensburg, 1983); A. Nocent, "Le quattro tempora," in *Anámnesis*, vol. 6, *L'anno liturgica: storia, teologia e celebrazione*, ed. M. Augé, et al. (Genoa, 1988), 263–66.

[3] "Only the Ember Days of September derive directly from the Jewish fast of Yom Kippur." ("Einzig und allein die H[erbst]Q[uatembertage] gehen direkt auf das jüdische Fasten des Versöhnungstages zurück.") Cf. Fischer, *Die kirchlichen Quatember*, 10. Fischer explicitly argued that only the Fast of the Seventh Month had a Jewish origin; this is in contrast to his predecessors, who, being mostly Protestant, were interested in making accusations of Judaizing against Rome and thus posited a Jewish origin for all the Ember Days (p. 7, n. 2).

[4] Cf. particularly Morin's review of Fischer in *Revue Bénédictine* 31 (1914–1919): 349–51.

[5] "La perspective d'un Romain du IVe siècle qui relirait l'Ancien Testament pour s'en inspirer dans la réglementation d'une célébration destinée à prendre place au cours du 'septième mois'," Chavasse, "Le sermon III de saint Léon," 81. The fourth century is probably too early a dating for the readings. Leo quotes only Mark 9:29 of all Epistle and Gospel readings (*Sermon* 87:2). But the general idea is valid also for the installation and promotion of the festival both in Leo's time and in the time before him. For the thesis regarding the pagan provenance, see below.

[6] Fischer calls the liturgy of the Ember Days "stark judaisierend"; however, he seems to regard this Judaization as an *internal* Christian development (Fischer, *Die kirchlichen Quatember*, 11). He does not refer to the Jewish reading cycle but only to the contents of the OT passages read on the Ember Days (see below).

influence, the only conceivable channel of a Jewish impact on Christianity *after* such a "Parting of the Ways."[7]

Against both theories, I will argue that direct contact between Jews and Christians left its traces in the development of the fast *after* the fourth century.[8] This direct contact encompasses polemic as well as non-polemic influence ("adoption") and therefore does not conform to the common conception of an early and absolute "Parting of the Ways."

I have chosen to approach the general question of the "Parting of the Ways" from the perspective of ritual rather than that of doctrine, which too often dominates the discourse on late antique religion. Investigating the emergence of the early Christian festival calendars and their relation to their Jewish counterparts can help foster our understanding of the emerging boundaries between Christian and Jewish identities.[9] Festivals are important cultural symbols that forge collective identities: "In [fasting and feasting rites] people are particularly concerned to express publicly – to themselves, each other, and sometimes outsiders – their commitment and adherence to basic religious values."[10] Moreover, their collective, public aspect makes festivals particularly apt objects of investigation in contrast to other rituals, such as dietary rules or circumcision. The ability of insiders and outsiders alike to perceive participation in festivals makes manifest otherwise invisible boundaries of collective identity, as Bell states with regard to Islam: "fasting [in Ramadan] sets Muslims off as a distinct community (*umma*) in contrast to their non-Muslim neighbors [who do not fast]."[11] In turn, the permeability of identity boundaries becomes visible, too: for example, when "Christians" observe "Jewish" festivals.[12]

---

[7] For a distinction between different types of influence, see pp. 5–7 in Daniel Stökl, "The Impact of Yom Kippur on Early Christianity" (Ph.D. dissertation, The Hebrew University of Jerusalem, 2001). The dissertation will be published in 2003 by Mohr Siebeck in the first series of *Wissenschaftliche Untersuchungen zum Neuen Testament*.

[8] This argument is based on Stökl, "Impact of Yom Kippur," 309–27.

[9] On ritual and its social functions, see Catherine Bell, *Ritual: Perspectives and Dimensions* (New York, 1997), 23–60 and 120–28. The work of Victor Turner in particular has established the foundations to this approach. For a recent sociological theory regarding the development process of collective identity and symbolic boundaries, see Michèle Lamont, "Culture and Identity," in *Handbook of Sociological Theory*, ed. Jonathan H. Turner (New York, 2001), 171–85.

[10] Bell, *Ritual*, 120.

[11] Bell, *Ritual*, 124.

[12] Cf. Daniel Stökl Ben Ezra, "'Christians' Observing 'Jewish' Festivals of Autumn," in *The Image of the Judaeo-Christians in Ancient Jewish and Christian Literature: Papers Delivered at the Colloquium of the Institutum Iudaicum, Brussels 18–19 November, 2001*, ed. Peter J. Tomson and Doris Lambers-Petry (Tübingen, 2003).

I will begin with a general introduction to the Fast of the Seventh Month and a comparison of it with Yom Kippur; next, I will discuss the possibility of a Jewish origin for the Christian fast; and finally, I will close with my main argument, which addresses the impact of Yom Kippur on Roman Christianity in the fifth and sixth centuries.

## The Fast of the Seventh Month

The Fast of the Seventh Month forms part of a series of fasts (in September, in December, during Lent, and after Pentecost) called the "Ember Days," which entail the abstention from food and work on Wednesday, Friday, and Saturday, culminating in a solemn vigil from Saturday evening to Sunday morning. Today the Ember Days are known mainly by specialists. From the fifth century through the Middle Ages, however, they were among the most solemn events of the liturgical year.[13] We are well informed about the rites and concepts attached to the fasts from three different sets of sources:

1.  Twenty-two sermons on the fasts by Pope Leo the Great, who led the Roman Church in the years 440–461.[14]

---

[13] This is shown by the great number of sermons on the Solemn Fasts written by Leo, the fact that in the Veronense the prayers for the Fast of the Seventh Month extend over as many pages as those for Christmas (and more than those for Pentecost), and by the fact that the lectionaries list the exceptionally high number of six epistolary lections for the fasts, an amount surpassed only by those for the Easter vigil.

[14] Chavasse, *Sancti Leonis*; Conway and Freeland, *St. Leo the Great: Sermons*; French translation with valuable notes by R. Dolle, *Léon le Grand. Sermons* (4 vols.; Sources chrétiennes 22, 49, 74, 200; Paris, 1964, 1969, 1971, 1973); German translation by Theodor Steeger, *Des Heiligen Papstes und Kirchenlehrers Leo des Grossen sämtliche Schriften* (2 vols.; Bibliothek der Kirchenväter 54–55; München, 1927).
A fresh study of Leo's life and thought is a *desideratum*. Most of the research concentrates on his pivotal role in the christological controversies. See most recently Lucio Casula, *La Cristologia di San Leone Magno. Il fondamento dottrinale e soteriologica* (Dissertatio Series Romana 27; Milano, 2000). For background information, see the introductions to the translations above; Basil Studer, "Leo I," *TRE* 20 (1990): 737–41; T. Jalland, *The Life and Times of St. Leo the Great* (London, 1941).
On the history of Christianity in Rome in the fourth and fifth centuries, see Charles Pietri, *Roma Christiana. Recherches sur l'Eglise de Rome, son organisation, sa politique, son idéologie de Miltiade à Sixte III (311–440)* (Bibliothèque des écoles françaises d'Athènes et de Rome 224; 2 vols.; Rome, 1976), especially pp. 575–95 on the papal liturgy and p. 594f on the Ember Days. Characteristically, "juives" or "judaisme" does not appear in his index. I could not consult S. Pricoco, *Il cristianesimo in Italia tra Damaso a Leone Magno* (Quaderni del Siculorum Gymnasium 12; Catania, 1983).

2. The two earliest Roman lectionaries, the *Epistolary of Würzburg* (seventh to eighth centuries) and the *Comes of Alcuin* (eighth century).[15]

3. The earliest Roman Sacramentary, the seventh-century Veronense (or Leonianum).[16]

The English term "Ember Days" is an abbreviation of the German *Quatember*, which, like the French *Quatre-Temps*, derives from the Latin term *quattuor tempora*, the "four times" of fasting. However, the fast in Lent was added later. In the fifth century, the series of fasts encompassed only three fasts in September, December, and after Pentecost – sometimes called *Trois-Temps* by French scholars.[17] In order to avoid anachronistic terminology, I will here adopt the terms employed by the earliest extensive source, Leo. Thus, "Solemn Fasts" refers to the whole series of three fasts, while "Fast of the Seventh Month," "Fast of the Tenth Month," and "Fast after Pentecost" refer to each of the three.[18]

Although all Solemn Fasts have an apotropaic and a placating function as well as a relation to the cycle of the agricultural year, each fast concentrates on a distinct theological theme. The themes of the Fast of the Tenth Month and the Fast after Pentecost are connected to their neighboring festivals in the *Christian* liturgical calendar, Christmas and Pentecost.[19] The Fast of the Seventh Month, however, is linked to the

[15] The lections of these lectionaries and of three others have been conveniently assembled in tables by A. Chavasse, *Les lectionnaires de la Messe au VIIe e VIIIe siècles* (2 vols.; Spicilegii Friburgensis Subsidia 22; Fribourg, 1993). See also G. Godu, "Epitres," *Dictionnaire de l'archéologie chrétienne et de la liturgie* 5/1 (Paris, 1922): 245–344; H. Leclerq, "Lectionnaire," *Dictionnaire de l'archéologie chrétienne et de la liturgie* 8/2 (Paris, 1929), 2270–306.

[16] The *Codex Verona Biblioteca Capitolare LXXXV (80)*, traditionally called *Sacramentarium Leonianum* or *Veronense,* preserves prayers older than the seventh century. I used L. Eizenhöfer, P. Siffrin, and L. C. Mohlberg, eds., *Sacramentarium Veronense* (Rerum Ecclesiasticarum Documenta, series maior Fontes [Sacramentarium Leonianum] 1; Rome, 1978[3]). See 108–14 for the prayers of the Fast of the Seventh Month.

[17] Some scholars regard not only the Lenten Fast but also the Fast after Pentecost as secondary and consequently speak of a *Deux-Temps.*

[18] For a similar decision, cf. Verstrepen, "Origines et instauration des Quatre-Temps à Rome." The lectionaries use yet another term to refer to the vigil: *sabbatum in duodecim lectiones,* which was used until the twelfth century. The name reflects the custom in the time of Greek rule over Rome (550–570 CE) of reading the six lections first in Greek Latin and then again in Greek translation. See A. Chavasse, *Le Sacramentaire gélasien (Vaticanus Reginensis 316), sacramentaire presbytéral en usage dans les titres romains au VIIᵉ siècle* (Bibliothèque de Théologie, série 4 / 1; Tournai, 1958), 107–10.

[19] The Fast of the Tenth Month is linked to Christmas through the theme of the Messianic prophecies of Isaiah and the Fast after Pentecost is linked to Pentecost through its focus on the giving of the Holy Spirit.

*Jewish* festivals closest to it on the calendar, Rosh Ha-Shanah, Sukkot, and especially Yom Kippur.

Any specific comparison of the Christian fast with Yom Kippur involves a major methodological *caveat*: the lack of local Jewish sources, particularly about the various reading cycles in Rome's synagogues in the fifth and sixth centuries.[20] Although archaeological finds have provided us with detailed sociological and geographical data about Judaism in late antique Rome,[21] we have no first-hand evidence about the rites and concepts associated with Yom Kippur as it was celebrated in Rome's Jewish communities.[22] Therefore, the following comparison is valid only under the assumption that rabbinic sources from Palestine and Persia are applicable for the study of the Roman Jewish community in Late Antiquity.[23] Unfortunately, the lack of local Jewish sources equally hampers our ability to research the possible contemporaneous effect of Christianity on Judaism in Rome. We will have to wait for a discovery of Roman Jewish lectionaries from Late Antiquity before we can investigate this side of the equation.

---

[20] On the history of Judaism in Rome, see Leonard V. Rutgers, *The Jews in Late Ancient Rome: Evidence of Cultural Interaction in the Roman Diaspora* (Religions in the Graeco-Roman world 126; Leiden, 1995); and the extensive and illustrative catalogue of an exhibition in Jerusalem's Bible Lands Museum edited by Joan Goodnick Westenholz, *The Jewish Presence in Ancient Rome* (Jerusalem: Bible Lands Museum Jerusalem, 1995). Also see the classic studies by Harry J. Leon, *The Jews of Ancient Rome* (rev. ed.; Peabody, Mass., 1994); and Abraham Berliner, *Geschichte der Juden in Rom* (2 vols.; Frankfurt am Main, 1893; republished as one volume; Heidelberg, 1987), especially vol. 1, pp. 3–104 on the time until 315 CE and vol. 2, pp. 3–7 on the Dark Ages, 315–800 CE. I could not consult Hermann Vogelstein and Paul Rieger, *Geschichte der Juden in Rom* (2 vols.; Berlin, 1895–96).

On the relations between Christians and Jews in first- and second-century Rome, see the various essays in Karl Donfried and Peter Richardson, eds., *Judaism and Christianity in First-Century Rome* (Grand Rapids, Mich., 1998); Karl Donfried, ed., *The Romans Debate* (Peabody, Mass., 1991[2]); Peter Lampe, *Die stadtrömischen Christen in den ersten beiden Jahrhunderten. Untersuchungen zur Sozialgeschichte* (WUNT, 2. Reihe; Tübingen, 1989[2]); Raymond Brown and John P. Meier, *Antioch & Rome: New Testament Cradles of Catholic Christianity* (New York: Paulist, 1983), 92–97. (This last has a clearly confessional interest but presents a very interesting approach to the Christian sources.) On later centuries, see Bernard Blumenkranz, *Les auteurs chrétiens latins du moyen age sur les juifs et le judaïsme* (École pratique des hautes études – Sorbonne. Sixième section: Sciences économiques et sociales; études juives 4; Paris, 1963); and A. Lauras, "Saint Léon le Grand et les Juifs," *Studia Patristica* 17/1 (1983): 55–61.

[21] On an evaluation of the archaeological data, see in particular Rutgers, *Jews in Late Ancient Rome*.

[22] But cf. our reading of Leo, *Sermon* 89:1, below.

[23] On the Christian side, we have to bear in mind that the readings come from sources about 200–300 years later than Leo's sermons.

The general characteristics of Yom Kippur and the Christian Fast of the Seventh Month are very similar. Both fasts take place in the same "relative time" (the seventh month of their calendars) and in the same "absolute time" (around September), and neither fast day is fixed to a particular day of the Julian calendar.[24] Moreover, both fasts connect the ideas of propitiation of God and purification to the practices of collective fasting, almsgiving, supplicative prayers, and abstention from work.[25] With regard to the Fast of the Seventh Month, Leo the Great emphasizes the extraordinary apotropaic and placating power derived from fasting collectively.[26] This is a new idea for Christianity, which at that time had only recently adopted Augustine's view of the church as a "school of sinners," and it recalls the importance of the communal fast on Yom Kippur.[27] Moreover, Leo and the Rabbis give their respective fasts sacrificial connotations.[28] Finally, both fasts are connected with ordination.[29]

There are, of course, notable differences as well. Whereas Yom Kippur is a single fast, the Fast of the Seventh Month, as it was observed in the fifth century, belonged to a series of three fasts. The Christian fast extends over several days, while the Jewish one encompasses only one day. Jews abstain completely from food, drink, and work on Yom Kippur; Christians abstain from these only partially during their autumn fast.[30]

---

[24] Today the Ember Day of September is celebrated in the week after Holy Cross Day, yet in Late Antiquity and the early Middle Ages until the eleventh century, the dates varied much more; see Chavasse, "Le sermon III de saint Léon."

[25] See the quotation below of *Sermon* 89:1.

[26] Cf. e.g. *Sermon* 88:2–4.

[27] Perhaps the emergence of another collective repentance ritual in the fifth century, the rogations in Gaul, may reflect this shift in ecclesiology. The rogations, however, probably developed out of local pagan rituals. See Geoffrey Nathan, "The Rogation Ceremonies of Late Antique Gaul: Creation, Transmission and the Role of the Bishop," *Classica et Mediaevalia. Revue danoise de philology et d'histoire* 49 (1998): 275–304; and William Klingshirn, *Caesarius of Arles: The Making of a Christian Community in Late Antique Gaul* (Cambridge Studies in Medieval Life and Thought, Fourth Series, 22; Cambridge, 1994), 177 and 240. I would like to thank Peter Brown for kindly drawing my attention to these connections.

[28] Cf. e.g. *Sermon* 88:5; 89:6; *Sacramentarium Veronense*, 895 (Eizenhöfer, Siffrin, Mohlberg (1978³), 112.

[29] Gelasius, Epistle 14 (PL 59: 138A). Cf. Chavasse, "Le sermon III de saint Léon." For the connection of Yom Kippur to priestly ordination, see Yisrael Knohl and Shlomo Naeh, "Ordination and Atonement," *Tarbiz* 62 (1993): 17–44 [Hebrew].

[30] See the quotation below of *Sermon* 89:1.

## A Jewish Origin for the Fast of the Seventh Month?

The traditional theory of a Jewish origin for the Solemn Fasts was replaced by the *opinio communis* established by Dom Morin (1897) and José Janini (1958). Morin argued that the Ember Days arose in competition with three pagan Roman festivals: *feriae sementivae, feriae messis,* and *feriae vindemiales.* Janini suggested that the Solemn Fasts originated in the time of Siricius I (384–399). Recently, however, Thomas Talley (1990) and Jean-Louis Verstrepen (1993) have refuted this consensus and revived the theory that the origin of the Solemn Fasts lies in the late second or early third century. Talley pointed out that the *feriae sementivae* take place at the end of January and not on a date parallel to the Fast of the Tenth Month.[31] Regarding the time of origin, Talley and Verstrepen show that Janini's late dating relies heavily on misreadings of Jerome. Talley's and Verstrepen's early dating of the Solemn Fasts is based on two passages, one in Tertullian and the other in the *Liber Pontificalis.* In his tractate *On Fasting,* the former contends with Christians who sometimes fast on Saturdays:

> Why do we devote to Stations the fourth and sixth days of the week, and to fasts the 'preparation-day?' Anyhow, you sometimes continue your Station even over the Sabbath, – a day never to be kept as a fast except at the Passover season, according to a reason elsewhere given.[32]

This passage is best understood as referring to (some) Roman Christians and their Solemn Fasts. Christian fasts on Saturday are rare in the West, and completely prohibited in the East.[33] The ecumenical exception is the pre-paschal fast, to which Tertullian explicitly consents. Some Christians in Spain seem to have fasted every Saturday, a practice opposed by the Synod of Elvira, yet this does not match Tertullian's statement about an occasional fasting (*si quando*), which implies a practice observed more than once a year but not every Saturday. Therefore, the Solemn Fasts are the most probable referent.

---

[31] While this suffices to overthrow Morin's hypothesis, there are other serious questions regarding the content of his argument and the method he used.

[32] *On Fasting* 14:2–3; translation by S. Thelwall in ANF 4:112. The Latin reads: *Cur stationibus quartam et sextam sabbati dicamus et ieiuniis parasceuen? Quamquam uos etiam sabbatum, si quando, continuatis, numquam nisi in pascha ieiunandum secundum rationem alibi redditam.* CCSL 1 (Gerlo), 1273:3–7.

[33] Cf. the critique of this fast in Canon 26 of the Synod of Elvira and in Hippolytus, *Commentary on Daniel* 4:20. Victorinus of Pettau, however, seems to belong to those who fasted every Saturday, cf. *On the Creation of the World* 5. See the brief discussion in Gerard Rouwhorst, "The Reception of the Jewish Sabbath in Early Christianity," in *Christian Feast and Festival: The Dynamics of Western Liturgy and Culture,* ed. P. Post, L. van Tongeren, and A. Scheer (Leuven, 2001), 255.

This interpretation of Tertullian's statement is corroborated by a legend in the *Liber Pontificalis* about the origin of the Solemn Fasts at the time of Callistus I, Bishop of Rome in 217–222: "He decreed that on Saturdays three times a year there should be a fast from corn, wine and oil according to the prophecy."[34] The part of the *Liber Pontificalis* dealing with the period before Anastasius II (496–498) is generally agreed to be late and of dubious historical value. However, that there are three fasts corresponds better to the time of Leo rather than to the sixth century, when the *Liber Pontificalis* was compiled and when the Solemn Fasts already included a fourth fast in Lent. A date of origin for the Solemn Fasts in the late second or early third century is therefore probable. Yet Talley and Verstrepen do not suggest a new theory for the origin of the fast.

If we can demonstrate that some Roman Christians observed Yom Kippur, a Jewish origin for the Fast of the Seventh Month becomes possible. However, common opinion holds that from early on the universal, "mainstream" form of "Christianity" had abandoned all Jewish festivals (already by 50–60 CE, according to some).[35] Only "marginal" Judaizers and Judeo-Christian communities continued to observe the Jewish festivals.[36] Such a view buys into the ideological argument of a

---

[34] Translation by R. Davis, *The Book of Pontiffs (Liber pontificalis): The Ancient Biographies of the First Ninety Roman Bishops to AD 715* (Translated Texts for Historians: Latin Series 5; Liverpool, 1989), 7. The Latin reads: *Hic constituit ieiunium die sabbati ter in anno fieri, frumenti, vini et olei, secundum prophetiam.* L. Duchesne, *Le liber pontificalis. Texte, introduction et commentaire* (reprint of original edition [1886–92] with addition of third volume; Paris, 1955–57), here 1:141. In the eyes of a later copyist the Latin phrase was too imprecise; he consequently added, "in the fourth, seventh and tenth months."

[35] E.g. Tim Schramm, "Feste. IV Urchristlich," RGG[4] 3 (2000): 91–93.

[36] I use the following nomenclature with as much consistency as possible without being stringent: "Jesus-followers" is the term for the first generations of adherents of Jesus, who were mostly Jewish, although there were some Gentiles. "Jewish Christians" is the general term for people of Jewish ethnicity who revered Jesus; since full proselytes joined the Jewish people, they were placed in the same category. Jewish Christians may have continued to be observant Jews, may have stopped being observant, or may have never been observant in the first place. "Christian Jews" revered Jesus and were part of Jewish communities that were not exclusively Christian Jewish. "Judeo-Christians," such as Ebionites and Nazoreans, were part of separate Judeo-Christian communities observing halakhot and revering Jesus. "Judaizing Christians" revered Jesus and were part of Christian communities but attended Jewish services from time to time or observed some halakhot in private. "Judaizing" in Christian literature is term used in inner-Christian debate to describe the deviant behavior of others (i.e., not that of the speakers/authors). In this respect the rhetorical use of the term is similar to that of "magic." What the author considers Judaizing, the Judaizer himself and others may regard as normal Christian behavior. On the term "Judaizing" see Shaye J. D.

number of second- and third-century Gentile Christian theologians who defined participation in Yom Kippur as "Jewish" and consequently un-"Christian," and thereby forged a distinction between Christianity and Judaism as mutually exclusive.[37] And yet the marginality of Judaizers and Judeo-Christianity in the second century is still open to debate. Moreover, some Gentile Jesus-followers, some of them probably from Rome, continued celebrating Yom Kippur, as can be shown from both Paul and Acts.[38] Paul writes in his Epistle to the Romans 14:5–6a:

> Some judge one day to be better than another, while others judge all days to be alike. Let all be fully convinced in their own minds. Who observes the day observes it in honor of the Lord.

According to most exegetes, Paul addresses a mixed audience and speaks of days sacred to Jews.[39] Doubtless, Yom Kippur is one of these days. While Paul does not consider the observance of Jewish festivals obligatory, he assumes that some among the Roman communities observe them and gives everyone the freedom to do so. There is no indication in the text that Paul distinguishes here between Jewish Christians who are allowed to observe festivals and Gentile Christians who are forbidden to observe them.[40]

In addition, a chronological expression in Acts 27:9 provides evidence that Luke and his audience kept the fast of Yom Kippur. Luke describes how on the way to Rome Paul and his guards discuss the dangers of shipping in autumn:

> Since much time had been lost and sailing was now dangerous, because even the Fast had already gone by, Paul advised them, saying, "Sirs, I can see that the

---

Cohen, *The Beginnings of Jewishness: Boundaries, Varieties, Uncertainties* (Berkeley, 1999), 175–97.

[37] Cf. *Diognetus* 4:1; Aristides, *Apology* 14:4; *Barnabas* 7; Tertullian, *Against the Marcionites* 3:7:7; *Against the Jews* 14:9–10; Justin, *Dialogue with Trypho* 15 and 40:4–5. For further texts see Daniel Stökl, "The Biblical Yom Kippur, the Jewish Fast of the Day of Atonement and the Church Fathers," *Studia Patristica* 34 (2001): 493–502.

[38] In addition, Gentile Christians from Syria-Palestine continued to celebrate Yom Kippur together with their Jewish neighbors until at least the fourth century, as sermons by Origen and Chrysostom prove. I have dealt elsewhere with the attitudes of Judeo-Christians and Christian Judaizers to Yom Kippur; see Stökl Ben Ezra, "'Christians' Observing 'Jewish' Festivals of Autumn."

[39] See Joseph A. Fitzmyer, *Romans: A New Translation with Introduction and Commentary* (The Anchor Bible 33; New York, 1992), 690; Ulrich Wilckens, *Der Brief an die Römer*, vol. 3, *Röm 12–16* (Evangelisch Katholischer Kommentar, VI/3; Zürich, 1982), 83.

[40] See Lampe, *Die stadtrömischen Christen*, 56–57, on the important role of Law-observing Christian God-Fearers.

voyage will be with danger and much heavy loss, not only of the cargo and the ship, but also of our lives."

Here, Luke employs "the Fast" as a chronological reference point, presuming that his readers understand "the Fast" as referring to Yom Kippur.[41] Apparently, Luke and his Gentile addressees consider the fast of the Day of Atonement as part of their own religious world and observe it.[42]

If the – possible but unverifiable – assumption is correct that Luke writes in Rome or addresses his work to a Roman audience, part of this Roman community observed Yom Kippur until at least 100 CE.[43] This would leave a gap of only 100 years between our latest evidence for Roman Christians observing Yom Kippur and our earliest allusion to the Fast of the Seventh Month.[44]

---

[41] See Stökl Ben Ezra, "'Christians' Observing 'Jewish' Festivals of Autumn."

[42] This deduction becomes clearer considering that the Peshitta introduces the gloss "the fast day of the Jews" into its version of the Luke passage. For the translators and the readers of the Peshitta, the fast already belongs to a distinct festival calendar "of the Jews."

On Godfearers as addressees of Luke-Acts, cf. Joseph Tyson, *Images of Judaism in Luke-Acts* (Columbia, SC, 1992), 19–41.

[43] Of course, a Roman provenance for Luke-Acts is only one of several possibilities. Elements pointing to a Roman provenance are the general plot of the story of Acts, telling the transition of the Gospel from Jerusalem to Rome, and the detailed knowledge of local Roman geography. Among the scholars placing Luke-Acts in Rome is F. Bovon, *Das Evangelium nach Lukas*, vol. 1, *Lk 1,1–9,50* (Evangelisch Katholischer Kommentar, III/1; Zürich, 1989), here p. 23 ("nächstliegend"). Cf. Irenaeus, *AH* 3:1:1; 3:14:1; Eusebius, *HE* 2:22:6.

[44] We lack other explicit references to Roman Christian observance or rejection of Yom Kippur. Implicit references are inconclusive. It is well possible that the various Roman communities each followed distinct liturgical habits. *1 Clement* 40:1–4, one of the prooftexts for Annie Jaubert's attempt to look for a levitical background of the letter, endorses an unspecified series of Christian festivals for Rome and Corinth, cf. *Clément de Rome, Épître aux Corinthiens* (SC 167; Paris, 1971), 48–50.

Dirk van Damme speculates that the pseudo-Cyprianic *Adversus Iudaeos* is a Gentile Christian tractate written in Rome at the end of the second century against Judeo-Christians who demanded that Gentile Christians observe *kashrut* (§14) and Jewish festivals (§41), cf. Dirk van Damme, *Pseudo-Cyprian, Adversus Iudaeos. Gegen die Judenchristen. Die älteste lateinische Predigt* (Paradosis, Beträge zur altchristlichen Literatur und Theologie 22; Fribourg, CH, 1969), here 10–16. However, van Damme's thesis has not been accepted, cf. Jean Daniélou, *The Origins of Latin Christianity* (Philadelphia, 1977), 31–39. Stewart Hall, in his review of van Damme in *JTS* 21 (1970): 183–189, regards this thesis as possible but not proved.

While Justin Martyr, despite Trypho's plea, refuses to observe Jewish festivals and polemicizes against the observance of Sabbaths and festivals (*Dialogue* 8–10; 15:1–4; 18:2–3; 23:3), he does *not* polemicize against the fast in his typological exegeses of Yom Kippur (*Dialogue* 40:4–5; 46:2; 111:1) and he only inveighs against the Temple ritual – unlike *Barnabas* 7 and Tertullian (*Against Marcion* 3:7:7), who employ the

Two questions can be raised concerning a Jewish origin for the Fast of
the Seventh Month. First, why did this festival develop only in Rome?
Second, how can we account for the fact that the most important day of
the Christian fast was the Sabbath? In my view, the answers to both may
be intertwined and do not preclude a Jewish background.

The exclusively Roman provenance of the Fast of the Seventh Month
has led scholars to look primarily for a pagan background. Yet Rome's
Jewish communities clearly had an impact on the development of early
Christianity. Particularly in Rome, Christian Jews seem to have been
prominent in the church for a long time.[45] At least until the mid-second
century, Roman Christian Judaism continued to produce important works,
such as *1 Clement* and the *Shepherd of Hermas*.[46] According to the *Liber
Pontificalis*, a Jew named Evaristus was bishop of Rome around 100 CE.
Even if this does not reflect historical truth, the fact that the *Liber*
considers it possible for a Jewish Christian to have held a leading position
in the church at that time reflects the Roman community's interest in
seeing its roots in Roman Judaism.

That the central fasting day of the Solemn Fasts is a Saturday is
usually interpreted as an expression of anti-Jewish sentiment and as a
sign of Christianity diverging from Judaism, and thus as evidence for the
"Parting of the Ways." Very tentatively, I would like to connect this issue
to the peculiar assertions by pagan authors living in Rome that Jews fast
on the Sabbath.[47] These statements are commonly understood as

---

same testimonial tradition (cf. also footnote 37). Therefore, Justin provides no evidence
that the Roman community of Luke-Acts discontinued their observance of Yom Kippur.
Justin probably did not know Acts (Cf. C. K. Barrett, *The Acts of the Apostles* [2 vols.;
International Critical Commentary Edinburgh, 1994, 1998], 1:41–44), and second, as
stated above, each of the various Roman communities probably followed its own
distinct liturgical habits.

[45] See, e.g., Raymond Brown and John P. Meier, *Antioch & Rome: New Testament
Cradles of Catholic Christianity* (New York, 1983), 92–97.

[46] On these works as products of Jewish Christianity, see L. W. Barnard, "The Early
Roman Church, Judaism, and Jewish Christianity," *Anglican Theological Review* 49
(1967): 371–84.

[47] Cf. M. Stern, ed., *Greek and Latin Authors on Jews and Judaism* (3 vols.;
Jerusalem, 1974–1984), who refers to Pompeius Trogus, *Philippic Histories, apud*
Justinus, *Epitome* 36:2:14 = vol. 1, #137 (Sabbath is a fast in remembrance of the end
of the hunger of the Exodus); Petronius, *frg.* 37 = vol. 1, #195 (fasts of Sabbath
imposed by law); Augustus(?) *apud* Suetonius, *Augustus* 76:2 = vol. 2, #303 (Augustus
claims to have fasted more than Jews on their Sabbath).

Cf. also Strabo, *Geography, apud* Josephus, *Ant.* 14:66 = Stern, *Greek and Latin
Authors*, vol. 1, #104 (Pompey takes Jerusalem on the fast); Dio Cassius, *Roman
History,* 37:16:2–4 = vol. 2, #406 (Pompey takes Jerusalem on a Sabbath); Lysimachus,
*apud* Josephus, *Apion* 308–309 = vol. 1, #158 (the "Israelites" fasted in the night before
the Exodus began); Martial, *Epigrammata* 4:4:7 = vol. 1, #239 (stench of a fasting
Sabbatizing woman); Horace, *Satyres*, 1,9:68–70 = vol. 1, #129 (30th Sabbath, or the

confusing Sabbath with Yom Kippur, the *Shabbat Shabbaton*.[48] However, it has long been remarked that the statements about Sabbath fasting come from *Roman* authors.[49] Is it not possible that these pagan authors generalized the observation that *some* Roman Jews fasted on *some* Sabbaths, such as *Shabbat Shuva*, which is celebrated just before Yom Kippur and closely connected to it?[50] This – very hypothetical – suggestion would allow us to take the pagan statements seriously as evidence for the practices of Roman Jews and to explain the specific Roman provenance of the Fast of the Seventh Month and the peculiarity of a Christian fast on Saturdays.[51]

---

30th, a Sabbath); cf. also Josephus, *Apion* 2:282–283 (fasts, seventh day, lighting of lamps, and food prohibitions spread to the Gentiles).

Yom Kippur, the only Jewish festival somehow known among second-century pagans besides Shabbat, is alluded to by Juvenal (see above) and by Plutarch, *Quaestiones Convivales* 4:6:2, 671D, cf. Stern 1, #557, and Stökl Ben Ezra, "Impact of Yom Kippur," 65–66.

Some of the statements may not refer to Shabbat. Strabo mentions only "the fast" (just read together with the parallel in Dio Cassius, the fast becomes a Sabbath). Lysimachus refers to the Exodus and not necessarily the Sabbath. Martial's poisonous pen might refer to a group of people (Sabbatizers) rather than the Sabbath.

[48] See the careful discussion in P. Schäfer, *Judeophobia: Attitudes towards the Jews in the Ancient World* (Cambridge, Mass., 1997), here p. 89–90, and footnote 63 on pp. 245–46; and Stern's comments on the various passages. See also Robert Goldenberg, "The Jewish Sabbath in the Roman World up to the Time of Constantine the Great," *ANRW* 19.1 (1979): 414–47, especially 435–41; L. H. Feldman and Meyer Reinhold, eds., *Jewish Life and Thought among Greeks and Romans: Primary Readings* (Minneapolis, 1996), 366–73; Max Radin, *The Jews among the Greeks and Romans* (Philadelphia, 1915); and Paul Lejay, "Le Sabbat juif et les poètes latins," *Revue d'histoire et de littérature religieuses* 8 (1903): 305–35. Regarding the recent book by Heather A. McKay, *Sabbath and Synagogue: The Question of Sabbath Worship in Ancient Judaism* (Religions in the Graeco-Roman world 122; Leiden, 1994), see S. J. D. Cohen's review in *JBL* 115 (1996): 736–37.

[49] Lejay, "Le Sabbat juif et les poètes latins," 312: "[C]e qui leur donne une cohésion et, par suite, une solidité bien digne de consideration, c'est qu'ils se réfèrent tous plus au moins directement à la juiverie de Rome."

[50] The passage from Horace about the 30th Sabbath (for which Feldmann and Reinhold give thirteen alternative explanations [*Jewish Life and Thought*, 368, n. 54]) brings to mind Shabbat Shuva in particular. A connection to Yom Kippur falling on a Shabbat (suggested by Radin, *Jews among the Greeks and Romans*, 399–402, n. 14) is unlikely, as this occurs only once in a while; however, if one counts thirty Sabbaths from the beginning of the Roman New Year on March 1st (and not from the first of Nisan) one often reaches Shabbat Shuva, or the Sabbath of Sukkot. Yet such a historical tradition is hard to distinguish from a satirical anti-Jewish remark.

[51] Goldenberg makes a similar suggestion ("The Jewish Sabbath in the Roman World," 440), referring to evidence from the Gaonic age that some Jews fasted on Shabbat Shuva (n. 109). While this parallel is obviously anachronistic, it proves that some Jews fasted on (at least one) Shabbat *despite* the well-established rules proscribing feasting and prohibiting fasting.

There exists, therefore, a slight possibility that Fischer is correct and that the Fast of the Seventh Month is a transformed Yom Kippur, just as Easter was adapted from Passover.[52] However, due to the lack of sources, any discussion of the origin of the Fast of the Seventh Month remains in the realm of speculation. Also, I want to state *expressis verbis* that it is not my intention to leave the impression that Yom Kippur and contemporary Judaism were the sole reasons for the emergence of the Roman Fast of the Seventh Month. As the appearance of the rogations in fifth-century Gaul demonstrates, internal Christian developments probably played a great part in the development of a communal ritual of penance.[53] Similarly, the promotion of the Christian fast in September probably also served to distance Romans from joyful pagan autumn festivals. However, we would gravely misunderstand the Christian fast without seeing it in its Jewish context. In any case, the conclusions to follow concerning material from the fifth and sixth centuries stand independent from these much more tentative suggestions on the fast's origin.

## The Fast of the Seventh Month and Yom Kippur in the Fifth and Sixth Centuries

In the eyes of ancient Christians such as Leo, the Fast of the Seventh Month and Yom Kippur were close enough to blur the boundaries between Christian and Jewish observance and thus to endanger the Christian collective identity. Chavasse and other defenders of the "bookish" model argue that the striking parallels between the two fasts are merely phenomenological in nature, the result of two groups reading the same Holy Writ. According to this view, Leo polemicizes against both an imaginary Judaism and his own vision of the biblical Yom Kippur. Similarly, this view holds that the readings of the Christian fast were reconstructed by a keen reader of the Old Testament who had no contact with the contemporary Judaism of Rome. We shall see, however, that competition with and influence from the contemporary celebration of Yom Kippur in Rome plausibly explains Leo's promotion of the Christian fast and some of the readings prescribed in the early lectionaries.

Leo's promotion of the Fast of the Seventh Month seems to have met with attacks from fellow Christians, who saw him as endorsing a Judaizing practice. Against this, Leo puts forward two main arguments to

---

[52] In this case, it would be likely that some of the parallels between Yom Kippur and the Fast of the Seventh Month derive from the origins of this fast as a Christianized Yom Kippur.

[53] Cf. footnote 27.

assert the Christian character of the fast. First, he portrays the Christian fast as an apostolic heritage. Like the Ten Commandments, the Solemn Fasts belong to those precepts of the Old Testament which have not been abrogated:

> The Apostles distinguished the Old Testament decrees, dearly beloved, in such a way that they might extract some of them, just as they had been composed, to benefit the teaching of the Gospel. What had for a long time been Jewish custom could become Christian observance (*obseruantiae*), for the Apostles understood that the Lord Jesus Christ had come into the world, "not to destroy the law but to fulfill it."[54]

Interestingly, Leo here articulates a concept of Christian law[55] and appeals to Matt 5:17, the Judeo-Christian prooftext par excellence.[56] Notably, he thinks of the Apostles as the ones who distinguished the Christian from the Jewish precepts in the Old Testament. Hence, for him, "Judaizing" is orthodox as long as it has apostolic roots. What makes a Jewish practice into a Christian one is its observance by Christians.

Leo's second argument in defense of the Christian character of the fast emphasizes the differences from the Jewish fast:

> When, therefore, dearly beloved, we encourage you on to certain matters set out even in the Old Testament, we are not subjecting you to the yoke of Jewish observance, nor are we suggesting to you the custom of a worldly (*carnalis*) people. Christian self-denial surpasses their fasts, and, if there is anything in common between us and them in chronological circumstances (*temporibus*), the customs (*moribus*) are different. Let them have their barefoot processions (*nudipedalia*), and let them idly show their fasts (*ieiunia*) in the sadness of their

---

[54] *Sermon* 92:1, Conway and Freeland, *St. Leo the Great: Sermons*, 385, CCSL 138A, 568: 1–6.

[55] In speaking of the OT decrees that the apostles "extracted," Leo likely means Lev 16:29–34, 23:27–32, and perhaps also Zech 8:19.

[56] Cf. *b. Shabb.* 116b; *Epistula Petri ad Jacobum* 2:3–7; Pseudo-Clementine *Homilies* 3:51–52; 'Abd al-Jabbār, who most probably used a Jewish-Christian source, quotes these verses. For the interpretation of the text as using a Jewish-Christian source, see the article by John Gager in this volume and Shlomo Pines, "The Jewish Christians of the Early Centuries of Christianity According to a New Source," in *Proceedings of the Israel Academy of Sciences and Humanities* (Jerusalem, 1966), 2:237–310, conveniently republished in *The Collected Works of Shlomo Pines*, ed. Guy G. Stroumsa (Jerusalem, 1996), 4:211–284. For the text, see Samuel M. Stern, "'Abd al-Jabbār's Account of How Christ's Religion Was Falsified by the Adoption of Roman Customs," *JTS* 19 (1968): 128–85, here 132–33, paragraph 3–4. The *Syriac Didascalia* 26 (syr. CSCO 407 [ed. A. Vööbus], 242–43; transl. CSCO 408 [ed. A. Vööbus], 224) seems to have polemicized *against* Jewish Christians using Mt 5:17–18; cf. U. Luz, *Das Evangelium nach Matthäus (Mt 1–7)* (Evangelisch-Katholischer Kommentar zum Neuen Testament 1:1, Neukirchen-Vluyn, 1985), 233–35, here 235. Cf. also A. von Harnack, "Geschichte eines programmatischen Worts Jesu (Mt 5,17) in der ältesten Kirche," in *Sitzungsberichte der preußischen Akademie der Wissenschaften* (Berlin, 1912), 184–207 (non vidi).

faces (*in tristitia uultuum*). We, however, show no change in the respectability of
our clothes. We do not refrain from any right and necessary work. Instead, we
control our freedom in eating by simple frugality, limiting the quantity of our
food, but not condemning what God has created.[57]

Clearly, the proximity of the Christian fast to Yom Kippur occupies Leo's
mind. "They," the fasting Jews, have barefoot processions, express
sadness, wear less respectable clothes, and abstain completely from work
and food. "We," the Christians, fast differently.

Defenders of the "bookish" model argue that Leo's description of the
Jewish rites reflects well-known topoi. The sadness and the clothes recall
Matthew 6. The differences regarding food and work reflect Christian
attitudes towards the alleged harshness of the Torah. Yet the *nudipedalia*,
the barefoot processions, cannot be fit readily into a "bookish"
explanation. They are usually explained as a pagan or Manichean
practice.[58] In my view, however, it is exactly this detail that exposes
Leo's personal acquaintance with contemporary Jewish ritual. The
prohibition against wearing sandals on Yom Kippur is found already in
*Mishnah Yoma* 8:1: "[On] Yom Kippur [it] is forbidden to eat, to drink, to
wash, to anoint, to wear sandals, and to have sex." It is unlikely that Leo
learned about this post-biblical practice from other non-Jewish authors,
who describe the same custom.[59] In fact, the existence of Leo's statement
contradicts my own remark above about the lack of any local Roman
sources on Jewish ritual. If Leo personally observed Jews in the custom
of walking barefoot on Yom Kippur, we can deduce that Leo's polemics
are in general not "bookish" statements against an imaginary Jewish fast
reconstructed from the biblical Day of Atonement and New Testament
polemics, but rather reveal traces of a real conflict between his Jewish
neighbors who observed their fast, those Christians who observed the Fast
of the Seventh Month, and those Christians who regarded this practice as

---

[57] My translation of *Sermon* 89:1, from the Latin in Chavasse, ed., *Sancti Leonis*,
551. The translation of Conway and Freeland misses aspects crucial to the comparison.

[58] Conway and Freeland, *St. Leo the Great: Sermons*, 368 (Manichean); Steeger, *Leo
des Grossen sämtliche Schriften*, 269, footnote 6 (pagan).

[59] The practice was noted by Chrysostom and by Juvenal, yet the formulations are
completely different from Leo's: "[This diamond] was given as a present long ago by
the barbarian Agrippa to his incestuous sister, in that country where kings celebrate
festal Sabbaths with bare feet, and where a long-established clemency suffers pigs to
attain old age." (Juvenal, *Saturae* 6:157–160, translation by G. G. Ramsay in LCL,
quoted by Stern, *Greek and Roman Authors*, 2:100). Cf. Chrysostom, *Against the Jews*
1:4:7; trans. Paul W. Harkins, *Saint John Chrysostom: Discourses against Judaizing
Christians* (The Fathers of the Church 68; Washington, 1979), 16: "Do you fast with the
Jews? Then take off your shoes with the Jews, and walk barefoot in the marketplace,
and share with them in their indecency and laughter." Unlike Leo, Chrysostom
describes the joyous aspects of Yom Kippur.

illicit Judaization.[60] Insofar as Leo promulgated the Christian fast in his capacity as Rome's bishop, and hence as the one responsible for decisions about the rites of the fast, it is plausible that some of the ritual differences between the Christian and the Jewish fasts were themselves introduced for the necessity of self-differentiation.

Further investigation into the details of the Christian fast reveals additional analogies to Yom Kippur. The choice of readings for the Fast of the Seventh Month betrays a connection to the readings for the Jewish autumn festivals in general and Yom Kippur in particular (see Table 1 at the end of this article).[61] The crucial question is whether these readings are related to contemporary Jewish practice or reflect the independent choice of a Christian in Rome reading the Old Testament. Whereas "bookish" influence accounts for some lections, others cannot be explained without an appeal to contemporary Jewish practice. This confirms what is implied in Leo's statement about the bare feet: that is, that Christians had some knowledge of what "real" Jews in Rome did on Yom Kippur.

Four of the readings refer explicitly to the three Jewish festivals of autumn: 2 Esd 8:1–10 refers to Rosh Ha-Shanah; Lev 23:27–32 describes Yom Kippur; Lev 23:34–43 concerns Sukkot; and Zech 8:14–19 mentions four fasts, one of them occurring in the seventh month and traditionally interpreted as the fast of Gedaliah. The main theological line of the remaining readings encompasses sin, repentance, propitiation, forgiveness, and restoration. Amos 9:13–15 and Hos 14:2–10 speak about the restoration of Israel or about its call to repentance; Mic 7:14–20 speaks of salvation and forgiveness and the protection of Israel against its enemies; and Ex 32:11–14 describes Moses' intercession on behalf of Israel after the sin of the Golden Calf. The language of Amos 9:13–15 and Hos 14:2–10 also resounds with agricultural reminiscences, which would well befit the atmosphere of any harvest festival. The reading from the New Testament Epistle to the Hebrews (9:2–12), describes the new atonement through Jesus Christ. Finally, the three Gospel readings discuss healing exorcisms connected to forgiveness of sins.

---

[60] After completing the research on this passage, I discovered that in 1963, Bernard Blumenkranz reached the same conclusion regarding the *nudipedalia* (pp. 31–32), a view adopted also by Lauras in "Saint Léon le Grand et les Juifs." However, Blumenkranz's conclusion has been overlooked in the research on the Ember Days.

[61] On the readings on Yom Kippur, see Stökl, "Impact of Yom Kippur," 52–56. Tannaitic sources give Lev 16; 23:27–32; Num 29:7–11 (*m. Yom* 7:1; *m. Meg* 3:6; *t. Meg* 3:7). Amoraic sources add Leviticus 18, Isa 57:15ff; and Jonah (*b. Meg* 31a) and hint to Hosea 14 (*b. Yom* 86a–b). In the Gaonic period, Rav Amram also mentions Obadiah and Mic 7:18–20; cf. D. Goldschmidt, ed., *Seder Rav 'Amram Ga'on* (Jerusalem, 1971), here pp. 166 and 168 [Hebrew].

On first glance, the choice of pericopes seems to confirm Chavasse's theory that the rites of the Fast of the Seventh Month were shaped by a Christian who combed the Old and the New Testaments for texts pertaining to September. There are, however, several problems with this approach. The "bookish" explanation does not account for the unusually large number of lections for this Christian fast. Nor can it explain the preeminence of Old Testament pericopes among the readings. Indeed, a Christian mining the Christian Bible for passages about repentance, propitiation, forgiveness, and restoration could find more than enough in the New Testament. Moreover, Chavasse (and Fischer) addressed only the content of the passages, without investigating their Jewish liturgical use. Analysis of the latter shows that other lections of the Christian fast betray connections with Yom Kippur, thus making it probable that some Christians were acquainted with Jewish liturgical habits.[62] Again, when comparing the readings of the Fast of the Seventh Month and Yom Kippur, we have to be aware that nothing is known about the readings in Rome's synagogues in the fifth or sixth century; thus, all of the following remarks are valid only if their liturgical practices on Yom Kippur agreed, at least in part, with the practices outlined in the Mishnah, Talmudim, and post-Talmudic literature. Likewise, we have to bear in mind that our evidence for the readings in the Christian fast postdates Leo by 150–300 years.

Four of the Old Testament passages of the Fast of the Seventh Month agree with readings used at about the same liturgical time in some synagogues. Two of the relevant passages (Lev 23:27–32 and Micah 7) were read on Yom Kippur itself,[63] while two others (Hos 14:2–10 and Lev 23:34–43) were read very close to Yom Kippur.[64] The passages from Micah and Hosea prove particularly interesting since neither text contains any references to the seventh month. According to the "bookish" explanation, these were adopted by Christians – independent of any

---

[62] These observations are also among the comparisons undertaken by L. Venetianer, "Ursprung und Bedeutung der Propheten-Lektionen," *Zeitschrift der Deutschen Morgenländischen Gesellschaft* 63 (1909): 103–70, especially 140–41; and by E. Werner, *The Sacred Bridge: Liturgical Parallels in Synagogue and Early Church* (New York, 1959), 80.

[63] In the time of the Mishnah, Lev 23:27–32 was read on Yom Kippur. Later this practice was abandoned. Mic 7:18–20 belongs to the Haftarah of Yom Kippur's afternoon prayer. Venetianer, "Ursprung und Bedeutung der Propheten-Lektionen," 140–41, argues that the Mishnaic reading of Lev 23:27–32 was abandoned as a reaction over and against its adoption in the Christian fast. This is overstretching the Roman evidence for the rest of the Jewish world.

[64] Hos 14:2–10 is the Haftarah on Shabbat Shuva, the Shabbat of the Yamim Noraim between New Year and Yom Kippur; Hosea 14 is also the scriptural focus of *b. Yom* 86a–b; Lev 23:34–43 belongs to the Torah-reading on Sukkot.

knowledge of the Jewish Yom Kippur – for their theological content. However, two factors (militate) against the likelihood of this. First, readings from the minor prophets are extremely rare in the Roman lectionary; Micah is read only here, while Hosea is read on only one other occasion. Second, these specific pericopes – Micah 7 and Hosea 14 – do not seem to have been well known among Latin authors.[65] In short, if a Christian reader were to have connected these texts to the fast, he would have been making an extremely atypical choice. A more plausible explanation is that the choice of Micah 7 and Hosea 14 as readings in the Christian services was connected to their use in some synagogues in September.

Furthermore, the final epistolary reading of the Saturday vigil, Heb 9:2–12, depicts Jesus Christ performing the high priest's ritual from the Day of Atonement, but includes no reference to September. Therefore, whoever chose this reading was likely aware of its typological and polemical connection to Leviticus 16, the main lesson of the Jewish festival (or the *Seder Avodah*). By virtue of its position after the Old Testament readings, Heb 9:2–12 is presented as the apex of the whole reading cycle, communicating to the hearer that Christ himself undertakes the atoning work of the *true* Yom Kippur. In light of the competitive situation attested by Leo, it is quite plausible that Heb 9:2–12 was chosen as a polemical, supersessionist substitute for Leviticus 16.

Direct contact between Christians and Jews, however, cannot explain all of the readings. Some readings of the Fast of the Seventh Month are not connected to the Jewish liturgy for the month of Tishri (e.g. Amos 9:13–15; 2 Esd 8:1–10; Ex 32:11–14; Zech 8:14–19). Moreover, many texts central to Yom Kippur are *not* read on the Fast of the Seventh Month (i.e. Leviticus 16; Num 29:7–11; Jonah; Isa 57:15ff).[66] Hebrews 9:2–12 may account for the omission of Leviticus 16 and Num 29:7–11, but it is difficult to give a reason for the neglect of Jonah and Isa 57:15ff.

---

[65] Cf. *Biblia patristica, index des citations et allusions bibliques dans la littérature patristique* (7 vols.; Paris: Éditions du Centre national de la recherche scientifique, 1975–); cf. also the index to the *translated* (and therefore incomplete) works of Augustine by James W. Siles, *A Scripture Index to the Works of St. Augustine in English Translation* (Lanham, 1995), which shows the equally meager use of the minor prophets by Augustine. A single verse, Hos 14:10, is used widely without any connection to repentance. The crucial verses about repentance, Hos 14:2–3, almost never appear in early Christian Latin literature. The exception proving the rule is the pseudo-Cyprianic *Exhortation to Penitence,* probably from Spain from about the same time as Leo; see C. Wunderer, *Bruchstücke einer afrikanischen Bibelübersetzung in der pseudocyprianischen Schrift Exhortatio de paenitentia* (Programm der kgl. Bayer. Studienanstalt zu Erlangen; Erlangen, 1889), here p. 34 for the dating.

[66] Neither does Leo quote them or allude to them. The reading of Leviticus 18 is strange in itself.

Christians combing the Old Testament for suitable texts surely
encountered these passages, which are very commonly used in Christian
literature, especially as prooftexts for Gentile groups who claim to fast
more piously than Jews do.[67] I cannot explain their absence, but neither
can the "bookish" model, since both texts would have matched the themes
of the Christian vigil of the Fast of the Seventh Month perfectly.

Particularly in light of Leo's familiarity with contemporary Judaism
and his references to the fast as part of the Jewish heritage of the church,
the theory of a completely independent development of these Christian
and Jewish readings seems highly unlikely. Competition with and
influence from the Jewish Yom Kippur plausibly explains the dominance
of Old Testament readings and the focus on repentance and propitiation.
The assumption that the Fast of the Seventh Month was shaped by a
completely internal Christian development (or a Christian development
responding only to pagan practices) does not suffice to explain these
distinctive features. Instead, I suggest a hybrid origin for the readings of
the Fast of the Seventh Month. Lections that appear in the Jewish reading
cycle and show no intrinsic connection to the Christian fast of autumn,
such as Hos 14:2–10 and Mic 7:14–20, could have been adopted from a
Roman Jewish liturgy via the mediation of Christian Jews, Judaizers, or
Christian–Jewish contact. It is more difficult to prove the adoption of
other readings such as Lev 23:27–32 from the Jewish liturgy, since
references to the seventh month may have attracted attentive readers of
the Old Testament apart from any contacts with Jews. However, I would
argue that Christian awareness of the Jewish use of Hosea and Micah
makes probable that the two readings from Leviticus 23 also reflect some
familiarity with Jewish practices on Yom Kippur. Other readings, such as
Heb 9:2–10, may have been selected as polemical responses to the
contemporary Jewish lections of Leviticus 16 or Num 29:7–11, or the
recitation of a *Seder Avodah*.[68] At the same time, some texts (e.g., 2 Esd
8:1–10; Zech 8:14–19; even Lev 23:34–43) may have been chosen by
attentive readers of the Old Testament for their references to September,
while yet others without close relation to the Jewish fast or the month of
September (e.g., Amos 9:13–15) may have been picked because of some
theological analogy.[69] Therefore, we should speak of a mixture of

---

[67] At least Isa 58:5ff is. Parts of Isa 57:15–58:14 are read during Lent, according to
most lectionaries in most churches. Parts of Jonah are usually read in the Easter vigil,
again according to most lectionaries. Of course, reading the whole book of Jonah or
Leviticus 16 would have been an exceptionally long reading, but this does not prohibit
the selection of some verses, *pars pro toto*.

[68] Lev 23:27–32 and Ex 32:11–14 can also fulfill polemical functions if read by
Christians mocking Jews.

[69] E.g., the special reading in the *Comes of Würzburg*, Jer 30:8–11, and the three
Gospels.

different types of Jewish "influence" on the Christian Fast of the Seventh Month: adoption, polemical reaction, and "bookish" biblical influence.[70]

It is difficult to draw any firm conclusions about *when* the lections were established. The complete absence of references to all lections in the sermons of Leo, however, suggests a late origin for them, i.e. after 460 CE.

If so, the ambiguous interaction between Roman Jews and Christians, which characterizes the context in which the liturgy of the Fast of the Seventh Month developed via adoption of certain lections and a polemical reaction to others, took place in a period much later than when the "Parting of the Ways" is usually set. Furthermore, this contact occurred in a geographical region usually neglected in investigations of the interactions between Christians and Jews, which tend to focus on areas such as Syria and Palestine.

## Conclusions and Implications

At least until the fifth century the Christian Fast of the Seventh Month developed both in contact with and competition to the contemporary Jewish holiday of Yom Kippur. The reference of Leo the Great to the Jewish custom of walking barefoot on the Day of Atonement reveals his acquaintance with contemporary Yom Kippur rites. It demonstrates that he promoted the Fast of the Seventh Month in competition with the contemporary "real" Yom Kippur, not an imaginary one. Competition with the contemporary practice of Yom Kippur corresponds with Leo's polemical statements as well as with the inclusion of Hebrews 9 in the readings for the Fast of the Seventh Month. The inclusion of at least two lections of the Fast of the Seventh Month, Hosea 14 and Micah 7, can be plausibly explained as the result of direct contact between Christians and Jews rather than an internal Christian development. It is not clear when the adoption of these liturgical habits occurred, but the period between Leo (the fifth century) and the canonization of the lectionary in the seventh century is the most likely.

A Jewish origin for the Fast of the Seventh Month is not impossible. Acts 27:9 provides evidence that Luke's community of Gentiles observed Yom Kippur, probably around 100 CE. If Luke-Acts reflects the provenance of a Roman Christian community and if Talley and Verstrepen are correct in dating the origin of the Fast of the Seventh Month to the second century, the Fast of the Seventh Month might be the

---

[70] Even "apostolic" influence is not ruled out – but the origin of the fast is too unclear.

transformation of a Christianized Yom Kippur, similar to Easter, which is an adaptation from the Jewish Passover. This, however, remains in the realm of speculation.

In a broader context, these conclusions speak against the conventional view of a once-and-for-all "Parting of the Ways" between Christianity and Judaism. Contrary to a model that assumes the total (or almost total) lack of interaction (except through polemic) after a single break-off point in the first or second centuries, we have seen that continuous contacts between Jews and Christians left their traces in the liturgical readings of the Fast of the Seventh Month. This, moreover, seems to have occurred after the mid-fifth century, since the lectionary system was not yet fixed in Leo's time.

The evidence for the development of the Fast of the Seventh Month also speaks against the view that the "Parting of the Ways" happened at the same time and in the same way in all geographical locales.[71] Considering, for example, the variation in martyr commemorations among early Christian calendars it would be odd not to observe local variation with regard to the relationship of Christian calendars to their Jewish counterparts. We have seen that at least one Roman Christian community continued to observe Jewish festivals longer than communities in other regions did. In order to understand the emergence of the early Christian festival calendars out of and in relation to Jewish festival calendars – and hence, the development of boundaries between Christian and Jewish identities – it is necessary to investigate each community separately.

Finally, the connection between the Roman fast and Yom Kippur counters the common prejudice whereby scholars look for Jewish–Christian contacts and for Judeo-Christianity mainly in Syria or Palestine and, to a lesser degree, in Semitic North Africa. The seeming scarcity of first-hand evidence in other locales should not mislead us into conflating the scope of the phenomenon with our own inability to reconstruct it. A reevaluation of the role of Roman Judeo-Christianity, which revisits Jean Daniélou's primary investigations – albeit with an equally revised methodology – might provide further results that refute this geographical preconception.[72]

---

[71] Regarding early Christian ritual, Paul Bradshaw has warned time and again not to fall victim to the temptation to reconstruct global linear developments by using data from distinct geographical areas, cf. e.g. "Ten Principles for Interpreting Early Christian Liturgical Evidence," in *The Making of Jewish and Christian Worship*, ed. Paul Bradshaw and Lawrence A. Hoffman (Two liturgical traditions 1; Notre Dame, Ind., 1991), 3–21.

[72] E.g., not only Hebrews, Romans, Luke-Acts, and Mark, but also *1 Clement*, the *Shepherd of Hermas*, Pseudo-Cyprian's *Against the Jews*, and the Pseudo-Clementine literature.

## Table 1: The Readings of the Fast of the Seventh Month in Relation to their Functions in Jewish Worship

| Function in Christian Worship | Text | Contents | Connection to Tishri in Jewish Thought | Function in Jewish Worship |
|---|---|---|---|---|
| Wednesday Epistle 1 | Amos 9:13–15 | Restoration of Israel using agricultural imagery, end of the book of Amos | | ((Haftarah to Qedoshim, sometimes falling together with Aharei Mot [Leviticus 16], usually read around Passover)) |
| Wednesday Epistle 2 | 2 Esd (Neh) 8:1–10 | Reading of the Law on New Year | Event takes place on New Year | |
| Wednesday Gospel | Mark 9:17–29[73] | Exorcism | | |
| Friday Epistle | Hos 14:2–10 | Call of repentance to Israel using agricultural imagery, end of the book of Hosea | Exultation of Repentance; *b. Yoma* 86ab | Haftarah on Shabbat Shuva (Repentance), the Shabbat between New Year and Yom Kippur |
| Friday Gospel | Luke 5:17–26 | Debate over forgiveness of sins and healing of the lame | | |

---

[73] This is the only text among the Epistle and Gospel readings quoted in the extant homilies of Leo (87:2).

| Function in Christian Worship | Text | Contents | Connection to Tishri in Jewish Thought | Function in Jewish Worship |
|---|---|---|---|---|
| Saturday vigil Epistle 1[74] | Lev 23:27–32 | Fast of Yom Kippur | Yom Kippur | Yom Kippur reading according to *m. Yom* 7, later abandoned |
| Saturday vigil Epistle 2 | Lev 23:34–43 | Sukkot | Sukkot | Sukkot |
| Saturday vigil Epistle 3 | Mic 7:14–20 | Prayer for protection and forgiveness, end of the book of Micah | | Mic 7:18–20 belongs to the Haftarah of Yom Kippur's afternoon prayer |
| Saturday vigil Epistle 4 | Zech 8:14–19 | Eschatological conditions and fourfold fast | One of the fasts is set for the seventh month[75] | |
| Saturday vigil Epistle 5 | Ex 32:11–14 | God is propitiated by Moses | Event happens just before the first Yom Kippur[76] | |
| Saturday vigil Epistle 6 | Heb 9:2–12 | Christ the High Priest performing atonement | | (typology of Leviticus 16, which is read on Yom Kippur) |
| Saturday vigil Gospel | Luke 13:10–17 | Releasing (on a Sabbath) the woman bound by Satan[77] | | |

[74] Additionally Jer 30:8–11 (an eschatological promise of salvation) appears only in the *Comes of Würzburg*, not in the *Comes of Alcuin*, as a second reading for the Saturday vigil.

[75] Cf. *m. Ta'an* 4; *y. Ta'an* 4:5 (20b); *b. RH* 18b.

[76] Cf. *y. Yom* 7:3 (44b), *LevR* 21:10 (Margalioth 1993:489–90)

[77] This exorcism leads to a discussion on the meaning of Sabbath; the passage is read on Saturday.

# Zipporah's Complaint

## Moses is Not Conscientious in the Deed!
## Exegetical Traditions of Moses' Celibacy

by

## NAOMI KOLTUN-FROMM

In the mid-fourth century the biblical Moses emerges as a central figure in late ancient Semitic Jewish and Christian discussions of holiness, sexuality, and religious identity. Jews and Christians explain their divine chosenness to themselves and others through their constructs of holiness. Sexuality and appropriate sexual behavior become focal points of difference. Some Jews stressed that God blesses the Jews (calls them holy, elects them to chosenness) because they marry and procreate, and condemns the Christians because they do not. Among their Christian contemporaries, the opposite claim was made: God favors the celibate because they stand prepared to enter God's presence and therefore God calls them holy. Moses' own sexual choices become foundational to this "conversation." Aphrahat, the Syriac-speaking "Persian Sage," claims that Moses provides the perfect example of holy celibacy, while Rabbis of the same general historic period and geographic location look to Moses to model their marriage and procreative strategies. Ironically, all of these late ancient Semitic exegetes focus their attention on the same biblical passages and share an extrabiblical tradition that Moses abandons wife and family to serve God.

The extrabiblical tradition of Moses renouncing sexual relations appears sporadically throughout early Jewish, rabbinic, and early Christian literature. This tradition, I argue, can be subdivided into two strains. The first evolves out of a more general notion that prophecy and family are incompatible, and the second derives from a particular reading of Ex 19.10–14. While this passage soon became a standard prooftext for celibate minded Christian readers, only Aphrahat, the fourth-century Syriac Christian homilist, and the early Rabbis provide similarly full-blown exegetical discussions of Moses' celibacy in the context of Exodus 19 (often coupled with Lev 11.44: "Be holy for I am holy"). Furthermore, the Rabbis and Aphrahat analogously promote and manipulate this particular Mosaic tradition within their respective discourses on sexuality, marriage, and holiness. In this study I pursue several interlinking exegetical traditions concerning Moses' sexual renunciation and show how the various biblical commentators engage in this exegetical discussion for their own ideological ends.

## Moses, Prophecy, and Sexual Restraint

*Aphrahat*

In the late 330s and early 340s CE, Aphrahat, a Syriac church father from Persian Mesopotamia, composed twenty-three *Demonstrations* outlining correct Christian faith and practice. The earlier homilies focus on defining the parameters of the true Christian life: love, charity, faith, belief in the resurrection, and celibacy fall into this category. Sexual renunciation especially embodies the true Christian vocation for Aphrahat. Nine of the later homilies come together as a systematic polemic against Judaism. In these *Demonstrations* Aphrahat finds himself in the position of defending his Christian faith and particularly his religious practice against the perceived critiques of contemporary Jews. While Aphrahat provides his own appraisal of contemporary Jewish practices and beliefs (e.g. Sabbath, dietary laws, and the gathering in of the exiles), he composes a pointed anti-Jewish polemic concerning the issue of holiness, which he equates with celibacy and virginity. The Jewish claim that Jews are somehow more holy or divinely blessed by God because they marry and procreate galvanizes Aphrahat's defense of celibacy. In his earlier homily on celibacy (*Demonstration* 6: "Concerning the Members of the Covenant [*bnay qyāma*]") addressed to other likeminded celibate Christians, Aphrahat does not need to underline or exegetically support the practice of sexual renunciation. Faced with Jewish condemnation of this practice Aphrahat fleshes out his anti-sexual hermeneutic of holiness in his polemical homily, *Demonstration* 18: "On Virginity and Holiness." The foundation for his exegetical support for celibacy, as noted above, lies in the tradition that Moses was celibate. Moses clearly remains authoritative in Aphrahat's world view for both Jews and Christians.

Among the various biblical figures Aphrahat treats as exemplars of the celibate life, Moses proves the most interesting and complex. Unlike Aphrahat's other models of celibacy, such as Joshua, Elijah, and Elisha, whose familial arrangements the biblical text generally ignores, Moses clearly has a wife and family. Yet Aphrahat offers Moses as his first and primary example of holiness (*qaddishutha*), that is, the act of giving up family life and sexual activity. According to Aphrahat, upon being called into service by God, Moses abandoned his wife and family. He explains:

From the time that the Holy One (*qaddisha*) revealed himself to him (i.e. Moses), even he (i.e. Moses) loved holiness (*qaddishutha*). And from the time that he was sanctified (*ethqaddash*) his wife did not serve him. Rather it is thus written: "Joshua bar Nun was a servant of Moses from his youth" (Num 11.28).[1]

Aphrahat implies a connection between God's first revelation to Moses and his abandonment of conjugal relations. Aphrahat deduces this from the "fact" that Joshua served Moses in place of Zipporah, for the Scriptures state, "Joshua bar Nun was a servant of Moses from his youth" (Num 11.28). From the moment that God first spoke to Moses he loved *qaddishutha*, that is, he chose to live a celibate life. *Qaddishutha* here is not simply celibacy or virginity, but the very act of separating oneself from family life.[2]

Several questions arise from this short notice in *Demonstration* 6 concerning Moses' celibacy. First of all, from where does this tradition arise, and how does Aphrahat come to it? I have already noted that it is not unique to Aphrahat but appears also in the early rabbinic literature. Second, what is the relation, if any, of Aphrahat's tradition to these other sources? Could Aphrahat's tradition be a separate but parallel development? Third, how do Aphrahat and these other authors deploy this tradition? And to what end? What is the relationship between Aphrahat's and the rabbinic usage of this tradition? The answers to the first question are less than certain. Nevertheless a suggestive "trace" can be placed on this tradition's development and transmission from its Second Temple attestation through its rabbinic and patristic flourishings. The second and third questions speak more directly to this comparative project and address issues of common exegesis and modes of interpretation, as well as notions of sexual and religious identity among third- and fourth-century Semitic Jews and Christians. Both Aphrahat and the Rabbis maneuver this tradition within their respective discourses on sexuality and family life in order to establish boundaries of acceptable behavior for

---

[1] Aphrahat, *Demonstrations*, 6.5/261.15–20. All citations to Aphrahat are according to J. Parisot's text ("Aphraatis Sapientis Persae Demonstrationes," in *Patrologia Syriaca*, ed. R. Graffin [2 vols; Paris: Firmin-Didot, 1894 and 1907]) and are in the following format: *Demonstration.chapter/column.line*. All translations are my own unless otherwise noted.

[2] While Moses is not technically a *btula*, a virgin, Aphrahat does not generally differentiate between those who are virgins and those who choose celibacy after marriage. All those who renounce celibacy at some point in their life are *bnay qyama* (members of the covenant) and *ihidaye* (single-minded ones). See my article, "Yokes of the Holy-Ones: The Embodiment of a Christian Vocation," *HTR* 94:2 (2001): 205–18 and Sidney Griffith's "Asceticism in the Church of Syria: The Hermeneutics of Early Syrian Monasticism," in *Asceticism*, ed. V. Wimbush and R. Valantasis (Oxford: Oxford UP, 1995), 220–45.

themselves and their followers. The tradition itself, however, does not originate in the fourth century.

## Philo

In order to address the question of where the tradition of Moses' celibacy arose and how Aphrahat came to it, it is necessary to return to the earliest-known citation of this tradition, which can be found in Philo's *On the Life of Moses*. This first-century Greek-speaking Alexandrian Jew, writing within a Hellenistic-philosophical framework, elaborates on all aspects of Moses' leadership. Moses is leader, friend of God, lawgiver, priest, and prophet. He is the ultimate Hellenistic philosopher king. He embodies numerous Greco-Roman virtues: humility, love of justice, hatred of iniquity, love of virtue, self restraint, continence, temperance, shrewdness, good sense, knowledge, evidence of toil and hardship, contempt of pleasures, justice, and advocacy of excellence.[3] Philo incorporates the tradition of Moses' celibacy into the preparatory process Moses undergoes to become high priest and the prophet of God. Philo focuses on Moses' overall control of his human passions as the means by which he achieves a purely spiritual life. Having previously addressed Moses' role as royal leader and legislator, Philo turns his attention to Moses' spiritual office – or what he calls his "priestly duties." Moses fulfilled his sacerdotal role in a most pious manner:

> But, in the first place [before assuming that office of priest], it was necessary for him [Moses] to purify not only his soul but also his body, so that it should be connected with and defiled by no passion, but should be pure from everything which is of a mortal nature, from all meat and drink, and from any connection with women. And this last thing, indeed, he had despised for a long time, almost from the moment when he began to prophesy and to feel divine inspiration [Loeb: possessed by the spirit], thinking that it was proper that he should at all times be ready to give his whole attention to God's commands [Loeb: receive the oracular messages].[4]

Philo draws a line between the corporeal/passionate life and spiritual pursuits: the one is necessarily incompatible with the other. As a prophet/priest of God, Moses understands that wine, women, and good food limit his ability to fulfill his divine duties; hence, he must distance himself from all these "mortal" things. From the moment God speaks to him, Moses "despises" his conjugal duties since they diminish his "attention to God's commands." Moses, as God's servant, priest, and

---

[3] David Dawson, *Allegorical Readers and Cultural Revision in Ancient Alexandria* (Berkeley: U. of California, 1992), 108–20.

[4] Philo, *Life of Moses* 2.68–69. This translation is by C. D. Young (*The Works of Philo* [Peabody, Mass.: Hendrickson Publishers, 1993]) and amended as noted from the Loeb translation.

prophet, clearly has no time for family, sex, or procreation, distractions that would undermine his devotion to God. Philo emphasizes the distractive nature of physical passion and lust. In fact, he practically ignores Zipporah, Moses' biblical wife, entirely.[5] For Philo, the issue is not based solely on temporal constraint – there is only so much time in the day to support a family and to serve God – but also on the question of the soul's focus, whether its attention is on the body or things spiritual. One can better concentrate on God's needs if one's own physical needs have been disciplined away (purified, nullified). Moses apparently appreciates this fact early enough to avoid the pitfalls of marriage. As far as Philo is concerned, Moses is to be lauded for his self-control and mastery of all bodily passions.[6]

In Philo's description Moses fits the paradigm of an ascetic Hellenistic philosopher who disciplines his body as well as his mind in order to better commune with the divine.[7] A true philosopher controls his desires and passions as a means to the fullest exercise of his mind. The Greco-Roman elite would have recognized in Philo's Moses a man who, like themselves, valued discipline and management of the body in the pursuit of wisdom and philosophy. They would have rated his manliness on his ability to master himself in this way.[8] Moses here exemplifies the Greco-Roman superman. As Clement of Alexandria would later note: "The human ideal of continence, I mean that which is set forth by the Greek

---

[5] Whereas Philo acknowledges Zipporah's existence elsewhere, he is quick to allegorize her into a non-physical reality. See *On the Cherubim* 5.41, 47; *On the Posterity and Exile of Cain* 77; *On the Change of Names* 120. In *Life of Moses* 1.59 Philo acknowledges Zipporah's existence, but there she remains nameless.

[6] Philo scholars continually discuss the extent to which Philo was a true Middle Platonist. A consensus seems to point to the more general notion that Philo, while sympathetic to many of the Hellenistic philosophical schools, never aligned himself wholeheartedly with one or the other. See Ellen Birnbaum's work, *The Place of Judaism in Philo's Thought: Israel, Jews and Proselytes* (Atlanta, Ga.: Scholars Press, 1996), especially the introduction. See also Robert M. Berchman, "Arcana Mundi: Prophecy and Divination in the Vita Mosis of Philo of Alexandria," *SBL Seminar Papers* 27 (1988): 385–423; John Pinsent, "Ascetic Moods in Greek and Latin Literature," in *Asceticism*, 211–19; and Jaap Mansfeld, "Philosophy in the Service of Scripture: Philo's Exegetical Strategies," in *The Question of "Eclecticism": Studies in Later Greek Philosophy*, ed. John M. Dillon and A. A. Long (Berkeley: U. of California, 1988), 70–107. Nevertheless, one can trace Platonic influence throughout Philo's work. For instance, the quote above in which Philo lauds Moses' self-control over lust and gluttony is reflected in Plato's *Phaedo* (64D) where Socrates makes similar claims.

[7] Steven D. Fraade, "Ascetical Aspects of Ancient Judaism," in *Jewish Spirituality*, vol. 1, *From the Bible through the Middle Ages*, ed. Arthur Green (New York: Crossroads, 1986), 256–57.

[8] Peter Brown, *The Body and Society: Men, Women and Sexual Renunciation in Early Christianity* (New York: Columbia UP, 1988), 19.

philosophers, teaches one to resist passion, so as not to be made subservient to it, and to train the instincts to pursue rational goals."[9] Interestingly enough, Clement further claims that Christians excel the philosophers in their espousal of permanent control over sexuality and partial control over gluttony and thirst. Ironically, but perhaps not surprisingly, Moses exemplifies for Clement the perfect continent. Clement continues to follow Philo when he posits that Moses could not have remained on Mt. Sinai for forty days had God's presence not stilled Moses' physical needs.[10] Once again, close contact with God necessitates that – and in this case provides the means by which – one overcomes physical needs such as hunger, thirst, and sexual contact.

Philo describes Moses here as both a prophet and a priest. Yet Moses was not an Israelite priest, that office having been conferred exclusively on Aaron and his sons in the biblical narrative. Nevertheless, because Moses is the leader of the Israelite people (whom the biblical text describes as a nation of priests) Philo casts Moses as the chief priest of a priestly nation.[11]

It is also likely that Philo had in mind a generic Greco-Roman priestly model. The Hellenistic priest ministered to the needs of the deity in the deity's temple but he also served as oracle and interpreter of the deity's words. Hence Philo aligned Moses' prophetic role with the Greco-Roman priestly role of "receiving oracular messages."

Philo provides the earliest extant example of the figure of Moses being used as a means for promoting a spiritual life in which celibacy plays a key role. Although Philo focuses on Moses' mastery of his passions, the result is the same as Aphrahat's: Moses foregoes his married life in order "to give his whole attention to God's commands." Moses, foreshadowing the Hellenistic philosophers, simply recognizes that succumbing to his physical needs or leading a family life distracts him from the higher pursuit of divine service to which God has called him. Better he should overcome those needs in order to perform God's demands more fully. In a sense, Philo's Moses takes Greco-Roman philosophical discipline to the extreme. Nevertheless, like Aphrahat, Philo holds up Moses' example as a model to be imitated.

Since Philo does not provide a prooftext either biblical or from some other source, there is no telling where he came across this specific Moses

---

[9] Clement, *Stromateis* 3.7.57.

[10] This midrash is found in Philo, *Life of Moses* 2.69, immediately following the above quote.

[11] See Philo, *Life of Moses* 1.149. Burton L. Mack, "Imitatio Mosis: Patterns of Cosmology and Soteriology in the Hellenistic Synagogue," *Studia Philonica* 1 (1972): 27–55; and Peder Borgen, "Moses, Jesus and the Roman Emperor: Observations in Philo's Writings and the Revelation of John," *NovT* 38 (1996): 149.

tradition.[12] If the notion of the incompatibility of family life and prophethood originates in the Greco-Roman sphere, Philo gives it a particular spin in advocating total renunciation for Moses. If the tradition of Moses' celibacy predates Philo, he dresses it up in Hellenistic garb. Yet the tradition might very well start with Philo. Or rather, he may have been the first to articulate this notion of incompatibility through the narrative of Moses' prophethood. Hence Philo could be the innovator of the celibate Moses paradigm. The tradition's appearance in Philo indicates its antiquity and perhaps speaks to its life outside the biblical text but does not give a clue to any earlier origin.[13] No matter where the tradition developed (or how it might have first been drawn exegetically from the biblical text – if at all) it shows remarkable popularity and versatility. Despite geographic, chronological, and linguistic distances, it surfaces repeatedly in later rabbinic and patristic literature.

*Early Rabbinic Traditions: Mekhilta*

Nowhere in the biblical text is it stated explicitly that Moses divorces or even abandons his wife. Nevertheless, this tradition is widespread in both Jewish and Christian literature, as Philo and Aphrahat clearly attest. Moreover, it appears several times within the rabbinic corpus. It may be founded on Ex 18.2, which states that when Jethro comes out to meet Moses and the Israelites after the exodus from Egypt he is accompanied by his daughter Zipporah and her sons. The text further states that Zipporah is in her father's company "after he (Moses) sent her" – presumably back to her father. The textual reference seems to point to some event earlier in the narrative, but we do not know from the biblical text when, where, or why that might have been. The *Mekhilta*, a third-century rabbinic commentary on Exodus, provides a plausible scenario. When Moses descends to Egypt with his family (Ex 4.20ff), and Aaron comes out to greet him, Aaron suggests to Moses that it would be too burdensome on the already oppressed people to assimilate yet another family into their suffering midst. Better Zipporah and the boys should remain with Jethro. Hence it is at this point in the narrative (chapter 4) that Moses sends Zipporah back.[14]

---

[12] While most Philo scholars tend to think of Philo as a biblical exegete first, the *Life of Moses* can be seen also as an encomium or biographic exposition which, while generally following the biblical narrative, sets out to explain Moses to the world in the terms most comprehensible to that world, in this case, first-century CE Alexandria. See Birnbaum, *Place of Judaism in Philo's Thought*, 16; and Philip Shuler, "Philo's Moses and Matthew's Jesus: A Comparative Study in Ancient Literature," *The Studia Philonica Annual* 2 (1990): 88.

[13] Daniel Boyarin, *Carnal Israel: Reading Sex in Talmudic Culture* (Berkeley: U. of California, 1993), 163.

[14] *Mekhilta*, Masekheta de-Amalek Yitro 1.26–29.

One could easily assume from the rest of the narrative in chapter 18 that Jethro expressly greets Moses with his (Moses') family in tow in order to reunite them. Although Zipporah now disappears from the narrative, the biblical text continues to refer to Jethro as Moses' father-in-law. Furthermore, at the end of this chapter Moses sends his father-in-law home – alone: "And Moses sent away his father-in-law and he made his way back to his country" (Ex 18.27). Zipporah presumably stays at her husband's side where she belongs. Nevertheless, the *Mekhilta* raises the issue of divorce in this context. In the same passage mentioned above, Rabbi Joshua suggests that this verse (Ex 18.2) parallels Deut 24.1, in which a man who is displeased with his wife divorces her with a *get* (a written document of divorce) and sends her from his home. There in Deuteronomy it says "send away" with a *get* – so here in Exodus it must mean "send away" with a *get* as well. The similarly deployed verb שלח (*shalah*) prompts Rabbi Joshua to conclude that a divorce must have occurred in Ex 18.27. Perhaps this reading appeals to Rabbi Joshua since there is no explicit statement in the biblical text that Moses and Zipporah are happily reunited at Sinai and, from that point forwards, Zipporah disappears from the narrative. Whether or not this reading is acceptable to the other Rabbis is not clear. It is certainly not refuted but rather followed – and perhaps opposed by – the aforementioned suggestion concerning Moses' encounter with Aaron upon returning to Egypt.

## Early Rabbinic Traditions: Sifre

The tradition that Moses divorces his wife might very well have developed from this interpretation of Ex 18.27. Yet this midrash does not provide a larger ideological context to explain the divorce. The question the *Mekhilta* seems to ask is not why Moses separated from his wife but whether he divorced her legally or simply sent her back to her father's house for the duration of his trip to Egypt. The Rabbis pursue neither the implications of, nor the motivations for, such a separation. Nevertheless, the tradition that Moses divorces his wife, or at least neglects his familial duties, is theorized in other rabbinic exegetical contexts where the Rabbis explore Moses' motivations and rationalize his action.

In the *Sifre*, another third-century tannaitic composition, Moses' marital difficulties arise from an inconsistency between the first two verses in Num 12.17. The biblical text states:

> Miriam and Aaron spoke against Moses concerning the Cushite woman whom he had married; for he had married a Cushite woman. And they said: Does God

speak only through/with (-בּ) Moses? Does God not also speak through/with (-בּ) us? [Num 12.1–2].[15]

The biblical text presents two seemingly unrelated reasons for Miriam and Aaron's complaint. The first verse suggests that the complaint has something to do with Moses' wife, Zipporah, the Cushite woman he married.[16] One might assume from the continuation of the first verse that Miriam and Aaron's complaint concerns the fact that Moses had married a Cushite (Ethiopian) woman and not a Hebrew woman, or at least that something particular about Zipporah bothered them, that she was in some way a bad or inappropriate wife. Yet the second verse expressly states that the complaint centers on Moses' sense of superiority over his siblings.

The Rabbis attempt to fuse the two complaints into one through the following midrash. Concerning Numbers 12.1 the *Sifre* expounds:

> *And Miriam and Aaron spoke against Moses* [*concerning his Cushite wife for he had married a Cushite woman* (Num 12.1)]: From where did Miriam know that Moses had abstained from procreation? She saw Zipporah, who was not dressed up in the ornaments of women. She said to [Zipporah], "What is wrong such that you are not dressed up in the ornaments of women?" [Zipporah] said to her, "Your brother is not conscientious in the deed." Thus Miriam knew and she spoke to her brother [Aaron] and the two of them spoke against him [Moses]. Rabbi Nathan says Miriam was beside Zipporah at the moment that it was said, "*And the youth ran* [*and told to Moses and said that Eldad and Medad were prophesying in the camp* (Num 11.27)]" because she [Miriam] heard Zipporah say, "Oy for the wives of those men!" And thus Miriam knew ... [*Sifre* 99].[17]

The language of the first verse allows for two contradictory readings; it can be understood to mean that Miriam and Aaron spoke *to* Moses *against* his wife, or, as the Rabbis prefer, that they spoke *against* Moses *on behalf of* his wife. This reading allows the Rabbis to combine the two complaints into one – which they do through the two midrashim on Miriam and Zipporah. The first part of the complaint concerns Moses' neglect of his conjugal duties. The biblical text itself may have suggested this line of reasoning, namely that the issue was Moses' marital behavior because of its repeated use of the word לקח "take" (in marriage). The Rabbis here emphasize "married" over "Cushite." The rabbinic authors then produce two scenarios in which Miriam discovers the problem. In the first, which is disconnected from the text and the narrative, Miriam comes upon a bedraggled Zipporah wandering around the camp and asks

---

[15] I prefer to leave in the various options of translations to help underscore the problematics of the Hebrew.

[16] The Rabbis note in this *Sifre* passage that Moses married a Midianite woman according to Ex 3.21. They then attempt to understand what "Cushite" really says about Zipporah, namely that she was dark-skinned and beautiful.

[17] All translations are my own unless otherwise noted.

her why she has not taken care of herself. Zipporah's accusatory cry, "Your brother is not conscientious in the deed," lets Miriam know that Moses has been neglecting his conjugal duties, but it does not inform us as to why he does so. That answer can be found only in the second midrash of Rabbi Nathan. Here Miriam happens to be standing with Zipporah when the spirit of prophecy lands on Medad and Eldad and the "youth ran" to tell Moses that they were prophesying in the camp. Zipporah's sympathetic reaction, "Oy for the wives of those men," gives the reader deeper insight into the anguish of her own situation. Those men, because of their newly found prophetic calling, will now also neglect their wives. From this, the reader and Miriam together deduce that Moses neglects Zipporah precisely because of his prophetic role. The first midrash gives a reason for Miriam's complaint concerning Zipporah, and the second connects this complaint to the next verse in which Miriam and Aaron grumble about Moses' leadership and prophethood. In both cases Miriam learns of the situation by observing her sister-in-law. Wives and families suffer when a husband/father presumes his divine calling supersedes his domestic obligations.

This gendered view of the effects of prophecy furthers the Rabbis' next contention that prophets (except for Moses) should not break with their families. Hence the midrash continues with an explication of the real complaint against Moses:

> *And they said, "Did God speak only through/with Moses?"* (Num 12.2): Did He not speak through/with the Patriarchs, and they did not withdraw from procreation? *Did God not speak also through/with us* (12.3), yet we did not withdraw from procreation?... [*Sifre* 100].

From this text we see that it is not just Zipporah's neglect which worries them, but the presumptive logic behind Moses' behavior, specifically, that because God speaks through/with Moses he necessarily must renounce procreation. The older siblings, including themselves among others who have spoken with God (or through whom God has spoken), do not renounce marriage, but rather strongly censure Moses' behavior. Miriam and Aaron take issue with what they perceive to be Moses' overreaching self-righteousness. Following the biblical narration, the midrash suggests that this is how God answers their question:

> *If there will be for you a prophet I will make it known to him in a vision* (Num 12.6): Perhaps just as I speak with the prophets in dreams and visions, so I speak with Moses, therefore scripture tells us, *"Not so is my servant Moses"* (12:7). *"In all my house he is entrusted"* (12.7) – except for the ministering angels. Rabbi Yose says, even more than the ministering angels. *Mouth to mouth do I speak to him* (Num 12.8): Mouth to mouth I told him to withdraw from his wife. [*Sifre* 103].

God hears their complaint and answers: Yes, with other prophets I appear in dreams and visions, but with Moses I speak directly. Moses is special –

in fact, he is equal to the ministering angels and hence God commands him specifically to separate from his wife. God may call others to prophecy, but only Moses is required to give up his family life. Yet the Rabbis do not flesh out the rationale for this requirement. Instead, they bestow an abstract notion of specialness on Moses: he is close (but not quite equal) to the ministering angels. God speaks "mouth to mouth" with Moses whereas all other prophets hear or see God indirectly through dreams or visions only and cannot talk back or respond to what they have seen or heard from God.

Starting from a position similar to Aphrahat's, the *Sifre* claims that Moses refuses his conjugal duties because of his service to God, that is, his prophetic calling. While Zipporah bemoans his conjugal neglect, Miriam accuses him of something more severe than neglect, for he has withdrawn from the act of procreating completely. Most importantly, he presumes to do so because of the demands of his prophetic role. Miriam is indignant not only on Zipporah's behalf but because Moses appears to be placing himself in a separate category from all other leaders of Israel who have had personal relationships with God. Miriam appears (in the rabbinic eye) just in her criticism of Moses on this account. Neither Miriam nor Aaron know of any other leaders of Israel who have been required to renounce their family, so why should Moses? Yet God comes to Moses' defense: not all prophets are made alike. Moses is special. Other prophets communicate with God through dreams and visions. Only Moses speaks directly to God. Moses does not presume to take leave of his family duties: rather, God has expressly commanded him to do so. Other prophets need not (nor should they) abandon their conjugal duties. Nevertheless the reason why Moses' special prophethood requires such a condition is never explored in depth. The Rabbis only state that his unique position warrants it. The *Sifre* authors construe Moses' renunciation not as an ideal, but as an exception that requires little explanation.

## A Comparison

The *Sifre* text does not seem to be familiar or concerned with the *Mekhilta* text because the issue of divorce is not at stake here. If Moses had already divorced Zipporah in Exodus 4 or 18, she would not have any right to complain about Moses in the desert. The *Sifre* text counters the notion (advocated by Philo and Aphrahat) that all prophets should abandon their family lives as part and parcel of their vocation, but does not deny the notion's applicability to Moses.

The major difference between the *Sifre*, Philo, and Aphrahat is in the value placed on Moses' example. The *Sifre* severely limits its applicability to Moses and Moses alone. It emphatically holds that other prophets should not renounce their families nor procreation whereas Philo and Aphrahat find Moses' life choices admirable and even worthy of emulation. Moreover, the Rabbis' emphasis on Zipporah's suffering (absent from both Philo and Aphrahat) highlights what they find problematic even in Moses' case. As Daniel Boyarin aptly notes, while the Rabbis reconcile two contradictory biblical statements they also take the opportunity to invest their response ideologically. That is, this midrash also addresses their own concerns about marriage and the spiritual life. The Rabbis recognize that their frequently long absences from home and lengthy days in the study house put enormous pressures on their families. Yet at the same time they admire Moses' audacity, if only from a great distance.[18]

This tannaitic text, as read against Aphrahat or Philo, certainly appears to be polemical. Yet it cannot be aimed at Aphrahat since he wrote his treatise at least a century later. Boyarin has suggested that the *Sifre* passage refutes an early Jewish variation, perhaps as represented by Philo.[19] The *Sifre* clearly questions the notion of an inherent incompatibility between family life and all prophethood or spiritual leadership. If the particular tradition that the *Sifre* authors had in mind was Philo's, they do not seem to be concerned with its more Hellenistic elements, that is, the notion of discipline and the managing of one's passions. The *Sifre*'s Moses neglects Zipporah either because God directs him to (for unknown reasons), or because he has no time for Zipporah due to the overwhelming attention needed by God, or because of some other unexplained nature of the job, but not out of a concern to discipline his body. As Boyarin notes, the *Sifre* focuses not on celibacy per se but on celibacy in marriage. This could be a reflection on any number of practices by contemporaries of the *Sifre* authors, Christians and Jews alike.[20] Certainly some Christian groups advocated giving up procreation at baptism.[21] In reality, this often happened late in life, after one had completed one's familial duties of procreation. Elderly celibate couples then continued to live together. Aphrahat makes use of the Mosaic tradition to counter this practice of "spiritual marriage" and to advocate abandoning one's domestic arrangements even if one's wife has also agreed to a celibate life.

In *Demonstration* 6 Aphrahat speaks to and for the already celibate. Moses here is more than an exemplar of celibacy; he is a model of the properly conducted continent life. The key is the separation of the sexes, which embodies a separation of the mundane from the spiritual. Celibate women should live with other women, and men with other men. Family

---

[18] Boyarin, *Carnal Israel*, 161.

[19] Boyarin, *Carnal Israel*, 163.

[20] Boyarin, *Carnal Israel*, 164, see especially note 47.

[21] In the Syriac tradition see the writings of Tatian and the Acts of Judas Thomas.

of any sort is inappropriate and untenable for the truly committed renunciants. Moses provides an excellent role model precisely because he has a family to abandon. The call to *iḥidāyutha* – the life in single-minded devotion to God – includes a physical as well as a mental element of separation.

While Pauline and the other New Testament texts promote leaving one's family in order to pursue spiritual goals, it would be limiting to suggest that this *Sifre* text argues specifically against Pauline or other early Christian claims. Rather, this rabbinic text demonstrates that Jews, too, were concerned with similar issues of balance in their lives. Boyarin suggests that the *Sifre* argues against a Jewish and rabbinic practice of "married monks," married Rabbis abandoning their families for long stretches at a time in order to study. The *Sifre*, which disapproves of this sort of practice, focuses on the women's suffering.[22] These Rabbis, Boyarin argues, would prefer their students to study before they marry. The *Sifre* authors manipulate this tradition about Moses to suggest that given the realities of life (i.e., family) compromises must be made in one's "spiritual" life. A balance must be struck.

Yet these same Rabbis never deny the tradition's associations to Moses. The possibility of an inherent incompatibility between family life and prophethood exists, but only in Moses' case. While the *Sifre* text seems to polemicize against an unknown earlier text or tradition, Aphrahat deploys a tradition similar to the one the *Sifre* attempts to counter, namely that Moses' celibacy provides an ideal model of religious behavior. What is his source – if he indeed has one? Except for the tradition itself, the textual associations do not seem to correspond. The Rabbis find sexual renunciation in Miriam's complaint against Moses and the prophesying of Eldad and Medad. Aphrahat, on the other hand, finds his proof in the "fact" that Joshua served Moses from his youth. However, textually and narratively these prooftexts are quite close. Aphrahat's prooftext, Num 11.28 ("Joshua was a servant of Moses from his youth"), follows immediately upon the *Sifre*'s – verse 27 ("*And the youth ran*" [and told to Moses and said that Eldad and Medad were prophesying in the camp]). Coincidence? Perhaps. Yet it is more likely that these prooftexts surface from a common exegetical matrix of traditions surrounding Numbers 11–12.

It is, of course, difficult to speak of sources when we have so little information about the texts, their date of composition, and the breadth of their readership. The *Sifre* to Numbers, a tannaitic commentary on the biblical book of Numbers, was most likely composed in the mid-third century in the Land of Israel. Similar to many of the rabbinic texts, this

---

[22] Boyarin, *Carnal Israel,* 164.

text is made up of earlier traditions that a later editor redacted into one volume. It is possible that some of these traditions had transmission histories, either written or oral, of their own and that they may also have come into non-rabbinic hands at one point or another. Some of these traditions may have emerged from non-rabbinic or pre-rabbinic circles, as the Philo text suggests. Aphrahat, who traveled the highways of fourth-century Persian Mesopotamia, may very well have come across any number of these sorts of texts and traditions without having a "*Sifre*" text, as we know it today, in his hands.

Aphrahat's training and background is even murkier than that of the tannaitic Rabbis. While he composed his 23 homilies in the mid-fourth century, we do not know with whom he studied, what sources he may have had at his disposal, or in what language(s) he pursued his scholarship. Though he has a Persian name, he writes in a Syriac minimally affected by Greek or Persian. One can only assume that his sources were limited to Syriac or other dialects of Aramaic. He may have learned and retained many of his sources orally from his teachers or from other itinerant preachers. There were probably former Jews and various Jewish Christians among his teachers and audiences. His Christian training may have come largely from Tatian-influenced circles. Yet his textual citation of this tradition is exegetically so close to the *Sifre* text it is hard to dismiss the possibility of a relationship of some sort, even as its exact nature may be difficult to pinpoint. At the very least, I suggest, Aphrahat and the fourth-century Babylonian Rabbis shared a common Aramaic "public" library; that is, they had access to similar compilations or collections of exegetical traditions[23]

Whether or not Aphrahat's source or inspiration is this *Sifre* text or something similar, he inverts the argument once again. If the *Sifre* counters an earlier notion that prophecy and family are incompatible, Aphrahat uses it to support that notion. Furthermore, he applies this logic to his own life. Prophecy and divine service are indeed incompatible with family and hence all *iḥidāye* – those who, in imitation of Jesus and the prophets, dedicate themselves to divine service – should separate themselves from family and women, even other celibate women. This is not to say that Aphrahat polemicizes against the *Sifre* text specifically; rather, he seems to me to be simply making use of traditions at his

---

[23] Even the exact nature of the biblical texts Aphrahat had at his disposal is far from clear. See J. R. Owens, *The Genesis and Exodus Citations of Aphrahat the Persian Sage* (Leiden: Brill, 1983). For a more in-depth discussion of Aphrahat's background see my dissertation, Naomi Koltun, "Jewish–Christian Polemics in Fourth-Century Persian Mesopotamia: A Reconstructed Conversation" (Ph.D. diss., Stanford, 1993) or my article of similar name, Naomi Koltun-Fromm, "A Jewish–Christian Conversation in Fourth-Century Persian Mesopotamia," *JJS* 47 (1996): 45–63.

disposal for his own purposes (as indeed the Rabbis do). In this case he uses a known tradition to convince wayward celibates to live alone, while the Rabbis deploy it to discourage others from staying away from home for extended periods of time. For obvious reasons Aphrahat is not concerned with the feelings of the abandoned wives – if anything, he feels they are better off without their menfolk so that they are free to pursue their own celibate lives. If Aphrahat were a direct participant in the rabbinic debate described by Boyarin, he might propose a third tactic – wholesale abandonment of the family by both men and women (after they had raised their children).

Aphrahat's emphasis on the root *Q-D-Sh* further differentiates him from the *Sifre* and Philo and may point to a different tradition entirely. Moses renounces sexuality (loves *qaddishutha*) because he is sanctified [*ethqaddash*] by God. As I noted above, the connection between sexuality and *qaddishutha* is assumed, not explained, by Aphrahat. While not explicit in the *Sifre* text (it might be inferred from his angelic disposition and the fact that he talks "mouth to mouth" with God) the link between *qedusha/qaddishutha* (holiness) and sexual abstinence is foundational to Aphrahat's claim. Yet this connection is not exegetically supported by Aphrahat's argument; rather, his prooftext speaks more to the tradition preserved in Philo and the *Sifre* that Moses does away with his marriage because of his prophetic calling. Nevertheless, the notion that Moses is somehow *sanctified* through or because of his celibacy is born out in later Aphrahatic texts and is reflected in other rabbinic Midrash.

## Moses at Sinai

### Aphrahat

Several years after his discussion of celibacy in *Demonstration* 6: "*Concerning the Members of the Covenant*,"[24] Aphrahat returns to this issue in *Demonstration* 18: "*Against the Jews Concerning Virginity and Holiness* (*qaddishutha*)." Here Aphrahat not only promotes celibacy, as he does in *Demonstration* 6, but defends it against what he considers to be the dangerously attractive Jewish arguments *for* procreation.[25] Of all the *Demonstrations*, holiness, or *qaddishutha*, appears as the central issue only in *Demonstration* 18, which is partly due to the fact that Aphrahat deploys *qaddishutha* here primarily as a technical term for celibacy. Yet

---

[24] *Bnay qyāma* can be translated either as "members of the order" or "members of the covenant." Aphrahat uses this title interchangeably with *iḥidāye*, "the single-minded ones," *qaddishe*, "holy ones," and *btule*, "virgins." With these names he refers to the celibate and spiritual core of his church community.

[25] See note 20 above.

as this treatise unfolds it becomes clear that *qaddishutha's* literal meaning, "holiness," is also central to Aphrahat's argument. Celibate "holiness" for Aphrahat excels other holy practices such as fasting, prayer, and charity. Holiness encompasses a sense of election, chosenness, and exclusive access to God. Like Ezra – who marks the returning Judeans as the "holy seed of Israel," the exclusive descendents of God's chosen people – Aphrahat marks his fellow celibates as "the holy ones" with whom God chooses to dwell. Thus, for Aphrahat sexuality and holiness are entwined. The celibate's holy status and special relationship with God is manifested through his sexual renunciation. The celibate *iḥidāye* (single-minded ones) not only perfect this spiritual separation from the mundane, but in so doing they imitate the *Iḥidāya* (only begotten): Jesus, the Son of God.[26]

Aphrahat uses this argument to counter what he considers to be the central Jewish claim against his own position. The Jews, he contends, make the following argument: "We are holy (*qaddishin*) and better, we who procreate and increase progeny in the world" (*Dem.* 18.12/841.3–9). Aphrahat here touches upon one of the stickiest points of contention between Jews and Christians in this era: namely, the manner in which sexuality (as opposed to circumcision, baptism, Sabbath observance, etc.) embodies God's holiness among the peoples. Once again Aphrahat turns to the celibate Moses to build his defense of celibacy as holiness and to counterattack the Jewish position. This time his exegesis is more clearly reflected in the rabbinic sources. Yet Aphrahat's manipulation of this textual reading complicates how we are to understand the rabbinic renditions. Commenting on Exodus 19:14–15, "And Moses went down from the mount to the people, and sanctified the people (*qaddesh l-'amma*); and they washed their clothes. And Moses said to the people, 'Be ready (*hwayton mtaybin*)[27] by the third day; do not go near a woman,'" Aphrahat writes:

> And concerning virginity and holiness (*qaddishutha*) I will persuade you that even in that nation [Israel] they [virginity and holiness] were more loved and preferred before God ... [for] Israel was not able to receive the holy text (*pethgāma qaddisha*) and the living words that the Holy One [*qaddisha*] spoke to Moses on the mountain until he had sanctified (*qaddsheh*) the people for three days. And only then the Holy One spoke to them. For He said to Moses: "Go down to the people and sanctify (*qaddesh*) them for three days" (Ex 19.10). And this is how Moses explained it to them: "Do not go near a woman" (Ex 19.15).

---

[26] See Griffith, "Asceticism in the Church of Syria," 224–25.

[27] Adam Becker pointed out to me in personal correspondence that the very use of "prepare" probably resonated and attracted Aphrahat to this Moses passage because it echoes the parable of the virgins in Matthew 25. Aphrahat refers repeatedly to this parable and the need to be prepared for the Bridegroom throughout *Demonstration* 6.

And when they were sanctified (*ethqaddash*) these three days, then on the third day God revealed himself .... " (*Dem* 18.4/824.25–27; 825.15–23)

In the biblical narrative, God commands Moses to sanctify the Israelites for several days before the Law is revealed and directs him to tell the people to wash their clothes and thus prepare themselves for three days. Moses, in transmitting these instructions, adds "be ready ... do not go near a woman." In other words, the people should abstain from sexual activity as part of the overall preparatory process. In the biblical text the action which *seems* to fulfill the requirements of *qaddesh l-'amma* is the washing of their clothing. Moses' additional "do not go near a woman" appears to be a precautionary prescription added to "be ready" in the next verse. Nevertheless, Aphrahat reads *qaddesh l-'amma*, "sanctify the people," and *hwayton mtayybin*, "be ready," as one. The directive "do not go near a woman" qualifies "sanctify the people" rather than, or perhaps in addition to, "be ready." Aphrahat assumes these two verses to mean: "Sanctify the people through sexual renunciation and be ready for the third day."[28] In his interpretation of this passage Aphrahat establishes a different paradigm: one sanctifies oneself through the act of sexual restraint. The intermediate details of "wash your clothing" are lost in this alternative reading. The sense of readiness or being prepared is also subsumed into the notion of sanctification. With this reading Aphrahat contends, against the Jews, that God "loves" *qaddishutha* (that is, celibacy) because God demands it of the Israelites at this point in the biblical narrative. Hence he can argue that celibacy is equal, if not superior, to procreation – the very act the Jews claim God has commanded and which they believe sanctifies them, i.e., makes them holy (*qaddishin*).

In contradistinction to the *Sifre* passages discussed above, this exegetical text does not claim that sex, marriage, or procreation is incompatible with prophecy. Rather it suggests that sexual abstinence is a required preparatory process for *anyone* before a divine meeting. In order for the people to hear God's word, they must be properly sanctified and, for Aphrahat, celibacy is the sine qua non of the preparatory process. That is, through Aphrahat's conflating of "sanctify" and "be ready," sexual abstinence is sanctifying. The preparatory and sanctifying processes coalesce in Aphrahat's interpretation of the biblical text. Aphrahat's understanding of this passage upholds what he already knows to be the truth: sexual abstinence and holiness go hand in hand. This is the

---

[28] The biblical Hebrew verb קדשׁ probably best translates here as "purify," rather than "sanctify," in that the Israelites are commanded to ritually purify themselves before the divine encounter. Semen, not the sexual act itself, was determined by the Levitical priests to be defiling (Leviticus 15). Yet it is unclear from Aphrahat's text whether he understands or knows of that particular connotation.

exegetical link that is missing from Aphrahat's earlier text in
*Demonstration* 6. While this passage supports his contention that holiness
is tantamount to celibacy, it says nothing particular about Moses. He then
continues:

> For Moses was speaking and God answered him with a voice. Israel stood on that
> day in terror, fear and trembling. They fell on their faces, for they were unable to
> bear it. And they said to Moses "Let not God speak with us so, that we may not
> die" (Ex 20.19). O hard-hearted one! Who is vexed by these things and stumbles!
> If the people of Israel, with whom God spoke only one hour (*da-ḥda shā'a
> balḥud*), were unable to hear the voice of God until they had sanctified
> (*ethqaddash*) themselves three days, even though they did not go up the
> mountain and did not go into the heavy cloud; how then could Moses, the man,
> the prophet, the enlightened eye of all the people, who stood all the time before
> God, and spoke with him mouth to mouth (*men pum l-pum*), how was it possible
> that he be living in the married state?! (*Dem.* 18.5/828.19–829.8)

Aphrahat here constructs a logical deduction from the narrative of the text
as he understands it. If the Israelites were required to be prepared and
sanctified (*ethqaddash*) through sexual restraint for three days just so
they could hear God's voice and receive God's word only once, how
could Moses, who stands continuously in God's presence, be sexually
active? He must necessarily refrain from sexual contact at all times. His
sexual activity is not inherently incompatible with his prophetic role, but
it has also become more than just a casualty of his duties to God.
Although Moses renounces his sexuality permanently because of his
constant proximity to God, Aphrahat does not link this specifically to
Moses' prophethood. In fact, Aphrahat opens up this possibility to all
Israel, for this is how he concludes the "midrash":

> And if with Israel, that had sanctified (*ethqaddash*) itself for only three days,
> God spoke, how much better and desirable are those who all their days are
> sanctified [*mqaddshin*], alert, prepared and standing before God. Should not God
> all the more love them and his spirit dwell among them? [*Dem.* 18.5/829.8–
> 14].[29]

Would it not be wonderful, he claims, if we all could be like Israel on
those three days, if not like Moses: prepared, sanctified, and continuously
standing before God? Would not God love us more (than the non-
sanctified, non-celibate) and dwell among us? Here Aphrahat lays out his
fundamental claim: not only does God demand celibacy prior to a
singular divine encounter, but through Moses' example God further
suggests that celibacy is the preferred status of God's beloved, elect,
chosen people, for God dwells among the holy, i.e. the celibate. Those

---

[29] This notion of preparedness clearly echoes the similar thesis in *Demonstration* 6
in which Aphrahat cajoles his fellow celibates to remember that they are akin to
Matthew's virgins who wait patiently but constantly for the Bridegroom's attention.

Jews then, Aphrahat contends, who claim they fulfill God's command-ments and claim to be God's holy people because they procreate are greatly mistaken. While Aphrahat will never condemn married procreation entirely (it too was created by God), God clearly prefers celibacy, for he calls it holy.[30]

Probably to Aphrahat's great frustration, the biblical text never explicitly commands, "Be celibate," in the same manner that procreation is so commanded: "Be fruitful and multiply." Yet with this exegesis Aphrahat comes as close as he can to a divine directive. Whereas Philo and the *Sifre* authors assume sexuality is a casualty of Moses' prophethood, Aphrahat not only construes celibacy as a divine commandment but strongly suggests that it is *the only*, or the most significant, commandment that also sanctifies a person. In this way Aphrahat establishes firm boundaries between "Jewish" holiness (marriage) and "Christian" holiness (celibacy). Moreover, by placing Christian marriage at an inferior spiritual level than celibacy he further undermines Jewish claims to holiness through marriage. In the end celibacy remains the only means to true sanctity and divine blessing. The Jews, by missing the significance of Moses' move, misunderstand the whole import of the biblical text. Holiness comes not through procreation, Sabbath observance, or dietary laws but by following the simple example of Moses' celibacy.

Although this interpretation of Exodus 19 appears only in Aphrahat's later work, one can assume that it lies behind his earlier statement that Moses "loved *qaddishutha*" and therefore was not served by his wife. In that context Aphrahat presumes he does not need to prove that Moses loved *qaddishutha*, nor that *qaddishutha* equals celibacy; rather, he wishes to show that once Moses became a practitioner of *qaddishutha* he did not live with his wife (for Joshua served him in her stead). Aphrahat's overarching purpose at that moment in *Demonstration* 6 is to undermine the practice of "spiritual marriage" in which celibate men and women share domestic arrangements.[31] Yet, because he constructs an exegetical paradigm of prophets who lead solitary lives, he must also cast Moses as a celibate prophet. Hence he deftly combines these two traditions in one – the one as represented by Philo and the *Sifre* and the other as laid out in *Demonstration* 18.

---

[30] Aphrahat, like many other early Church fathers, creates a spiritual hierarchy in which marriage is acceptable but inferior to celibacy. See Elizabeth Clark, *Reading Renunciation: Asceticism and Scripture in Early Christianity* (Princeton: Princeton UP, 1999).

[31] The other problem with "spiritual marriage" is that it does not fit the image of the celibate as a bride of Christ. The imagery of true spiritual marriage (a celibate union with Jesus) pervades *Demonstration* 6.

## Avot de Rabbi Nathan

This particular reading of Exodus 19, and specifically this understanding of the relationship between *qaddishutha*, readiness, and sexual abstinence, is not lost on the Rabbis, many of whose exegetical works were in the process of composition and redaction around the time that Aphrahat wrote and in the same geographic location in which he ministered. Perhaps it should not be too surprising, therefore, that a remarkably similar reading of Exodus 19 appears several times within the rabbinic corpus. In these texts – all variations of the same midrash – the rabbinic authors establish a direct link between holiness/preparation before divine encounter and sexual renunciation. The following midrash comes from *Avot de Rabbi Nathan* (*ARN*) 2.3 but can be found also in the Babylonian Talmud tractates *Shabbat* (87a) and *Yevamot* (62a), as well as in the midrash *Exodus Rabbah* 19.3 and 46.13.[32] Whereas the *Sifre* text is not as obviously exegetically similar to Aphrahat's Moses tradition, the thematic, linguistic, and terminological affinities, as well as the parallels in logical progression, between the *ARN* text and Aphrahat's are hard to deny:

> This is one of the things that Moses did on his own and his opinion matched the opinion of God .... He separated from his wife, and his opinion agreed with the opinion of God. How so? [Moses] said, "What if Israel, who are not sanctified [נתקדשו *nitqadshu*] except for the hour [לפי שעה *le-fi sha'ah*], and are not called but in order to receive upon themselves the ten commandments from Sinai (for the Holy Blessed One, said to me, 'go to the people and sanctify them [וקדשתם *ve-qiddashtem*] today and tomorrow'); and I, who am called to this every day at every hour and I do not know when God will speak with me – in the morning or in the night – isn't it more important for me to separate from my wife?" And his opinion agreed with the opinion of God ...
>
> [However] R. Yehudah ben Batira said ... as it is said (Num 12.8): "Mouth to mouth [פה אל פה *peh el peh*] I will speak to him," "mouth to mouth I said to him separate from your wife" and he separated ... and his opinion agreed with the opinion of God.
>
> Some say: Moses did not keep away from his wife until he was told so by the mouth of the Almighty; for it is said, Go say to them: *Return ye to your tents* (Deut 5:27), and it is written, But as for thee, *stand thou here by Me* (Deut 5:28). He went back but kept away from his wife. And his judgment coincided with God's.[33] [*ARN* 2:3].

---

[32] Martin Jaffe (*Torah in the Mouth: Writing and Oral Tradition in Palestinian Judaism 200 BCE–400 CE* [Oxford: Oxford UP, 2001]) has recently argued that when a midrash appears in several versions, no one of them necessarily is the original; they may all be variations on a theme, created in rhetorical exercises in the academy. If there was an original it may very well be lost to us. See his chapter 7.

[33] This last paragraph follows the translation by Judah Goldin, *The Fathers According to Rabbi Nathan* (New Haven: Yale UP, 1955), 19.

Like Aphrahat, the Rabbis read the commandment to sanctify in vv. 10 and 14 in conjunction with the commandment to "be ready" in 11 and 15. They conclude, like Aphrahat, that when God said "sanctify" he meant, as Moses claims, "Prepare yourselves through sexual restraint." Furthermore, they contend, as does Aphrahat, that Moses deduces from this that he must refrain from sexual contact permanently, since he would not necessarily have three days for proper preparation every time God called on him. In both texts Moses speaks to God "mouth to mouth" and Israel stands but for an "hour" interview with God. The deductive analogies made by the exegetes are the same: Moses models his behavior on Israel – only more so.

The biggest difference between the texts is in the literary structure. Whereas in Aphrahat's rendering it is Aphrahat who makes a deduction concerning Moses, in the rabbinic telling Moses draws his own conclusions. This difference is not insignificant, for Aphrahat wants only to support his previous contention that celibacy is divinely desired, even commanded, that is, it is better than marriage and a key element in holiness (*qaddishutha*). The Rabbis, however, by making Moses' celibacy a result of his own choice, question that very choice. The two closing addenda introduce a tension into the rabbinic discourse and suggest that Moses did not decide, but was commanded by God to leave his wife. Whereas Aphrahat eagerly imitates Moses' move, the Rabbis equivocate. They do not resoundingly conclude to follow Moses' example, nor do they equate celibacy with a universally desired behavior. Finally, although the Rabbis and Aphrahat similarly elide the meanings of "sanctify" and "prepare," the Rabbis emphasize the latter while Aphrahat focuses on the former. Aphrahat's whole exegesis hinges on his understanding that *qaddishutha*, "holiness," does indeed equal celibacy.

The rabbinic Midrash on Exodus 19 is significantly different from the *Sifre*'s, even as it "cites" the *Sifre* text. The *ARN* focuses on universal sexual restraint before a divine encounter. It shows no particular concern for prophecy and celibacy. Aphrahat's conclusion – that Moses' move is exemplary – is a logical conclusion drawn from this reading of the text and has little to do with Moses' prophethood. Yet the Rabbis do not follow through on this idea and again limit its application to Moses alone. Nevertheless, Rabbi Yehudah's addendum seems to refer back to the *Sifre* text in its citation of Num 12.8: God spoke to Moses "mouth to mouth"; "mouth to mouth" God told Moses to separate from his wife. This citation reaffirms the conclusions drawn from the *Sifre* discussion that Moses is in a separate category of people altogether. In the *Sifre* he is a super-prophet; in the *ARN* he distinguishes himself from the rest of Israel. Furthermore, in the *ARN*, the central issue is not specifically prophecy, but a more general encounter with God. The *Sifre* suggests an inherent incompatibility between Moses' role as a prophet and his obligations as a

husband and father. The *ARN* affirms only that sexual restraint is
incumbent upon all Israel before an extraordinary encounter with God –
such as the revelation of the Torah at Sinai – and that Moses' peculiar
position within Israel necessitates total withdrawal from his sexual life.
Most significantly for this discussion in the *ARN* this preparatory process
(i.e. sexual restraint) is linked to *qedusha/qaddishutha* by both the Rabbis
and Aphrahat. While Aphrahat builds his theological case from this
apparent connection, the Rabbis make no such broad conclusions
concerning *qedusha* and celibacy. In fact, they make every effort to
downplay it. Moses' celibacy is unique, and its connection to holiness is
contested as the addenda attest. For in reference back to the *Sifre*, Rabbi
Yehudah suggests that it was a command of God, *not* a decision on
Moses' part, which caused Moses to give up his sexuality. Moreover,
after the revelation of the Torah the people are "commanded back to their
tents," whereas Moses is directed to stay where he is at God's side. The
Rabbis acknowledge the link between *qedusha* and temporary celibacy
for Israel before the revelation, but they hesitate to apply *qedusha* to
Moses' permanent abstinence or extend the possibility to the rest of
Israel. These added references reaffirm Moses' unique situation while at
the same time they subvert the original exegesis.[34]

Daniel Boyarin reads this midrash in its Babylonian talmudic
incarnation (*b. Shabbat* 87a) as supporting a particular Babylonian
rabbinic marriage pattern. He places this midrash in opposition to the
earlier *Sifre* version within an internal yet "global" rabbinic debate
concerning marriage practices for Rabbis. As noted above, Rabbis early
and late, Palestinian and Babylonian, recognized the tensions between
family duties and full-time study – that very activity which they
considered to be analogous to the work of the prophets and priests of
ancient Israel. In Babylonia the debate, which perhaps started with Philo,
came almost full circle. Unwilling to give up on family life and
procreation, the Rabbis construct two opposing models: either a scholar
should marry young and then leave home to study for extended periods of
time, or he should put off marriage until his education is well under way
(the modern graduate student model!). Both solutions posed their own
problems, which the Rabbis continuously critique. The *Sifre* midrash
seems to censor the marry-early study-late model in that these "married
monks," as Boyarin labels them, cause undue harm and anxiety to their

---

[34] The Rabbis' obvious discomfort with a generalized link between *qedusha* and
celibacy is further played out in the other midrashic variations in which the preparation
before Revelation excludes any notion of *qedusha*. It is unclear to me at this point,
before further research, whether the Rabbis understand קדש here to connote primarily
"sanctify" or "purify" (as the biblical Hebrew would) or some combination of the two. I
hope to answer that question in a future study.

abandoned or neglected womenfolk; thus the *Sifre* focuses on Zipporah. The later midrash, devoid of any female voices (or complaints), does not clearly condemn the practice of married monks and so leaves the door open to emulating Moses. While the *Sifre* differentiates between Moses and all other prophets (read: spiritual leaders of all sorts), the other midrashim differentiate Moses from the *hoi polloi* of Israel – nothing is said about the other leaders of Israel, that is, the Rabbis.[35]

Supporting Boyarin's theory of internal polemic, the version from *b. Shabbat* 87a that he quotes appears again in *b. Yevamot* 62a within a discussion of procreation. To Aphrahat, Moses' actions here are clearly a positive precedent; the Rabbis, not able to make the exegetical leap of faith made by Aphrahat, resolve to emulate Moses in a different fashion. Their emulation contains an important element: they, like Moses, procreate before withdrawing from married life. Moses may have separated from his wife, but he at least had a wife, Zipporah, who produced two sons from their conjugal union. *Mishnah Yevamot* 7:6, in discussing the issues of procreation and children, states: "A man shall not do away with procreation, unless he already has children. Shammai adds that he should have two male children; Hillel says one male, one female." The Babylonian talmudic commentary to this passage (also found in *Tosefta Yevamot* 8:2–3), elaborating on Shammai's qualification, reasons that because Moses had two sons, Gershom and Eliezer, the same should be required of all Jewish men. Moses certainly is not the only biblical character with two sons, but it is Moses that the Rabbis most wish to emulate. Having fulfilled his duties as a father, Moses is free to pursue his relationship with God. Similarly, the Rabbis allow themselves the luxury of spending most of their lives studying God's word, following the model of Moses, the "proto-rabbi," only after they have produced at least two children. Howard Eilberg-Schwartz argues that this mishnaic ruling should be seen as a maximum number, as opposed to a minimum. One needed to produce only two children, not two or more children.[36] Hence these Rabbis use Moses' procreative model, *followed* by his celibate one, to allow themselves extended study-breaks from home, as Boyarin suggests. So while Aphrahat builds a hermeneutic of celibacy from the sanctification and divine commandment he believes to be present in scripture, the Babylonian Rabbis understand Moses' celibacy simply to be a guideline for how to manage the conflicting demands of procreation and study. Nevertheless their detailed discussion of Moses' celibacy reveals their deep ambivalence toward their own marriages and sexuality.

---

[35] Boyarin, *Carnal Israel*, 165.

[36] Howard Eilberg-Schwartz, *God's Phallus and Other Problems for Men and Monotheism* (Boston: Beacon Press, 1994), 216.

## Conclusion

Whichever solution these late ancient scholars and spiritual leaders adopted – marrying early or late, or abandoning family life altogether – Moses remains central to their notions of sexual practice and spiritual pursuit. Moses serves as a focal point for contemplating the perceived conflicts between sex, marriage, and divine calling for Philo, the Rabbis, and Aphrahat. While Philo prefers to see Moses as the embodiment of Hellenistic virtues such as self-discipline, the authors of the *Sifre* understand Moses' special prophethood (but no one else's) as necessitating his distancing himself from domestic life. Within the Jewish–Christian polemic, however, Moses' celibacy becomes the exegetical foundation for constructing religious identities based on sexual behavior. Through his exegetical construct of holiness-as-celibacy, Aphrahat both polemicizes against Jewish marriage practices and establishes a hierarchy of spirituality for his Christian readers. Celibacy is holiness and therefore remains the ultimate manifestation of true Christian living. Aphrahat wears his celibacy with pride for it marks him as holy, divinely blessed, and chosen. While the Rabbis never specifically counter Aphrahat's conclusions, Moses' sexual history, both procreative and celibate, allow them to construct their own sexual and religious identities. Never forgoing marriage, they struggle to create a balance between their domestic lives and their spiritual pursuits, basing their choices on Moses' example.

# Rabbi Ishmael's Miraculous Conception

## Jewish Redemption History in Anti-Christian Polemic

by

RA'ANAN BOUSTAN

אשרי עין שראתה כך ואשרי הגבר שזכה לכך תתברך האם שחבלה אדתו אשרי המעים
שגדל בהם אשרי דדים שינק מהם אשרי האב שהולידו ולמדו תורה אשרי עין
שהציצה בו אשרי זרועות שחבקוהו אשריך ר' ישמעאל שזכית לכך
– MS NY JTSA ENA 3201 folio 1a/39–40

Embedded in the early medieval Hebrew martyrological anthology *The Story of the Ten Martyrs* is a curious "annunciation" scene that recounts how Rabbi Ishmael's mother, the unnamed wife of Elisha the high priest, became pregnant after encountering an angel sent to her by God.[1] More remarkable still, Rabbi Ishmael is said to have inherited the angelic messenger's beautiful appearance. Within the martyrological cycle, the physical embodiment of the sage's unique kinship to the divine permits him unparalleled access to the heavenly realm from which his efficacious beauty derives. Each one of the episodes of Rabbi Ishmael's *vita* recounted in *The Story of the Ten Martyrs* – his ascent to heaven to determine whether it is the will of God that the ten sages should be martyred, his own gruesome execution during which the skin of his

---

[*] This paper has been enormously enriched by both the written work and conscientious mentoring of Peter Brown, Shaye Cohen, Martha Himmelfarb, and Peter Schäfer. I would like to thank Annette Yoshiko Reed and Adam H. Becker for their keen editorial suggestions. I offer this paper with love to Leah Platt, whose tender strength and searching intellect have come to infuse every aspect of my life.

[1] This pericope appears in two distinct versions in Gottfried Reeg's synoptic edition of the text, *Die Geschichte von den Zehn Märtyrern* (Tübingen: Mohr Siebeck, 1985): I.15.10–19 and V, VII–VIII.11.10–23. All translations of *The Story of the Ten Martyrs* are mine. In addition to Reeg's German translation of this unit (*Geschichte*, 63 and 93), English translations can be found in Micha Joseph bin Gorion, *Mimekor Yisrael* (3 vols.; ed. E. bin Gorion; trans. I. M. Lask; Bloomington: Indiana UP, 1976), 547; David Roskies, "The Ten *Harugei Malkhut*," in *The Literature of Destruction* (Philadelphia: JPS, 1988), 61–62; David Stern, "Midrash Eleh Ezkerah, or The Legend of the Ten Martyrs," in *Rabbinic Fantasies* (ed. D. Stern and M. J. Mirsky; New Haven: Yale UP, 1990), 148–49. The narrative also appears in a number of medieval Jewish sources (see n. 12 below for citations).

beautiful countenance is peeled off, and the subsequent use of this "death mask" as a relic in a ritual that portends the ultimate fall of Rome and redemption of Israel – is intimately bound up with the special circumstances of his birth.[2] In fact, it is this hagiographic account of Rabbi Ishmael's life and death that lends a semblance of narrative unity to the otherwise disjointed literary traditions of which the anthology is composed.

The centrality of this narrative to the highly polemical collection of martyr stories certainly seems an intentional provocation. After all, in conferring upon this Jewish martyr semi-divine status through the agency of an angelic messenger at his birth, the anthology elicits automatic comparison between its protagonist and the prototypical Christian martyr Jesus, whose birth, death, and afterlife serve as the cornerstones of a very different history of redemption. It is certainly striking that, like the Christ of the NT Letter to the Hebrews, Rabbi Ishmael is imagined in the dual role of heavenly high priest and atoning sacrifice offered on the celestial altar. At the same time that the author/redactors of the anthology were painting a graphic portrait of the bleak experience of late antique Jews under Roman and, later, Christian domination, they thus chose to claim for themselves a set of highly charged literary motifs that were at odds with the more conventional scholastic orientation of their rabbinic source material. The recent work of Daniel Boyarin and Israel Yuval, among others, has taught us not to be surprised at such seemingly precarious fusions of polemical and apologetic aims: even where it is possible to speak of Jews and Christians as two distinct communities, they shared many common discursive categories, ritual practices, and literary forms, despite, or perhaps especially while, maintaining a rhetoric of difference and, at times, overt hostility.[3]

---

[2] It perhaps goes without saying that this hagiographical cycle is legend and not biography. Indeed, even the actions and statements attributed to Rabbi Ishmael the high priest in earlier rabbinic sources (e.g., *t. Hal.* 1:10; *b. Ber.* 7a; *b. Ber.* 51a; *b. Git.* 58a; *b. Hul.* 49a–b) are entirely unusable for biographical purposes, although they do constitute a relatively coherent corpus of material concerning this figure. On a note of caution, Rabbi Ishmael ben Elisha the high priest should not be facilely identified with the early-second-century Tanna Rabbi Ishmael, whose priestly identity remains uncertain (Gary G. Porton, *The Traditions of Rabbi Ishmael* [4 vols.; Leiden: Brill, 1982], 4.212–14, esp. n. 2). Compare, however, the discussion of Rabbi Ishmael's distinctively priestly orientation in Menaḥem Hirshman, *Torah for the Entire World* (Tel Aviv: Hakibbutz Hameuchad, 1999), esp. 114–49.

[3] For the use of Christian imagery in the Jewish martyrological literature produced in the wake of the Crusades, see Israel Yuval, "Christliche Symbolik und jüdische Martyrologie zur Zeit der Kreuzzüge," in *Juden und Christen zur Zeit der Kreuzzüge* (ed. A. Haverkamp; Sigmaringen: Jan Thorbecke, 1999), 87–106. See also idem, *Shene goyim be-vitnekh: Yehudim ve-Notsrim – dimuyim hadadiyim* (Tel Aviv: Am oved, 2000); idem, "Easter and Passover as Early Jewish–Christian Dialogue," in *Passover*

Of course, the trope of "miraculous conception" was never the sole province of Christian authors.[4] The Hebrew Bible itself offers clear precedent for the link between a figure's exceptional origins and his or her extraordinary life.[5] Greco-Roman biographers and hagiographers similarly viewed the visions and portents that accompanied the conception or birth of an exceptional figure as signs of future greatness.[6] For instance, in his imaginative biography of Apollonius of Tyana, the early-third-century writer Philostratus recounts how the mother of that quintessential first century *theios aner* ("divine man") has a vision of the actual physical form of the god Proteus while she is pregnant. Like the angel in the Rabbi Ishmael tradition, Proteus is so strongly identified with the child he has heralded that he passes on to him his special abilities and

---

*and Easter: Origin and History to Modern Times* (ed. P. F. Bradshaw and L. A. Hoffman; Notre Dame: U. of Notre Dame, 1999), 98–124; idem, "Vengeance and Damnation, Blood and Defamation: From Jewish Martyrdom to Blood Libel Accusations," *Zion* 58 (1993): 33–90 [Hebrew]. On the mutually constituting histories of Judaism and Christianity, see Daniel Boyarin, *Dying for God: Martyrdom and the Making of Christianity and Judaism* (Stanford: Stanford UP, 1999); idem, "Martyrdom and the Making of Christianity and Judaism," *JECS* 6 (1998): 577–627; idem, "A Tale of Two Synods: Nicaea, Yavneh and Rabbinic Ecclesiology," *Exemplaria* 12 (2000): 21–62; also his "Semantic Differences; or, 'Judaism'/ 'Christianity'" in this volume.

[4] The secondary literature on Christian annunciation, nativity, and childhood narratives is naturally quite vast. See the updated commentary in Raymond E. Brown, *The Birth of the Messiah: A Commentary on the Infancy Narratives in Matthew and Luke* (rev. ed.; New York: Doubleday, 1993) and the compendious bibliography there. I speak here and throughout the paper of *conception* and not *birth*, since, unlike the accounts of Jesus' (and Mary's) conception, nativity, and childhood in the canonical gospels (Matthew 1–2; Luke 1–2) and in some apocryphal texts (e.g., *Odes of Solomon* 19:6–10, *Protevangelium of James* 11, and *Ascension of Isaiah* 11:8–9), the tradition of Rabbi Ishmael's supernatural origins does not address the circumstances of his birth or early life, instead restricting itself to the actual process of procreation. Notably, this emphasis conforms to the biblical prototype; see the excellent summary of this paradigm in Athalya Brenner, "Female Social Behavior: Two Descriptive Patterns within the 'Birth of the Hero' Paradigm," *VT* 36 (1986): 258–59.

[5] God is said to intervene in the process of procreation, either directly or through the agency of an intermediary, in the conceptions of Isaac (Gen 18:9; 21:1–3), Samson (Judg 13:2–7), and Samuel (1 Sam 2:21). On the "annunciation" motif in biblical literature generally, see especially Robert Alter, "How Convention Helps us Read: The Case of the Bible's Annunciation Type-Scene," *Prooftexts* 3 (1983): 115–30.

[6] For a useful discussion of many of these sources and their relationship to early Christian literature, consult Charles H. Talbert, "Prophecies of Future Greatness: The Contribution of Greco-Roman Biographies to an Understanding of Luke 1:5–4:15," in *The Divine Helmsman* (ed. J. L. Crenshaw and S. Sandmel; New York: Ktav, 1980), 129–41. On the specific theme of supernatural conception, see Plutarch, *Theseus* 2.6.36; *Romulus* 2.5; 4.2; *Alexander* 3.1–2; also Quintus Curtius, *History of Alexander* 1; Pseudo-Callisthenes, *Alexander Romance*.

knowledge.[7] The Jewish historian Josephus, who often employed the stock motifs of the biographical genre,[8] likewise availed himself of the notion that the appearance of an angel to a barren woman could transmit unusual beauty to her child.[9]

Nevertheless, the story of Rabbi Ishmael's conception is not just one more example of this near-ubiquitous impulse. Rather, the narrative, while exhibiting discursive commonalities with the broader cultural milieu, represents a pointed rejoinder to Christian accounts of Jesus' divine nature and of his uniqueness within human history. This bold act of appropriation cannot be considered in a cultural vacuum; nor is it merely a symptom of intercommunal polemic. In his incisive work on the use of common liturgical forms in related, but distinct, religious communities, Lawrence Hoffman has developed a model for conceptualizing precisely this sort of contested cultural idiom:

> Instead of viewing society as a series of already sharply defined conflicting religious groups, vying with each other, I suggest a model in which all are presumed to share equally in a generally pervasive cultural backdrop. This cultural backdrop is what everyone takes as normative, and within which everyone takes some stand or another. In their liturgy, people declare themselves to stand within the commonly accepted boundaries of the religious enterprise, sharing certain generally accepted cultural characteristics along with everyone else – that is, censoring themselves in; at the same time they preserve the boundaries of their own integrity by censoring out those cultural characteristics which they have chosen not to accept.[10]

Hoffman cautions against an overly general and undifferentiated notion of shared cultural space. In his view, the act of participating in a common culture automatically entails marking out where one stands on that terrain. The trick is to locate the precise strategies by which the elements of a common idiom are fashioned into an exclusionary practice – or, in this case, narrative.

---

[7] Philostratus, *Life of Apollonius* I.4.

[8] For signs accompanying the birth of heroes in the writings of Josephus, see, for example, *A.J.* 2.9.6–7; 2.10.1–2. Josephus even highlights the special circumstances of his own birth in *Life* 1. For a similar impulse in Philo, see *Mos.* 1.5.20–24; 1.6.25–29. See also Daniel J. Harrington, "Birth Narratives in Pseudo-Philo's Biblical Antiquities and the Gospels," in *To Touch the Text: Biblical and Related Studies in Honor of Joseph A. Fitzmeyer* (ed. M. P. Horgan and P. J. Kobelski; New York: Crossroad, 1989), 316–24.

[9] See the retelling of Samson's conception at *A.J.* 5.276–285; cf. Pseudo-Philo's *Biblical Antiquities* 42; *b. B. Bat. 91a*; *Num. Rab.* 10:5. On the relationship between Josephus' account and the biblical Samson cycle, see especially Adele Reinhartz, "Samson's Mother: An Unnamed Protagonist," *JSOT* 55 (1992): 25–37.

[10] Lawrence Hoffman, "Censoring in and Censoring Out: A Function of Liturgical Language," in *Ancient Synagogues: The State of the Research* (ed. J. Gutman; Chico, CA: Scholars Press, 1981), 22–23.

What sets the Rabbi Ishmael material apart from comparable late antique hagiography, then, is its use of the notion of ritual purity to understand and articulate its hero's special status. The narrative constructs Rabbi Ishmael as a more-than-human figure who, by virtue of his angelic paternity, is exempt from the impurity that inheres in all human existence. It is worth noting that in the *Toledot Yeshu* literature, the Jewish anti-Gospels that flourished in numerous versions and languages throughout Late Antiquity and the Middle Ages, Jesus' mother is said to have conceived during her *menses*.[11] Jesus is thus the quintessential offspring of impurity (בן נידה), whose illegitimate power and destructive nature reflects his improper origin. Rabbi Ishmael is his mirror opposite, a rabbinic figure who belongs to the heavenly realm because he is truly of it. Indeed, the conception narrative attributes his mother's decisive encounter with the angelic messenger to her rigorous and even extreme practice of ritual bathing following the period of her menstrual impurity. Of course, the story of his conception does to some extent operate according to a theory of sexual reproduction that was widely accepted by late antique Jews, Christians, and "pagans" alike. Nevertheless, the narrative follows the conventions of a specific strain of Jewish purity discourse that developed in Byzantine Palestine toward the end of Late Antiquity and assumed its clearest statement in the unusual halakhic rulings of the *Beraita de Niddah*. A close reading of the unit's relationship to the two separate discursive contexts in which it evolved – Jewish purity practice and Jewish martyrology – is thus essential to a proper understanding of Rabbi Ishmael's place within the history of salvation put forward in *The Story of the Ten Martyrs*.

The argument of the paper will proceed as follows: I first situate the conception narrative within the broader discourse of late antique gynecological science, both Jewish and non-Jewish. I then analyze the intimate relationship between this vignette and the distinctive understanding of Jewish purity practice current among Byzantine Jews. The conspicuous formal and ideological affinities between the "annunciation" scene and this purity discourse demonstrate that the unit assumed its present form as a narrative dramatization of its stringent

---

[11] I cite here only a very partial list of the many versions of *Toledot Yeshu* that characterize Jesus in these terms: Samuel Krauss, *Das Leben Jesu nach jüdischen Quellen* (Hildesheim: Georg Olms, 1977), 38–40 (MS Strassburg), 64–69 (MS Vindobona), 118 (MS Adler); Günter Schlichting, *Ein jüdisches Leben Jesu: Die verschollene Toledot-Jeschu-Fassung Tam ū-mū'ād* (Tübingen: Mohr Siebeck, 1982), 65–67, 87–89, and 99. On the development of this literature as a whole, see especially Jean Paul Osier, *L'évangile du ghetto* (Paris: Berg International, 1984); R. Di Segni, *Il Vangelo del Ghetto* (Magia e religioni 8; Rome: Newton Compton, 1985); William Horbury, "A Critical Examination of the *Toledoth Yeshu*" (Ph.D. diss., University of Cambridge, 1970).

system of purity practice. Yet, at the same time as the unit adopts the theoretical terms set out in the purity literature, it draws its narrative content from the martyrological tradition. I show that the central episodes of Rabbi Ishmael's life recounted in *The Story of the Ten Martyrs* all directly hinge on the radical claims put forward in the "annunciation" scene concerning his angelic purity and beauty. Finally, I offer some concluding reflections on the significance of this narrative tradition for our understanding of the complex and, at times, paradoxical nature of Jewish cultural expression in the Byzantine period.

## Visuality and Gynecological Science in Late Antiquity

Before considering the literary and ideological origins of the "annunciation" scene in *The Story of the Ten Martyrs*, I will first present the relevant text in its entirety.[12]

VII.11.10. [Every time Rabbi Ishmael wished to ascend to heaven (לעלות לרקיע), he would ascend. 11. Why was Rabbi Ishmael worthy of this (ולמה זכה ר' ישמעאל לכך). The reason is because (-מפני ש)][13] his father was Elishah the

---

[12] I translate and number the text following *Ten Martyrs*, VII.11.16–23 (Reeg, *Geschichte*, 19*). The unit also appears at I.15.11–30; V and VIII.11.16–23. I.15.11–30 seems to represent a relatively independent textual form, whereas the versions in recensions V, VII, and VIII stand in close relationship to each other as well as to the variations found in other medieval sources: *Liqute ha-Pardes* (attributed most likely to R. Solomon ben Isaac's disciple Rabbi Shemaya), Amsterdam 1715, 4a; Munkács, 1897, 6b–7a; *Sefer ha-Miqtso'ot*, 13–14; Eleazar of Worms, *Sefer ha-Roqeah*, "Hilkhot Niddah," 317; Isaac ben Moses of Vienna, *'Or Zaru'a*, Alpha Beta 29; Isaac of Dura, *Sha'are Dura*, "Hilkhot Niddah," 2:23; Menaḥem Tsioni, *Sefer Tsioni*, 78a; Azariah de Fano, *Sefer Gilgul Neshamot*, 8–29; MS New York-JTSA ENA 3021, fol. 1a (entitled *Zehirut ha-Tevillah*); MS Paris-BN 1408, fol. 67a; MS New York-JTSA Mic. 1842, fol. 192a–b (entitled *Ḥayye Nefesh* by Isaiah ben Joseph). See also the version in Moses Gaster, *Ma'aseh Book: Book of Jewish Tales and Legends Translated from the Judeo-German* (Philadelphia: Jewish Publication Society, 1934), 237–39; "Shivḥe R. Ishmael Kohen Gadol," in *Ḥadashim gam yeshanim* (ed. A. M. Haberman; Jerusalem: R. Mas, 1975), 86. These attestations have been collected from Ch. M. Horowitz, *Tosefta 'Atiqta* (5 vols.; Frankfurt am Main, 1889), 4.7–15 and 5.VIII–IX (several of the versions are transcribed at 5.43–54, 57–61); Bin Gorion, *Memekor Yisrael*, 3.106 n. 5; Elliot R. Wolfson, *Through a Speculum That Shines* (Princeton: Princeton UP, 1994), 212–14, esp. n. 96; Michael Swartz, *Scholastic Magic: Ritual and Revelation in Early Jewish Mysticism* (Princeton: Princeton UP, 1996), 162–65, esp. n. 66; Evyatar Marienberg, "Etudes sur la Baraita de Niddah et sur la conceptualisation de la menstruation dans le monde juif et son echo dans le monde chrétien de l'époque medieval à nos jours" (Ph.D. diss., EHESS Paris, 2002), 485–514.

[13] The material in brackets is a redactional frame that appears only in recensions V, VII–VIII.11.11 and is not integral to the pericope.

High Priest.[14] None of his children lived (ולא היו מתקיימין לו בנים), since, at the moment when his wife would give birth, the child would die (היה מת אותו ילד).[15] 12. His wife said to him: "Why do those wholly pious people have sons who are pious like them (מפני מה להללו צדיקים גמוריי יש להם בנים גמורים כמותם),[16] whereas we do not have even a single son who remains alive?" 14. He answered her: "They always purify themselves in the ritual bath before sexual intercourse (הם נוהגין בנפשותיהן טהרה וטבילה בשעה שהם עולים למטה בשעת תשמיש),[17] whether or not the law prescribes it (בין בדבר ובין שלא בדבר),[18] both they and their wives (הם ונשיהם)." 15. She said: "If that is so, then we too shall adopt this practice." They immediately did so.

16. One time, this pious woman went down to the bathhouse (לבית הטבילה) and immersed herself (וטבלה). But when she emerged (ועלתה), she saw (וראתה) a pig in front of her.[19] She returned (חזרה) to the bathhouse and (again) immersed herself. When she emerged, she saw a camel. She returned, immersed herself, emerged, and saw a leper (חזרה וטבלה ועלתה וראתה מצורע). She returned and immersed herself forty times.[20]

17. After the fortieth time, the Holy One blessed be He said to Metatron:[21] "Descend and stand before that pious woman (רד ועמוד לפני הצדקת הזאת) and tell her that tonight she will become pregnant with a son (תתעברי בן זכר) and his name will be Rabbi Ishmael." 18. Metatron straight away descended in the form of a human being (דמות בן אדם). He clothed himself and adorned himself (ונתעטף והקשיט את עצמו) and stood at the opening of the ritual bath

---

[14] In recension I alone Rabbi Ishmael's father is R. Yose and not Elisha the High Priest.

[15] In all the versions of the story, Rabbi Ishmael's mother is not barren, but instead has lost all of her children during childbirth. Only in recension I is it at all possible that she is barren: "We have not had success with children, since we have no heir, neither son nor daughter (ואנו לא הצלחנו בבנים כי אין לנו יורש בן או בת)."

[16] The other recensions read צדיקים rather than גמורים.

[17] בשעת תשמיש is, of course, an unnecessary gloss. Recension VIII offers the more straightforward formulation: מפני שנותני מטוהיהן בטהרה.

[18] This enigmatic phrase is difficult to interpret, but seems to indicate that these "righteous people" have exceeded the required practice.

[19] In some versions, a dog and a camel are added to this list of impure animals, and in some she also encounters an "ignoramus" (*'am ha-aretz*).

[20] The number of repetitions is highly variable. Recension VII agrees with recension VIII (and with *Liqute ha-Pardes*) that she repeated the procedure forty times. Recension I doubles the number to eighty times. *Sefer ha-Miqtso'ot* reports that she did so ten times. Recension V restricts the number to "several times" (כמה פעמים).

[21] In most versions of the narrative (including recensions VII and VIII), the angelic messenger is named Metatron. By contrast, in recension I and *Liqute ha-Pardes* the angel is named Gabriel. In recension V, which initially casts Metatron in the role of the angel (V.11.17), Gabriel joins Metatron outside the bathhouse (V.11.18) and entirely displaces Metatron in the latter half of the narrative (V.11.20–23). Even here in recension VII, Gabriel makes an appearance at the end of the unit (VII.11.23), where he seems to have been carried over into this recension from one of the other versions. In the *'Or Zaru'a*, the angel is identified as the *Sar Torah*, which may indicate that this version was once incorporated into magical material.

(על פתח המקוה). [19. From this you learn that a man must adorn himself in fine clothing and go stand before his wife when she emerges from immersion.][22] 21. She emerged, saw him, went home, and became pregnant that very night with Rabbi Ishmael. His form was beautiful like the form of Metatron (והיה דמותו כיופיות דמות מטטרון), the god-father (סינדיקנוס) of Rabbi Ishmael, 22. so that every time that Rabbi Ishmael wished to ascend to the heavens he would pronounce the divine name (היה מזכיר השם) and, when he ascended, 23. Gabriel (sic)[23] would tell him anything he wanted.

Because of the aggressive process of redactional adaptation to which the unit was subjected in the course of its transmission, it is nearly impossible, if not methodologically irresponsible, to try to deduce which of its many extant versions, if any, might represent its original formulation.[24] Gottfried Reeg, however, has convincingly argued the unit developed and circulated independently from the martyrological anthology and was incorporated into it only at a relatively late point in its transmission.[25] He bases this insight on the unit's relative infrequency within the manuscripts of *The Story of the Ten Martyrs* – it appears in only four of the ten recensions of the text (i.e., I, V, VII, VIII) – as well as on its shifting redactional context. The unit appears in two different locations within the anthology's narrative progression. In each case, it serves a different function: recension I links the unit to a discussion of Rabbi Ishmael's beautiful appearance, while recensions V, VII, and VIII situate the narrative immediately before Rabbi Ishmael's heavenly ascent, thereby transforming the narrative into an aetiology of his unique powers. Moreover, the peculiar ethical form of the story – its overt encouragement of proper behavior and its promise of reward – is awkward in the martyrological context and, as we will see, more naturally conforms to the ethical (*Musar*) literature from which it likely emerged.

Despite this considerable textual instability, all the versions of the narrative share a common understanding of Rabbi Ishmael's miraculous conception, merging rigorist purity practice and pietism with a visual theory of procreation. In this amalgamation, impurity and divine favor are both mediated through the medium of sight. The narrative puts the very act of seeing an unclean animal or an impure skin blemish on par with the standard regulations concerning actual physical contact with the sources of impurity, thus going far beyond the normal strictures surrounding

---

[22] This hortatory statement, which treats the surrounding narrative as an elaborate *exemplum*, is found in the martyrology only in recensions V and VII. It is common in the purity literature (e.g., MS New York-JTSA ENA 3021, fol. 1a/9).

[23] See n. 21 above.

[24] Horowitz, *Tosefta 'Atiqta*, 4.14 tentatively suggests that *Liqute ha-Pardes*, *Sefer ha-Miqtso'ot*, and *Sefer ha-Roqeah* preserve the earliest form of the narrative and that the versions in the martyrological anthology represent secondary revisions.

[25] Reeg, *Geschichte*, 40.

contact impurity in conventional Jewish law. Strikingly, the same mechanism that exposes Rabbi Ishmael's mother to the dangers of impurity and the associated threat to her newborn children bestows upon him his distinctive character and appearance. Although the angel does not adopt the appearance of a specific human being, the narrative's emphasis on the angel's capacity to assume "human form" (דמות בן אדם) highlights the physical concreteness of the theory of visual procreation it assumes.[26]

The theory of visual "impressions" operative in the narrative would not have struck the late antique reader as remarkable.[27] Indeed, its basic premise, that visual stimuli can influence the process of gestation, was a commonplace in certain branches of Greek and Latin gynecology.[28] It is already prefigured in the patriarch Jacob's exercise in eugenics through which he produced mottled sheep by placing striped twigs in front of the flock during breeding: "The rods that he had peeled he set up in front of the flocks in the troughs .... Their mating occurred when they came to drink, and since the goats mated by the rods, the goats brought forth streaked, speckled, and spotted young."[29] In his commentary on this biblical passage, Jerome goes to great lengths to explain the narrative in terms of contemporary genetic theory.[30] Augustine, too, cites this biblical precedent in his only partly-successful attempt to provide scientific grounding both for his theory of original sin and his conception of the relationship between body and soul.[31] *The Testaments of the Twelve*

---

[26] Recension I departs from the majority tradition when it says that the angel (Gabriel) took on the appearance of the husband, in this case Rabbi Yose (I.15.16–17): לה כדמות ר' יוסי בעלה והיה נדמה (cf. MS New York-JTSA ENA 3021, 1a/8). The idea that angels could assume the form of a particular human being is discussed in Wolfson, *Speculum*, 212–13, although he nowhere indicates that recension I diverges from the majority tradition precisely on this matter.

[27] An impressive number of ancient, medieval, and even modern sources that attest to the endurance of this theory in the medical tradition are collected and discussed in M. D. Reeve, "Conceptions," *Proceedings of the Cambridge Philological Society* 215 (1989): 113–43. See also the interesting observations concerning the place of this theory in Western notions of human imagination in Silvio Curletto, "L'immaginazione e il concepimento: Fortuna di una teoria embriogenetica e di un mito letterario," *Maia* 52 (2000): 533–64.

[28] Galen, *De theriaca*, 11; Soranus, *Gyn.* 1.39; Caelius Aurelianus, *Gyn.* 1.50. On the place of this branch of gynecological theory in Greek medicine, see G. E. R. Lloyd, *Science, Folklore, and Ideology: Studies in the Life Sciences of Ancient Greece* (Cambridge: Cambridge UP, 1983), 174–80.

[29] Gen 30:25–39. All citations from the Hebrew Bible are from the JPS translation.

[30] The relevant passage is translated in C. T. R. Hayward, *Saint Jerome's Hebraicae quaestiones on Genesis* (Oxford: Clarendon Press, 1995), 66–68.

[31] I cite here only one example of Augustine's argumentation: "In other animals, whose bodily bulk does not lend itself so easily to such changes, the fetus usually shows some traces of the passionate desires of their mothers, whatever it was that they gazed upon with great delight. For the more tender and, so to speak, the more formable

*Patriarchs* employs a similar notion to explain how the "sons of God" (בני האלהים) of Gen 6:1–4 were able to procreate with human women after descending to earth:

> It was thus that they (human women) allured the Watchers before the flood; for, as a result of seeing them continually, the Watchers lusted after one another, and they conceived the act in their minds and changed themselves into the shape of men and appeared to the women when they were having intercourse with their husbands. And the women, lusting in their minds after their phantom forms, gave birth to giants (for the Watchers seemed to be them tall enough to touch the sky).[32]

Although the descending angels here intrude in the course of the sexual act itself rather than during the elaborate preparations for it, there are obvious affinities between Rabbi Ishmael and the monstrous progeny of this episode of primeval transgression. Yet, whereas their angelic paternity dooms them to drag humanity down into sin, Rabbi Ishmael's represents its opposite, the legitimate and even redemptive unification of the heavenly and the earthly realms.

This same theory of visual conception, however, can be found much closer to the cultural context in which the Rabbi Ishmael legend developed. Midrashic sources explicitly employ this theory in order to elucidate these early Jewish traditions about the "sons of God:"

---

the original seeds were, the more effectually and the more capably do they follow the inclination of their mother's soul, and the fantasy which arose in it through the body upon which it looked with passion. There are numerous examples of this which could be mentioned, but one from the most trustworthy books will suffice: in order that the sheep and the she-goats might give birth the speckled offspring, Jacob had rods of various colors placed before them in the watering-troughs, to look at as they drank, during that period when they had conceived" (*De Trinitate*, II, 5; trans. in Stephen McKenna, *The Trinity* [Washington, DC: Catholic University of America, 1963], 321–22). Cf. *De Trinitate*, III, 15; *Against Julian*, V, 51–52; *Against Julian*, VI, 43; *Retractatio* II, 62, 2. On the importance of this issue in Augustine's thought, see Elizabeth A. Clark, "Vitiated Seeds and Holy Vessels: Augustine's Manichean Past," in *Ascetic Piety and Women's Faith: Essays on Late Antique Christianity* (Lewiston, NY: E. Mellon Press, 1986), 291–349.

[32] *T. Reu.* 5:6–7 (Translation by Marinus de Jonge in *The Apocryphal Old Testament* [ed. H. F. D. Sparks; Oxford: Clarendon, 1984], 519–20). There are numerous allusions to the story of the Watchers in early Jewish literature (e.g., *1 En.* 6–16 and *passim*; *T. Naph.* 3:5; *Jub.* 4:15–22, 7:21, 8:3, 10:5; *CD* 2.18). Compare the counter-tradition concerning the miraculous birth of Noah in which Lamech's apparently erroneous concern that his son's angelic visage is a sign of his fallen-angelic parentage is assuaged (*1 En.* 106–7; 1QapGn ii–v). On the place of the fallen-angel myth in late antique Judaism and Christianity, see Annette Yoshiko Reed, "What the Fallen Angels Taught: The Reception-History of the *Book of the Watchers* in Judaism and Christianity" (Ph.D. diss., Princeton University, 2002).

*It was then, and later too, that the divine beings cohabited with the daughters of men* (Gen 6:4). Rabbi Berekhiah said: A woman would go to the marketplace, see a young man, and desire him (מתאוה לו). She would then go have sexual intercourse and give birth to a child just like him (היתה מעמדת בחור כיוצא בו)."[33]

In a similarly vein, a narrative unit contained in a number of midrashic works recounts that the "cushite" King of the Arabs came to Rabbi Akiva for advice after accusing his wife of adultery because she had given birth to a white child.[34] Without further prompting, the rabbi immediately asks whether the figures painted on the wall of the couple's house are black or white (צורות ביתך שחורות או לבנות). When he learns that they are white, he reassures the anxious father that his wife must have been looking at them when she conceived. Interestingly, this brief rabbinic tradition offers an almost perfect précis of Heliodorus' vast novel, *The Aethiopica*, which similarly turns on the problem of skin color. Through myriad narrative twists and turns, the novel's protagonist, Charikleia, learns that, despite her white skin, she is in fact the daughter of the King and Queen of Ethiopia.[35] Apparently, the royal couple has given birth to this remarkable child because the Queen gazed at the beautiful image of Andromeda painted on the wall of their bedroom during sexual intercourse, an event that has stamped their child with the exact appearance of the Greek heroine. Fearing that she will be accused of adultery, Charikleia's mother arranges for her to be cared for by others and tells her husband that the newborn has died during childbirth. While the midrash and Heliodorus may simply reflect a common folk motif, Rabbi Akiva's question regarding the existence of the painted figures – a detail that is not otherwise accounted for in the midrashic sources – suggests that *The Aethiopica* itself or, more likely, its underlying narrative kernel somehow exerted an influence on the rabbinic authors. Whatever the channels of influence, it proves significant that Charikleia's inheritance of the specific appearance of a heroic figure from the mythic

---

[33] *Gen. Rab.* 26:7 (translation mine); cf. *Tanh. B, Bereshit* 40. I would like to thank Annette Yoshiko Reed for calling my attention to this tradition.

[34] *Gen. Rab.* 73:10; *Num. Rab.* 9:34; *Tanh., Naso'* 7. These sources are collected in Horowitz, *Tosefta 'Atiqta*, 5.55–56. I follow the narrative sequence and language of the *Tanhuma* version. In some versions, this figure is identified as the king of the Arabs, while in others simply as "an Ethiopian" (כושי אחד). Just as in Jerome's *Quaestiones hebraicae* on Gen 30:35–43, the predicament of the Ethiopian king is used in each of these versions to provide validation for Jacob's strange breeding technique. Jerome and the Rabbis may here be transmitting a common exegetical tradition, although it is also possible that this interpretative strategy developed independently in the two contexts.

[35] Heliodorus, *Aethiopica* 4.8; 10.14. On the function of this theme within the novel's complex narrative, see especially Michael J. Anderson, "The Sophrosyne of Persinna and the Romantic Strategy of Heliodorus' *Aethiopica*," *Classical Philology* 92 (1997): 303–22.

past comes very close to Rabbi Ishmael's physical kinship with Metatron. Heliodorus shared with the Jewish texts that we have been looking at a common set of literary motifs and scientific knowledge from which to build his narrative.

Rabbinic literature, however, often viewed this theory of "maternal impression" through the lens of purity regulation. In fact, the story about Rabbi Ishmael draws explicitly on Rabbi Yoḥanan's unusual practice of standing outside the ritual bath so that the women who saw him after purifying themselves would have children as handsome as he.

> R. Yoḥanan used to go sit outside the ritual bath (הוה אזיל ויתיב אשערי טבילה). He said: "When the daughters of Israel come out from the bath, let them meet me (מצוה לפגעו בי)[36] so that they will have children as beautiful as I am (דשפירי כוותי)." The Rabbis said to him: "Are you not afraid of the Evil Eye (מעינא בישא)?" He answered: "I am of the seed of Joseph, our father, of whom it is said, *Joseph is a fruitful bough, a fruitful bough by a spring* (Gen 49:22)."[37]

Rabbi Ishmael's story echoes the specific terminology of this description of Rabbi Yoḥanan's curious form of public service: both passages use the root פגע to describe the encounter outside the bathhouse.[38] It is this distinctive mixture of gynecological science and purity practice that connects the story of Rabbi Ishmael's conception to these earlier rabbinic traditions. At the same time, the interest in purity sets them both apart from the general cultural discourse in which they participated.


## Purity, Piety, and Procreation: *Beraita de Niddah*

When the narrative of Rabbi Ishmael's conception is not found in the context of the martyrological literature, it appears in a number of instructional manuals and legal texts as a freestanding narrative

---

[36] The parallel version at *b. Ber.* 20a reads "they look at me" (מסתכלן בי).

[37] *b. B. Metsia* 84a (I have slightly modified the translation in Daniel Boyarin, "Talmudic Texts and Jewish Social Life," in *Religions of Late Antiquity in Practice* [ed. R. Valantasis; Princeton: Princeton UP, 2000], 136). Compare the parallel text at *b. Ber.* 20a. Rabbi Yoḥanan also discusses the importance of ritual bathing for procreation at *b. 'Erub.* 55b. On Rabbi Yoḥanan's eroticized relationship with Resh Lakish (*b. B. Metsia* 84a–b) and the importance of this narrative for the formation of rabbinic scholastic culture, see Daniel Boyarin, "Rabbis and their Pals: Rabbinic Homosociality and the Lives of Women," in *Unheroic Conduct: The Rise of Heterosexuality and the Invention of the Jewish Man* (Berkeley: U. of California Press, 1997), 127–50.

[38] The term פגע is also found in a similar context at *b. Pes.* 111a, where the dangers of encountering a woman immediately after she has completed her ablutions are described.

exhortation to proper purity practice.[39] The stringent form of Jewish purity law reflected in these texts was particular to the Franco-German cultural sphere in the later Middle Ages, but seems to have spread along with so much else in medieval Ashkenazi culture to these nascent centers of Jewish life from the Land of Israel; hence, this branch of Jewish purity law is best viewed not as a deviation from a firmly established norm but rather as a later refraction of what was originally a legitimate local practice.[40] This mode of purity practice is most fully described in the enigmatic text *Beraita de Niddah* (*BdN*).[41] The text, consisting of a collection of legal statements and narrative *exempla*, seems to have its origins in the Jewish community of Byzantine Palestine in the sixth and seventh centuries and, according to Shaye Cohen, reflects that community's new tendency to equate the synagogue with the Jerusalem Temple.[42] Whether or not *BdN* actually existed as a literary whole as

---

[39] See the sources listed in n. 12 above, especially *Liqute ha-Pardes, Sefer ha-Roqeah, Sha'are Dura, Zehirut ha-Tevillah*.

[40] On the purity practices of Ashkenazi Jews, see especially Israel Ta-Shma, "On Some Franco-German Niddah Practices," *Sidra* 9 (1993): 163–70 [Hebrew]; also idem, *Early Franco-German Ritual and Custom* (Jerusalem: Magnes, 1992), esp. 57 [Hebrew]. On polemical responses to the diversity of purity ritual practiced throughout the medieval Jewish world, see Shaye J. D. Cohen, "Purity, Piety, and Polemic: Medieval Rabbinic Denunciations of 'Incorrect' Purification Practices," in *Women and Water: Menstruation in Jewish Life and Law* (ed. R. Wasserfall; Hanover: Brandeis UP, 1999), 82–100.

[41] A version of the text is available in Horowitz, *Tosefta 'Atiqta*, 5.1–34 (all citations of the text follow Horowitz's chapter divisions and page numbers). The sources collected and discussed by Horowitz have been thoroughly reevaluated in Marienberg, *Beraita de Niddah*. Marienberg is currently preparing a critical edition of the text with French translation.

[42] Shaye J. D. Cohen, "Menstruants and the Sacred in Judaism and Christianity," in *Women's History and Ancient History* (ed. S. B. Pomeroy; Chapel Hill: U. of North Carolina, 1991), 285: "By the time of *Beraita de Nidda*, however, the synagogue was becoming a surrogate temple, a development confirmed by archaeology. In the sixth and seventh centuries synagogues were regularly outfitted with an ark, an eternal flame, and representations of temple vessels ...." Cohen calls special attention to the description of Palestinian purity practice in *Differences between the Jews of the East and the Jews of the Land of Israel*, 79 sect. 11. This date and provenance are supported in Saul Lieberman, *Sheqi'in* (Jerusalem: Bamberger & Wahrmann, 1939), 22. See also Shaye J. D. Cohen, "Purity and Piety: The Separation of Menstruants from the *Sancta*," in *Daughters of the King: Women and the Synagogue* (ed. S. Grossman and R. Haut; Philadelphia: JPS, 1992), 103–15; Sharon Koren, "'The Woman from whom God Wanders': The Menstruant in Medieval Jewish Mysticism" (Ph.D. diss., Yale University, 1999), esp. 102–26; idem, "Mystical Rationales for the Laws of *Niddah*," in *Women and Water: Menstruation in Jewish Life and Law* (ed. R. Wasserfall; Hanover: Brandeis UP, 1999), 101–21; Yedidyah Dinari, "The Customs of Menstrual Impurity: Their Origin and Development," *Tarbiz* 49 (1979–80): 302–24 [Hebrew].

early as the Geonic period,[43] the traditions attested therein do conform to earlier Palestinian practice.

Although the "annunciation" scene does not occur in *BdN*, it is this collection that offers the most sustained source for understanding this story. It presents a wide range of para-halakhic strictures that severely limit the activities of the menstruant: one could not enjoy the fruits of her labor (*BdN* 1:2); she could not enter the synagogue or house of study (*BdN* 3:4); one could not greet her or say a blessing in her presence lest she respond with "amen" or with the name of God, thereby desecrating it (*BdN* 2:5). Her social exclusion was absolute. Even the speech of the menstruant was considered impure (*BdN* 2:3). She could not comb her hair or shake her head lest a hair fall out and convey impurity to her husband (*BdN* 1:4). Finally, contrary to standard Talmudic sources (*b. Bek.* 27a and *m. Niddah* 10.7), *BdN* ranks the maintenance of its purity laws above a woman's other obligations, barring the menstruant from the commandments of *hallah* (separating the priestly offering from dough) and of lighting the Sabbath candles. For *BdN*, menstrual impurity had become a dangerous state from which public life had to be assiduously guarded.

Amongst its idiosyncratic (though influential) rulings *BdN* includes explicit discussion of the role of visual stimuli in the process of procreation. One such passage reports in the name of Rabbi Hanina[44] that "at the time when she immerses, if she encounters (פגעה) a dog, if she is wise and has fear of heaven, she will not allow her husband to have intercourse with her that night. Why? Lest her sons be ugly and their faces resemble a dog's, she returns and immerses again."[45] The passage continues by listing similar cases concerning a donkey and an ignoramus (עם הארץ). The tendency to enumerate such encounters in a series of parallel cases is a distinctive feature of this literature, one employed in the "annunciation" scene to great effect. Like the sources of impurity encountered by Rabbi Ishmael's mother, these dangerous types of people and animals pose a threat to a woman's capacity to conceive a healthy child.

Oddly enough, however, the notion of visually transmitted danger described in these texts does not coincide fully with the categories of ritual impurity that have their roots in biblical, or perhaps better, levitical,

---

[43] Prof. Shaye Cohen has suggested to me the possibility that, as with so much late antique Jewish literature, the existence of this work as a redactionally unified composition may be no more than a scribal fiction of the later Middle Ages (oral communication).

[44] Perhaps to be identified with Rabbi Hanina ben ha-Qanah (=Rabbi Nehuniah ben ha-Qanah). On this identification see below.

[45] *BdN* 1:1 (Horowitz, *Tosefta 'Atiqta*, 5.2).

purity concerns. In fact, in the same passage, *BdN* instructs that, if a woman sees a horse, she and her husband should have sex that night: "Happy is one whose mother came upon a horse; her sons are beautiful in carriage and speech, hearing, understanding and learning Torah and Mishnah ...."[46] This detail represents an important inconsistency in the text's discursive logic since, after all, a horse is no more or less pure than a dog. At least in this case, *BdN* is concerned wholly with the animal's impact on the "ethical" attributes of the child and does not view the horse through the lens of ritual purity. This reasoning should apply equally to the dog and the ignoramus. Just as in non-Jewish sources, these are ethical types and not potential carriers of ritual impurity. What we find here, then, is that *BdN* has wed the conventional theory of visual "impressions" to its basic framework of levitical regulations. Just as ritual immersion removes impurity in conventional Jewish law, in the context of this hybrid discourse it is said to erase, as it were, the damaging images that have become imprinted in the woman. Yet, despite the tensions between these systems, it is virtually impossible to separate them out once they have been integrated, however incompletely, within the purity literature. Indeed, as we will see, the boundary between levitical purity and other forms of purification, such as those that precede ascent and adjuration in late antique Jewish and non-Jewish magical literature, is impossible to fix in this material. *BdN*'s kitchen sink approach to ritual purity lumps together what we might prefer to imagine as wholly separate systems of purity or simply procreative science. The creators and consumers of this "post-levitical" purity discourse seem not to have been interested in strict categorization. For *BdN*, just as for the account of Rabbi Ishmael's conception, purity, piety, and procreation are inextricable.

In fact, even in sections of *BdN* that do not explicitly relate to conception and procreation, vision serves as the principal medium through which impurity is conveyed. The text recounts that a certain Rabbi Ḥanina ben ha-Qanah, likely the same Rabbi responsible for the list of dangers discussed above, "was once walking on the road and came across a woman. He covered his eyes and distanced himself from her three paces."[47] The Rabbi seems to have an almost preternatural sensitivity to impurity; he senses her impurity even before she has approached him. More importantly, he carefully covers his face so that her impurity will not enter him through his eyes. Scholars have long noticed the strong similarities between this figure in *BdN* and the almost identically named Rabbi Neḥuniah ben ha-Qanah of the Hekhalot

---

[46] *BdN* 1:1 (Horowitz, *Tosefta 'Atiqta*, 5.3).

[47] *BdN* 1:7 (Horowitz, *Tosefta 'Atiqta*, 5.9).

corpus,[48] whose disciples famously bring him back from before God's chariot-throne using a piece of cotton tainted with a minuscule trace of menstrual impurity.[49] Indeed, this rigorist brand of purity practice in which "magical" practice and halakhah are interwoven seems to be at the heart of the many ideological affinities between *BdN* and the Hekhalot literature. Within the context of the Jewish mystical and magical literature of Late Antiquity, practices to achieve a heightened state of ritual purity are most commonly intended as preparation for revelatory adjuration (and not primarily for heavenly ascent).[50] This notional background may very well have informed the conception narrative's description of Metatron's appearance to the mother of Rabbi Ishmael. As in so many adjurational texts, the power to draw down an angel for specific practical aims is here predicated on the attainment of proper levels of ritual purity.

Interestingly enough, angels do not play only constructive roles in *BdN*'s understanding of conception. In its description of the causes of birth defects, the text attributes a malevolent aspect to angelic intervention as well:

When the father has intercourse with the mother, if he thinks of her as a prostitute (חושבה כזונה), and neither of them act with the fear of heaven, and he has sex with her light-heartedly (בליצנות), and both of them laugh during the time of their pleasure (בשעת הנאתן), what does the Holy One blessed be He do to the fetus? Before the fetus has left the mother's womb, He summons (lit. hints to: רומז ל-) an angel, who takes blood of menstrual impurity (דם נידה), places it

---

[48] This identification was first pointed out in Saul Lieberman, "The Knowledge of Halakha by the Author (or Authors) of the *Heikhaloth*," Appendix 2 of Ithamar Gruenwald, *Apocalyptic and Merkavah Mysticism* (AGJU 14; Leiden: Brill, 1980), 241–44.

[49] *Hekhalot Rabbati*, §§224–228. Hekhalot paragraph designations are given according to Peter Schäfer's *Synopse zur Hekhalot-Literatur* (Tübingen: Mohr Siebeck, 1981). This well-known passage has received a great deal of scholarly attention, most notably, Lawrence H. Schiffman, "The Recall of Rabbi Neḥuniah Ben Ha-Qanah from Ecstasy in Hekhalot Rabbati," *AJS Review* 1 (1976): 269–81; Margarete Schlüter, "Die Erzälung von der Rückholung des R. Neḥunya ben Haqana aus der *Merkava*-Schau in ihrem redaktionellen Rahmen," *FJB* 10 (1982): 65–109.

[50] On purity practice in the Hekhalot corpus and especially its primary connection to angelic adjuration, see Peter Schäfer, "Engel und Menschen in der Hekhalot-Literatur," *Kairos* 22 (1980): 201–25 (rev. and repr. in *Hekhalot-Studien* [TSAJ 19; Tübingen: Mohr Siebeck, 1988], 250–76); Martha Himmelfarb, *Ascent to Heaven in Jewish and Christian Apocalypses* (Oxford: Oxford UP, 1993), 106–14; Swartz, *Scholastic Magic*, 153–72; idem, "'Like the Ministering Angels': Ritual and Purity in Early Jewish Mysticism and Magic," *AJS Review* 19 (1994): 135–67; Rebecca Macy Lesses, *Ritual Practices to Gain Power: Angels, Incantations, and Revelation in Early Jewish Mysticism* (Harrisburg, PA: Trinity Press, 1989); idem, "Speaking with the Angels: Jewish and Greco-Egyptian Revelatory Adjurations," *HTR* 89 (1996): 41–60.

in the mouth of the fetus so that it enters its body, and it is immediate struck (לוקה) [with a defect].[51]

Here we find the text's familiar tendency to conflate ethical and cultic categories at its most extravagant. The deleterious effects of immoral thoughts are put on par with failure to attend to one's condition of ritual impurity. Whereas Rabbi Ishmael's parents demonstrate their piety by embracing the strictures of purity law and are duly rewarded, the parents in this passage bring harm to their child through decadent attitudes towards sexual intercourse. Not surprisingly, the medium of punishment is menstrual blood.

Other portions of the text betray a similar interest in the notion of divine intervention in the process of procreation. Basing itself on biblical precedent, the text asserts that the miraculous fruitfulness of each of the matriarchs, Sarah, Rachel, and Leah, should be attributed to her careful maintenance of purity regulations.[52] More interesting still, its account of Samson's conception in Judges 13 emphasizes the added element of angelic intervention. The text reports that, despite her female neighbors' (שכינותיה) advice to employ a magical remedy involving the hide of a fox (עורו של שועל) as a cure for her barrenness, Manoah's wife chooses instead simply to continue being vigilant about her state of ritual purity: "Although they led her astray (אעײפ שהיו מכזבות בה), the Holy One blessed be He heard her voice. Immediately, an angel appeared to her and said to her: 'Take care not to eat any impure thing (הזהרי ואל תאכלי כל טמא).' And, because she maintained her purity (ועל ידי ששמרה את נדתה), she immediately conceived (מיד נפקדה)."[53] In this "annunciation" scene, it is not her piety in general that is rewarded, but her steadfast dedication to the purity laws in particular, coupled with her refusal to engage in magical practice. Whatever the tangible similarities between this form of rigorist purity practice and late antique Jewish magic, *BdN* vigilantly insists on a firm boundary between them.

Although the purity discourse, of which *BdN* is the most developed example, accounts for the formal logic and vocabulary of Rabbi Ishmael's conception, the larger context of this narrative unit still demands elucidation. In other words, where does the literary fabric of this brief *exemplum* – its characters and its dramatic setting – come from? As we have seen, the presence of the "annunciation" scene in *The Story of the Ten Martyrs* presents us with a paradox. On the one hand, in strictly formal terms this narrative unit achieved its present literary form outside of the martyrological tradition – the story reflects the practical, ethical, and ritual concerns of the purity literature in which it developed. On the

---

[51] *BdN* 2:7 (Horowitz, *Tosefta 'Atiqta*, 5.20).
[52] *BdN* 2:6 (Horowitz, *Tosefta 'Atiqta*, 5.19).
[53] *BdN* 2:6 (Horowitz, *Tosefta 'Atiqta*, 5.19).

other, its narrative content is so integrally connected to the later events of
Rabbi Ishmael's life that it is difficult to imagine how these motifs could
have been generated and orchestrated in so coherent a manner without
presupposing a tradition concerning his miraculous origins. Nevertheless,
the complex process of redaction through which the martyrological
anthology was assembled belies any overly elegant solution to this
tension. In what follows, I argue that, while this narrative tradition was
incorporated into the anthology only after it had already become
crystallized in another literary context, its thematic content is essential to
understanding the figure of Rabbi Ishmael within *The Story of the Ten
Martyrs*.

## Rabbi Ishmael's Angelic Purity and Beauty in *The Story of the Ten Martyrs*

Despite being set during the "Hadrianic persecutions" of the second
century CE, the martyrological anthology as a fully formed literary
composition dates to the Geonic period (seventh to tenth centuries).
Jewish historians have long endeavored to isolate the historical kernel
concealed in the multiple and shifting versions of this legend.[54] More
recent scholarship, however, has come to reject the positivist assumptions
of these earlier attempts, preferring instead to emphasize the literary
nature of the cycle.[55] According to these scholars, the text is only of

---

[54] See especially Heinrich Grätz, "Die Hadrianische Verfolgung und die zehn
Märtyrer," *MGWJ* 1 (1852): 307–22; M. Auerbach, "Asarah Haruge Malkhut,"
*Jeschurun* 10 (1923): 60–66; idem, "Zur politischen Geschichte der Juden unter Kaiser
Hadrian," *Jeschurun* 10 (1923): 398–418; idem, "Zur politischen Geschichte der Juden
unter Kaiser Hadrian," *Jeschurun* 11 (1924): 59–70, 161–68; Samuel Krauss, "Asarah
Haruge Malkhut," *Hashlah* 44 (1925): 10–22, 106–17, 222–33 (repr. in *Bar-Kokhba*
[ed. A. Oppenhiemer; Jerusalem: Zalman Shazar Center, 1980], 239–77); N.
Wahrmann, "Zur Frage der 'Zehn Märtyrern,'" *MGWJ* 78 (1934): 575–80; Louis
Finkelstein, "The Ten Martyrs," in *Essays and Studies in Memory of Linda R. Miller*
(ed. I. Davidson; New York: JTSA, 1938), 29–55.

[55] This literary approach was inaugurated in Solomon Zeitlin, "The Legend of the
Ten Martyrs and its Apocalyptic Origins," *JQR* 36 (1945/6): 1–16. See also Joseph Dan,
"The Story of the Ten Martyrs: Its Origins and Development," in *Studies in Literature
Presented to Simon Halkin* (ed. E. Fleischer; Jerusalem: Magnes, 1973), 15–22; idem,
"The Story of the Ten Martyrs: Its Origins and Development," in *The Hebrew Story in
the Middle Ages* (Jerusalem: Keter, 1974), 62–66 [Hebrew]; idem, "Pirke Hekhalot
Rabbati ve-Ma'ase Asarat Haruge Malkhut," *Eshel Be'er Sheba'* 2 (1980): 63–80
[Hebrew]; Reeg, *Geschichte*, 1–2. For detailed analysis of the full range of rabbinic
sources related to this period of conflict and alleged persecution, see especially Peter
Schäfer, *Der Bar Kokhba-Aufstand. Studien zum zweiten jüdischen Krieg gegen Rom*
(Tübingen: Mohr Siebeck, 1981), 194–236. Schäfer's emphasis on the ongoing literary

historical value for understanding the experience of the Jews under East-Roman (Byzantine) rule in the period of its actual literary formation, not the earlier community from which its characters are drawn.[56]

The story weaves together a unified tale from pre-existing martyrological material found scattered throughout the Babylonian and Palestinian Talmuds as well as the vast midrashic corpus, together with a number of units that seem to have been generated specifically for the anthology itself.[57] The result is a new form of martyrology. Classical rabbinic literature, for instance, nowhere recounts the contemporaneous deaths of ten rabbinic martyrs, but instead restricts itself to brief narrative complexes that typically narrate the death of one martyr, and at most two or three.[58] By contrast, the anthology situates the executions of all ten sages within a single literary framework that offers a common explanation for their deaths, namely, the sin committed by Joseph's brothers when they sold him into slavery (Genesis 38).[59] Basing itself on the

---

transformation of these traditions in later rabbinic sources is an important corrective to the more positivist interpretation of the evidence in Saul Lieberman, "The Martyrs of Caesarea," *Annuaire de l'Institut de Philologie et d'Histoire Orientales et Slaves* 7 (1939–1944): 395–446; idem, "Religious Persecution of the Jews," in *Salo Wittmayer Baron Jubilee Volume on the Occasion of his Eightieth Birthday* (Jerusalem: The American Academy of Jewish Research, 1974), 213–45 (repr. in *The Bar-Kokhba Revolt* [ed. A. Oppenheimer; Jerusalem: The Zalman Shazar Center, 1980], 205–37) [Hebrew]; Moshe David Herr, "Persecutions and Martyrdom in Hadrian's Days," *Scripta Hierosolymitana* 23 (1972): 85–125.

[56] This insight was first suggested in Philip Block, "Rom und die Mystiker der Merkabah," in *Festschrift zum siebzigsten Geburtstage J. Guttmanns* (Leibzig, 1915), 113–24.

[57] On the use of earlier rabbinic sources in *The Story of the Ten Martyrs*, see Reeg, *Geschichte*, 49–51. Otherwise unattested material is used in the martyrological accounts of Rabbi Judah ben Bava (I.43), Yeshevav the Scribe (I.50; III–VII.44), Rabbi Judah ben Dama (I.46); Rabbi Ḥanina ben Ḥakhinai (I, III–V.49); and Rabbi Elazar ben Shammua (I–II, IV–VII.51).

[58] E.g., for the death of Rabbi Akiva: *y. Ber.* 9,7 (14b); *Mek. Y., Shirata* on Exod 15:2; *b. Ber.* 61b; *b. Erub.* 21b; *b. Ber.* 66a; *b. Pesaḥ.* 50a; *b. B. Bat.* 10b; of Rabbi Ḥananya ben Teradyon: *b. 'Abod. Zar.* 17b–18a; of Rabbi Yehudah ben Bava: *b. Sanh.* 14a and *b. 'Abod. Zar* 8b; of Judah the Baker: *y. Ḥag.* 2,1 (77b); of Rabbi Ḥutzpit the Interpreter: *b. Ḥul.* 142a; *b. Qidd.* 39b; of Lulianus and Pappus, "the Two Martyrs of Lod": *b. Ta'an.* 18b; *b. Ketub.* 77a; *b. Pesaḥ.* 50a; *b. B. Bat.* 10b.

[59] This motif appears in earlier Jewish literature (e.g., *Jub.* 34:10–20; *Gen. Rab.* 84:17; *Song Rab.* on Song 1:3; *PRE* 38; *Midrash Mishle* 9, 2; cf. *Test. Gad* 2:3; *Test. Zeb.* 1:5). Lists of the ten martyrs are found in *Lam. Rab.* 2,4; *Ekha Rabbati* 2,2; *Mid. Ps* on Ps 9:13. Versions of this list are also found in the body of the *Story of the Ten Martyrs* (I.21.12; II–III.4.3; IV–V, IX.10.32; VIII.22.27) and in some manuscripts of *Hekhalot Rabbati* at §109 (MS N8128 and in a gloss in V228). These lists vary greatly from text to text and even within the different recensions of the anthology. It is important to note that several recensions of *The Story of the Ten Martyrs* suggest one of two alternative explanations of the sages' deaths: either Israel's sin of teaching Torah to

scriptural authority of Ex 21:16 ("He who kidnaps a man – whether he has sold him or is still holding him – shall be put to death"), the text argues that their actions constituted a capital crime. The deaths of the ten sages are intended as atonement of the "original sin" committed by the progenitors of the tribes of Israel.

While there are many versions of *The Story of the Ten Martyrs*, they all share a common literary structure provided by a highly elaborate account of the twin executions of Rabban Simeon ben Gamaliel and Rabbi Ishmael, into which the motif of ten rabbinic martyrs has been incorporated.[60] This frame narrative (*Rahmenerzählung*) served as a relatively flexible literary structure within which future redactors of the anthology could organize and reorganize shifting configurations of thematically related martyrological material. Moreover, the individual versions of this collection differ wildly in their application of the frame narrative. The number and content of the martyrological units included in each recension is highly unstable; in fact, recensions II and VIII do not even bother to attach any additional martyrological material to the frame narrative.[61] Therefore, the subsequent martyrological material, whether drawn from earlier rabbinic sources or attested first within this collection, often seems no more than the obligatory realization of the literary structure established in the frame narrative. Rabbi Ishmael's *vita*, then, not only dominates late Jewish martyrology in a thematic sense, but also functions as its literary anchor.

### Rabbi Ishmael's Heavenly Ascent

As we have seen above, several recensions of *The Story of the Ten Martyrs* offer the story of Rabbi Ishmael's miraculous origins as an explanation for his ability to ascend to heaven. He makes this celestial visit to learn if the executions of the ten sages are in accordance with the

---

the Roman Emperor or the Gentiles (IV–V, VIII–IX.8.6) or the hubristic belief that the wisdom of the sages can fully compensate for the destruction of the Temple (I.8.5). These aetiologies, however, are merely ancillary to the sin of Joseph's brothers, which is found in every recension of the text and is clearly central to the literary development of the anthology.

[60] On the form of the open frame narrative, see Reeg, *Geschichte*, 33–34. This frame narrative more or less occupies I–X.10–22, V–VII.25–28, and IX–X.28, although the different recensions differ considerably. An early version of this passage is contained in *Midrash Shir Hashirim* on Song 1:3 (L. Grünhut, *Midrash Shir Hashirim* [Jerusalem: Wilhelm Gross, 1897], 3a–4b). The account of their twin deaths is found in its more rudimentary forms without being connected to the motif of ten martyrs at *Mek. Y.* on Exod 22:22; *Semaḥot* 8:8; *AdRN* A 37 and 38; *AdRN* B 41; and *SER* (30) 28, p. 153.

[61] See Reeg, *Geschichte*, 54.

will of God and, more importantly, whether the decree can be repealed.[62] Immediately following the account of his conception, these versions of the text continue:

> At that time Rabbi Ishmael recited the name of God and a storm wind lifted him up and brought him to heaven (וקבלתו רוח סערה והעלהו לשמים). Metatron, the Prince of the Countenance, met him (פגע בו) and asked him: "Who are you?" He answered him: "I am Rabbi Ishmael ben Elishah the High Priest." He said to him: "You are the one in whom your Creator takes pride each day (אתה הוא שקונך משתבח בך כל יום) saying, 'I have a servant on earth, a priest like you [Metatron]; his radiance is like your radiance and his appearance is like your appearance (יש לי עבד בארץ כהן כמותך זיו כזיוותך ומראהו כמראך).'" Rabbi Ishmael answered: "I am he." He asked him: "What is your business in this place of pure ones (מה טיבך במקום טהורים)?" "A decree has been passed that ten noble ones of Israel will be executed (גזירה נגזרה עלינו עשרה שיהרגו מאבירי ישראל) and I have ascended to learn whether this is the will of heaven or not (ועליתי לידע אם גזירה זו מן השמים ואם לאו)."[63]

Metatron answers Rabbi Ishmael with a detailed description of the proceedings in the heavenly court during which the angelic prosecutor successfully demands from God that he exact the punishment due Israel for the crime of their forefathers. This account satisfies Rabbi Ishmael, who returns to earth to instruct his colleagues to accept their collective fate. The coupled descriptions of Rabban Simeon ben Gamaliel and Rabbi Ishmael's gruesome deaths immediately ensue, followed by the sequential reports concerning the deaths of the other martyrs.

Of course, Rabbi Ishmael's encounter with an angel in heaven seems familiar enough. In the Hekhalot literature, Rabbi Ishmael is portrayed numerous times as the favored disciple of the great master of secret lore, Rabbi Neḥunya ben ha-Qanah. He serves as the prototype of the aspiring mystical initiate who, through careful preparation and technique, gains access to the heavenly sphere above. Like his colleagues in the mystical fellowship, his powers derive from the secret teachings transmitted within the human community of scholars.[64] The act of heavenly ascent is typically described in the Hekhalot literature using the technical phrase "to descend to the chariot-throne" (לירד למרכבה).[65] By contrast, *The*

---

62 *Ten Martyrs*, V, VII–VIII 11.11. Recension I.15.10, however, links the conception narrative to Rabbi Ishmael's exceptional beauty.

63 *Ten Martyrs*, I–X 15.1–4; cf. Grünhut, *Midrash Shir Hashirim*, 4a. The translation follows recension VII. This unit is relatively stable within the manuscript tradition.

64 The *locus classicus* for this instructional style of literature is the *ḥavura*-account in *Hekhalot Rabbati* (Schäfer, *Synopse*, §§198–259).

65 See most recently the comprehensive study of its technical vocabulary of "descent to the chariot" (*yeridah la-merkavah*) in Annelies Kuyt, *The 'Descent' to the Chariot* (Tübingen: Mohr Siebeck, 1995); idem, "Once Again: Yarad in Hekhalot Literature," *FJB* 18 (1990): 45–69. See also the important analysis of this phenomenon in Elliot R. Wolfson, "Yeridah la-Merkavah: Typology of Ecstasy and Enthronement in Ancient

*Story of the Ten Martyrs* employs the more conventional verb "to ascend" (עלה) in order to characterize Rabbi Ishmael's journey.[66] This terminological discrepancy is not incidental, but signifies the differing ideological and literary contexts of the two accounts. Whereas the Hekhalot corpus portrays Rabbi Ishmael gaining his powers through a process of study, piety, and ritual performance that can be replicated by others, the martyrological tradition presents Rabbi Ishmael's power as radically unique, deriving from his special kinship with the angel Metatron.

In fact, rather than drawing on the Hekhalot literature, the description of Rabbi Ishmael's journey to heaven has a striking number of verbal and conceptual affinities with the well-known midrashic tradition concerning Moses' ascent to receive the Torah.[67] Like Moses, who in almost all the

---

Jewish Mysticism," in *Mystics of the Book: Themes, Topics, and Typologies* (ed. R. A. Herrera; New York: Peter Lang, 1993), 13–44.

[66] There are several notable exceptions where versions of the martyrology do employ the technical terminology of *yeridah*. These, however, are unquestionably later adaptations of the original formulation in the martyrology. The version of the story of the ten martyrs contained in *Hekhalot Rabbati* (Schäfer, *Synopse*, §§107–121) reports: "When Rabbi Neḥunya ben ha-Qanah saw this decree (גזירה זו), he rose and led me down to the Merkavah (עמד והורידני למרכבה)" (Schäfer, *Synopse*, §107). However, the causative (*hif'il*) form of the verb *yarad* used here is found only in this one instance throughout the entire Hekhalot corpus (Kuyt, *Descent*, 150–52). This anomalous formulation suggests strongly that this version of Rabbi Ishmael's ascent was adapted to conform to the literary/ideological context of the Hekhalot literature. Similarly, recension III of the martyrological anthology, which is represented by a single Italian manuscript family, employs the same technical terminology (e.g., at 12.9 and 31.1). Reeg, *Geschichte*, 43–44, however, rightly argues that this recension represents a relatively late and highly modified version of the anthology into which a great many passages from the Hekhalot corpus have been interpolated. *Pace* Dan ("The Story of the Ten Martyrs," 15–22; idem, "Pirke Hekhalot Rabbati," 63–80), recension III is not the earliest extant version of the anthology from which the Hekhalot literature derived its version of the martyrology.

[67] For detailed discussion of this material, see especially David Halperin, *The Faces of the Chariot: Early Jewish Response to Ezekiel's Vision* (TSAJ 16; Tübingen: Mohr Siebeck, 1988), 289–322; Karl-Erich Grözinger, *Ich bin der Herr, dein Gott! Eine rabbinische Homilie zum Ersten Gebot (PesR 20)* (Bern: Herbert Lang, 1976). Differing versions of this narrative tradition are contained in the following sources: *b. Shabb.* 88a–89a; *Pesiq. Rab.* 20, §§11–20 (ed. Rivka Ulmer, *Pesiqta Rabbati: A Synoptic Edition of Pesiqta Rabbati Based upon All Extant Manuscripts and the Editio Princeps* [vol. 1; SFSHR 155; Atlanta: Scholars Press, 1997], 422–35); MS Oxford Or. 135, 357a–358a (printed in Grözinger, *Ich bin der Herr*, 12*–16*); *Ma'ayan Hokhmah* (Adolf Jellenik, *Beit ha-Midrash* [3rd ed.; 6 vols.; Jerusalem: Wahrmann Books, 1967], 1.58–61; *Haggadat Shema' Yisra'el* (Jellenik, *Beit ha-Midrash*, 5.165–66); T-S K 21.95.A, 1a–2a (fragment 21 in Peter Schäfer, *Geniza-Fragmente zur Hekhalot-Literatur* [TSAJ 6; Tübingen: Mohr Siebeck, 1984], 171–81); *PRE* 46; *Midrash ha-Gadol* to Ex 19:20. The narrative also appears in *piyyut* form as *'El 'ir gibborim* by

versions of this tradition is conveyed to heaven within a cloud (ונשאתו ענן),[68] Rabbi Ishmael is said to ascend within a storm-wind (רוח סערה). Indeed, precisely the same phrase – "he encountered him" (פגע בו) – is used in both literary traditions to describe their audience with the angel who meets them immediately upon their ascent.[69] Moreover, the image of heaven in both of these traditions is horizontal, not vertical as in the Hekhalot literature.[70] This horizontal orientation is given expression through the description of Rabbi Ishmael walking about in heaven (והיה מהלך ברקיע),[71] which uses almost identical language to the characterization of Moses' own movement – "he was walking in heaven like a human being walking on earth" (והיה מהלך ברקיע כאדם שמהלך בארץ).[72]

Yet the affinities between these two accounts go beyond these verbal echoes. Upon ascending, both figures are interrogated by the angelic host concerning their presence in heaven. Just as Metatron asks Rabbi Ishmael, "What is your business in this place of pure ones (מה טיבך במקום טהורים)?" the angels who confront Moses demand to know, "what business does one born of woman have in this place of purity, in this place of holiness (מה טיבו של ילוד אישה כאן במקום טהרה במקום קדושה)?"[73] An even more dramatic formulation of this protest is found in the brief textual unit known as "The Seventy Names of Metatron."[74] Here the angels oppose God's decision to reveal the secrets of the universe to Moses, who, as the representative of mankind, is

---

Amittai ben Shephatiah (Yonah David, *The Poems of Amittai* [Jerusalem: Akhshav, 1975], 100–2).

[68] E.g., *Pesiq. Rab.* 20, §11 (Ulmer, *Pesiqta Rabbati*, 422–23).

[69] E.g., *Pesiq. Rab.* 20, §11 (Ulmer, *Pesiqta Rabbati*, 422–23).

[70] On the layered vertical cosmology of the Hekhalot literature, see most recently Peter Schäfer, "In Heaven as it is in Hell: The Cosmology of *Seder Rabbah di-Bereshit*," in *Heavenly Realms and Earthly Realities in Late Antique Religions* (ed. R. Abusch and A. Y. Reed; Cambridge: Cambridge UP, forthcoming).

[71] I.20.1.

[72] *Ma'ayan Hokhmah* (Jellenik, *Beit ha-Midrash*, 1.57). Cf. *Pesiq. Rab.* 20:11–12; MS Oxford Or. 135, 357a (§11,2).

[73] T-S K 21.95.A, 1b/13–14 (Schäfer, *Geniza-Fragmente*, 174). Most versions of the narrative use the shorter phrase מה לך (e.g., *b. Shab.* 88b; *Pesiq. Rab.* 20, §11), instead of the more explicit מה טיבך. However, since all of these versions include the phrase "one born of woman" (ילוד אישה), it is reasonable to assume that both formulations are similarly intended to address the impropriety of human entry into heaven. In most versions, this question is asked by Kemuel, the first angel encountered by Moses, rather than by a group of angels.

[74] Schäfer, *Synopse*, §§71–80. On this unit, see Claudia Rohrbacher-Sticker, "Die Namen Gottes und die Namen Metatrons: Zwei Geniza Fragmente zur Hekhalot-Literatur," *FJB* 19 (1991–92): 95–168; Joseph Dan, "The Seventy Names of Metatron," *Proceedings of the Eighth World Congress of Jewish Studies, Division C* (Jerusalem: World Union of Jewish Studies, 1981), 19–23.

described as "born of woman, blemished, unclean, defiled by blood and impure flux," and who like all men "excretes putrid drops (of semen)."[75] Unlike Rabbi Ishmael, who is immediately granted a detailed answer to his request, Moses is met with the unbridled hostility of the angelic host, which is evidently displeased that God plans to entrust to flesh and blood what he has withheld from His beloved angels.[76] The angels view Moses' arrival in heaven as an unacceptable invasion of their domain and wage a near-fatal battle against his perceived aggression. Their challenge does not primarily address the content of his mission, but rather his right to be present in heaven at all.

The phrase מה טיב- constitutes far more than the pragmatic (and relatively neutral) question: "What is your business here in this place?" Instead, this interrogative formula signals a pointed challenge to the interlocutor: "What business do you have being here at all?" – or, perhaps even better, "Should not the very nature of this human being bar his entry into our realm?"[77] The question insists on the radical disparity between human existence and the wholly pure status of the heavenly realm. The angels' complaint against Moses is based on their unshakable conviction that for a human being to enter the angelic realm constitutes a grave transgression of the cosmic order.

What, then, accounts for the contrasting receptions that these two figures are given upon arriving in heaven? In order to answer this question, we should first turn to the Hekhalot literature, which similarly employs the phrase מה טיב- as its standard formula for expressing alarm at the potential mixing of these two apparently antithetical domains, the angelic and the human.[78] The formula is used most frequently in *3 Enoch*, which directly addresses the problems associated with the transformation

---

[75] Schäfer, *Synopse*, §79 (translated in Philip S. Alexander, "3 (Hebrew Apocalypse of) Enoch," in *The Old Testament Pseudepigrapha* [2 vols.; ed. J. Charlesworth; New York: Doubleday, 1983], 1.315). Cf. *b. Shabb.* 88b; *Pesiq. Rab.* 20:11–12; *Lev. Rab.* 14:2. At *m. Avot* 3, Akabya ben Meḥalalel reflects on the lowliness of humanity using the same terminology: "Consider where you have come from – a putrid drop (מטפה סרוחה)."

[76] On the motif of conflict between angels and human beings and its bearing on the Moses ascent traditions, see especially Peter Schäfer, *Rivalität zwischen Engeln und Menschen: Untersuchungen zur rabbinischen Engelvorstellung* (Berlin: de Gruyter, 1975), 207–16.

[77] This last rendering of the phrase reflects the literal meaning of the word טיב as "form, nature, character, or peculiarity" (s.v. Jastrow, 523).

[78] In his recently published study *A Transparent Illusion: The Dangerous Vision of Water in Hekhalot Mysticism* (Leiden: Brill, 2002), esp. 118–23, C. R. A. Morray-Jones applies a similar analysis to the enigmatic question "What is the nature of this water?" (המים האלה מה טיבן) that appears in the well-known "Water Vision Episode" in the Hekhalot corpus (Schäfer, *Synopse*, §§258–259 and §§407–408; cf. *b. Hag* 14b). I arrived at my conclusions prior to reading Morray-Jones' discussion.

of the human Enoch into the angelic figure Metatron.[79] In a passage that is highly reminiscent of the Moses material, the text puts the phrase in the mouths of the distraught angelic trio, Uzzah, Azzah, and Azael, who vocally oppose Enoch's arrival in heaven and subsequent elevation to angelic status:

> Then three of the ministering angels, Uzzah, Azzah, and Azael, came and laid charges against me in the heavenly height. They said before the Holy One blessed be He, "Lord of the Universe, did not the primeval ones give you good advice when they said, Do not create man!" The Holy one, blessed be He, replied, "I have made and will sustain him; I will carry and deliver him." When they saw me they said before him, "Lord of the Universe, what right has this one to ascend to the height of heights (מה טיבו של זה שעולה למרום מרומים)? Is he not descended from those who perished in the waters of the Flood? What right has he to be in heaven (מה טיבו ברקיע)?" (§6 = 4:6–7)[80]

In response to their charges, God turns the tables on them, rebuking the angelic rebels with a curt reminder of the strict boundaries that severely circumscribe their influence on his judgment: "What right have you to interrupt me (מה טיבכם שאתם נכנסים לדברי)?" (§6 = 4:8) As a thematically related passage later reports, it is Enoch's odor that has apparently been the cause of the angels' distress. Like Moses' opponents, these angels complain, "What is this smell of one born of woman (מה טעם של ילוד אישה)? Why does a white drop (of semen) ascend on high (ומה טיפת לבן שהיא עולה לשמי מרום) and serve among those who cleave to the flames?" (§6 = 4:2) Finally, in a passage that belongs to the literary frame of *3 Enoch*, this same complaint is lodged against Enoch/Metatron for permitting his interlocutor in the text, Rabbi Ishmael, to visit him in heaven: "Then the eagles of the chariot, the flaming ophanim, and the cherubim of devouring fire asked Metatron, 'Youth, why have you allowed one born of women to come in and behold the chariot (מה הנחת ילוד אישה שיבא ויסתכל במרכבה)? From what nation is he? From what tribe is he? What is his character (מה טיבו של זה)?'" (§3 = 2:2). In *3 Enoch*, unlike the martyrology, the angelic host does not recognize Rabbi Ishmael's special status.

In each case, the phrase -מה טיב is used to assert that everything must have its proper place – God, the angels, and human beings – reaffirming

---

[79] On Enoch's angelification as Metatron, see esp. Nathaniel Deutsch, *Guardians of the Gate: Angelic Vice Regency in Late Antiquity* (Leiden: Brill, 1999), 27–77; Wolfson, *Speculum*, 82–85; C. R. A. Morray-Jones, "Transformational Mysticism in the Apocalyptic-Merkabah Tradition," *JJS* 43 (1992): 1–31. On the somewhat anomalous place of *3 Enoch* with the Hekhalot literature, see Peter Schäfer, *The Hidden and Manifest God* (New York: SUNY, 1994), 123–38.

[80] On the relationship of this passage to the fallen angel traditions in *1 Enoch*, see Annette Yoshiko Reed, "From Asael and Semihazah to Uzzah, Azzah, and Azael: 3 Enoch 5 (§§7–8) and Jewish Reception-History of 1 Enoch," *JSQ* 8 (2001): 105–36.

the cosmic order in the face of these repeated breaches. Indeed, it is used not only to challenge the over-reaching ambitions of lesser beings, whether human or angelic, but also to safeguard the divine from being tainted by the human sphere. In a passage again found in *3 Enoch*, the angels complain that because of idolatrous sins committed by the generation of Enosh it is no longer fitting for God to remain among human beings.[81] More germane to our purposes, however, is a striking adjurational text that is appended in some manuscripts to *Hekhalot Rabbati*, in which the Prince of the Torah (שר תורה) rebukes the young Rabbi Ishmael, here age thirteen, for having improperly called him down to earth:

> I stood and afflicted myself for forty days, and I recited the Great Name, until I caused him [the Prince of the Torah] to descend. He came down in a flame of fire, and his face had the appearance of lightning. When I saw him, I trembled and was frightened and fell back. He said to me: "Human being! What is your business that you have disturbed the great household (בן אדם מה טיבך שהרעשת את פמלייא גדולה)." I said to him: "It is revealed and known before Him Who spoke and the world came into being that I did not bring you down for [my] glory, but to do the will of your master." Then he said to me: "Human being, son of a stinking drop, worm and vermin (בן אדם טפה סרוחה רמה ותולעה)!"[82]

The text then proceeds to instruct the reader on the proper preparation for angelic adjuration: "Whoever wants it to be revealed to him must sit fasting for forty days, perform twenty-four immersions every day, and not eat anything defiling; he must not look at a woman, and must sit in a totally dark house."[83] As we have noted above, the rigorous practices prescribed here are typical of the Hekhalot literature: the state of ritual purity that is a prerequisite for interacting with the divine is an achieved state. Like Moses and Enoch, the Rabbi Ishmael of the Hekhalot literature is neither exempt from the contamination inherent in normal human existence nor from the dangers this impurity poses for the person attempting to gain access to divine knowledge.

Thus, despite the many literary and conceptual connections between *The Story of the Ten Martyrs* and the Hekhalot corpus, they offer radically different solutions to the predicament created by their common notion of a selectively permeable cosmos. The Hekhalot corpus' Rabbi

---

[81] Schäfer, *Synopse*, §8 = 5:10–12: "'Lord of the Universe, what business have you with men (מה לך אצל בני אדם)? ... Why did you leave the heaven of heavens above ... and lodge with men who worship idols? Now you are on earth, and the idols are on the earth; what is your business among the idolatrous inhabitants of earth (מה טיבך בין דרי הארץ)?'"

[82] Schäfer, *Synopse*, §313. (I have slightly modified the translation in Swartz, *Scholastic Magic*, 69.) Cf. §292.

[83] Schäfer, *Synopse*, §314 (translated in Swartz, *Scholastic Magic*, 70).

*threshold*

Ishmael must labor to achieve the proper state of purity and to learn the necessary practices for encountering the divine, but the martyrology posits a very different type of liminal figure. Rabbi Ishmael's angelic status and purity seem to derive directly from Metatron himself. In Metatron's words, Rabbi Ishmael is the one in whom God "takes pride each day saying, 'I have a servant on earth, a priest like you (Metatron); his radiance is like your radiance and his appearance is like your appearance (יש לי עבד בארץ כהן כמותך זיו כזיוותך ומראהו כמראך)."[84] Quite simply, he is a hybrid of the divine and the human, his nature structurally analogous to the porous cosmos he traverses. His encounter with Metatron is more a recognition scene of kin than a confrontation between two dissimilar beings.

It is hardly surprising that Rabbi Ishmael's kinship with his angelic progenitor is embodied in his luminous face, since Metatron's own bond with the divine is regularly expressed in similar terms. One particularly evocative passage from the Hekhalot corpus, which takes the form of a midrashic exegesis of two verses that mention God's face, Ex 33:15 (אם אין פניך הולכים ...) and 23:21 (השמר מפניו), relates how God warned Moses to beware of the dangerous force exerted by His countenance (ואדון כל העולמים הזהיר למשה שישמור מפניו).[85] The unit then explicitly identifies God's face with the angelic name Yofi'el (lit. "beauty of God") and finally with Metatron himself. Nathaniel Deutsch has rightly pointed to this passage to support his conclusion that "some sources understood Metatron to be the hypostatic embodiment of a particular part of the divine form, most notably the face of God .... It is likely that this tradition underlies the title *sar ha-panim*, which is associated with Metatron. Rather than 'prince of the face [of God],' this title is better understood as 'prince who is the face [of God]."[86] Rabbi Ishmael's angelic appearance is thus synonymous with God's own hypostatic countenance. It is, therefore, understandable that in one of the recensions of the martyrological anthology, the relatively late *Midrash Eleh Ezkerah*, Metatron explicitly comments on the resemblance between Rabbi Ishmael and God: "You are Ishmael in whom your Creator takes pride each day, since he has a servant on earth who resembles the countenance/beauty of his own face (שדומה לקלסתר פניו)."[87] Although this formulation is a

---

[84] *Ten Martyrs*, I–X 15.1–4; cf. Grünhut, *Midrash Shir Hashirim*, 4a.

[85] Schäfer, *Synopse*, §§396–397.

[86] Deutsch, *Guardians*, 43. See Deutsch's fuller discussion of this material in *The Gnostic Imagination: Gnosticism, Mandaeism, and Merkabah Mysticism* (Leiden: Brill, 1995), 99–105.

[87] *Ten Martyrs*, I.15.3. קלסתר = Greek κρύσταλλος, "countenance or beauty" (s.v. Jastrow, 1379). For the dating of this recension and its relationship to the *piyyut Eleh Ezkerah*, see Reeg, *Geschichte*, 48–52.

minority tradition, it puts a suitably fine point on the matter: Rabbi Ishmael is God's special servant, whose more-than-human purity and beauty are tokens of the divine nature that ensures his safe reception in heaven and affords him an unparalleled place in Israel's history.

## Rabbi Ishmael's Execution

Just as Rabbi Ishmael's heavenly ascent hinges on the motifs of angelic purity and beauty, so too does the elaborate account of his execution that is at the heart of *The Story of the Ten Martyrs*. In addition to the allusions to his angelic beauty in both the conception and ascent narratives, the martyrology explicitly reports that Rabbi Ishmael belongs to a long succession of beautiful Jewish men: "They said concerning Rabbi Ishmael ben Elisha the high priest that he was among the seven beauties the world had seen (אחד משבעה יפים שהיו בעולם). And these are Adam, Jacob, Joseph, Saul, Absalom, Rabbi Yoḥanan, Rabbi Abbahu, and Rabbi Ishmael."[88] A variation on this motif, which is also contained in the anthology, reports even more succinctly: "There was no beauty in the world from the days of Joseph the son of Jacob except Rabbi Ishmael (שלא היה נוי בעולם מימות יוסף בן יעקב אלא ר״י)."[89] These competing formulations, which both seek to link rabbinic figures with biblical prototypes of masculine beauty, effectively situate Rabbi Ishmael within a specific tradition found in rabbinic literature concerning this eugenic genealogy that wends its way through Israel's history.

Indeed, the list of the "seven beauties" to which Rabbi Ishmael is added seems to draw much of its material from the very same passage cited above in connection with Rabbi Yoḥanan's public service of transmitting his beauty to the next generation:

> Said Rabbi Yoḥanan: "I have survived from the beautiful of Jerusalem (משפירי ירושלים)." One who wishes to see the beauty of Rabbi Yoḥanan should bring a brand new silver cup and fill it with the red seeds of a pomegranate and place around its rim a garland of red roses, and let him place it at the place where the sun meets the shade, and that vision is the beauty of Rabbi Yoḥanan. Is that true? But haven't we been taught by our master that, "The beauty of Rabbi Abbahu is like the beauty of our father Jacob and the beauty of our father Jacob is like the beauty of Adam," and that of Rabbi Yoḥanan is not mentioned. But (the editor objects) Rabbi Yoḥanan is not included here because he did not have a beard (lit. "splendor of face," i.e. had a different sort of beauty). Rabbi Yoḥanan used to go sit outside the ritual bath. He said: "When the daughters of

---

[88] This statement appears in variety of formulations and locations in the different recensions of *The Story of the Ten Martyrs* (in some cases several times within a single recension): I.15.10; IV–V.22.6–7; IV.22.32; VI–VII.37.1–2; VII and IX–X.28.1–2.

[89] *Ten Martyrs*, II–III.22.33. A slightly different form of this tradition occurs at V–VII.22.33: "They said (of Rabbi Ishmael) that from the days of Joseph there was no beauty like him (אמרו מימות יוסף לא היה יפה כמוהו)."

Israel come out from the bath, let them meet me so that they will have children as beautiful as I am." The Rabbis said to him: "Are you not afraid of the Evil Eye?" He answered: "I am of the seed of Joseph, our father, of whom it is said, *Joseph is a fruitful bough, a fruitful bough by a spring* (Gen 49:22).[90]

Although Rabbi Ishmael's beauty is explicitly mentioned on a number of occasions elsewhere in earlier rabbinic literature (e.g., *t. Hor.* 2:5–7; *y. Hor.* 3,7 [48b]; *b. Giṭ.* 58a.), the inclusion of Rabbi Abbahu and Rabbi Yoḥanan in the list further emphasizes Rabbi Ishmael's genealogical bond to the one biblical figure most renowned for his beauty, Joseph.[91] Indeed, it may be possible to hear an echo of this kinship in the martyrology's account of Rabbi Ishmael's arrival in Rome for execution: "When they brought Rabbi Ishmael to Rome all the women who gazed upon him began to bleed because of his great beauty."[92] Rabbi Ishmael's damaging effect on the women of Rome is strikingly similar to medieval versions of the Joseph narrative in Genesis 39, which describes how Potiphar's wife and her friends were so astounded at Joseph's beauty when he entered the banquet room to serve them that they mistakenly cut the palms of their hands with the knives they were holding.[93]

---

[90] *b. B. Metsia* 84a (Boyarin, "Talmudic Texts," 136). For the beauty of Rabbi Abbahu, see also *b. B. Batra* 58a; *b. Sanh.* 14a. On Rabbi Abbahu's important leadership role in the Jewish community of Palestine and his deep acculturation in Greco-Roman society, see Lee I. Levine, "R. Abbahu of Caesarea," in *Christianity, Judaism, and Other Greco-Roman Cults: Studies for Morton Smith at Sixty* (ed. J. Neusner; Leiden: Brill, 1975), 56–76.

[91] Gen 39:6; cf. *T. Jos.* 3:4, 18:4; *T. Sim.* 5:1; *Jos. Asen.* 5:1–7; Philo, *Joseph* 40; Josephus, *A.J.* 2:9; *Gen. Rab.* 87:3. On Joseph's beauty, see especially James L. Kugel, *In Potiphar's House: The Interpretive Life of Biblical Texts* (Cambridge: Harvard UP, 1994), 28–93; Joshua Levinson, "An-other Woman: Joseph and Potiphar's Wife. Staging the Body Politic," *JQR* 87 (1997): 269–301; Ra'anan Abusch, "Eunuchs and Gender Transformation: Philo's Exegesis of the Joseph Narrative," in *Eunuchs in Antiquity and Beyond* (ed. Shaun Tougher; London: Duckworth, 2002), 103–21.

[92] V.22.8; VI.37.3; VII, IX–X.28.3: בשעה שהביאוהו לרומי כל הנשים שהיו רואות אותו היו שופעות דם מרוב יופיו.

[93] This motif was current in late antique and medieval midrashic sources: *Tanḥ., Va-yeshev* 5; *Midrash ha-Gadol* on Gen 39:14; Moses Gaster, *The Chronicle of Jerahmeel* (repr. H. Schwarzbaum; New York: KTAV, 1971), 94; *Sefer ha-Yashar* (ed. Lazarus Goldschmidt; Berlin: Benjamin Harz, 1923) 159–60; *Maḥzor Vitry* (ed. Simeon Hurwitz; Nürnburg, 1923), 342. It also appears in the many of the versions of the Joseph narrative found in Islamic/Arabic literature and art, most notably *Qur'an*, Sura 12:22–53 (of Late Meccan provenance), where the women exclaim that Joseph is "no human being, but a noble angel" (12:30–32). For discussion of these sources, see Kugel, *Potiphar's House*, 28–65. See also Shalom Goldman, *The Wiles of Women/The Wiles of Men: Joseph and Potiphar's Wife in Ancient Near Eastern, Jewish and Islamic Folklore* (Albany: SUNY, 1995), 31–54; Barbara Freyer Stowasser, *Women in the Qur'an, Traditions, and Interpretation* (New York: Oxford UP, 1994), 50–56; Fedwa Malti-Douglas, *Woman's Body, Woman's World: Gender and Discourse in Arabo-Islamic Writing* (Princeton: Princeton UP, 1991), 50–51. See also the Islamic sources

Whatever the cultural and literary background of these traditions, each is carefully situated within the martyrology's account of Rabbi Ishmael's gruesome death. Some recensions even report that the Roman Emperor decides to execute Rabbi Ishmael precisely in response to the violent reaction the martyr's beauty provokes in him: "When they brought him before the king, he asked him: 'Is there anyone in your nation more beautiful than you?' He answered: 'No.' He immediately decreed that he should be executed."[94] Later in the same scene, however, his beauty has precisely the opposite effect on the Emperor's daughter, who spies him through the window of the imperial palace[95] after hearing the baleful cries of the martyr for his decapitated colleague Rabban Simeon ben Gamaliel. The text continues:

> She went to her father and said: "Father, I have one request from you." He said to her: "My daughter, I will grant whatever you ask, except for sparing Ishmael and his colleagues." She responded: "But that *was* my request!" He responded: "You can't have your way on this matter." She said: "If that's the case, then at least give me permission to remove the skin of his face (לפשוט עור פניו)." He immediately ordered that the skin of Ishmael's face be removed while he was still alive (בעודו חי).[96]

Rabbi Ishmael's death is cruelly enacted precisely through the removal of the very token of his special status, his beautiful face.

---

collected in *Joseph and Potiphar's Wife in World Literature* (ed. John D. Yohannan; New York: New Directions, 1968), 158–220.

[94] *Ten Martyrs*, V.22.9; VI.37.4; VII, IX–X.28.4. I here translate recension V.

[95] *Ten Martyrs*, I–VII.22.31; IX–X 28.5. Compare *Jos. Asen.* 5:1–7, where Asenath catches sight of Joseph from a high window in the tower her father has built to help her safeguard her virginity and is immediately captivated by his beauty. Later in the text, Asenath mistakes an angel who has appeared before her for her beloved Joseph, whose beauty was apparently angelic like Rabbi Ishmael's (*Joseph and Asenath*, 14.1–17.6). For mention of how the women of Egypt look at Joseph from walls or windows, see *Jos. Asen.* 7:3–4; *Tg. Neof.* Gen 49:22; *Tg. Ps.-J.* Gen 49:22; Vulgate Gen 49:22. On the biblical motif of the woman at the window, see Nehama Aschkenasy, *Woman at the Window: Biblical Tales of Oppression and Escape* (Detroit: Wayne State UP, 1998), esp. 23–41.

[96] *Ten Martyrs*, I–VII.22.35–40; IX–X 28.7–11. I here translate recension V. The version of this pericope in Grünhut, *Midrash Shir Hashirim*, 4b, differs considerably from the ones found in *The Story of the Ten Martyrs*. Here, the female figure is identified as a Roman matron (מטרוניתא) rather than as the Emperor's daughter. In addition, the figure of the Emperor is entirely absent from the scene, leaving the Roman matron to engage in an explicitly sexual dialogue with the martyr – she tries to seduce him into looking directly at her in exchange for saving his life. He rebuffs her, explaining that he is far more concerned with his ultimate reward than with his earthly existence. I believe that this version is earlier than the one found in the martyrology, where the Emperor preemptively refuses his daughter's request to save Rabbi Ishmael even before she has articulated it.

Rabbi Ishmael remains impassive throughout the procedure until the executioner reaches the site where he wears his *tefillin* (מקום תפילין), at which point he lets out a loud and bitter scream. When the executioner asks him why he has only started to cry now, he responds that he is not mourning his own life (נשמתי) but rather the loss of his capacity to fulfill the commandment of putting on *tefillin*. This curious detail may be an allusion to the anthropomorphic notion that God himself dons *tefillin*, which is attested in both the Babylonian Talmud and the Hekhalot literature.[97] If, as it seems, Rabbi Ishmael possesses a replica of the divine visage, then it is no wonder that the amputation of the holiest portion of his face threatens the divine order itself. Indeed, the text reports that the cries that Rabbi Ishmael utters at precisely this point in the procedure reach up to heaven, threatening to return the world to primordial chaos and even to overthrow the throne of God.[98] In the face of this unleashed power, however, God insists that the angelic host not intervene to stop his death, since it will seal a contract between Him and His people on earth: "Let him alone so that his merit may endure for generations (שתעמוד זכותו לדור דורים)."[99] In a similar statement elsewhere in the martyrology, God makes this promise even more explicit: "The Holy One blessed be He said: 'Because of the merit (of the martyrs) I will redeem Israel and exact revenge from the enemies of God.'"[100]

## The Ritual of Rabbi Ishmael's Mask

Furthermore, the very flesh that embodies Rabbi Ishmael's unique relationship to the divine will serve as a physical guarantee of God's enduring promise to Israel. According to the narrative, after Rabbi Ishmael's execution, the mask of his face is preserved in the treasury at Rome in defiance of the forces of decay and is brought out of safekeeping every seventy years for use in a truly bizarre ritual:[101]

---

[97] *b. Ber.* 6a; Schäfer, *Synopse*, §582. Other citations that express this same notion have been collected in Lieberman, *Sheqi'in*, 11–13. For an excellent discussion of this and other related material, see Arthur Green, *Keter: The Crown of God in Early Jewish Mysticism* (Princeton: Princeton UP, 1997), 49–57.

[98] *Ten Martyrs*, I–VII.22.52–53: ועוד זעק שנייה ונזדעזע כסא הכבוד ובקש הבׄיׄה להפוך את העולם לתוהו ובהו.

[99] *Ten Martyrs*, I, III–V 22.50; VI–VII 37.10; IX–X 28.14

[100] *Ten Martyrs*, VI.36.4: אמר הקבׄׄה בזכותן אני עתיד להושיע את ישרׄ ולעשות נקמה באיבי השם. Cf. VII.27.4.

[101] *Ten Martyrs*, II, IV–V, VII.22.65–73; IX.54.1–6. I translate here recension VII. A longer version of this passage also appears at *b. 'Abod. Zar.* 11b, where this alleged description of a Roman festival is attributed to Rav Judah in the name of Samuel. The variations between these versions are considerable. Recension IX is closest to the *Bavli* text, although somewhat more condensed. IV and V, which are almost identical, similarly have the same sequence of phrases as the *Bavli*, although their phraseology is different on a number of occasions. II and VII are closely related, since both similarly

They take a healthy man and have him ride on [the back of] a cripple
(מביאין אדם שלם ומרכיבין אותו על חיגר); they summon a herald who proclaims
before them: "Let him who sees, see; and anyone who does not see, will never
see (כל מי שיראה יראה וכל שלא יראה לא יראה)." They place the head of Rabbi
Ishmael in the hand of the healthy man (ונותנין את ראשו של ר׳ ישמעאל ביד
האיש השלם).[102] They call the healthy man Esau and the cripple Jacob because of
his limp (בשב׳ שהוא צולע על יריכו). And they proclaim: "Woe to him when this
one rises up for the sin of the other. Woe to Esau, when Jacob rises up for the sin
of Rabbi Ishmael's head (אוי לעשו כשיקום יעקוב בעון ראשו של ר׳ ישמעאל),[103] as
it is written: *I will wreak my vengeance on Edom through My people Israel* (Ez
25:14).

The ritual is deeply obscure, although it seems to reflect Jewish
perceptions of Roman barbarism. Another passage in the Babylonian
Talmud reports that "every Roman legion carries with it several scalps
and do not be surprised at this, since they place the scalp of Rabbi
Ishmael on the heads of their kings (קרקיפלו של ר׳ ישמעאל מונח בראש
מלכים)."[104] More than a century ago, Samuel Rapaport read the version of
this passage in *Avodah Zarah* as an allusion to a carnivalesque practice
introduced into the *Ludi Saeculares* by the Roman emperor, Philip the
Arab (244–49 CE), around 247 CE in which a normal man rode upon a
limping dancer wearing a mask. According to this explanation, the
ritual's symbolism reflected the internal political struggles between Philip
and his rival, Decius.[105] Indeed, the customary formula used by the herald
to proclaim the start of the *Ludi Saeculares*, at least according to the
Roman historian Suetonius, is strikingly close to the crier's phraseology
in the mask ritual: "The herald invited the people in the usual formula to
the games which 'no one had ever seen or would ever see again (*quos nec
spectasset quisquam nec spectaturus esset*).'"[106] Yet, whatever the

---

Hebraize what must be the Aramaic original of certain portions of the text. I note only
those textual variations that are significant for my argument.

[102] IV–V.22.67 reads: "They dress him in the clothes of the first man; they bring out
the face of Rabbi Ishmael and place it on his head (ומלבישין אותו בגדו של אדם הראשון
ומביאין קלסתר פניו של ר׳ ישמעאל ומניחין אותו על ראשו)." In this formulation, Rabbi
Ishmael's face is spoken about precisely in the manner of God's countenance (i.e.
קלסתר פניו). In *b. 'Abod. Zar.* 11b and IX.54.3, the word used for the mask is קרקיפלו.

[103] IV–V.22.71 adds: "and when God destroys evil Edom (והב״ה יאבד אדום הרעה)."

[104] *b. Ḥul.* 123a.

[105] Samuel Rapaport, *Erekh Millin* (Warsaw, 1852; repr. Jerusalem: Makor, 1970),
57–63 (s.v. איד). However, the medieval commentator Rashi, clearly familiar with *The
Story of the Ten Martyrs*, interpreted the passage in light of the martyrology's narrative
of redemption (*b. 'Abod. Zar.* 11b, ד״ה קרקיפלו של ר׳ ישמעאל).

[106] Suetonius, *Claud.* 21.1 (J. C. Rolfe, trans., *Suetonius* [vol. 2; LCL; Cambridge:
Harvard UP, 1997], 39). Cf. Herodian 3.8.10: "So heralds traveled throughout Rome
and Italy summoning all the people to come and attend the games the likes of which
they had never seen before and would not see again" (C. R. Whittaker, trans., *Herodian*
[vol. 1; LCL; Cambridge: Harvard UP, 1969], 313). These sources as well as several

historical origins of this material, *The Story of the Ten Martyrs* clearly presents this macabre pageant as a Roman celebration of the Jews' bad fortune, and not as a struggle within the imperial family. Moreover, by redeploying this material within this narrative context, the martyrology seems to be making the case that the Romans' hubristic display of Rabbi Ishmael's face is bound to backfire. They mistake the meaning of their own actions: rather than signifying their power, the ritual in fact enacts the long-held wish that Jacob avenge the crimes of Esau, the legendary ancestor of Edom, which is systematically identified with Rome throughout late antique and medieval Jewish literature.[107]

Earlier in *The Story of the Ten Martyrs*, Rabbi Ishmael has foreseen that it will be his fate to serve as an instrument of God's redemption of Israel. As he is moving about in heaven, led by his angelic guide Metatron, he comes across an altar. Puzzled, he asks the angel: "What do you sacrifice on this altar? Do you have cows, rams, and sheep in heaven?" When the angel responds that they "sacrifice the souls of the righteous on it (אנו מקריבין עליו נפשותיהם של צדיקים)," Rabbi Ishmael says: "I have now learned something I have never heard before."[108] In fact, it is this final piece of revealed knowledge that seals Rabbi Ishmael's decision to return to earth to report to his colleagues what he has learned, apparently now satisfied that his death at the hands of the Roman authorities will not be in vain. He immediately descends and bears witness to what he has just seen in heaven.[109] A passage in the medieval midrashic compilation *Numbers Rabbah* expresses this sacrificial theology in strikingly similar language:

> Another explanation of the text, *Setting up the Tabernacle* (להקים את המשכן; Num 7:1) – Rabbi Simon expounded: When the Holy One, blessed be He, told Israel to set up the Tabernacle, He intimated to the ministering angels that they also should make a Tabernacle, and when the one below was erected the other was erected on high. The latter was the Tabernacle of the "youth" (הנער), whose name is Metatron, and therein he offers up the souls of the righteous to atone for Israel in the days of their exile (שבו מקריב נפשותיהם של צדיקים לכפר על ישראל בימי גלותם). The reason scripture says "(את) the Tabernacle" is because another tabernacle was erected simultaneously with it. In the same way it is

---

others are cited in Saul Lieberman, *Greek in Jewish Palestine* (New York: JTS, 1942), 145 n. 7.

[107] On the symbolism of Edom/Esau in Jewish culture, see esp. Gerson D. Cohen, "Esau as Symbol in Early Medieval Thought," in *Jewish Medieval and Renaissance Studies* (ed. A. Altmann; Cambridge: Harvard UP, 1967), 19–48; Yuval, *Shene goyim*, 18–34.

[108] *Ten Martyrs*, I–IX.20.1–5.

[109] *Ten Martyrs*, I–X.21.1–3.

written, *The place, O Lord, which you have made for yourself to Dwell in, the Sanctuary, O Lord, which your hands have established* (Ex 15:17).[110]

The phrase נפשותיהם של צדיקים (or in some variants נשמותיהם של צדיקים) runs like a red thread through the numerous passages in contemporary Jewish sources that describe this heavenly cult of the martyrs.[111] Yet, unlike these loose units, *The Story of the Ten Martyrs* integrates this notion into a coherent narrative framework. As the human manifestation of the purity and beauty of heavenly high priest Metatron, Rabbi Ishmael is both the elected high priest and atoning sacrifice of the people of Israel.

## Preliminary Conclusions

Although it is impossible to fix with any confidence the precise social and historical context within which late Jewish martyrology developed, its direct literary and ideological relationship to the purity literature of the Jewish communities of late antique Palestine – coupled with its unequivocal anti-Roman imagery – strongly suggests that it is the product of Byzantine Jewish culture. Certainly, its vivid portrayal of Rabbi Ishmael as a redeemer figure who is fated to be play an instrumental role in the liberation of Israel from the yoke of Roman rule resonates with the apocalyptic writing that flourished among Jews in this period.[112]

---

[110] *Num. Rab.* 12:12 (I have slightly modified the translation in Judah J. Slotki, *Numbers Rabbah* [2 vols.; London: Soncino, 1939], 1.482–83).

[111] E.g., *Midrash aseret ha-dibrot* (Jellenik, *Beit ha-Midrash*, 1.64); *Seder gan eden* (Jellenik, *Beit ha-Midrash*, 3.137); *Midrash Adonai be-hokhma yasad ha-aretz* (Jellenik, *Beit ha-Midrash*, 5.63). Compare *b. Menaḥ.* 110a; *b. Ḥag.* 12b; *Yalq. Sh.* 189 (376b); *Yalq. Sh.* 339 (417c), where the heavenly altar is discussed although the notion of human sacrifice is absent. See also the fascinating Tosafist gloss that cautiously weighs the burning question of whether it is "the souls of the righteous" or "fiery sheep" (כבשים של אש) that are sacrificed on the heavenly altar (*b. Menaḥ.* 110a, קרבן ד״ה מיכאל שר הגדול עומד ומקריב עליו). On the atoning blood of the martyrs in Jewish tradition, see Yuval, *Shene goyim*, 110–16 and 159–69.

[112] See the material collected in Yehudah Even Shmuel, *Midreshei Geulah* (2nd ed.; Jerusalem: Mosad Bialik, 1954); A. Wünsche, *Kleine Midraschim zur jüdischen Eschatologie und Apokalyptik* (vol. 3 of *Aus Israels Lehrhallen*; Hildesheim: Olms, 1967). On the historical circumstances of the emergence of this literature, see most notably Joseph Dan, *Apocalypse Then and Now* (Hertzeliya: Yediot Aḥronot, 2000), 49–92 [Hebrew]; idem, "Armilus: The Jewish Anti-Christ and the Origins and Dating of the Sefer Zerubbavel," in *Toward the Millennium: Messianic Expectations from the Bible to Waco* (ed. P. Schäfer and M. Cohen; Leiden: Brill, 1998), 73–104; idem, *The Hebrew Story in the Middle Ages* (Jerusalem: Keter, 1974), 43–46 [Hebrew]; Martha Himmelfarb, "Sefer Zerubbabel," in *Rabbinic Fantasies* (ed. D. Stern and M. J. Mirsky; New Haven: Yale UP, 1990), 67–70; Robert L. Wilken, "The Restoration of Israel in

Moreover, the martyrology's use of the "annunciation" scene in *The Story of the Ten Martyrs* betrays an interest in the origins of the messiah akin to the portrait of Menaḥem son of Amiel and his mother Ḥephtzibah in the seventh-century Hebrew apocalypse *Sefer Zerubbabel*.[113] Read within this cultural context, the martyrology offers a similarly incisive critique of Byzantine Christian society in this period, as well as of the place of the Jewish community within it. It is tempting to see its virulent anti-imperial polemic as the Jewish counterpart of Christian–Jewish debates of the Late Roman and Byzantine periods.[114]

---

Biblical Prophecy: Christian and Jewish Responses in the Early Byzantine Period," in *"To See Ourselves as Others See Us": Christians, Jews, and "Others" in Late Antiquity* (ed. J. Neusner and E. S. Frerichs; Chico, Calif.: Scholars Press, 1985), 443–71, esp. 453–61; Abba Hillel Silver, *A History of Messianic Speculation in Israel* (Boston: Beacon, 1959), esp. 36–57; M. Buttenwieser, *Outline of the Neo-Hebraic Apocalyptic Literature* (Cincinnati: Jennings, 1901). On the use of this material for historical reconstruction, see Joseph Yahalom, "On the Value of Literary Sources for Clarifying Historical Questions," *Cathedra* 11 (1979): 125–36 [Hebrew].

[113] Martha Himmelfarb has rightly suggested that "the figure of Hephtzibah should be understood as a counterpart to the figure of the Virgin Mary in contemporary Byzantine culture" ("Sefer Zerubbabel," 69). On the relationship between Hephtzibah and the Virgin Mary, see Himmelfarb's fuller discussion in "The Mother of the Messiah in the Talmud Yerushalmi and Sefer Zerubbabel," in *The Talmud Yerushalmi and Greco-Roman Culture* (vol. 3; ed. P. Schäfer; Tübingen: Mohr Siebeck, forthcoming). See also Peter Schäfer, *Mirror of His Beauty: Feminine Images of God from the Bible to the Early Kabbala* (Princeton: Princeton UP, forthcoming 2002); Israel Lévi, "L'apocalypse de Zorobabel et le roi de Perse Siroès," *Revue des etudes juives* 71 (1920): 60. The birth narrative of the Davidic messiah Menaḥem is found in a number of classical rabbinic sources (e.g., *y. Ber.* 2,4 [5a]; *b. Sanh.* 98a). For the text of *Sefer Zerubbabel*, see Even Shmuel, *Midreshei Geulah*, 55–88; Jellenik, *Beit ha-Midrash*, 2.54–47; Solomon A. Wertheimer, *Batei Midrashot* (2nd ed.; Jerusalem: Mosad ha-Rav Kook, 1954), 2.497–505. For English translation, see Himmelfarb, "Sefer Zerubbabel," 71–81.

[114] For the flourishing of *Adversus Iudaeos* literature specifically in the seventh to ninth centuries in Byzantium, see especially Averil Cameron, "Disputations, Polemical Literature and the Formation of Opinion in Early Byzantine Literature," in *Dispute Poems and Dialogues in the Ancient and Medieval Near East* (Orientalia Lovaniensia Analecta 42; ed. G. J. Reinink and H. J. L. Vanstiphout; Leuven: Peeters, 1991), 91–108; Gilbert Dagron and Vincent Déroche, "Juifs et chrétiens dans l'Orient du VIIe siècle," *Travaux et Mémoires* 11 (1991): 17–273; Vincent Déroche, "La polémique anti-judaïque au VIe et au VIIe siècle, un mémento inédit, les *Kephalaia*," *Travaux et Mémoires* 11 (1991): 275–311; M. Waegemann, "Les traités adversus Iudaeos: aspects des relations judéo-chrétiens dans la monde grec," *Byzantion* 56 (1986): 195–313; Peter Hayman, "The Image of the Jew in the Syriac anti-Jewish Literature," in *To See Ourselves as Others See Us*, 423–41; David M. Olster, *Roman Defeat, Christian Response, and the Literary Construction of the Jew* (Philadelphia: U. of Pennsylvania Press, 1994), 116–83. For Jewish anti-Christian literature in this period, see Wout Jac. van Bekkum, "Anti-Christian Polemics in Hebrew Liturgical Poetry of the Sixth and Seventh Centuries," in *Early Christian Poetry* (ed. J. Den Boeft and A. Hilhorst;

Ironically, however, the narrative's repudiation of Byzantine political power reflects the same fascination with the nature of visuality that was at the stormy center of the iconoclastic debates of seventh- to ninth-century Byzantium. Indeed, the martyrology – and in particular its view of the capacity of Metatron's human form to bridge the gap between the upper and lower worlds – seems to engage fully the central questions of the acrimonious debates that shook the Byzantine Christian world concerning the role of physical representation of angels and saints in enabling human beings to come into contact with the divine.[115] Peter Brown has recently noted how "Jewish criticisms of Christian image-worship as a form of idolatry play a significant role in the literature of the 630s and 640s."[116] However, is it also possible that, far from giving voice to any ideological predilection for aniconic modes of representation that this literature so often attributes to the Jews, the redactor(s) of *The Story of the Ten Martyrs* framed the ritual of Rabbi Ishmael's mask precisely in terms of the theoretical assumptions that underlay the widespread use of iconic relics in Christian worship? Certainly its vivid account of how the Romans preserved the skin of Rabbi Ishmael's face for ritual purposes bears an uncanny resemblance to the haunting images – and the stories that surrounded them – of Christ's face that circulated throughout the East in this period, in particular the Mandylion and other similar representations on fabric and wood.[117] Like the meticulous portraits of various NT figures that filled the Christian apocrypha, the image of Rabbi

---

Leiden: Brill, 1993), 297–308; Nicholas de Lange, "A Fragment of Byzantine Anti-Christian Polemic," *JJS* 41 (1990): 92–100; idem, "Jewish Attitudes to the Roman Empire," in *Imperialism in the Ancient World* (ed. P. Garnsey and C. Whittaker; Cambridge: Cambridge UP, 1978), 255–81. See also the analysis of Jewish–Christian relations in this period in Gedaliahu G. Stroumsa, "Religious Contacts in Byzantine Palestine," *Numen* 36 (1989): 16–42.

[115] On the liturgical function of representations of angels and the significance of these images within the Iconoclastic debates, see especially Glenn Peers, *Subtle Bodies: Representing Angels in Byzantium* (The Transformation of the Classical Heritage 32; Berkeley: U. of California, 2001); idem, "Hagiographic Models of Worship of Images and Angels," *Byzantion* 68 (1998): 407–20; idem, "Imagination and Angelic Epiphany," *Byzantine and Modern Greek Studies* 21 (1997): 113–31; Ernst Kitzinger, "The Cult of Images in the Age before Iconoclasm," *Dumbarton Oaks Papers* 8 (1954): 85–150.

[116] Peter Brown, *The Rise of Western Christendom* (Oxford: Blackwell, 1996), 245. For considerations of the possible role of the Jews in the iconoclastic controversy, see also Averil Cameron, "The Language of Images: The Rise of Icons and Christian Representation," in *Changing Cultures in Early Byzantium* (Aldershot, UK: Variorum, 1996), 95–137, esp. 35–40; Vincent Déroche, "Léontios de Néapolis, *Apologie contre les juifs*," *Travaux et Mémoires* 12 (1994): 43–104; Robin Cormack, *Writing in Gold: Byzantine Society and its Icons* (London: George Philips, 1985), 106–18.

[117] See the photographs of these images that appear on cloth and wood and the essays discussing them in *The Holy Face and the Paradox of Representation* (ed. H. L. Kessler and G. Wolf; Villa Spelman Colloquia 6; ed. Bologna: Nuovo Alfa, 1998).

Ishmael painted by the martyrology can be characterized, in Gilbert Dagron's words, as "an icon in words in response to an immense desire to visualize."[118] It is fair to say, then, that at least some Jews and at least some Christians could agree that the possibility of redemption is bound up in the ritualized manipulation of these repositories of "otherworldly" presence. It would, of course, be wrong to view the martyrology's narrative of collective redemption through atoning human sacrifice as a mere derivative of the regnant Christian paradigm. Instead, what we have seen is a pointed attempt to appropriate salient elements of Christian sacred history, while still formulating innovative and even idiosyncratic claims about Rabbi Ishmael's (semi)-divine nature in distinctive literary and cultural terms.

---

[118] Gilbert Dagron, "Holy Images and Likeness," *Dumbarton Oaks Papers* 45 (1991): 25 and the primary sources cited there in n. 17.

# Jews and Heretics – A Category Error?

by

AVERIL CAMERON

The mutual relations between Christians and Jews in Late Antiquity, particularly in relation to issues of representation, cannot be taken out of the wider context of the development of early Christianity. I wish to draw attention in this paper to a tendency which might to a modern mind seem somewhat strange, even inappropriate, namely, the juxtaposition, elision, or even identification of Jews and "heretics" in a range of early Christian writing. Sometimes heretics (to adopt a simplistic term for the sake of brevity) are simply called "Jews"; often the two are juxtaposed, whether in texts or, later, in visual art, and quite often the portrayal of "heretics" is mapped onto established Christian ways of writings about Jews.[1] It can hardly be that the perpetrators did not understand that heretics and Jews were different. Rather, we face a phenomenon that is, I shall suggest, at times a deliberate strategy, at times an almost subconscious way of writing or of thinking, part of an early Christian cast of mind the origins of which can be seen at a very early date and which, once having taken root, became ever more strongly established. As has often been noted, the very pervasiveness of these ways of expression make the task of finding heresy, insofar as it really existed, or assessing the "real" relations between Christians and Jews and the "real" Jewish presence in the early Christian and late antique periods extremely difficult.[2] When, therefore, Christian authors seem to equate Jews and heretics, to call heretics "Jews," or to include the Jews within the lists of heresies set out in Christian heresiologies, they are not guilty of a category error, as we

---

[1] The latter practice is well argued in the case of Ephrem the Syrian by Christine C. Shepardson, "'Exchanging reed for reed': Mapping contemporary heretics onto Biblical Jews in Ephrem's *Hymns on Faith*," *Hugoye: Journal of Syriac Studies* [http://syrcom.cua.edu/hugoye] vol. 5, no. 1 (2002).

[2] For Jewish and Christian relations see also Shepardson, "Exchanging reed for reed"; for the same problem at a later period see my paper "Blaming the Jews: the seventh-century invasions of Palestine in context," *Travaux et Mémoires* 14 (2002), 57–78.

might at first think.[3] Rather, a more complex and more insidious process is going on, whereby both groups are made to partake of the same range of characteristics, with predictable results.

Examples can be found across a wide chronological range of early Christian and patristic writing. Heretics had long been objectified and made the subjects of condemnation and ridicule when, as reported in a late-eighth-century text, Theodosius II erected statues of heretics in the forum of Constantinople so that they could be mocked and dishonored by passers-by.[4] In the ninth-century Byzantine psalters the failed iconoclasts, assimilated to the category of heretics, are depicted in caricature fashion in the act of attacking images.[5] Heretics had acquired a visual presence in Byzantine art.[6] But they were also conflated with Jews. The same sets of manuscript illustrations include stereotyped depictions of Jews; contemporary texts portray Jews attacking Christian icons and rejecting the image of Christ.[7] In these iconographic programmes, as Kathleen Corrigan noted, the opponents most often attacked are not the iconoclasts but the Jews.[8] The arguments implied in the visual illustrations are the same as those in the *Adversus Iudaeos* literature, of which there is a rich amount surviving from the pre-iconoclastic and into the iconoclastic period. Perhaps, then, it simply made sense as a technique of abuse to draw on this now fully worked out tradition and to collapse iconoclasts, branded as "heretics," into the category of "Jews."[9] In the late eighth century an iconophile pamphlet says of the iconoclasts that they have "perpetrated the work of the Jews."[10] They are likened to the Jewish priests conspiring against Christ. In the same work we find a familiar

---

[3] Famously, John of Damascus added Islam to the list of Christian heresies which he had inherited from many previous heresiologists, not least Epiphanius; the salient feature is not so much whether Islam was in fact a Christian heresy, or whether it could be regarded as one, but that this was the natural way of writing about a sect of any kind of which one disapproved. For the text see R. Le Coz, *Jean Damascène. Écrits sur l'Islam*, SC 383 (Paris, 1992), with discussion.

[4] *Parastaseis Syntomoi Chronikai* 39, in fact so that passers-by could "shit, piss and spit" on them; see Richard Lim, *Public Disputation, Power and Social Order in Late Antiquity* (Berkeley, 1995), 148, n. 209.

[5] See Kathleen Corrigan, *Visual Polemics in the Ninth-Century Byzantine Psalters* (Cambridge, 1992) and further below.

[6] C. Walter, "Heretics in Byzantine art," *Eastern Churches Review* 3 (1970), 40–49.

[7] For a discussion see Corrigan, *Visual Polemics*, 29 ff. After the end of iconoclasm in 843, artists like the illustrator of the Chludov Psalter depicted the defeat of the iconoclasts, whom they characterized as "simoniacs, sorcerers who are inspired by demons, and, especially, [whom they] likened to the Jews" (Corrigan, *Visual Polemics*, 27).

[8] Corrigan, *Visual Polemics*, 5.

[9] See Corrigan, *Visual Polemics*, 5.

[10] *Adv. Const. Caball.*, PG 95.333A–336B in Corrigan, *Visual Polemics*, 31, n. 23.

motif: the very idea of iconoclasm was put into the minds of the Byzantine emperors by the Jews.

Kathleen Corrigan asks why it was that the illustrations in the ninth-century psalters concentrate so heavily on Jews: "one wonders what purpose such an anti-Jewish polemic would have served in the ninth century."[11] Others have wondered why the Christian writers of the period continued to focus on arguments against Judaism rather than on Islam.[12] But we are concerned here not with that issue but with Jews and heretics, and Corrigan shows well how particular passages in the Psalms, such as Ps 68.22, were turned against the iconoclasts by adapting familiar anti-Jewish themes. In the illustration in the Chludov Psalter of the verse at Ps 68.22, "they gave me also gall for my food and made me drink vinegar for my thirst," "Jewish" figures hold the lance and offer the sponge to Christ on the cross, while in parallel two iconoclasts obliterate an image of Christ below.[13] By this date a dense texture of anti-Jewish argument had evolved, and it was therefore perhaps to be expected that this should be utilized in relation to the highly tendentious argument over Christian images. A well-established repertoire of scriptural passages and interpretations relating to Jews and Judaism could be drawn upon to suggest much more wide-ranging and sometimes not obviously relevant Christian lessons. That this was so in visual art as well as in literature, is also argued by Leslie Brubaker in her recent book on the Paris MS of the homilies of Gregory of Nazianzus.[14] Anti-Jewish themes, rhetoric, and vocabulary had certainly become a standard feature, not only in the *Adversus Iudaeos* texts, but also in almost every other kind of Byzantine text.[15] It is easy to see how the confusion, or rather the strategic conflation, between "heretical" iconoclasts and Jews arose in the minds of writers and artists alike. Modern discussion is prone to focus on the question of what, if anything, this can tell us about the actual Jewish presence in the period of iconoclasm, but the prior need is to explore how and why anti-Jewish and anti-heretical themes were so closely intertwined.

The combination can be found from a very early stage. Eusebius takes it for granted, stating in the opening paragraph of the *Ecclesiastical History* that an avowed aim of his is to write about both heretics and

---

[11] See however G. Dagron, "Judaïser," *Travaux et Mémoires* 11 (1991), 359–80; Averil Cameron, "Byzantines and Jews: Some recent work on early Byzantium," *BMGS* 20 (1996), 249–74, at 270–74.

[12] See Cameron, "Blaming the Jews," 77.

[13] Fol. 67r; Corrigan, *Visual Polemics*, 30, with fig. 42.

[14] Leslie Brubaker, *Vision and Meaning in Ninth-Century Byzantium* (Cambridge, 1999).

[15] See Cameron, "Blaming the Jews," especially part III.

Jews, to record "the names, the number and the age of those who ... have heralded themselves as the introducers of knowledge, falsely so-called, ravaging the flock of Christ unsparingly, like grim wolves. To this I will add the fate which has beset the whole nation of the Jews from the moment of their plot against our Saviour."[16] Heretics and Jews are linked as purveyors of false knowledge and enemies of the truth. It is the aim of the *HE*, as of Eusebius' two later apologetic works, the *Praeparatio Evangelica* and the *Demonstratio Evangelica*, to expose how this conjunction worked in practice. The first four chapters of *HE* I set out the role of Moses and the Old Testament history of Christianity, fore-shadowing the argument developed more fully in these later works.[17] The association of Jews and pagans is endorsed by Eusebius, when he retells the story of the martyrdom of Polycarp in Smyrna and recalls the role of the crowd of pagans and Jews who pressed for Polycarp's death.[18] Eusebius can stand as the exemplar of other fourth-century writers: Jews, heretics and pagans are grouped together to represent three kinds of error, with the "blindness" of the Jews in relation to their own Scriptures being adduced as proof.[19]

Christian attempts to brand and refute wrong belief, whether in the form of paganism, "heresy," or Judaism, developed in tandem. In the mid-second century, Justin was one early Christian writer who composed a treatise against the Jews, in his *Dialogue with Trypho*, as well as apologies or refutations of pagan belief. Eusebius mentions a whole string of works by him and cites praise of him by Irenaeus in his *Adversus Haereses* for his arguments against Marcion in the late second century.[20] Arguments against paganism, against Jews, and against heretics thus go hand-in-hand.[21] The same is true when Eusebius reaches Hegesippus,

---

[16] *HE* I.1, translation from Eusebius, *The Ecclesiastical History,* vol. 1, translated by Kirsopp Lake, Loeb Classical Library (Cambridge, 1926).

[17] In general see A. Kofsky, *Eusebius of Caesarea against Paganism* (Leiden, 2000).

[18] *HE* IV.15.26–29.

[19] The connection, and the development, is well put by C. R. Phillips, "The sociology of religious knowledge in the Roman Empire to AD 284," *ANRW Prinzipat* II.16.3 (1986), 2677–2773, at 2733–52.

[20] *HE* IV.18.

[21] A helpful work among the extensive literature on Christian attitudes towards Jews is Judith Lieu's "History and theology in Christian views of Judaism," in *The Jews among Pagans and Christians in the Roman Empire*, ed. Judith Lieu, John North and Tessa Rajak (London, 1992), 79–96. For the permeability between apologetic and polemical writings in relation to pagans, Jews, and heretics see Averil Cameron, "Apologetics in the Roman empire – a genre of intolerance?" in *"Humana sapit": Études d'Antiquité tardive offertes à Lellia Cracco Ruggini*, ed. Jean-Michel Carrié and Rita Lizzi Testa, Bibliothèque de l'Antiquité Tardive 3 (Paris, 2002), 219–27. The same feature is noted by Judith Lieu, *Image and Reality: The Jews in the World of the*

another second-century author: five books by him are mentioned. Hegesippus, says Eusebius, set out the sects (*haireseis*) of his time; these included some fairly exotic ones, as well as Marcionists, Valentinians, and Basilidians. But Hegesippus also described the sects among the Jews: "Essenes, Galilaeans, Hemerobaptists, Masbothei, Samaritans, Sadducees and Pharisees."[22] Melito of Sardis (d. ca. 190) is another writer who combined writing about the Jews and about "heretical" sects.[23] There are also Apollinarius' five books: *Against the Greeks*, two *Against the Jews*, and a treatise against the sects of the Phrygians and the Montanists.[24] Tatian, another who wrote *Against the Greeks*, included the soon-to-be-standard Christian argument that Moses and the Hebrew prophets preceded the Greek philosophers.[25] He was himself regarded as a heretic, founder of the Encratites, but that did not stop Eusebius from praising him for his writings.

Book IV of Eusebius' *Ecclesiastical History*, where he records all these writers, concludes with Bardesanes and his Syriac writings against the Marcionites. In Book V he reaches Irenaeus, whose work *Adversus Haereses* he has several times quoted already. It would be tedious to continue further, except to reiterate that the works of earlier writers who had attempted to combat "error" feature very largely indeed in the *Ecclesiastical History*, a work whose main aim is to record the triumph of true belief over error, whether that error is pagan, Jewish, or sectarian. Thus Eusebius approvingly quotes from a predecessor who had linked together in one passage Justin, Miltiades, Tatian, Clement, Irenaeus, and Melito as writers who "announced Christ as God and man."[26] The range of the opponents attacked by these writers was wide: those who needed to be refuted included, for example, some who turned to logic and geometry for the truth; they, too, are called "heretics" (followers of a *hairesis*).[27]

Jews and Judaism are absent from the index of a recent book on Eusebius by Doron Mendels, *The Media Revolution of Early Christianity*, though it contains a relevant chapter on Eusebius' treatment of orthodoxy and heresy. Mendels draws compelling attention to Eusebius' rhetorical strategies, to his perception of the need to "sell" Christianity in a

---

*Christians in the Second Century* (Edinburgh, 1996), e.g. 104 ff., 160, an excellent discussion, pointing out at p. 105 that Tertullian, for instance, reused earlier anti-Jewish material in his *Against Marcion*.

[22] *HE* IV.22.7.
[23] *HE* IV.26.1–2.
[24] *HE* IV.27.
[25] *HE* IV.29.7.
[26] *HE* V.28.5.
[27] *HE* V.28.13–15.

competing market environment for religion in the Roman Empire.[28] Not only heresiology but also this new "history" of the church sought to impose a master narrative or success story of Christianity. The techniques by which Eusebius highlights true belief and castigates sects of all kinds have been well described in Mendels' book and elsewhere. We should note however that all that Mendels says about Eusebius' treatment of heresy applies equally to Judaism and indeed also to paganism. What may seem now to be distinct and separate sets of issues – Christianity versus Judaism, Christianity in relation to polytheism, and true as opposed to "false" belief within Christianity – were close together in the minds of early Christians and approached in very similar ways. Naturally the edges became blurred.

In particular, the same language was employed. Mendels argues that Eusebius' techniques in relation to heretics involve a resort to a "rhetoric of hysteria," which Mendels identifies as equally common in modern media and communication.[29] It involves labeling and the use of negative vocabulary, terms, and concepts such as "filth," "disease," "poison," "insanity," "fanaticism," "corruption," "evil," and so on. In fact, this is the language of binary opposition that is standard when labeling one's enemies as "the other": the language of disqualification.[30] We can add to this the habitual resort to genealogies of heresy and to the concept of the "arch-heretic" from whom all others are descended.[31] This is the language of polemic, which we find employed in possibly even more strident terms in relation to the iconoclastic/iconophile texts with which I started this

---

[28] D. Mendels, *The Media Revolution of Early Christianity: An Essay on Eusebius's Ecclesiastical History* (Grand Rapids, Mich., 1999); cf. R. Stark, *The Rise of Christianity: A Sociologist Reconsiders History* (Princeton, 1996).

[29] Mendels, *Media Revolution*, 145–47.

[30] See Lieu, *Image and Reality*, 147; see also Judith M. Lieu, "The forging of Christian identity," *Mediterranean Archaeology* 11 (1998), 71–82. For a discussion of theories of deviance, including labeling-theory, see Jack T. Sanders, *Schismatics, Sectarians, Dissidents, Deviants: The First One Hundred Years of Jewish–Christian Relations* (London, 1993), 129–51; on the "other," see M. de Certeau, *Heterologies: Discourse on the Other*, trans. Brian Massumi (Manchester, 1986).

[31] In general, see A. Le Boulluec, *La notion de l'hérésie dans la littérature grecque, IIe–IIIe siècle*, 2 vols. (Paris, 1985); and e.g., V. Burrus, *The Making of a Heretic* (Berkeley, 1995). For the genealogical argument, see especially D. Kimber Buell, *Making Christians: Clement of Alexandria and the Rhetoric of Legitimacy* (Princeton, 1999) and S. Elm, "The polemical use of genealogies: Jerome's classification of Pelagius and Evagrius Ponticus," *Studia Patristica* 33 (1997), 311–18; this is of course the mirror image of the idea of an unbroken apostolic tradition: cf. Lieu, *Image and Reality*, 177 ff., 241, 253 ff.

paper.[32] It applies with equal frequency, and often in the same contexts, to writing about the Jews. To take only one closely related example, Gohei Hata has recently analyzed Eusebius' own techniques in connection with Jews, and specifically his polemical and tendentious handling of Josephus, in the *Ecclesiastical History*.[33] If we looked more closely at some of the writers mentioned above we would find similar resemblances.

So we have conflation between the groups: Jews, heretics, and "Greeks," or pagans. It is also striking that, as Le Boulluec argues, the problem tended to be posed in moral, historical, and psychological terms rather than in terms of doctrine.[34] Such groups are seen as a danger threatening the Christian community, and it is this moral and psychological understanding that stands behind the constant terminology of disease, bestiality, and irrationality.[35] It is the same with Ephrem's representation of the Jews[36] and with the genealogical model already mentioned. While the literature talks of groups and "sects," emphasizing their moral threat to the Christian community, it also focuses on individuals: heresy was personalized.[37]

Given such a background, it becomes easier to understand how Jews had come to be included among heretics in later heresiological writings. One such example can be found in the work of Filastrius of Brescia, writing in the late fourth century, perhaps in AD 385, whose work on heresies seeks to refute twenty-eight Jewish and one hundred and twenty-eight Christian heresies. In his recent book on northern Italy in this period, Mark Humphries refers to this as "a familiar trope in anti-heretical works: the association of Jews and heretics as a common enemy."[38] Interestingly, though, he is unwilling to draw the obvious conclusion. He refers to the feature as "harping on the Jews and their faults" and accuses Bishop Zeno of Verona of constantly returning to the

---

[32] See Averil Cameron, "Texts as weapons: polemic in the Byzantine dark ages," in *Literacy and Power in the Ancient World*, ed. Alan K. Bowman and Greg Woolf (Cambridge, 1994), 198–215.

[33] G. Hata, "Eusebius and Josephus: the way Eusebius misused and abused Josephus," *Patristica: Proceedings of the Colloquia of the Japanese Society for Patristic Studies*, supp. 1 (2001), 49–66.

[34] Le Boulluec, *La notion d'hérésie*, II, 414–38.

[35] On bestiality, see Le Boulluec, *La notion d'hérésie*, II, 317 f.; on irrationality, 332–60; on the psychological portrait of heretics, 414–16.

[36] Shepardson, "Exchanging reed for reed."

[37] See F. Wisse, "The use of early Christian literature as evidence for inner diversity and conflict," in *Nag Hammadi, Gnosticism and Early Christianity*, ed. Charles W. Hedrick and Robert Hodgson Jr. (Peabody, Mass., 1986), 177–90.

[38] Mark Humphries, *Communities of the Blessed: Social Environment and Religious Change in Northern Italy, AD 200–400* (Oxford, 1999), 212, citing Ambrose, *De Fide* 2.15.130.

theme. He then goes on to ask what, if anything, can be deduced from Filastrius about actual Jewish–Christian relations in the region in the late fourth century. Quoting Robert Markus, but with evident reluctance, he says that "it is hard to see the use of the Jews here as anything other than a 'hermeneutical device [used] to define a premature closure of biblical discourse.'"[39] I have not singled out Humphries for particular criticism: the dilemma (whether to take the texts as representing "real" conflict or "real" situations) is only too familiar to anyone who has studied the formal anti-Jewish dialogues.[40] Or, indeed, to anyone who has studied Christian–Jewish relations in the Roman Empire since the classic work by Marcel Simon.[41] Humphries just happens to provide a good example: like many other scholars before him, when faced with a text such as that of Filastrius and by similar passages in contemporary treatises and homilies such as those by Zeno, he asks himself first and foremost what they might tell us about real Jews and real Christian heresies, even though he is well aware of the role of literary patterning and tropes. He goes on in the same passage to refer to a tenth-century *Life* of Innocentius of Tortona, which refers to the conversion by the saint of many pagans and Jews, but again reluctantly discards it as "riddled with anachronisms." These "anachronisms" turn out to include the notorious story of Constantine's baptism by St. Sylvester, hardly an "anachronism" so much as an interesting but in no way historical unfolding of Christian legend.[42]

It is not unnatural that historians find themselves struggling with the later texts. Yet the intertwining of Jews and heretics as equally representative of error starts very early in Christian writing. The process is also more complex than has been suggested so far. Jews, Christian heretics, and pagan philosophers alike are subjected to analysis as sectarians, that is, as groups to be identified and classified, over whom the superiority of orthodox belief has to be asserted.

I will start with the apologists, though the New Testament texts can also offer instructive examples. Christian apologetic and anti-Jewish writing developed together: in Justin's *Dialogue with Trypho*, for example, the presentation of Christianity as the best philosophy slides into a denunciation of Judaism, while in the *Epistle to Diognetus* pagans

---

[39] Humphries, *Communities of the Blessed*, 213. Cf. R. Markus, *Signs and Meaning: World and Text in Ancient Christianity* (Liverpool, 1996), 24.

[40] See also Shepardson, "Exchanging reed for reed."

[41] Marcel Simon, *Verus Israel: A Study of the Relations between Christians and Jews in the Roman Empire (AD 135–425)*, trans. H. McKeating (Oxford, 1986), originally published in 1948.

[42] Humphries, *Communities of the Blessed*, 213–14.

and Jews are attacked together.[43] Tertullian writes of an "alliance" between Marcion and the Jews.[44] Clement of Alexandria likens heretics to pagans in the *Stromateis*, and Hippolytus accused heretics of plagiarizing the Greeks (that is, pagans).[45] As noted above, Judith Lieu has pointed to numerous examples where apologetic writers draw on a common stock of argument and terminology whether writing of Jews or of heretics. Christian texts thus constantly elided what to a modern reader may seem obviously different categories.

Part of the explanation certainly has to do with the Greek word *hairesis*, meaning "sect" or "group," rather than "heresy" in the fully developed sense of wrong belief. *Hairesis* was of course applied to philosophers and used in medical texts, especially Galen's *De Sectis*. In the New Testament it is already used for factions within the church (in Galatia, for example).[46] Equally, it is used in the Acts of the Apostles for groups within Judaism: Nazarenes, Pharisees and Sadducees.[47] The same phenomenon is found in the work of Philo and Josephus. The latter likens the "three sects of Judaism" – the Essenes, the Pharisees, and the Sadducees – to philosophical groups – Stoics and Pythagoreans.[48] Justin is another who uses *haireseis* of the Jews.[49] Christians themselves are referred to as a *hairesis* at Acts 28:22; soon it became vitally important to transfer the label elsewhere in order to counter the accusation that Christianity was itself a sect of Judaism. During the second century the word is used both neutrally and pejoratively, though Heinrich von Staden writes of a change which gave rise to "elaborate new taxonomies of doctrinal and institutional error."[50] The change was not, however, a simple chronological one; neutral uses of the term continued alongside pejorative ones. When Eusebius uses it in the *Ecclesiastical History* he is therefore drawing on a substantial earlier body of usage. It has been

---

[43] For Justin, see Tessa Rajak, "Talking at Trypho," in *Apologetics in the Roman Empire: Pagans, Jews and Christians*, ed. Mark Edwards, Martin Goodman, and Simon Price, in association with Christopher Rowland (Oxford, 1999), 59–80.

[44] *Adv. Marc.* III.6.2, cf. 23.1.

[45] See Le Boulluec, *La notion d'hérésie*, II, 312 f.; for Hippolytus see G. Vallée, *A Study in Anti-Gnostic Polemics: Irenaeus, Hippolytus and Epiphanius*, Studies in Christianity and Judaism I (Waterloo, Ont., 1981), 48.

[46] Gal. 5:20; cf. 2 Peter 2:1, Tit. 3:9 (*hairetikos*), 1 Cor. 11:18–19 (*schismata* at Corinth). See H. von Staden, "Hairesis and heresy: the case of the *haireseis iatrikai*," in *Jewish and Christian Self-Definition*, vol. 3, *Self-definition in the Graeco-Roman world*, ed. Ben F. Meyer and E. P. Sanders (London, 1982), 76–100, at 99; for the term see also M. Simon, "From Greek *hairesis* to Christian heresy," in *Early Christianity and the Classical Intellectual Tradition*, ed. W. Schoedel and R. Wilken (Paris, 1979), 101–16.

[47] Von Staden, "Hairesis and heresy," 96 f.

[48] Le Boulluec, *La notion d'hérésie*, I, 37 f.

[49] Le Boulluec, *La notion d'hérésie*, I, 38 (Justin, *Dial.* 80.2–4).

[50] Von Staden, "Hairesis and heresy," 98.

argued, for instance by Robert Markus, that Eusebius saw a change towards corruption and error in the church as being marked first by the reign of Trajan and then evident again in the third century;[51] this explains why the concept of heresy in the *Ecclesiastical History* is particularly developed in relation to the third-century church. However even at this point there is still some conflation between a Christian "heresy" and "sects" of other kinds. According to Eusebius' later *Life of Constantine*, Constantine himself addressed the problem of heresy, or perhaps better, "sects," in similar language.[52] He names his targets as Novatians, Valentinians, Marcionites, Paulians, and Cataphrygians. They are "the enemies of the truth," guilty of crimes, a kind of disease, and so on. In his own introduction to the emperor's words Eusebius calls them false prophets and ravening wolves (Matt 7:15-16), and in his conclusion to it he calls them "heterodox" and "schismatic." The penalty imposed by Constantine is confiscation of their churches and a ban on assembly; the language is equally harsh. It is interesting to note that Constantine himself refers to them both as "heretics" and as "those who constitute the *haireseis*." According to Eusebius, the world now having been settled in the direction of right belief after the Council of Nicaea, the emperor logically turned to the remaining sects, which like wild animals were attacking the civilized community. In the early stages of the Arian controversy, before the Council, when Constantine had written his famous letter to Alexander and Arius, he urged the parties to come together and likened them to philosophers who disagree: here, again as quoted by Eusebius in the *Life of Constantine*, he used the language of medicine and cure, but as yet he explicitly denied the existence of a new *hairesis* or schism.[53] We seem to be witnessing terminology in transition.

With this background I want to turn to a well-known text which can otherwise seem rather puzzling. This is the *Panarion*, or "Medicine Chest" against heresy, an aggressive condemnation of deviation from orthodox Christianity written in the 370s by Epiphanius, bishop of Constantia (Salamis) in Cyprus.

The *Panarion* was preceded by an earlier but less elaborate doctrinal treatise by Epiphanius known as the *Ancoratus*, or "Well-Anchored Man," and claims to be a compendium of remedies against heresy on the pattern of classical treatises against poisonous snakes. It follows in part the example of earlier works of Christian heresiology, though it is more ambitious and in some ways more complex in scale. It was to prove

---

[51] R. Markus, "The problem of self-definition: From sect to church," in *Jewish and Christian Self-Definition*, vol. 1, *The Shaping of Christianity in the Second and Third Centuries*, ed. E. P. Sanders (London, 1980), 1–15.

[52] *VC* III.63–66.

[53] *VC* II.64–72, esp. 70.

highly influential for later heresiologists and is for example the basis of the classic compilation on heresies by John of Damascus. Eighty heresies are enumerated, after the number of concubines in the Song of Songs,[54] Epiphanius' point being that the concubines are alien to the one undefiled "dove," or lawful wife, which is the church. However Epiphanius is not consistent in his use of the two models of medical treatise and scriptural antecedent, and scholars have commonly complained of his failure to follow through as well as about his flat literary style and his disagreeable and quarrelsome mentality.[55] He was clearly a difficult person, and he occupied a place in the forefront of contemporary church rivalries.[56] Critics have not been kind to him. A not infrequent view is that he was "narrow" and not very well trained in Christian *paideia*.[57] He was certainly forthright: his imagery applied to heretics likens them to snakes, weeds, and poisons; he also accuses them of being proud and of being seducers.[58] In relation to heresy, one scholar says "he has no equal in the history of heresiology for the art of insulting."[59] Epiphanius' inconsistency is noted in the main study of him by Aline Pourkier, who suggests that he has not understood his sources properly.[60] These and other contradictions in the work have also contributed to an uncertainty as to his actual intentions. But before writing him off we ought surely to give him the courtesy of a more sympathetic reading.[61]

---

[54] Song of Songs 6:8–9; *Pan.*, Proem I.1.3.

[55] On his style, see R. Lyman, "The making of a heretic: The Life of Origen in Epiphanius, *Panarion* 64," *Studia Patristica* 31 (1997), 445–51, at 446. She connects this with Epiphanius' ascetic aim, and sees it in part as representing an alternative to reliance on *paideia*. See R. Lyman, "Origen as ascetic theologian: orthodoxy and heresy in the fourth-century church," in *Origeniana Septima. Origenes in den Auseinandersetzungen des 4. Jahrhunderts*, ed. W.A. Bienert and U. Kühneweg (Leuven, 1999), 189–84; also R. Lyman, "Ascetics and bishops: Epiphanius and orthodoxy," in *Orthodoxie, christianisme, histoire*, ed. S. Elm, E. Rébillard, and A. Romano, Collection de l'École française de Rome 270 (Rome, 2000), 149–61.

[56] See Elizabeth A. Clark, *The Origenist Controversy: The Cultural Construction of an Early Christian Debate* (Princeton, 1992).

[57] Lyman, "Ascetics and bishops," 154 f.

[58] Lyman, "The making of a heretic," 448, n. 16.

[59] Vallée, *A Study*, 73.

[60] Aline Pourkier, *L'hérésiologie chez Épiphane de Salamine* (Paris, 1992), 96; Frances Young, "Did Epiphanius know what he meant by 'heresy'?" *Studia Patristica* 17.1 (1982), 199–205. J. F. Dechow, in *Dogma and Mysticism in Early Christianity: Epiphanius and the Legacy of Origen* (Macon, Ga., 1988), focuses on issues of spirituality and especially on the topic of Origenism, for which *Pan.* 64 is central. For uncertainty surrounding the interpretation of Epiphanius, see however Pourkier, 95. For Epiphanius and Origen see also Lyman, "Origen as ascetic theologian."

[61] F. Williams, *The Panarion of Epiphanius of Salamis*, 2 vols. (Leiden, 1987), I, xix–xxvi is a fair assessment.

The puzzling passages come in the first preface, *Anacephalaeosis* I (or "Contents"), and the second preface to the work, where Epiphanius refers to the "mothers of heresies" from which all the rest have sprung. These are defined chronologically and are named in order as "Barbarism" (comprising the ten generations from Adam to Noah), "Scythianism" (from Noah until the building of the Tower of Babylon, and then until the migrations to Europe), Hellenism (the time of idolatry, from the father of Abraham to classical Greece), and Judaism, which came through Moses. The fifth, Samaritanism, derived from Judaism.[62] Epiphanius discusses each of these in more detail before launching into the individual Christian sects or heresies which make up the total number of eighty. Again, he is not consistent even with himself. Samaritanism is counted, but differs from the rest in that it is not cited in the ultimate source (as named at *Anaceph.* 4.2), which is Colossians 3.11: "In Christ there is no barbarian, Scythian, Greek nor Jew, but a new creation."[63] This text also required that Epiphanius name the mothers of heresies in the same order. But Samaritanism was needed in order to arrive at the number of eighty, the total that includes the "mothers of heresies" as well as the heresies themselves, and it has to be placed here since it is clearly a Jewish and not a Christian sect. It is named as one of the five in proem I, but separated from the first four in the summary and in proem II. At proem I.5.2 it is included as one of the "mothers." Within the categories of "Greeks," or Hellenism, and Judaism specific *haireseis* are mentioned: Pythagoreans, Platonists (as though they are all in the past), Stoics and Epicureans, and seven sects among the Jews: Scribes, Pharisees, Sadducees, Hemerobaptists, Ossenes (Essenes?), Nasareans, and Herodians. Again, at other passages in the text Epiphanius changes the order and is therefore inconsistent again.[64] From his sources, which are partly lost (they include Hippolytus and Hegesippus), he has taken the Jewish "sects" from different authors, and mixed them up in the process; the same is true of the Greek "sects." Vallée comments on the "problematic" inclusion by Epiphanius of pre-Christian errors or sects, on the grounds that they are historical periods rather than sects or heresies: hitherto, he says, "nobody has explained why this is included."[65] He

[62] See *Pan.*, proem I.3.2–3; *Anaceph.* I.1–4, 9; proem II.1–4, 9, *Epiphanius* I, ed. K. Holl, GCE 25 (Leipzig, 1915); cf. trans. Williams (n. 61). The structure of Epiphanius' work is certainly far from straightforward. It has seven *Anacephalaeoseis* arranged at various points through the work, though these may not be authentic.

[63] Cf. Gal. 3:28 for another version.

[64] Pourkier, *L'hérésiologie*, 96.

[65] Vallée, *A Study*, 75 f., citing for opposing views E. Moutsoulas, "Der Begriff 'Häresie' bei Epiphanius von Salamis," *Studia Patristica* 8, TU 93 (Berlin, 1966), 86–107: E. Riggi, "Il termine 'hairesis' nell'accezione di Epifanio di Salamina (*Pan.*, t.1; *De Fide*)," *Salesianum* 29 (1967), 3–27.

suggests that Epiphanius has "broadened" the concept of heresy to include Jews and pagans, by turning heresiology into a type of history.[66] One could argue that Eusebius had already done the same, and more overtly. But the overall point is sound: in Epiphanius' mind, heresy represents all deviation from the primeval unity, represented by Adam. In other words, heresy is part not so much of history as such but of the sinfulness of humanity.

Adam, Epiphanius says, was "simple and innocent, without any other name. He had received no surname derived from any doctrine or view or distinction of life, [but] was called simply 'Adam,' meaning 'man'."[67] The "mothers of heresies" are the alien influences which in chronological order demonstrated deviation from the original state.[68] More than that, they themselves were the origin of, and gave rise to, the Christian heresies which succeeded them; in other words, we have here a *traditio* or *successio haereticorum*, an expanded genealogy of error traceable from the time of Adam to the present, Epiphanius' own day.[69] According to a recent study, it was not until Theodoret of Cyrrhus in the fifth century that heresies were grouped doctrinally rather than genealogically.[70] In Epiphanius we see, as it were, the apogee of the earlier scenario. The first twenty chapters of the *Panarion* deal with pre-Christian heresy, the first sectarian after Christ being Simon Magus, who is discussed in ch. 21. In a sense, allowing for Epiphanius' certainly clumsy presentation, we are given a more personalized version of Eusebius' view of religious development, the latter having prefaced his history of the church from the time of Christ in *HE* I.2–4 with an exposition of the antiquity of Christianity beginning from the creation of the world, whereas Epiphanius' story of heresy, or rather of error, begins explicitly and in detail with Adam, the first man.

As I have argued, Epiphanius certainly had antecedents, even if not in exactly the same formulation. The "mothers of heresies" recall Hippolytus, and the historical view of Christian development is already presaged in the second-century apologists. In a similar vein, Hippolytus'

---

[66] Lyman, "Ascetics and bishops," 157, also suggests that Epiphanius has extended the traditional model, but in a different way: he "has extended the traditional juridical opposition of orthodoxy and heresy as right and wrong belief into a strategic opposition of heresy and disobedience."

[67] *Pan.* 1.1 (Holl I, 173); for Adam and his sinful descendants, see Eus., *HE* I.2.

[68] Vallée, *A Study*, 67.

[69] Vallée, *A Study*, 70. On succession, see *Pan.* 9.1.1; 46.1.1. For "Ketzergeschichte," see A. Hilgenfeld, *Ketzergeschichte des Urchristentums* (Leipzig, 1888). For the genealogy idea applied to Greek philosophers, see J. Mansfeld, *Heresiography in Context. Hippolytus's* Elenchos *as a Source for Greek Philosophy* (Leiden, 1992).

[70] Helen Sillet, *Culture of Controversy: The Christological Disputes of the Early Fifth Century*, Ph.D. Diss., University of California, Berkeley (1999), 144.

*Elenchos* of heresies argues that the Greek philosophical sects were the origin (in genealogical fashion) of later heresies. Neither the Jewish nor the Greek philosophical sects are new with Epiphanius. Nor is the idea of heresies as serpents or snakes.[71] Tatian likened heresies to the devil, as later did Ephrem, and this idea is already deep-rooted in Eusebius. It is also Tatian, in his work *Against the Greeks*, who develops the theme of the dependency of Greek culture on Moses, specifically the idea that Moses came before Homer: this is the theme of "ancestral culture" which Frances Young highlights as a major theme in Christian apologetic. What we have in Epiphanius, I suggest, is not so much a broadening of earlier tendencies as a kind of consolidated statement, or development, of them.

The debate between pagans and Christians as to the primacy of Moses or Greek culture has been much discussed, and there is no need to revisit those arguments here.[72] It serves my argument, however, that in this particular instance Christians found themselves on the side of the Jews and against the pagans. Eusebius in his apologetic works, as Epiphanius here, separates the periods before and after Moses. Moses as the bringer of Judaic law stands for Judaism, whereas the time before Moses could be regarded by Christians as their own. But Epiphanius, it is worth noting, has placed "Hellenism" before "Judaism." This seems odd against the existing context, and the reason, I have suggested, is to keep to the Pauline formula which he explicitly evokes. It does not help his overall argument from a rational point of view, but it reinforces the point that while this section is in a sense historical, it is in an even deeper sense ideological. Epiphanius' Hellenism is not the same as Tatian's. For the latter, it represents not merely Greek philosophy but also the gods, mythology, drama, and legislation. For Epiphanius, Hellenism is constituted by the philosophical schools. Tatian also places Moses in the category of "barbarian wisdom," which again is not the "barbarism" of Epiphanius. In Tatian, "barbarian wisdom" embraces the story of Moses,

---

[71] See R. M. Grant, "Eusebius and Gnostic origins," in *Mélanges offerts à Marcel Simon: Paganisme, Judaisme, Christianisme* (Paris, 1978), 195–205, at 196–97; Lyman, "Origen as ascetic theologian," 189. Epiphanius is likely to have obtained his knowledge of classical treatises through a handbook or handbooks, see J. Dummer, "Ein naturwissenschaftliches Handbuch als Quelle für Epiphanius von Constantia," *Klio* 55 (1973), 289–99.

[72] See John Gager, *Moses in Greco-Roman Paganism* (New York, 1972); R. Mortley, *The Idea of Universal History from Hellenistic Philosophy to early Christian Historiography* (Lewiston, 1996), 105–16; A. Droge, *Homer or Moses? Early Christian Interpretations of the History of Culture,* Hermeneutische Untersuchungen zur Theologie 26 (Tübingen, 1989); D. Ridings, *The Attic Moses: The Dependency Theme in Some Early Christian Writers* (Göteborg, 1995); J. Waszink, "'Philosophy of the barbarians' in early Christian literature," in *Mélanges offerts à Mlle. Christine Mohrmann* (Utrecht, 1963), 41–56.

older than the Greek poets and historians, and even older than writing; Clement too has the conception of Christianity as "barbarian philosophy," which quickly gives rise to the argument from ethnicity or genealogy. Thus Christians were a people, even a "third race," whose growth was natural, a product of nature, stemming from the "simple" Adam whom Epiphanius gives us.[73] Epiphanius' model is rather different, reminding us that there could always be different formulations. But he too was sharing in the Christian project of rewriting the history of culture, which entailed engaging with all three groups – pagans (or "Greeks"), Jews and Christian heretics.

If, then, Epiphanius appears willing to place both pagan philosophy and Judaism in the category of *hairesis*, as wrong belief, this is perhaps not so strange as it first appears.

Christian writers assembled various histories from pagan, Jewish and Christian components, and I would suggest that they were more inclusive in their willingness to incorporate diverse elements than the modern usage of "heresy" will allow. It is no accident that the contributors to the recent collection edited by Mark Edwards, Martin Goodman, and Simon Price on *Apologetics in the Roman Empire*[74] found it hard to designate a distinguishable genre that could be called "apologetic." Similarly, my sense is that Christian writing about Jews and about heretics often came close together. With the passage of centuries and many more examples of Christian polemic, together with the Christian reinvention of history led by Eusebius of Caesarea, the categories merged even more. The Jews were both part of and a model for writing about Christian deviants.

We are not, then, in the presence of a category error after all, and any sense of discomfort is our own. The question therefore presents itself: what the advantage lay in such an elision?

Recent scholarship has emphasized Christianity's role among the variety of religions that characterized the Roman Empire, and the jostling for position that this necessitated.[75] My opening example of the iconophile texts from the eighth and ninth centuries vividly demonstrates how long this continued, and the extent to which, even then, Christians continued to exist in a context of religious competition. There was no comfortable moment when this situation ceased to exist; for the eight or so centuries covered in this paper, Christians went on continually reinventing their own Christian past and labeling their rivals in the hostile

---

[73] See G. G. Stroumsa, *Barbarian Philosophy: The Religious Revolution of Early Christianity* (Tübingen, 1999); Ridings, *The Attic Moses*, 24–27; on the "third race," see also Lieu, *Image and Reality*, 166 (on Aristides).

[74] Mark Edwards, et al., eds., *Apologetics in the Roman Empire* (n. 43).

[75] E.g. Stark, *The Rise of Christianity* (n. 28), and "Rodney Stark's *The Rise of Christianity*: a discussion," in *JECS* 6.2 (1998), 161–268.

or trivializing ways which were indeed often intended to make them seem quite straightforwardly demonic or ridiculous. This is as true for their picture of the Jews as it is for that of those whom they labeled Christian "heretics." It is a mistake to think that we are in the presence of three distinct strands, let alone genres, of Christian writing, concerned respectively with pagans, Jews, and heretics. Rather, I have been describing a mode of thinking, a kind of mindset and a way of describing, that informed Christian self-identity.[76] Not only were the techniques used the same, but often enough the different groups were simply mixed together in the Christian texts. It is therefore no surprise if Epiphanius' heresiology also became a model for anti-Manichaean writing, or that "Manichaean" became a label for later heretics.[77] I have argued elsewhere that at a later date anti-Jewish writing and modes of expression spilled over more and more into types of Christian writing ostensibly directed in other ways.[78] These writers at least (and there were very many of them – an increasing number as time went on) were sustained by their dogged unwillingness to accept that the ways had never parted and by their determination to take every opportunity to make sure that they did.

[76] For the latter, see Stroumsa, *Barbarian Philosophy*, chs. 9–13, "Shaping the person," especially ch. 10; connected with this is the important issue of tolerance and intolerance in early Christianity, for which see chs. 1 and 5. Also see G. Stanton and G. G. Stroumsa, eds., *Tolerance and Intolerance in Early Judaism and Christianity* (Cambridge, 1998); Cameron, "Apologetics in the Roman empire."

[77] See G. Stroumsa, "Aspects de la polémique anti-manichéenne dans l'antiquité tardive et dans l'Islam primitif," in *Savoir et Salut* (Paris, 1992), 355–77; cf. C. Riggi, *Epifanio contro Mani* (Rome, 1967).

[78] See Cameron, "Blaming the Jews," part III.

# Did Jewish Christians See the Rise of Islam?

by

## JOHN G. GAGER

My goal in this paper is to cover two related topics: (1) an epic academic controversy over a possible Jewish-Christian anti-Christian pamphlet from the tenth century, and (2) the relevance of this controversy to our understanding of Jewish Christianity in whatever form and from whatever period and how this relates to the broader question of the "Parting of the Ways."

## The Controversy: Pines, Stern, and Crone

In the 1960s, two great scholars, Shlomo Pines and Samuel Stern, came upon a little-known Muslim treatise attributed to a Mutazilite author of the late tenth century, 'Abd al-Jabbār. In 1968[1] Pines published a study of one section from al-Jabbār's treatise and summarized his results as follows: "this Moslem theologian adapted for his own purposes ... writings reflecting the views and traditions of a Jewish-Christian community."[2] This Muslim text – or better, collection of texts – consists of several parts: an attack on those Christians who, under the noxious influence of Paul, have abandoned the religion of Christ, rejected the commandments of the Mosaic law, and adopted alien Roman customs as part of their quest for power and domination; a series of polemics against a variety of Christian groups, including Jacobites, Nestorians, and orthodox Christians; a Jewish-Christian version of early Christian history; malicious stories about monks, priests, and Christian laymen, including a version of the apocryphal tale of Constantine's leprosy; and a number of gospel quotations, some canonical and others apocryphal.

---

[1] S. Pines, "The Jewish Christians of the Early Centuries of Christianity According to a New Source," in *Proceedings of the Israel Academy of Sciences and Humanities*, vol. 2 (Jerusalem, 1968), 2:237–309. The original, Hebrew version of the paper was delivered in 1966; the English version of the paper was published in 1968.

[2] Pines, "Jewish Christians," 237.

Pines concluded that the level of detailed knowledge revealed in these texts made it unlikely that they could have originated in Muslim circles. In his own words, "they could only derive from a Jewish-Christian community and were rather maladroitly and carelessly adapted by al-Jabbār for his own purposes."[3] Pines dated the production of these Jewish-Christian texts rather loosely to the late fourth, fifth, sixth, and early seventh centuries.[4] From various place-names in the texts, he located their place of origin in Mesopotamia. As he put it, the "author or authors had some connection with the region of Harran (and perhaps also with the district of Mosul)."[5] The texts were written in Syriac and later translated into Arabic.

Perhaps the most striking of Pines' claims is that some Jewish-Christian groups had managed to survive in a kind of clandestine existence throughout the Byzantine period, only to resurface briefly under the protective umbrella of early Islam. And, while he wavers somewhat, Pines is inclined to the view that these late groups represent an unbroken line of continuity with those whom he calls the earliest Jewish Christians in first-century Jerusalem: "their positions derived without hiatus, though probably ... not without some modification, from the early (or earliest) Jewish Christians."[6] As for the overall question of the "Parting of the Ways," Pines sums up their view as follows: "these Jewish-Christian authors ... had not yet quite reconciled themselves to the historical trend which led to the split and deep antagonism between Judaism and Christianity."[7]

In 1968, Pines' original collaborator on this text and one-time friend, Samuel Stern, published his own study in the *Journal of Theological Studies*.[8] In it, he asserts that Pines is "entirely wrong"[9] and that his conclusions are "based on an erroneous reading of the text."[10] Stern

---

[3] Pines, "Jewish Christians," 238.

[4] Pines, "Jewish Christians," 271.

[5] Pines, "Jewish Christians," 272. For evidence of Jewish-Christian and/or Judaizing groups in the region in the tenth century, see the discussion in P. Crone, "Islam, Judeo-Christianity and Byzantine Iconoclasm," *Jerusalem Studies in Arabic and Islam* (Jerusalem, 1980), 2:87–94. The attestation of pagan survivals in Harran deep into the Islamic period provides further evidence of the possibility of Jewish-Christian continuity in the region; see P. Chuvin, *A Chronicle of the Last Pagans* (Cambridge, 1990), 138–41.

[6] Chuvin, *Chronicle of the Last Pagans*, 269. On p. 256, Pines uses slightly different language: "the people ... *thought of themselves* as lineal descendants ...." [emphasis added].

[7] Chuvin, *Chronicle of the Last Pagans*, 257.

[8] S. Stern, "'Abd al-Jabbār's Account of How Christ's Religion was Falsified by the Adoption of Roman Customs," *JTS* n.s., 19 (1968), 128–85.

[9] Stern, "'Abd al-Jabbār's Account," 129.

[10] Stern, "'Abd al-Jabbār's Account," 129.

speaks of "Pines' fantasies,"[11] his "regrettable act of folly,"[12] "his [own] somewhat coarse imagination,"[13] and his "absurd theory about a Judaeo-Christian text in Syriac."[14] He expresses his confidence that "breaches made by my own [Stern's] analysis are sufficient ... to destroy any credit he [Pines] may have found ... There will always be people ready to believe the craziest theory, but I trust that everybody of sound judgment will be convinced that Pines' publication must not be taken seriously."[15]

This is powerful medicine. Little wonder that this volley of insults marked the end of the two men's friendship and scholarly collaboration, although the break seems to have come primarily from Stern's side.[16] As for the substance of Stern's reply, these are the essentials: certain elements in al-Jabbār's text stem from sources that were not known to Pines. Stern places great emphasis on the story of Christ's temptation by Satan, which, he insists, was taken by al-Jabbār from Muslim sources, notably Ali b. Rabban al-Tabari and al-Hasan b. Ayyub.[17] This claim forms part of Stern's larger argument that virtually all of al-Jabbār's material, including its anti-Pauline elements, finds parallels in Muslim anti-Christian polemics, some of which were based on information provided by Christian converts, while others derived from Jewish sources, most notably the *Toledoth Yeshu*.[18] As to the possible survival of Jewish Christians in the Byzantine world and beyond, Stern is simply dismissive. He refers to "Judaeo-Christians" as a despised minority group soon to disappear after the first generations.[19] And, while he holds open the theoretical possibility of Jewish-Christian sources, he regards them as improbable and un-provable.

A number of years passed before Pines returned to the controversy. In 1985[20] and 1987[21] he published two lengthy articles, the obvious goal of

---

[11] Stern, "'Abd al-Jabbār's Account," 129.

[12] Stern, "'Abd al-Jabbār's Account," 129.

[13] Stern, "'Abd al-Jabbār's Account," 183.

[14] Stern, "'Abd al-Jabbār's Account," 183.

[15] Stern, "'Abd al-Jabbār's Account," 130.

[16] This observation is based on personal conversations with Steven Wasserstrom, who has spoken with Pines' family about the controversy. Richard Walzer, a close friend of Stern's, has noted that the controversy "saddened [Stern's] life during the years 1966–1969"; quoted from R. Walzer, "Samuel Stern: In Memoriam," in *Israel Oriental Studies* II (1972), 13.

[17] Stern, "Christ's Religion," 147.

[18] Stern, "Christ's Religion," 184f.

[19] Stern, "Christ's Religion," 177.

[20] S. Pines, "Studies in Christianity and in Judaeo-Christianity based on Arabic Sources," *Jerusalem Studies in Arabic and Islam* 6 (1985), 107–61.

[21] S. Pines, "Gospel Quotations and Cognate Topics in 'Abd al-Jabbār's *Tathbit* in Relation to Early Christian and Judaeo-Christian Readings and Traditions," *Jerusalem Studies in Arabic and Islam* 9 (1987), 195–278.

which was to strengthen his position against Stern's criticisms. In his 1985 article, Pines argues that the anti-Pauline themes of the *Tathbit* show no trace of a distinctively Muslim environment and derive instead from Christian and Jewish-Christian anti-Pauline traditions, among them parodic readings of the canonical Acts of the Apostles.[22] In his 1987 article, Pines argues that a number of gospel quotations in al-Jabbār's text "appear to derive from a very early tradition which is by-passed in the canonical New Testament."[23] After showing that "one of the historical sections in the *Tathbit* contained correct information concerning an important characteristic of the Gospel according to the Hebrews," Pines concludes, against Stern, that this material "could not have been written exclusively on the basis of elements provided by the Moslem tradition on the one hand, and by the canonical Gospel and the literature of the main Christian churches on the other ...."[24]

Who, then, can we say is the winner and who the loser in this unpleasant battle? Thus far, it would appear that Stern's views have carried the day – at least in England. What I have in mind here is a brief comment by J. Carleton Paget, in his recent contribution on Jewish Christianity in *The Cambridge History of Judaism*: "Evidence of the existence of such [Jewish-Christian] sects beyond the fifth century is almost non-existent and attempts to discover such evidence, particularly in Arabic sources [referring specifically to Pines' article of 1966], has [sic] in general found few supporters."[25] However, apart from his own work, Paget is able to cite only Stern's response from 1968 and a brief essay in the same year by Ernst Bammel.[26] Hardly a mountain of scholarship! More to the point, Paget appears to have missed entirely several basic contributions to the debate: the 1985 and 1987 articles of Pines cited above, and an important essay by Patricia Crone, "Islam, Judeo-Christianity and Byzantine Iconoclasm," published in 1980.[27]

---

[22] Pines, "Arabic Sources," 142f. Pines makes hardly any direct reference to Stern in either of these articles. The one exception occurs in a footnote of the 1985 article ("Studies in Christianity," n. 124 on p. 143) in which Pines explicitly refutes Stern's claim (Stern, "Christ's Religion," 176ff.) that all of the anti-Pauline elements in the *Tathbit* find close parallels in Muslim sources. Against this criticism Pines insists that the Muslim authors cited by Stern show none of the "basic tendencies of the *Tathbit* account [such] as solidarity with the Jews ...."

[23] Pines, "Gospel Quotations," 243.

[24] Pines, "Gospel Quotations," 243.

[25] J. Carleton Paget, "Jewish Christianity," in *The Cambridge History of Judaism*, vol. 3: *The Early Roman Period*, ed. William Horbury, W. D. Davies, and John Sturdy (Cambridge: Cambridge UP, 1999), 750f.

[26] E. Bammel, "Excerpts from a new gospel?" *NovT* 10 (1968), 1–9. The only other response to Pines' 1968 article that I have been able to find is a review by F. Dreyfus, *Revue biblique* 77 (1970), 148–49.

[27] Crone, "Islam," 59–95.

Crone's main concern is with the impact of Islam on Byzantine iconoclasm. In arguing for a direct influence of Muslim iconoclasm on the Christian world, she pauses to consider what she calls the "case for an intermediary milieu" between Islam and Byzantine Christianity.[28] In her words, this intermediary vector consisted of "Judaizers who had," in her charming definition, "gone over the edge to become Judeo-Christians."[29] Against Stern and others, she points to evidence of such groups not just from the fifth century but from much later, even as far as the thirteenth century.

The evidence for a renaissance of Jewish-Christian groups under Islam, and their common cause against mainstream Christianity, lends support to Pines on a number of points. While Crone is prepared, with Stern, to see traces of the *Toledoth Yeshu* in al-Jabbār's treatise, she notes other elements in the treatise that could not have come from this source. These she locates "in a Syriac-speaking environment, none earlier than the fifth century."[30] She further characterizes these elements as "adaptations of the same Judeo-Christian polemic against Christianity."[31] Groups who would have produced or preserved such stories (here she is careful not to portray these groups as a unified phenomenon) existed in Mesopotamia and are attested as late as the tenth century, the time of al-Jabbār. Unlike Pines, she states that there is little likelihood of an unbroken chain reaching back to the first century. As she puts it, "Jewish Christianity can ... appear wherever Christianity exists, particularly where it coexists with Judaism."[32] While it is certainly true, as Pines states early in his 1968 article, that these later Jewish-Christian groups "thought of themselves as lineal descendants"[33] of primitive Jewish Christianity and as the only true Christians – thus mirroring the self-understanding of all Christian groups, including those in the mainstream – Crone is not at all inclined to infer from this that such a lineage actually exited. She clearly prefers a model of renaissance to one of continuity. On balance, she seems to get it just about right. In the end, Pines is largely vindicated, though with certain modifications.

---

[28] Crone, "Islam," 73.
[29] Crone, "Islam," 74.
[30] Crone, "Islam," 86.
[31] Crone, "Islam," 86.
[32] Crone, "Islam," 93.
[33] Pines, "Jewish Christians," 256.

## Ideology and the "Parting of the Ways"·

There are lessons to be learned in all of this. First, we are often the
victims of our own expertise. The deeper the ditch we dig, the less we are
able to see what is happening in the larger field. Specialists in the New
Testament are ignorant of later Christianity, while specialists in Islam are
ignorant of Judaism, and so on. Second, we need to be conscious of what
recent cultural critics have called "master narratives," in particular their
power to distort our picture of the past. In the present case, the master
narrative is well known, widely circulated and deeply rooted in Western
scholarship (e.g., Stern). As concerns the history of Jewish Christianity,
the master narrative can be summarized as follows: Jewish Christianity is
defined as an early movement of Torah-observant followers of Jesus; this
movement, typically seen as uniform in its beliefs and practices, quickly
became a tiny minority, swept aside by the rising tide of Gentile
Christianity; the figures of Peter and Paul played prominent roles in the
triumph of Gentile over Jewish Christianity; after all, Paul repudiates
Judaism totally, thus depriving Jewish Christians of any claim to validity
in their adherence to Jewish customs, and Peter famously abandons his
prior commitment to the laws of *kashrut*.

What is more, the source of this master narrative is unmistakable – the
canonical book of Acts – and the message of Acts is unmistakably clear:
Stephen breaks decisively with Judaism (ch. 7); Jesus' early, Torah-
observant followers – known universally as Jewish Christians – disappear
from the narrative definitively in ch. 11, following Peter's revelatory
vision which convinces him to abandon his Jewish practices. From that
point onward the narrative focuses entirely on Gentiles as the new people
of God and moves inexorably toward Rome, the new holy city. No more
Jerusalem, no more Jewish Christians, no Syria, no Egypt. Thus, in the
canonical account of Christian origins, both Judaism and Jewish
Christians are superseded and annulled, with Paul serving as the primary
spokesman for this message.[34]

But recent scholarship has, with much effort, begun to break free from
this master narrative and to challenge it at every point. Some of these
revisions are as follows:

- The early, Torah-observant followers of Jesus and their successors were not
  uniform in belief or practice.

---

[34] In general, see L. Gaston, "Anti-Judaism and the Passion Narrative in Luke and
Acts," in *Anti-Judaism in Early Christianity*, ed. P. Richardson (Waterloo, Ont., 1986),
1:127–53.

- Jewish Christians do not quickly disappear from the historical scene nor, in the regions of Syria and beyond, are they even a tiny minority or a heresy.[35]

- The evidence for the persistence of various strands of Jewish Christianity is overwhelming. Stern's view that "the Judaeo-Christians constituted a despised minority group soon to disappear altogether"[36] and Carleton Paget's claim that "Evidence for the existence of such [Jewish-Christian] sects beyond the fifth century is almost non-existent"[37] are manifestly without merit, as Crone and numerous others have shown.[38]

- Contrary to the ideologically determined picture of Acts, early Christianity did not move uni-directionally toward Rome but multi-directionally into every corner of the Mediterranean world and beyond; in Syria, the evidence rather points to the conclusion that "Jewish Christianity occupied a dominant 'orthodox' position superior to 'catholicism'."[39]

- Contrary to the portrait in Acts, Paul did not repudiate Judaism – or those whom we call Jewish Christians; instead, he focused entirely on his mission to Gentiles, insisting simply that Gentile believers had no need to observe the customs and practices of the Torah.[40] The author of Acts has deliberately drafted Paul to serve for his own anti-Jewish and anti-Jewish-Christian message. Here it is worth noting that just as Paul advocates a "two-door" road to salvation, with different paths for Jews and Gentiles, so at least some Jewish-Christian groups advanced a similar "two-doors" scenario.[41]

- Largely due to this proto-orthodox image, Paul became the arch-enemy among most Jewish-Christian groups;[42] he was seen as the apostle who had repudiated the Torah for all followers of Jesus and thereby undermined the validity of Jewish Christians. Thus, the anti-Jewish image of Paul in the *Tathbit* finds its most natural source and trajectory in the long history of Jewish-Christian anti-Paulinism.

---

[35] See the discussion of G. Strecker, "On the Problem of Jewish Christianity," in *Orthodoxy and Heresy in Earliest Christianity*, by W. Bauer, trans. R. A. Kraft and G. Kroedel (2nd ed.; Philadelphia, 1971), 241–85

[36] Stern, "Christ's Religion," 177.

[37] Paget, "Jewish Christianity," 750.

[38] Among earlier authors, see A. Harnack, *Lehrbuch der Dogmengeschichte* (4th ed; Tübingen, 1909), 2:534ff. and H. J. Schoeps, *Theologie und Geschichte des Juden-christentums* (Tübingen, 1949), 334–42. See also, A. F. J. Klijn and G. J. Reinink, *Patristic Evidence for Jewish-Christian Sects* (Leiden, 1973).

[39] So G. Strecker, "Jewish Christianity," 257.

[40] In general, see L. Gaston, *Paul and the Torah* (Vancouver, 1987); S. Stowers, *A Rereading of Romans* (New Haven, 1994); and J. Gager, *Reinventing Paul* (New York, 2000).

[41] See the remarkable and little-noticed passages in the Pseudo-Clementine writings, e.g., *Recognitions* 4.5.8 – "It is therefore the particular gift bestowed by God upon the Hebrews that they believe Moses; and the particular gift bestowed upon the Gentiles is that they love Jesus"; compare also the parallel passage in the *Homilies* 8.7.

[42] See G. Luedemann, *Opposition to Paul in Jewish Christianity* (Minneapolis, 1989).

- In similar fashion, the image of Peter, and especially of his abandonment of Jewish observances (Acts 11), reflects not historical reality but the theological interests of Acts and its author. Indeed, a radically different and fully Torah-observant image of Peter appears in the later Pseudo-Clementine writings where, in an apocryphal letter from Peter to James, Peter complains that "some have undertaken to distort my words, by certain intricate interpretations, into an abolition of the Law, as if I myself thought such a thing – God forbid! For to take such a position is to act against the Law of God which was spoken through Moses and whose eternal endurance was attested by our Lord ...."[43] Here it is difficult not to conclude that the target of "Peter's" wrath is the canonical Book of Acts!

At this point I would like to consider some of the implications of this controversy for the "Parting of the Ways." My own view is that the expression "Parting of the Ways," on the face of it a simple phrase, covers, or even obscures, a much more complex set of issues. How often do we ask the sociologist's question, "parting for whom?" Who is it, in any social system, whose interests are served by drawing sharp lines of differentiation? Sectarian groups are well known for their tendency to draw sharp lines between insiders and outsiders. But who else does so? Or, to put the matter differently, where do we encounter the rhetoric of separation in early Christian literature, whether it be separation from heretics, from pagans, from Jews, or from Jewish Christians? The answer, I would contend, is to be found in the overall message of the New Testament, at least as it has been understood in the mainstream of historic Christianity, and in the theological literature of emergent orthodoxy as embodied in the New Testament canon. We need to remind ourselves that this canon was produced several centuries after the birth of the Jesus movement and that it consciously retrojects a picture of much later times into its presentation of sacred origins. In other words, all too often we have become the victims not so much of our expertise but rather of history's winners, those who not only sought to erase the voices of the losers from our records but who also rewrote the surviving records in such a way that these others – in our case Jewish Christians of every stripe – were made to appear either as a tiny minority, or as an evanescent trace on our historical map, or as a deviation from the straight line that moves from Jesus to the position of the winners – in short, as a despicable heresy. We now understand that none of this was true in the beginning, or in neglected regions beyond the fringes of the West, but we also understand that every effort was made to make it appear as though this was the case from the very beginning. To be blunt, it was very much in the interest of triumphant Christian elites – theological as well as ecclesiastical – to stress separation and to create the image of a definitive

---

[43] See the translation and discussion in W. Meeks, *The Writings of St. Paul* (New York, 1972), 178f.

"Parting of the Ways." Here I would add that, in many cases, this rhetoric of separation needs to be seen as a defensive response to criticisms and attacks against the legitimacy of Gentile Christianity from Jewish Christians themselves. This is clearly the case, I believe, for the New Testament book of Acts.

Thus we have no choice but to read against the grain. And we can. Once we look behind the historical and theological smoke screen released by these elites, what we find among what I will call (for lack of a better term) "ordinary Christians" is plenty of evidence to suggest that for them there was no such parting at all. There is no need to rehearse here the multitude of references to the widespread and long-lasting phenomenon of Christian Judaizers.[44] How do these numerous references fit the image of a "Parting of the Ways"? In them we find Christians, most of them not heretical at all, participating in the life of synagogues well into the fourth century and beyond.

Moreover, there is every reason to suppose that most synagogues welcomed these Christian visitors. Of course, some may object that I am thinking here not about Jewish Christians but about Christian Judaizers, and others will point to Jewish texts that are distinctly unfriendly toward Jesus and his followers. As a preliminary rejoinder, I would defend my case by pointing out that, just as there was a wide range of views among Christians about Jews and Judaism, a similar diversity of opinion existed among Jews toward Christians and Christianity. The evidence of John Chrysostom's anti-Jewish sermons and the decrees of various church councils stand against any view that would see a univocal stance among Jews toward Christians. And whatever else is going on in these unfriendly Jewish texts, they clearly do not speak for all Jews, perhaps not even for many. Given this, we simply cannot speak of "Judaism" and "Christianity" as uniform entities; we must speak, rather, of Jews and Christians at different times and in different places. This may sound trivial, I know, but it is a simple lesson that gets lost all too easily. Just as in the case of Christian elites (or would-be elites), we need to be on guard against Jewish elites (or would-be elites) and their views of the "other."

Still, the question about the distinction between Christian Judaizers and Jewish Christians does raise interesting questions. How does the "Parting of the Ways" look from this perspective? Is there reason to suppose that Jewish communities might have been less open to Jewish Christians than to Christian Judaizers? Is it possible that Jewish Christians confronted mainstream Jews and Christians with a dilemma that was qualitatively different from the presence of Judaizers? Were Jewish Christians more likely to generate a response that stressed

---

[44] See J. Gager, *The Origins of Anti-Semitism. Attitudes toward Judaism in Pagan and Christian Antiquity* (New York, 1983), 117–33.

separation and produced rhetoric of parting? Recent work on the *birkat ha-minim* (especially the early versions from the Cairo Geniza that include the words *ve ha-notsrim*) has suggested that the target of this *berakhah* (blessing) was never intended to be Christians in general but only Jewish Christians, perhaps even those known as Nazarenes.[45] If this be so, is it also possible that those versions of *Toledoth Yeshu* with the bizarre story of Paul working as an undercover agent of the sages to bring about the separation of Jesus-worshippers from Jews – and thus restore peace to Israel – are about the separation not of Jews in general from all Christians but instead of some (possibly rabbinic) Jews from some (possibly Jewish) Christians?[46] The reference to Jesus-believers as those who "claim Yeshu as the Messiah," i.e., as Jewish Christians, may point in this direction, as may those rabbinic texts discussed most recently by Daniel Boyarin in his book, *Dying for God*.[47] Boyarin seems inclined to take these texts as evidence for the appeal of Christianity – writ large – in rabbinic circles, but to me these passages have always seemed to point more specifically in the direction of interactions between Jews and their close, and thus dangerous, relatives, Jewish Christians.[48]

Two further considerations may serve to buttress the general point that I am trying to make, namely, that Jewish Christians posed a greater threat to Jewish and Christian elites than did Christian Judaizers. The first is a rule drawn from the sociology of conflict: the rule holds that the closer the relationship between two parties, the greater the potential for conflict. In other words, whenever we encounter polemical language or the rhetoric of separation, we should look close to home for its source. And Jewish Christians certainly stood close to both homes: they claimed to be the only true Christians ("After all," they were fond of saying, "Jesus observed the Law and so do we!") and the only true Jews (they observed the Law and worshipped the Messiah). In any case, they insisted that there was no need to choose between being Christians or Jews. Indeed, for them it was an altogether false choice.

---

[45] See R. Kimelman, *"Birkat Ha-Minim* and the Lack of Evidence for an Anti-Christian Jewish Prayer in Late Antiquity," in *Jewish and Christian Self-Definition*, ed. E. P. Sanders (Philadelphia, 1981), 2:226–44.

[46] See the version cited by M. Goldstein, *Jesus in the Jewish Tradition* (New York, 1950), 154f. Ancient versions attribute this role sometimes to Paul, sometimes to Peter. For a more recent treatment of the *Toledoth Yeshu*, see Hillel Newman, "The Death of Jesus in the Toledot Yeshu Literature," *JTS* 50 (1999), 59–79.

[47] D. Boyarin, *Dying for God: Martyrdom and the Making of Christianity and Judaism* (Stanford, 1999).

[48] See Boyarin's discussion under the heading "When Rabbi Eli'ezer was Arrested by Christianity" in *Dying*, 26–41. But it may well be that Boyarin intends to designate here what others refer to as Jewish Christianity.

The second consideration comes from those gospel passages (especially in Matthew and John) which speak of Jesus-believers being tossed out of local synagogues.[49] Clearly, these Jesus-believing Jews sought originally to live within their local synagogues, no doubt proclaiming their message about Jesus. But at some point the tensions proved too great and they were expelled. Of course, we cannot speak of these early Jesus-believers as Jewish Christians; they were just – I hesitate to use this term, but it is fitting – first-century messianic Jews. However, they do provide a concrete model for the sorts of difficulties that Jewish Christians offered in later times. In a word, they were just too close for comfort.

In the end, my reflections on the fate of Jewish Christianity lead me to the conclusion that our phrase, "The Parting of the Ways," says both too little and too much. Too little, in that it can mask the negative potential of the parting for the losing side. That is, the two ways – again, at least from the triumphant and triumphalist Christian side – do not just go their separate directions, each to a happy end. One way leads to salvation, the other to condemnation or, in more recent terms, to what Peter Berger and Thomas Luckmann have called conceptual nihilation.[50] Crone hints at this in the final sentence of her article where she speaks of Islam's impact on the "plausibility structures of the world in which it made its impact felt."[51] In other words, Islam, like Jewish Christianity, represented "an alternative symbolic universe" which posed "a threat because its very existence demonstrates that one's own universe is less than inevitable."[52] Thus too little, also in the sense that the phrase minimizes the extent to which Christian identity, from the very beginning, was inextricably tied to Judaism. There appears to be an inverse relationship between the recognition and acceptance of these ties on the one side and the need to engage in conceptual nihilation on the other. At one extreme stand the various forms of Jewish Christianity, with their cousins the Christian Judaizers, who seem by and large to have avoided most forms of anti-Judaism. At the other extreme, I would argue, stand John Chrysostom in the fourth century and Nazi Germany in the twentieth. In these cases, the denial of all ties between Christianity and Judaism led to the most violent forms of anti-Judaism, and worse.

But our phrase also says too much, in that it seduces us into taking the views of certain elites as if they represented the views of all. As the later history of Jewish Christianity forces us to admit, the voices of these elites

---

[49] See, for example, Matt 10.17, 23.24; John 9.22, 12.42, 16.2.

[50] P. Berger and T. Luckmann, *The Social Construction of Reality* (New York, 1967), 159.

[51] Crone, "Islam," 94.

[52] Berger and Luckmann, *Social Construction of Reality*, 108.

reveal by their very existence the presence of other voices for whom the "Parting of the Ways" was nothing less than a historical tragedy. And the recovery of these voices, some of which survived well after the rise of Islam, has become one of the most exhilarating tasks in rewriting the history of ancient Judaism, Christianity, and Jewish Christianity.

# Beyond the Spatial and Temporal *Limes*

## Questioning the "Parting of the Ways" Outside the Roman Empire

by

## Adam H. Becker

Since its inception church history has been under the (at times) baneful influence of the *Ecclesiastical History* of Eusebius, a writer who saw the culmination of Christian history in the figure of the Roman emperor Constantine and thus privileged developments in the Roman Empire.[1] The effects of this bias are evident even in the scholarly discussion concerning Jewish–Christian relations in Late Antiquity. Scholars often restrict their inquiries to the West, and the discussion is usually divided between pre-Constantinian Jewish–Christian relations and events after Constantine.[2] Whereas some scholars argue that there was a "Parting of the Ways" between Jews and Christians in the late first or early second century, others – including many of the contributors to this volume – contest this. However, from as far back as James Parkes in the 1930s to Daniel Boyarin in the 1990s and present, scholars have agreed that the conversion of Constantine and the Christianization of the Roman Empire caused the communal boundaries between Jews and Christians to harden, eventually leading to their divergence into completely separate religious communities.[3] This line of scholarship, however, has generally failed to examine the relationship between Jews and Christians not living under a Christian empire. By introducing material which comes geographically and temporally from outside the Roman Empire, I hope to contribute to

---

 * I would like to thank Leyla B. Aker, Sebastian Brock, Annette Yoshiko Reed, and Jeffrey Rubenstein for taking the time to read and comment upon this paper.

[1] For a discussion of the negative influence Eusebius has had on the history of Christianity in the East, see Sebastian Brock, "Christians in the Sasanian Empire: A Case of Divided Loyalties," *Studies in Church History* 18 (1982): 1–2; repr. in *Syriac Perspectives on Late Antiquity* (London: Variorum, 1984), ch. 6.

[2] Cf. Marcel Simon's explanation for the periodization of his study, *Verus Israel: A Study of the Relations between Christians and Jews in the Roman Empire, AD 135–425* (trans. H. McKeating; London: Littman Library of Jewish Civilization, 1996), xvi–xvii.

[3] James Parkes, *The Conflict of the Church and Synagogue: a Study in the Origins of Anti-Semitism* (London: Soncino, 1934), e.g. 119; Daniel Boyarin, *Dying for God: Martyrdom and the Making of Christianity and Judaism* (Stanford: Stanford UP, 1999), 18.

the discussion concerning how the development of a Christian empire affected communal dynamics and, more broadly, to further question the scholarly model that has been termed the "Parting of the Ways."

This paper is composed of three parts. First, I look at the history of the Church of the East and the very different conditions under which the East Syrians lived vis-à-vis both the state and the Jewish community. The history of Christianity in fourth- through sixth-century Sassanian Mesopotamia – where the Christian community continued to suffer persecution despite its semiformalized status as a recognized minority – problematizes the nascent scholarly model which holds that, if a decisive break did occur between Jews and Christians, the moment of this fracture must be pushed forward from the first and second centuries to the fourth and fifth, when the development of a Christian empire helped determinatively to differentiate between the two religious communities. Second, I will look at how the increase in anti-Jewish literature in the period after the Arab conquest may help to confirm this aforementioned model of separation based upon assertions of power through the state, albeit only in those regions previously under Roman rule. Finally, I discuss one instance from the early Islamic period when "the ways" actually approached each other; that is, when, for lack of a better term, what we might call a "shared discourse" developed between Jews and Christians.

## Parting Ways East of Rome: The Church of the East

The conversion of Constantine did not end the persecution of Christians everywhere; Christianity outgrew the limits of the Roman Empire from the British Isles to Ethiopia, and it spread to Mesopotamia through various vectors, including trade, the taking of Western captives in times of war, and the previous existence of a large Jewish community in the region.[4] Mesopotamia never saw the triumph of the church of the fourth

---

[4] The question regarding the relationship with earliest Christianity in Mesopotamia depends on the authenticity of the *Chronicle of Arbela*. For a brief summary of the problem and references, see Sebastian Brock, "Syriac Historical Writing: A Survey of the Main Sources," *Journal of the Iraqi Academy* (Syriac Corporation) 5 (1979–80): 23–25; repr. in *Studies in Syriac Christianity* (Aldershot, Great Britain: Variorum, 1992), ch. 1. For Christianity in the Syriac milieu in general, the ongoing scholarly discussion has located the origins in either a local Jewish community or a Hellenized community with connections to Antioch, the latter position most strongly supported by H. J. W. Drijvers in much of his work. Unfortunately, this debate often relies on "Hellenism" and "Judaism" as mutually exclusive categories, which no longer hold in other fields. For a discussion of this question in the study of Judaism in the Greco-

century. In fact, the Church of the East continued to offer up martyrs and compose martyrological literature into the Islamic period. To quote from a letter of Timothy I, the Catholicos of the Church of the East in the eighth and early ninth centuries:

> We never had a Christian king. First it was the Magians for about four hundred years; then the Muslims. Neither the first nor the second ever attempted to add or subtract anything from our Christian faith, but took care not to suppress our faith, especially the blessed kings of the Muslims who never imposed anything in religious matters.[5]

Despite its rosy depiction of East-Syrian relations with the state, Timothy's letter demonstrates that the imperial church of the fourth and fifth centuries has no place in our discussion of the events in the East. Furthermore, if, as some scholars have suggested, the formation of a Christian empire played a significant role in the drawing of more distinct communal boundaries between Christians and Jews,[6] how are we to understand what happened to Christians and Jews who never lived in the Roman Empire, namely, those living in Sassanian Mesopotamia? I am not suggesting that Christians and Jews in the Persian Empire were somehow frozen in time somewhere in the late third century CE, but rather that we must be wary lest we impose Western imperial developments on realms outside of the Roman Empire. The Church of the East had its own internal history that led to the distinct communal identity we find in the early Islamic period.[7]

It has been suggested that the conversion of the Roman emperor to Christianity marked Christians within the Persian realm as potential fifth columnists, always a possible threat to the Sassanian state.[8] In the East, instead of ending persecution, Constantine's conversion may have actually increased it. In fact, some scholars have noted that the main periods of Persian persecution of Christians occurred during times of war between the two empires.[9] Furthermore, the restructuring of the Zoroastrian priesthood and the development of a Zoroastrian "orthodoxy"

---

Roman world, see Lee I. Levine, *Judaism & Christianity in Antiquity: Conflict or Confluence?* (Seattle: U. of Washington Press, 1998), 3–32.

[5] Translation from Thomas Hurst, *The Syriac Letters of Timothy I (727–823): A Study in Christian–Muslim Controversy* (Ph.D. diss., Catholic University of America, 1986), 242; text from Raphaël Bidawid, *Les Lettres du Patriarche Nestorien Timothée I*, Studi e Testi 187 (Città del Vaticano, 1956), 121. This letter is addressed to a community of Christian monks.

[6] E.g., Daniel Boyarin, *Dying for God*, 18; Charlotte Elisheva Fonrobert, "The *Didascalia Apostolorum*: A Mishnah for the Disciples of Jesus," *JECS* 9.4 (2001): 485.

[7] Michael G. Morony, *Iraq after the Conquest* (Princeton: Princeton UP, 1984), 332–83.

[8] Brock, "Christians in the Sasanian Empire," 5, 7.

[9] Brock, "Christians in the Sasanian Empire," 5, 7.

– possibly in reaction to events in the West – may have spurred on this antipathy. Thus, in contrast to the ending of persecution in the West and the subsequent state support of Christianity, persecution may be one of the differentiating factors in the East, driving a wedge between Jewish and Christian communities. Interestingly, this has been an explanatory device used in the past for the "Parting of the Ways" in the West; scholars have argued that Roman persecution, in conjunction with formal attempts to remove Christians from the synagogue by means of the *birkat ha-minim*, led to the development of two distinct religious communities.[10] Perhaps this very phenomenon, which has been challenged in recent scholarship on the West, actually did occur in the East.

Significantly, the most important literary witness to Christianity in fourth-century Sassanian Mesopotamia, Aphrahat, the so-called Persian Sage, only begins to attack Judaism once the persecution under Shapur II begins.[11] Aphrahat dates his own works in two different collections:[12] the first, from 337, contains little anti-Jewish polemic in contrast to the collection from 344, the majority of which consists of whole treatises devoted to arguments against Judaism. As the work of Naomi Koltun-Fromm in this volume (and elsewhere) demonstrates, the method and content of his exegesis and argument seem to place him in the same discursive sphere as near contemporary Rabbis, even despite his anti-Jewish stance.[13] While Aphrahat shows an interest in Rome – in fact, he interprets Daniel as predicting the apocalyptic victory of Rome over the Persian empire, thereby revealing his perfidy towards the Sassanian state (*Demonstration* 5, *On Wars*)[14] – the major purpose of the later treatises is the defense of Christianity in the face of Jewish criticisms and the demonstration of the error of the Jews.

One way of understanding the chronology of Aphrahat's treatises – specifically, the fact that the treatises attacking Judaism appear only *after* Christianity is threatened – is to set his literary production in a context in

---

[10] This understanding of the function of the *birkat ha-minim* has been rejected. See Reuven Kimelman, "*Birkat Ha-Minim* and the Lack of Evidence for Anti-Christian Jewish Prayer in Late Antiquity," in *Jewish and Christian Self-Definition*, vol. 2, *Aspects of Judaism in the Greco-Roman Period*, ed. E. P. Sanders, Albert I. Baumgarten, and Alan Mendelson (Philadelphia: Fortress, 1981), 226–44, 391–403.

[11] An English translation of Aphrahat's anti-Jewish writings (with the exception of *Demonstration* 20) can be found in Jacob Neusner, *Aphrahat and Judaism: The Christian–Jewish Argument in Fourth-Century Iran* (Leiden: Brill, 1971).

[12] *Demonstration* 22.25.

[13] See also Sebastian Brock, "Jewish Traditions in Syriac Sources," *JJS* 30 (1979): 212–32; repr. in *Studies in Syriac Christianity*, ch. 4. Brock notes that the rate of transferal of material decreases sharply after the fourth century.

[14] Timothy Barnes, "Constantine and the Christians of Persia," *JRS* 75 (1985): 126–36, puts the fifth *Demonstration* in its contemporary political context.

which the local Jewish and Christian communities were not fully distinct and separate from one another. Once persecution began, Christians may have flocked to the synagogue. To be sure, one might suggest that Aphrahat's is merely a theodical response to adversity, but if we are to allow ourselves to posit a sociological reality behind his anti-Judaism, it would seem to be a situation in which Christians (whether of Gentile or Jewish background we do not know) were doing things that seemed "Jewish" to Aphrahat, and in all likelihood were so. The exegetical proximity, mentioned above, also points to this social proximity. I have argued elsewhere that Aphrahat's *Demonstration* 20, *On the Care of the Poor*, may be read as evidence that such a situation was occurring: that is, when the persecution began, Christians who were affiliated with the Jewish community, whether by background or as Judaizing Gentiles, flocked to the synagogue and received aid.[15] Shapur's persecution destabilized whatever existing balance there has been between the Jewish and Christian communities at the time and would have resulted in a different intercommunal dynamic. In other words, Aphrahat was indifferent until a lack of difference made a difference. When persecution began, Aphrahat turned to the prescriptive description of "Judaism" and "Christianity" common to anti-Jewish literature.

The story of the martyrdom of Simeon bar Sabbaʿe (Catholicos of the East until his death in 344 CE)[16] is a source dated later than Aphrahat's writings that also addresses events under Shapur II's persecution. This story provides an example of the gulf between Jews and Christians that the persecution may have caused, but it also hints at the deeper connections that held the communities together in the first place. Gernot Wiessner has shown that the two versions[17] of Simeon's martyrdom go back to an original source, which in turn was composed of two earlier documents.[18] The first of these, the *Steuerquelle*, describes the Shah's imposition of a double head-tax on Christians and how Simeon's refusal to aid the Shah's authorities in the collection of this tax led to his death.

---

[15] Adam H. Becker, "Anti-Judaism and Care for the Poor in Aphrahat's *Demonstration* 20," *JECS* 10.3 (2002): 305–27.

[16] For a discussion of the dating and various sources, see R. W. Burgess and Raymond Mercier, "The Dates of the Martyrdom of Simeon bar Sabbaʿe and the 'Great Massacre'," *Analecta Bollandiana* 117 (1999): 9–66.

[17] The shorter version A and the longer version B, referred to as the *Martyrium* and the *Narratio* in the *Patrologia Syriaca* edition. *S. Simeon bat Sabbaʿe*, ed. and trans. Michael Kmosko, in *Patrologia Syriaca* 2.659–1055 (Paris: 1907) (=*PS* 2).

[18] Gernot Wiessner, *Untersuchungen zur syrischen Literaturgeschichte I: Zur Märtyrerüberlieferung aus der Christenverfolgung Schapurs II*. Abhandlungen der Akademie der Wissenschaften in Göttingen, philologisch-historische Klasse, Dritte Folge 67 (Göttingen: Vandenhoeck & Ruprecht, 1967). See also the useful review of this book by Sebastian Brock in *JTS* 19 (1968): 300–9.

The second, the *Judenquelle*, describes how the Jews' accusations against the Christians of being in cahoots with the Roman Empire are the cause of the persecution. These two sources have been combined in the *Vorlage* of the two recensions of the martyrdom of the patriarch.

After a list of the leading figures killed during the persecution, the longer version of the martyrdom begins with a discussion of how persecution in the West ended under Constantine and how Shapur II began to persecute Christians upon his western rival's death.[19] The text apologizes for the permission God seems to have given for the suffering of his followers with the common explanation that persecution helps to keep the church strong.[20] The text describes the beginning of the persecution and the imposition of the double head-tax.[21] After this, it turns to the Jews, the eternal enemies of the Christians:

> But the Jews, those who are at all times against our people, who murdered the prophets, crucified the Messiah, stoned the apostles, and continually thirst for our blood, found for themselves an opportunity to slander,[22] and because they had freedom of speech (*parrhesia*) due to their proximity to the queen because she was of their opinion, they began to attack the glorious Simeon with slander.[23]

This text, Aphrahat's treatises, and others rely on the idea of the Christian community as a "people." For example, the shorter version of the martyrdom (A) begins with an extended comparison of Simeon with Judah Maccabee: "One saved his people in war, the other saved his people in death."[24] While the mere title, "the people" (Syr. *'amma*), can be used in Syriac to refer to the Jews,[25] the idea of "peoplehood" developed among Syriac Christians at the same time.[26] After the introduction of the motif of Jewish slander, the longer version of the

---

[19] Paul Bedjan, *Acta Martyrum et Sanctorum* (Paris: Otto Harrassowitz, 1890–97; repr. Hildersheim: Georg Olms, 1968), vol. 2 (=*AMS* 2), 131–2.

[20] See Ephrem, *Hymns against Julian* 1, stanzas 12–13; Aphrahat, *Demonstration* 21; for a later Syriac example, see *The Life of John of Tella* in *Vitae virorum apud Monophysitas celeberrimorum*, ed. and trans. E. W. Brooks, CSCO 7–8 (1907), 38.18 ff (cf. Prov 3.11–12).

[21] *AMS* 2.135.

[22] The idiom translated as "slander" (*ekhal qartze*), also found in Jewish sources, is commonly used to refer to Satan in Syriac.

[23] *AMS* 2.143.5–10.

[24] *PS* 2.727.26–27.

[25] This appellation is ubiquitous. For example, Jacob of Sarug's seventh *Memra* (Homily) against the Jews begins, "If the people were willing to read lucidly, they would learn of the Son of God." (M. Albert, "Homélies contre les Juifs par Jacques de Saroug," in *Patrologia Orientalis* 38.1 [Turnhout: Brepols, 1976]).

[26] Brock, "Christians in the Sasanian Empire," 15: "In Sasanid Iran, then, as far as Christians themselves were concerned, religion and 'national' identity can be said to have coincided, in that the nation concerned was the 'Nation, or People, of God'."

martyrdom goes on a brief excursus concerning fourth-century events, particularly the Roman emperor Julian the Apostate's attempt to rebuild the Temple. Like the anti-Jewish literature that will be discussed later in this paper, the martyrdom dwells on Jewish failure: the Temple will not be rebuilt.[27]

Up to this point the text reveals the developing dichotomy between the Christians who are persecuted by the Sassanian state and the Jews who are protected by it. The text clearly is trying to resolve the theodical problem of persecution and how the worst enemies of the Christians, the Jews, are permitted to get away with their malignant behavior. At first glance the text seems to be, among other things, a meditation on the problem of Christian minority existence in an empire that clearly favors the Jews. However, certain passages serve as evidence that the relationship between the Jewish and Christian communities in the fourth century was more complex than the simple division between Jews and Christians depicted by the text:

> And right away there was a great commotion in the cities, Seleucia and Ctesiphon, after the persecutors came to uproot the church. Then the members of the orders (*qyāma*) were hidden and the flock was hidden and Simeon, who was the head, was taken. And there was an occasion for the evil ones. The church was filled with the uncircumcised (*'urle*)[28] and instead of the sound of prayer and splendor there was heard at that time the sound of upheaval and perturbation – with the roof of the church which was damaged – and instead of sweet incense the dust of the walls which were being uprooted ascended to the sky. There was a great commotion and fear for all the churches everywhere.[29]

That the distinguishing characteristic of the "evil ones" destroying the church in this passage is their lack of circumcision seems to suggest that the Christians whose church it was were circumcised. The text is silent about this fact, even as this reference to the uncircumcised points to it. Perhaps some of these circumcised Christians, members of this "flock" who were "hidden," whether Judaizing Gentiles or Christians of an originally Jewish background, went to the synagogue, where they would have had less to worry about during persecution because, despite being Christians, they also belonged to a licit and protected group of people: the Jews – or rather, they bore the differentiating mark of the Jews. If the above-suggested context for Aphrahat's anti-Jewish polemics is accepted, evidence such as this would make even more sense in light of Aphrahat's *Demonstration* 11, which is a historico-ethical etiology of circumcision that aims to relativize its value in the audience's eyes.

---

[27] *AMS* 2.143–45.

[28] *PS* 2.819 translates this as: *et ecclesia repleta est incircumcisis.*

[29] *AMS* 2.148.18–149.6.

Even more striking is the fact that several Syriac martyrdoms from the same time report in a matter-of-fact way that the persecutors of Christians would commonly seek to make these Christians engage in an activity abhorrent to Jews. In the story of Anahid, a martyr under Yazdgard II (438–57; persecution c. 446–48), we are told how soon after her conversion, "She refused to eat in the presence of her parents in case they would thereby discover that she was now a Christian."[30] That Anahid was refraining from eating blood seems to be confirmed by the references to the Christian refusal to eat blood in a number of martyr acts from the persecution under Shapur II.[31] It seems that even Aphrahat may not have eaten blood, since he takes for granted in his critique of Jewish dietary law that the eating of blood was forbidden long before the reception of the Mosaic legislation (*Demonstration* 15.3). That Christians were not sanguine about consuming blood proves to be a point of difference/similarity shared by Jews and Christians. To us it looks particularly Jewish, but in its day this practice may have seemed to Christians who actually concerned themselves about these things a practice not delegitimized by the Pauline abrogation of the Law,[32] while for some Jews it was one of the few acts in which even Gentiles should not engage (cf. *b. Sanhedrin* 56a). The Persian authorities were imposing on Christians a practice that both Christians and Jews could not perform; thus, a practice that is recognized by many both in antiquity and today as a point of Jewish difference in this case reveals Jewish and Christian proximity. In addition, it might be noted that the deaths of martyrs in the Persian Martyr Acts are dated according to a Jewish calendar.[33]

---

[30] *AMS* 2.569; translation from *Holy Women of the Syrian Orient*, trans. with an introduction by Sebastian P. Brock and Susan Ashbrook Harvey (Berkeley: U. of California Press, 1987), 84. See also Brock, "Christians in the Sasanian Empire," 9 (n. 37).

[31] *AMS* 2.303, Barba'šmin; *AMS* 2.307, Jacob and Mary; *AMS* 2.314, Barhad-beshabba; *AMS* 2.308, Thekla and Companions (see also Brock and Harvey, *Holy Women of the Syrian Orient*, 78); *AMS* 2.387, Aqebšma; *AMS* 4.138, Jacob and Azad. I would like to express my gratitude to Sebastian Brock for sharing this list of references with me.

[32] For Aphrahat on Paul, see Stephen S. Taylor, "Paul and the Persian Sage: Some Observations on Aphrahat's Use of the Pauline Corpus," in *The Function of Scripture in Early Jewish and Christian Tradition*, ed. Craig A. Evans and James A. Sanders (JSNTSup 154; Sheffield: Sheffield Academic Press, 1998), 312–31. For some earlier western examples of this avoidance of eating blood, see Acts 15:20; Tertullian, *Apology* 9.13; Minucius Felix, *Octavius* 30.6.

[33] Burgess and Mercier, "The Dates of the Martyrdom of Simeon bar Sabba'e," 63: "While a number of dates in the Acts remain unresolved, many which resisted earlier approaches can be understood when the date is interpreted according to the Jewish calendar."

At one point in the martyrdom of Simeon bar Sabba'e, the Shah is informed that Simeon has again refused to pay the double head-tax; he is enraged and consequently "set the land in commotion with his vehement response."[34]

> And he gave orders concerning the Priests and the Levites (*kāhne w-lewāye*) that there immediately be a slaughter by the sword of them and that the churches be uprooted and holiness defiled and the (liturgical) service be despoiled.[35]

It is striking that this text apparently relies on the term "Levites" to refer to the lesser clergy of the church, such as deacons. This usage, which may be considered a form of archaizing, reflects the Christian understanding that what goes on in a church is equivalent to the liturgy of the Jerusalem Temple of old. The appellation takes on even greater significance in light of the continuing preoccupation with priestly and levitical descent that we know the Babylonian Amoraim had.[36] This passage, then, would be one of the numerous examples of how Christians and Jews share the same metaphors and historical self-understanding.[37] While clergy are referred to as "Priests and Levites" in later Syriac literature, the use of "Levite" for "deacon" is uncommon enough – particularly in early literature – that we should ask ourselves if it is not our own categories that are compelling us to regard the martyrdom's reference to "Priests and Levites" as a metaphor. Is it not possible that Christians of Jewish descent in the local communities of Seleucia–Ctesiphon and nearby Karka d-Ladan had the same concern for pedigree as their Amoraic contemporaries? We certainly do not have much evidence for this – aside from the Jewish origins of the community posited by the highly problematic *Chronicle of Arbela*. However, neither do we have much evidence to the contrary, only the assumption that it can not be the case.[38]

---

[34] *AMS* 2.147.18.

[35] *AMS* 2.147.18–148.3.

[36] Jeffrey Rubenstein, *The Culture of the Babylonian Talmud* (Baltimore: The Johns Hopkins UP, forthcoming), ch. 5; see also the comparison between Palestinian and Babylonian concerns for genealogy in Richard Kalmin, *The Sage in Jewish Society of Late Antiquity* (New York: Routledge, 1999), 51–67.

[37] Chapter VIII of the *Didascalia Apostolorum* uses the discussion of responsibilities of Priests and Levites and the portions they receive at Num 18:1–32 to justify the gifts priests may receive. However, here only an analogy is drawn.

[38] S. Pines has argued that in Pahlavi, New Persian, and Sogdian the one indigenously formed word for "Christian," based on the root "tars," meaning "to fear," seems to derive from the appellation "God-fearer" attested across the ancient Mediterranean. This etymology would serve as further evidence of a Judaizing group among Persian Christians. S. Pines, "The Iranian Name for Christians and 'God-Fearers'," *Proceedings of the Israel Academy of Sciences and Humanities* 2 (1967): 143–52. Josephus' description of the conversion of the kingdom of Adiabene is further evidence of God-fearers in this same region, but in an earlier period (cf. *Ant.* 20.2).

The question of Jewish–Christian relations in the East has great bearing on the two fields of Syriac Studies and Rabbinics. Assumptions about a clear and easy separation between Jews and Christians in the East have contributed to the closing off of these fields of scholarship from one another.

For example, in one article a well-known scholar has suggested that the disproportionate number of references to disputes with *minim* ("heretics") in the Babylonian Talmud (in contrast to the Palestinian Talmud) derive from the "entertainment value" such stories would offer to the Babylonians – who "enjoyed the relative peace and security of life without such virulent pests in Persia" – because there was an "absence of a significant scripturally based challenge" (i.e. there were no pesky Christians).[39] These references to *minim* in the Babylonian Talmud may be a product of the rabbinic imagination; polemical statements are often aimed at straw men. However, it is clear that the traditional model of the "Parting of the Ways" not only condones the ignorance within some corners of rabbinic studies of the massive corpus of Syriac literature composed in the same milieu as the Talmud but also threatens to leave the evidence from a significant proximate culture out of scholarly discussion.[40]

## Anti-Judaism in the Post-Conquest Period

Whereas in the previous section I questioned the application of a nascent scholarly model for the history of Jewish–Christian relations to the Church of the East, in this section I will support a qualified version of this model, that is, one limited to the Roman Empire. For in the early Islamic period the production of anti-Jewish literature by Christians appears to have increased particularly in those areas that had only

---

[39] Richard Kalmin, "Christians and Heretics in Rabbinic Literature of Late Antiquity," *HTR* 87.2 (1994): 166. This claim is repeated in *The Sage in Jewish Society of Late Antiquity*, 70, but then he adds, "Nevertheless, Babylonian rabbis could have interacted with Bible-reading non-Jews and heretics had they so desired," and then mentions the East Syrians and Manichees in the region. Apparently, his prior claim is qualified in the second work, but the conclusions are basically the same. While he need not have given an extensive summary of research in the field, it is striking that, given the abundance of primary and secondary sources on Syriac Christianity, his only citation here, n. 12 (p. 138), is Yeshayahu Gafni, *Yehudei Bavel b-Tekufat ha-Talmud* (Jerusalem: Merkaz Zalman Shazar le-Toldot Yisrael, 1991), 137–48.

[40] This is also the case for Syriac Studies, which, like Jewish Studies, under the pressure of nationalist motivation and practical institutional requirements often treats culture as an insular phenomenon.

recently been under Roman rule.[41] The same question that has been asked with regard to anti-Jewish literature from earlier periods can be asked of this literature. In recent years scholarship on Christian anti-Judaism has been divided into two different but not mutually exclusive approaches.[42] The former, which has been termed "conflict theory," works with the sociological assumption that the greater the social proximity, the greater the strife. The ire of anti-Jewish literature is attributed to an environment in which Jews and Christians are living in proximity and therefore must compete with one another, as well as continually concern themselves with the threat of porous community boundaries. The second approach, what has been called "Christian discourse theory," argues that anti-Jewish polemic is an intra-Christian tradition, an autonomous discourse that must be examined in itself and not used to reconstruct some kind of "real" situation on the ground.

Both of these approaches to the material have their flaws. Conflict theory often contextualizes Christian literary compositions in real-life social situations for which we have little evidence.[43] It assumes that a social reality can be extrapolated from anti-Jewish literature. By contrast, Christian discourse theory founders when it is presented with the evidence we actually do have for Christian and Jewish competition with, and attacks upon, one another – as well as for the boundary problems caused by such phenomena as Gentile Christians attending synagogue. In focusing on anti-Judaism as an autonomous discourse one risks treating all texts as disembodied entities outside of real social situations. To paraphrase the title of Judith Lieu's now well-known book, "Christian discourse" forgets that there is a "reality" behind the "image."[44]

Whatever their flaws, these two approaches can still be used to examine the apparent increase in anti-Jewish polemic from the seventh century onwards. The question to be asked is: was the increase in anti-Jewish polemic in the post-conquest period a discursive, intra-Christian response to recent events, or was it an attempt to address social problems,

[41] For a survey of some of this literature, see Vincent Déroche, "La polémique anti-judaïque au VIe et au VIIe siècle. Un mémento inédit, les *Képhalaia*," *Travaux et Mémoires* 11 (1991): 275–311.

[42] For a summary of these two perspectives, see Guy G. Stroumsa, "From Anti-Judaism to Anti-Semitism in Early Christianity?" in *Contra Iudaeos: Ancient and Medieval Polemics between Christians and Jews*, ed. Ora Limor and Guy G. Stroumsa (Tübingen: Mohr Siebeck, 1996), 1–26, as well as Andrew S. Jacobs' contribution to this volume.

[43] David Satran, "Anti-Jewish Polemic in the Peri Pascha of Melito of Sardis: The Problem of Social Context," in *Contra Iudaeos*, 49–58.

[44] Judith M. Lieu, *Image and Reality: The Jews in the World of the Christians in the Second Century* (Edinburgh: T&T Clark, 1996). Lieu's book is a useful attempt at going beyond the simplistic division between "rhetoric" and "reality."

particularly those related to community boundaries, as caused by a shift
in community dynamics? At first glance the unreality of these literary
debates leads one to think that post-conquest Christians were creating an
imaginary world where Christians always won their debates with Jews
and Muslims did not even exist. Furthermore, several of these texts may
have been composed before the conquest. The title one modern scholar
gives to his chapter on three of the anti-Jewish texts from this period
sums up this reading of them: "We Are Still Better Than You."[45]

The fall of Jerusalem, the destruction of the Second Temple, and the
subsequent suffering of the Jews make up one of the major themes of this
new trend in anti-Jewish literature.[46] To be sure, Christians had always
used this theodically persuasive argument against Jews, but it moved
closer to center stage in some of the literature of this period. This focus
on Jerusalem and the Temple fits not only the early-seventh-century
Persian capture of the city, but also the continuing Muslim occupation
that culminated with the construction of the Dome of the Rock in 691 CE
by the Umayyad caliph 'Abd al-Malik (reign 685–705).

In conjunction with this harping on the Jews' permanent loss of
Jerusalem, apocalyptic texts of the day, both Christian and Jewish, use
Jerusalem as a central theme in their attempts to explain the tumultuous
events of the seventh century.[47] The date of composition of both the
*Apocalypse* of Pseudo-Methodius and the apocalyptic *Gospel of the
Twelve Apostles* has been established as being soon after the foundation
of the Dome of the Rock.[48] The monophysite *Gospel of the Twelve*

---

[45] David M. Olster, *Roman Defeat, Christian Response, and the Literary Construction of the Jew* (Philadelphia: U. of Pennsylvania, 1994), 116–137. For a broader
discussion beginning with a review of this book, see Averil Cameron, "Byzantines and
Jews: some recent work on early Byzantium," *Byzantine and Modern Greek Studies 20*
(1996): 249–74

[46] Averil Cameron, "Byzantines and Jews," 258–59.

[47] For material on Jewish Messianism in Late Antiquity, especially in reaction to the
Arab conquest, see Steven M. Wasserstrom, *Between Muslim and Jew: The Problem of
Symbiosis under Early Islam* (Princeton: Princeton UP, 1995), 47–89.

[48] G. J. Reinink, "Ps.-Methodius: A Concept of History in Response to the Rise of
Islam," in *The Byzantine and Early Islamic Near East (I): Problems in the Literary
Source Material*, ed. Averil Cameron and Lawrence I. Conrad (Studies in Late
Antiquity and Early Islam 1; Princeton: Darwin, 1992), 149–87; p. 185: "The
hypothesis that the *Apocalypse* of ps.-Methodius was composed in reaction to 'Abd al-
Malik's foundation of the Dome of the Rock on the site of the Jewish Temple is very
attractive." H. J. W. Drijvers, "The Gospel of the Twelve Apostles: A Syriac
Apocalypse from the Early Islamic Period," ibid., 189–213; p. 213: "The *Gospel of the
Twelve Apostles* was thus written after 692, when ps.-Methodius wrote, and before 705,
when 'Abd al-Malik's reign ended." Also on the *Gospel of the Twelve Apostles*, see H.
J. W. Drijvers, "Christians, Jews and Muslims in northern Mesopotamia in early Islamic
times. The Gospel of the Twelve Apostles and related texts," in *La Syrie de Byzance à*

*Apostles* addresses the different issues of the day in each of its parts. After the introductory "gospel," the text consists of three apocalypses. The Apocalypse of Simeon Kepha deals with the wretched state of the church due to Chalcedonian orthodoxy. The second, the Apocalypse of James, focuses on the destruction of the Temple because of the Jews' refusal to believe in Jesus and their subsequent banishment (presumably under Hadrian).[49] The apocalypse then describes the coming of Constantine and the construction of the basilica where the Temple once stood. It ends with a reference to the descendent of Constantine, the *Endkaiser* of other texts such as the *Apocalypse* of Pseudo-Methodius, who would come and set things right. Finally, the third apocalypse offers a description of the end-time, the conquests of the Arabs, and their eventual defeat. The structure of the *Gospel of the Twelve Apostles* reveals that some Christians, even while addressing contemporary events, felt the need to remind themselves of the Jews' permanent loss of Jerusalem and of the glory days of the Christian city under Roman rule.

Another manner of dealing with the painful loss of Jerusalem is to be found in the *Discourse on Priesthood*, an anti-Jewish text still only in manuscript form in the British Museum.[50] The *Discourse* consists of two chapters. The first, which takes up the majority of the work, is a dialogue between a Christian and a Jew on the priesthood of the Messiah and the abrogation of the ancient Israelite priesthood. While avoiding *ad hominem* attack, this dialogue depicts the Christian as attempting to logically demonstrate his argument to his interlocutor. The second, much briefer chapter is a list of reasons why the Israelite priesthood has been superseded by the priesthood of the Messiah. The author of this text has taken most of his arguments from the Epistle to the Hebrews; however, interestingly, he never quotes from this text nor does he ever allude to the New Testament. He emphasizes the loss of the Jewish priesthood and the supersession of the earthly Temple by the heavenly one, in which Jesus is high priest. In this way, the text tacitly accepts the Christian loss of Jerusalem, while reminding us that the Jews do not possess the city either. The text's priestly focus may also be understood as reacting to the contemporary Jewish messianism, which foresaw the rebuilding of the Temple and reinstitution of the priestly order at the end of time. As with

---

*l'Islam, VIIe–VIIIe Siècles*, ed. P. Canivet and J. P. Rey-Coquais (Damascus: Institut Français de Damas, 1992), 67–74; repr. in *History and Religion in Late Antique Syria* (Aldershot, Great Britain: Variorum, 1994).

[49] Drijvers, "The Gospel of the Twelve Apostles," 196–97.

[50] British Library Add. 18295, 137b–140b; text, translation, and introduction are forthcoming. This text is difficult to date. In this future publication I will go through my arguments for placing it in the early Islamic period. Certain technical terms and the use of particular philosophical texts give it a *terminus post quem* of c. 600 CE.

other anti-Jewish texts from this period, considering its post-conquest composition it is perhaps telling how the *Discourse* focuses on the Jews and their disenfranchisement and completely ignores the new political environment.

In conjunction with the increase in anti-Jewish polemic, another striking feature of Christian literature in the post-conquest period is the failure of Christians to produce any substantial polemic against Islam through most of the first century of Arab rule.[51] Concerted efforts to intellectually debunk Islam did not begin until the eighth century, when they arose particularly from the Melchites, who lost the most from the changeover to Arab rule.[52] It has been argued that in the earliest decades after the conquest, Muslims "were not yet seen by Christian polemicists as a clearly defined, distinct religious community."[53] This focus on Jews and the general lack of awareness that a new player had entered the religious field occurred elsewhere as well. For example, after the Arab invasion of Spain in 711, Christian chronicles generally ignore Islam, focusing instead on heresy and problems with Judaizers. It is only in the early ninth century, after Christians began to convert to Islam and assimilate to Islamic norms, that Spanish Christians began to polemicize against Islam.[54]

As events in Spain suggest, post-conquest anti-Jewish literature may not be just cheap consolation for crushed Christian pride. If we consider the communal boundary problems that plagued Jews and Christians

---

[51] Sebastian P. Brock, "Syriac Views of Emergent Islam," in *Studies on the First Century of Islamic Society*, ed. G. H. A. Juynboll (Carbondale-Edwardsville: Southern Illinois UP, 1982); repr. in Sebastian P. Brock, *Syriac Perspectives on Late Antiquity* (London: Variorum, 1984), ch. 8. Sidney H. Griffith, "Disputes with Muslims in Syriac Christian Texts: from Patriarch John (d. 648) to Bar Hebraeus (d. 1286)," in *Religionsgespräche im Mittelalter*, ed. B. Lewis and F. Niewöhner, Wolfenbütteler Mittelalter-Studien 4 (Wiesbaden: Harrassowitz, 1992), 251–73; G. J. Reinink, "The Beginnings of Syriac Apologetic Literature in Response to Islam," *Oriens Christianus* 77 (1993): 165–87; J. Lamoreaux, "Early Christian Responses to Islam," in *Medieval Christian Perspectives of Islam*, ed. John Victor Tolan (New York: Routledge, 1996), 3–31.

[52] Melchites (deriving from the Syriac word for "king") were those Christians in the newly conquered territories who remained in communion with the Byzantine emperor (i.e. Chalcedonians).

[53] Quotation from Fred Donner, "From Believers to Muslims: Patterns of Communal Identity in early Islam," in *The Byzantine and Early Islamic Near East 4: Patterns of Communal Identity*, ed. Lawrence I. Conrad (Princeton: Darwin, forthcoming). Donner begins with the scholarship on Christian responses to Islam but then goes on to argue that a distinct Muslim communal identity did not exist until some decades after the conquest.

[54] Kenneth Baxter Wolf, "Christian Views of Islam in Early Medieval Spain," in Tolan, *Medieval Christian Perspectives of Islam*, 85–108.

before the triumph of the church in the fourth century and how the Arab conquest in some ways, especially with respect to the political dynamic (i.e. dhimmitude), set the clock back three hundred years, the increase in anti-Judaism may not have been mere flight into fantasy, but rather an attempt to reaffirm differences which were seen to be in danger of fading. Further confirmation of this can be found in the fact that, of the various anti-Jewish texts extant from this period, most are attributed to Melchites, Christians who were living under and benefiting most from the Roman Empire. None are attributed to the East Syrians, that is, Nestorians living under the Persian Empire.[55]

Understanding this rise in anti-Judaism in the post-conquest period as a reaction to the new political situation in which community boundaries were (or at least were perceived to be) under threat would fit with those scholarly arguments pushing a more systemic divergence between the two communities forward in time to the fourth and fifth centuries, a period when clearer lines were being drawn, as opposed to the traditionally posited first or second century.

## The Discursive Common Ground within the Arena of Reason

So far I have argued for and against a model which sees the intermingling of Christianity with the imperial government as an impetus that would have facilitated and made necessary a clearer differentiation between Jews and Christians. First, I argued against the application of this model to Christians in the East, who did not live under Roman rule. Second, I suggested that the increase in anti-Jewish literature in the post-conquest period could be used to argue for the validity of this model. Once the Christian state disappears, the status quo ante threatens to return.

Finally, I would like to examine the development of "shared discourses" between Jews and Christians, cases in which, as I mentioned in the beginning of this essay, the "ways" may in fact come together. The sociological premise that the realm of ideas is a reflection of the social world means that shared social worlds will entail a shared realm of ideas, and this is just what we find in the intellectual culture which evolves in the Islamic *oikoumene*.

In examining the aforementioned *Discourse on Priesthood*, I have come across several instances that seem to suggest that the author relied

---

[55] John of Fenek, the East-Syrian historian whose work belongs to the contemporary resurgence in apocalypticism, addresses events of the seventh century. See the introductory comments in Sebastian Brock, "North Mesopotamia in the late seventh century: Book XV of John bar Penkaye's *Rish Melle*," *Jerusalem Studies in Arabic and Islam* 9 (1987): 51–75; repr. in *Studies in Syriac Christianity*, ch. 2.

on formulations from Aristotelian logic, or that he at least came from a context where this logic was studied. Note, for example, the manner in which the Christian in the text attempts to convince the Jew that Christ's self-sacrifice was in fulfillment of his priestly office:

> *Jew*: But how is it possible for a person to be a priest of himself?
>
> *Christian*: If he is called a priest who sacrifices other things, all the more so is he who offers himself to God the Father on behalf of everyone.
>
> *Jew*: Then everyone who kills himself is a priest?
>
> *Christian*: According to your definition[56] then again even everyone who slaughters a sheep is a priest. But if not all slaughterers are priests, but (only) those who slaughter and offer according to the commandment of God, by this very definition, not everyone who hands themselves over to death are reckoned (as) priests, but rather (only) those who are guided because of God according to the will of God.[57]

Here the Christian first responds to the Jew with an *a fortiori* or – as it is commonly known in Jewish texts – a *qal va-ḥomer* argument. When the Jew responds to it, the Christian refutes him with a *reductio ad absurdum* that clearly evidences an awareness of a fallacy based on genus and species, a problem addressed by Aristotle in the *Topics*.[58]

Another example of this reliance on philosophical logic is apparent when the Jew asks how exactly the Messiah, if he is a priest and priesthood entails sacrifice, has actually made offerings. The Christian responds:

> As I said, he too is shown to be a priest by (his) priestly power,[59] both if he sacrifices and if he does not sacrifice. . . . For not even a priest of the Law, when he sacrificed, was a priest after he brought (it) to an end, that is, his priesthood, but only once per year would he enter the Holy of Holies and when he served in the inner sanctuaries, this alone was sufficient to demonstrate that he was the high priest continually within Israel.[60]

The argument that a priest is characterized by his "priestly power" – or, perhaps more accurately, his capacity or potential to act as a priest – also seems to derive from an Aristotelian notion,[61] and the author here

---

[56] *Meltha*, lit. "word," is equivalent to the Greek *logos*.

[57] British Library Add 18295 138b column 2, line 14–139a column 1, line 1.

[58] "It is clear then that the species take part in the genera, but the genera do not take part in the species; for the species admits the definition (lógon) of the genus, but the genus does not admit the definition of the species" (121a12–14). There are several other points in book IV of the *Topics* where this and similar issues are raised.

[59] The Syriac reads: *a(y)k d-'emret kāhna 'o(w) hāna bhayla kāhnāya meṭhawe*. The reading of *kāhna* could alternatively be *bhāna*. I have emended *'o(w)* to *'āp*.

[60] 137b column 2.

[61] For the use of this notion in dialectical discussion, see *Topics* 126a30ff, 138b27ff, 139a1ff.

employs the word *ḥayla*, the Syriac word often used to translate Aristotle's *dúnamis*.[62] The use of such logic in the *Discourse on Priesthood* raises the issue of the relationship between logic and polemic and the common ground created by them within the arena of rational disputation.[63]

By the sixth century Aristotelian logic was already popular in Syriac, especially via the Syriac translation of Porphyry's *Isagoge*, and was used for questions pertaining to language and epistemology. However, it is not until the seventh century that we see the systematic translation of Aristotle's logical works.[64] Of these, the ones that come later in the traditional ordering of his works, particularly the *Topics* and the *Sophistic Refutations*, were significant weapons for debate. These two works were translated into Syriac by Athanasius of Balad, some time before his death in 686. Approximately a century later, the Abbasid caliph al-Mahdī (d. 785) commissioned the Nestorian patriarch Timothy I (mentioned above), in conjunction with Abū-Nūh, a Christian underling of the governor of Mosul, to translate the *Topics* into Arabic.[65] As Dimitri Gutas has argued, "the exigencies of inter-faith discourse" were one of the main impetuses behind the translation of secular Greek literature.[66] It does not, then, seem to be a coincidence that Timothy I was also responsible for composing a long pro-Christian, anti-Muslim dialogue extant in both Arabic and Syriac.[67]

---

[62] See, e.g., a Syriac version of Aristotle's *De Interpretatione*, where *katà dúnamin* is rendered as *bḥayla* (J. G. H. Hoffman, *De Hermeneuticis apud Syros Aristoteleis* [Leipzig, 1873], 36.7=19a17; see also 52.6=23a4).

[63] In the quotation above, one is in fact tempted to translate the word that I have rendered as "definition" as "logic," given the Syriac *meltha*'s relationship to the Greek *lógos*.

[64] Sebastian Brock, "The Syriac Commentary Tradition," in *Glosses and Commentaries on Aristotelian Logical Texts: The Syriac, Arabic and Medieval Latin Traditions*, ed. Charles Burnett (London: The Warburg Institute, 1993), 3–18

[65] Sebastian Brock, "Two Letters of the Patriarch Timothy from the late Eighth Century on Translations from Greek," *Arabic Sciences and Philosophy* 9 (1999): 233–46.

[66] Dimitri Gutas, *Greek Thought, Arabic Culture: The Graeco-Arabic Translation Movement in Baghdad and Early 'Abbāsid Society (2nd–4th/8th–10th centuries)* (London: Routledge, 1998), 61 (section heading); "A concrete indication of the significance of inter-faith disputation is provided by the disproportionately high number of apologetic and polemic treatises written in Arabic during the period of the translation movement," 66.

[67] Syriac version and translation: Alphonse Mingana, "The Apology of Timothy the Patriarch before Caliph Mahdi," in *Christian Documents in Syriac, Arabic and Garshuni, Edited and Translated with a Critical Apparatus* (Woodbrooke Studies 2; Cambridge: W. Heffer & Sons, 1928), 1–162; Arabic version and translation as well as general treatment of Timothy: Hans Putman, *L'église et l'islam sous Timothée (780–*

It has been argued by several scholars that the roots of *kalām*, Islamic dialectical or systematic theology, lie in this culture of dispute.[68] Gutas argues that even obscure sciences, such as physics, in the Abbasid period often derived from the context of controversy. For example, the Greek physical sciences were useful for disputing with the many dualists of the day (e.g. Manicheans).[69] In turn, as *kalām* developed it was increasingly taken up as a tool of disputation by the non-Muslims who were beginning to compose in Arabic. This close relationship between logic and inter-religious disputation continued. Polemics were composed in which one would try to show the reasonableness of his own faith and the irrationality of others'. In the process, these intellectuals ironically developed a common ground in which their disputation could occur.[70] The fact that teachers and students could come from different religious backgrounds and even engage in polemic with each others' faiths, yet could still maintain their academic relationships, demonstrates the proximate intellectual space that they shared.

The rationality of *kalām* would become a shared discourse between Jews and Christians (and of course Muslims) in the East.[71] In this shared discourse members of different faiths engaged in activities that differentiated their faith from that of others, but by engaging in this shared sphere they were also committing themselves to being similar to one another.[72] This space of rationality opened up a link between the

---

823), *étude sur l'église nestorienne au temps des Premiers 'Abbasides* (Beirut: Dar el-Machreq éditeurs, 1975).

[68] M. Cook, "The origins of *kalām*," *BSOAS* 43 (1980): 32–43; S. Pines, "An Early Meaning of the Term *Mutakallim*," *Israel Oriental Studies* 1 (1971): 224–40; repr. in his *Studies in the History of Arabic Philosophy* (Collected Works III; ed. S. Stroumsa; Jerusalem: Magnes, 1996), 62–78.

[69] Gutas, *Greek Thought, Arabic Culture*, 70–71.

[70] Pines, "An Early Meaning of the Term *Mutakallim*," 71: "In debates among people professing different religions and obeying different authorities reason was the only possible arbiter, and the *Mutakallimūn*, who engaged in such debates, and also their opponents, must have recognized this."

[71] "Those Christians and Muslims (and Jews) who met and worked together in the grand projects of translation and Arabic philosophical inquiry came to share an intellectual world: they had a common formation, common modes of discourse and argument, and a common library of the authoritative works of past sages." Mark Swanson, "Early Christian–Muslim Theological Conversation among Arabic-Speaking Intellectuals," paper presented in Yogyakarta, Indonesia, July 1998, 10–11 [http://www.luthersem.edu/mswanson/].

[72] "It was precisely their participation in *common* intellectual currents that provided Muslim and Christian thinkers with the tools with which they could defend and commend their *particular* beliefs"; Swanson, "Early Christian–Muslim Theological Conversation," 14. A negative example of this response in kind can be seen in the West, where individual philosophical anti-Jewish arguments, but not a truly philosophical anti-Jewish polemic, were used. In turn, according to Daniel J. Lasker, "Jewish

different faiths and made intellectual conversion possible.[73] Representative of this is the story of Dāwūd ibn Marwān al-Muqammiṣ, who converted from Judaism to Christianity under Nonnus of Nisibis, a Christian intellectual and *kalām*-influenced apologist,[74] only to return to his original faith and compose the first *kalām*-inspired critique of Christianity. Al-Muqammiṣ apparently embraced and rejected Christianity within the same realm, that is, the realm of reason. Thus, points of difference and similarity share the same loci.

Furthermore, although the progressive arabicization of the Near East went along with and allowed for conversion to Islam, it also created a *lingua franca* for theological dialogue.[75] Christians under Arab rule eventually developed their own Arabic Christian literary culture, thus succumbing to the Arabic language yet not yielding to Islam.

One contemporary analogy may help to convey my point, which is perhaps quite obvious. In the Fall of 2001, when the recent terrorist attacks put Islam at the center of much public discussion, the head of the Southern Baptist Convention asked its members to pray and fast during the Muslim holy month of Ramadan so that "God will miraculously reveal himself through Jesus Christ to Muslims."[76] Ironically, in order to attack Islam, it seems that Christians were being asked to engage in one of the "Five Pillars" of Islam: fasting during Ramadan. Attack entails at least some form of engagement. Thus, I would argue that, in tandem with whatever models we develop for the interaction of Jews and Christians – whether they be living in a Christian, a Persian, or a Muslim empire – we must remain aware of the continuing possibility of their participation in common realms, whether it be the rationality of *kalām*, the ancient vernacular of magic, the shared scripture of the Hebrew Bible, or eventually the shared Arabic language.

---

Philosophical Polemics in Ashkenaz," in *Contra Iudaeos*, 213: "Philosophical arguments against Christianity existed in Ashkenaz; a philosophical critique of Christianity did not."

[73] S. Stroumsa, "On Jewish Intellectuals Who Converted in the Early Middle Ages," in *The Jews of Medieval Islam: Community, Society, and Identity*, ed. Daniel Frank (Leiden: Brill, 1989), 179–97. For al-Muqammiṣ' critique of Christianity, see S. Stroumsa, *Dawud ibn Marwan al-Muqammis's Twenty Chapters* (Leiden: Brill, 1989).

[74] For Nonnus' own work, see Albert Van Roey, *Nonnus de Nisibe, traité apologétique* (Bibliothèque du Muséon vol. 21; Louvain: 1948). Sidney Griffith, "The Apologetic Treatise of Nonnus of Nisibis," *ARAM* 3.1&2 (1991): 115–38

[75] Mark Swanson, "Beyond Prooftexting: Approaches to the Qur'ān in Some Early Arabic Christian Apologies," *The Muslim World* 88 (1998): 305–8; idem, "Arabic as a Christian Language?" paper presented in Yogyakarta, Indonesia, July 1998, 9–12 [http://www.luthersem.edu/mswanson].

[76] "Baptist Head Urges Prayers for Muslim Conversion," *New York Times*, 27 Nov. 2001, A10.

## Conclusion

In this essay I have made several suggestions, the summation of which is that we need to look outside of our disciplines and the particular time periods on which we work in order to formulate a model for Jewish–Christian relations. My main point by now should be clear: a different model of Jewish–Christian relations, arising from a better knowledge of the mutual sources, may contribute to a better understanding of phenomena that have been examined distinctly in the past; furthermore, the model of separation we develop for the West should not be summarily (and presumptuously) imposed on the East. Our assumptions about the lack of any interrelationship between the Jewish and Christian communities in late antique Mesopotamia have too often limited our capability of imagining how to use our wealth of textual evidence in new ways.

The evidence, a sample of which was used in this paper, puts into question the possibility of our speaking of a simple "Parting of the Ways" without constantly having to qualify our terms. There were, in fact, many "partings," and they happened in different places at different times in different ways; furthermore, the Jewish and Christian communities continued to be intertwined in certain ways at certain times. However, with so many qualifications appended to its meaning, perhaps the expression the "Parting of the Ways" is not particularly useful for characterizing the trajectory of Jewish–Christian relations at any time in any place. Models can only be refined so far before they collapse in upon themselves. If we are to maintain the metaphor of "the ways," then in the end, it seems, they were ways that never parted.

# List of Contributors

RA'ANAN S. ABUSCH (BOUSTAN) is a doctoral candidate in the Religions of Late Antiquity at Princeton University. He is completing his dissertation on the literary and ideological relationship between the Hekhalot corpus and Jewish martyrological literature. He has published articles on the development of Hebrew mystical poetry as well as gender in ancient Judaism.

ADAM H. BECKER was one of the organizers of the Princeton workshop and the joint Oxford–Princeton conference on "The Ways That Never Parted." He is presently a doctoral candidate in the Department of Religion at Princeton University and a visiting lecturer at New York University. His dissertation is an intellectual and institutional history of the School of Nisibis.

DANIEL BOYARIN is Taubman Professor of Talmudic Culture at the University of California, Berkeley. He is currently completing a book about the discursive means by which the separation of Judaism from Christianity was effected in the second to the fifth centuries, entitled *Border Lines: "Heresy" and the Emergence of Christianity and Judaism.*

AVERIL CAMERON is Warden of Keble College, Oxford, and Professor of Late Antique and Byzantine History. She is a member of the Steering Committee for the Princeton–Oxford partnership, under whose auspices the Oxford contributors attend the 2001 conference at Princeton.

PAULA FREDRIKSEN is the Aurelio Professor of Scripture in the Department of Religion at Boston University. She studied theology at Oxford University and earned her doctorate in Religion at Princeton. Fredriksen specializes in the social and intellectual history of Mediterranean Diaspora Judaism and ancient Christianity, from the Late Second Temple period to the fall of the Western Roman Empire. Her latest book, *Augustine and the Jews*, will appear next year.

DAVID FRANKFURTER is Professor of Religious Studies and History at the University of New Hampshire. He is the author of *Elijah in Upper Egypt: The Apocalypse of Elijah and Early Egyptian Christianity* and *Religion in Roman Egypt: Assimilation and Resistance*, as well as articles on magic, popular religion in antiquity, and Christian apocalypticism.

JOHN G. GAGER is William H. Danforth Professor of Religion at Princeton University. His work covers relations between Christians and Jews in the early centuries of the Common Era. His most recent book is *Reinventing Paul*.

E. LEIGH GIBSON is a graduate of the Department of Religion at Princeton University and has taught at Oberlin College. Her first book, *The Jewish Manumission Inscriptions of the Bosporan Kingdom*, appeared in 1999. She is currently at work on *Thinking with Jews: the Christian community of Ancient Smyrna*.

MARTIN GOODMAN is Professor of Jewish Studies in the University of Oxford, and a Fellow of Wolfson College and the Oxford Centre for Hebrew and Jewish Studies. He has written books on both Jewish and Roman history, and on the history of mission and conversion in Late Antiquity. He was joint convener, with Simon Price, of the Oxford seminar which participated in the Oxford–Princeton project on "The Ways that Never Parted."

ANDREW S. JACOBS is an Assistant Professor of Religious Studies at the University of California, Riverside. He is completing a study of Christian writings about Jews in the late ancient holy land (forthcoming from Stanford University Press) and continues his studies of the cultural history of early Christianity and late ancient religious identity in various contexts, such as the family, biblical interpretation, and gender studies.

NAOMI KOLTUN-FROMM is an Assistant Professor of Religion at Haverford College. Her interests include ancient and late ancient Jewish history, the early Church, the Syriac Church, Jewish–Christian polemics, and comparative biblical exegesis.

ROBERT A. KRAFT is Berg Professor of Religious Studies at the University of Pennsylvania. His main areas of academic focus have been Greek Jewish scriptures and the "edges" of Jewish and Christian canonical collections, especially "apocrypha and pseudepigrapha" in both traditions and early Christian appropriation and adaptation of Jewish materials.

SIMON R. F. PRICE is CUF Lecturer in Ancient History in the Faculty of Classics at Oxford University and a Fellow of Lady Margaret Hall. His books include *Rituals and Power: The Roman imperial cult in Asia Minor*, *Religions of Rome*, and *Religions of the Ancient Greeks*. He inaugurated the broader Oxford–Princeton project on "Culture and Religions of the Eastern Mediterranean," together with Fritz Graf, and he convened the Oxford seminar on "The Ways that Never Parted," together with Martin Goodman.

ANNETTE YOSHIKO REED is an Assistant Professor in the Department of Religious Studies at the University of Pennsylvania. She is the author of *Fallen Angels and the History of Judaism and Christianity* and co-editor, with R. S. Abusch (Boustan), of *Heavenly Realms and Earthly Realities in Late Antique Religions*. She is presently working on a book on "Jewish Christianity."

ALISON SALVESEN'S main research interests are early translations and interpretations of the Hebrew Bible in Greek, Latin, Aramaic, and Syriac. She is Fellow in Jewish Bible Versions at the Oxford Centre for Hebrew and Jewish Studies, and a University Research Lecturer at the Oriental Institute, Oxford University.

PETER SCHÄFER is the Ronald O. Perelman Professor of Jewish Studies and Professor of Religion at Princeton University. His latest book, *Jesus in the Talmud*, examines the anti-Christian rhetoric of the Babylonian Talmud within a Sasanian imperial and thus predominantly non-Christian context. He oversaw the organization of the Princeton workshop and the joint Oxford–Princeton conference that forms the basis of the present volume.

DANIEL STÖKL BEN EZRA studied comparative religion, Jewish Studies, and Theology in Bochum, Bern, and Jerusalem. Since 2006 he is serving as Permanent Research Fellow for Qumran at the National Center for Scientific Research (CNRS) in the Centre Paul-Albert Février, Aix-en-Provence, France.

AMRAM TROPPER is a Lecturer in Ancient Jewish History in the Department of Jewish History at Ben-Gurion University. He recently published *Wisdom, Politics and Historiography: Tractate Avot in the Context of the Graeco-Roman Near East*.

# Modern Author Index

# Subject Index

exodus of Israel from Egypt 271–72,
290
*Exodus Rabbah* 303
Ezra-Nehemiah (1 Esdras) 235, 298
4 Ezra 138, 211
5 and 6 Ezra 136, 138, 139, 141
Fast of the Seventh Month 259–67,
269–72, 274–81
fasting 262, 264, 266–67, 271–72,
275, 299, 333, 392
Filastrius of Brescia 351
fourth century, as critical era for
Jewish and Christian self-definition
12, 17, 22, 66, 44, 87, 94, 204, 226–
29
Franks 62
Gaius Julius Philippus 148
Galen 315, 353
Galilee 80, 114, 115, 205
Genesis 51, 55, 27, 95, 105, 209, 253,
317, 319, 326, 336
*Genesis Rabbah (Bereshit Rabbah)*
230, 318, 326, 338
"Gentile Christianity," 4, 5, 35, 56, 92,
200, 201, 203, 231, 366, 369
Gentiles
– and "Jewish" observances 42, 18, 54,
60, 221, 230, 262, 268–70, 280–81
– attraction to Judaism 47, 50–52, 384
– Christian missions to 52–53, 111,
193, 206, 208
– Jewish missions to 43, 49–52, 225
– Jewish perceptions of 54–55, 92, 370
– perceptions of Jews and Judaism 37–
42
– salvation of 141–42, 111, 215–19,
222–23, 225
Geonic period 181, 321, 292
Germanicus 151
God-fearers 49, 51, 219–20, 223, 230,
381
Golden Calf 208, 275
Gospel of John 5, 95, 96, 71, 152
Gospel of Luke 152, 166, 173, 215,
281, 310
Gospel of Mark 206, 261, 248
Gospel of Matthew 15, 132, 140, 148,
166, 194, 275, 299, 301, 310, 355,
372
– and "Jewish Christians," 206, 174,
215–17, 274
– on Pharisees, 50, 25, 207

*Gospel of the Twelve Apostles*, 384
gospels
– canonical 37, 28, 150, 310
– "Jewish-Christian" 194
Gregory of Nazianzus 347
*hairesis* 350, 354–55, 327
halakhah 45, 84, 100, 137, 142, 151,
158–59, 197, 210, 285, 302, 311,
316, 320–22, 367
heavenly ascent 136–38, 308, 282,
322–23, 328–29, 331, 335
*Hebraica veritas* 242, 249, 217, 252–
54, 257
Hegesippus 173–75, 178, 194, 203,
348, 356
Hekhalot literature 322–23, 328–29,
297, 331, 333, 338
*Hekhalot Rabbati* 328, 332
Heliodorus 317
Hellenismos 67, 68
Hellenistic Jews 41–43, 60, 236–39
Hemerobaptists 349, 356
Heracleon 201
heresiology 37, 85, 180–86, 187, 189,
192–94, 198–99, 231, 351–52, 355,
357, 360
"heresy" 59, 92, 97, 172, 180, 184,
186, 202, 231, 345–46, 348–51, 353–
55, 357, 359, 367–68, 386. *See also*
*haireses*; *minut.*
Hermippus of Smyrna 42
Herod 45, 91, 122
Herodians 356
Hexapla 238, 240–41, 245–46, 248,
251, 253, *See also* Origen
Hillel 91, 161, 162–63, 165–66, 169,
305, 370
Hippolytus 143, 174, 266, 353, 356–57
Holocaust 7, 11, 100, 101
Homer 238, 358
Honorius (emperor) 53
hybridity 67, 75, 75
Hephtzibah 341
Iberia 63
iconoclastic controversies 342–44,
346, 347, 365
idolatry 208–10, 218–19, 223, 342,
356
Ignatius 2, 72, 136, 151, 154
*ihidāye, ihidāyutha* 285, 296–99
Innocentius of Tortona 352
*Ioudaios, Ioudaioi* 45, 33, 96